UNTIMELY PASSAGES

Anonymous (French School), *The Colporteur (Merchant Selling Various Books and Almanacs Dated 1623)*, seventeenth century

ALSO BY JERRY ZASLOVE

A Dossier against Cynicism: Two Essays for Robert Chaplin

Federalism-in-the-Making: Contemporary Canadian and German Constitutionalism, National and Transnational (with Edward McWhinney and Werner Wolf)

The Ideology and Poetics of "Poshlost": The Work of Nikolai Gogol and Its Importance in Our Time

The Insurance Man: Kafka in the Penal Colony (with Bill Jeffries)

Jeff Wall, 1990 (with Gary Dufour)

ON JERRY ZASLOVE'S WORK

Anarcho-Modernism: Toward a New Critical Theory in Honour of Jerry Zaslove (edited by Ian Angus)*

*Published by Talonbooks

Untimely Passages

DOSSIERS FROM THE OTHER SHORE

by Jerry Zaslove

Foreword by Samir Gandesha

Talonbooks

Talonbooks
9259 Shaughnessy Street, Vancouver, British Columbia, Canada V6P 6R4
talonbooks.com

Talonbooks is located on xʷməθkʷəy̓əm, Sḵwx̱wú7mesh, and səlilwətaʔɬ Lands.

First printing: 2022

Typeset in Minion
Printed and bound in Canada on 100% post-consumer recycled paper

Cover and interior design by Typesmith
Cover image via Flickr: Édouard Riou, "Ripples left by the waters of the Old
World," fig. 19 in Louis Figuier, *La Terre avant le déluge* (1863)

Talonbooks acknowledges the financial support of the Canada Council for
the Arts, the Government of Canada through the Canada Book Fund, and the
Province of British Columbia through the British Columbia Arts Council and
the Book Publishing Tax Credit.

LIBRARY AND ARCHIVES CANADA CATALOGUING IN PUBLICATION

Title: Untimely passages : dossiers from the other shore / by Jerry Zaslove ;
foreword by Samir Gandesha.

Names: Zaslove, Jerald, 1934–2021 author. | Gandesha, Samir (Samir Suresh),
1965– writer of foreword.

Description: Includes bibliographical references and index.

Identifiers: Canadiana 20210354607 | ISBN 9781772012606 (softcover)

Subjects: LCSH: Modernism (Literature) | LCSH: Postmodernism (Literature)
| LCSH: Modernism (Literature)—Europe. | LCSH: Postmodernism
(Literature)—Europe. | LCSH: Modernism (Literature)—North America. |
LCSH: Postmodernism (Literature)—North America.

Classification: LCC PN56.M54 Z37 2021 | DDC 808.8/0112—dc23

CONTENTS

Epigraphs are lifebuoys.
They show the ways to the other shores.

—JERRY ZASLOVE
from an early draft of the prologue

FOREWORD

Journeying towards Other Shores

by Samir Gandesha

This extraordinary volume of essays is structured by a constellation of *Stichwörter* (catchwords) and proper names that, taken together, form the politico-philosophical itinerary of a beloved teacher and colleague, scholar, public intellectual, art critic, community organizer, and virtuoso institution builder whose career spanned several decades at Simon Fraser University in Vancouver, Canada. Jerry Zaslove was the founding director of the Institute for the Humanities at SFU. It will celebrate its fortieth birthday in just over a year. This is a significant legacy.

Readers of this volume will come across: exile, colportage, Panzaic Principle, pariah, parvenu, *Nachträglichkeit* (afterwardness), materialism, chronotope, among others. They will also encounter, *inter alia*, proper names such as: Franz Kafka, Bertolt Brecht, Walter Benjamin, Siegfried Kracauer, Theodor W. Adorno, Fyodor Dostoevsky, Sigmund Freud, Herbert Read, Hannah Arendt, Simone Weil, Bohumil Hrabal, Mikhail Bakhtin, Jeff Wall, Karl Marx, G.W.F. Hegel, and Joy Kogawa.

The two most crucial such *Stichwörter* form the volume's title and are closely connected to two equally significant proper names. The first echoes *Untimely Meditations* (*Unzeitgemässe Betrachtungen*) which was published in 1876. This was Friedrich Nietzsche's early aesthetico-philosophical quartet of essays which were to prove so influential for postwar French writers such as Michel Foucault and Gilles Deleuze. The second *Stichwort*, "passages," is inspired, in part, by Walter Benjamin's vastly ambitious and promising, though tragically unfinished, interwar magnum opus on the Paris passages or arcades, which is often referred to simply as his *Passagen-Werk*, or *The Arcades Project*. In the image of the Paris arcades, Benjamin discerned capitalism's dream about its own self-overcoming through a paradoxical form of awakening.

Against certain historicist or teleological readings of Hegel and Marx respectively, Nietzsche and Benjamin deliberately sought to rupture the temporal continuum of history. Like the Roman god Janus, these two master stylists of the German language looked simultaneously backward and forward; they looked to past ages as a way of imagining radically different futures that broke decisively with a present they found impoverished. With Jacob Burckhardt, Nietzsche looked back to the Renaissance of Machiavelli, centred on the virtuosity of audacious and innovative form-bestowing activity, and forward, through a kind of history writing motivated not by an antiquarian interest in the past, even less in the monumental representation of political power, but an enhancement and amplification of the feeling of *life* he would later call the "will to power." In the baroque *Trauerspiel* or "mourning play," Benjamin discerned a conception of "natural-history" and a powerful allegorical vision fastened upon disorienting dialectical images, in which natural events, like the setting of the sun, presaged historical ones.

As the essays in *Untimely Passages* demonstrate, Jerry Zaslove shared very deeply Nietzsche's and Benjamin's aspirations. Like them, and in a manner that few have the courage to do, he defiantly resisted an increasingly manic compulsion to fall into lockstep with the times, with the apparent unfolding of historical "progress." And such dark, terrible times, filled with xenophobia, racism, the uncanny return of fascism, unceasing war, and impending ecological collapse, were eminently worthy, as Brecht might have said, of being out of step with. The red thread running throughout this diverse yet eminently coherent collection of essays is precisely a utopic horizon that could not be more antithetical to a world characterized by "capitalist realism," in which "it is easier to imagine the end of the world than the end of capitalism."* The times are dark, in part, because of the impoverishment of the imagination. The riches contained in this book constitute an antidote.

Zaslove's *untimeliness* is perhaps best summed up by his embrace of a commitment to what he called, in connection with Herbert Read, "anarcho-modernism." This peculiar term is not so strange or discordant as it may, at first, sound. Both anarchist politics and modernist aesthetics maintain an irrepressible impulsion towards independence and autonomy. This is an impulsion towards obeying no law other than one's own, be it the law that we legislate together collectively or the law fashioned by an artist (or artists) in their atelier.

The secret hope, of course, is that, as Marx put it in his *Grundrisse*, production would, itself, be organized according to the law of beauty, which is to say, beyond the estranged division of the world into artists and non-artists and the consequent ugliness of the seemingly inexorable law of value. Marx held out the promise that the law of the community would itself, one day, become beautiful and embody harmony and peace. In this achievement, the negation would, in other words, finally, be negated. This possibility of living in a world that was "*anarkhos*" or beyond any form of aliened authority was, I think, Zaslove's guiding spark, impulse, and spirit.

Anarcho-modernism, moreover, could be understood, to use a term Arendt borrowed from Bernard Lazare, as the "conscious pariah's" rebellion against the necessity of conforming to a

---

* This widely cited apophthegm is attributed by Mark Fisher to both Fredric Jameson and Slavoj Žižek; see Fisher, *Capitalist Realism: Is There No Alternative?* (Winchester, UK: Zer0 Books, 2009), 2.

timeliness that would make us all into parvenus – those sad, tired souls trying, usually with the use of sharp elbows, to get ahead, no matter the cost nor the consequences. The contemporary university, as Zaslove often made known, although not necessarily in so many words, is managed precisely by such types who will stop at nothing to advance their careers; conscious pariahs like Jerry Zaslove are few and far between and, doubtless, very much on the retreat. But if you look carefully enough, one can find them in the deep recesses of an institution that wants them gone. Just as it wanted him gone.

If he could be described, in his artistic, philosophical, and literary predilections and enthusiasms, as "cosmopolitan," a word best used advisedly, Zaslove was very much what Kwame Anthony Appiah has called a "*rooted* cosmopolitan."* He was grounded in the cultural landscape of his adopted hometown, Vancouver, the city in which he lived so much of his life. Like many of us fellow Vancouverites, he never lost an opportunity to register his profound "ambivalence" about the place. As one *passes* through the concrete and glass structures of the city, home to some of the most rapacious extractive industries on the face of the earth, the malingering symptoms of its violent roots in settler colonialism lurk around every corner from forced displacement and homelessness, bad drugs, brutally racist policing, and disposable architecture. As Zaslove showed over and again, "civilization" and "barbarism" could never be properly disentangled.

The idea of "passage," is not just spatial but also, of course, deeply temporal. Just as we pass through the environs of the city, time also passes us by. But let's be careful, however, not to understand time as simply passing in uniformly empty measures such as hours and days, months and years. Time is, rather, qualitative, filled with colour and darkness, melancholy, longing,

---

*   Kwame Anthony Appiah, "Cosmopolitan Patriots," in Martha C. Nussbaum, *For Love of Country? A New Democracy Forum on the Limits of Patriotism*, ed. Joshua Cohen for the *Boston Review* (Boston: Beacon Press), 22.

expectation, and hope. Present time is always being interrupted by the repressed and unfulfilled time of the past. Such unfulfilled time was the time of the *vanquished*; compare Lucan's epic poem *Pharsalia*: "The victorious cause pleased the gods, but the vanquished cause pleased Cato." The vanquished are not necessarily the *vanished*. The vanquished have not vanished precisely because they remain alive through their defeated hopes. Such hopes are bequeathed to us. Our solidarity with them is, therefore, anamnestic. The present is always, then, being disrupted by the utopian and redemptive longings of what both Martin Luther King Jr. and Walter Benjamin called the time of the "now" (*Jetztzeit*) that shatters those empty vessels and points somewhere else. This is what Jerry called "another shore."

In that very special other shore called Prague, one also finds passages, which is to say, arcades, albeit ones that do not shine quite as brightly as those that so fascinated Benjamin. Václav Cílek, a friend of Jerry's and a friend of mine, a veteran of the Prague Spring, a geologist by training, a surrealist by heart, and one of the most important contemporary Czech public intellectuals, would explain the significance of these arcades to visiting students in SFU's Prague Field School that Jerry founded.

Cílek would explain that the tourists walk through the passages like "this" (gesturing in a vertical axis); but we Czechs walk like "that" (gesturing in a horizontal axis). In Cílek's psychogeography lurked an existential question that each one of the students had to answer for themselves. How would *they* walk the passages? North to south or east to west? How would *they* pass the time? Would they swim in their schools with the current or against it? In every aspect of his *Leben* and *Lehre*, his life and his teaching, these were Jerry Zaslove's decisive questions.

To think of the passage of time and place together is to remember or hold in mind (*Eindenken*) that what is familiar or homely is always at the same time strange or uncanny. To truly experience home, one must also experience its loss, one must live the fate of the exile. "The past," as L.P. Hartley wrote in

The Go-Between, "is a foreign country; they do things differently there." To know our own place, our own shore, is to be oriented, as Zaslove reminds us repeatedly, to *another* shore, indeed, perhaps to *many other shores*.

In *Minima Moralia*, his brilliant collection of aphorisms on what he called "damaged life," Theodor W. Adorno notes in connection with Nietzsche's statement about his good fortune of never having owned a home: "For he who has no homeland, writing becomes a place to live." While in interwar exile, staying in an incongruous and disorienting Santa Monica, Adorno ultimately disavows the idea that it would ever be possible to live in one's writing. It must be said that Zaslove was never more alive than in his *teaching*, which was also, as one can see here, his *writing*.

Jerry Zaslove may have recently passed on to that ultimate "other shore," but in the scintillating pages that follow, he is very much still alive to us his friends, his colleagues, his students. He is very much still alive, above all, to his readers on whichever other shores they may dwell and to whichever other shores they may, ultimately, be journeying.

Editor's Note

Jerry Zaslove died on June 23, 2021, shortly after we had worked together on the final versions of all dossiers and chapters that comprise *Untimely Passages* and while we were completing editorial work on the following prologue. All efforts were made to respect Jerry's wishes and preferences with regard to final edits.

—CHARLES SIMARD

River Crossings

As for me, I do not want to stop being angry or suffering; this is so much a human right that I should not dream of surrendering it; my indignation is my protest; I do not want to make peace.

—ALEXANDER HERZEN, *From the Other Shore* ([1850] 1956), trans. Moura Budberg

This *Manual of Piety* is intended for the reader's use. It should not be senselessly wolfed down.

—BERTOLT BRECHT, *Manual of Piety* (1966), trans. Eric Bentley

Which ink is used to sign the death sentences – chemical ink, the India ink used in passports, the ink of fountain-pens, alizarin? No death sentence has ever been signed simply in pencil ... Only the simple, black graphite pencil is permitted. In Kolyma, graphite carries enormous responsibility.

—VARLAM SHALAMOV, *Kolyma Tales* (1994), trans. John Glad

A well-thought-out story doesn't need to resemble real life. Life itself tries with all its might to resemble a well-crafted story.

—ISAAC BABEL, "My First Fee" (ca. 1930), trans. Peter Constantine

Thesis I

A dedication and vade mecum as prologue to the building blocks of *Untimely Passages*

The organizing design of this collection of essays is shaped by compiling my essays into "dossiers." This prologue introduces the dossiers through thirteen theses, a strategy based on Wallace Stevens's undaunting conviction that there are "Thirteen Ways of Looking at a Blackbird."

> Among twenty snowy mountains,
> The only moving thing
> Was the eye of the blackbird. [1]

So then, the dossiers are a record of many of the essays I wrote over several decades, essays that relate to each other and can now be viewed as bridges across time. Some essays follow from invitations to contribute to collections, and some were initially conference presentations that were later revised for publication. While they may appear to be diverse essays, they are united by a common cause – romantic anti-capitalism informed by anarchism as a form of resistance and interventions into a culture that has come to be dangerous for humankind. Each "dossier" is an imaginary bridge for the river crossings that take the literature to the students and readers who are part of the journey. The thematic arrangement into theses here is intended to show some of the key ideas and figures that have shaped the essays; they are not meant as summaries, but as a palimpsest and primer.

The entire collection can also be imagined as a kind of *Bildungsroman*: not only a collection, but a recounting of a life in teaching and writing. It should be read as a double-sided humanist anarchism, in which the autonomy of the individual comes up against the institutions we live with, and which informs our responses to literature, but do not fully control our responses in the world of reaction, counterfeit, and bureaucratism.

Epigraphs in the prologue and within the dossiers are meant to stand as signpostings to the bridges. They can be likened to what readers find in Dickens's *Oliver Twist* are like short synopses to the chapters, small prologues to the dossiers, telling the reader what is coming. I think of them like the boards with texts used by a *Moritatensänger*, or barrel-organ singer, who announces to the street audience what is to follow in the play about to be performed, and reminds the spectators to pay attention to what is coming, especially to what can be learned along the way. The *Moritatensänger* points, shows, teaches, and also can improvise and intervene with commentaries or gestures, showing that there is always the unstaged in what is being staged.[2] The essays that make up *Untimely Passages* are a dramaturgical organization that "stages" the unstaged of a record of writing over a period of time. The essays are intended to be a record of writing and should also be understood as pedagogy resisting the critical positions that, over the years, tended to displace the works themselves in favour of critical preoccupations and critical schools.

Writing is an aesthetic praxis that comes out of my reading and teaching both as an aesthetic and personal journey, searching for the readers on the "other shores." I hoped the students (as readers) would come along with me. It is in this regard that I imagine the collected essays as a *Bildungsroman* that stresses the dialogue with the readers, who happen to be students (through a turn of time and through no fault of mine or theirs). Their presence is dialogical. They came; we studied and talked. So then again, this "pedagogy" on the bridges crossing rivers is also an accounting for *why we write*. Teaching the literature I loved, reread, and often taught again and again, along with the artworks I often brought into the aesthetic, is the groundwork of these untimely passages.

We live within the reality that teaching leaves behind no record of our crossing the rivers, because it is the material of a life-journey recorded just as it takes place. Teaching is the invisible prologue to the writing. The good fortune: to reread literature that one knows makes a difference in one's life if the reader is prepared to follow the author. This is what Wayne Burns, in one of the essays in this collection, calls the "Panzaic" illumination after Sancho Panza, always turning Don Quixote's ideals into actual, lived experiences. In an exemplary passage reflecting Cervantes's aesthetic, Sancho describes and instructs Don Quixote about how goats cross a river rather than speculating on how many there are, which Don Quixote wants him to; what is important to Sancho: *Let's get on with the story*. Sancho lives with what Siegfried Kracauer describes in *History: The Last Things before the Last* as the "side-by-side principle":

> Sancho Panza succeeded in the course of years, by devouring a great number of romances of chivalry and adventure in the evening and night hours, in so diverting from him his demon, whom he later called Don Quixote, that his demon thereupon set out in perfect freedom on the maddest exploits, which, however, for the lack of a preordained object, which should have been Sancho Panza himself, harmed nobody. [3]

The present prologue identifies many of the "dramaturgical motifs" in the spirit of Kracauer's side-by-side principle. It is meant to be read novelistically, in which the storyteller is unannounced in each of the numbered "theses." While it is true, according to Heraclitus, that we can't "step into the same river twice," we can still cross to the other shores and watch the river flowing and can even cross back again and again. We build bridges to the other sides, where there are paths.

In chapter 14 of *Oliver Twist*, the young ward arrives at Mr. Brownlow's safe harbour and the following conversation occurs:

"How should you like to grow up a clever man, and write books, eh?"

"I think I would rather read them, sir," replied Oliver.

"What! wouldn't you like to be a book-writer?" said the old gentleman.

Oliver considered a little while; and at last said, he should think it would be a much better thing to be a bookseller ...

"Well, well," said the old gentleman ... "Don't be afraid! We won't make an author of you, while there's an honest trade to be learnt, or brickmaking to turn to."[4]

The authors in my life are the lifebuoys that point to the other shores where readers and writers lived. Others have been here before me and have left the lifebuoys, marking how the history we read also reads us. The German language has a word to designate someone's personal reading history: *Belesenheit*, the reading in us, which is like memory coming back nameless again and again. These authors – to change to another metaphor – were resistances to the culture that formed us. I also think of the essays as radical reflections on the history of art and literature, in the spirit of those who influenced me and the students who came along with me and the authors.

I like to think that in years of reading, writing, and teaching, one becomes something of a *colporteur* (see below). One reads books, speaks through them, they speak through us, then, if fortunate, we write about them, and if more fortunate, we read them again and again. Because teaching can also be compared to how artists look at painters who came before them and are influenced by them, not by imitation, but by learning through them. Again, and again.

Books may, on rereading them, become strange to us. We are colporteurs of our own reading. Have we read this before? And do we write about our reading and put our name to what we write? Siegfried Kracauer, about whom I write, by my rough count, used thirty-one different pseudonyms in signing his essays and articles in Weimar Germany's *Frankfurter Zeitung*. He fled the Nazis and, going into exile in the United States at a late age, he avoided mentioning his birthday or his age. He described a life lived in the regions of the "exterritorial." In my writing, life, and thinking, exile becomes a conceptual and aesthetic "thesis."[5]

So then, this "prologue" does not point to a "method," but bears witness to the passages in time, to the writing and teaching about the long history of crises of modernism that accompanied me. Tolstoy wrote a diary during the 1840s he named "A History of Yesterday"; it was also the history of the day before yesterday, and the day before that, because integrating his personal history as a record is lived more fully – Panzaically – through the characters in the novels he brings to life. "Yesterday" failed the test of time because there were too many of those yesterdays, too many digressions to account for, too many delusions to unpack, too much staging to "plot" and "unplot." While reading a novel, Anna Karenina suddenly sees Vronsky, and that novel's ending will change for her because of her unexpected encounter with Vronsky and what the encounter will tell her and the reader about reading novels and about her inner life. The reader who looks for critical principles will find them working against the grain by my resisting the call of professionalism.[6]

Recounting one's reading and writing, then, is a process in which we think about reading and writing in our lives. Recounting is not reversible time or time that has prognostic value, but reveals the "unpast" – that is, a sedimented history. We can call it the Anna Karenina principle.

How does one become a "collector" of one's own writing? Collecting one's own works is an exercise in living with distance and nearness, not unlike the *flâneur* whose purpose, in Walter Benjamin's words, is the very purpose of life, to ask implicitly: "What do you think has gone here?"[7] The question opens the breeding grounds of collecting as a form of memory-making and recounting.

I write about "posthumous memory" in several essays. In this prologue, I mark out the configurations and motifs as if it were a musical score or prelude, laying out the themes and chords that remind me how, in my own writing, I "constantly wish to start over," as André Green, one of my "lifebuoy markers," writes below.

This prologue is then an antechamber. It can be understood, as well, how these essays have been informed and influenced by my teaching and my relationship to the subject and the classes, and the weight of both the city and university where I have lived since leaving the United States for Canada in 1965 to a new Simon Fraser University. Other essays, written more directly about "teaching the city," are another story of river crossings and may one day comprise a separate collection of essays.

I think of the collection in the fashion of a tableau that reflects on the turning points in the crises of modernism, which marks the basis of my aesthetic. That is why I often express how the "unpast" and "posthumous memory" are markers of time and memory, loss and reparation, living in the transition zones of modernism that inform my reading.

The "untimely meditations" understood in a Nietzschean spirit are writings by a stowaway in the Institutions, with leanings towards anarchistic other shores. They do not resist the polemical. They speak to the idea that all writing is composed of an "authorial mask" of the "dialogical-poetic" relationship with the reader, which Mikhail Bakhtin expresses as the aesthetic "authorial mask": "It is customary to speak about the authorial mask. But in which utterances (speech acts) is there a face not a mask, that is, no authorship?"[8] Lessons in remembrance do not mean becoming "gravediggers of the present, knowing the right time to remember and forget."[9]

With *Speech Genres and Other Essays* (1979), Bakhtin became an influence and inspiration not only for the aesthetic of the novel, but his language world; the "image of language" is the expression of the individual who thinks within the novel as a form of being. Bakhtin lived through the crisis in the aesthetic of the novel and the humanities from Rabelais to Dostoevsky. Bakhtin's understanding of the author's doubleness lies in

> the sense that [the author] directs all words to others' voices, including to the image of the author (and to other authorial masks). Perhaps any literal, single-voiced word is naive and unsuitable for authentic creativity. Any truly creative voice can only be the second voice in the discourse. Only the second voice – pure relationship – can be completely objectless and not cast a figural, substantive shadow. The writer is a person who is able to work in a language while standing outside language, who has the gift of indirect speaking. [10]

Similarly, on looking at one's writing and thinking about authorship and the critical emotions that became the "figural" bridging from one author to another, one also looks at paintings through the painters who have looked at other painters. On looking back, it can appear that the written may be likened to a recording listening to "someone else," even while that someone else is familiar but seems alien. By showing correspondences in these essays, continuities and departures, we also see the alibis we construct, trying to make sense of the world with readers who are "on other shores" – the addressees. For this reason, I was always interested in how reading shaped cultural life, thus my interest in Bakhtin, the novel, the Menippean world of the comic grotesque, and the leaking boundaries explored in the essays in dossier III, "Streets and Borders: Vancouver and Elsewhere."

So then, the essays of *Untimely Passages* are not ordered chronologically. Chronology is inevitably found throughout the entire book, if the reader wishes to see that happen. However, the image I use gathering the essays is that of the colporteur – a ragpicker who sorts the goods according to some principle that becomes apparent in time, but isn't staged. In this regard the collection is a memoir in a time of unrelenting capitalist expansion, when romantic libertarian anarchism risks being relegated to a historical backwater.

To be sure, there is an academic "through line" in the essays: teaching and research in comparative literature in a broad framework of world literature grounded in European literature and the aesthetics and politics of critical theory of the Frankfurt School and proto-anarchist thought. The collection is a chronicle bearing witness to the crises of modernism that accompanied my teaching and writing about European literature.

Because I have been a settler in Canada since 1965, the tableau reflects on the turning points and breeding grounds in the crises of modernism, the basis of my anarcho-modernist aesthetic – a chronicle of writing that peers across the passages to the "other sides" against the grain of the times. "Against the grain" means resistance to the deadly history of capitalism that accompanies us in life adjacent to and within the institutions of literature. The "dossiers" gathered here hope that writing is not written on blotting paper. The assumption: that the outside is also inside.

Time writes into the essay as a form of memory-construction: my essays are presented as a form of remembrance or *Eingedenken*, which in German roughly translates as "bearing in mind," or "let's remember" – and we had better not forget that memory lives in and changes over different periods of time and leaks through boundaries of time, reflecting time and place. So then, the collection should also be understood as a tableau of "*untimely meditations*" through a lifeline that connects apparently distinct essays to each other. [11]

Meditations are also mutations! Time is the most "modern" of aesthetic conditions: the flight of the "modern" into time past and not knowing what is yet to be foreseen is the *crisis* of historicism which cannot predict the present. Indeed, the crisis of modernity lies squarely where it becomes apparent that history could not predict the violence of states and violence-making societies, especially as humans formed liberal institutions that, while inventing forms of protective colouration, legitimated powerful states. Thus, the essays are constellations against domination, related to the crisis of the individual facing the sedimented violence of modern life.

I often reflect upon time, memory, and inbuilt violence with reference to Theodor W. Adorno, Walter Benjamin, and the categories of thought that relate to the commodity becoming commodity fetishism under the star of exchange value, and the interlocking nature of the present with what has been lost in the sedimented crises of modern times.

So, while *Untimely Passages* is a chronicle that peers across the passages to the other sides, integrating reading and writing into one's life, my "against the grain" is a form of anarchism and bears footprints of resistance to the deadly history of capitalism that accompanies us. However, the reader deserves a little more.

Assembling is itself a construction of form, a building. In the words of psychoanalyst André Green, writing is "a strange act, as unnecessary as it is unpredictable, but for the writer writing is also as tyrannical as it is inevitable." [12] I recall the great American literary critic Alfred Kazin saying that writing is a "burning into the world ... I write in order to become that which I write. I write in order to lay claim to what I would like to become. The hand I write with is already flexed to take possession." [13] That says it well, and also fits for those writers I write about. Viktor Shklovsky can help. He points out that Dante's "circles of the inferno" are not just a literary structure, but "are traces of the various perceptions of time during the era of the great city of Florence"; [14] Shklovsky means that people lived within the form of the city as if in delusion and confinement. Form recapitulates and demands expression of delusion and confinement.

Writing these essays, however, has meant living side-by-side with the bureaucratic institutions of Universities that only seem to be "anti-bureaucratic" when we feel free inside the classrooms. We try to hold on to the freedom of the autonomous artwork and the protective colouration it gives to us when we learn that the subjective element is in the individual author, which can also be understood, in a somewhat Darwinian sense, as camouflage forming a protective barrier against the merging of thing and nature; put another way, the work of art struggles against becoming a "thing."

We are embattled in a damaged culture in which we might not recognize the defeated from the victors, the radical humanists from the false prophets, the diagnostic from the expressive, and the limits of accommodation and resistance to the twists and turns of culture, even while we are wondering about those theories of literature that make some authors obsolete and some worth defending and rediscovering. In this regard, I write against the commodification of writing and schooling and the bureaucratization of literacy. [15]

So then, the essays are diagnostic commitments to the subjects that were important to me and which, by their very nature, will always feel unfinished. They address what may appear to be different subjects, but they are about authors and subjects that draw me to them and that I have come back to again and again, just as memory comes back again and again, often without a name. In the allotted teaching "hours" given to us as privileged teachers, each course was like a book in the making. The "hours" given to teaching were shadowed by unfinished time. One might feel like Emma Bovary looking towards Paris, the promised land: there is always more, always something on the other side of the river. There was always a Monsieur Homais in the hallways.

On the other hand, the essays are my *Stundenbuch* or *Hauspostille*, a "breviary." I'll explain.

A *Stundenbuch* is in German a book of hours, a personal and secular "breviary" that is both a history and memoir of lived experience. Breviaries are carried by the book peddlers, those who, metaphorically and historically, carry and deliver books in order to distribute the objects fallen by the wayside as debris, and which can be picked up and collected for a while. A likeness of the novelist's "*I* voice" is in this prologue, as well as the image of the colporteur. Breviaries are the subject of dossier V, a postlude. The "thematic" organization of the prologue which shows the raw materials in the essays is a guide and a friendly negotiation with the readers.

The image of the colporteur is a thin disguise for my "radical humanism" loosely informed by anarchism – a thread in my politics which I apply to the critique of traditions of culture where I have found traces of a live natural anarchism. In other words: resistances.

Some alert readers might see in Hegel's "Owl of Minerva" – the marvellous image of the owl that opens its wings and flies only at dusk. [16] At dusk, we realize an image of time in the construction of historical consciousness *in oneself as a historical being* who, in life, is more than the sum of its parts. About one's life in writing, one might often foolishly feel it has been a prognostication of what was and what will come, because prognostication can't be helped in searching for readers and students. Children and authors of Enlightenment: prognostication also means coming to terms with the repressed, the unpast, because Hegel's "owl" emerges in order to carry literature and both conscious and unconscious qualities of the aesthetic that mark how literature becomes resistance to the inevitable, even by fooling us through the formulaic at every level of culture.

Bertolt Brecht published a book of "devotions," *Hauspostille* (1927). They were "instructions for living" in dark times. In this book, the headnotes to each of the dossiers act as my "Breviaries." [17]

Thesis II

A pause for Hegel's Owl: We need a meta-dedication to imaginary readers – to those ideal readers we might never know

The ideal readers of the essays: the service nomads, chimerical patriots of the local neighbourhoods; the exiles, migrants, strangers, members of the intelligentsia who are not bureaucrats; apprentices who were at one time other than what they are now; the unemployed and poorly served/employed; those whose work barely counts; those who carry the cultural memory of smaller nations and the outlying regions within their hearts, the insiders who are really outsiders but can't change their jobs; hybrids, dropouts, anarchists, tricksters, utopians, visionaries, mystics, psychoanalysts, parasitic and natural anarchists; also those who once were and might still be called "humanists," who are in peril now for using that name; and those who do not know they are anarchists until something strange happens and they think that they will be stopped in their tracks for thinking like that; those who make pictures, and those restless with the arts and culture, and those who in the name of the dearth of cultural memory are building cities while searching for what is missing and might know where to look for it and the children of the next generation; those who don't know what they might create when we are not looking.

Thesis III

So then: Yes, I know that the imaginary readers listed above were produced in a university – the university that is a calling card for entrance and exit in and from the wandering institutions of culture.

Institutions of Enlightenment are the calling card of "advanced" capitalism that provide protective colouration for literature teaching. The avant-garde has always had to reinvent modernism, despite the self-consciousness of its failure to release culture from the unpredictable shadowing of history and culture. We know that "avant-garde" feeds and thrives on unpredictability and has different histories depending on national traditions. Russian futurism and constructivism, for example, "were utopian and linked to the mechanical age, and in this sense, they played the negation game, and yet affirmed at the same moment the autonomy of art." [18] This is also true of many others, namely Duchamp, Brecht, Chaplin, Vertov, Malevich, Akhmatova, Faulkner, Lawrence, Woolf, Stevens, Adorno, Benjamin, Klee, Jeff Wall ... – all have been artistic models for me. [19] The spectres of experience and memory become the mark of the not-yet-final nature and praxis of modern art. Dossier V in this collection recounts the *situations* of writing into my preoccupation with anarchism and the inbuilt world of culture. [20]

But wait: If this text "recounts," then it is also a memoir of a way of reading and a manual of survival – the protective colourations that enabled me to locate those moments illuminating the specific intellectual experience I am compelled to recall. The essays on Boris Pasternak, W.G. Sebald, and Siegfried Kracauer address the essay and novel genres as a literature of unmasking, combining memoration and this book's dossiers as "constellations." [21] The imaginary addressees are Mercurians, a "chronotope" in Bakhtin's aesthetic, a time and place that lives through the power of resistance and openness to experience that may be hidden, and they are breathing holes as well. The fragments are like individuals which the literature picks up and assemble in time in the aesthetic of the novel. [22] In 1967 I wrote an essay titled "Counterfeit and the Use of Literature," which came out of my study of Nikolai Gogol and *poshlost*, meaning self-satisfied mediocrity or moral cheesiness in Russian and European literature. [23] I wrote then:

> Artistic experience is neither imitation of reality nor symbolic projection, but is an unmasking and a negation in bitter conflict with all those repressive and inhibiting experiences whose nature is never fully known until artistic creation disturbs the surfaces of assent to the bad infinity of a society in which the formalist idealization of ambiguity retreats from this conflict by creating a dualism between opposing forces, and reveals modes and contents of thought which transcend the codified patterns of use and validation. Dialectical thought does not invent these contents ... it recovers tabooed meanings and thus appears almost as a return to the conscious liberation of the repressed. [24]

While I have often changed the register of what I wrote in 1967, it is a good place to remind the reader of the embattled breeding grounds and the demands to understand the individual, and the taboo on the individual, and to note what does not "fit in." Paramount in this context is the influence of Adorno, who opposed the total domination of "method" and the use of concepts "to expunge the untamed sphere placed under a taboo by the world of concepts." [25]

Thesis IV

So then. There's the classroom: a working place, a salon, in the streets' vicinity, although it remains contained in the university – a monastery perched on a hill. The classroom is about the "past in the future": one eye on the future in the past, and a defence against compartmentalization because of the interventions into the present that speak through the work of art. If the classroom is only academic intellectual experience, only theory, *so be it.* It's not my fault we need to address theory because – *on the other hand* – there are movements and theoretical figures who have accompanied me. Could it be otherwise? Yet, this is not a book about theory. More to the point, I engage an unfashionable, humanistic *Bildung* and how the novel works out the autonomy of the vanishing individual that Wayne Burns addresses in *The Panzaic Principle*. Sancho Panza is one of the figurative ideas in Adorno and Horkheimer's *Dialectic of Enlightenment* that I used in my 1967 study of Gogol and the ideology of *poshlost*.[26] The nature of the "untimely" present of the individual is a constant undercurrent in modernism, in which we witness the demise of individuals and the "coldness that permits a person to watch even the most extreme actions because, in accordance with the principal of individualism, it is felt to be of no concern to himself or herself; an attitude which culminates in Auschwitz and everything associated with it, events that would not be possible in the absence of such a principle."[27] Preoccupation with accommodation, resistance, and the administered world that produced Auschwitz has accompanied me throughout these essays.

The titles of the dossiers extend the "untimely meditations" of Adorno's and Horkheimer's Enlightenment Project, shadowed by Nietzsche's own *Untimely Meditations*, as well as by Kierkegaard, the subject of Adorno's *Kierkegaard: Construction of the Aesthetic* (1933), his first philosophical study. The study appeared on the day Hitler declared a national emergency, as if to prove Adorno's thesis that history turns our temporal inner lives into "power protected inwardness"[28] – a matter undertaken in many of my essays.

The "inner person" became the subject of the ideological and experiential substance of the novel form. The *I* voice, even in its various forms, felt as an experience of fate. As Adorno says in many essays: "The course of the world is still essentially one of individuation. We learn that the individual with impulses and feelings is still the equal of fate, that the inner person is still directly capable of something,"[29] even as the individual becomes a subject of cheap by-products of the culture itself. So then, there are dossiers here on Exiles, Pedlars, Tricksters, Utopians.

The reader is forewarned: Do not expect a final "blow" as recounted in the Brothers Grimm's prescient fable, "The Brave Little Tailor," in which a tailor kills seven flies with one blow to prove to his sons how to succeed in life forever after. The tailor in the fable is the "*I* narrator." While telling everyone his story, he begins to realize that when his sons grow up to be men and become tailors like himself and are able to kill seven flies with one blow, they might conquer the world as victors – but they will survive only when they learn to improvise. It is the story of an anarcho-trickster mentality that protects us from our ideals and what has been done to children by adults who initiate children, knowingly or not, into the culture. The essays cross and recross this river of initiation into authority and improvisation against authority.

Thesis V

The aesthetic of the "shudder" of and in "marginal domains"

My essays side with the world's trickster stories, which are, as Benjamin and others famously mused: "History written by the victors, not the vanquished." For the underdogs of history, if they survive "history as it really is," history will not be provided with providential hope. Benjamin's image of the historical underdog reads history as writing on a blotting pad, blurring the outlines of emotion and value; the blotting pad signifies loss of the outline, the realization that capitalism will never die of its own natural death. If it does, it may take us all with it, unless we understand how art will tell us whether we are victorious or vanquished, and whether or not we act "differently from how it was planned or hoped … [or] if history is made in the short run by the victors, [or whether] historical gains in knowledge stem in the long run from the vanquished." [30]

Along the way are many vanquished art movements. Cubism, montage, collage, architectonic arrangements of music are examples of the art movements that, in Adorno's words, give us a "shudder," by overcoming pre-re-established harmonies which aim to possess us. We experience the disharmonies by living restlessly with the freedom of the autonomous work; but one is compelled to resist, being embattled by a philosophy that by definition cannot succeed, that is, a philosophy that takes aim at oneself. Nietzsche and then Adorno allied against the "ratio" of the bourgeois class that "had smashed the feudal order and its intellectual reflex, scholastic ontology [and] panicked at the sight of subsequent ruins, its own creation ... fears shaped its response."[31] Adorno, again, in his *Aesthetic Theory*:

> Ultimately, aesthetic comportment is to be defined as the capacity to shudder, as if goose bumps were the first aesthetic image. What later came to be called subjectivity, freeing itself from the blind anxiety of the shudder, is at the same time the shudder's own development; life in the subject is nothing but what shudders, the reaction to the total spell that transcends the spell. Consciousness without shudder is reified consciousness. That shudder which subjectivity stirs without yet being subjectivity is the act of being touched by the other. Aesthetic comportment assimilates itself to that other rather than subordinating it, [joining] eros and knowledge.[32]

Mikhail Bakhtin became an inspiration in thinking about the novel, Russian literature, and an image of language in which the novel as a form of life is answerable to the reader who is in dialogue with the novel. The "passage of time" in the novel leads us to the work of art as an image of reality that is by definition "untimely." Literature and writing about literature and art is not a theodicy or a last judgment, even though critical schools may make final judgments.

History shadows the dreamworld of the image. I bear in mind that "image" is related to the *eidos*, which points to the "idea" as both a *figuration* and *fragmentation*. "Figurations" come alive artistically in the interstices and resistances; they are places of experiences where the intangible lurks and lives. We can call these epochs of time "topistic structures of mutual immanence." Immanence points to "radical doubt" and the autonomy of the work of art, which is a foundation of my aesthetic.[33]

> Here it becomes evident that the hallmark of the new type of researcher is not the eye for the "all-encompassing whole" or the eye for the "comprehensive context" (which mediocrity has claimed for itself), but rather the capacity to be at home in marginal domains. [34]
>
> Focus on the "genuine" hidden in the interstices between dogmatized beliefs of the world, this establishing tradition of lost causes; giving names to the hitherto unnamed. [35]

Thesis VI

Each thesis leads to the dossiers as imaginary companions

The headnotes to the dossiers are like Benjamin's "architectonics" of quotations or building blocks in his unfinished *Arcades Project*. I imagine them as a user's manual of sorts, a breviary. They remind me of Osip Mandelstam's phrase in *The Noise of Time*, that writing is the "phenomenon of the impulse and the text." [36] I should hope that in the future, scholars will indeed study the coordination of "the impulse and the text":

> Dante's cantos are scores for a particular chemical orchestra in which the external ear can easily distinguish comparisons identical with the impulses and solo parts, that is, the arias and ariosos, peculiar self-avowals, self-flagellations or autobiographies, sometimes brief and capable of fitting into the palm of the hand, sometimes lapidary, like a tombstone inscription, sometimes unrolled like a certificate awarded by some medieval university, sometimes well developed, articulated, and capable of achieving a dramatic, operatic fullness. [37]

Think of essay writing side by side with peddling and colportage. Essays travel well in periods of migration and exile, and they accompany itinerant readers who come as strangers: imaginary companions. A new kind of research. Think of booksellers who are eagerly awaited by villagers and city dwellers along with the books for sale; they bring the news from the "other shores." Even the guilds wanted to ban the pedlars who arrived as strangers: who knew how trustworthy they were or the bad news they brought as what Mandelstam called "rancid, poisoned honey."

Book readers are also untimely: they come and go, momentarily taking leave from books and writers, then come back. Leave-taking and returning is the threshold of the inner life of reading, as well as of exile, a subject of dossier IV.

There is a gnostic element of loss attached to reading and writing: how we recover what is lost marks both the anarchism and Marxism in my life and times, as well as the feeling of a leap into "new time" and a new concept of the human. The eschatological nature of this leap into new time from exhausted, used-up time (in other words, to free "frozen time" from failed time) is an idea that has not been "lost" on many untimely readers.[38] Nietzsche, in *Untimely Meditations*, writes that "a man who wanted to feel historically through and through would be like one forcibly deprived of sleep, or an animal that had to live only by rumination and ever repeated rumination."[39]

Ruminations about essayistic writing are also "meditations," thinking about thinking, which is why in this prologue I use refrains like "So be it," "So then," and other similar phrases, links, transitions, and pauses. Thinking in writing, writing in thinking is, as Benjamin felt throughout his writing, pointing to the fact that life is a form of collecting and working in an archive of memory built like an archival drawer, where the materials in the "drawers" of memory are ways to "preserve and catalogue everything," all within the struggle against "dispersion" of the interior experience of memory and the productive disorder of the *mémoire involontaire*. Benjamin's manifesto on "The Collector" in the *Arcades* explains why dispersive connections open meanings:

Perhaps the most deeply hidden motive of the person who collects can be described this way: he takes up the struggle against
dispersion. Right from the start, the great collector is struck by the
confusion, by the scatter, in which the things of the world are found.
It is the same spectacle that so preoccupied the men of the Baroque;
in particular, the world image of the allegorist cannot be explained
apart from the passionate, distraught concern with this spectacle.
The allegorist is, as it were, the polar opposite of the collector ...
The collector, by contrast, brings together what belongs together,
by keeping in mind their affinities and their succession in time, he
can eventually furnish intonation about his objects. [40]

Thesis VII

So sein. Let us move on.

The structure of the prologue can be seen as an architectonics
of building blocks – a user's manual about "the act of writing
[which] is a strange act," to quote André Green once more. For
Green, writing is a materialist act in the world: writing thought in
images is both a wound and a loss, like composing music whose
origins and completion in time remain unknown until the composition; this is not language as such, because writing and music
do not emerge out of concepts.

> The act of writing is a strange act, as unnecessary as it is unpredict-
> able, but for the writer it is also as tyrannical as it is inevitable ...
> the work of writing presupposes a wound and a loss, a work of
> mourning, of which the text is the transformation into a ficti-
> tious positivity ... Pseudo, because this victory can only last for
> a limited time, because it is always contested by the author ...
> who constantly wishes to start over, and thus to deny what he has
> already done, to deny in any case that the result, satisfying as it
> might seem, should be taken as the final product ... And we will
> then have to begin anew with another work by the same author

> or by another. Reading and writing constitute an uninterrupted work of mourning. [41]

The bridges help us find lost objects. We begin anew. Back and forth. Bridging silences, they are guides like the "periegetes," the Greek tour guides "who led people around, giving commentaries on whatever was worth seeing." [42] It is transference of lost objects stamped by time. [43] It is crossing many rivers where exiles tread, crossing the Russian rivers where the exiles went, east, west, south, and north, and where, in the midst of the revolution, Victor Serge, the anarchist and social-revolutionary exile, returned to Russia and Stalingrad, carrying his river-history with him from East-West to Mexico:

> One could no longer believe that there was still war, death, hunger, fear, lice. The river, immensely free between its granite banks, carried along huge blocks of ice. [The floes] moved with soft crunching sounds downstream from northern lakes toward the sea now reopened to the lapping waves, to the living lights beading the foam, to the warm Gulf Stream breezes which starting from the Yucatan and the Floridas, passed over the Atlantic, the fjords of Norway and the plains of Sweden, and came to rest on our icy shores. Atop the golden spire of the Admiralty Building a tiny gilded ship, as light and distinct as an idea, sailed through the sky. The colors of the red flags revived. [44]

Serge thinks always of the political revolutionaries, together with poets like Anna Akhmatova and Osip Mandelstam, who crossed many Russian rivers, and the Russians who, like Dostoevsky, did not "survive the Revolution and the political scruples and incomplete massacres." [45] Throughout, I link the idea of "other shores" with expressions such as *on the other hand*, which imply of course *on the one hand* and *on the other hand*. I also use the German phrase *so sein*, which means, in the way I use it, "so be it," or "so there it is now," or in the vernacular, "wait, let's try this for a while." These expressions are intended to show transitions, and I play with transitions because alive-openness is part of the story of essay writing: *Well, so be it!* The dossiers are *situations of writing*, what Adorno named "negative dialectics," whose "musicality" can take different forms:

> So when I speak here of negative dialectics ... what you should be on the lookout for [is] not a kind of intellectual scaffolding that in fact you will seek in vain ... and in this respect Marx was undoubtedly right to maintain that the forces of production, in other words human energies, and their extension in technology, have a tendency of their own to overcome the limits that have been set by society. [46]

Adorno's devastating attacks on culture are linked to Hobbes's *Leviathan* and to the Party State as an arm extending into mass culture. This leads to the betrayals of the intellectuals as such – the intelligentsia acting as a class. Therefore, I had to ask: Why do we write and link writing to the readings we love? We search for that productive understanding. Our readings must be unsettled because the reader is addressed not as that which is missing, *but as that who is listening* for the "maybe so" through their mutual resistance to the culture. We do that, provisionally, by withholding assent to the culture. Following Adorno, writing for the unpast in the present is work in "productive understanding." This is also the "Mercurian understanding" that does not yield to ideology a helping hand, either to blind obedience or to apocalyptical fantasies.

Thesis VIII

Leave-taking and exile

Leave-taking and exile express the need to keep questions open in order to find our resistance to things as they are; I have always looked at the counterfeit that passes as mere existence in order to find the genuine and live with it as long as we can. Writing searches through sublimation, and is an *affect*, a *feeling*. André Green writes: "The aims of both the unconscious and the ego come together in the compulsion to write ... [One] feels hardly free to write or not to write: I must write to contribute to the increase of knowledge and to maintain a self-image that I can recognize" – a discipline that imposes on us the goals that are not always freely chosen when the work of writing is also work against the culture industry. [47] This, as I say in many different ways, is a way to think with and about romantic anti-capitalism: an anarchism by another name, or a semantics of an anarchist aesthetics, one can say. Green's and Adorno's aesthetics influence how we can think of art as double-voiced resistance to culture; we are both in and out of culture. *Minima Moralia* is Adorno's exile testament about the situation of writing in exile. For writing is a guide to understanding the exile's living as a stranger and bystander in culture; his words explain why I have written on exile, and return, or no-return, to institutions of culture. *Yet, wait:* one is more than a bystander.

[*Protection help and counsel assistance and advice:*]
Every intellectual in emigration is, without exception, damaged, and if one does not wish to be taught a cruel lesson behind the airtight doors of one's self-esteem, would do well to recognize ... Between the reproduction of one's own life under the monopoly of mass culture and impartial, responsible work, there yawns irreconcilable breach. One's language has been expropriated, and the historical taproot from which one derived their powers of cognition has been sapped ... Only a very few have, of course, an appropriate craft at their disposal. Most of those who climb aboard are threatened with starvation or madness. [48]

Making music "erases singularity, but making writing knows something else: that writing is part reverie, dream, and historical emergency, yet is situational in its enigmatic immediacy to the unrecounted historical events that come to view after the writing is done."[49] Did I know that Kafka's mother died one day before the day I was born? If Kafka had lived as long as my grandfather, he would have been a contemporary in my life. In other words, writing creates forbearers and missing links. Other analogies could be made here with the outsides that are also insides; these do come along with the unpast and the non-contemporary and the continuum of striving for presentation, not just representation. My generation came into history and life when Hitler became Nazi Chancellor of Germany; the Soviet State became the ideal for many in my lifetime. That world casts a shadow over my teaching and writing.

Thesis IX

Climbing aboard the ship of the institutions

Does one do that? Thomas Bernhard calls writing "gathering evidence"; he despised writing an autobiography, but he did write an account of his writing.[50] Kafka knew well the torment of writing and lived out his "sense of failure" in the face of the world. Writing in Kafka's life was both an obstacle and a comic form of redemption. Paul Valéry, a touchstone for both Adorno and Benjamin, wrote:

> It often occurs that a poet constructs a lengthy poem on the basis of a single line … The line comes to him in a state of mind resembling a dream, as a discrete unit … Now it is a matter of making a poem out of this line. And this is where the novel begins. There is the process of elaboration, fitting the parts together, etc., and the difficulty lies in finding one's way back to the state of mind that is worthy of the beginning. The devil is in the continuation.[51]

So then: Kafka is a guide and stands often at the door of the essays. "Mr. Kafka is at the door," writes Bohumil Hrabal:

Every morning my landlord enters my room on tiptoe. I can hear his footsteps. The room is so long that you could ride a bicycle from the door to my bed. My landlord leans over me, turns, signals to someone in the doorway and says: "Mr. Kafka here" ... Sometimes after such an awakening, I get to thinking: supposing my landlord came to wake me and announce my presence and I weren't there? [52]

It is inevitable that the institutions that house modern life "gather evidence" for what is left over *for the future of the past.* They are at the door. What is "left over" is the "what is missing" that we know is "at the door." Does that make me a Hegelian? Yes and no. Brecht thought Hegel was a great comedian. It is "the magnitude of the task" facing the writer of the "novel" when the "novel" becomes the coded word for the agony and fulfillment of self-creation.

Thesis X

Verbal-ideological speech in transient time

So then: Writing lives in shelterlessness. [53] We are exposed. Self-reflections about modernism and modernity without a critique of Institutions is not possible. This is the essayist's fate: it is the "situation of writing" as Sartre lived it. The reader will see that Bakhtin's vision of writing and language cannot be separated from speech; Bakhtin describes writing "in a Russian way" as the world of the "semiosphere," that is, an "image of language." Writing is the bastard brother and sister of the novel. The actuality of language is its "*so sein,*" the shifts in its here-and-now presence in the world; *so sein,* or "so be it," works its way into what is said but also reveals what cannot be said quickly, which becomes visible in the totality of the image of language. Following Bakhtin, I call the essays in this volume examples of "verbal-ideological speech."

Every essay written over these years is related to the courses that walked through the door with actual students. They are my public world. Courses are essays in waiting: genres of "verbal-ideological speech." Each course I have taught gave me the freedom to explore *along* the other shores with the students who came with me. Teaching links us to the hearts of the works we read. This is the discourse of the verbal-ideological, in which the speech and the literature come to performance of "ideological time" within the chronotope of the classroom. The classroom is both in time and out of time. It is a place of transience, and manifests the double-sidedness of time. Nietzsche gazed at the herds of animals watching him; the beast, he observed, is not speaking of its happiness, because the beast forgets what it wished to say, so "the man is left to wonder that he has not learned to forget and hangs onto the past." [54]

Here's the historical point: in the "age" of modernism, when we dared to believe in the promise that through literature and art there was an anthropology of the modern, both the weight of the past and of resisting the past feared to become "the gravedigger of the present," methods experiencing the art of the modern itself and the crisis of historical understanding of the "sedimented" nature of time and an emerging crisis of social nothingness – a social death caused by the Institutionalization of "crisis" itself. No theory of history before the Enlightenment could account for the nature of this crisis that permeated the humanities and the immanence of the work of art as a form of life. This is in relationship to the individual, which is how the Hungarian German art historian and sociologist Arnold Hauser, a major influence on how I think about the individual and the social history of art, puts the issue to the dialectics of the modern:

> In no other field of spiritual activity does the individual, with his [*sic*] own particular aims and powers, play so important and striking a part as he plays in art. Nor is there any other field in which we have such well-tried means and methods for tracing general tendencies and describing collective factors in the development. The circumstance that so many works of the visual arts have

survived without the names of their authors or any information regarding their date caused historians relatively early to look for signs of their place in the order of development, and on that basis to seek for some indications regarding their origin. [55]

Thus, there is the problem for the historian of ideas and movements who sees history as a problem of prognostication and/or historicism.

Thesis XI

The factor of spontaneity

So then: There is always unfinished time. Adorno took pains to explain why he could not make the person become identical with the objects of this world. This idea of non-identity can also be found in Benjamin's ideas about language. There can be no identity of subject and object, because what is created in and through language is also sublimated by language. Here is a thinking which identifies use value only through the exchange process, which is living in forgetfulness of the origin of the object and of the experience of making the object. This notion of the abuse of "history" returns in Benjamin's notorious "loss of aura." [56]

I began studying Russian and European literature and sailed with it to other shores. This formed my thinking about alien time, frozen time, or what Bakthin called "epochal time," linking authorial and novelistic times to "chronotopes" and the memory of long time. Time is one of the "sails" on the ships sailing to the other shores of the speaking and writing individual; inside the life of the person is a figure or a "chronotope."

> My memory of the other and of the other's life differs radically from my contemplating and remembering my own life ... [but] Memory of someone else's finished life (although anticipation of its end is possible as well) provides the golden key to the aesthetic

> consummation of a person ... Memory is an approach to the other from the standpoint of his axiological consummatedness. In a certain sense memory is hopeless, but on the other hand, only memory knows how to value – independently of purpose and meaning – an already finished life, a life that is totally present at hand. [57]

This is the chronotope of "autobiographical" time, preserving what has been put there in time. Remembrance comes at the moment when we fear it will be forgotten. So, memory work hunts and – if we are lucky – consummates what is lost; we fear finishing and we write inside of the reparation of lost time. Time, then, is the illegitimate "childhood of memory" where we hold onto and retrieve situations without giving them a name; and yet, the situation of memory has a historical life that acquires names. Time is "epochal": it collects struggles against "frozen time." In the age of what might be named after Deleuze and Guattari the "deterritorialization" of time in absence and mourning of the loss, the fear of loss of even mourning – the "loss of loss," the feeling of total abandonment – is replaced by the "phantasmagoria." We pick up the fragments that are strewn by the wayside. Or picked up and made into another delusional camouflage of ideology as reality, of reality as ideology. The canonization of death. The fear becomes: that the inner prognosis of time is the eternal repetition of the same. [58]

Thesis XII

Hold on now, there's Hegel's Owl of Minerva

We give names to Memory. Memory bags up the "aftermath-ness" of memory. In German, *Nachträglichkeit* means the life and death of memory, its aftermathness. The childhood of memory holds onto "loss" that seeds time. Loss is sedimented into time. It "comes after." *Nachträglichkeit* carries another meaning too: "resentment." Resentment appears when we least want it: having lost time, we lose what memory has failed us. We "have time" which means repairing and containing time and memory. We pass from "I" to "you" and we annex and supplement *I and You* to what is here and now and to what is missing. We live in reparation of what is missing. We live in the time zone of Hegel's Owl of Minerva, where philosophy paints grey on grey and can't be rejuvenated, only understood. Again: "The Owl of Minerva first takes flight with twilight closing in."[59]

Time brings the multiplicity of persons and things into view. Dissonance is a chronotope of "alien time." That is what the *situation of writing* is about – see Sartre's "Why Write" chapter in *What Is Literature?* (1948). Furthermore, Thomas Mann in *Doctor Faustus* writes that there is a "historical element in dissonance" which is "the emancipation of dissonance ... the polyphonic dignity of every chord-forming note [being] guaranteed by the constellation."[60]

So then, in writing the past faces us. This is Bakhtin's "axiological," which ties aesthetics to ethics and the loss of time. Bakhtin's essays followed me, along with Russian literature and what Osip Mandelstam referred to as "the noise of time" and the attrition of time and poetry: the fate of standing against the attrition of time.[61] Thus, writing is in feeling and forms noise that becomes "polyphonic." This is what psychoanalysts call "thing-representations," that is, the work of the negative in the unconscious. There, writing and reading begins.

Could there be an "anarchist-like" approach to language and to language as our own property, the way a painter paints? This question haunted me in my reading and writing. The Bakhtinian idea of the image of language helped me understand the ideological refractions of the "word" as an extension of institutions and the struggle to understand class and literacy.[62] Language, then, illuminates the fourth wall of the yet-to-be-uttered words of the "addressees" in a world that does violence to the objects of thought: language and commodity.[63] *So then, moving on:* The

numbered "theses" in this prologue are signposts that point to
the dossiers as a "user's manual."

Thesis XIII

On the other hand: fate, geography, time, and rivers

In Canada I became a settler: dossiers pose questions of crossings yet unsettled. I was born on Lakeview Road in Cleveland,
Ohio, which intersects Lake Erie [64] – or does it rather begin or
end there? Canada is an "other shore" across stormy Lake Erie.
One learns early that fate is the memory of a place. It is a principle of the geography of fate that one doesn't choose where one
enters the world. I call this the "Antigone chronotope," because
Antigone's memory is destiny and the place where she can't bury
memory. Destiny, as the ancient Greeks knew, is a "built-world,"
that is, a world shaped and assimilated to become "Creonic."
From there comes the "inbuilt" world, which is a *map to self-
creation*. But what "maps" drive in the repeatable conditions of
structures of repetition given to us by culture? Another dilemma
of modernism!

So then, living on the Cuyahoga River. [65] The lake connected
the trade routes from New York State on the Atlantic via the Erie
Canal that linked Lake Erie to the Ohio River and the Mississippi
River and then to the Gulf of Mexico. [66] Linkings and fate.

The city of Akron on the canal was the home of every brand
of tire that could be made. The air was rubber; just as the air of
Warhol's Pittsburgh was coal. Native American Peoples inhabited,
and still inhabit, the region. Here was the Connecticut Western Reserve, "owned" by the State of Connecticut, and what the
Eastern settlers of the first Atlantic colonies named the Great
Lakes region. The fate of the canal: heritage history. Time is only
a tributary.

The word "reserve" meant territory; the settler Connecticut people intended that they would own the land all the way to the Pacific. That covers territory! However, the territory was already peopled, inhabited. Native American Peoples living in the area at the time and whose Ancestral Lands it had been for millennia were *eventually* allowed "allotments." So, is time "eventually" part of the map? Work is required to see bridges here.

The region was settled by European immigrants and later by migrants from the Southern States in flight from the Civil War. It became home to Christian evangelicals; churches perched on every block. Tent revivalists came to the door telling us that God told them they could use our bathroom. When the suburban movie houses failed, the churches settled in the buildings. Downtown movie houses simulated baroque mansions with names like The Palace. South to north, the Underground Railroad flowed with Mercurians, escaped slaves. The illegal traffic of slaves marks Ohio history just as labour and industrial conflict mark cities.

Poor whites were also stigmatized. The teacher in my grade-seven class shouted "White trash!" at a student who acted out. I asked my mother, "What is white trash?" I worried. Were we also white trash? Because I was his friend? Chippewa Lake, Ohio, became an amusement park. Did we know, coming of age, that the "Mound Builders" were the Adena, Hopewell, and Fort Ancient Cultures native to the fertile Ohio Valley? Did we know of the settlers' extreme violence, marauding, and war crimes in the Ohio Valley and "Indian country"? Do we know now? [67]

I lived in this primal-industrial Midwest city with a network of neighbourhoods, which were class and economic enclaves. Class consciousness came with the territory. There was even class consciousness to be found in the elegiac, rural town of Wooster, Ohio, where the Amish came to shop in horse-drawn wagons. Hybrid Bakhtinian polyphonic existence meets merchant class.

Another river domain: the Tennessee (Tanasi) River, the southern "Appalachia," located on Tsoyaha (Yuchi) and

Aniyvwiya?i (Cherokee) Native American Territories. Civil War monuments populated Missionary Ridge. My classroom included "Appalachians" who came to school barefoot. Edward, Ira, and Ronald fought with me to remind me I was an intruder from the Civil War and this was "their Place." Jim Crowe and World War II were other shores, and "Negro" and "White" were different hardships embedded inside the cultured, urban prosperity of the city. These placeways of memory are bridges of the memory of the separate "Negro" water fountains. The seats at "back of the bus" were nearby "other shores," *but not for us*, as a bus driver said when my friends and I wanted to sit there because the view "to the other shore" was better from the back of the bus. African American people lived near the quarry. Faulkner's South is a "Placeway" of immanence whose traces remain.

Cleveland and northern Ohio appeared in my life again as an undergraduate at Western Reserve University on Cleveland's Euclid Avenue, near Lakeview Drive. Euclid Avenue led straight downtown to one of the largest city libraries in the nation and to Lake Erie and the Municipal Stadium of the Cleveland Indians, who had played for years in League Park. That a team named the "Cleveland Lake Shores" is defunct, as are the "Cleveland Indians," as is the "Chippewa Lake" amusement park, speaks to the amnesia about historical violence and the silence of the enigmatic disavowal of that violence. Teams are not named "Aphasia."

The university was adjacent to the Cleveland Museum of Art where I could look at pictures and study aesthetics. It was here that I developed a passion for the social history of art in a city of settlers, immigrants, industry, social inequality, and exorbitant wealth. A Hungarian professor and an Armenian-raised literature professor seemed to understand what others didn't. It was in this time and years later that social philosophers of art like Arnold Hauser and Ernst Gombrich, originally so opposed to each other, came together in the anarchist-romantic aesthetics of Herbert Read, along with approaches to aesthetics influenced by psychoanalysis. This mannerist prologue expresses in many ways my aesthetic credo, my commitment to art history and the historical process in literature and art and the historical origins of modernism – where Hauser found the origins in primitive, mannerist, and baroque art.

> If one eliminates or purposely neglects the complexity of the work of art, interweaving motifs, ambiguity of symbols, polyphony of voices, mutual dependence of form and content, unanalyzable fluctuations of cadence and emphasis, then the best of what art offers us is gone. Still, sociology is not alone in incurring this sort of loss, for all scientific treatment of art has to pay for knowledge gained by destroying the immediate, ultimately irretrievable, aesthetic experience ... The work of art is not only a source of complex personal experience, but also has another kind of complexity, being a nodal point of several different causal lines. It is the outcome of at least three different types of conditions: psychological, sociological and stylistic. As a psychological being, the individual retains not merely the freedom of choosing among the various possibilities permitted by social causation; he is also always creating for himself new possibilities in no way prescribed by his society ... The creative individual invents new forms of expression, does not find them ready-made. [68]

Hauser became one of the aesthetic building blocks around the idea of polyphony in art as an experience of time and place. His thinking about conventions in art echoes through these dossiers, most importantly his capacity to think about ideology and the ideological origin of art as a cultural institution with a history of its own that could illuminate the "bewildering strangeness and ambiguity of things." The artwork and its conventions semantically illuminated the inseparability of unconscious intentions and the irreducible artistic qualities that come together when elements of mystery and the symbolic emerge through semantic richness that may shift and change. [69]

I learned how neither art history nor laws of epochs or periodicity can take away the concrete individuality of the work of art arising from the work and the continuous and discontinuous nature of spontaneity in art-making. The non-contemporary features of the contemporary work and the cross-over to the older and the newer in time cannot be reduced to the social preconditions of its development, nor its estrangement from the social context surrounding the work. A historiography of progress in the arts cannot explain the work of art that has been influenced by other works of art, or by the individuality of the individual who, while in thrall to a humanism of the will, is struck dumb by the "incarnation of the totality" and "intoxication of delusion" in the "strident claims" that the totality of life can be evinced in the single work of art. [70]

The great Severance Hall was in Cleveland, too, and I was lucky to take tickets and listen to the concerts with George Szell and other famous conductors. The ticket takers were fraternity boys that I knew from my basketball life; they didn't like to take tickets and farmed the job out to others.

Not far from this high cultural centre were the Hough Avenue neighbourhoods, ex-location of the Cleveland Indians, and the "Negro league" Cleveland Buckeyes played in League Park, where in 1966 riots occurred. I worked in the Hough neighbourhood when it was an enclave of African Americans and migrants from the South. A woman I worked for had Senator Robert A. Taft on her living room wall, one of the Republicans who authored the infamous 1947 Taft–Hartley anti-labour-union act, vetoed by President Truman. I wonder now whether she was the first Republican I had ever met face to face. Politics was that way.

Thesis XIV

Moving on, from a graduate-school outpost at the University of Michigan, Ann Arbor, the soon-to-be home of the Students for a Democratic Society, my Ohio "friends and neighbours" drafted me into the Army. I told the Induction Centre that I was con-scientiously opposed to serving, I would not shoot anyone; but that didn't count with them. *So then*: From outposts of basic train-ing across the Ohio River in Kentucky and then Georgia south of the Tennessee River and the Appalachians to Germany the Rivers and Shores merged in a small town, which during the war had housed General Rommel's tanks. It was – naturally – named Panzer Kaserne ("tank barracks"). Nearby the Neckar River, flowing along the Black Forest, was Tübingen, one of Hölderlin's "other shores." He lived in his Yellow Tower in Tübingen where he was unprotected from the world. The anarcho-utopian Ernst Bloch taught in Tübingen after leaving East Germany. It was in Stuttgart in 1958 that I saw Brecht's *Resistible Rise of Arturo Ui*, its first German performance after the war.

Thesis XV

In 1958, war rubble was piled in the centre of the city of Stuttgart, a thirty-minute train ride from Schiller's birthplace in Marbach am Neckar, where I returned many years later to the archives of the German National Library to read Siegfried Kracauer's papers. Kracauer was Adorno's teacher of Kantian philosophy and his close friend. So then I returned to "A National Archive of Writing on the Neckar River"! The library had just received the manuscript of Kafka's *Trial*. A consortium of German insti-tutions outbid the Bodleian in London for the manuscripts, which had been saved by Max Brod. A train and a postage stamp were named after Franz Kafka. Another train was named after Hannah Arendt.[71]

I was transferred to Mannheim on the Neckar River a short distance from Heidelberg, the home of Max Weber's philo-sophical salons in the pre–World War I years. György Lukács's coming-of-age *Theory of the Novel* originated there. In 1962 he disavowed his own book. His accusation: the failure of trying to synthesize "left" ethics and "right" epistemology, in other words a Marxist fusion of left politics and Kantian autonomy of art displaced his romantic anti-capitalism. Impaled on his own Hegelian sword, and keeping with metaphors of the other shores, he floundered on the shoals by naming his book a call for "a radical revolution coupled with a traditional-conventional exegesis of reality."[72]

For Lukács, the Adornian intelligentsia took up residence in the "hotel abyss." It was to be the introduction to his Dostoevsky book. However, Lukács went to Moscow and then returned to Budapest – to his own Hotel Abyss where, in 2017, the right-wing government of Viktor Orbán removed his statue. Throughout his work one finds a sense of guilt about his formative anarcho-utopian outlook. I see his theory of the novel as his fearful resistance to the comic-grotesque which I have named "graffiti on the walls of monuments."

Influenced by Lukács, I wrote a dissertation on the theory of the novel in 1965, centring on Nikolai Gogol. The epigraph to Brecht's *The Resistible Rise of Arturo Ui* was one inspiration to the study of Gogol: "The womb is still fruitful from which he crawled." As I wrote thinking of Russia, Germany, and the US, Adorno and psychoanalysis were another way for me to relate the Russian characterology of *poshlost*, or self-righteous mediocrity, to other novelists, to "counterfeit," and to American culture.

The first Brecht play I saw was in 1954 in Cleveland, performed by the renowned all–African American Karamu House and Theatre. Brecht had testified not long before, in October 1947, at the House Unamerican Activities Committee (HUAC). Eric Bentley was translating his plays and later produced the recording of Brecht's interrogation by the HUAC committee. I used some of the transcript when I produced Brecht's *The Measures Taken* (*Die Maßnahme*) at Simon Fraser University in 1973. I saw the *Resistible Rise of Arturo Ui* several times over the years in East Berlin at the Brecht Ensemble Theatre, on the shore of the river Spree, with its many bridges.

Thesis XVI

But wait: Brecht is an epigone for writing in different forms. Writing about the capacity for annihilation of the world, Walter Benjamin, in 1934, sensed terror when he listened to Brecht talk about the coming war (in the year I was born). Brecht was in exile in Svendborg when Benjamin visited him. Benjamin's fear was prophetic: "While he spoke I felt a force acting on me that was equal to that of fascism; I mean a power that has its source no less deep in history than fascism. It was a very curious feeling, new to me. It was matched by the direction Brecht's thought now took."[73] The terror was making Brecht's satire into what Brecht called "coarse thinking," what I call essayistic, verbal-dialogical thinking. In 1989 I returned to the Neckar River and to the town of Marbach to do research on Kracauer; the Wall had just fallen. I remember an East German editor of a Marxist literary journal doing research in Marbach weeping; we were sitting on a park bench and he told me his story.

Over the years I have seen more than twenty Brecht productions. Brecht and his wife, actor Helene Weigel, are buried adjacent to the Brecht House and a Huguenot cemetery, Dorotheenstädtischer Friedhof. Huguenots are "Mercurians" in their own biblical ways. Brecht too had read and used the Bible liberally. Hegel, Marcuse, and others are buried there.

Thesis XVII

So then, later, other rivers: the Main River in Würzburg, Germany, where late Gothic and early Renaissance Tillman Riemanschneider, another mannerist and Mercurian, created his wooden sculptures. Legend says authorities chopped Riemanschneider's hands off because of his loyalty to the peasants; but legend is also fearful prophecy of future violence. Würzburg and its baroque palace, the Würzburg Residence, were bombed at the end of World War II, because the Gestapo were housed there. Also housed: Giovanni Battista Tiepolo's frescoes on the ceiling of the Residence, which became a central image for me when teaching courses on "reading the city reading us."

I lived for many summers teaching on the winding Vltava River in Bohemia and in the city of Prague, alongside Mercurians like Kafka and Bohumil Hrabal, Jaroslav Hašek (and his character Švejk), who were themselves at home with many writers and maverick philosophers such as Karel Kosík and Jan Patočka. It was the heart of Czech surrealism, like that of Jan Švankmajer and his comic-grotesque films, and of great Czech filmmakers and masters of polyphony in music, like Leoš Janáček.

The Vltava, or Moldau in German, winds from the Bohemian Forest northward. It is one of a few European rivers that define places, shores, and crossroads where one might change a national or ethnic identity so often that "identity" confuses; borders get invaded and ethnic nationalism replaces the local.

The shadow of the feudal order hovers too. This is also the heartland of the austere religious "Mercurians," the Taborites and Hussites, who left their mark on the history of Czech-speaking dissidence and martyrdom that lead to burning people and churches and to immolation. This is a region of apocalyptic terrorism, the Protestant Church, the Thirty Years War, razed earth, and death. Brecht's 1939 play *Mother Courage and Her Children* sardonically showed how war, business, and the business of extermination could combine.

Thesis XVIII

Speaking of Rivers and Borders: There are the fjords and inland waters of the "Northwest" in Washington State where, from Puget Sound, we could look at Mount Rainier (Tacoma) on one side and the Olympic Mountains on the other. From the summit of Rainier, the shadow of the mountain could be seen stretched west over the Olympic Peninsula's Hoh Rainforest. One points to the map in one's head and thinks, "Northwest" – but northwest of what? *Yet, take note:* there are always those who need to have a geographical "centre" in their lives, so they named this region accordingly, framed by the wandering Skagit, Columbia, and Fraser Rivers. The "Northwest"? *Where do we place the Northwest, and in relation to which centre?* What is the "Mid"west? Seattle was settled by Wobblies and Industrial Workers of the World resistance movements. I then moved across the forty-ninth parallel and the Fraser River. The inland seas stretch through the enclosed fjords all the way to Alaska, alongside these trade routes and "placeways." Migrants came to British Columbia from other shores: west, east, north, and south, following rivers or the Pacific trade routes. The Similkameen, my favourite river, flowing from British Columbia across into Washington State, appears in dossier III's "Geological Poetics" essay about borders.

The Vancouver that I came to in 1965 seemed a timeless city: it was not unlike American cities that I knew. It had beautiful historical footprints on its streets, its buildings, and in many of its diverse neighbourhoods, some with stucco houses, the "Vancouver Specials." Why and when did cities become "the enemies of the people" is a question underscoring many of my essays, including in my co-edition of *Unfinished Business*, a 2005 collection of essays on the "ruins" of a city.[74] A dossier on "Streets and Borders: Vancouver and Elsewhere" is a chronotope of modern dilapidation. The photographs of Jeff Wall and Fred Herzog, in different ways, portray that period for me. Jeff Wall's photographs inspire many essays about place, time, and the crossover of literature and image.[75] Is Vancouver, as it is now and was before, similar to a baroque play of mourning?[76]

Thesis XIX

Tableaux

Such was the mood of a recounting. Now I pause to consider how the essays are "critical models" and together form a tableau and an assembly of writing. *Untimely Passages* is an assembly, a tableau. One writes with many hands and speaks in many voices when one collects one's work: one hand in the past, the others in the present. The essays are "double-voiced" because writing moves through time and across time. Collecting the essays crosses time zones in my life. I wrote them then as "essays" in the older sense of that word: by learning how one thinks in writing of situations of tumult and fragmentation. Of course, any assembly or collection is a "construction" personal to the writer. They stand also as an archive. I hope that the total work is what in psychoanalytical aesthetics can be referred to as figurability, understood both as a critique of ideology and the search for truth value.

They are passages through which I have walked with others. They are scholarly because I use my reading of others who have walked these passages; they are critical models, and also patterns of my experience. They write me when I see connections among them as I have put them together in these dossiers as forms of time. As I have said, the "dossiers" are organizational principles, an architectonic. Architectonics are alive for me in writing, teaching, and in the references to the city as a form of reality that includes exile as one of the dominant motifs emerging in my later writings. I take up writers who are not "consciously" writing "theory" as the literary establishment used "theory" in my lifetime; the mania for theory became a narrow passage of rocky shoals one had to pass through to reach the other shores. This book is not a theoretical collection, although I am conversant with theory.

On the other hand, there are risks I take with the theoretical, risks which are inescapably bound to the creative utterances of art itself. Art moves "essayistically" into the world and becomes a dialogue that is active in the world. This is my form of radical humanism, if one needs a name for it, or the anarcho-humanism that is a motif throughout. Compare Sartre: "The notion that one might help [the masses] become self-conscious ... the homogeneity of the public banished all contradiction from the author's soul ... [Then] the writer questions [them]self about [their] mission only in ages when it is not clearly defined and when [they] must invent and re-invent it." [77]

Thesis XX

Anarchism in the tableau's "Untimely Passages"

The quotations herein framed in blocks are exiled quotations looking for home, and finding it here. It is not how I lived anarchism looking down on life, but how I thought of anarchism as a multiple-voiced humanism fighting against domination. I was born when war became the breeding grounds. War was a "bowstring" that affected everyone during the period of writing these essays in a manner of self-formation. That "bowstring" shot me across many inner horizons, almost like a painting by Malevich. How does one "take leave" when "leaving" is always with us? "Leave-taking" is a chronotope; memory comes back again and again without a name; it is there when we are recounting in the acts of writing and reading. I was born when the fascist dictatorships were close at hand, in the year when Russian poet Osip Mandelstam wrote his "Ode to Stalin" which got him entry into the Gulag, where he died. Mandelstam's 1925 book *The Noise of Time* could be a subtitle.

One needs a glossary for all the synonyms of "war" that go unrecounted in one's life. All the best titles about war have been taken. [78] *On the other hand:* Anarchism, as an ideology and "poetics," accompanies me in this entangled life of writing and teaching; anarchism was more of a lighthouse from the "other shore," perhaps a life jacket. The epigraphs used for the dossiers of this book are islands: the essays in retrospect become like notes in a bottle washed ashore. One never knows the fate of one's writing. *So then:* The dossiers recount the books I loved to teach; books and authors become landmarks and signposts. They orient me towards the shores where one finds the surplus meanings and the breathing holes. I think of them as in the spirit of the opening lines of Peter Weiss's 1975 *The Aesthetics of Resistance,* discourses written in the "urgency" of the act of writing, marking the heat of the times that places us into intellectual engagements taking place in the shadows of the ruins of the cities:

> All around us the bodies rose out of the stone, crowded into groups, intertwined, or scattered into fragments, hinting at their shapes with a torso, a propped-up arm, a burst hip, a scabbed shard, always in war-like gestures, dodging, rebounding, attacking, shielding themselves, stretched high or crooked, some of them snuffed out, but with a freestanding, forward-pressing foot, a twisted back, but the contour of a calf harnessed into a single common motion. A gigantic wrestling, emerging from the grey wall, recalling perfection, sinking back into formlessness ... When the sculptural fragments that had lain buried under the deposits of Near Eastern power changes came to light, it was once again the superior, the enlightened who knew how to use the valuable items, while the herdsmen and nomads, the descendants of the builders of the temple, possessed no more of Pergamum's grandeur than dust. [79]

Weiss's dirge-like song illuminates the horror of the displacement of the Pergamon Altar from Greece to Berlin. Weiss adapted the ancient Greek frieze to the terror thoughts of the permanence of war and his own attachment to the Spanish Revolution of 1936.

Likewise, my essays are intended to lighten the load of living with domination; by showing that load, I throw a light onto the load itself. If the form of *Untimely Passages* has a model, there are two, for sure: Peter Weiss's study of his life and writings, *The Aesthetics of Resistance* (1975); and Walter Benjamin's tableau of memory built inside the baroque city, *The Arcades Project* (1927–1940).

Our quest for archaic shapes of experience passes through "strange seas of thought": exploring the work of periegetes, antiquaries, and choreographers where sometimes it is possible to find a holistic, integrated *theoria.* We need a "restitution of decayed intelligence ... a fundamental change in the form of mutual immanence."[80] When Hungarian author and Nobel Prize winner Imre Kertész was asked by an interviewer if he could be more specific about what he meant by a "tower of Babel," Kertész replied it was a situation in which not only others' languages aren't understood, but also our own.[81]

So then, this collection attempts to live with the past and anticipate the future, keeping the utopian dimension alive as a productive understanding about resistance and emancipation. Ultraviolet rays of anarchism pervade these essays through authors and issues of culture and creation that compelled me to treat each course as a situation from which a new consciousness could emerge – the students' and mine. Can one have a "calling" for creative dissonance? Teaching is itself the shock of looking at the world in which one is always coming of age. Teaching, the world feels like the world can go on forever; yet because the world is fragile and frightened, teaching can end any time.

So then also, posthumous memory and the shudder. The problems of the limits of autonomous art, of the labour of the individual, will not go away and they never did for me, even though the fragility of art facing the culture spoke of hard lessons to be learned when artists working in oppressive regimes faced the "situation of art."

Sartre reminds us that *situating the muse of writing* means that essays speak to each other. Sebald and Benjamin are not concerned with remembering "how history really was," but how thoughts come back to us again and again even when nameless, in the name of this kind of memory which I call, perhaps redundantly, "posthumous memory." Writing rekindles *considered memory* of what one has created and how memory can be arranged and configured. Not all memory of what one has done in the past as creative work represents the actuality of what was and has been, but the actuality of recounting, which is an untimely form of "thinking with," and "thinking in," is itself a configuration. The inner image is a tableau. *They write me when I see connections among them.*

Epigraphs in this collection are meant to show breathing holes; they float like notes in a bottle, washed ashore with other notations from other authors: "Recountings." Events in a life of writing are commensurate to one another, come closer, and yet may become distant from the shores from which we set out; they may become incommensurate in our existence under the pressure of the shudder of new readings of literature and art. Virginia Woolf's *To the Lighthouse*, for one, is about the incommensurability of *now-and-then*. The shores become visible in the act of writing and recounting. When the *Lighthouse*'s Lily Briscoe looks at the other shore, she tries to paint the inner recountings, which in the novel are unknown and yet known to her when she is, in novelistic time, recounting her life "from the other shore."

The reader, the writer, and the character come into life where the truth of the work of art gives us a "shudder," just as Adorno shudders as he writes:

> The forms of reaction that are subsumed under the concept of feeling become futile enclaves of sentimentality as soon as they seal themselves off from their relation to thought and turn a blind eye to truth; thought, however, approaches tautology when it shrinks

> from the sublimation of the mimetic comportment. The fatal separation of the two came about historically and is revocable ...[82]

I intend that the reader in the work be immersed in the recountings and the unrecounted. The warm stream of an anarchist aesthetics, finished and yet unfinished, is as Lily Briscoe's painting speaks to her, and to the reader as well, if they are willing to follow her.

Finally, the epigraphs of *Untimely Passages* are for the readers who will find them to be important *markers*; they are lifebuoys marking the passages among the essays. Lily Briscoe, Woolf's "untimely" visitor, stares towards the lighthouse while she paints. Her memories interrupt the painting *because her life means that painting*. Does she know it? The wanderer to and from the other shores can ask where one came from and where one is going. One is always in the midst with her, and her paintings, and the "shudder" of the artwork.

PROLOGUE: ENDNOTES

THESIS I

1 Wallace Stevens, *The Collected Poems of Wallace Stevens*, ed. John N. Serio and Chris Beyers (New York: Alfred A. Knopf), 1954. I am also thinking about Ralph Ellison's "Prologue" to the *Invisible Man* (1952), which I taught for many years in courses on the novel. There, Ellison describes the room in which the novel is conceived and written, siphoning power from the electric company while maintaining his invisibility.

2 The "staged and unstaged" in film and photography is an aesthetic concept derived from the works of Siegfried Kracauer. See Kracauer, *Theory of Film: The Redemption of Physical Reality* (Princeton: Princeton University Press, 1997), 60 and *passim*.

3 Siegfried Kracauer, *History: The Last Things before the Last* (New York: Oxford University Press, 1969), 216.

4 Charles Dickens, *Oliver Twist* (London: Penguin Classics, 2003), chap. 14.

5 See, in dossier II, the essay on Kracauer's "cosmopolitan homelessness" and his aesthetic of the film age.

6 On digressive writing, see Viktor Shklovsky, *Energy of Delusion: A Book on Plot*, trans. Shushan Avagyan (Champaign, IL: Dalkey Archive Press, 2007). Tolstoy had no plan for the novel; it was "unstructured": "He wanted to create a real work that would untie the main knot of life, that would uncover something absolutely new and indispensable, but he had no concrete plan on how to write it. This 'unstructured' novel was a sort of blind search for truth, but without his 'energy of delusion' the real work would be impossible for Tolstoy" (12). Shklovsky's aesthetic, as related to writing which he calls "delusional energy," shows how experimentation and mistakes can lead writing to older forms and to the reinvention of new ones. The effect becomes the famous theory of "enstrangement," or *ostranenie*, variously translated as the "alienation" or "defamiliarization" technique or the "sideways view" of literature that negotiates and guides the reader into the enigmatic nature of reading.

7 Walter Benjamin, "The Flâneur," in *The Arcades Project*, "Section M," trans. Howard Eiland and Kevin McLaughlin (Cambridge, MA: Harvard University Press, 1999).

8 Mikhail Bakhtin, *Speech Genres and Other Late Essays*, trans. Vern W. McGee, ed. Caryl Emerson and Michael Holquist (Austin, TX: University of Texas Press, 1986), 152.

9 Friedrich Nietzsche, *The Untimely Meditations (Thoughts Out of Season, Parts I and II)*, trans. Anthony M. Ludovici and Adrian Collins (New York: Digireads, 2009), 98–99.

10 Bakhtin, "The Problem of the Text," *Speech Genres and Other Essays*, 110.

11 Dossiers III and IV further document how the aura of memory informs the essays.

12 André Green, "The Double and the Absent," in *Psychoanalysis, Creativity and Literature* (New York: Columbia University Press, 1978), 281.

13 Alfred Kazin, *A Lifetime Burning in Every Moment: From the Journals of Alfred Kazin* (New York: Harper Collins, 1996), 155.

14 Viktor Shklovsky, *Energy of Delusion* (Champaigne, IL: Dalkey Archive Press, 1985), 25.

15 See, in dossier I, "*Einbahnstrasse* or the 'One Way Street': The Legacies of Formalism and the Dilemmas of Bureaucratic Literacy."

16 Hegel's famous Owl of Minerva: "When philosophy paints its gray on gray, then has a form of life grown old, and with gray on gray it cannot be rejuvenated, but only known; the Owl of Minerva first takes flight with twilight closing in" (G.W.F. Hegel, "Preface," in *Philosophy of Right*, trans. T.M. Knox [Oxford: Oxford University Press, 1967], 13).

17 See dossier V, the postlude, for more on "Breviaries."

THESIS III

18 Peter Bürger, *The Decline of Modernism*, trans. Nicholas Walker, Literature and Philosophy series (University Park, PA: Pennsylvania State University Press: 1992). See also Bürger's *Theory of the Avant-Garde*, trans. Michael Shaw (Minneapolis: University of Minnesota Press, 1984).

19 See essays on Herbert Read in dossier I and on Jeff Wall in dossier II.

20 I have addressed "anarchism" more directly in essays on Wayne Burns, Herbert Read, and their aesthetic. I see Benjamin and Adorno likewise, through a troubled anarchist-Marxist critique of culture and a defence of the dying out of the "individual" in the ever-same of exchange value.

21 For an understanding of essays as "constellations," nothing better exists than Adorno's "Essay as Form," in *Notes to Literature*, vol. 1, trans. Shierry Weber Nicholson (New York: Columbia University Press, 1991).

22 See here the essays on Wayne Burns (dossier I, chapter 3), Herbert Read (I, 4), W.G. Sebald (II, 3), Franz Kafka (II, 4 and IV, 2), and Bohumil Hrabal (III, 4).

23 The study centred on the virtually untranslatable Russian word *poshlost* – self-satisfied mediocrity, sometimes rendered "moral cheesiness," as it appears in *Dead Souls*, *The Inspector General*, and other works by Gogol, and relates his aesthetic to Theodor W. Adorno, Hannah Arendt, William Empson, Arnold Hauser, and Wolfgang Kayser.

24 Jerry Zaslove, "Counterfeit and the Use of Literature," *West Coast Review* 3 (Winter 1969): 5–6. The essay owes its inspiration to Wayne Burns and extends his "Panzaic Principle" into other domains.

25 Adorno, *Lectures on Negative Dialectics: Fragments of a Lecture Course, 1965/1966*, trans. Rodney Livingstone (Cambridge, UK: Polity Press, 2008), 192.

THESIS IV

26 See in this collection dossier I, chapter 3, my introduction to Burns's *A Panzaic Theory of the Novel* (2009).

27 Adorno, "The Concept of Progress," in *History and Freedom: Lectures, 1964–1965*, trans. Rodney Livingstone (London: Polity Press, 2006), 155. Needless to say, Adorno comes back to this form of pitiless unfreedom informed by Nietzsche throughout his writings.

28   Adorno, *Kierkegaard: Construction of the Aesthetic*, trans. Robert Hullot-Kentor (Minneapolis: University of Minnesota Press, 1989). Adorno dedicated the study to Kracauer. See here the essays on Sebald and Kafka in dossier II and on Hannah Arendt and Robin Blaser in dossier IV.

29   See Adorno, "The Position of the Narrator in the Contemporary Novel," *Notes to Literature*, vol. 1, 31.

THESIS V

30   Benjamin, "Theses on the Philosophy of History," in *Illuminations*, trans. Harry Zohn (New York: Harcourt, Brace and World: 1968), 255.

31   Adorno, *Lectures on Negative Dialectics*, trans. Rodney Livingstone (London: Polity Press, 2008), 194. The central idea of Adorno's philosophy is the consciousness of "untruth immersed in the consciousness of that untruth. It is precisely this that constitutes the idea of negative dialectics" (218). The individual, for Adorno, carries the seeds of "negative dialectics."

32   Adorno, *Aesthetic Theory*, trans. Robert Hullot-Kentor (Minneapolis: University of Minnesota Press, 1997), 81.

33   "Chronotopes" and "placeways" are topistic or spatial structures that identify phenomenological places (*khōra*) of experience, as well as ideas that have enough expressive intelligibility to bring fragments together into a new configuration. This is formulated brilliantly by E.V. Walter in *Placeways: A Theory of the Human Environment* (Chapel Hill, NC: University of North Carolina Press, 1988).

34   Benjamin, "The Rigorous Study of Art," in *Selected Writings*, vol. 2, part 2, *1931–1934*, trans. Rodney Livingstone and others (Cambridge, MA: Harvard University Press: 1999), 670. Benjamin's "epistemo-critical prologue" to *The Origin of German Tragic Mourning* is an influence on beginning a collection of essays with a "prologue" rather than an "introduction."

35   Kracauer, *History: The Last Things before the Last*, ed. Paul Oskar Kristeller (New York: Oxford, 1969), 219.

THESIS VI

36   Osip Mandelstam, *The Noise of Time: Selected Prose*, trans. Clarence Brown (Evanston, IL: Northwestern University Press, 2002).

37   Dante is a touchstone for Mandelstam's Russian poetic of poetry as an expression of wandering: see "Conversation about Dante," in Osip Mandelstam, *The Complete Critical Prose and Letters*, trans. Jane Gary Harris and Constance Link (Ann Arbor: Ardis, 1979). In these pages, Mandelstam hears Ugolino's tale of starvation as the "cello-like sound of rancid, poisoned honey" (427).

38   The work of Herbert Marcuse and how the "alienated intellectual" speaks as both ideologue and organizer of movements is a strong influence here.

39   Nietzsche, *Untimely Meditations*, 97.

40   Benjamin, "The Collector," *The Arcades Project*, 211.

THESIS VII

41 André Green, *On Private Madness* (Madison, WI: International Universities Press, 1993), 322.

42 E.V. Walter's essay "Road to Topistics" relates periegesis to "travellers to strange places, who do not departmentalize" and who do not "discard subjective collective experience." Simply, they are "place-lovers" (Walter, *Placeways*, 19–20).

43 See Adorno, "Music, Language, and Composition," in *Essays on Music*, trans. Susan Gillespie, ed. Richard Leppert (Berkeley: University of California Press, 2002), 113. Adorno there refers to Kafka, who did not "imitate music but wrote parables resembling life through broken, signifying language" (115). See also Shierry Weber Nicholson, *Exact Imagination, Late Work: On Adorno's Aesthetics* (Cambridge, MA: MIT Press, 1999) for a deep reading of the "shuddering" that strikes us in reading and writing, that brings us "alive," and gives us a language to speak from somewhere in ourselves. This is mimesis through "semblance," with the process that enables reading and writing as a dialectic of the will to resist the darkness of violence at the heart of language.

44 Victor Serge, *Conquered City*, trans. Richard Greeman (New York: New York Review of Books, 2011), 105; translation slightly modified.

45 Serge, *Conquered City*, 104.

46 Adorno, *Lectures on Negative Dialectics*, trans. Rodney Livingston (Cambridge, UK: Polity Press, 2008), 6.

THESIS VIII

47 André Green, *On Private Madness*, 3.

48 Adorno, *Minima Moralia: Reflections from a Damaged Life*, trans. E.F.N. Jephcott (London: New Left Books: 1951), 33. I have altered the translation slightly.

49 Adorno, "Music, Language, and Composition," 125.

THESIS IX

50 Thomas Bernhard, *Gathering Evidence: A Memoir; My Prizes: An Accounting*, trans. David McLintock and Carol Brown Janeway (New York: Vintage International, 1985). The "accounting" explains Bernhard's rejection of his many prizes and why giving up on writing and starting again *is the music of and in his life*. See his "Speech at the Awarding of the Georg Buchner Prize," where he denounces prizes in order to "get work done ... advancing over all one's inner resistances and evident mindlessness" (406).

51 Quoted in Reiner Stach, *Kafka: The Decisive Years*, trans. Shelley Frisch (New York: Harcourt, 2005), 246.

52 Bohumil Hrabal, "Mr. Kafka," in *Mr. Kafka and Other Tales from the Time of the Cult*, trans. Paul Wilson (New York: New Directions, 2015), 1. Hrabal's writing, films, and literature accompanied me on my seven semesters teaching at the Prague Field School.

THESIS X

53 See, in dossier II, "Siegfried Kracauer's Cosmopolitan Homelessness: The Lost Cause of an Idea."

54   Nietzsche, "The Use and Abuse of History," *Untimely Meditations*, 97.

55   Arnold Hauser, *The Philosophy of Art History* (Chicago: Northwestern University Press, 1958), 248.

THESIS XI

56   Dossier IV continues to explore this idea through the means by which aura is lost and remains unconsummated and unfinished.

57   Mikhail Bakhtin, "Author and Hero in Aesthetic Activity," in *Art and Answerability: Early Philosophical Essays*, trans. Vadim Liapunov, ed. Michael Holquist and Vadim Liapunov (Austin: University of Texas Press, 1990), 107.

58   The essays in dossiers II and IV express the paradigms of loss, mourning, and phantasmagoria.

THESIS XII

59   Hegel, *Philosophy of Right*, 13.

60   Thomas Mann, *Doctor Faustus*, trans. H.T. Lowe-Porter (New York: Random House, 1948). Mann's novel was influenced by Adorno's reflections on music, Wagner as the counterfeit of musical understanding and dissonance, and how music can't be translated into any other form, just as the work of memory cannot be translated into any other form beyond its own discordances. Mann and Adorno discuss music and decadence in late bourgeois society (see *Doctor Faustus*'s pp. 92–103).

61   Osip Mandelstam, *The Noise of Time*, trans. Clarence Brown (Evanston, IL: Northwestern University Press, 1986), 32.

62   I first encountered Bakhtin through *Rabelais and His World* in 1967. I had finished writing a dissertation on "The Ideology and Poetics of *Poshlost*: The Work of Nikolai Gogol and Its Importance in our Time." Bakhtin's work on the grotesque and the Menippean paralleled my approach to Gogol and the novel and the grotesque. Valentin Voloshinov's *Marxism and the Philosophy of Language*, likely written in collaboration with Bakhtin, appeared in English translation in 1971. This work influenced my engagement with the "literacy" question in history and experience: see, for example, my text "Bureaucratization of Eros," in *Explorations in Comparative Literature*, ed. Makoto Ueda (Lanham, NY: University Press of America, 1986), a Festschrift for Frank Jones, translator of Sophocles, Brecht, and Hölderlin.

63   See Ferruccio Rossi-Landi, *Language as Work and Trade: A Semiotic Homology for Linguistics and Economics*, trans. Martha Adams and others (South Hadley, MA: Bergin and Garvey, 1983). This study brings to the foreground the struggle between semiotics of a social matrix for language as an institution and social capital, and the semantic "labour power expended" by we who speak and consume language in the form of commodities.

THESIS XIII

64   [Editor's note.] Lakeview Road, Cleveland, Ohio, stands on the unceded, Traditional, and Ancestral Lands of the Kaskaskia, Mississauga, and Erie Native American Peoples. Lake Erie's pre-colonial Iroquoian names include Kanahnòk:ke ("where it is replenished"), Teióhoserare ("basswood around it"), Anòn:warore ("hat"), and

Aanikegamaa-gichigami ("chain of lakes sea"). *Erie* is a shortened form of the Northern Iroquoian ethnonym Erielhonan ("long tail").

65 [Editor's note.] Perhaps from the Onödowá'ga:' (Seneca) word *Gayó'ha'geh*, "on the chin."

66 [Editor's note.] The Native American names of the Ohio River include: Ohi:yo' (from an Onödowá'ga:' word meaning "good river"), Mosopeleacipi ("river of the Mosopelea people" in the myaamia language, a.k.a. Miami-Illinois), and pelewa thiipi / spelewathiipi / peleewa thiipiiki (other forms of the former in Sawanwa, a.k.a. the Shawnee language). The Native American names for the Mississippi River are numerous and include: Misi-ziibi in the Anishinaabemowin language (Ojibwe), Mníšošethąka in Dakhótiyapi (Dakota), Mihsi-siipiiwi in myaamia (Miami-Illinois), Ma'xee'ometãá'e in Tsêhésenêstsestótse (Cheyenne), Xósáu in Cáuijògà/Cáuijò:gyà (Kiowa), Beesniicie in Hinóno'eitíít (Arapaho), and Kickaátit in Pawnee.

67 On "Ohio Country" and military conquest, see Roxanne Dunbar-Ortiz, *An Indigenous Peoples' History of the United States* (Boston: Beacon Press, 2014), 71–74. The defunct Chippewa Lake Amusement Park should remind us of the inbuilt history of the forgetting of violence.

68 Arnold Hauser, *The Philosophy of Art History*, 15.

69 Hauser, 25.

70 This formulation derives from Adorno's *In Search of Wagner* (1966) which locates Wagner in the crisis of time in modernism, where the "bourgeois" individual is the incarnation of the very totality that has produced the "magical effect inseparable from the same process of production that it attempts to exorcise": Adorno, *In Search of Wagner*, trans. Rodney Livingstone (London: New Left Books, 1981), 110.

THESIS XV

71 See the essay on Kracauer in dossier II, and references throughout.

72 György Lukács, *Theory of the Novel*, trans. Anna Bostock (London: Merlin Press, 1971), 20–21. Radical in nature, Lukács wrote novelistically, with naive utopianism.

THESIS XVI

73 Walter Benjamin, "Conversations with Brecht," in *Reflections*, trans. Edmund Jephcott, ed. Peter Demetz (New York and London: Harcourt Brace Jovanovich, 1978), 218. Dossier IV in this collection goes further into "coarse thinking."

THESIS XVIII

74 Bill Jeffries, Glen Lowry, and Jerry Zaslove, eds., *Unfinished Business: Photographing Vancouver Streets, 1955 to 1985* (Vancouver: Presentation House Gallery and West Coast Line, 2005), a collection of writing related to Vancouver as an agon, an agonistic *placeway*.

75 See also, in my monograph on Jeff Wall, "Faking Nature and Reading History: The Mindfulness toward Reality in the Dialogical World of Jeff Wall's Pictures," in *Jeff Wall, 1990* (Vancouver: Vancouver Art Gallery, 1990).

76 See in dossier III "Talking through This Space around Four Pictures by Jeff Wall."

THESIS XIX

77   Jean-Paul Sartre, "For Whom Does One Write?," in *What Is Literature?*, trans. Bernard Frenchman (London: Methuen & Co, 1950), 67.

THESIS XX

78   In a review of Wayne Burns's *Resisting Our Culture of Conformity: In the Hills of Southern Ohio and in the Groves of Academe* (*Rain Review* 5, no. 1 [Summer 2007]: 2–3), I quoted Mandelstam, writing in 1935, while in exile in Cherdyn, Northern Ural: "I have to live, breathing and bolshevescent, laboring with language, disobeying, I and one other." Russian literature has accompanied me since writing my dissertation on Gogol.

79   Peter Weiss, *The Aesthetics of Resistance*, vol. 1, trans. Joachim Neugroschel (Durham and London: Duke University Press, 2005), 1–20. Weiss's novel takes up three volumes and can be called his "untimely history."

80   Walter, *Placeways*, 41. "Mutual immanence" (see the final dossier for a discussion of this concept) is Walter's own "other shore" throughout the book.

81   Imre Kertész, *Dossier K.*, trans. Tim Wilkinson (New York: Melville House, 2006), 155.

82   Adorno, *Aesthetic Theory*, 331.

Breeding Grounds
Looking Back

Dossier I consists of essays on an aesthetic literacy that brings novels into conflict with the political Institutions of culture. Essays on Boris Pasternak, Herbert Read, and Wayne Burns show my relationship to anarchism as a "breeding ground." They belong to my earliest criticism of American literary formalism by turning my attention to authorship during times of the institutional teaching practices of what was named the New Criticism. Essays in this dossier relate to counterfeit and to the use of literature within the bureaucratic institutions. They were influenced over the years by critical theory and show knowledge of Russian formalist aesthetics and a growing awareness of Mikhail Bakhtin's work and the aesthetics of "digressive writing."

If Sancho Panza isn't Tolstoy's favorite hero, then at least he represents the absence of the main hero. When Chekhov wrote "The Darling," Tolstoy read this fascinating non-moralizing story and said that the Darling had to become as popular a character as Sancho Panza ... [Anna Karenina's] lover asks her, Are you unhappy? And she replies – no, I am not unhappy, I'm like a person, a hungry person who is given something to eat ... Her feelings are described with a frankness that doesn't exist in any of the most explicit romance novels.

—VIKTOR SHKLOVSKY, *Energy of Delusion: A Book on Plot* ([1981] 2007), trans. Shushan Avagyan

Artistic experience is neither imitation of reality nor the symbolic projection of another (deeper version of that) reality: it is an unmasking and a negation in bitter conflict with all those repressive and inhibiting experiences whose nature is never fully known until artistic creation disturbs the surfaces of assent to the "bad infinity" [Adorno's phrase] of a society that has in the Anglo-formalist idealization of ambiguity retreated from this conflict by creating a dualism between opposing forces. It reveals modes and contents of thought which transcend the codified patterns of use and validation. Dialectical thought does not invent these contents ... it recovers tabooed meanings and thus appears almost as a return, or rather a conscious liberation, of the repressed.

—JERRY ZASLOVE, "Counterfeit and the Use of Literature," *West Coast Review* (1967)

DOSSIER I – CHAPTER 1

Doctor Zhivago and the Obliterated Man: The Novel and Our Time and Literary Criticism[1]

... that if you kill a man he dies, whatever your intentions were; that if your convictions are leading you into officially sponsored acts like Dachau and the atom bomb, you are, humanly speaking, insane; that it is to the person under your own feet that you owe responsibility. The seekers of pure form, such as the constructivists, produce work, often of great merit, but which ultimately imprisons them ... There is no way round or out of this *impasse* of choice any longer. The novelist cannot now restrict his field to a small area into which history does not intrude. If he does, as some of the earliest social novelists did, the steady migration of the novel-form into wider and wider issues will catch him, and the quality of major achievement will fail to appear. Anything today which is smaller than life-size is too small, inadequate, and becoming irrelevant.

—ALEX COMFORT, *The Novel and Our Time* (1948)

I

Almost from the time *Doctor Zhivago* created an international crisis upon its publication in 1957, the novel presented a difficult critical and ideological front for readers. Easily compared with Tolstoy's novels or Alexander Blok's symbolic ecstasies, the novel grew as a meta-artifact that transcended the critical pronouncements on Pasternak's intense protest against the life which he and his generation found so oppressive to the creative process in the period of revolution. Pasternak's individualism was praised and critics seemed to identify with this individualism in the face of the novel's deep-seated confusions and often bewildering simplifications.

The critics stood over the political and aesthetic scene and, in the manner of Tolstoy's General Kutuzov in *War and Peace*, pronounced all to be "quite right," if a bit messy in spots. *Doctor Zhivago* struggles with both a poetics of the present and a Tolstoyan sense of historical time; the crisis of the novel as both a chronicle of the revolutionary times and the crisis of literary culture is its subject. However, I argue that Tolstoy's sense of reality would show how the novel struggles with its own failure to recognize the exact nature of Pasternak's response to life and art. This is a comment on the state of criticism and aesthetics in our time.

Turning to *War and Peace*'s General Kutuzov, we might begin with what Tolstoy does with the character's self-righteous blindness. Tolstoy's General Kutuzov coolly watches two armies slaughter each other and believes that all is going according to plan; the battle illustrates his theories of war. In that scene Tolstoy casts a net of lunacy over the whole event, never allowing us to forget for a second that that is certainly the way things are. The attitude towards the war we are watching, which blossoms like a hardy perennial out of the General's rich authoritarian fantasies and dominates the landscape, suddenly appears inhuman and insentient when Tolstoy's brutally rendered details of the suffering bounce from the General's consciousness like so many pebbles off a sidewalk. The scenic details are commonplace, yet we feel the power of lunacy pervading the General, whose fantasy spreads over the surface of the smug cultured life of the few, infecting the many with maladies of helplessness and powerlessness – in short, the fate of a class and a people. The scene stops short of dream or reverie – Tolstoy stops it short, perching us on the abyss of our own resistance to the logic and horror of the scene – because we are made to feel how life must be despiritualized and deritualized if we are ever to seize events and their inner meaning. The scene does not expose men (Tolstoy is contemptuous of personalities) but the banality of their fantasized control over life. [2]

A similar scene occurs in *Anna Karenina* when Vronsky, urged on by inner demons and Tolstoy's own ascetic ideology, breaks the back of his horse while Anna watches. She watches, is traumatized, and feels the quick of life in her very body respond to the horse. For a brutal moment we experience the reality of Anna's desire to live, but also how the vengeance code breaks that desire into pain, judgment, and guilt. We know at this point how vital and necessary pleasure and autonomy are to her soul. We see on a very emotional level what Julian Moynahan has described as one of the qualities of Lawrence's novels: "To clarify the relationships of 'inhuman selves' to social roles on the one hand and vital forces on the other." [3]

Tolstoy's humaneness lies in his vision of libidinous forces; a new definition of the novel became problematic for Pasternak. We learn what inhuman selves are and what responsibility Tolstoy feels to the person under foot who is not symbolic. Ursula Brumm in "Symbolism and the Novel" shows how this scene (but with a different interpretation) contains no symbolic device like Henry James's cracked golden bowl, which requires an arbitrary value if we are to understand the place it occupies in James's 1904 novel. [4] Tolstoy's beings encounter the banality (again, this is not Brumm's interpretation) of eternal and changeless truth – indeed those arbitrary values themselves – in the face of the immediacy of desires and passions. Ursula Brumm writes, theorizing:

> The realistic novel is against types, against the changeless decked out in varying guises, against the authority of the eternal and the accepted. The presuppositions for a symbolic literature in our time are two, an imagination hungry for images, and a vague idea that our lives are somehow determined by indefinable principles which operate outside the domain of cause and effect but which have a hidden meaning that manifests itself in external phenomena.

Implications in this statement for the relationship between art and life – between the aesthetic and the socio-political – are many;

namely, that for Tolstoy, and all great novelists, to be on the offensive against the "authority of the eternal" is to push implications outward, extensively, and not seal them into a hermetic inner life. Comfort speaks about the wider issues which will catch novelists if they have not reached for them themselves. Returning to *Doctor Zhivago*, I would put official statements on Pasternak's individualism into the context of Tolstoy's great novels this way: Tolstoy shows that individualism cannot be a meaningful issue, political or artistic, if the greater issue is to stay human before great annihilating forces destroy the individual. One cannot worry about the spirit of things as Tolstoy's General does, because everything he touches is spiritualized. So Tolstoy does not worry about annoying principles; he just levels everything in sight. But in *Doctor Zhivago* we only *apparently* have this Tolstoyan method, for at no time does someone's fantasy extend out over the surroundings to implicate inhuman behaviour in depth; at no time do we implicate asocial politicians, Marxist or capitalist, in the pattern of action which Pasternak's comments on art and politics set forth. In Tolstoy we cannot separate aesthetic from socio-political alienation, because he has penetrated so deeply into the roots of fantastic behaviour that we see how the politics of everyday life and war come from the same source as aesthetics: he has implied that when you detach yourself however ironically or technically from either, you increase the distance, human and aesthetic, between yourself and your fellows. All share the same life of lunacy and nightmare and self-deception. Tolstoy's Vronsky and General have detached themselves, and they are lunatics somehow in the sense that "All that makes a lunatic are very ordinary ideas of mankind shut up very tight inside a man's head."[5]

On this, Tolstoy and Céline had common cause. In the words of George Woodcock, Tolstoy's "refusal to obey … is [his] greatest weapon,"[6] and in terms of Isaiah Berlin's *Two Concepts of Liberty*, I would translate Tolstoy's art into a fictional version of this insight: "If I consent to be oppressed, or acquiesce in my condition with detachment or irony, am I the less oppressed? If I sell myself into slavery, am I the less a slave? If I commit suicide, am I the less dead because I have taken my own life freely?"[7]

Because Tolstoy did not obey, he disturbed deeply the ideals of civilized institutions, which aroused such hatred in him towards all that had determined people to suffer and even towards himself for somehow collaborating in the suffering. His pages are not saturated with symbolic life but with persons trying to shed the decreating fabrics of eternal assumptions, which lead them away from life and towards a life that inflicts pain on themselves and others. Tolstoy saw this conflict as animal (not only epic or historical): the General's fantasy is enfeebled but real, and his will is crippled, but still functions as a human will to self-creation; Vronsky's feelings are crippled, but in the way the locomotion of an animal is crippled when it has been injured. Vronsky, at that moment of insane impulse, could not tell the difference between the horse and the woman, between the object and his fantasy. But Tolstoy tells the difference, although he may give the appearance that he does not in pretending authorial naïveté. Tolstoy plays the primitive who proves he knows the difference between symbols and reality. So Tolstoy becomes the primitive that Lawrence felt he really was. Lawrence criticized Tolstoy for not admitting the phallic nature of his insights into life; Tolstoy, Lawrence felt, finally could not lie to himself in the novel form in spite of all his ethical teachings.

Lawrence's version of Tolstoy's art may not be the real Tolstoy (although I think it is), but it is clearly true that the novelist in capitulating to his assertions will not escape the demands of his demonstrations – he will not be able to subdue, with the truncheon of the literary symbol, his private desires which want to spring out and accuse whatever keeps his novel from coming alive.

Tolstoy shows that there are no sides of good and bad to be taken in matters of human experience. His novels show the effects of a powerful mind virtually insane with a desire to live, and thus his brutally rendered scenes are saturated with homicidal impulses (towards the General) and frustrated passion (towards Anna); because of this skirting of the abyss, we get the pressure of life and we feel that it is right to scream in anger and horror at "officially sponsored acts," including those deriving from imaginative or societal life that defy emotional reaction.

* * *

War and Peace is not an "officially sponsored act." But *Doctor Zhivago* struggled with officially sponsored literature officers, although critical commentary puts it on equal or near-equal ground with *War and Peace*. Moreover, the theory of the novel which I think is represented in Tolstoy's novels, which are full of digressive material crucial to the crisis of the novel form, also poses this problem raised by Alex Comfort in *The Novel and Our Time*: "The artist is forced at an early stage to make up his mind whether he regards himself as a man or a disguised quadruped, and in the novel his choice is revealed with astounding clarity. The bigger the conception and the higher the attempt, the more total the revelation of the outcome of the writer's decision."[8]

The question for the artist is perhaps rhetorical, because Comfort does not imply that we are always either one or the other, for in a barbarian society, he writes, the artist like everyone is both patient and explorer. The reader will not be embarrassed by this situation because the novel, as a form historically and psychically, starts from the realization of a common human ground that is both material and changing. Once this is realized, the reader will find that the novelist cannot be autonomous (like the lyric poet) unless, realizing his own sickness, he can explore and liberate the subject matter. Such a creative process defines what Raymond Williams, in his social Marxism, defines as the function of art in the struggle for human domination of matter and oppression:

Art reflects its society and works a social character through to its reality in experience. But also, art creates, by new perceptions and responses, elements which the society, as such, is not able to realize. If we compare art with its society, we find a series of real relationships showing its deep and central connections with the rest of general life. We find ... in certain characteristic forms and devices, evidence of the deadlocks and unsolved problems of the society: often admitted to consciousness for the first time. Part of this evidence will show a false consciousness, designed to prevent any substantial recognition; part again a deep desire, as yet uncharted, to move beyond this ... And at this point we find ourselves moving into a process which cannot be the simple comparison of art and society, but which must start from the recognition that all the acts of men compose a general reality within which both art and what we ordinarily call society are comprised ... we compare both with the whole complex of human actions and feelings. [9]

However, all artists of any greatness know that "all the acts of men compose a general reality" and artists who have stumbled over this obstacle will prevent this "general reality," this deepest revelation of vital forces, from speaking to them and their own "deep desire," will not turn towards the "uncharted" but towards more culturally sanctioned possibilities, that is, towards cultural reverie instead of personal fantasy.

Therefore, let us turn to *Doctor Zhivago*'s critics and see what they say or what they do not say. Life, the "idea of the free personality and the ideas of life as sacrifice," militates against "the deadness of abstraction and the tyranny of governmental control." "Again and again," says Edmund Wilson, "the characters are entombed and rise from the tomb." [10] Zhivago, or Pasternak's muse, is shown in growth from childhood to manhood, pushed before the onrushing forces of history with its entombing abstractions into a mind-oriented life devoted to poetry and the recording of images. In another sense he represents Pasternak's own problems of merging his lyrical poetry to the life of an internal exile that must somehow come to terms with his conception of life as "vital," "Christian," "personal," and "tragic as *Hamlet* is tragic."[11] Wilson describes it as a great moral act because it expresses a love of life through spiritual sacrifice and through Woman, demonstrated, he says, by a mind that astonishes us as if we came upon "mammoths preserved in Siberian ice … their flesh still intact."[12] The equation – novel equals preserved mammoth – is revealing for unintentional content. To Wilson, the novel represents a monument, an act of "faith in art and the human spirit," worthy of standing in that Eternal Museum where all such gigantic acts rest, flesh dead, but intact, reminding us of their power to heat the blood of readers through their bloodless, symbolic presence.

Yet I would question whether the mammoth could be resurrected, whether this modern novel can even be compared to the mammoths of nineteenth-century fiction. The ice surrounding the novel is not melting, although the temperature of the criticism is high. Entombment, I would like to show, is caused by Pasternak's own ideological limitations and by a central character who turns life into cultural reverie, and who finds reconciliation with the very forces he wishes to transcend.

Such charges will seem perverse at this date, especially since the criticism of the novel has moved into the arena of symbolic explication, the content and greatness of the novel having been taken for granted. Wilson himself elucidated symbols and significant puns in the *Nation* five months after his first review article. Well aware that "symbol hunting is fashionable," he still did not stumble over a comparison of *Doctor Zhivago* with Joyce's *Finnegans Wake* because the novel is so "plotted and planned by the author."[13]

Thus the tradition, which begins in "instant liberation," ends in "instant classic" – or great moral event, with only small, pitiful voices murmuring in protest, understandably muted by the "courage" of Pasternak's spiritual protest.[14] Whatever is meant by "courage" as distinct from "cowardice" (whose?) is never quite clear. But the moralistic assumptions underlying the use of the word *courage* are clear enough – there are collaborators and there are Pasternaks, the collaborator who survives is a ready scapegoat and better off dead – and while we might hope for some human understanding in the implied assumptions of collaboration, another version of "humanity" – the *true* life of the spirit – canonizes Pasternak and the novel.

But criticism that makes *Doctor Zhivago* a moral act in linking Zhivago's "passion ... for individual freedom"[15] with the Hungarian Revolution is difficult to understand, given the nature of the two Hungarian Revolutions, 1918 and 1956, which were put down.

In this critical land of limbo we have our side's and another side's officially sponsored revolution: Pasternak is plainly against the dry-as-dust "Marxists" in his novel, but he is not against people dying for a cause, so long as Zhivago can remain detached from it. To assume that we can enlist literature on the side of revolutions as we have known them to work out in history distorts the egalitarian radicalism at the heart of any great novelist who has shown – like Dickens, Dostoevsky, Tolstoy, or Lawrence have – that revolutions are finally caused by human beings and not governments in the abstract, that the life we have to consider is the person and not the cause. For if we can use *Doctor Zhivago* as a "moral act" for Radio Free Europe, certainly Aleksandr Chakovsky, the editor of *Literaturnaya Gazeta*, can claim *Doctor Zhivago* is an immoral act because it opposes the October Revolution.

And when Chakovsky asks whether we would approve an American novel written against the American Revolution we are obligated to show that there is a level in *The Sound and the Fury* or *Moby-Dick* or *Huckleberry Finn* which is not *for* anything and certainly denies the commercial-class ethics of the 1776 insurrection;

neither, one might add, are these novels waving banners of God, personality, poetry, myth, whole-man, nor, least of all, crying idealistic affirmations to Paul Revere in the heat of the American revolution – they are, in fact, quite disloyal to the American Dream of its founding Revolution.

The issues are relevant to literature and life, aesthetics and socio-political values, because if Tolstoy, for one, is correct, then the novel that supports our most cherished assumption about our most cherished ideals is a counterfeit novel. It is a capitulation to ideal values – either in the name of the status quo, or in the name of eternal verities – and the tacit recognition of the leader's cause of the moment. In what sense, then, is the novelist writing a novel that does not annotate authoritarian Marxism? In the sense of human community – not society – that allowed Dickens to understand criminality and the ghettos of Victorian England from his own position of his illusion of respectability, or that allowed Dostoevsky to approach an understanding of the political irrationalism, as criminal from his own position of mystical nationalism, conservative ideology, and redemptive suffering. And although Irving Howe and Edmund Wilson would be the first to see this, even though Howe's cautious appraisal of Céline finally does Céline in for his political buffoonery – and politics – and even though Wilson acts as if *Doctor Zhivago* were the last word on Marxism – has he never read Wilson's *To the Finland Station*? – they have made their criticism of Pasternak's novel testify to high moral ideologies without showing that *Doctor Zhivago* can be read as a doctrinaire and ideological novel, unredeemed by either Céline's or Marx's understanding of unbearable suffering.

II

Recently, a Soviet critic of children's books was asked about the criteria she used in evaluating books for publication. She answered: "The main qualities are: high, fine storytelling qualities, cognitive values and high ideological content. These books should help to educate children, extend their outlook and teach them to behave decently and for the good of society." [16] Now the horror I experience in reading this has nothing to do with communist ideology, for we are familiar with the righteous exemplars who teach children – we know them from the pedagogical tyrants of the English novels' Allworthies and Gradgrinds, or in the dogmas of schooling in the Party-minded reforms that reached into the naive revolutionary classrooms as the cultural Front against prescriptive bourgeois morality. Yet the criteria are really similar to the pastoral tones and ideological preachings handed down by the Cold War readers of *Doctor Zhivago*, a fundamentally decent novel and not very threatening to the "good of society." If you are dealing in sublime ideologies you will honour whatever does your own a great service, and Yuri Zhivago's own ideology is sacrificial and saintly enough to serve, even though his papers may not be in order. Irving Howe has eloquently described the novel: "Through his doomed yet exemplary struggle to maintain the life of contemplation, through his proud insistence upon the autonomy of his inner 'organic' being, Zhivago comes to represent … all that which in human life must remain impervious to the manipulation of the party state and its ideology. [*Doctor Zhivago*] is … a testament for the silent and suppressed. And then [it] persuades us that the yearning for freedom remains indestructible. And, finally, *Doctor Zhivago* is no facile spirituality [because Pasternak] knows how easy it is to debase and kill a man, how often and needlessly it has been done." [17]

I do not believe that Zhivago, the character in the novel, does know what it means to "kill a man," even as the novel may struggle with the ambivalence of the ideological content of such remarks that reward a novel written in the service of good as "sacrifice," and suffering as "suffering for inner life." Yet Howe's reading of the novel *is* the right reading, but only insofar as he has accepted the novel at face value even more than Pasternak does.

What does all of the yearning and inward music sound like? Some comments by Zhivago's Uncle Kolia, the major influence on Zhivago.[18] "Yes, there are gifted men," said Nikolai Nikolaevich, "but the fashion nowadays is all for groups and societies of every sort. Gregariousness is always the refuge of mediocrities, whether they swear by Soloviev or Kant or Marx. Only individuals seek the truth ... How many things in the world deserve our loyalty? Very few indeed. I think one should be loyal to immortality, which is another word for life, a stronger word for it. One must be true to immortality – true to Christ! ... history as we know it now began with Christ ... what is history? It is the centuries of systematic explorations of the riddle of death, with a view to overcoming death ... Now, you can't advance in this direction without a certain faith. You can't make such discoveries without spiritual equipment. And the basic elements of this equipment are in the Gospels ... [and] the idea of free personality and the idea of life as sacrifice" (12–13).[19]

This explicit ideology of a life of sacrifice becomes the ideology of the novel later repeated to Zhivago's approval by a peasant woman and by Zhivago himself in the name of poetry. The ideology becomes the point behind the ever-receding camera, where the controlling intelligence of the novel watches, where cultural reverie – almost a pastoral consciousness – substitutes for an awareness of men and dying people. Yet this faith, or drama of consciousness as many critics have named it, makes the rather astonishing, sententious assertion that: "It was not until after the coming of Christ that time and man could breathe freely. It was not until after Him that men began to live towards the future. Man does not die in a ditch like a dog – but at home in history, while the work towards the conquest of death is in full swing; he dies sharing in this work" (13).

History becomes the spiritualization and abstracting of events that push men into the ditches because Zhivago attempts to make the contemplating, meditating consciousness the *proper* form of a liberating consciousness. Yet the novel chokes off life in the name of this consciousness that we are to believe gives "ordinary experience ... a halo of sanctity." [20]

Zhivago says:

> Wait, let me tell you what I think. I think that if *the beast who sleeps in man* could be held down by threats – any kind of threat, whether of jail or of retribution after death – then the highest emblem of humanity would be the lion tamer in the circus with his whip, not the prophet who sacrificed himself. But don't you see, this is just the point – what has for centuries raised man above the beast is not the cudgel but an *inward music*: the irresistible power of unarmed truth, the powerful attraction of its example. It has always been assumed that the most important things in the Gospels are the ethical maxims and commandments. But for me the most important thing is that Christ speaks in parables taken from life, that He explains the truth in terms of everyday reality. The idea that underlies this is that communion between mortals is immortal, and that the whole of life is symbolic because it is meaningful. (39)

Consciousness, "inward music," is quite plainly used to keep down the "beast who sleeps in man" – to render, still later in the novel, wolves into material for poetry and not into threats against starving people. Thomas Merton matches Zhivago inward-life for inward-life, simple parable for simple parable:

> Pasternak stands first of all for the great spiritual values that are under attack in our materialistic world. He stands for the freedom and nobility of the individual person, for man the image of God, man in whom God dwells. For Pasternak, the person is and *must* always remain prior to the collectivity. He stands for courageous, independent loyalty to his own *conscience*, and for the refusal to compromise with slogans and rationalizations imposed by compulsion. Pasternak is fighting for man's [*sic*] *true freedom*, his *true creativity*, against the false and empty humanism of the

Marxists – for whom man does not yet truly exist. Over against the technological jargon and the empty scientism of modern man [*sic*], Pasternak sets creative symbolism, the power of imagination and of intuition, the glory of liturgy and the fire of contemplation. But he does so in new words, in a new way. He speaks for all that is *sanest* and most *permanently vital* in religious and cultural tradition, but with the voice of a man of our own time. [21]

I have italicized words that sing with the tones latent to the spiritualism of contemplation: a Marxist cannot love a man; an idealist is a judge of sanity; there is true freedom and true creativity. But whether the tone is Merton's or Pasternak's or Zhivago's, the importance of this tone is not spurious to the novel itself, for Zhivago turns his resentment towards threats to his poetic life into culturally decent reverie and one-dimensional, imagistic encounters with reality, troubled musings that do not testify to the man dying in a ditch.

The novel begins with Zhivago's father dying in a ditch, a suicide from a moving train. The novel ends with Zhivago himself, a victim of heart disease, grasping at the windows of a tram for air and finally dying on the roadside, an unsung hero of the protest against the commissars with revolvers. Ironically we are to perceive that man does die in a ditch; yet by the end of the novel we are also to feel that this new Russian Christ is a man who has organized the death and *ditchness* of life onto a plane of perception and transcendence far above those who really do die in ditches, far above the sleeping beasts who are not superintendents of consciousness: the gregarious, the mediocre, the fanatic, the brutal, the sensual, the compassionate, the collaborator – those truly superfluous to the genuine, new Russian superfluous man, Zhivago. The effect of this higher orthodoxy is to integrate the ideals of sacrifice and renunciation with individuals whose sole concern is "the truth." Aesthetically, this is accomplished by the obliteration of fact and persons and the imposition of the Text itself as a historical symbol of literariness or, as Zhivago says:

> Resurrection. In the crude form in which it is preached to console the weak, it is alien to me. I have always understood Christ's words about the living and the dead in a different sense. Where could you find room for all these hordes of people accumulated over thousands of years? The universe isn't big enough for them; God, the good, and meaningful purpose would be crowded out. They'd be crushed by these throngs greedy merely for animal life ... Consciousness is a poison when we apply it to ourselves. Consciousness is a light directed outward, it lights up the way ahead of us so that we don't stumble. It's like the headlights on a locomotive – turn them inward and you'd have a crash ... and now listen carefully. You in others – this is your soul. This is what you are. This is what your consciousness has breathed and lived on and enjoyed throughout your life – your soul, your immortality, your life in others ... This will be you – the you that enters the future and becomes part of it ... There is nothing to fear. There is no such thing as death. Death has nothing to do with us. (60–61)

Crudeness, the ditch, and fear are alien concepts to sacrifice and, moreover, the doctrine of "you in others," which is as decent and socially respectable as any Soviet or Western ideology, does not illuminate the "sleeping beast" in Zhivago or the "throngs greedy merely for animal life." Consciousness is poison when it is admitted as *personal*, but it is light – God, the good, and purpose. The locomotive keeps us from stumbling; it lights the way, it overcomes the *merely* greedy, the *merely* animal. That Zhivago's own life is conducted on an ideological track cannot be justified by the allusions to the stock-railroad symbolism which crisscrosses the novel, apparently representing crossed lives, crossed purposes, density, dirt, and stink, which are filtered out until the reader has little more than the sense of an interminable symbolic journey of reverential proportions. Yet the image of the train is a prophetic image conceived to look back at events in order to project them into the future as material for a superfluous consciousness, but which eliminates along the journey all that the merely animal looks for.

When Anna Ivanovna Gromeko dies (she is the mother in the family where Zhivago lives as a boy), Zhivago recalls the "half-animal faith" of childhood when God comes out of the forest and lodges in his nurse's skirt; while the insight is genuine, it remains a virtuoso effect because it is tucked safely away in the past, only describing a boy's God-centred sensibility which will soon evolve into the *moral* stuff of a mature poet; more vividly than ever he realized that "art has two constant, two unending concerns: it always meditates on death and always creates life. All great, genuine art resembles and continues the Revelation of St. John ... With joyful anticipation he thought of the day or two which he would set aside and spend alone, away from the university and from his home, to write a poem in memory of Anna Ivanovna" (78).

The human animal is sublimated until life becomes meaningful as art, belief, and the aesthetic world; in short, cultural reverie replaces a demonstrated concern for persons. The argument is that we can of course read the poems in the appendix, which begs the question of the reality presented in the novel; although not quite: "And yet, no matter how the night / May chain me within its ring of longing, / The pull of separation is still stronger / And I have a beckoning passion for the clean break." This is how the novel shows the suffering for the poet's loss of poetic form; it is the fear the novel struggles to show as the terror of the contemporary period.

In the novel, however, the "clean break" takes on details that cannot be dismissed as the privileged sanctuary of a lyric poet. When Zhivago's wife bears a son – she is a woman about whom we are to feel a tender connection – she is hardly pictured beyond the immaculate "like a Botticelli" with which Larissa (Lara) labels her. We are to feel Zhivago's poetic connection to vital forces. This sensitive, allegedly pagan poet "rushed headlong to the hospital":

As he walked down the passage to the door which by mistake had been left half open, he heard Tonia's heart-rending screams; she screamed like the victims of an accident dragged with crushed limbs from under the wheels of a train ... Raised higher, closer to the ceiling than ordinary mortals usually are, Tonia lay exhausted in the cloud of her spent pain. To Yurii Andreievich she seemed like a barque lying at rest in the middle of a harbour after putting in and being unloaded, a barque that plied between an unknown country and the continent of life across the waters of death with a cargo of immigrant new souls. One such soul had just been landed, and the ship now lay at anchor, relaxed, its flanks unburdened and empty. The whole of her was resting, her strained masts and hull, and her memory washed clean of the image of the other shore, the crossing and the landing: And as no one had explored the country where she was registered, no one knew the language in which to speak to her. (88–90)

We connect these passages to trains and ineffable states of being and, typically, we leave the human being in the bed in the unexplored country of the merely animal: a baby immaculately conceived, a Botticelli, a barque, inward music of violence which we are to associate with pain, a birth which becomes a poem. The child who never utters a sound in the novel (or barely one in a sentimental passage) is a cause. Love is a cause. Death is a cause. That his consciousness is cluttered with cultural objects and gates is a tragic ignorance and is a quality that the novel does not wish to explore.

Zhivago is fighting in the Czar's army and an old friend visiting him wonders about an incredible smell:

"I know what you mean. That's hemp – they grow a lot of it here. The plant itself has that nagging, clinging, carrion smell. And then in the battle zone, the dead often remain undiscovered in the hemp fields for a long time and begin to decay. Of course the smell of corpses is everywhere. That's only natural. Hear that? It's the Bertha again." In the past few days they had talked of everything in the world. Gordon had learned his friend's ideas about the war and its effect on people's thinking. Zhivago had told him how hard he found it to accept the ruthless logic of mutual extermination, to get used to the sight of the wounded, especially to the horror of certain wounds of a new sort, to the mutilation of survivors whom the technique of modern fighting had turned into lumps of disfigured flesh. (99)

The sentiment is decent but troubled; Zhivago's theories are in the right place, but the intellectuality protects us from understanding what flesh and pain really are. Hemp, fields, and the dead are to be equated with fields of mice when we run up against that symbol later in the novel. When we do see a wounded man, we are to equate his wounds (of the mouth) with a revolutionary who learns to talk although he is deaf and dumb. The effect is a virtuoso performance, but made at the expense of human beings and human concern. It is literary prophecy with a vengeance. Only compare Pierre Bezukhov who wanders through a field hospital as a naive – but not holy – idealist. We understand his shock because we feel his defencelessness, and we feel how indelible the experience is to Pierre, how it changes him. Zhivago cannot change because his principles will not let him. When he complains that a roving journalist does not really comprehend war, a bomb explodes sending Zhivago to a hospital. But this is a bomb that cannot kill, it is a lever to get him into the hospital where he can meet the haunting Lara whose moral beauty is to fructify Zhivago's poetic beauty.

She had noticed a sharp change around her recently. Before, there had been obligations of all kinds, sacred duties – your duty to your country, to the army, to society. But now that the war was lost (and that was the misfortune at the bottom of all the rest) nothing was sacred any more … Everything had changed suddenly – the tone, the moral climate; you didn't know what to think, whom to listen to. As if all your life you had been led by the hand like a small child and suddenly you were on your own, you had to learn to walk by yourself. There was no one around, neither family nor people whose judgment you respected. At such a time you felt the need of committing yourself to something absolute – life or truth or beauty – of being ruled by it in place of the man-made rules that had been discarded. You needed to surrender to some such ultimate purpose more fully, more unreservedly than you had ever done in the old familiar, peaceful days, in the old life that was now abolished and gone for good. (108–109)

I am not concerned particularly with the moral feeling here, but with the sense of reality it invokes in relationship to the presented reality in the novel; for nowhere in the novel do we feel a sense of the cruelty, brutality, or savagery that preceded life before the revolution in Russia. The warm glow evoked by lost horizons aesthetically falsifies history and the sufferings of persons, and a moralizing of the "life itself" for which Zhivago's *life force* is always searching under the guise of "human understanding rendered speechless by emotion" (118).

Such pronouncements may seem to masquerade as human insight and have been described by Nicola Chiaromonte as the very dimension of consciousness, more important than any single person in the novel. Pasternak himself claimed he was effacing the characters in order to show the "liberty of being." The problem, however, is not whether or not the characters are effaced, or why, but when and to what ends, and whether this will convince us that effacement of people represents "reality itself [with] freedom and choice."[22] Chiaromonte says that "They [the characters] are defined by an attitude to life instead of by a sequence of revealing insights into their nature," and "the final impossibility for such characters (and for the author through them) to conceive of their own identity as a mere sequence." Yet this attitude to life, which is defined for many critics by the books Zhivago reads – Pushkin, Chekhov, etc. – as if we know what he thought or understood in these books, must be defined by *sensibility* in the Jamesian sense of the verbalization of reality into symbols and ambiguities. Sensibility as an ideal is also affirmed in the novel itself when Zhivago claims that people without sensibility massacre others, an observation which contradicts the entire historical Tolstoyan vision, which found that the people with the most sensibility were liable to massacre the most. But the problem of sensibility ought to be detailed by scenes from the poetic structure of the novel when finding one's voice is the soul of Zhivago's voices in him. The novel searches for the form-giving experience, which will enable the reader to find a transcendental position of a poetic epochal sensibility.[23]

A famous scene is the "wild duck" scene; Zhivago has returned home from the war. The revolutionary, whom we mentioned before as the one who found his voice in time to participate in the revolution, has given Zhivago a duck, and the family prepares a feast in the middle of Moscow's pre-Revolutionary gloom, only to find themselves unable to eat it: "And so it turned out that only a life similar to the life of those around us, merging with it without a ripple, is genuine life, and that an unshared happiness is not happiness, so that duck and vodka, when they seem to be the only ones in town, are not even duck and vodka. And this was the most vexing of all" (148).

The didactic selflessness of the passage is a clear voice, and the duck, which sticks in their mouth and throat, becomes the symbol for ineffable states of being of a genuine life, which would surely be destroyed if one were to eat the fowl. Sir Walter Raleigh once remarked that a child in *Paradise Lost* would do something radical to the illusion, and Lawrence wanted a water closet on the premises in *Hamlet*, something that would express and not idealize emotions.

The problem of Zhivago's duck is that you cannot eat a symbol, the merely animal, and still have a symbol; you cannot manipulate reality where your assumptions have told you that you are eliminating cause-and-effect relationships from your novel.

I do not believe the objects come alive in the novel because human beings feel things with their hands. Lara's cut finger is a reverie for a tainted past; when a dog tears her stocking, it is a prophesy for hungry wolves which appear later in the novel; Zhivago's medical career is a self-imposed ashamed mask for being a "healer"; Komarovsky, Lara's seducer, is a capitalist sinner whose motives are never intelligible, not even when he is synthesized into the higher organicism of Zhivago's consciousness; trees are not trees but woman's breasts, but when you encounter woman's breasts they are trees; Marxists are stupid because, paraphrasing, they ignore the truth and we know that Zhivago doesn't like people who don't care about the truth.

I have no quarrel with novels of images and dramas of historical consciousness of the alien world of the contemporaneity of the living revolution, but such novels *can* create an image of human nature by the transparency of their images and their explicit comments on life. And in this novel whose surface technique wants to deny causal relations – and in this sense intentionally defies socialist realism – we find symbol after symbol, one consequent on the other, so that in the end the reader cannot understand the novel without making an arbitrary causal connection between the ducks and the frustrated feasts.

A second very famous scene occurs after the Red partisans have captured Zhivago. During a pitched battle with the Whites, he is caught near the battle zone and is forced to fight, although "according to the Red Cross International Convention" he thinks he must not. At first he only watches the battle, and then the latent principles of sacrifice and heroism overcome his passivity. "It was not a question of loyalty to the side that held him captive or of defending his own life, but of submitting to the order of events, to the laws governing what went on around him. To remain an outsider was against the rules" (278–279).

But instead of firing at persons, he fires at a tree stump – that tree again – in order to sympathize, somehow, with the Whites. However, the White attackers, who are mostly children, move into his firing line "every now and then" and Zhivago wounds two; one apparently is dead. The scene materializes with reluctance, for we are watching the shooting from a point outside of involvement somewhere in the interstices of a man's soul. We do not worry about Zhivago; he is always safe because he is always in sorrowful baroque reverie that verges on allegory. The plunge into life is not an encounter but a recapitulation of symbols – trees, children, and an amulet with a Biblical passage, which saves the boy Zhivago from being shot, the amulet deflecting the bullet. The assertion that savagery is wanton in the fields is dismissed in one line, because, I assume, of Zhivago's principle that to the revolutionaries "the fate of the universe is less important than the victory of the revolution" (283).

The battle, the bullets, and the revolutionary represent a lag between the soldiers' own poor conceptions and Zhivago's poetic intellect which sees fate and universal truth, making him the sanest and most vital creature on earth. This separation of mind from reality is, in the terms of the constantly invoked spiritual values, quite sane, because it is quite in harmony with the projected values of sacrifice and the ethics of pre-revolutionary good; but the conflict between persons and history, which critics claim is resolved, is resolved only on a level of resignation to orthodox aesthetic forms; and the moving camera eye which jams the vision of the beholder is so full of images that no breakthrough into the terrible or dangerous is possible; there is no regression into fantasy but only a digression into baroque melancholy reverie where the "sleeping beast" is thoroughly obliterated. Such allegedly anti-Marxian ideological statements as: "Men who are not free, he thought, always idealize their bondage. So it was in the Middle Ages, and later the Jesuits always exploited this human trait" (407); "And do you know why these never-ending preparations are so futile? It's because there are men who haven't any real capacities, they are incompetent. Man is born to live, not to prepare for life" (248).

This is a very Gogolian defiance of mediocrity and involvement with the emotional problems and conflicts of people trying not to annihilate themselves with history.[24] The self-indulgent "So it was" serves to shift the issue into the past, as if the suffering of some remote people can illuminate our own "idealized bondage," which Pasternak leaves on the level of a harmless, decent, and sententious reverie on the Universe.

Bondage is not caused by the competence or incompetence of men – Tolstoy's General uses a different textbook of history but cannot alleviate suffering, although he might redefine it. Kutuzov is a general who fails although he is competent in shrewd understanding which verges on disloyalty – but his deep lack of insight into the insanity of collaboration begins with the inability to accept responsibility to the man under foot. The passages quoted above are, in fact, the typically moralistic statements of the detached observer, even more moralistic because the referents for Zhivago's opinions are never shown. Certainly, with slight shifts of emphasis indicating how there are "good" and "bad" Marxists, the novel can be shown to mean that Zhivago will side with a government or society that reflects his particular sense of competence – life as solidarity and self-abnegation in the name of something else. The tragedy of the Revolution and the irony of the limited consciousness of the hero come together.

III

The scenes given the most loving dramatic care concern the developing love affair between Zhivago and Lara, a woman Frank Kermode gallantly described as "difficult to speak of … without vulgarizing the conception."[25] It is not difficult to detect in such comments the idealizing critic's self-identification with a novel that worships the highest ideals. Or there is Edmund Wilson, the otherwise hard-nosed American critic, who when speaking broadly of the episode in which Zhivago allows Lara to leave Russian soil with her old seducer Komarovsky, says: "The last episode of life in love is unlike anything else in fiction: full of the tension of anguish and terror yet also of nobility and exaltation." The search for nobility and exaltation is certainly an emotional quality in the novel, but how can we really care about such a search? Can these words mean anything at all but embellishments to codes of sacrifice grandly linking misery and detachment?

In a cloying scene, Zhivago describes his newly awakened awareness of Tonia, his soon-to-be wife. Is his nobility convincing? We are soon aware that this relationship with Tonia is exalted in the way Don Quixote's windmill is exalted: "She [Tonia] had become a woman. By a stretch of imagination he could visualize himself as an emperor, or a hero, a prophet, a conqueror, but not a woman" (70). Even if we feel that the words are spoken with boyish archness, the imaginative deadness cannot revitalize Tonia, the idealized Victorian housewife – loyal, devoted, immaculate, in short, a product of Zhivago's reverie:

> Tonia and I have never drifted apart, but this year of work has brought us even closer together. I have noticed how efficient, strong, and tireless she is, how cleverly she plans her work, so as to waste as little time as possible between one job and another. It has always seemed to me that every conception is immaculate and that this dogma, concerning the Mother of God, expresses the idea of all motherhood. At childbirth, every woman has the same aura of isolation, as though she were abandoned, alone ... It is the woman, by herself, who brings forth her progeny, and carries it off to some remote corner of existence, a quiet, safe place for a crib. Alone, in silence and humility, she feeds and rears the child. (234–235)

This *Good Housekeeping* Madonna has no relationship to the sense of flesh or mysterious vital forces that surround the characters in Tolstoy. This is a version of allegory and emotional reverie that recreate life onto stock scenes and use traditional imagery to superintend the decency of it all, showing the aesthetic limitations of the historical drama. Later, when an image of light transposes Zhivago into reverie and "the gift of the living spirit ... [comes] out at his shoulders like a pair of wings," his mind turns to the other woman, Lara, who compels "his inward face, his personality" to transform "the forest, the afterglow, and everything visible ... into a similarly primordial and all-embracing likeness of a girl" (286–287). But Zhivago, like Frank Kermode, does not want to vulgarize the conception-female; when Zhivago finally turns his reverie into reality we find:

> Their subdued conversations, however casual, were as full of meaning as the dialogues of Plato. Even more than by what they had in common, they were united by what separated them from the rest of the world. They were both equally repelled by what was tragically typical of modern man, his textbook admirations, his shrill enthusiasms, and the deadly dullness conscientiously preached and practiced by countless workers in the field of art and science in order that genius should remain a great rarity. Their love was great. Most people experience love without becoming aware of the extraordinary nature of this emotion. But to them – and this made them exceptional – the moments when passion visited their doomed human existence like a breath of eternity were moments of revelation, of continually new discoveries about themselves and life. (329)

Or when put into the words of Lara:

> The whole human way of life has been destroyed and ruined. All that's left is the naked human soul stripped to its last shred ... shivering and reaching out to its nearest neighbor ... You and I are like Adam and Eve, the first two people on earth who at the

beginning of the world had nothing to cover themselves with –
and now at the end of it we are just as naked and homeless. (335)

The passage continues to search for mediating forces which
acknowledge the violence of history and which affirm the ascetic,
weeping heroism of Adam and Eve, but which deny, while reaching for, an imaginative rendering of the meaning and terror of the
"human soul stripped to its last shred."

That Zhivago is fully clothed and wrapped in protective
orthodoxies is apparent in the way he sublimates and experiences what we are to experience as nakedness:

> The dominant thing is no longer the state of mind the artist seeks
> to express but the language in which he wants to express it. Lan-
> guage, the home and receptacle of beauty and meaning, itself
> begins to think and speak for man and turns wholly into music,
> not in terms of sonority but in terms of the impetuousness and
> power of its inward flow. Then, like the current of a mighty river
> polishing stones and turning wheels by its very movement, the
> flow of speech creates in passing, by virtue of its own laws, meter
> and rhythm and countless other forms and formations. (363)

Pasternak the poet may work "directed by a superior power which
was above him ... namely the movement of universal thought
and poetry in its present historical stage" (364), but Zhivago
the presented character has admitted too much, said too much
explicitly, and has shown that a theory of purity, exclusion, and
Adam and Eve postlapsarianism is not compensation enough for
allowing the mammoth and sleeping beast to remain undisturbed
and decently intact.

It comes as no great surprise when Zhivago, as "maturing"
poet, "allows" Lara to leave Russia, for his consciousness has
already refused to permit a believable union which would have
forsaken reverie and joined them to the processions of greedy in
the streets, the hungry wolves who are starving but not ascetic.

After Lara departs, Zhivago stands leaning against the balustrade in Hamlet-like introspection, soliloquizing in as banal a passage of emotional detachment and reverie as the worst passages in Victorian melodrama. Worse still, the scene must dramatize the *literary* nature of the separation, and Zhivago moves from grief to poetry in one leap that intends to join life and art. However emasculated the farewell passage may be, and critics like Lionel Abel have worried over it,[26] I find it less disturbing, in fact more honest, than the passage which follows and which self-confessionally justifies as art and experience what are imaginative and emotional chains:

> The reason for his revision and rewriting was his search for strength and exactness of expression, but they also followed the promptings of an inward reticence that forbade him to disclose his personal experiences and the real events in his past with too much freedom, lest he offend or wound those who had directly taken part in them. As a result, his feeling, still pulsing and warm, was gradually eliminated from his poems, and romantic morbidity yielded to a broad and serene vision that lifted the particular to the level of the universal and familiar. He was not deliberately striving for such a goal, but this broad vision came of its own accord as a consolation, like a message sent to him by Lara from her travels, like a distant greeting from her, like her appearance in a dream or the touch of her hand on his forehead, and he loved this ennobling imprint. (377)

Finally, he concludes what the underlying form of the novel has been telling us: "History cannot be seen ... art always serves beauty, and beauty is delight in form, and form is the key to organic life, since no living thing can exist without it, so that every work of art, including tragedy, expresses the joy of existence" (378). This is the baroque philosophy of tragedy superimposed on a willed orthodoxy of life: his own knowledge about his situation is limited, almost by choice, by the fabric of his images. His life is identified with the aura of the creative and spiritual, the life of sacrifice and heroic self-abnegation which cannot cover up vast areas of insentience: you sacrifice "your" woman or the screaming misery around you in order to stare out of the window and meditate yourself into the Bible, or the literary tradition; or you scoop off the froth from the reservoirs of self-accusation that you find still potent enough to make castigation of the ignorant and insensible gratification for the reveries which mask your own unmediated desires for reconciliation with the play of sorrow that comes with the historical tragedy of the revolution.

But in this novel's poetry, or drama of epic consciousness, freedom is confused with a version of an egalitarian unconscious that relegates the slaughters and conflicts of life to "wholeness," and "form." And we cannot say that Pasternak is dramatizing this particular problem because he does not draw on the sleeping beasts and the unknown, the catastrophic, the irreconcilable, the irrational: a preformed idea of inward music however fine and coherent has stopped him from disturbing the sleeping beasts.

When Prince Andrei in *War and Peace* fantasizes his own death in eternity, he has experienced the painful isolation of man from man. His famous oak tree puzzles him because it gives the illusion of sensuality, of autonomous singleness in the face of his own perceived sensuality and potential inner deadness. For a brief moment Andrei makes the tree his own, but then he drops it because he understands where he is and that the tree will not tell him anything that humans will not know and feel through life and passion. He can make the distinction between people and nature. Zhivago cannot transform his perceptions of nature, which are passionless and cerebral, by seeing them for the first time as Andrei does. For Zhivago, they do not mean what they are since Zhivago makes them mean some private concept which never touches ground on earth. Zhivago merges into history. He cannot see the difference between tree and woman – leaving one is leaving the other; between himself as Adam, or St. George, and himself as poet; between Lara and Plato; between butchery and blood-coloured rowan berries. His own rage for order seems a fearful unawareness of persons, or liberation, or compassion for people or enemies, or shame at inequality of treatment, or understanding of those greedy in the streets who must fight the poets to get onto the same stage with Hamlet. And when Zhivago returns to Moscow to die an unsung poet, the magical reunion with the forces of political and imaginative control has been accomplished in a world of the utter abandonment of any commensurability of art and history.

Tolstoy wrote in his 1897 book *What Is Art?* that "all compromise with institutions of which your conscience disapproves – compromises which are usually made for the sake of the general good – instead of producing the good you expected, inevitably lead you, not only to acknowledge the institution you disapprove of, but also to participate in the evil that institution provokes."

I should be sorry to appear frivolous and make Pasternak's novel imply political collaboration with a political movement. It is a novel of dissent. Yet the novel he has written is the conventionally penitential novel that makes peace with history on a high level of ideology, where conflict and brutalization of persons are dissipated in the name of controlling unsavoury imaginative impulses. Zhivago never articulates, and thus Pasternak never recognizes, threats to bodily and imaginative autonomy, and Zhivago /Pasternak's addiction to poiesis, however understandable, remains a poeticized and spiritualized abstracting of life. His own aesthetic reveries are incanted only to exhaust the novel of any human potential and thus the ever-receding (or epical) camera frustrates Zhivago himself and leaves orthodoxies unaccused and the controlling intelligence of the novel hermetic and banal. He lacks insight into his shabby idealism which hurts others because the novel shows he has no sense of human connection; his allegedly defiant treatment of codes and Marxist-ideological doctrine is hardly critical, analytical, emotional, or amoral, but ascetic, for he has never let anything penetrate into his inward music with enough force to allow a personal fantasy or vision to develop.

Pasternak has written a novel which so confuses art with life and demands such spiritual goodness that it ought to be resurrected in the idealistic Soviet Union – and praised in the moralistic West – as the odyssey of a man who leaves the revolution, rewrites it into poetry in his exile, and who then comes back with his novel to inspire the society on to new, more decent heights, for example, the patriotic heights of World War II, where the novel ends in impending heroic glory.

If *Doctor Zhivago* presents a radical criticism of society, as Wilson and others claim, then it does so for reasons Pasternak does not understand in the way Tolstoy or Lawrence understood that you kill your inward music and yourself when you compromise with anything but the entire sun.

Chiaromonte has said approvingly that the novel is written "To move out of the 'fragmentary' and the 'personal' to dominate his lyrical impulse in order to render the sense of human experience …"[27] Exactly. The lyrical impulse, which was his own, capitulates to guilty "sense," and the self-accusatory feeling that pervades the novel reveals uneasiness, something wrong, with the fragmentary and the personal; that it is, in fact, personal. Thus the novel does not respond to the person under foot or create a sense of life that connects people to history in the sense in which Theodore Roszak says, and which great novels demonstrate:

> The function of morality is (to channel motivations rather than create them) … Don't we all dimly realize that it isn't a series of "bad breaks" that has descended upon us in the years since 1914, driving the proud self-confidence of the Enlightenment from our society? Nasty things like world wars and concentration camps and Hiroshimas don't just happen. Human beings, the same decent human beings who build cathedrals and draft constitutions and subscribe to symphony orchestras, make them happen and for reasons that sound far-fetched. That is to say, for reasons that challenge our conventional perception of things. And what is far-fetched is easily dismissed.[28]

The decent *Doctor Zhivago* does not "challenge our conventional perception of things" because its commitment to organic, symbolic form relegates the living human community to a secondary role. The baroque longing for a human community is not formed at a level of abstraction, but at a level where the artist sees spirituality as cheap compensation for the human indecency and imaginative irresponsibility of "decent human beings." The liberator may have courage and sensitivity, but he is still obligated to give us more than nobility, exaltation, and spirit as his own personal vision before we let him lead us by the hand to fight the 1918 Hungarian Revolution or rewrite the Bolshevik revolution on a level of cultural reverie which allows us to feel that our vicarious complicity in other people's lives is our own reward for never having been there. If the author gives us a personal vision as Tolstoy and Lawrence have, we are, moreover, not going to enlist our services quite so quickly. One does not have to dominate the lyrical impulse to represent the human beings under the artist's foot – Lawrence and Brecht were lyric poets.

The novel in Tolstoy's and Lawrence's romantic-realist theory of and for the novel – and I mention both with Pasternak because all avow to protect "life" – keeps people and art separate, but only in the sense that good art can never be a substitute for people or a capitulation to forms artistic or cultural which people create to control other people; moreover, the novel is a way of perpetuating life in people by implicating the dead reverie – found in life or art as the way of life which obliterates the human being in life or art. *Doctor Zhivago* never implicates the dead reverie, and if it is wrapped in the same package that living mammoths come in, I do not think it should be confused with the living beast for reasons that are very crucial to how we evaluate a novel: blindly setting up as we do separate categories for life and art, and blindly merging the two with ideal, spiritualized values, all participating in a cozy, unified, conflictless organic form.[29]

Einbahnstrasse or the "One Way Street": The Legacies of Formalism and the Dilemmas of Bureaucratic Literacy[30]

Only a speaking that transcends writing by absorbing it, can deliver human speech from the lie that it is already human.
—THEODOR W. ADORNO, *Minima Moralia: Reflections on a Damaged Life* (1951), trans. E.F.N. Jephcott

If ... ideologies have a special relationship to written objects and to writing, this necessarily implies that ideologies will also have a special relation to those places in which writing and writers are to be found in some density.
—ALVIN GOULDNER, *The Future of Intellectuals and the Rise of the New Class: A Frame of Reference, Theses, Conjectures, Arguments, and an Historical Perspective on the Role of Intellectuals and Intelligentsia in the International Class Contest of the Modern Era* (1979)

Karl Marx in "Critique of Hegel's Doctrine of the State" sharply draws out the how the State and bureaucracy are like a haruspex: in order to understand the State, one must first look at the "entrails" of the Priests of Bureaucracy and the Intellectual work in the capitalist mode of production that reproduces itself through cultural institutions.[31] Its universalizing tendencies are the phenomenal condition of the expression of bureaucracy; and in the realm of social and political needs, these tendencies struggle with writing, speaking. We look for the addressees for our work in culture. In the realm of cultural creation, "literacy" is a form of imaginary performance, and bureaucratic criticism dominates this performance, giving to struggle and critique an aura of pedagogy and spectacle. The hopes which the Enlightenment saw in the autonomy of art objects, and which lead to the objectification of art as a disinterested form of knowledge and nature, provided the reading public with an appetite for skills and technology, as well as arguing the need for reading habits that created the groundwork for bureaucratic discourse. Autonomy, then, became the *false* subject of one's thought and speech, the false totality itself. So, in this way, autonomy becomes totality by *not* delivering on Adorno's hope in *Minima Moralia* to reveal "speech from the lie that it is already human."

The dilemmas of a literate culture – the intellectual division of labour into structure and technique – are revealed at two levels in modern attempts to formulate a post–World War II formalist literary theory. On the one hand, literature departments are burdened by the Anglo-American legacy of formalism, which functions as a blind law in teaching and writing about "texts." Where the laws of formalist criticism are challenged, literary studies still fall back on ahistorical methods of explication and interpretation; this is fully visible in the fields of semiotics, structuralism, response-criticism, linguistic analysis, and the like. On the other hand, the laws of textual criticism reside in culture, too, for culture in times of crisis turns to the ahistorical, "neutral" terrain of "skills" and demands that civil society read and write according to certain, but unmeasurable, levels of how to measure literacy. [32]

However, there's a cultural issue here: Are literary scholars prepared, either by training or inclination, to deal with literacy as an aspect of the social history of art or the art of reading? One answer is that they are little prepared to question or probe the common myths behind the cultural demands and claims that a literate populace can predict democratic publics. The attempt to apply the formalist legacy of literary analysis to teaching reading and writing suggests that literary criticism can participate in "curing" all social problems.

The domination of culture – as if culture and nature are the same – is also the domination of intellectual needs by mass culture and the transformations in the nature of literacy and the production of literate culture driven by the assimilation of the individual into the marketplace. The conceptualization of literacy has commonly been a sub-specialization of sociology, education, and history or, more recently, communication theory. English studies, insofar as they are a branch of cultural studies and the humanities, have only by default been concerned with literacy. That is because literary "science" has failed to find a social or historical rationale for its existence outside of normative language, or national culture, or analytical functionalism: symbol hunting, close reading, myth decoding, and the like. Literary science is an ideologically fixed form of the more fluid and dynamic cultural context in which it finds itself, in which real history exists outside of its domain – the worldly domain of connoisseurship, skills, and humanism as ideological constructions of knowledge.

Therefore, from this point of view, recent critical thought that claims reading and writing are *primary* human traits which can be naturalized as "discourse" reveals the dilemmas of bureaucratic literacy and mirrors a more general crisis of alienation in bourgeois culture. This is a crisis in the cultural bureaucracy's ability to define, control, and utilize the thought and creativity of its young.

The same culture that makes a value of literacy overreacts to claims of illiteracy in the public sphere. A reading and writing pedagogy in the academy emphasizes technique, discourse, process, and product; in short, literacy becomes a delivery system. The guardians of literate culture have invaded *both* the public and private realm of the individual in the name of reading and on the subject, described by Dieter Richter as a "double reading morality": "In the reading institutions they behave like critical readers, once outside of them they behave quite differently … They develop amazing skill at this schizoid mode of behaviour (like their teachers, by the way)." [33]

The cultural sphere where the intellectual works and where the concrete experiences of becoming a literate individual take place reflects the ambivalent and anxious demands of cultural consumption. "Discourse" becomes a mediating concept and stands above and distant from expression and experience of individuals as creative beings. As an artifact or a grammatical or semantic system, discourse or "literacy" assumes a higher, more valued meaning than the lived totality that conditions meaning in both oral and written speech forms.

The early formalist thinkers in the American literary schools of the postwar period sought to make tradition and history unnecessary, or, minimally, to subordinate the reading and writing subject to the "ideal" text, and thus to dispense with both modernity and tradition. Literacy became part of neo-formalist thinking in which both the author and the critical reading subject were made obsolete by subordinating creation to the concept of a total language or grammar, or a procedural "strategy" that should be considered to be mentalist and idealist in its form, functional in its operation. It is "yoked," as Marvin Harris writes, "to a grammarian's paradigm." [34] While Harris's reference is to idealist schools of cultural anthropology, it could equally apply to the modern literary forces that treat the classroom as if it were populated with illiterates who are learning literacy. Students relate to texts as if they are peoples without history. [35]

This pedagogy has rejuvenated the enervated critical community whose grammarian work reveals a "massive ideological occlusion associated with solidarist, structuralist, and grammarian principles" because, while engaging in left-liberal or radical politics, their practice in the classroom, and in theory, institutionalizes mentalism and structuralism. No longer traditionally humanistic, literary science became a specialized cultural, philological practice. The study of the production of literacy, then, transcends sociologically oriented content analysis or ideology-critique to the extent that we recognize literacy as a principal form of cultural formation.

It is, moreover, a problem in the culture of modernity and the humanities to the extent that the secularization and democratization of culture throughout the twentieth century have been accompanied by the decimation of cultural elites and the destruction of the aura and tradition associated with nineteenth-century cultural ideals. The self-image of the humanist critic so completely atomized by modernist art and literature is now repudiated in principle and discarded by structural-idealist critical philosophy.

Herbert Marcuse claims that our fate as modernists is to observe how the "apparatus becomes ... the subject" and takes upon itself an independent existence as "form." Marcuse's "affirmative Culture" means the culture of bureaucratic domination. In this he follows Marx's reading of Hegel where bureaucracy and the state form a common bond in creating the institutions of the bourgeoisie and culture as itself an autonomous and separate agent of society. This is counterpart to the modernist destruction of experience (*Erfahrung* in German); on the one hand, experience, lived in its continuities with culture, and on the other, the sublimation of lived experience into instantaneous pleasure (*Erlebnis*) as in "having an experience."

For the humanities, then, the "literacy problem" is a problem of understanding culture as a spiritual dimension of life that is autonomous from the state or bureaucracy. In Hegelian language, "culture" is spirit, or "Geist." We do not realize that "culture" is not opposed to the state but is an extension of the forms of life, the praxis, that give the state its meaning; bureaucratic formalism. The study of literacy calls into question the very aesthetic and cultural forms of cultural creation and reception; the sociological qualities of mass elaboration and assimilation of literacy are the way we measure "culture." Literacy is the way we measure social performance. The dynamic of culture is its "delivery system" of *Abbildung*, the picturing through the systems of reproduction, distribution, and assimilation of reason through a "delivery system" which is the educational system, or "Bildung," human creativity with its own internal laws which must be integrated into civil society, and above all be "civilly expedient"; that is, useful for creativity, in a particular place and time. "Literacy" is education for maturity.

Literacy understood through this dialectical and critical lens cannot be separated from particular conceptions of cultural creation and humanization: in short, the constitutive and integrative aspect of culture. Literacy should be understood as a form of "Bildung"; cultural creation and education for autonomy, expressed through writing and reading the works of individuals, carries the responsibility of education for autonomy. [36]

However, conflict with disturbing aesthetic forms in which we reproduce ourselves *within* the pleasure principle and the search for happiness is included and is assumed to be innate to development of the self and emancipation from powerlessness. Culture is both friend and foe. Turning literate culture over to the institutional forces of and by the intelligentsia has conditioned how modernist reading practices are incorporated into pedagogy and education. Because these forces mirror bureaucratic forms common to social groups, they correspond to politicized forms of capitalist, bureaucratic anti-bureaucracies or anti-bureaucratic bureaucracies which struggle *within* the contemporary forms of the aesthetization of politics, in the very sense in which Benjamin discovered that "Fascism seeks to give the masses an expression while preserving property ... the logical result of Fascism is the introduction of aesthetics into political life." [37]

Thus, the importance of a dialectical understanding of literacy, which is by definition argued here, is a cultural problem that lies in understanding how the mechanical reproduction of culture at the level of aesthetics – art, spectacle, and propaganda – has created new non-human, abstract, and fetishistic culture. Benjamin named this cultural phenomenon "the spectacle," which conditions the mental life of the individual's assimilation into the cultural production which we can call "the public sphere."

Robert Weimann's critique of structuralism in literary theory has much in common with Marvin Harris's judgment, although Weimann does not speculate about classroom culture. Weimann tellingly points out that Roland Barthes's and Michel Foucault's rejection of "humanism" does not lead to a more complex view of the historical situation of literature but leads to a "formaliz-ation of some of its aesthetic and sociological ingredients." [38] The bureaucratic and business communities should applaud a notion of discourse that eliminates creativity, reception, memory, character, genesis, genre, and social responsibility. In short, the aesthetic preconditions for literacy as a form of cultural dom-ination dominates modern capitalism! Atomized communities, spectacles, and commodified art and literacy are not theorized in a dialectical manner by the neo-formalist ideology. [39]

When Barthes and Foucault and their younger successors argue that the text is an imaginary sign, we are led – by Fredric Jameson for one – to the view that literature is only an interpret-able artifact that must be rewritten and eventually replaced by the way in which we experience its structure. Paradoxically this new science of culture does not seek the truth value of the relationship of culture to origins, truth, and use that motivates the demands of science itself; nor does it place the production of meaning and value into an explanatory historical framework of labour and use value. The intelligentsia, reflecting the industrial process, turns mental processes into the production of rootless articles of language whose primary mediating factor is the attempt to make pedagogy stand for human service.

Institutionalized, the performance of criticism becomes an end in itself, neither able to break the spell that industrial capital-ism casts over cultural creation, nor able to provide the culture of the modern classroom with conditions of learning that are historically responsive to value or political change. A bureau-cratic pedagogy internalizes all opposition to administered truth by schooling students in the counterfeit criticism that mirrors rationalistic bureaucratic attitudes. Because the social individual is reified by and through the technological, linguistic, or textual forms that have replaced the traditional humanistic concerns of bourgeois art and letters, the social being of the readers and writ-ers in our classrooms is equated with the activity of their reading and writing about language and texts, thus forcing students to recapitulate the reading and writing experiences of their formalist teachers who have repressed their own history by passing on formalist techniques to the young.

Insofar as criticism of this kind can have an effect on us, it is to "improve" us as taste-making consumers. It provides universal norms for the standardization of culture. The use of structure, myth, or form in the formalist repertoire must impress the reading public that critical discourse, and "the text," have risen above the conditions of our industrialized literacy with its ever-pressing demands for skills. Bureaucratic criticism, in the way I argue, hones our consciousness of the text as an artifact. This convergence of literate culture with the hegemony of text-consciousness enables middle-class culture to assimilate readily available myths until the tougher, pragmatic functionalist critic comes along to reintegrate literature, with all of its contradictions, into the mentalist and cognitive structures of the mind. It is no wonder that Cornelius Castoriadis wrote in the 1950s that "art and culture have become simple objects of consumption and pleasure without any connection with human or social problems. Formalism and the Universal Museum become the supreme manifestations of culture."[40]

Formalism, then, has become institutionalized into literary studies as if it is by definition a human science, and while it has yet to produce a social theory or a conceptualization of literacy beyond "communication" of texts, it remains an intellectual resource. Formalism itself becomes a form of cultural creation but does not frame a world view or vision of how its origins reflect historical problems of reception, which the controversies of aesthetics and poetics did in the origins of Russian formalism in the pre-Revolutionary period which connected reading, writing, speech, and visual art to a common project of emancipation from sovereign forms of discourse.[41]

The formalist reading practice, when the practice does not connect to the cultural conditions of reading and writing as a historical problem, claims to be a creative moment in history.[42] It is not a cultural critique nor a consciously held aesthetic ideology, as in the work of the original Russian Formalists that wanted to change our problematic historical dependence on culture as the single most effective transcendent moral or mediating quality of reading.

However, formalism practised in the Anglo-American world *is* more like class *un*consciousness that works itself out through ideology but exists through its absolute dependence on pedagogy and institutions. Yet its order of existence requires that it remain separate from life and experience. Cursed by the demands of modern consciousness, it must establish itself as an *independent* language, an autonomous technique, a practical criticism. Or, in its more flamboyant forms, it becomes scholastic and a form of subculture departing from the aesthetic discourse developed in the Russian formalist movements. The Anglo-American academic culture, which is now embedded in the ritual of criticism, is not a language of a shared ethnological or social responsibility where literacy evolves from social performance based on critical emancipation from institutions. In the current phase of cultural crisis, the criticism of a figure like the American critic Fredric Jameson must be judged as a dramatic performance of his own flight from literature, rather than as an expression of his openness to creation or value. His attraction to mass culture, huckster language, and politically conservative writers reinterpreted as symptoms of capitalism (Balzac, Joyce, Conrad, Wyndham Lewis) is a symptom to be overcome. Like many critical paragons, he attempts to explain alienation to itself by wearing the mask of redemption and myth, form and ritual in the role of the anti-bureaucratic bureaucrat. This speaks to Max Weber's despair that modern culture cannot be rationalized as value.

The sociologist Alvin Gouldner comes to this problem in a different way. In describing the bureaucratized language of the intelligentsia, Gouldner wrote that the "culture of critical discourse that characterizes intellectuals" involves two sides of a contradiction both at the centre of rational discourse within representatives imposing a critical, i.e., an organic, cultural language onto the classroom. [43] Formalism spins its wheels, producing critical languages, but tears apart the total activities of people only to expose our intellectualized activities in all of their divided and raw forms, while in turn providing these activities with abstract drives, power, and undifferentiated forces of causality loosened from representation of the class conflict which forms culture as the "spirit of the age." [44] Quite different is the older, landed-gentry class of critics who accepted their subordinate socio-political and ideological roles while assuming a privileged moral and religious life, and a superior but partisan critical attitude towards all of culture. Expansionist economies have transformed this class into advocates of production and process in the realm of cultural creation as itself a transcendent autonomous institution of truth value.

Put another way, illumination of human relationships and the social production of memory are not objects of modern formalist thought. The homeless advocate for a modernist literacy has become, in a deliberate and programmatic way, a technologist of literate culture in the sense that both reading and writing usage are assumed to be synonymous with *cultural creation as such*. Yet, insofar as reading and writing, whether at the level of skills or hermeneutics, have replaced the older immanent humanist aesthetic, the attempt to cure the modern curse of intellectual fragmentation through "interdisciplinary" knowledge constructions is still centred in the concept of textual studies and in the aura of language-bound autonomous artifacts.

Propertyless in culture, the intelligentsia owns "texts" while state ownership of the means of cultural production resides in education. But whereas in the nineteenth and early twentieth centuries the artwork still contained the means of its own reception and had social significance for the audience, regardless of the problematic quality of the reader's relationship to "art," current critical theory renounces and repudiates both representation and the critical searching out of humanistic and social correspondences. It is as if there exists a fatalistic quality in our anxiety about art – because we sense that culture can never reproduce the "autonomy" of artistic works, or fully explain art in the conditions of art creation. This, by the way, is the creative condition of modern art as such.

This latent philistinism admits utilitarian concerns into the aesthetic dimension that are universalized and instrumentalized as intellectual "tools" – process, mind, or rational communication of knowledge.

The British theoretician of literacy and the history of literacy as a form of reason, Jack Goody, writes approvingly that "literacy and the accompanying process of classroom education bring a shift towards greater 'abstractedness,' towards decontextualization of knowledge." [45] Oral transmission in primitive culture is not rational because it "tends rapidly to incorporate or reject outright a new element in the body of knowledge … and the absence of writing means that it is difficult to isolate a segment of human discourse … and subject it to the same highly individual, highly intense, highly abstract, highly critical analysis that we can give to a written statement." [46] Preliterate contexts, according to Goody, cannot be critical of the reified literacies practised by elites and in institutions. Abstraction is good for culture. Goody's formulation of "individual" cultural creation does not show awareness of the work of anthropologists like Stanley Diamond, Paul Radin, and Dell Hymes who represent another view of traditional society by focusing on the dialogical, spoken, and conditioning of meaning in cultures without writing. Bakhtin's view of language as living utterances that struggle with culture against man is closer to the anthropological understanding of culture in the figures I refer to here.

The encounter of public, cultural, and aesthetic literacies in the simultaneity of everyday life under modernist culture is itself a totality that is reproduced in all of its complexity in the work of art. A theory of literacy, then, that incorporates a conception of critique and cultural dominance must also recognize that literacy is not neutral but is an ideologically overdetermined form of ideologically grounded expression. As Arnold Hauser says, "The occurrence of different art forms and stylistic trends at one and the same time corresponds for the most part to a stratification of society into several classes of wealth and culture, or else it is the harbinger of a coming split between the leading social class and the cultural elite."[47] At the present time, when it appears that the hierarchical, critical views of the cultural elite are obsolete, it is assumed that critical schools, for all their differences, still share a neutral and formal method of reading, writing, speaking. At worst this is "theorized" as an "interdisciplinary" reading practice.

This unity, I am arguing, is a unity of practice vis-à-vis the classroom, but it is a pseudo-unification in terms of the theory and practice of literacy; for whereas the traditional intelligentsia with its humanistic critique was able to distance itself from the state, even as the state was representing cultural institutions, and could even subject the state to bitter criticism, because it felt cultural criticism recognized government's position towards the individual and private property. The *contemporary* guardians of culture not only insist on their traditional critical independence, they divorce cultural creation from everyday life by, in Alvin Gouldner's words, criticizing "the mystified form of asserting the dominance and autonomy of impersonal technology."[48]

"Technology," in the case of the academic guardians of literate culture, refers to the language of utility and instrumentality, "educationally acquired technical competence," reflected in the socioeconomic privileges of those who reinforce the culture industries.

The culture industry is in partnership with the state, already recognized historically by Marx and Hegel. The correspondence between the cultural bourgeoisie and the business and bureaucratic interests grow closer to each other, in particular when the transition from an economy of wealth and distribution can no longer discriminate between value and the control of the supply and demand for cultural artifacts. The weak democratic system of education is part of the culture industry and camouflages the strong political economy of culture. [49] At the same time that the image of a working culture disappears, culture provides the means to professionalize, manage, and process images and words in the form of a critical apparatus that requires a hierarchically organized discourse and formalistic, skill-oriented techniques. Culture and administration are intertwined.

Cornelius Castoriadis's statement that "capitalism imposes its logic on the whole of society [so that] the ultimate objective of human activity (and even human existence) becomes maximum production" [50] must be applied to the semi-hallucinatory state of modern literate culture where, in the flight from sordid, entrepreneurial, and middle-class critical values of modernity and mass culture, the modern critic recognizes all the anxiety and ritual, theatricality and fetishism of modern consciousness, but establishes as a critical mode a vocabulary of textual analysis that emphasizes both process and production. This critical vocabulary becomes refined, scholastic, and ahistorical; it is mechanistic, professional in tone, iconophobic, scientist, and ultimately managerial in the way it standardizes and professionalizes its objective to affirm culture.

The problematic state of modern literacy needs to be related to questions of capitalist modernity, to the historicized myth of process and production, and to the role that the intelligentsia plays in cultural creation. [51] Anglo-American literary or cultural criticism has long been afflicted by an inability to formulate and use historical and class consciousness while not being able to resist the call of a National Culture.

In England, the peculiar deficiencies and strengths of I.A. Richards, Raymond Williams, Christopher Caudwell, Richard Hoggart, or George Orwell can in part be explained by their strict nationalistic point of view which, in comparison to their European counterparts, gives one the impression that they are not familiar with European movements. [52] In this period, the work of Gordon Childe, Herbert Read, Jack Lindsay, or E.P. Thompson is scorned, minimized, or ignored: true, neo-formalism grafts textual analysis onto European intellectual and political trends, French-Catholic ontology and existential positions; but the underlying tendencies have not changed, even though at the present time the speech and writing associated with public literacy and mass culture have been levelled by economic forces and political crises of unprecedented violence, bureaucratic controls, and power to expand cultural production and consumption.

In the face of this, the literacy of the critical avant-garde makes of the non-human a virtue: structuralists ask students to "imagine a culture where discourse would circulate without any need for an author."[53] And when Michel Foucault, who *did* author this statement, offers that "the subject should not be entirely abandoned," he rewards us with the warning that the subject's "freedom" should not be posed, and "meaning" should not be applied to the "density of things."

But how does the "subject appear in the order of discourse"? By being "stripped of its creative role and analyzed as a complex and variable function of discourse." And as "discourse unfolds in a pervasive anonymity," the tiresome questions of origin and representation are eclipsed by the higher discourse. Should this drama of aggression against the "subject" remind the reader of the Grand Inquisitor, or of his bureaucratic successors in Kafka's anti-capitalistic and conceptually rich and dense social world, then, in spite of Foucault, the world of human meaning has not disappeared. The word "subject" dissolves itself into the enigmatic elimination of the "individual" who is on trial.

In attempting to provide a historical and theoretical hypothesis for conceptualizing modern literacy struggles, I am suggesting that the classroom culture of the Cold War has not receded from view.

The postwar close-reading ideology, which was dominant in the 1950s and which has been consigned by the critical movements of the 1970s and 1980s to a feudal past, has returned with renewed force. But the contemporary historical conditions that we are witnessing may be likened to a "literacy crusade" not unlike the one mounted immediately after the war. Just as the war and its economic aftermath contributed to the formation of a new class of intellectuals that came to power in universities so, today, a new class of scholar-critic has emerged wearing a formal language of criticism with a pastoral passive-aggressive outlook towards learning conditions.

Our new bureaucratic populism, where everyone will be reading and writing "cultural texts," links cultural idealism, ambivalent acceptance of mass culture, and teaching "skills" to rational approaches to culture as process and product. This formative pedagogy is redistributed at higher academic levels by technical and pseudoscientific or psychologistic categories of thought, or in its softer structural varieties by mythical thinking that rivals the renaissance of Jung in America during the postwar period.

Whereas we can demonstrate that historically, literacy, speaking anthropologically, is controlled by priests, prophets, lawgivers, and cultural chieftains, we appear today to accept literacy as a given of modernity so that today's major literary critics speak in the language of either social science or its Faustian variants, including academic Marxist theory, without facing the problem that industrialization has not only increased literacy but may have reduced the opportunities for schooling, while alienating literacy from human needs. [54] Human capital is absorbed into cultural creation for ends other than aesthetic literacy.

Subjecting the material expressions of culture to the uneven forces of history and culture, bureaucracy not only replaces industrialization as a force upon individuals but reproduces culture and organizes it in forms that return creativity to us in unrecognizable representations of the human – whether in post-modernist prose, unemployment compensation offices, terroristic politics, or crude economistic solutions to warfare and "progress" that all depend on the technological-media-driven culture. The *false* materialism of "text" and "structure" hides the intimate relationship that still exists between economism and humanism and hides the relationship of intellectual to manual labour.

The neo-formalist dichotomies of discourse and textuality, product and process, theory and interpretation, practice and instrumentality, really comes down to two rationalized manifestations of the bureaucratic transcendence of market economy contradictions: learning skills and the cultural authority of interpretive reading signify the nonmaterial needs expressed by humanistic education. If the object of nineteenth-century humanism was the study of economic individualism (Marx), the object of literate culture should be the study of the bureaucratic forces that form our non-material needs. But this tabooed relationship is covered over by the ever-shifting cultural concerns that link literacy to the state, the school, the church, and to commerce. Yet, in the study of "literacy" it is not enough to demonstrate that "crises" are relative to the demands of technocratic economies and administered schooling; we must demonstrate how pre-bureaucratic, historical elements in cultural creation link ideology, world view, mass media spectacle, and classroom culture, and ever-new critical outlooks to the work place.

If, as Harvey J. Graff argues, the "environment in which students acquire literacy has a major impact on the cognitive consequences of their possession of the skill and the uses to which it can be put," [55] then both a culturally committed formalism (whether a Roman Jakobson, Northrop Frye, or I.A. Richards), and a technologically advanced formalism (Foucault, etc.) have missed the historical juncture of literacy and cultural creation. Simply using a politicized nihilistic vocabulary of process in a classroom divorced from history and society reduces use value to the bureaucratic consciousness implicit in formalism and modern cultural creation itself. Put another way, it suppresses a theory of bureaucracy for bureaucratic theory – that is, it co-opts for theory the already existing institutional bureaucracy.

"Literacy" is a dynamic concept known to the artists and thinkers of the nineteenth century *through* the forms of literary reception that expressed the problematic, cultural assimilation of meaning within the radical transformations of class consciousness, historical movements, and ideologies of creation. Today, however, the intelligentsia with its vast resources of culture-making techniques, propaganda, art business, education, image processing, icon producing, entertainment, and publishing, is no longer simply charged with preparing students and readers to enter the heavenly city of culture or preparing them for vocations or professions as enlightened democratic citizens. Today's culture guardians must also formulate, process, rationalize, and project culture as both an inwardly resigned and thus fatal affirmation of *itself*, and as a product that can be assimilated into the rational activities of mass culture. In other words, the creators of an aesthetic culture must originate, elaborate, and constitute the means of reception for cultural objects on the basis of an entrapped and crippled literacy, or as Theodor W. Adorno expressed it: "What is trapped within, therefore, comes to appear to itself as its own otherness – a primal phenomenon of idealism." The social subject, then, the entrapped subject of bureaucracy, is treated as social property by the terms of the discourse. Just as the need for cultural reproduction is internalized in the subject, the means for reproducing culture and consuming it is taken from the experiencing subject and is replaced by an abstract category, at times called "language" (Orwell, Jameson, Derrida), or technology (Goody), or discourse (Foucault), or form (Barthes). These categories are in fact attributes of culture, secondary formations or reifications; they have become the dominant formal tools of criticism. Using these as formal tools, the intelligentsia, uncritical and unaware of itself as an ideological community, cannot speak its own history and is thus doomed to repeat it as a cultural institution.[56] It *can* only formalize it, exploit the emerging reader's innocence and ahistorical sensibilities by dominating response, what has been called our "autonomous intentional capacity," [57] through instrumental logic and language consciousness.

Formalism as a technique of literary criticism cannot break the spell of industrial capitalism, which has turned social needs into spectacle and community into the *reproduction* of needs "stored" in cultural capital by the nature-less quality of the technicized images produced by the solely economic relationships of production. Formalism, then, does not abolish, through critique, the differences between art and life, but draws firmer the link between form, spectacle, and product by denying the ultimate realization of radical difference and alternative experience. Michel Foucault, for example, in "What Is an Author?" (1969) treats contexts as devoid of participants, and replaces the human with power, desire, and language, transitory categories that produce no picture (*Abbildung*) of human relations except as they are predetermined through institutionalized languages.

A historical concept of literacy would fill the void in theory currently filled by formalistic or structural vocabularies. The aesthetic act itself, particularly in its narrative or novelistic form, provides a legacy of public, cultural, and sensual literacy that remains *in* history by advancing the concept of the individual and the audience. The neo-formalist tendency to reduce literature, for example, to a manifestation of culture or ideology, or the structure of the unconscious, or the mirror of production, leads us into the old formalist claim that the particular "literariness" of the literary artifact has a higher reality than its social meaning. The potential literacy in the artwork is subsumed into the abstract role of the fictiveness or the arbitrary language of cultural process. Literature becomes illusion as an appendage, not as a utopian emancipatory effort to take control of illusion. Insofar as the novel (or myth) contained a *critical* literacy within the problematic of its creation of readership, character, and intention, it provided culture with a means to name and connect, to remember and relate, to act on and develop the sensual relationships of men and women.

In short, reading and writing as activities need to be grounded in a historical theory of literature as the generic form par excellence of the history of literacy. It is no accident, for example, that three of the most important artistic theorists of the crisis of modern consciousness, Freud, Brecht, and Kafka, reacted against formalism, positivism, cultural bureaucracy, and the bourgeois ideology of "theatre" and situated their critique of culture in the cultural institutions of "performance." The story of their relationship to modern literature, carefully reconstituted in Benjamin's understanding of the spectacle of production, consumption, and dependence on external authority as a mode of performance, leads to the Crisis of Everyday. The forms of public life expressed the needs of the soon-to-be-liquidated workers' parties, unorganized wage earners, and war victims. These groups and their experiences would soon be organized into the forces administered by the propertied classes who would repress the old cultural forces underlying the capacity to experience a literacy of cultural freedom.

The literary intelligentsia of the postwar period, New Critics, maintained America's traditional independence from European thought and created an Anglo-American alliance of religion, language, and political conservatism by teaching form, myth, and structure in the increasingly professionalized study of English. Close reading or textual studies in general do not require the teacher in the classroom, nor the literary historian to reflect on the social totality which provides the basis of historical meaning. The tradition, with a few notable exceptions, did not have to face the classic questions of the nature of literacy and community, class and institution, state and bureaucracy. Criticism itself was an institution, or in its most fervent moments, a New Jerusalem where the redemptive qualities of close reading would provide the student with an inner cultural resource. In the 1940s, '50s, and early '60s, American criticism, at first a local aberration happily and complacently fortifying its neo-formalism with the new specialty of "English," became the dominant mode of analysis, perception, and experience.

As prestige and status accrued to English studies, the New Criticism conceded that their linguistic methods and aspirations to participate in the intellectual hegemony enjoyed by philosophy or science were immune from and should remain untouched by either history or other disciplines in the humanities or mass culture.

No other humanistic discipline could assert that its inner logic must exclude other forms of knowledge-making in order to claim for itself cultural authority over literacy. The history of the effects of "close reading" on classroom culture and literate culture, and the history of the literary intellectual's absorption into the rationalizing economic and cultural system of capitalism, have yet to be written, even though the current crisis in literate culture has produced some studies of the deficiencies of the New Criticism.

It is important to state that post-Vietnam arguments against the University's economic affiliation with corporate capitalism, like Richard Ohmann's *English in America: A Radical View of the Profession* (1976), use moralizing historicist variants of the New Criticism to question the historical genesis of formalism in America. His approach concedes the institutionalization of English studies by attacking the apolitical tendencies of this movement which, he neglects to point out, began as early as the 1930s in the theological backyard of America as a reaction to liberal humanism and left-cultural criticism.

Without here analyzing Ohmann's response, we can say that such ahistorical approaches unfortunately allow the reader to believe that the history and development of American literate culture can be explained by an analysis of English departments, and that a reformed literary intelligentsia would convert English studies into political content and enlightenment. Ohmann's work needs to be criticized from the viewpoint of radical thought itself, not the least because his own sense of history and politics does not recognize that Anglo-American formalism in its essence sought to level and relativize modernist cultural differences, not deepen the contradictions of history and politics.

Formalism was not apolitical, but had a mission, the same one as Ohmann's: "We must humanize the *machinery* [*sic*] of literary study."[58] This "machinery" and the "we"-authority turn out to be the same old institutionalizing cultural bureaucracy, maybe with a new face. The new New Criticism assumes that meaning and use will ultimately converge in the production of students who will directly influence the system. How the "machinery" reflects the system and how culture remains an instrument that transcends the "institution" of "English" is never discussed, and the absence of that discussion is characteristic and symptomatic of the idealistic quality that still pervades American critical methods. Ohmann himself says, "The humanities are not an agent but an instrument."[59] He thus provides a version of the neo-philological, process-oriented approach which was already on the way to becoming entrenched in the universities in 1975. His structuralism is a universal theory and science of culture which is supposed to replace the deficiencies of individual perception with clerical power.[60]

Arguments about the falling rate of literacy do not typically analyze the cultural conditions that have totalized response into either the ethics of community norms or the class and cognitive hierarchies of bureaucratic educational goals. The truth content of art and the humanizing qualities of cultural creation are subsumed into the activities of the alienated intellectual who lives out the dilemma of becoming conscious of privatized reading, having to *both* criticize cultural conditions, and sell schooling and products of schooling. Attacks on the failure of Literacy fall into authoritarian criticism that patronizes reader, culture, and writer by claiming there are redemptive qualities in learning new "techniques" to read and write. And we assume the correct "receptive" attitude towards the "text" will turn literate experience from the private into the politically social. Brecht's own experience of his transformation from the intellectually alienated forms of Weimar expressionist cultural literacy to his sense that the "commodity character of the intellect" separates imaginary activities from self-criticism is an appropriate critique of the tendency of intellectuals to crave a merger between the ruling classes and its reading habits:

> The legitimate mistrust of the proletariat puts intellectuals into a difficult situation. They frequently attempt to merge with the proletariat, and precisely this proves that there are not different kinds of intellectuals, two types as it were, proletarian ones and others who are bourgeois, but that there is only one type. For haven't they continually tried to merge with the ruling class? Wasn't this the reason why intellect took on a commodity character in the first place? [61]

The key idea: critiques of literacy must consider the "commodity character" of the intellect and the ideological conditions that underlie the creation, reception, and assimilation of the "text" into culture. Culture is the "delivery system" and rests its case on the *harmony of the reader's subjectivity with the culture.* The discontinuity between knowledge and literate culture, which in part is expressed in the aesthetic forms that reveal the uneven development of culture and language – put another way, the uneven development of domination and cultural capital – is not understood as part of the process but is muted by forgetting that the artwork *itself* posits, questions, and resolves the problem of discontinuity at a level of understanding more concrete than language. The reader's mental, linguistic "ideas" cannot be the reader's *whole* mental existence. [62]

Benjamin's reflections on Weimar culture refer to the obsessive silences in everyday life: the fear of industrialization and revolution, and the aesthetic that trivializes everyday life with bad art and design. These silences have no "language" but produce literacy nonetheless by filling the streets with half-educated gossip about money, ego, power, and status. Everyday literacy could not cope with the sorrows and helplessnesses of individuals, nor could the humanistic tradition, with its didactic and philological capital, fully comprehend the transcendent State then in the process of successfully instrumentalizing political and military power. Weimar's fearful silences were soon replaced by the false totalities of communal "consensus," and the silent images loosened from the world of culture and freed from the domination of hierarchical authority; human relationships were administered by the rationality of the instrumental State that processed the voice of "reason." The obsolete materiality of process is industrialized and bureaucratized and becomes text, discourse, and authority. The spoken "word" that does not listen to its listeners' responses is, in Benjamin's and Adorno's response, in administered culture reduced to the expressions of the losers in history.

The modernist accounts of the nature and development of literacy as an explanatory and constitutive concept featured the work of Jack Goody, Eric Havelock, Walter Ong, and others.[63] Their historical-structural approach can be examined alongside of reception theorists who attempt to create a theory of reading based on the relationship of the text to an ideal reader who is a hypostasized subject without a past and without freedom.

Although these remarks may appear too sweeping, the intention is to open up the relationship between the study of the history of literacy and the aesthetic and cultural contexts that inform and influence our normative definitions of the concept of "literacy." This is an aesthetic problem. Moreover, I am suggesting that the recent literacy crusade in North America, with its emphasis on skills, process, and social adaptation, acts out the same solution proposed at a "higher" level of theory and practice where the hermeneutical, structural, and deconstruction discourses are not informed by the controversies in aesthetics or the philosophy of art; but they function as methods of avant-garde criticism.

Avant-gardism in literature or art-making has always been struck with the formalist dilemma, namely: How to find a historical ethic and logic that will explain the alienation of meaning from use value? And how to find a means of cultural creation that will integrate the "uneducated" subject into contemporary problems of culture? Posed in another way, this question would be: How can the bureaucratic and commercial, that is, the business and state orientation of secular life, be recognized in the totality of the culture that it creates? The terrorized humanist tradition has, we have been told, been reduced to debris: there's no totality, only fragmentation.

For theory to simply use the concept of *production* as a synonym for form and the complex interrelationship of creation, reception, elaboration, and assimilation of meaning to life makes a farce of Marx's silence about the role that art and cultural creation play in the lives of sensual creatures. Marx's silence about language may be uncanny, even repressed, because he assumed, in the Hegelian manner, that we must in the future piece together the totality of cultural creation out of the totality of life itself. Giving over cultural creation to the masters of interpretation and the legislators of skills allows the legitimating ideologies to adapt the bureaucratic educational structure to competency testing, literacy testing, and skills analysis. The makers of policy and the publishers of manuals conscript students into the "iron cage" of textual studies without our providing the means to question the assumption that literacy equates with progress, intellectual development, change, and modernization. Reinforced by technical formalism, pedagogy actually stands for culture, while pretending to speak for education – repressing the legacy of the Enlightenment critique of culture.

If literacy is understood as a socially constituted activity, a reproduction and illumination of the imaginary events in sensuous human relationships, we can see how fragile its mode of being can be, and how fundamental to life and the very constitution of literacy and its social reproduction. Linking economism to humanism based on cultural property, rather than real property, the intelligentsia controls the technical reproduction of life and not only reifies and fetishizes that life for cultural consumption, but returns it to us in a form that we do not recognize. Literacy must mean the constitutive capacity to experience. For the

humanities, the principal issue is not just the mechanical reproduction of culture or even the destruction of tradition, or "aura,"
even though this is necessarily involved in cultural transformation
and conflict. Today, to conceptualize about literacy raises the spectral issue of the democratization of culture, the institutionalization
of power, death, and aggression. Here we are talking of the creation of ideological communities. Culture, which has traditionally
been marked by the struggle to constitute social relationships in
forms that maintain and conserve meaning, is sensual reception
on a material base. But because this value cannot be determined
rationally, the creation, through the humanities, of ideological
communities based on texts, language, discourse, or interpretation
abolishes the social basis of the aesthetic subject – the individual.
The drive to reproduce ourselves in images and to represent those
images as cultural creations suggests that affirmative, permission-
giving drives are integral to the process of individuation.

The socialization and institutionalization of affirmative culture discussed in Herbert Marcuse's "The Affirmative Character
of Culture" (1937) and *One-Dimensional Man* (1964) describe
how the ethic of formalism and the spirit of bureaucracy have
abolished the element of protest integral to cultural creation.[64] To
determine whether this view is fatalistic, elitist, and catastrophic
would require an examination of the secularizing potential of
modernist literate culture, sped up, as it were, by mass media,
using the technical forces of administered bureaucratic literacy,
into new modes of reception.

What does this mean as a critique of culture? It means the
intellectual division of labour fragments and intensifies at the
same time. Everything is drawn into the labour force of everyday
toil. The separation of cultural managers, who are no longer separate elites, becomes forces for integration into the "affirmative
culture." We all become managers and learn to write about the
demands that money, inflation, wretchedness, and violence make
on our silences; this is not is a problem just of national cultures
but of world literature and literary creation as such.

But this relearning must occur outside of the legacy of formalist culture while acknowledging why and how it arrived on the scene and does not go away. The hopes which the Enlightenment saw in the autonomy of art objects, and which lead to the objectification of art as a disinterested form of knowledge and nature as a human need, provided the reading public with an appetite for skills and technology and for reading habits that created the groundwork for academic bureaucratic discourse, as well as the need for autonomy of art and the education of the person who reads. Autonomy, then, became the *false subject* of one's thought and speech, the false totality itself. So, in this way, autonomy becomes totality by *not* delivering "speech from the lie that it is already human." [65]

DOSSIER I – CHAPTER 3

Why Are We Afraid of the Panzaic Principle? One Road through the Wilderness of Institutions [66]

Wayne Burns began his long road through the institution of literature as a student in the 1930s. He describes the relationship of his life, his aspirations, and formative years in a three-volume autobiography published between 1986 and 2006. [67] He describes the third instalment as a "sketch" in order to distinguish it from a typical autobiography that delves into all aspects of a life. In my review of it, titled "The Outsider's Outsider," I referred to Burns's Socratic method of writing about his life through his vigilance towards the culture we live in and what it does to the individuals who are blind to what the culture is doing to them and they to themselves. In order to maintain his own mindfulness to his own place in the worsening cultural conditioning of the university and intellectual life, I wrote that his life and work revealed "an exemplary lesson to the writer as autobiographer and to the reader who may not have the understanding or cultural memory to see how things have gotten worse since 1968 when Burns dates the great divide between then and now." [68]

Burns's 2003 book *In Defense of Panzaic Contextualism* brings years of thinking to revising the concept and providing illustrations of the Panzaic. I hope to show that Burns's approach to the novel as a microcosm of the whole of our contemporary culture releases the individual from that whole, while defending, not only the Panzaic Principle as he defines it, but also the novel as a revolutionary form of art. The reader will find that the Panzaic Principle is not a system, a symbol, a method, but a way of reading.

"Mindfulness" means the way reading and writing changes our relationship to literacy and the created word. Mindfulness means not only care and attention to details but attention to the person (the reader) one is addressing. Mindfulness is also sensitive to remembering what has been lost, forgotten, and has vanished into an exterritorial place; being mindful is about memory and traces. But what, outside of one's own character and person, would contribute to the mindfulness necessary for survival in our mass culture? For Burns it is the novel, and it is this "mindfulness" towards the novel and its worlds that distinguishes *In Defense of Panzaic Contextualism* from other theories of the novel.

The defence of the "Panzaic" is from beginning to end a dialogue with the novel, with readers who can, and with those who cannot or will not, understand the importance of the novel for the individual who can read novels. Burns has been writing about this principle related to the novel since he began to think about the nature of literature as a life project, not as a profession or career. In Max Weber's words, intellectual life consists of "callings," and in Burns's life there is an instinctive calling to find holes in the system of culture and the institution of literature to enable him to carry on, come through, as he explains again and again in *In Defense of Panzaic Contextualism*. [69] This book is a calling. Burns often wonders himself why it is necessary to keep on explaining the relationship of this calling in regard to the novel to those who apparently don't want to understand it, choose to reject it, or who, for various life reasons, cannot understand it. His short explanation of the Panzaic in the novel goes like this:

> In life the rightness of the guts (as against the mind) will depend on one's point of view. In Lawrence's as in other novels, however, the guts are always right; it is an axiom or principle of the novel that they are always right, that the senses of even a fool can give the lie to even the most profound abstractions of the noblest thinker. And it is this principle that I have designated the Panzaic principle. [70]

The threshold period for the rise of *The Panzaic Principle* began at the time when the principles of the New Criticism were just appearing on the critical horizon. These principles of reading had not yet become the pieties internal to the critical principles that defined the formal approach to texts. The study of the novel was not a popular academic subject. Novelists wrote about the novel, but the "modern" in literary and cultural studies was reserved for the poets that stretched us back to the seventeenth century and forward to T.S. Eliot. Even Romantic poetry was suspect. While individual emotions, feelings, and confusions about life and death are the signature vision of the romantics, the controversies over romanticism lead to idealistic readings of the novel, in the hope that a comprehensive ethic of moral conduct could be promised for individual readers. The "Panzaic" took on the New Critical Express Train with its Institutionally driven locomotive speeding through the Universities making a few token stops at the theory of the novel; when it did stop, as Burns points out, the formal doctrines of the New Criticism dominated in one formist moral theory or another. Groupthink was clearly the order of the day. Henry James was the pre-history, and James Joyce became the contemporary paragon; they were the main examples of the novel's forays into the modern. English departments would be on the train as entrepreneurs of the modern. One way seemed to be to make *Finnegans Wake* the Valhalla of critical theory. The other way: to dismiss alternative views that grew apart or against the New Criticism and were labelled as Marxist or Freudian or, if part of the romantic expressive tradition, were given a berth on the train only to be told to hang around at the whistle stops where the bumpkins could listen to them until the students matured.

We were told that we needed taxonomy and a map as Critical Givens to inoculate ourselves against various critical fallacies. The issues in Wellek and Warren's *Theory of Literature*, published in 1949 but originated in 1942, provided that map by placing literature into either a taxonomy of forms or into the notorious "extrinsic and intrinsic" dichotomy that dominated the organization of what would soon become an encyclopedia of forms that everyone had to refer to. Of course, it wasn't a theory at all but a system of classification that, to be sure, included aesthetic and linguistic questions, but these were there to be answered as instruments for applied criticism. The theory opened the age of "Theory." It also opened up many questions but closed down others that Burns addressed about how he encountered this movement and its afterlife in postmodern literary and cultural criticism.

In this sense, this book describes a "Panzaic" relationship of criticism to the public life of intellectuals in the institution of literature – public life understood as the classroom – and how the emerging literary intelligentsia had its own problems defining itself. The choice was between packaging techniques of reading culture for students who were suspicious of literature anyway or opening up other ways of experiencing literature. The New Critical movement was nothing less than a shift in the nature of literacy itself and was, therefore, more than just one more chapter in literary history. However, it is clear from my own reading of Burns that if anyone finds and reads him now, or in fifty or one hundred years, his ideas will make inroads into their consciousness in ways the early forms of criticism could not. My introduction is intended to be an "Introduction to the Reader of the Future," in the spirit of Burns's concern that readers in the future will not know how to read novels.

In the spirit of posing questions about the future, I write about what affects me as a reader in the future *and* the past. I am one of those who remember the past. I believe Burns's book has a life in the future apart from the dust that Burns says remains on it because, he feels, it belongs to the "dustheap of history." Perhaps the present introduction, placing his book in the context of the times in which he composed it, could be a way of sweeping the dust away.

It is necessary for the future reader to realize that we live in an age of "criticism" that has ignored this voice of the Panzaic. In a larger sense, which cannot be described here, the culture that has moved from a historical market economy to a market society has endowed itself with the power to remove different voices of critical intelligence from the domains of the struggle of individual and society. Literature departments have too easily become adjuncts to market society. The suppression has not been deliberate – the death of the novel, a perennial claim during the age of criticism, has always been the sound of the alarm bell in the night when the Owl of Minerva spreads its wings at dusk – and here Burns addresses *the death of readers* who might not understand when and how the death of the novel itself became a reality in the name of the New Criticism.

Burns's provocative notion of the novel as a revolutionary moment of dissidence in literary history began to bear critical and personal fruit in the period after World War II. Soon translations of the Europeans began to articulate the crises in modernism and modernity in earnest – modernity often being a code word for a liberal culture buttressed by the cleavage between culture and the capitalist realities. And when Proust, Kafka, and Beckett began to appear, little magazines like the *Partisan Review* brought the novel and modernism into an alliance with the possibility of reading literature and the novel as if the individual counted and revolutionary possibilities for the individual were possible. Burns refers to his two essays on Kafka written at the time when there were no theories or methods to read Kafka, which put the burden of insight and judgment squarely on the individual reader. But this was not without some difficulty, as Burns points out in his further writings and discussions of Louis-Ferdinand Céline, D.H. Lawrence, the Brontës, Charles Dickens, and Thomas Hardy. The tour of great subjects would not work to bring the novel to performance as the struggle of the ideal and the real. If the novel were to retain the cultural privileges given to poetry or the epic, something had to be done to domesticate its tendencies, if it were to come into the canon and be blessed with an institutional identity. The ghost of "The Death of the Novel" was always around the critical corners, but the protean labyrinth in which the novel lived did not disappear so easily.[71]

The search for an aesthetic or ethic that would illuminate the individual's responses to the novel was always shadowed by the ideal of the canon on the one hand and the search for an ultimate reading method on the other.

For example, in Wellek and Warren's canonical *Theory of Literature*, a text of the times, the chapter on "the mode of existence of a literary work" wanted to solve questions that other theories could not resolve. The end result? Wellek and Warren constructed a theory of the autonomy of the text that dismissed the individual from the system of reading. *Theory of Literature* prepared and addressed the conventional reader who would be the groundwork for a mass response to literature midwifed into existence by the creation of overwhelmingly powerful doctrines of forms. Forms of literature would create the ideal of a homogeneous text integrating its cultural forms into the world as is. In theory this was to be a house with many mansions, but in actuality the rooms existed under the ideological shelter of form or genre or other "objective" categories of critical theory.

In the chapter on "Psychology and Literature," René Wellek pronounces that it is a given that Kafka is "neurotic in his themes."[72] This is said in passing and with such authority and confidence that no naive reader could possibly have disagreed. The novel as a personal project – indeed a personal project of the intimate and personal sovereign individual of the author – would remain a liability because the novel resisted, if read properly, incorporation into the Coming of the Institutions. How does one teach a "loose baggy monster" except by emptying it? James's loose baggy monsters contained explosive chambers. The "theory of literature" was not a theory at all, some of us knew, but a taxonomy, a map that lead right into the academy, not into the dark woods of literature. The classificatory critical guidebook was the beginning of a *nomenclatura*. But somewhere one has to confront Nietzsche in *Human, All Too Human* that the inversion of good and bad can turn idealistic "good things" into "Panzaic" bad things, by which Burns and Nietzsche mean that the god Nemesis comes back to haunt us. The novel always comes back to haunt literary theory. This is one of Burns's messages among others, that the novel remains a "Panzaic" nemesis whose "Untimely Meditations" can be seen as "thoughts out of season" in the way Nietzsche reads culture against itself. [73]

There were exceptions of course, for example Erich Auerbach's *Mimesis: The Representation of Reality in Western Literature* (1946), an essay comparable to Burns that actually discussed the novel and the individuals who struggle to detach themselves from the culture and the received authorial ideals. [74] The equivocation at the heart of the formalist doctrines was the need to make the text identical with itself. The individual becomes a phantasm of a "subject" subjected to the reified identity that the individual wants to cast off. Today, "identity," "subject position," and "subject" have redefined the now archaic "individual."

Burns's defence of the "Panzaic Principle" is a personal testimony. It is a Nietzsche-like working out of his own world view through his encounter with novels; as well it is a theory of the novel that consists of a set of principles that introduce the problems of reading novels. I attempted to point out the relationship of his world view to his practice of reading in my review of his *Resisting Our Culture of Conformity*, the third volume of his autobiographical trilogy. There I wrote that Burns knew that "tacit knowledge based on Panzaic qualities seemed to wait for events to show how one might resist the grain of the culture and the management of symbols of religion." This meant criticism as a religion as much as it meant religion itself. I felt that Burns aligned himself in life and teaching with those who defended the self and the individual when Burns created and developed his Nietzschean autobiographical "I" voice in his critique of culture. I extended the idea of the "voice" of the "I" and compared his way of writing his life to others who also wrote about the origin of their world views and consciousness. I wrote:

Similarly, Montaigne created "Montaigne" and discovered his own emerging humanist-I, contradictory character in a deadly feudal culture that made the inner life taboo. Diderot created Rameau's Nephew and realized that the doubleness of a baroque boutique culture was leading to the death of the spirit. Dostoevsky created the "I monologist," the Underground Man, an epiphenomal "I" voice that taught the "author-hero-I" how the culture had made him crazy. Freud in *Interpretation of Dreams* created "Freud" the dreamer who had to learn about the sixth sense that supported the speaking I narrator internal to the self. Even Theodor W. Adorno's wartime essayistic "memoir," *Minima Moralia: Reflections from a Damaged Life*, repaired his damaged self "I-narrator" by finding those breathing holes and reparation against the lethal culture of fascist conformity – American culture notwithstanding. A paradigmatic form, retarded awareness, could be said to emerge in the encounter of the "I-narrator" with, what Burns in his case, calls his "Panzaic Contextualist anarchist view of the world."[75]

In Defense of Panzaic Contextualism is, as he acknowledges, both a critical manifesto that clears the air and opens windows to experiencing the novel, and it is also the testament to his own vision and to his own voice that emerges through the novels discussed. However here the voice of the critic, the teacher, the reader, and the novel join in a discourse of individual selves who are thinking through the experiences and feelings of self-understanding. Socratically questioning what is Panzaic in the work and hopefully within the reader, the double-voiced nature of "remembrance of things past" is a way of thinking about how the novel illuminates the present. This thought turns the clock back to those times when it was possible to sail against the winds of the emerging critical movements.

This is done by showing how the novel brought the reader into an encounter with the ideals by which our culture insists we live. Burns frequently puts his own views to the test of the Panzaic Principle. He at first applauded Kundera's *The Unbearable*

Lightness of Being (1984) as an example of how the Panzaic worked in the novel, but changed his mind when *The Art of the Novel* (1986) appeared to go against his own novelistic vision of what he named the "Panzaic." The reader will discover that he revises his own principle, for example in regard to how one defines and uses "contextual." In this regard this is not a book about the past *but about the future in the past.* I know of no other critical study related to the novel where a teacher-critic's own critical preoccupations and presumptions are scrutinized for their history, their changes, and their encounters with other readers and students. Burns subjects his theory to the critical controversies that define both the private and public world of the critic such that the controversies illuminate the novel and him as reader. [76]

✻ ✻ ✻ ✻

Since the end of World War II, the critical intelligentsia has contributed to the explosion of criticism as a field in itself; the breakneck speed of change of critical positions has transformed criticism into vocabularies that line the shelves of the Walmart literary marketplace with terms and concepts. A market economy has incorporated what I have heard named "criticality" and "narrativity" as modes of intellectual fetishized parlance that must catch up to the standards of the market society for new brands, new phrases for the anxious and gullible believers. The attempt to turn critical minds towards some form of proletarian-minded populism related to the emerging cultural issues of mass-universities has been done without the proletariat, unless one considers the student the new proletariat class subject to the literacy and internet wars. The mass market of academe that Harold Rosenberg, the art critic, prophetically called "the herd of independent minds" has expanded to such an extent that it became necessary for Wayne Burns to review his entire thinking in order to be able to understand why he, and those sympathetic to his position, could possibly want to read novels and in turn understand why a critical theory of the novel was necessary and could, if possible, in the age of deconstruction, be a matter of life or intellectual death. [77] A theory that could be described as a "weak explanation" would be feared – if by "weak" we understand the self-reflecting consciousness of the critic who is unafraid to look back to what the work of the novel does in correcting the theory in order to undercut our "professional" or academic desires and fortunes. We live in an age of strong explanations with schools and labels and brand names: the word to use is Antonio Gramsci's "hegemony," where institutional arrangements and our idealistic presumptions come into alignment with our desire to find consensual loyalty in what Burns calls our enchantment with "the crystalline orb" of our ideals.

Burns illustrates his Panzaic Principle with readings that clarify his principles. In particular he stares the counterfeit novel in the face and names it for what it is, the assimilation of kitsch into complicity with the culture of accommodation to the institutions of market cultural capitalism. Philistinism in criticism is even worse.

The issue is not whether the novelist or the critic is politically reactionary, but whether the writer, like Burns, Kafka, and Adorno, sees kitsch miles away. He does this with great agility and familiarity with contemporary critical positions. One has the sense that these movements are force-feeding us with practices of hope for the future of an entire culture; Burns's comments about Edward Said or Terry Eagleton, for example, describe them as paragons of what might be called "Just Culture Theory" (as in "Just War Theory") and who justify their side of the critical wars by revising and rewriting novels as Edward Said did in reading novels for what is missing and making cultural value judgments on what is not there but should be there according to some doxa.

I could have pointed out the affinities of Burns's critical project to aspects of Adorno's critiques, for example, or Nietzsche's, or, relevantly, to Freud's. He makes these allusions himself. One could find anarchist affinities as he himself points out in his description of himself as a "parasitic anarchist," or one could have become a critical postmodern zealot by claiming, as many contemporary critics do, from J. Hillis Miller to many others, that literature must be, indeed ought to have been, and must now advance, the Just Cause. And if literature doesn't conform to the Just Cause, or, put in a way more flattering to us, give us hope for the species, or the underclass, or the subaltern, then literature must be interpreted in such a way that it will give us the ideological commitments by which we can live.

In an age obsessed by representations and critical vocabularies that represent representations, literature becomes the source of countless affirmations of these reproducible responses, as if literature were one media-driven commodity among other cultural artifacts. Its "mode of existence"? To become institutionalized. [78]

One might here show the affinity of the Panzaic to Bakhtin's metaphysics of the novel, but Burns himself brings this problem of critical affinities to our attention when he writes that the Panzaic Principle is about experience that is situated in regard to the novel and the reader, in the contemporary, and the reader's own autonomy in conflict with cultural ideals. Bakhtin uses the novel as a life or death mode of existence of the writer responding to the traditions of cultural controls that create novels written in extreme circumstances; for Bakhtin, the novel exists among the ruins of a history littered with cultural ideals. It is also the case that Bakhtin's "prehistory" of the novel – his term – develops from the ancient world of storytelling and the "genre creating principle" of a "prosaics" based on the post-Cervantes novel that challenges forms like epic and storytelling. Bakhtin's philosophical anthropology based on ethics and his view of the "semiosphere" of languages has this in common with Burns's Panzaic Principle: the reality of self-censorship, or overt censorship in Bakhtin's case, required him to develop a theory that opened up cultural criticism to the analysis of the subreal – the Menippean grotesque.

But it is not always clear in Bakhtin, except perhaps in his book on Dostoevsky, that he is opening up the novel to readers as individuals, even though the novel in Bakhtin confronts the always-existing situation of the reader in a conscious and unconscious response to a specific work not as a linguistic "text" but as a work in the making informed by readers' ethical worlds, in which answerability and dialogue are intrinsic to the novel. In the final analysis, Bakhtin's work is as much a theory of culture – he writes about the novelization of culture – as it is about the novel. Perhaps this is a point of difference with Burns's Panzaic Principle. Burns writes, in explaining the uses of the Panzaic with all of its variables:

> There is a difference between asking someone to see something and asking him [sic] to do something – even if in some instances asking someone to see something may be tantamount to asking him to do something. In the classroom it's the difference between a teacher's lecturing and a teacher's conducting a class discussion in which he and the students are exploring intellectual possibilities and he can do no more than make suggestions. And the same difference holds for the Panzaic theorist in his relationship to readers, since he wishes to present himself to readers, not as an arbitrary ideologue telling people that they should give up their crystalline orbs but as a critical theorist offering them a theory of the novel that may enable them, as readers, to see all that genuine novels can and do express. That is how, as a Panzaic theorist, I wish to be seen because that is how, insofar as I am aware, I am presenting Panzaic theory. Nor does it matter if, deep down, I am a raging anarchist who would like to smash all the crystalline orbs in the Western world. As long as my anarchist impulses do not affect my theorizing they are of no consequence. And my being aware of the impulses, and making allowances for them, should be the best possible guarantee of their not adversely affecting either my theorizing or my presentation of my theorizing. As long as students and readers are free to reject what they see, the theorist is justified in asking them to see all that is textually there. [79]

By creating a contextual-epistemological critical framework, *The Panzaic Principle* is in Burns's words a contextual theory of the Novel. It is a heretical theory of the novel in the sense that it is difficult to understand its implications in contemporary criticism without accepting that the novel is for individuals reading as individuals who can relate to others as individuals. One could of course bring psychoanalysis into the picture at this point and write a fully developed theory of the novel in regard to unconscious intent. Even if one is sympathetic with the "theory of the Panzaic," applying it to many critics and novels is the basis of Burns's many examples in the study.

My intention here in bringing Bakhtin into the picture is to show the affinity with his view that Don Quixote and Sancho Panza are Copernican forerunners of a theory of the novel which was on the table. With this "novel," there is the beginning of the "modern" in contact with the common situations, the birth of scientific thinking, the unrealized surplus of emotion in characters, feeling and life in the language that cannot be categorized in socio-historical genres like the allegorical, pastoral, or epic genres. The novel is genre-breaking. Yet these conventions are there, and Bakhtin was subversive because of the way he used the novel, which was one of the primary causes for his banishment from the Stalinist schools. But the issue that Burns puts before us lies in the way we understand the word "revolutionary" in the context of the individual, not as an honorific term, but as a concept that allows the discerning reader to link to Freud and the cultural criticism of those generations that did not shy away from Marx, communism, or anarchism. This was all a part of the cultural baggage in Burns's own "untimely meditations" and what I call his "romantic anti-capitalism."

The basic critique of the novel in Bakhtin, as for Burns, and even allowing for their differences, is turning to the novel in a capitalist culture that has, today, already destroyed the institution of literacy as we knew it and hoped for. Burns developed his ideas about the "counterfeit novel" and "counterfeit" postmodern criticism from the standpoint of the "Panzaic." Put another way we exist in the culture of the *tertium datur* – the mediating institutions that exist in some shabby outpost (that is, if they are visible at all), and in that regard Burns describes us as pariahs. This view of culture can be backed up with anthropological and sociological evidence, of course, but that is not the point. I don't think the Panzaic can exist in Burns's terms without the wholesale dismissal of bourgeois culture. The *tertium datur* is that a rescue mission for culture is absent.

Adorno, similarly, defended his own aesthetic as an outpost: a message in a bottle from a pariah who was addressing his work to outcast readers.

Burns's own critical readings of novels are reasoned with the reader in mind, with great skill and understanding worthy of Freud himself; he does not write as a programmatic radical. One could even turn Burns's theory into a call for a populist reading of litera-ture where the reader joins with other would-be Sancho Panzas or Marxists or New Dealers or Beats or New Agers or multi-culturists who fear that their organizations and post-traumatic communities or utopian alternatives will fall into neo-neo-liberal capitalism. Burns does not do that, but instead addresses the counterfeit escape hatches throughout the book. Here I will only point out for the reader entering this book that his defence of the "autonomy" of the novel as a work of art for the individual is also a defence of, or illumination of, what might be called the unconscious, which Burns addresses in key places. [80]

He has spent many years defending "the Panzaic Principle" and the authentic novel against counterfeit literature and counter-feit criticism. He avoided being eaten up by the movements that came with the legacy of the New Criticism, and although aware of them, Burns remained at the dividing lines all these years with his incorrigible desire to maintain what I want to call the measured actualities of the novel's encounter with cultural forces that deny the individual the experience of what Burns calls the "basic critical premises" that "differ so radically from present day theories of the novel."

The Panzaic Principle is a palimpsest of issues about the novel. It can be understood in Nietzsche's sense of how a work of art can serve life; or, put another way, if Falstaff or E.M. Forster or D.H. Lawrence or Virginia Woolf epitomize the Panzaic Principle one might draw an extended analogy of the *Panzaic* to Georg Simmel's essay "The Stranger." Simmel defines strangers as those who come into our midst today and stay tomorrow who do not by their very nature fit into the system of the state, the nation, the culture, or the community. [81] The critical premises about the novel and the reader's immanent experience of the novel as outlined in Burns's sixteen premises that introduce the book are not a full theory, yet they cannot be dislodged from the critical debates that accompanied Burns in his own conflict between one's own self, or nature, and the cultural "second nature" that, in Nietzsche's words, struggle with the reader's first nature. Burns makes this point through his early essay on Kafka's "In the Penal Colony," a point that is addressed again and again throughout the encounters with novels, their readers, and the critics:

> Whether or not something is Panzaic in a novel therefore depends not on what it is like (it may, in itself, be "inert and insignificant") but on what it does. More specifically, what it does to the abstract, the ideal, the "crystalline orb," the "imaginary halo." The two fine ladies' handkerchiefs that Kafka's Officer wears under the collar of his uniform (in "In the Penal Colony") may, for instance, be more Panzaic than "the seven bronze verges ... to which the dancing women offered flowers and furious caresses ... [until] shouting and howling, seven women suddenly hurled themselves upon the seven bronzes ..." in Octave Mirbeau's *The Torture Garden*. The handkerchiefs may be more Panzaic because, "inert and insignificant" as they may be in themselves, they nevertheless function in such a way, in context, as to bring out the discrepancy between the officer's impulses and his professed ideals; whereas Mirbeau's seven verges bear little if any relationship to the ideal: they merely express his notion of female lust. [82]

Freud sees in Greek drama a living legacy for a modern knowledge of the unconscious; Burns sees the novel as a living legacy whose existence lies in the Proustian sense of uncovering what culture camouflages.

Burns at this point speaks about the novel as the art form that carries the burden of opening us to the "the vanishing individual," words used in his autobiographical trilogy. It is as if Burns is showing the novel as the Great Barrier Reef whose fate is to be eaten away by the critical movements that he describes. The best that can be said of where the novel went after the New Criticism is to acknowledge that the novel surfaced suddenly in the critical history of ideas in literary history, radicalized in part by György Lukács's Kantian *Theory of the Novel*, or, in Walter Benjamin's case, the novel is pictured as being in conflict with "The Storyteller"; or, in Benjamin's approach to Proust, the novel became important as a philosophical-anthropological genre, critically important in the urban spectacle and a culture of consumption, kitsch, and violence. But while Adorno turned to music and Benjamin to other genres of modern literary creation, neither turned to a fully developed theory of the place of the novel in the emancipatory project of modernism. Yet both Adorno and Benjamin saw the historical task was to save the individual self from the appearances in which the self struggles to maintain a connection to the real. This is Burns's project as well.

Adorno's one extended essay on the novel, for example, argues, in a similar vein to Burns, that "If the novel wants to remain true to its realistic heritage and tell how things really are, it must abandon a realism that only aides the façade in its work of camouflage by reproducing it."[83] Adorno, in order to maintain his own aesthetic theory of the novel, still believed in the utopic motive to alter reality, yet at the same time admitted that "the contemporary novels that count, those in which an unleashed subjectivity turns into its opposite through its own momentum, are negative epics. They are testimonials to a state of affairs in which the individual liquidates himself, a state of affairs which converges with the pre-individual situation that once seemed to guarantee a world replete with meaning."[84] It was absolutely necessary to go the entire way and to "discover" what Burns names the Panzaic Principle in order to see how the novel works against the liquidation of the individual.

There were of course others like Lionel Trilling, R.P. Blackmur, D.H. Lawrence, Virginia Woolf, and E.M. Forster whose works formed an alliance to this contextualism, but never became central; contextualism never became the last critical word either. Erich Auerbach's *Mimesis* was not translated until 1971. Wellek and Warren were useless on the novel. György Lukács rejected his *Theory of the Novel* for his brand of Leninism, and his attack on Kafka and the modern novel in *Realism in Our Time* only made this intelligent, protean Marxist look pious and foolish, however much he defended Thomas Mann and the bourgeois realist prose forms. Philosophers like John Dewey or Stephen Pepper helped out along the way, only to be discarded as too constricting. To be sure, the critical locomotive picked up avant-garde travellers along the way, like Alain Robbe-Grillet and his *For a New Novel* (1971), and many others, like Edward Said, Fredric Jameson, or Terry Eagleton, who are likewise brought into view through the lens of the Panzaic. Burns writes that

> the Panzaic is not synonymous with the sexual, or the Dionysian, or the Rabelaisian, or, for that matter, any of the current forms of postmodern philosophizing. The Panzaic principle is *not* an attempt to elevate or idealize the Panzaic or Panzaic characters at the expense of the idealistic or the heroic. By their very nature Panzaic characters cannot be so elevated – and still remain Panzaic. Inevitably they become heroic. And when this happens they can no longer function like Sancho Panza or like Schweik. They cease being undercutters of the ideal and become embodiments of the ideal, i.e., they cease being Sancho Panzas and become spiritual Sancho Panzas or sensual Don Quixotes or, more positively, Tristans or Don Juans.[85]

The revolutionary potential of the Sixteen Basic Premises, which Burns outlines, is not about changing the University in regard to the social process or the spreading of art and literature into politics or a postmodern playground, theatrical, democratic, decorative, and ornamental, but is the potential to finally see the rise of the middle-class culture in all its complexity and horror that the avant-garde smelled and were often repelled by. [86] The novel goes closer to the odours. The autonomy of the self, the individual, the freedom of the mind became revolutionary because it did not matter whether the ecclesial world view of an Eliot, the canonization of this or that cultural movement, or the heroic and secular return to myths of the classical period, or a scientific determinism that smelled of something absolute. For Burns the individual is referred back to themself, and the intellectual autonomy where the novel makes this crossing over of individual and culture thinkable. This nexus is not possible without a theory of the novel that has its origins in how Kafka redefined the modern reader or reminded the modern reader what it meant to be affected emotionally and cognitively by novels.

Burns's chapter "Some Final Words" are about the fear of the novel. He turns to Kafka's now well-known letter about the novel in life and letters. In 1904, Kafka writes:

Altogether, I think we ought to read only the kind of books that wound and stab us. If the book we are reading doesn't shake us awake like a blow to the skull, why bother reading it at all? So that it can make us happy, as you [Oskar Pollak] put it? My God, we'd be just as happy if we had no books at all; books that make us happy we could, in an emergency, also write ourselves. What we need are books that hit us like misfortune that pains us, like the death of someone we loved more than we love ourselves, that make us feel as though we had been banished to the woods, far from any human presence, like suicide, a book must be the axe for the frozen sea within us. That I believe. [87]

Kafka was nineteen when he wrote these words, which are *not* cast upon the flames of *Weltschmerz*, but anticipate the responses of a much older reader in their commitment to Kafka's own inner project that shows how literature has an unconscious relationship to a concrete individual's life. In Kafka's case the writing that he carried out in his stories, diaries, and letters linked his fictional world to his Promethean efforts to make writing an aesthetic act of the kind Burns describes as "revolutionary." The meaning of "revolutionary" in Kafka's case is exactly the relationship of Kafka's own novels and stories that will define the nature of writing against the grain – namely that authorship and work are not "texts" – Kafka actually parodies the idea of "text" in several of his stories – but are works that cannot be assimilated into cultural theory or religious or moral convictions, not even those that want to represent the novel through Marxist or Freudian eyes.

As if anticipating a creative manifesto or credo about novels not being just books like any other books, the part of the letter that supports what Burns has written is the phrase, "The novel is the ax for the frozen sea within us." In explaining this haunting phrase, sinister to some, Kafka refers to his reading of Hebbel's diaries that he has been reading in bits and pieces (eighteen hundred pages!). When he reads the diaries "consecutively," he writes, the "game" of reading piecemeal, something begins to happen to him and he realizes what constitutes the "wound." In short, he turns the diaries into an experience *like* the novel and writes in the same letter:

> Eventually I came to feel like a caveman who rolls a block in front of the entrance to his cave, initially as a joke and out of boredom, but then, when the block makes the cave dark and shuts off air, feels dully alarmed and with remarkable energy tries to push the rock away. But by then it becomes ten times heavier and the man has to wrestle with it with all his might before light and air return.

Burns has created a theory of the novel that distances the reading of novels from other forms of writing and authorship in order to create more closeness, more intimacy to the inner world of the readers of novels, those cave dwellers.

It is this effort, this project, this building of a novel, that wants to roll the block of stone from the front of our caves by allowing the novel to illuminate "Panzaically" the idealist underbelly of our attachment to culture; the novel – here I am referring to Burns's "Ninth Critical Premise of the Novel" – "through 'vision' ... cuts through readers' ideas and ideals to show them who they are and what they are up against in the real world."[88]

Burns fires a salvo across the bow of the twentieth-century debates around the canonization of authors who cannot recognize that the novel cannot be conflated with poems or plays. This dividing line between the novel as the bright book of life (Lawrence), and the turn away from poetry as the dominant measure of literary value, may well be one of the most revolutionary aspects of the theory of the novel advanced here.

The Copernican effort to turn from poetry and redefine the novel joins Kafka with many defences of the novel at the beginning of the twentieth century; Kafka's manifesto-like statement cannot be equalled for its audacity and truth-telling, as we all become figurative Sancho Panzas or, to put it more crudely, "cavemen," wrestling with our ideals that require us to defend, rescue, and redeem culture in the face of the barbarism underwritten by that culture.

Kafka's statement is Critical Premise Nine in Burns's sixteen steps towards a revolutionary theory of the novel. But Burns goes even farther than Kafka when he writes that

> among other things, ... the novelist must be free to follow his [sic] "madness" (or as I prefer to designate it, his "difference") wherever it leads. He must because, as Proust explained, "Only that which issues from ourselves is unknown to others ... Intuition for the writer is what experiment is for the learned, with the difference

that in the case of the learned the work of the intelligence precedes and in the case of the writer it follows." In other words intuition, or "difference," always comes first, always exercises directive control. The function of intelligence or technique is not to deny or restrict "difference" but to give it the fullest possible expression that can be achieved within the limits of fictional form. [89]

By throwing Burns's words back at the argument of the book, we see in its development first the intuition of a revolutionary moment in the history of literature and then the integration of genuine novels into a world view – a way of knowing the unthought known in a psychoanalytical sense of the "known and unknown" – that does not deny or restrict "difference" but gives "it the fullest possible expression that can be achieved within the limits of fictional form." [90]

Throughout his life Burns has written about the novel as if it were a matter of life and death. His own theory of the novel is laid out for the reader willing, with Kafka, to see the details and not play the "game" of mere academic criticism. Burns joins with the first generation of romantic, anti-capitalist revolutionaries, enumerated and discussed in the book: Lawrence, Woolf, Proust, and those he identifies as ones who attempt to roll the rock from the cave, but who in his view fail the test of the Panzaic:

> The final test of a novel, according to James himself, is the quality of mind of its creator; and by this test, Dickens and Brontë take their places alongside Eliot and James and the other genuine novelists of the period. The novelists eliminated are the counterfeiters who denied both the conscious and unconscious aspects of their "difference" [which is] "unconscious intention" corresponding to "alien vision." ... Furthermore, [they] cannot avoid working from and through his beliefs in an attempt to give form and meaning to his "difference." ... Since "difference" totally abstracted from "roots" ... are what the novelist moves from, not towards,

in keeping with the demands of the creative process ... And these are the lessons that every modern novelist must learn, regardless of whether he [sic] tends towards "conscious" or "unconscious" modes of fictional expression. [91]

These are lessons for the future of readers, for individual readers, and for the future of the novel, if it has a future. We are on unknown territory here predicting the future of culture. On the one hand, I am tempted to write that the future of the novel is linked to the future of culture, or there is no future at all. On the other hand, there is *The Panzaic Principle* leading the Don Quixotes out of the Dark Woods where anticipating a future would be too much like the ones we have had even when – in Burns's view – the novels show the way out. Lucky for us, he has "taken a pen in hand" to remove the block of stone in front of the caves, as Kafka puts it.

Burns, in my view, understands what Theodor W. Adorno saw about the warm and cold streams of humanity, the struggle of the genuine and counterfeit so difficult to theorize about. "Making poetry after Auschwitz" is the infamous statement so often misunderstood to mean that one could not write poetry after Auschwitz. Adorno meant that the rupture into barbarism lies in the breaking down of the cultural formations and institutions. *Dichtung*, which is the making of an artwork, includes "poiesis," the struggle for creative difference which itself has been a struggle for liberation during the period between the wars when fascism burned into the individual's struggle for "self-preservation." Both *Kultur* and violence are integrated into inner caves of what we now call the "subject," an admixture of the culture industry. Adorno is clear in *Negative Dialectics* that he is defending what Burns names as "the Panzaic individual." [92]

We Shall Act, We Shall Build: The Nomadism of Herbert Read and the 1930s Legacy of a Vanished Envoy of Modernism[93]

Through all the mutations of these years I have relied upon a weapon which I found in my hand as soon as I was compelled to abandon my innocent vision and fight against the despairs of experience. This weapon was adamantine: and invincible, like the sickle which at the beginning of legendary time Earth gave to Cronus and with which he mutilated the divine father. The Furies were born from the drops of blood which fell in that fray.

—HERBERT READ, "The Adamantine Sickle," *Annals of Innocence and Experience* (1940)

Wounds dried like sealing-wax upon the bond but time has broken the proud mind.

—HERBERT READ, "Envoy," *The Contrary Experience* (1973)

Herbert Read's reputation and linking of aesthetics and anarchism seemed to vanish sometime after his death in 1968. "Neglect" is too honorific when we think about how his reputation drifted away. This, along with several other essays I have written on Read's anarcho-modernist critiques, is an attempt to rescue and redeem his work.[94]

His achievements in his own time might still be remembered, but have been discounted, minimized, even assimilated into the traditions of obsolete modernism which claim to be superseded by a more adequate *political aesthetic* of modernism. But this is not the case. He is not "the last modern," the title of a comprehensive biography of Read by James King, but an archetypal lost modern. A retrospective examination of the historical vagaries of British modernism since World War I, which would attempt to locate Read within the controversies over modernism and postmodernism, must account for the almost total amnesia which settled over the remains of this poet, anarchist, and partisan of a radical, aesthetic modernism that touched on continental modern art history, the social history of arts, sculpture, surrealism, and education through art in the tradition of libertarian, romantic anti-capitalism. [95]

Understanding the shape of Read's literary work in the 1930s, which were his formative political years, allowed him to break with his past. In the 1930s, he began the writing of his autobiography *The Innocent Eye* (1933) and constructed his aesthetics of memory only by staying close to the ruins of the past, themes clearly shaped in his 1926 *Collected Poems*, and in his 1930 study of Wordsworth. In the latter Read made peace in his personal synthesis of Wordsworth and Godwin by turning his thoughts to the creative process without sacrificing his political outlook, noting as he does that Wordsworth became more conservative. Read's march through the 1930s ends with the publication of *To Hell with Culture: Democratic Values Are New Values* (1941). The war itself confirmed Read's choice of anarcho-pacifism as the resolution of his engagement with the policies of modernity. [96] But the militancy of his postures does not reveal at first glance the nature of his *inner pilgrimage* into the world of modernism, which started with his discovery of poetry and philosophy at Leeds before World War I. This aesthetic-political pilgrimage carried him through the philistine and conventional British art worlds, where the formation of a national literature based on the values of Arnold or Ruskin – the rites of passage that would lead either to honour and gentlemanship or to Cardinal Newman's world of intellectual power and the cultivation of an elite – had been forever damaged by turn-of-the-century modernisms and the mutilation, death, and homelessness suffered by over a million people in Europe during World War I. [97] It is not an overstatement to say that a quality of inner nomadism marks Read's life and also marks his way of looking at pictures as objects torn from the catastrophic violence of World War I, in which he participated as a soldier. [98]

This is characterized in the way he ascribes both a sense of foreignness and hermetic rationality to both art and literature. [99] The picture for Read was a situation, an event, not unlike wandering into a Talmudic book, which both located and resisted authority, power, and insight at every turn. Art and poetry for Read always maintained a condition of separateness and individuality that has something to do with the sacredness of the image, conceived as if it were a person. Read revered the almost taboo quality of the individual utterance or image that he claimed was a spiritualized otherness. To anti-romantics, this often looked like mysticism or religion.

By the 1930s, Read was at the centre of the new revolutionary movements where gallery, museum, and the publishing press were working together to constitute a new art public. The world of the vanguard contemporary art journals like *Unit One*, *Axis*, *Art Now*, and *Circle* enabled artists, educators, and left-wing, politically engaged intellectuals to form a community, a syndicalist-inspired intelligentsia with roots in the constructivist and surrealist, antifascist art movements of England and continental Europe. Read's own aesthetic values were tempered by a deep self-scrutiny of his own artistic curiosity about form and a continued preoccupation with the relevance of the *failed* revolutionary British social movements to effect social transformation based on artistic practices in England and Europe.

In his own way, Read became part of the impulse to reconcile the art and political movements of the 1930s. He recognized that any revolution would ultimately have to be communicated through a thorough knowledge of the laws of the visible and material universe, as revealed in the way particular communal conditions must evolve out of the reciprocity of nature and praxis. The urban grotesque as a violent pictorial norm for the phantasmagoria of modernity would have to be reconsidered through the influence of psychoanalysis on an aesthetic view of art as form of life: the thing-representations of the unconscious. "Thing-representations" for Read are "forms" or depictions, not representations. The unconscious would be a process related to abstract art, and abstractions could then conceptualize art itself as a representation of the social history of the individual. Thus, Read finds the term "superrealism" useful to displace "surrealism." His objective: to illuminate the social misery also linked to the beautiful rationality of our art-susceptible inner selves and worlds. This enabled him to develop a new theory of the abstract in art and the phantasmagoria of modern life, based on a new receptive attitude toward non-representational subject matter (see Henry Moore and Barbara Hepworth). For Read, art movements are the historical expression and depiction of the history of modernity itself.

At his death in 1968, Read was arguably the most significant international literary figure that the English-speaking world had produced since the romantic movements in art and literature. Moreover, the economic analysis that accompanied his aesthetic – wrongly conceived by many commentators as a brute synthesis of pure literary romanticism and classicism – enabled him to critique the post-romantic aesthetic social pragmatism of Ruskin, Morris, or Fabian-styled Bloomsbury, although this aspect of his thought has been widely ignored, sadly and most centrally by Raymond Williams, who is paradigmatic of critics who attempt to place him into a unitary, single modernist tradition. Williams's rejection of Read, and E.P. Thompson's silence about him, is in fact exemplary of the narrow sectarianism of the British modernist tradition that saw culture subsumed into the labourist traditions, which were in turn historically placed as a struggle between Morris and Marx. [100]

This vanished legacy of a cultural revolution is deeper than the venerable clash between two cultures, or between Christianity and guild socialism that surfaced since the crisis of European

Marxism played out in the British schools of cultural studies, whose roots clearly can co-exist with Read's own populist, communitarian, and regional modernism. The historical consciousness we find in cultural studies is far more indebted to purely academic institutions and their languages than it is Read's tradition of libertarian aesthetics.

His fellow anarchists inevitably scorned his knighthood that was awarded in 1953 for his contribution to literature and to the cultural role that literature had played in England. This episode in Read's life certainly plays a role in the perception of him as an establishment figure. This condescending stereotype was maintained by those who never recognized that his pacifism and anarchism were deeply philosophical and moral forms of subversive anarchism. His pacificism turned him into the public intellectual who spoke against the liberal state while protecting and nurturing artists and artistic practices which were seen by the public as cultural Bolshevism or appeasement. Often pacifism is rendered as being synonymous with being pro-Nazi, an accusation levelled at Alex Comfort by George Orwell in an exchange in *the Partisan Review* in 1942.[101] Read's anarchism[102] was not compatible with a knighthood. But his quixotic and perhaps opportunistic choice to accept the knighthood did not stop him from speaking out against what his fellow anarchist and poet, Alex Comfort, named in *Art and Social Responsibility* our "megalopolitan civilisation living under a death sentence" which, for Read and Comfort and their fellow anarchists like Louse Berneri, Vernon Richard, Nicolas Walter, and George Woodcock, included a cultural struggle against professionalizing art in the name of sycophantisms of all kinds.[103]

Ironically, Read has been accused of being a conformist modernist. Yet, Read's form of anarchism is grounded in his experience of a consensus about the widespread denunciation of the social and political barbarisms active in the dictatorships and mass cultures of the 1930s, which were developing new forms of obedience and accommodation to the very state which liberal cultural epigones thought would safely steer a welfare state through capitalism and fascism. While Read never accepted liberal solutions to the psychopathology of power, he never made the step to becoming an absolute enemy of society. Read felt more at home in traditions of Utopic modernism in art that was a visionary critique of culture represented by William Godwin, William Morris, Peter Kropotkin, and the broken roots in the Russian Revolution that destroyed the anarchist movements that preceded it. [104] He was always restless with "ideologies of Britishness." [105]

Read's search for a radical humanist intellectual tradition which would enable him to bridge his pre–World War I Nietzscheanism found in artistic iconoclasm, which was in the air, a home. The search for the roots of proto-utopian mentalities is illustrated, for example, in *The Sense of Glory: Essays in Criticism* (1929), where figures as diverse as Jean Froissart, Thomas Malory, Descartes, Swift, Luc de Vauvenargues, Sterne, Hawthorne, Walter Bagehot, and William James are linked to a personalist theory of authorship and consciousness, for Read probably rooted in Nietzsche, Morris, Hegel, and Whitehead. The book consists of essays originally published in the *Times Literary Supplement* and comes equipped with epigraphs from Hölderlin and Ernest Renan which plumb the terrible depths of glory and hope in the unconscious. Read argues that images and languages of literature cannot exist in artistic form without individuals who rebel against the cultural forms themselves, long after the violent state, in Read's view, created violent civilizations that have produced a culture without mind. However, traces of emancipatory, poetic, and visual images continue to exist within the literary mind which fights against the pathological delusions and illusions of capitalist society.

For this reason, Read reissued *The Sense of Glory* in 1938 during his most productive period when he was linking surrealism, montage, and futurism to his defence of the essayistic, compositional style as the highest form of a Baudelairean or in his eyes Freudian, culturally engaged writing suitable for a critically engaged modernism: by using science, observation, and self-analysis we would avoid any possibility of being seen to be in collaboration with journalistic, professional, or academic culture.

The expressed thesis of Read's *Collected Essays in Literary Criticism* (1938) articulates a more unpopular defence of psycho-analytic understanding and the psychoanalytically oriented creative mind, and was, by definition, a challenge to the cultural conservatism of his friend, T.S. Eliot, even as he accepted Eliot's poetic modernism. [106]

In this period, Read's major literary effort, *The Green Child: A Romance* (1934), which he wrote quickly, in an almost trancelike state, is a side-by-side counterpart to his essayistic, partisan essays of the 1930s. All are grounded in conflict between the artist and the intellectual. *The Green Child* represents the torment of this struggle in a fictionalized Blakean / Freudian, even Lawrentian, allegory-like fable. The conflict in *The Green Child* illustrates the libidinal depth of Read's search for an aesthetics of self-creation beyond mortality and death, which he pursued through his pro-tean writings in the 1930s. This is the dominating thesis: that art and Eros cannot be disentangled and that together they consti-tute the *kairos* of revolutionary art's capacity to make autonomy and self-repair intelligible for a damaged life in a damaged society.

In the postwar period when Read became something of a celebrity with the American literary establishment – incurring the wrath of Clement Greenberg as well as an irritated response from Barnett Newman, who considered himself an anarchist – he was both lionized and tolerated in America, displaying his own willingness to join the symbolist, Jungian, and Suzanne Langer / Ernst Cassirer traditions.

By the 1950s any indigenous British surrealism which had survived the 1930s was either discredited because of its links to communism, or had been superseded by other movements, even though Read had already abandoned surrealists like E.L.T. Mesens, who had himself abandoned Read. The demise of his thought and his partisanship for an anarchist aesthetic can partially be explained by noting the anti-romantic formalist biases in literary culture, formulated by the epigones of cultural criticism like Frye, Leavis, Eliot, or the leaders of the American new criticism, like Alan Tate or John Crowe Ransom. The New Criticism's reading practices ensured that any contextual or psychological criticism would not be welcome.

Tate's editing (in 1963) of a volume of Read's essays notwithstanding, [107] Read's political aesthetics did not fit snugly into any new critical formalist mode. When his romantic-anarchist reception is seen in the light of the virulent Cold War antisocialism and the mood of despairing accommodation of cultural criticism to American capitalism, the now-canonical depoliticization of the modernist emancipatory aesthetic that Read championed in the 1930s was already part of a postwar minority culture.

From the vanishing point of Read's reputation, his visionary aesthetic project, formulated so carefully in the 1930s was already in decline, eclipsed by new forms of academicism and patronage, along with the growing influence of Eliot and Leavis as the normative modernist forces in the institutionalization of *textual* explication in the universities as the primary mode of reading. The hegemony of abstract expressionism after the war, which became the major American discourse about the avant-garde, mirrored the politics of the end of ideology. The futurist world of pop art mimicked suburban conformism, and early conceptual and abstract art flirted in a triumphant manner with the successes of British liberalism and American consumerist democracy: both gleamed with a falsely popular, egalitarian façade.

Read's disillusionment with the early stages of postmodern art was grounded as much in his commitment to the emancipatory ethics of 1930s surrealism, as in his fear that purely autonomous art would end up becoming distanced from the labile, plastic, iconic, and imagistic *roots* of art. Art as revolution was a form of thinking with art about the socio-historical progress of consciousness towards freedom. For Read, art was always *revealed* as thought in action. This was a philosophy of the act, and this meant that art was by definition a process that engaged the irrationality of capitalism: art would have to communicate the democratic character of its deepest impulses in order to avoid the cultic formalization circulating among the elite as post-utopian despair. The emergence of a monolithic view of modernism based solely on technical experimentation, which might be described as a text-centred, also gave to the reader or artist a de-authored and depersonalized view of the creative process. Read was aware that the industry of art could also produce counterfeit and high-kitsch art. For Read, this was understood as the last gasp of the British bourgeoisie in the face of the triumph of an alienating industrial culture.

This attentiveness to the flux and concreteness of artistic practice is reflected in all of Read's socially conscious writings about art and literature. *A Letter to a Young Painter* (1962), *The Forms of Things Unknown* (1963), *The Redemption of the Robot* (1966), which reprinted several of his most demanding anarchist essays on education through art, and *Art and Alienation* (1967), all demonstrated that the 1930s had constituted laboratory work on "the forms of things unknown."[108]

Read's work in the 1930s vanished into the postwar historical ash can, but for him they remained realistic *strategies* in aesthetic syndicalism and emancipatory, utopian modernism. The aesthetics of self-creation he self-advertised in the 1930s would continue to show a brave face of social responsibility in the face of the conformist nature of art buying and reputation marketing. Just as his work in the 1930s engaged adversaries and allies alike, his postwar work engaged Lukács, Sartre, Arendt, Marcuse, and Weil among others performing on the historical stage of "the great refusal": the refusal to accept that the tragic sense of life *organically* depicted in the way modernity reified and alienated our innate need for abstraction. Art as "thing-representations" linked to the unconscious, those "forms of things unknown," turned us both away from and towards a hunger for *natural* aesthetic life forms.

Capitalism thrives on prolonging chaos, and a new naturalism would have to isolate and analyze the forces that were leading to the construction of a second nature that would inevitably force the masses into reconciliation with capitalism. The alternatives, that the natural forms of the mind would become virtually synonymous with religion or fatalistically redemptive and violent art forms, lead, for Read, to a perverse form of humanism which became complicit with the vocabulary of the pseudo-humanist critic who asked the vast majority of mankind to become guinea pigs for culture.

While the artwork might paradigmatically represent a symbolic and communicable hypermodern experience, as in Henry Moore's depictions of the shattered torso of an exiled humanism, Read's 1930s anarcho-Freudian outlook stubbornly maintained that the desensualized and mechanical world of brutal labour can only depict and reproduce horror and misery. This world could not be reconciled with the idea of a society without art.

Almost all of Read's work after World War II addressed his fear that the existing social order had sold out to Cold War capitalism, which he saw as a preview of an emerging society without art, or a society without the possibility of individual transformation mediated by aesthetic experience. The rational style of his mind subjected his political and aesthetic emotional allegiances to a continuous and rigorous, almost monastic, self-examination. No other critical and pivotal figure of the modern British intelligentsia can be said to have constructed a personal aesthetics of self-creation that used the model of artistic practice as a social model.

This anarcho-rational model of the mind at its limits would enable cognition to *register* ontologically grounded representations of psychological forces in the unconscious. This internal world of the artist constituted a mimesis of self-creation which was based in a powerful phenomenological, revolutionary artistic tendency: the dialectic which contained the dissonant and the fragmented *co-existed* with a deep need in humans to project an erotically and compositionally constructed subjectivity. This aspect of Read's thought is reflected in his struggle to historicize his own political vision without subjecting art history to a *systematic* Marxist or formalist historicism. The following comment in *Poetry and Anarchism* (1938) is a redaction of many of his ideas about the erotic and sensual basis of consciousness, and was clearly the product of both anarchism and psychoanalysis formed in the crucible of surrealism's claims to have a special knowledge of the taboos and sublimations at the basis of artistic creation:

> What in the attitude of our between-war socialists probably repelled me most directly was their incapacity to appreciate the significance of the artist's approach. To me it seemed elementary that a belief in Marx should be accompanied by a belief in say, Cézanne, and that the development of art since Cézanne should interest the completely revolutionary mind as much as the development of social theory since Proudhon. I wanted to discuss not only Sorel and Lenin, but also Picasso and Joyce. But no one saw the connection. Each isolated on his [*sic*] separate line denied the relevance of the force animating the other lines. [109]

Here Read's ideological critique echoes Trotsky, as well as Kropotkin, Stirner, Tolstoy, and Kierkegaard, and reflects his deep awareness of many exiled Hegelian and Marxist art historians and aestheticians in the 1930s like Carl Einstein, Max Raphael, and later other radical humanist critics like Karl Mannheim, Martin Buber, Arnold Hauser, and Sigfried Giedion. [110]

The social significance and existential reality of this *antifascist intellectual community* in exile is never lost on him. In the postwar years he attempted, perhaps quixotically, to define an aesthetic of anarchism in terms of a radically contingent attitude towards human nature, positioned in relationship to a social history of art and design. This introduced a social history of art to England, in what he called a culture of highbrow bad taste. Read's intellectual project in the 1930s was nothing less than a conscious and deliberate attempt to ground artistic practice in a social history of the present. Yet it was the contingencies of the art practices and their relationship to the social movements to which he felt a clear sympathy. He saw that the contingencies of modern methods of art reflected not only his personal crisis of belief in the efficacy of art, but his commitment to a new kind of artist and the education of intelligence away from the class-oriented affectations of British cultural values: literature and modern art were really laboratories and studios where non-rational and pre-rational forms become reflected in the autonomy of the work itself.

The politics of this pan-revolutionary humanism for which he sought a vocabulary in the 1930s is demonstrated in his hundreds of commentaries about the radical nature of this project. In order to function socially, artistic abstraction and dissonance, in an age of brutal and criminal social transformation, must stimulate the organic possibilities of a revolution in perception, which was *already* going on in the minds of educated and uneducated beholders alike who had not given up their desire to become free and spontaneous individuals. As a mediator and envoy for this public role of revolutionary art, Read serves as the transmitter of the particular values of artistic experimentation to the public, who are themselves alienated but not devoid of innate or natural values. He saw himself as representative of working-class connectedness to former craft and vernacular cultures. However, these separate and indigenous working class and pastoral cultures from which Read emerged, whose sympathies were with these cultures, are in trouble because of the social domination in which they are immersed. The primitive and discursive mythical roots of earlier forms of social organization have been all but obliterated, and no amount of utopian news from elsewhere, not Ruskin, not Morris, not even Marx, could redeem a natural perception of forms from the crisis of culture into which the masses of peoples had been propelled and then exiled.

Read was himself almost morbidly aware of the pressures of historical change on his own personality, and in this respect, his analysis of the creative process in *The Green Child*, his single work of fiction, should be understood to be contiguous with his project of an aesthetic of self-creation that redeemed the perversity of the social for a personal vision.

The pathos of his allegorical romance, *The Green Child*, is not only the search for an ideal community of virtue in which a romance and love story carries the burden of disclosing the loss of nature and home. Here Read faces the problem of the loss and reconstruction of both personal and historical memory. Memory is conditioned by a yearning for an ideal world in which an absolute love which cannot be – the surrealist's artistic desire for abstraction that wills elimination of all taboos – reconciles sexual taboos by rescuing an unknown person, the Green Child, the immaculate girl-child who becomes iconic; she claims existential rights over the male quester. The quest: the male's odyssey must free him of archaic forms of symbolic identities.

The only source of peace would be to purge the will to power of the political quester, power which is connected to our tendency to indulge ourselves in political abstractions, unmediated by art, that is innate in the human mind. Only concrete aesthetic experiences can alleviate the misery of an endless search into symbolic systems of knowledge. The anarcho-social aesthetic therefore demands a sensual connection, reciprocity and mutuality as a condition of artistic formation and humanness. Continually aware of the way artists subjected abstractions of space, time, and the conceptual situation of art itself to a continuing critique of contemporary life, artistic activity was for Read a self-reflexive act, grounded in the natural world, which worked against convention and the assimilation of the artist into an authoritarian and dehumanizing society. His last works were, as David Thistlewood argues, a critique of painting "that in its post Existentialist manifestations … had abandoned the Modernist project." [111]

This critique, however, is not a postwar affectation of pessimism; Read was maintaining a project already underway in the 1930s. It is not difficult to see his deep affinity with the other European aesthetic modernists who formed their dialectical organicism in the period between the wars, and who continued the controversies of the 1930s, well into the postwar period of modernism. The critiques of Adorno and Benjamin come to mind, and' these would have to be compared to Read's, who also saw in the collapse and assimilation of the avant-garde into capitalism's cultural accumulation the failure to provide either a political, cognitive, or aesthetic practice that would sustain the critique that had been fundamental to the origins and continuity of modernism's deep critique of capitalism. [112] If modernism was now driven by an economic and political theology – a will to power controlled by massive industries which degraded the will to resist – then the art historian and critic and the formative institutions of modernism would have to be measured by their absorption into an anonymous society which had surrendered its historical memory to a self-absorbed reconciliatory aesthetic attitude without art. Kitsch would infect art.

> If the aesthetic attitude as such is now ineffectual, the reason is to be found in our conscious and sceptical attitude to works of art. A deep rift divides the poetic consciousness from the collective instincts of mankind. The poet is an outcast, isolated. As a result, he has become introspective and analytically self-destructive. The mass does not resist him – it ignores him. [113]

Read writes in *The Contrary Experience* (1963) that

> Actually, there was an unfailing continuity in my political interests and political opinions. I would not like to claim that they show an unfailing consistency, but the general principles which I found congenial as a young man are the basic principles of the only political philosophy I find congenial. In calling these principles Anarchism I have forfeited any claim to be taken seriously

as a politician and have cut myself off from the main current of socialist activity in England. [114]

The relationship of life to memory and Read's construction of a philosophy of the artistic act can be understood in the mysterious work, *The Green Child*. This elusive romance, which fascinated Jung and a younger generation of poets, like Kenneth Rexroth, reveals how his surrealist turn, in thought, poetry, and intellectual action struggled against the forces of sensual atrophy, and how an adversarial ideology of "Forward from Liberalism" beyond Fascism and Communism would be an emotional swamp for any art and aesthetic self-creation. In order for Read to transform "this life" into "this art" – Merleau-Ponty's representation of Cézanne's experiential life in the immediacy of his paintings – it was necessary to render the psychological image into a political one without losing the essential aesthetic perception that resided in the forms of memory.

※ ※ ※ ※

Now, Olivero had never forgotten this strange event – in his mind it had the significance of an unresolved symbol, obscurely connected with his departure, and connected, too, with the inevitability of his return.

—READ, *The Green Child* (1963)

We shall act
We shall build
A crystal city in the age of peace
Setting out from an island of calm
A limpid source of love.

—READ, *A World within War* (1945)

Surrealism was not only an art-historical movement. It is a mimetic event of the always possible misrecognition of both the erotic core of love and the fear of images inside our morphic forms of creation. For Read, not knowing this fear destroys the mind and wrecks the impulse to combine images with life in order to keep memory alive: dreams are "figurations" or "thing representations" in the unconscious and haunt both art and life.

Read's early love affairs with surrealism and with the philosophy of the act are emotionally and formally rendered in his fable, *The Green Child*. The Green Child is a girl, a strange translucently fleshly creature who "comes from a world" from which her Odyssean lover, Olivero, "has no knowledge": "She had never been able to describe that world to anyone, because there were no earthly words to exchange for her memories" (59). The abstractions in quester Olivero's mind must protect him against the erosion of everyday life and the memories which she hauntingly evokes as he engages on a rescue mission of this tabooed creature. The two characters are then subjected to the mysterious forces of symbolic nomadism. They represent otherworldly peoples whose only baggage is their words and stories – "too many words," Olivero feels, that cannot convey the loss of life found in traditional communal forms that are now wholly imaginary. Read's surreal fable constructs the childhood of memory by fusing the imaginary past and the memory of an *immaculate* love together into an André Breton, Nadja-like image of an extreme happiness. The Childhood of Memory is an aesthetic world in itself, where memory exists as both experience and construction, not just as recollection of the events in childhood.

The woman-child is both an image and a body that accompanies the Odyssean hero back to otherworldly, Blakean mythologies where persecution, rape, repression, and ugliness dominate. Surreal memory formation is equated with artistic formation, and the search for form passes through dream imagery. Olivero, the Green Child's protector, lover, and intellectual companion, comes alive during the final, deathly phase of his adventures, because he "found it advisable to suppress his knowledge of another world and all his other worldly experience."

This is an anamnestic fall into sensuality that allows him to recover his mind, but only "by keeping his knowledge to himself, regarding it as a secret store of dream imagery ... [can he have] ... a great advantage over his companions in his discussions" (184).

The non-human peoples who have created a surreal community based on geologic principles could not understand the laws of the natural world, since they "regarded the organic and vital elements of their bodies as disgusting and deplorable" (175) and worshipped death. "Their sole desire was to become solid – as solid and perdurable as the rocks around them" (175). The source of their misery: deprivation of experience and the loss of nature, which becomes the loss of the knowledge of eternity embedded in Read's notions of aesthetic nature as a world of "thing representations" or dreams. The consequence of the allegory as dream is the knowledge that the harmony of artistic creation with the surreal fantasies created in the world by power-driven individuals is a new form of brutalist contingency and necessity. This degradation creates this world of half-creatures who live with totemistic knowledges and who have no capacity to mourn the past.

In Kafkaesque parabolic form, without metaphor and without colour or description, Read's fable of human abstraction documents the derealization of the powers of the imagination. The fable combines rational analysis with dreamlike everyday life sequences in order to create a powerful sense of Read's knowledge of the place of repression in the construction of abstract art and imagist poetry. However, this process causes everyday life to disappear like the mirage that it comes to be. The artistic people discovered at the end of Olivero's journey do not know any source for their music, geometry, or worship of crystals. They attach no value to change; they have no knowledge of "sensuous anticipation" (*The Green Child*, 189). Their goal in life: to prepare for death. Olivero prepares for his death by rigours of contemplation which ritual-ize his body through ecstasies "of objective proportions" and anticipation of the "objectivity of death" (191). Read seems to recognize that the elimination of desire cannot be allegorized into form without a distancing formal technique, which in the fable is the awareness that the laws of sight and memory are somehow entwined in a labyrinthine logic of the repressed body of memory, where departure and return, recovery and loss occur.

The stream that flows backward without a source becomes the sign of the living unconscious of memory and mourning, of grief and absence and reparation in art. The conflict between Olivero's memory that was "a long thread, stained with ... multi-coloured experiences" and which "coiled up in ... [his] brain," symbolizes his encounter with political tyranny when he turns towards polit-ical liberalism in an obscure Latin American nation on the verge of revolution; Olivero becomes an apologist for assassination.

In passages which will remind the reader of Rex Warner's *Professor* and *Aerodrome*, or Orwell or Golding, Read flirts with the seductive power of allegory as he contemplates the nature of absolute power. However, there is a substantial difference between Read's fable and Warner's or Orwell's allegories: Read's is an anarchist's deeply personal parable, not a tragic one, nor a liberal one, nor one grounded in Golding's cultural despair that equates children with original sin and politics with animal behaviour. [115]

Read's fable is fully non-representational. Read has no faith in a culture without aesthetic experience, and Olivero discovers that, in spite of his liberal pretensions, he carries a Jesuitical col-onizing frame of mind adjacent to his Platonic and republican ideals: "Try as I would, I could not solve my personal problem in social terms" (150). All of his ideal reformist plans would shatter the serenity of the primal peoples. No matter how "civilized" his schemes, he is obsessed with the presence of the mystery of the green children in his past. How did they appear? Who were they? This failed revolutionary longs to know how that mystery had been solved, what had become of them in the course of the years. I began to create an ideal image of them as they had grown up in our alien world: being half-human and half-angel, intermediate between the grossness of earth and the purity of heaven. (*The Green Child*, 151)

The parable questions the personal and could be compared to Orwell's *flight* from the personal and the intimate in *Homage to Catalonia*.

Olivero's longing for the past, and his attempt to regain a sense of real experience not governed by power or ideals, reflects the crisis of Read's own spiritual and political odyssey: How to overcome the deathly complicity of art with a history of oppression? How to go back to Norse gods without succumbing to cultic mythology?

By creating a parable that describes the failures of revolutions, Read changes from a believer hopeful for a political revolution to a philosophical anarchist who, like Godwin, Stirner, Tolstoy, Nietzsche, Dostoevsky, and later epigones like Gandhi and Weil, must live as an anonymous figure compelled to read history backward: there would be no solution until the personal and the political – that superreal undertaking of self-creation – found new sources of imaginary representations. Behind this literary fable are Schiller, Marx, and Hegel, and Read's manifestos about surrealism, which were the harbinger of the Art Now movement of new sources of association, complementarity, and contiguity of thought and feeling in his political aesthetic of the 1930s. A natural tendency of human creativity not yet immune to the powers of appropriating and delineating objects for artistic purposes – his later works on art education for children – are prefigured in this fable. [116]

Behind *The Green Child* there also lies a Freudian fable about the end of the superego's attempts at philosophical transformation of collective memory into personal history. At the beginning of the fable, Olivero returns to the sources of his intelligence in the foreign land of his childhood; Read understood that memory and the construction of the aesthetic self cannot be separated – alienated – from the personal, the subject-in-the-making. The characters in the fable die twice: once, in order to overcome their self-appropriation as rational beings when they dive into the unconscious, and then, in order to represent that journey, they leave life to confront the powers of objectification. Read understands that surrealism performs the ideal: "nothing else than the material world reflected by the human mind and trans-lated into images. But 'reflection' and 'translation' are not, for us today such simple mechanical processes as perhaps Marxist aesthetics implies. For us the process is infinitely complicated: a passage through a series of distorting mirrors and underground labyrinths" (*Surrealism*, 42).

Read's discomfort with the mystical nature of ideal images is reflected in his statement that "surrealism demands nothing less than such a revaluation of all aesthetic values ... it has no respect for any academic tradition, least of all for the classical-capitalist tradition of the last four hundred years" whose conventions in reality are the "extensions of the personality" (*Surrealism*, 43–44); however these extensions carry the risk of eliminating the person. The surreal doubleness of the feel-ingful person embodies an awareness of the social powers of relativization. Experience works through the emotional need for aesthetic experience, of necessity not the mind of culture-bred artists, but a mind that understands that "the more irrational the world the more rational the art object," which Read cites as if it is his own manifesto in his chapter on Paul Klee in *A Concise History of Modern Painting*. [117]

In this mood, then, in Read's manifesto on surrealism which accompanied the 1936 International Surrealist Exhibition in Lon-don, he rashly announced that it was "his ambition someday to submit Hegel's *Aesthetik* to a detailed examination – to do for the realm of art on the basis of Hegel's dialectic something analogous to what Marx on the same basis did for the realm of economics."[118] Read's claim that surrealism's, Marx's, and Hegel's re-evaluation of the conventions of art would also necessitate a re-evaluation of the romantic tradition, and therefore of the treason of the intellectual clerisy, is in many circles today considered to be archaic polemics, even though Read's position is grounded in knowledge of the traditions of subversive art. His plan is to liberate conventions from the will to power, the abnormal conditions of his times – socialist realism, racial purity, and nationalism are equal menaces – which requires that the artist ally themself with whatever "promises intellectual liberty." Read's poetry in this period expresses this sentiment in deeply personal terms where "the contradictions of the personality are resolved in the work of art."[119]

Is this personal sentiment only justifying Read's love of the archive and the gallery? Read's role in the London reconstruction of the Nazi "Degenerate Art Exhibit" which installed Picasso's *Guernica* might be one answer, although it is too easy to assume that surrealism was automatically a liberating political movement. His political disagreements with the militant communist surrealists show his independence and his resistance to ready-made truths for understanding the complex questions about the fate of emancipatory modernism in the 1930s.

It is important to note that in Raymond Williams's *Culture and Society*, which has become a kind of bible for contemporary cultural studies, revision of the romantic and communitarian traditions in English modernism, Read is patronized and misrecognized as a follower of T.E. Hulme's anti-romanticism. This is an error of fact and judgment, in the cases of both Hulme and romanticism, but in Read's case it is a misrepresentation. Williams's critique of romanticism characterizes Freud and Read as defenders of the artist's "abnormality," which is either willfully obtuse or misinformed. Instead of the artist as revolutionary, Williams offers Read as liberalistic reformer. Here we have the beginnings of a cultural studies shorn of anarchism, surrealism, and the experiential. To be sure, Williams's work that follows

Culture and Society is substantial. But his version of the politics of modernism hides an anti-romantic melancholy. Read had dismissed this anti-modernism, which he already had abhorred, in his work of the 1930s: what Williams described in *Culture and Society* as a work of "disgusted withdrawal." [120] Further, In *Politics and Letters*, Williams returns to Read and *Culture and Society*: his publisher had to shorten the book, and Godwin and the Freud–Read nexus had to go: "I was sorry to let Godwin go. I was so hostile to Read that I was less distressed about that; although I regret it now because it would have been relevant to the sixties, when the whole question of Freud became so important in the discussions of art." [121]

However, Freud was equally if not *more* important in the 1930s when Read engaged Freud, Freudians, and Jungians along with Wilhelm Worringer and Alois Riegl, as well as Godwin, Marxism, and popular education about surrealism, communism, and anarchism. And while Williams did discuss the Marxian Rex Warner in *Culture and Society* (see 288–289), who is a benchmark for the failure of 1930s Marxism, afterwards Williams had ample opportunity to return to Read and to the problem of a modernist aesthetic which would have included anarchism and surrealism. The key question raised by Williams's dismissal of Read and an entire tradition in English modernism is the fate of liberalism.

Charles Harrison, the historian of modern art, wrote that it would be hard to overestimate Read's importance, but Harrison gives the standard shrug about Read: "Read's stress on the essentially non-rational or pre-rational nature of the origins of art was an effective prescription for liberalism in response to the eccentricities of modern art." [122] Read's transgressive aesthetics is reduced to liberal, cultural accommodation, and even a superficial reading of his essayistic, personal encounters with art, his poetry, and *The Green Child* as I read it here, shows his deep antagonism to any "off to Arcadia" natural culture, to the market economy, and to liberal subservience to misery. "Only misery is collective," he wrote, establishing this principle as a basis in the 1930s for the debate about the origins and erosion of British modernism into an anti-romantic liberalism.

Read's 1930s studies of art and literature examined both the accommodating and reactionary tendencies in modernism, in order to show the limits of *British* modernism and of the *British* reception of modernism, and his way was to show how modernism assimilated the failures of the various revolutions since the Middle Ages: the revolt against humanism by culturist Anglican populism; the failure of the Industrial Revolution to provide a standard of living or meaningful work; the slicing off of popular democracy from the French Revolution; the Chartist movement's failure to include art and culture; and the 1887 Bloody Sunday uprising in London which petered out into despair; the tyranny of the Russian Revolution and the violent elimination of the German Munich Council Communist Republic which had anarchist implications; and the ultimate failure of the anarchist Spanish Revolution.

Only an ethics and aesthetics of modernism could keep the image of the "Green Child" as an allegory of failed revolutions alive as a symbolic, non-representational image of non-identity with England's past, and with England's tendency to surrender to the spirit of the times, by constructing a cultural theology out of the existing class system.

This was Read's clearly voiced message against liberalism. Read felt that the 1930s were the opening into another world – towards a tainted "crystal city" of revolutionary but fragmented hope. In the 1930s, he foresaw the future in the self-reproduction of capital, in its ability to maintain the empire and an effete domestic counterfeit culture without either a strong state apparatus or a nationalized gentry. He knew that a class-controlled society was being governed by a culture-bearing class that would always resist finding its own image in either literature or painting.

The success of British capitalism until the 1960s resided in its ability to fuse aristocratic privilege and the educated bourgeoisie into new institutions of culture, capital, and welfare. His is a *semantic-idealistic* model of art, derived from the traditions of the educated yeoman. For all its failings in the eyes of the current postmodern critiques of an academic clerisy, his anarchist-modern aesthetics must be recognized. It is not liberalistic but is expressive of a cry of pain against the erosion of sociality, social being, habituation to a mass culture, and attention to aesthetic detail – all of which are loosened by capitalism and in danger of being lost forever.

Like his central character in *The Green Child* who settles his account with both a narcissism of loving art too much, and a longing for the historical reconstruction of memory, Read wanted to repair the damages caused by the absent reality of ideal forms by dissolving these forms into the presence of the now, into a loose network of pragmatic associations which are governed by deep relationships which would shine through the ruins of forms. Read's controlled use of phantasmagoria and abstraction in the discovery of his imaginary world in the 1930s came together in his love poems and political poems, like "Herschel Grynspan," expressing solidarity with "this beautiful assassin," "your friend" who delivered "love" by shooting Ernst vom Rath in Paris on November 7, 1938. This brings his anarcho-aesthetics to our edge of consciousness.

Read seemed to have a premonition that he and his thought would vanish, and with him the emancipatory modernism of the period between the wars – "a world within a war" he wrote in a 1944 poetry collection of that name. We can sum up this aspect of his own self-war with his self-awareness in his Klee-like fable poem "Picaresque," where he depicts fragmented bodies, limbs, and bourgeois picnickers "tented above the impious pools of memory": the nomadic figure "cannot disentangle / The genesis of any scope" and, in turn, "His limbs / Dangle / Like marion-ettes / Over / a / mauve / Sea." [123]

DOSSIER I: ENDNOTES

CHAPTER 1

1   This essay was originally published as "*Dr. Zhivago* and the Obliterated Man: The Novel and Literary Criticism" in *The Journal of Aesthetics and Art Criticism* 26, no. 1 (Autumn 1967): 65–80. It shows my interest at the time in the counterfeit and genuine described in this volume's prologue: an interest that came from my study of the Russian novel itself. The Russian novel struggles with the aesthetic and political problem of the crisis of the novel and poetics common throughout Russian literary history. The ideology and poetic of the novel informs my writings. Pasternak's letters at the time of writing *Doctor Zhivago* show his deep immersion in his aesthetic of commitment, how the political violence of Russian life continued through the hope that came with the revolution into his life and the life of other poets and writers who were always in dialogue with each other. In Russian literature "presentness" and "contemporaneity" are lived side by side. This became the bedrock of Bakhtin's dialogical "prosaics" that became familiar to me at the time in Bakhtin's study of Rabelais and the roots of the novel in the Menippean nature of dialogue. Bakhtin's and Russian dialogical writing constructs the reader, and is what can be called "compilational" writing, as in the film form itself of Soviet film director and theorist Sergei Eisenstein. This dialogical intervention as an aspect of the voice of the author in the text is a hallmark of Russian writing. The Cold War reception did not permit withdrawal from what seemed the extraordinary confusion of the age of revolution, exile, death, or imprisonment in his generation, which Viktor Shklovsky and others of Pasternak's contemporaries write about. The Gulags, wars, revolution, and civil war, then Hiroshima and Auschwitz, are embedded in the situation of writing that lived side by side with this epoch of catastrophe.

2   In a 1965 study of Gogol titled *The Ideology and Poetics of "Poshlost": The Work of Nikolai Gogol and Its Importance in Our Time* (Ann Arbor: University Microfilms, republ. 1974), I argued that Gogol's caricatures of Russian life became the heart of the Russian novelistics, or poetics of the novel. His humorous stories and *Dead Souls* gave Gogol the freedom to show how life and art merged in the cheap freedom, humorously won, that deflected us from the nature of what counterfeit is and how deeply penetrating are its grotesque-*making* powers. Gogol's adversary – *poshlost*, self-righteous mediocrity – is not conquered but opened up, aggrandized. *Poshlost* life materializes rapidly and grimly *through* humour towards the grin of actuality; but the final result is not a *rictus*. It is, instead, the grotesque face of normality. Deadening institutions lurk behind the scenes, every bit as real as the non-existent souls. These formations project their repressive power onto the people, thus degrading them and monopolizing their lives and making them grotesques or parodies of life impulses. Tension is maintained within the dialectical alternatives wherein brutality and superficiality are seen as normal events mirroring their opposites, paralysis and acquiescence. The accommodation to stability and the integration of reason with madness counterfeit order and peace. This attitude of wilful acquiescence to what is pervaded the art of Dostoevsky, Tolstoy, and Chekhov, as well as the essays of Alexander Herzen. James was allergic to the Russians'

"loose baggy monsters," which he used to decry their openness to the reader and the form of writing that is the *Skaz*. He didn't understand, or chose not to understand, that the Russian novel is immersed in a readership and authorship of the *Skaz* that imitates speech discourse. I discuss digressive writing in the prologue. Among the best discussions of "digressive writing" is Viktor Shklovsky's in *Bowstring: On the Dissimilarity of the Similar*, trans. Shushan Avagyan (Funks Grove, IL: Dalkey Archive Press, 1985).

3   Julian Moynahan, *The Deed of Life: The Novels and Tales of D.H. Lawrence* (Princeton, NJ: Princeton University Press, 1963), 71.

4   Ursula Brumm, "Symbolism and the Novel," *Partisan Review* 35 (Winter 1958): 331.

5   Diane Arbus, *Notebook* (1960), quoted in Patricia Bosworth, *Diane Arbus: A Biography* (New York: Knopf, 1984); sometimes attributed to Louis-Ferdinand Céline.

6   George Woodcock, "The Prophet," in *Anarchism: A History of Libertarian Ideas and Movements* (Cleveland: World Publishing Co., 1962), 233.

7   Isaiah Berlin, *Two Concepts of Liberty: An Inaugural Lecture Delivered before the University of Oxford on 31 October, 1958* (Oxford: Clarendon Press, 1958), 49.

8   Alex Comfort, *The Novel and Our Time* (*London:* Phoenix House Publishers, 1948), 19.

9   Raymond Williams, *The Long Revolution* (London: Chatto & Windus, 1961), 69.

10   Since *Doctor Zhivago* appeared in 1957 it has been virtually the unanimous opinion that it is what Wilson said it was: "It is a book about human life, and its main theme is death and resurrection." See Edmund Wilson, "Doctor Life and His Guardian Angel (On *Doctor Zhivago* by Boris Pasternak)," in *The 50s: The Story of a Decade*, ed. Henry Finder (New York: Random House: 2016), 488, originally published in *New Yorker*, November 15, 1957.

11   Edmund Wilson, "Doctor Life and His Guardian Angel," 489.

12   Wilson, 489.

13   Wilson, "Legend and Symbol in *Dr. Zhivago*," *Nation* (April 25, 1959): 363.

14   For dissents, see: Lionel Abel, "Letter to Nicola Chiaromonte," *Dissent* 5 (Autumn 1958): 334–341 [and Chiaromonte's answer in *Dissent* 6]; Isaac Deutscher, "Pasternak and the Calendar of the Revolution," *Partisan Review* 26 (Spring 1959): 248–266; Edgar H. Lehrman, "A Minority Opinion on *Doctor Zhivago*," *Emory University Quarterly* 16 (Summer 1960): 77–84; R.H. Powers, "Ideology and *Dr. Zhivago*," *Antioch Review* 19 (Summer 1959): 224–236; Phillip Toynbee, *Twentieth Century* (October 1958): 404–406; and Edward Wasiolek, "Courage but Not Excellence," *Chicago Review* 13 (Winter/Spring 1959): 77–83.

15   Irving Howe, "Of Freedom and Contemplation," *New Republic* 139 (September 8, 1958): 16.

16   Oktyabrina Voronova, "Interview," *Times Book Review* (June 14, 1964): 22.

17   Howe, "Of Freedom and Contemplation," 270.

18   Pasternak's aesthetic of the contemporaneous is a hallmark of the Russian historical novel that always struggled to illuminate a poetic of the digressive of the novel and the grotesque, the Rabelaisian streams in Russian literature. The combination of these

streams is discussed in Viktor Shklovsky's writing on film and literature, in particular his own formation in his *Sentimental Journey: Memoirs, 1917–1922* (trans. Richard Robert Sheldon [Ithaca : Cornell University Press, 1984]). His chapter entitled "The Writing Desk" illuminates the revolutionary circumstances and political shifting of the political risks in the schismatic period of the Revolution. I have adapted his metaphor of the Writing Desk in the prologue to explain the nature of my own aesthetic in this collection of *Untimely Passages*.

19   Page references in the text refer to the 1960 Signet edition of *Doctor Zhivago*, translated by Max Hayward and Manya Harari.

20   Howe, "Of Freedom and Contemplation," 16.

21   Thomas Merton, "The Pasternak Affair in Perspective," *Thought* 34 (Winter 1959–1960): 490. Italics mine.

22   There have been few full-scale "attacks" on *Doctor Zhivago*. The prologue to the dossiers explains my view of the relationship of writing to reading, teaching and exile, which drives the *utopian aesthetic* of Pasternak's novel, as well as Russian writing before and after the Revolution. Reading and writing are political acts by definition.

23   This essay was written under the influence of György Lukács's baroque *Theory of the Novel* (1916), and so was articulating Pasternak's attempt to write an epic work that told a terrible story of the totality of men and their events searching for lived experience without falling back into the world of conventions. In essence, the Russian novel can be considered in the light of its baroque roots in the psychology of melancholy and a world violently torn into fragments, and the destruction of historical ethos which Walter Benjamin describes in *The Origin of German Tragic Drama* (1928).

24   See in the prologue my comments on digressive writing, which Pasternak does, but at the same time the digressions, on the one hand, make the character a case study for historical events and, on the other, show the "mediocrity" of the character in the face of understanding the cataclysmic changes happening. Zhivago represents both sides of the historical narrative, the Revolution and Shklovsky's "writing desk." Writing and the Revolution are inextricably combined in creating historical and aesthetic situations of writing.

25   Frank Kermode, "Pasternak's Novel," *Spectator* (September 5, 1958): 315.

26   Lionel Abel, "Letter to Chiaromonte," 339; Nicola Chiaromonte, "*Doctor Zhivago* and Modern Sensibility," *Dissent* 6 (Autumn 1958): 39.

27   Nicola Chiaromonte, "Pasternak's Message," *Partisan Review* 25 (Winter 1958): 128.

28   Theodore Roszak, "The Historian as Psychiatrist," *Nation* (November 24, 1962): 343–344.

29   The world-forsakenness created by the historical tragedy that Zhivago the poet experiences in trying to write an "epic" that *forms*, and yet transcends, catastrophic events through the actuality of Pasternak's voice, which lives in the work as author – the word "Zhiv" equals "life" in a melancholic-allegorical sense – opens the novel to thinking about writing, authorship, and the poetics of the novel form. Other essays in this collection pursue the problems of authorship in times of historical and cultural crisis.

CHAPTER 2

30   This essay appeared in German in the Berlin journal *Leviathan* (1985) and in English for the Italian collection *Filosofia e scienze sociali: Nuove prospettive,* ed. Michele Schiavone (Genova: Bozzi, 1985). While this particular essay was written in the 1980s I place it into this dossier because it shows my interest in the "breeding grounds of modernity" and the social history of art and literature in the work of Arnold Hauser, Jean Duvignaud, Theodor W. Adorno, and Herbert Read.

31   Karl Marx, *Early Writings,* ed. Lucio Colletti (New York: Penguin, 1992).

32   See Harvey J. Graff, *The Literacy Myth: Literacy and Social Structure in the Nineteenth Century City* (New York: Academic Press, 1979).

33   Dieter Richter, "Teachers and Readers: Reading Attitudes as a Problem in Teaching Literature," *New German Critique* 7 (Winter 1976): 36.

34   Marvin Harris, *Cultural Materialism: The Struggle for a Science of Culture* (New York: Alta Mira Press, 1979), 156–157.

35   See Eric R. Wolf, *Europe and the People without History* (Berkeley: University of California Press, 1979).

36   See Mikhail Bakhtin, "The *Bildungsroman*" [The novel of education], in *Speech Genres and Other Essays,* trans. Vern M. McGee, ed. Caryl Emerson and Michael Holquist (Austin: University of Texas Press, 1986). We are speaking here of a historical typology of the formation of the literate, self-conscious individual who becomes enlightened through a process of becoming, always unfinished, searching for the significance of one's own mortality.

37   A more detailed elaboration: bureaucratic anti-bureaucracies are political and economic forces that operated within state and corporate capitalism. The policing forces and banking trusts are dramatic examples. These forces exist side by side with the state, dialectically shifting the "emphasis in the nature of domination (*Herrschaft*) … from the labor process and the legal system to the realm of dictatorial political power"; see Tim Mason, "National Socialism and the Working Class, 1925–May 1933," *New German Critique* 11 (Spring 1977). It is Marx in the *Critique of Hegel's Doctrine of the State* for whom the bureaucracy is the "imaginary state alongside the real state" which is then treated as the essential spirit of formalism. Anti-bureaucratic bureaucracies are modern cultural *institutions* that attempt to give a concrete historical practice to the sensuous constitutive qualities of creation: schools, universities, museums, etc. Within these bureaucracies a war for cultural literacy – that is literacy about conflict and self-knowledge – is waged over criticism itself. George Konrad and Ivan Szelenyi argue that on the margins of the intelligentsia "the class character of the intelligentsia" can be recognized. On the other hand, "the class culture of the intelligentsia is well suited to co-opt any transcendent criticism which the marginal intelligentsia can offer, and since this class is the first one whose marginal members represent the element of transcendence within the class and its culture, rational redistribution finds it easy to appropriate any transcendent analysis for its own purposes, just as the capitalist elite can put any immanent critique to its own uses" (*The Intellectuals on the Road to Class Power* [Brighton: Harvester Press, 1979], 249–250). For Benjamin's statement, see *Illuminations* (New York: Schocken Books, 1968), 24. "Bildung" is expressed here as "cultural literacy" and is often taken as synonymous with aesthetic education. The

critique of "Bildung" centres on the not-so-hidden assumptions about class conflict in the idea of a strengthened rationality and self-discipline at the heart of joining reason and culture as a critical common cause.

38   Robert Weimann, *Structure and Society in Literary History: Studies in the History and Theory of Literary Criticism* (Charlottesville: University of Virginia, 1977), 156–157.

39   I am taking a position here articulated by Arnold Hauser in *The Sociology of Art* (Chicago: University of Chicago Press, [1973] 1983) that is based on the view that the crises of art are a problem of art-creation and reception that can be understood through understanding conventions of art-making; the delivery systems of art can be addressed sociologically. See also Jean Duvignaud, *The Sociology of Art*, trans. Timothy Wilson (London: Paladin, 1972).

40   "Modern Capitalism and Revolution," in *Cornelius Castoriadis: Political and Social Writings*, ed. D.A. Curtis, *vol. 2, 1955–1960: From the Workers' Struggle against Bureaucracy to Revolution in the Age of Modern Capitalism* (Minneapolis: University of Minnesota Press, 1988), 70. (I thank David Wallace for bringing this statement to my attention.)

41   There is a different formalism: I have been influenced by Mikhail Bakhtin's *Speech Genres and Other Late Essays.*

42   By Marshal Sahlins, in his struggle to argue a materialist theory of meaning that relates nature to culture: see his book *Culture and Practical Reason* (Chicago: University of Chicago Press, 1976).

43   Alvin W. Gouldner, "Revolutionary Intellectuals," *Telos* 26 (Winter 1975–1976): 24. See also Gouldner, *The Future of Intellectuals and the Rise of the New Class* (1979). For a discussion of the "redistributive" power of intellectuals, see Konrad and Szelenyi, *The Intellectuals on the Road to Class Power* (1978). The transformation of humanist and Enlightenment values into a materialist and aesthetic form would have to be discussed in the various historical manifestations that gave rise to the novel. The work of Bakhtin explores this subject of the dialogical in many ways, just as surely as do Lukács's and Benjamin's, which I explored in "The Bureaucratization of Eros: Formalist Culture and the Spirit of Modernity," in *Explorations: Essays in Comparative Literature*, ed. Makoto Ueda (New York: University Press of America, 1986).

44   Again, an exception is Bakhtin whose 1965 *Rabelais and His World* derives from formalist legacies but departs from formalist values by recognizing that the genre of the grotesque is a culture-shaping genre. Even Bakhtin's *The Dialogic Imagination* (written between 1934 and 1941, published in 1981) is anti-formalist.

45   *The Domestication of the Savage Mind* (Cambridge, UK: Cambridge University Press, 1977), 13.

46   Goody is uncritical of the role played by intellectuals in the formation of cultural forces and the rationalization of knowledge. See *The Domestication of the Savage Mind*, 32–35.

47   Arnold Hauser, *The Sociology of Art* (New York: Vintage Books, 1982), 25.

48   Gouldner, *The Future of Intellectuals and the Rise of the New Class,* 24.

49   See Christopher Lasch, "The Democratization of Culture: A Reappraisal," *Change* 7, no. 6 (Summer 1976): 14–23.

50   Cornelius Castoriadis, "Modern Capitalism and Revolution," 61.

51   This is a question about writing and reception, but it is also a question of how writers are bribed with culturally sanctioned good feelings that lead to authority in the cultural sphere.

52   See Raymond Williams, *Politics and Letters* (London: Verso, 1979), 97: "I first started to look at the idea of culture in an adult education class, and it is very significant that the writers I discussed then were Eliot, Leavis, Clive Bell and Matthew Arnold. They were all I knew." Williams also reflects on his hostility to Herbert Read's romantic anti-capitalism. This hostility is still apparent in Williams's *Marxism and Literature* (Toronto: Oxford University Press, 1977), but is assimilated in his structuralist- and "language"-oriented epistemology even as Williams's Marxism is clearly his distinguishing mark as a modern critic. Not only does this tendency weaken Williams's earlier interest in D.H. Lawrence, it renders modernity into a framework where the uneven development of art, culture, and institutions are confounded with the "even" development of language: "Language is the articulation of this active and changing experience; a dynamic and articulated social *presence* in the world" (38). Language is "a means of production"; however, Williams's understanding of "language" is so opaque it is difficult to know whether he is affected by the hallucinatory, tormented, grotesque and pathological condition of language today as a "means of production" which enables his work to fit into communication theory.

53   Michel Foucault, "What Is an Author?," in *Language, Counter-Memory, Practice: Selected Essays and Interviews*, trans. Daniel F. Bouchard and Sherry Simon, ed. Daniel F. Bouchard (Ithaca: Cornell University Press, 1977), 130–138. As confirmation: the International Association for the Evaluation of Educational Achievement (IEA) reports that students do not have "a way into a text." "Less able readers" persist in asking questions "about the author, about the similarity of the text to other texts that they know, or about the relations that characters or incidents have to their own lives." The commentator remarks that meaning and moral questions seem to interest students, but formal or stylistic questions do not. He and the test conclude that meaning and moral questions are "peripheral" matters, but the most able students (who are likely to go on to university) overcome this deficiency and learn to find the "hidden meaning" (*Bulletin of the Association of the Departments of English* 72 [Summer 1982]: 1–3).

54   See Harvey J. Graff, *The Literacy Myth: Literacy and Social Structure in the Nineteenth-Century City* (Cambridge, MA: Academic Press, 1979) and *Literacy Myths, Legacies, and Lessons: New Studies on Literacy* (London: Routledge, 2017). Graff's work on literacy and its historical contexts may be the most important critical and analytical work on the subject. Aesthetic and socio-aesthetic considerations related to literacy are not touched on but are neither negated nor repudiated by Graff's historical analysis.

55   Harvey J. Graff, "The Legacies of Literacy," *Journal of Communication* 32, no. 1 (March 1982): 15. Also see Graff, "Reflections on the History of Literacy: Overview, Critique, and Proposals," *Humanities and Society* 4, no. 4 (Fall 1981): 303–333.

56   Bakhtin's term for this process, which is familiar to the Russian formalists, is the "aesthetics of verbal creation" as an ongoing event. This position is spelled out in Bakhtin's *Art and Answerability* (Austin: University of Texas Press, 1990).

57   By Marshal Sahlins, in his struggle to argue a materialist theory of meaning that relates nature to culture: see Sahlins, *Culture and Practical Reason* (Chicago: University of Chicago Press, 2013).

58   Richard Ohmann, *English in America: A Radical View of the Profession* (Middletown: Wesleyan University Press, 1976), 20.

59   Ohmann, *English in America*, 303.

60   Ohmann's equation of Bloomsbury and R.M. Forster with the New Criticism is wrong (*English in America*, 75), as is his lumping of the personal and erotic with mass culture and pornography (334).

61   Bertolt Brecht, "Intellectuals and the Class Struggle," *New German Critique* 1 (Winter 1973): 29.

62   For further discussion about a contextual theory of language: Roman Jakobson, *Verbal Art, Verbal Sign, Verbal Time* (Minneapolis: University of Minnesota Press, 1985); Ferruccio Rossi-Landi, *Language as Work and Trade: A Semiotic Homology of Linguistics and Economics* (Cambridge, MA: Bergin and Garvey, 1983); and Maurice Merleau-Ponty, "Indirect Language and the Voices of Silence," in *Signs* (Evanston, IL: Northwestern University Press, 1964).

63   See: John Oxenham, *Literacy: Writing, Reading and Social Organisation* (London: Routledge, 1980); David Cressy, *Literacy and the Social Order: Reading and Writing in Tudor and Stuart England* (Cambridge, UK: Cambridge University Press, 1979); Eric Havelock, *Origins of Western Literacy: Four Lectures Delivered at the Ontario Institute for Studies in Education, Toronto, March 25, 26, 27, 28, 1974* (Toronto: Ontario Institute for Studies in Education, 1976); and Walter J. Ong, *The Presence of the Word: Some Prolegomena for Cultural and Religious History* (New Haven: Yale University Press, 1967).

64   Herbert Marcuse, "The Affirmative Character of Culture," in *Negations: Essays in Critical Theory* (Boston: Beacon Press, 1968), 88–133. In *One-Dimensional Man*, Marcuse provides a framework for the way affirmative culture has socialized aggression, but he has not provided examples of aesthetic images of the institutionalizing *forces* or human *agents* of this transformation. The spirit of bureaucracy in modernity drives us to reproduce ourselves in abstract images and to represent those images and cultural creations in mass forms that dehumanize needs and desires. Whether "communicative rationality" is a concept that explains modern literacy would require a more extended discussion. However, Habermas acutely identifies the conservative features of modernist and postmodernist thought as a legacy of Enlightenment thinking, in "Modernity versus Postmodernity," *New German Critique* 22 (Winter 1981), 3–14, co-written with Seyla Ben-Habib. A more radical approach to modern literacy would have to confront Russell Jacoby's *Social Amnesia: A Critique of Contemporary Psychology* (Boston: Transaction Publishers, 1975) with the work of Adorno. John Berger's work, on the other hand, is part of the problem and does not present a satisfactory solution to modern literacy structures; but that would require another essay explaining Berger's place in the tradition of formalist semiotic traditions where economism has replaced humanism without realizing the radical potential of humanism. Berger reduces iconography to emblem and allegory and avoids the implications or the dialectics or iconomania and iconophobia in modern art and literature. Modernity *has* produced its non-Nietzschean exponents or a critically conscious vanguard in areas *outside* of

the predictable surrealism and postmodernism or the film age: in Brecht, Kafka, and Benjamin, for example, whose works add a radical marginality to major twentieth-century trends. See also: Cliff Slaughter, *Marxism, Ideology and Literature* (London: Humanities Press, 1980), for an anti-structuralist, pro-Marxian-humanist approach to modernist writing and reading practices.

65   Adorno, *Minima Moralia*, trans. E.F.N. Jephcott (London: New Left Books, 1951), 102. Adorno adds: "If the written language codifies the estrangement of classes, redress cannot lie in regression to the spoken, but only in the consistent exercise of strictest linguistic objectivity." While this puts class conflict in the foreground, the vernacular idioms common to all cultures – Bakhtin's concept of language as unfinished discourse – is not addressed here since in exile all language is damaged discourse and is symptomatic of homelessness and the loss of the origins of language in our childhood experiences of reading. Language for Adorno was synonymous with music, and listening was subject to atrophying.

CHAPTER 3

66   Previously unpublished.

67   *Journey through the Dark Woods* (Vancouver: Howe Street Press, 1982), *The Vanishing Individual: A Voice from the Dustheap of History or How to Be Happy without Being Hopeful* (in *Recovering Literature* 21, special issue [1995]), and *Resisting Our Culture of Conformity: In the Hills of Southern Ohio and in the Groves of Academe* (Alpine, CA: Blue Daylight Books, 2006). By including this essay in dossier I, titled "Breeding Grounds Looking Back," I am showing the early influences on my writing and reading about anarchism, the counterfeit, and Panzaic materialism in the novel. I refer to Theodor W. Adorno, for example, in this essay. I began reading Adorno in the 1960s; he appears often in these dossiers.

68   "The Outsider's Outsider: A Review of Wayne Burns, *Resisting Our Culture of Conformity: In the Hills of Southern Ohio and in the Groves of Academe*," *Rain Review of Books* 5, no. 1 (Summer 2007).

69   This is the "call" from D.H. Lawrence from *Look! We Have Come Through!* (1917) which I used as the title of an afterword to Burns's essay "The One Bright Book of Life," published in *West Coast Line* 13, no. 4 (April 1979): 3–13.

70   Wayne Burns, *A Panzaic Theory of the Novel* (Seattle: Howe Street Press, 2009), 12.

71   This was the subject of George Lukács's *Theory of the Novel* (London: Merlin Press, 1971), which appeared at a time when continental theories of literature were being translated into English in the search for critical models for the novel.

72   René Wellek and Austin Warren, *Theory of Literature* (San Diego: Harcourt, Brace and Company, 1948), 82.

73   Nietzsche's *Untimely Meditations* (or *Thoughts Out of Season*, 1873–1876) accompanies my reading of Burns.

74   Erich Auerbach is an exemplum of the many ways that realism pervades the novel's awareness of the growing reality of the individual coming into existence in the novel and in essays in writers like Montaigne. Unencumbered by critical baggage, Auerbach's exile in Turkey gave him the distance to become "Panzaic" in his outlook about the novel. His view of the individual as more than a random atom struggling for a sense

of totality in individual life does not name this struggle as the Panzaic, but he does not eliminate it from "mimesis": he intensifies the struggle to see it and know it.

75   Zaslove, "The Outsider's Outsider."

76   For a very different retrospective of one's life as a critic and teacher from Burns's one might compare George Steiner's *Lessons of the Masters* (Cambridge, MA: Harvard University Press, 2003). Steiner rages against mediocrity in the name of the masters of culture and against "democratization in the mass-consumption system" (183); his subject is "mastery and discipleship" in teaching and he almost sees a Don Quixote–Sancho Panza cultural paradigm in the way "Eros and teaching are inextricable" (140), connected to "discipleship" as a paradigm in literary relations. Yet for all Steiner's erudition, and despair over mediocrity, he does not see how the novel destroys our idols or limits our attachment to them; we always bring our ideals.

77   Harold Rosenberg, "The Herd of Independent Minds," in *Discovering the Present: Three Decades in Art, Culture, and Politics* (Chicago: University of Chicago Press, [1948] 1973).

78   It's time for me to confess. There are readers of this book who will refute Burns's argument by asking: What about Fredric Jameson or many others? Let me refer to Adorno's essay "Reading Balzac" since Jameson pretends to know Adorno. Balzac is clearly a novelist in whom Adorno is at pains to find Panzaic qualities. He begins the essay by writing that when the "peasant comes to the city everything says 'closed' to him. The massive doors, the windows with their blinds, the innumerable people to whom he may not speak under penalty of seeming ridiculous, even the shops with their unaffordable wares – all turn him away … in the eyes of the newcomer, everything that is locked up resembles a brothel, mysterious and enticingly forbidden." Jameson's criticism, overdetermined, pretentious, drenched with name-dropping, enticingly up-to-date, and swollen with critical platitudes, exists behind those doors, and no Panzaic Peasant, or Panzaic anyone, can find in Jameson more than an insider. See Theodor W. Adorno, "Reading Balzac," in *Notes to Literature I*, trans. Shierry Weber Nicholson, ed. Rolf Tiedemann (New York: Columbia University Press, 1991), 121. For a critique of Jameson, see Robert Hullot-Kentor, *Things beyond Resemblance: Collected Essays on Theodor W. Adorno* (New York: Columbia University Press, 2006), 220–233.

79   Burns, *A Panzaic Theory of the Novel*, 67.

80   Just as Burns's *The Panzaic Principle* has been misunderstood as a defence of only certain kinds of subject matter in novels that conform to a type based on content – issues he discusses – Bakhtin's views on Tolstoy are misunderstood as a dismissal of Tolstoyan poetics. Tolstoy would understand Burns's principles of the novel. Bakhtin complains about the later Tolstoy and the later Dostoevsky, both of whom turned the novel into idealistic attempts to find that "official authoritative truth, images of virtue (of any sort: monastic, spiritual, bureaucratic, moral, etc.) [which] have never been successful in the novel" (*The Dialogical Imagination*, ed. Michael Holquist, trans. Caryl Emerson and Michael Holquist [Austin: University of Texas Press, 1981], 344). Bakhtin further writes that we need to know the "inner monologues of developing human beings, the monologue that lasts a whole life" (345). He names this process of self-examination "monologue," but it is clearly a way of writing about what should be called "character." This has to include a sense that the novel is the living-breathing legacy of the discovery

of the unconscious in art and literature. Character is a slippery term and Freudian views of the developing person would have to caution us about making character into a benchmark for theory in all novels or of realism – what does one do with Kafka, for example? The novels of Dostoevsky become the basis for Bakhtin's view of character as Hardy's and Lawrence's novels are the ground for Burns's view of character. Bakhtin explains his view of Tolstoy's "deheroization" of "pathos" (398–399) where he praises Tolstoy's way of alienating readers' expectations. This is Tolstoy's version of Panzaic understanding. Bakhtin poses this against the formalists of the time but also against the "unitary" world of poetry. In my experience of teaching Bakhtin, the students complain more about his critique of poetry than they accept his view of the novel. They just don't get the difference in the "Copernican" divide that poetry, as we know it, and the novel, as Burns and Bakhtin understand it, inhabit different worlds. They fear his Rabelais book about the body, especially as it inspires phallic bodies over women's bodies. But fear is exactly what Bakhtin wants to dispel! Fear and the novel could be a subtitle of both Burns's and Bakhtin's approach to culture and the novel, even though they differ; however on *Don Quixote* they share the view that we have there the seeds of the sentimental, idealist Don Quixote facing off against the "brute discourse of life," ending up in a "hopeless dialogic conflict with the actual heteroglossia of life" (398). My reading of the word "heteroglossia" points towards Burns's Panzaic principles and the material many-sided nature of undercutting the ideal.

81 Georg Simmel, "The Stranger," in *On Individuality and Social Forms: Selected Writings*, ed. Donald N. Levine (Chicago: University of Chicago Press, 1971). ·

82 Burns, *A Panzaic Theory*, 6.

83 Theodor W. Adorno, "The Position of the Narrator in the Contemporary Novel," in *Notes to Literature I*, trans. Shierry Weber Nicholson (New York: Columbia University Press, 1991), 32.

84 Adorno, "Reading Balzac," 34.

85 Burns, *A Panzaic Theory*, 10.

86 On the question of "democracy," see David Wallace, "In Search of a Democratic Aesthetic, or Does the Novel Still Matter?," in *Anarcho-Modernism: Towards a New Critical Theory in Honour of Jerry Zaslove*, ed. Ian Angus (Vancouver: Talonbooks, 2001), 87–98. Burns's Panzaic Principle in Cervantes and literature has affinities to Bakhtin and the "carnivalesque," also noted in Howard Mancing's *The Cervantes Encyclopedia*, vol. 1, *A–K* (Westport: Greenwood Publishing, 2004), 89.

87 Franz Kafka, letter to Oskar Pollak, January 27, 1904, in *Letters to Friends, Family, and Editors*, trans. Richard and Clara Winston (New York: Schocken Books, 1977).

88 In the spirit of his theory Burns introduces sixteen "critical premises" for the "Principle" by quoting from Stendhal: "In all ages, the base Sancho Panza triumphs, you will find, in the long run, over the sublime Don Quixote" (epigraph to chapter 1).

89 Burns, *A Panzaic Theory*, 136.

90 The reference to "the unthought known" is to Christopher Bollas's formulation of the nature of the unconscious as an aesthetic and dialogical figuration in *Being a Character: Psychoanalysis and Self Formation* (New York: Farrar, Strauss and Giroux, 1992). The "Panzaic" is an illumination of this struggle of the ideal in the culture and, as Burns says in concert with many of the figures and novels he musters on behalf

of the "principle": "To be fully illuminating a genuine novel must oblige readers to undertake a full consideration of who they are and what they are doing in the world that they have chosen to live in or have been forced to live in" (*A Panzaic Theory*, 75).

91   Burns, "Appendix A: The Genuine and Counterfeit: A Study in Victorian and Modern Fiction," in *A Panzaic Theory*, 132.

92   Adorno, *Negative Dialectics*, trans. E.B. Ashton (New York: Continuum, 1973), 362–385. I see Adorno's negative dialectics as a materialist defence of the "Panzaic" individual and as Adorno's underlying anarchist stream in his patterning of genuine aesthetic thought against the identity of subject and object. Adorno is clear that the rescuing of semblance is the gate through which one passes towards reparation and repair and is a defence of the individual whose expressive acts break apart the subjectivization of the individual into fragments, into the subjectifying delusions – the hallucinations of our quixotic accommodation to domination. The Panzaic struggle broadly considered is the utopian will to self-creation and the "rescue" of the intelligible sphere even when that means "the poetry after Auschwitz" must be understood by thought about reparation and yearning for a better life. Many of my other essays in this collection refer to versions of this struggle in difficult authors writing in difficult situations.

CHAPTER 4

93   First published in Patrick J. Quinn, ed., *Recharting the Thirties* (Selinsgrove, PA: Susquehanna University Press; London: Associated University Presses, 1996), 17–39. This essay is dedicated to Wayne Burns and Alex Comfort; in different ways both enabled me to think about Read in the early 1960s after I had discovered his work a decade earlier. Read's writing stimulated many anarchist and libertarian writers: Alex Comfort, Murray Bookchin, David Goodway, George Woodcock, Lewis Mumford, Vernon Richards, and the social anarchists associated with Freedom Press and the journal *Anarchy*. His aesthetics and philosophy of art are informed by psychoanalysis; his is a world view that in his later years took in Carl Jung and hermetic symbolism, Herbert Marcuse and contemporary figures who wrote on art and alienation.

94   Over the years I have published several essays on Herbert Read and his defence of modern art in the spirit of my romantic anarchism and guild socialism. One not collected here is "Herbert Read and Essential Modernism," in David Goodway, ed., *Herbert Read Reassessed* (Liverpool: Liverpool University Press, 1998). Read's attempts to find a way to bring anarchism as a politics and philosophy, including psychoanalysis, informs my essays. This essay in this dossier reflects my writing on literature, counterfeit, and the crisis of modernity. In an essay titled "Counterfeit and the Use of Literature" (*West Coast Review* 3 [Winter 1969]: 5–19), I wrote: "Artistic experience is neither imitation of reality nor the symbolic projection of another (deeper version) of that reality: it is, for the writers to be mentioned here, an unmasking and a negation, in bitter conflict with all those repressive and inhibiting experiences whose nature is never really known until artistic creation disturbs the surfaces of assent."

95   Recent literature on modernism would fill a small warehouse. Those that fail to mention Read are Raymond Williams, *What I Came to Say* (London: Hutchinson, 1989) and *Politics of Modernism* (London: Verso, 1989); Paul Woods, Francis Frascina, Jonathan Harris, and Charles Harrison, *Modernism in Dispute: Art since the Forties*

(New Haven: Yale University Press; London: Open University, 1991); and John Carey, *The Intellectuals and the Masses: Pride and Prejudice among the Literary Intelligentsia, 1880–1939* (London: Faber and Faber, 1992). Carey's is symptomatic; he describes the tradition of class-based elitism inside of British modernism, but his omission of Read is inexcusable not only because Read can't be placed within the tradition Carey creates, but because Read represents another tradition entirely which Carey seems oblivious to.

96 Read's *To Hell with Culture and Other Essays on Art and Society*, a seminal collection, has been reissued with an introduction by Michael Paraskos (London: Routledge Classics, 2002).

97 On the subject, see Tom Steele, *Alfred Orage and the Leeds Arts Club, 1893–1923* (Aldershot, UK: Scolar Press, 1990).

98 *Naked Warriors*, Read's first volume of poems, was published in 1919.

99 David Thistlewood's many essays on Read's aesthetics are unparalleled in working out Read's development of an aesthetic. See in particular chapters 2–4 of *Herbert Read: Formlessness and Form; An Introduction to His Aesthetics* (London: Routledge & Kegan Paul, 1984). James King's study of Read's life and intellectual development – *The Last Modern: A Life of Herbert Read* (London: St. Martin's Press, 1990) – does not really address the question of his aesthetics. King reads Read's aesthetics, as do many, as a synthesis of romanticism and classicism. My own view is that this is limited and reduces a complex and evolving aesthetic attitude to simple contexts of influence or affinity. This shows the difficulty in finding the roots of British modernism. Read's several essays on D.H. Lawrence show why he goes outside of the polarity of romantic / classic.

100 The nature of Read's anarchism as it compares to others in the 1930s or in the history of anarchism would require more comment than I can give here. David Goodway has recently, and correctly, written that "Read's anarchism was not peripheral to his other, varied activities. Rather it was – knighthood and all – at the core of how he viewed the world in general" (Goodway, *Introduction to Hubert Read: A One-Man Manifesto and Other Writings for Freedom Press* [London: Freedom Press, 1994]). Goodway, however, believes that Read was not able "to extend his professional concern with the visual arts into a generalized theory of human emancipation" (15). George Woodcock believes that Read's anarchism doesn't stand up to others, like Nicholas Walter or Paul Goodman's, and Woodcock's now canonized views on anarchism do not see how Read's visual modernism is connected to his anarchism; Woodcock's views on art and anarchism, and anarchism itself, would have to be assessed along with his view of Read's limitations. Woodcock's views on Read are in *Herbert Read: The Stream and the Source* (London: Faber and Faber, 1972), and "Herbert Read: The Philosopher of Freedom," in *Anarchism and Anarchists: Essays by George Woodcock* (Kingston, ON: Quarry Press, 1992). Another of Woodcock's low-key, cool assessments of Read is "Herbert Read: Contradictions and Consistencies," in *Drunken Boat: Art, Rebellion, Anarchy*, ed. Max Blechman (New York: Autonomedia; Seattle, Left Bank Books, 1994). My own view is that Read's anarchism contains the seeds of a Stirnerite "parasitic anarchism," a term Wayne Burns uses in "The Vanishing Individual: A Voice from the Dustheap of History, or How to Be Happy without Being Hopeful," in *Recovering Literature* 21, special issue (1995).

101   George Orwell, "London Letter," January 1, 1942, in *Partisan Review* (March–April 1941).

102   Most commentators interpret Read's acceptance of the knighthood as selling out of his anti-state, anarchist ideals. His acceptance is, indeed, odd considering his pacifism during the war and his anti-bomb militancy and his work with the Freedom Defence Committee which defended deserters and those whose civil rights were violated by the state. Woodcock finds his life to have been "curiously bourgeois" (*Herbert Read: The Stream and the Source* [London: Faber and Faber, 1975], 262). His accepting the knighthood was perhaps a failure of nerve, but Read did not read BBC propaganda during the war, which Orwell found himself capable of doing, to me a larger failure of responsibility to humanity.

103   Alex Comfort's *Art and Social Responsibility: Lectures on the Ideology of Romanticism* (London: Falcon Press, 1946) is dedicated to Read.

104   See Miguel Abensour, "William Morris: The Politics of Romance," in *Revolutionary Romanticism: A Drunken Boat Anthology*, ed. Max Blechman (San Francisco: City Lights Books, 1999), and Richard Stites, *Revolutionary Dreams: Utopian Vision and Experimental Life in the Russian Revolution* (New York: Oxford University Press: 1989). The war on machines, the sense of the future, and the future in the past marked his anarchism.

105   Versions of my essays on Read appeared in the Vancouver journal *Collapse: The View from Here* 1 (1995).

106   Herbert Read, *The Green Child* (New York: New Directions, 1971).

107   Alan Tate wrote the introduction to a selection of essays chosen by Read. The introduction is very complimentary but does not see the continuity of Read's 1930s poetics of art within Read's poetic development. Tate makes Read into a wholly Jungian symbolist, misinterprets Freud, and assumes that Read's anarchism is like the American new agrarian movement, which Tate claims is also a form of anarchism. See Herbert Read, *Selected Writings* (New York: Horizon Press, 1964). Tate did not see how Read's anarchism is also a radical humanism.

108   For a provocative argument that reflects some of the same concerns of Read's, namely how to defend modernism against the avant-garde's mythologizing of art as everyday praxis, see Boris Groys, *The Total Art of Stalinism: Avant-Garde, Aesthetic Dictatorship, and Beyond*, trans. Charles Rougle (Princeton: Princeton University Press, 1992), or the many works of Peter Bürger on the ambiguities of the avant-garde and radical modernism. Read's works in the 1960s that reflect his struggle with the ethical basis of avant-garde art are: *A Letter to a Young Painter* (London: Thames and Hudson, 1962); *The Forms of Things Unknown: An Essay on the Impact of the Technological Revolution on the Creative Arts* [subtitled on the frontispiece: *Essays towards an Aesthetic Philosophy*] (Cleveland and New York: World Publishing Company, 1963); *The Redemption of the Robot: My Encounter with Education through Art* (New York: Trident Press, 1966); and *Art and Alienation: The Role of the Artist in Society* (New York: Horizon Press, 1967). Epigraphs in the latter book are from Wordsworth and Marx. The young painter referred to in *Letters to a Painter* is the artist Ruth Francken.

109 Read, "Essential Communism," in *Anarchy and Order: Essays in Politics* (Boston: Beacon, [1954] 1971); the essay "Essential Communism" was first published in Herbert Read, *Poetry and Anarchism* (1938).

110 During Read's tenure as editor for Routledge, Kegan Paul facilitated the publication of Arnold Hauser's monumental *Social History of Art* (1951). It has been translated into at least a dozen languages.

111 David Thistlewood, "Herbert Read's Paradigm: A British Vision of Modernism," in *A British Vision of World Art*, ed. Benedict Read and David Thistlewood (Leeds: Leeds City Art Galleries, 1994), 91.

112 I argue for the continuity and difference in Read's work with Adorno, Benjamin, Marcuse, and Hauser in another essay on Read: "Herbert Read as Touchstone for Anarcho-Modernism: Aura, Breeding Grounds, Polemic Philosophy," in *Re-Reading Read: New Views of Herbert Read*, ed. Michael Paraskos (London: Freedom Press, 2007).

113 Read, "The Reconciling Image" (1963), in *The Forms of Things Unknown*, 91.

114 Read, *The Contemporary Experience* (New York: Horizon Press, 1963), 392.

115 Both George Woodcock and David Goodway cite Read's letter to Woodcock about Read's admiration for Orwell but overestimate the letter's praise of Orwell. In my understanding of Read there is little affinity between the two figures. Read's comment is that of a sick and dying man who was simply accepting his own demise and Orwell's as well. See the letter reprinted in part in David Goodway's *Herbert Read: A One-Man Manifesto and Other Writings for Freedom Press* (London: Freedom Press, 1994), 22. One also has to bear in mind to whom Read was writing, Woodcock, who was determined to redeem Orwell as a saviour for our times. This could not have failed to impress Read, but I am not convinced that Read saw Orwell as a great man or as a great writer. In addition, most commentators on Read's romance assume it is Jungian inspired. It is *both* Jungian and Freudian. In essence *The Green Child* is a self-criticism and his coming-to-terms with his own tormented libidinous idealism.

116 Read's *Education through Art: A Revolutionary Policy* (1943), a treatise on children's understanding of art and art-making is annotated with marginal comments by T.S. Eliot. Eliot irascibly and vigorously objects to Read's educational views for children.

117 Paul Klee, *A Concise History of Modern Painting* (London: Thames and Hudson, 1961).

118 Read, *Surrealism* (London: Praeger, 1971), 22–24.

119 Read, *Surrealism*, 90.

120 Raymond Williams, *Politics and Letters: Interviews with* New Left Review (London: Verso Books, 2015), 106.

121 Williams, *Politics and Letters*, 99.

122 Charles Harrison, *English Art and Modernism* (New Haven: Yale University Press, 1981), 99.

123 Read, "Picaresque," *New Coterie* 5 (Spring 1927): 53.

Errants and Exiles on the Banks of Rivers

This dossier includes writing that negotiates with exile. Writing that doesn't always fit in well in its times. These essays stretch the use and meaning of "genre." They ask: What is the situation of writing? The era of the crisis of modernism opens up the anticipatory illumination of Ernst Bloch in his utopian political aesthetic of the "contemporaneity of the non-contemporary." Thinking about exile yields a thinking about loss and return, and no return. Exile affects generations to come and has become an epical form of literature about refuge, loss of home, and no return.

Will anyone doubt that I am aware how incomplete and debatable these analyses are? Exceptions abound, and I know them, but it would take a big book to go into them … One cannot write without a public and without a myth – without a certain public which historical circumstances have made, without a certain myth of literature …

—JEAN-PAUL SARTRE, *"What is Literature?" and Other Essays* ([1948] 1950), trans. Bernard Frechtman

Which ink is used to sign the death sentences – chemical ink, the India ink used in passports, the ink of fountainpens, alizarin? No death sentence has been signed simply in pencil … Only the simple graphite pencil is permitted. In Kolyma, graphite carries enormous responsibility.

—VARLAM SHALAMOV, "Graphite," *Kolyma Tales* (1994), trans. John Glad

DOSSIER II – CHAPTER 1

Siegfried Kracauer's Cosmopolitan Homelessness: The Lost Cause of an Idea[1]

In sum, the whole assumption examined here stands and falls with the belief that people actually "belong" to their period. This must not be so. Vico is an outstanding instance of chronological exterritoriality ...

—SIEGFRIED KRACAUER, *History: The Last Thing before the Last* (1969), trans. Paul Oskar Kristeller

Kant's First Principle

All natural faculties of creatures are destined to unfold completely and according to their end. But the end has been prophesied by the very society that wishes always to begin again.

—IMMANUEL KANT, *Critique of Pure Reason* (1781)

The title of this essay raises a terrifying question: Can one be both cosmopolitan and homeless? To begin again with Kant's idea of cosmopolitan peace: what a delusion it appears in the twentieth century, which some call the century of total violence. Where is the geographical boundary of this idea that has no map? Does it have a linguistic boundary? Does it mean a German, Central European, and German colonization, a Hitler-fantasy already beginning when Kracauer began writing his essays on film as witness, an observing mirror of everyday life in Berlin and of white-collar workers? The fantasy of European intellectuals and politicians for a national state of Europe that would have its capital – where? in Berlin, Vienna, Paris, Prague, or Budapest? – shows how cosmopolitanism has its geographical axis drawn around and through boundaries that are redrawn and vanish like the various peoples which inhabit boundaries. The period between World War I and the rise of the Third Reich was already being identified by the "aliens" moving across borders, staging the "shelterlessness" in which Kracauer saw a fate that would overtake us after World War I, with its devastating technical and military brutality. It takes a great risk to speak of cosmopolitanism at the end of the twentieth century after a century of total war and the unspeakable atrocities waged by "civilized" nations. [2]

How is any idea of a "Kantian Universality" constructed, and to what end do its subjects believe in it?

Kracauer studied the everyday lives of working people in his Berlin essays entitled "The Hired Workers," which in the English translation became *The Salaried Masses: Duty and Distraction in Weimar Germany*. [3] Kracauer was one of the first to look at everyday life from the standpoint of work and labour, the construction of the "stranger" in film, and the revelation of a "state of mind" as an "act of seeing." [4] His essayistic writings were almost novelistic; his writing gave working people a voice, but a voice that they didn't know they had – a voice that would be taken from them and used in the coming years by the Third Reich. [5] It is no exaggeration to say that his approach to analyzing social phenomena shows how reification and experience are interlocked in the reverence shown by the workers for authoritarian society.

But at the same time, Kracauer's sympathies were with those in the offices and bureaus. He saw the coming of the war against them and how they lived in a state of effacement and accommodation: "It is only in this state of self-effacement, or homelessness, that the historian can commune with the material of his [*sic*] concern ... A stranger to the world evoked by its sources, he is faced with the task – the exile's task – of penetrating its outward appearances, so that he may learn to understand that world from within." [6]

Kracauer had studied Kant deeply. His Kantian-inspired essays on the estranged cultural boundaries in Weimar culture speak of Berlin and of *anderswo* (elsewhere). His idea in this study is that the cosmopolitan intellectual suddenly comes face to face with the double-edged sword of the impossible dream of the idea of universality itself. Cosmopolitanism had become part of class war and was equated with the rootless intellectual, already separated from Kant's revolutionary idea that cosmopolitan peace was a natural human desire. Who speaks for whom about cosmopolitanism? In an age of globalism and transnationalism there can be no refuge for an idea that once had its moment of Enlightenment glory. But today it is one of a number of formerly utopic ideas that have become part of the inbuilt violence of the century: Is there an Asian cosmopolitan imaginary? An African one as well? A cosmopolitan humanism? A cosmopolitan pathos and sorrow?

For Kracauer the "Cosmopolitan" is a new kind of "person" who is living in a dream world, hoping for security, and who feels like being a stranger to the world is the beginning and end of history. Dreaming is a form of thinking, thinking and dreaming and wandering go together for the "strangers" and pariahs, which is an extended definition of Georg Simmel's "The Stranger" as a meta image of "strangers." The stranger is a new "cosmopolitan," so important for Kracauer and Simmel, especially in the tableau of the "Metropolis" which contains the "origins of modern life." Later, Kracauer in *Theory of Film* explores film as the artform of the "Metropolis," which shows "unstaged reality" – modern life as the staging and unstaging of life itself. The dream, however, is a shelter for our feelings of omnipotence and the omnipotence of thought. But the dream is also a construction, a form of thinking, thinking about thinking without our knowing that we are thinking.

Who is the "parvenu"? The parvenu is a social type who lives to the order of things as they are. The parvenu exploits the stranger, and both "parvenu" and "adventurer" are social types in the "Metropolis." The parvenu would be the trader, the capitalist entrepreneur, who arrives on the scene with early capitalism. The parvenu learns, as characters in Brecht's plays, which are populated with "parvenus," to fit in, accommodate to the real. Charlie Chaplin's Tramp is a prototype of the "stranger among us." Chaplin and the stranger must always begin life again and again, each day, as if the "new" becomes old again and again before it can be lived. The Chaplin character lives with fragments of life but picks up the fragments and tries to make them into a "whole"; thus, Chaplin is the "stranger who becomes the adventurer," another of Simmel's cosmopolitan social types. Brecht's plays and his dramaturgical concept of "estrangement" (*Verfremdungseffekt*) exploit the social types of the theatregoer, the consumer in the theatre, in order to change the consumer into a spectator-observer who sees how something is made and so resists emotional exploitation. [7] Kracauer sees the "cosmopolitan" as paradigm of a new type of person. Brecht's "paradigmatic" character types fall into the portrayal of "ideological" types who cling to their lives in deteriorating social institutions.

Kant's essay is magisterial and yet feels archaic. Its visual corollary might be the famous *vedute* ("views") of Giovanni Paolo Panini *Modern Rome* (1757) and *Ancient Rome* (1758). The large-scale paintings portray the dream of universal justice, justice as the universal wish of mankind framed in a cosmopolitan view of universal history. Here is the utopic artistic view of history seen through the struggle for peace within the ruins of the decline of civilizations. Allegory wins the historical game. But its axis is Greece and Rome, supreme in relationship to other cultures. Where are the Slavs, the Scandinavians, the Africans, and the Asians? The Origins of Europe hover over what is "cosmopolitan." The subtitle of the English translation of *The Salaried Masses*, "Duty and Distraction," calls forth the Kantian ideals of obligation, responsibility, and reasonability. Yet Kant imagined a "cosmopolitan" Archimedean point – a turning point and axis – where all needs and desires are transformed into the "ought" of the axiom that the end cannot justify using other persons as means justifying an end.

For Kracauer the new cinema and photography were both an expression and extension of the emergence of a culture of modernity. Film and photography arrived on the scene with capitalism and the emergence of a political and economic system that conditions the political and cultural conditioning of life itself as "exterritorial" and as a universal process of reification under the principle of the exchange of images that had no name. [8] Writing itself must represent not only life in the present but how a life of writing is in the present as an epochal situation. Kracauer and Benjamin both understood writing as detecting "the main things that appear puzzlingly embedded in the phantasmagoria ... from which long-forgotten echoes arise ... in the dexterity of the shorthand typist the petit-bourgeois desolation of the piano étude ... his essay is a landmark on the road to the politicization of the intelligentsia." [9]

Kracauer wrote in his last book, *History: The Last Things before the Last* about history as a tableau of disconnected images. We look at the contemporary scene from the distance of the camera: "History resembles photography in that it is, among other things, a means of alienation ... [We are] evicted from our familiar surroundings ... and as the world is shrinking ... it extends beyond our control [and we] ... scramble for the shelter of unifying and comforting belief." Cosmological abandonment is the nascent state – the other shores – of both the ideological wars and the lost fragments hidden in the interstices of modernity. Kracauer's "cosmopolitanism," which he said later during his exile he had already begun in his study of "The Hired Workers," searched for the ways to "rehabilitate" objectives and modes of being which still lack a name and hence are overlooked or misjudged, "a region of reality which despite all that has been written about them are still largely *terra incognita* ... focus on the 'genuine' hidden in the interstices between dogmatized beliefs of the world, thus establishing tradition of lost causes; giving names to the hitherto unnamed." [10]

Modernity, however, deliciously described by Georg Simmel as the nervous love of the wanderer for the *very* metropolis that provides no peace at all if one's heart and eyes are open, becomes the carrier of European cosmopolitanism.[11] The city was its geophysical location, whether through the Habsburgs, Bismarcks, Hitlers, or Stalins, who all desired to root out all non-national, republican spirits. The association of cosmopolitanism with the modern movement of the arts and technology centralized the idea of the modern around the architectural and mechanical advances associated with the city and the new internationalism of styles and fashions. If Rome was the capital of visual arts, Vienna of music, Paris of literature, Prague and Budapest of rising national aspirations, Russia the capital of futurist manifestos, then the axis of a Central Europe balanced on an Archimedean fulcrum of an imaginary power which needed a political capital.

Cosmopolitanism can be understood not only as an idea about intellectual and cultural history, but as an imaginary space in which cultural alienation will be placed on a *continuum* with the ancient world. Greece was the city-state and Roman law was the gate keeper that provided Kant with a space-time image, a chronotope, of a world that transcends history and exists without borders or boundaries, without economy or politics – in short the path to that transcendental republican consciousness – the cosmopolitanism of the unspoken and hidden tendencies of a liberated humanity that travels the road through sociability as the consciousness of a collectivity of individual beings whose atomization can never fully define their humanity.[12]

This was the problem that Kracauer anticipated in the 1920s when he began writing an ethnography of the city as a form of reality and then followed with his study of Weimar film. Indeed, Weimar cinema would become the unconscious as the new "totality" – the transcendental loci – of the wage and service workers. These culture workers were formed in and by this epochal "firmament" of the film age. Transparencies did not always show the interstices, but the film would try.

His book *Die Angestellten: Aus den neuesten Deutschland* (Suhrkamp, 1971) should have been translated as "The Hired Service Workers (From the Newest Germany)." However, it was translated by Quintin Hoare as *The Salaried Masses: Duty and Distraction in Weimar Germany* (Verso, 1998). This translation is not right. Kracauer never saw them merely as "masses." The salaried worker was a segment of a larger whole. The worker was the harbinger of a new phenomenon of flight *into* mass-minded fear and distraction. The salaried workers were standing alongside the dispossessed bourgeoisie who also longed for a politics that would protect them from the destiny which was being imposed on them. Ideally, the wish was for a politics that would eliminate politics entirely. Kracauer witnessed a new kind of modernity of the shelterlessness of the politically homeless who seemed to merely exist in a "nature reserve" of the authoritarian state. The State would soon create the means to spread its "sovereign territory" throughout Europe. The spirit of the title should be in the spirit of Kracauer's aesthetic: "The Masses Are Their Own Ornament." [13]

Kracauer wrote it as a serial publication in 1929 in the Feuilleton section of the *Frankfurter Zeitung*, one of Germany's national newspapers. He shows empathy for the people, especially the women, working in the department stores, the shops, offices, and administration, union members who go out at night into the streets and boulevards to relieve their anxieties and fears under the clouds of the still-existing ravages of war and the failure of the economic system to save them. He wrote: "The flight of images is a flight from revolution and death … The movie industry's products serve to legitimize the existing order by concealing both its abuses and its foundations." [14]

Kracauer wrote this study for the widely read *Frankfurter Zeitung*. He conceived it as an ethnography by conducting interviews, going to the businesses and enterprises, workplace schools, labour unions, apprentice orientations, court rooms, looking at the social stratifications, hierarchies, and boards of directors.

He writes:

> If literature usually imitates reality, here it precedes reality. The
> works of Franz Kafka give a definitive portrait of labyrinthine
> human big firm – as awesome as the pasteboard models of intri-
> cate robber-baron castles made for children [Kafka was barely
> in his grave and Kracauer already knew his work! – JZ] and the
> inaccessibility of the supreme authority. The complaint of the
> impoverished petite bourgeoisie, whose very language seems bor-
> rowed from Kafka, undoubtedly concerns an extreme case; yet it
> points with extreme accuracy to the mid-level boss – i.e., usually
> the head of a department – in the modern large-scale enterprise ...
> They are the necessary result of the abstractness of the prevailing
> economy which is moved by motives that seek to escape the real
> dialectic with the people kept busy in the business. [15]

This goes beyond what Adorno or even Benjamin wrote at the
time. Here, one should refer to Kracauer's essays in the collection
The Mass Ornament ("The Ornament of the Mass" would be
more accurate, because it's the people becoming ornaments.) [16]

Cosmopolitanism means to live in the interstices that replace
the millennial preoccupation of Christianity with the end of history and its messianic preoccupation with the symbolic rupture
of time by revolutionary and redemptive transformations. At the
same time, cosmopolitanism anticipates the future as a utopic
place of a post-revolutionary dream of peace of an untrammeled
freedom from a national-ethnic destiny. The dream is imagined
and materialized in the city where aesthetic design and invention
materializes as the renewal of life forces. There are two sides to
modernity as the carrier of the cosmopolitan: on the one hand
the kairos of exile and homelessness; on the other hand, yearning
for images – *Denkbilder* in Walter Benjamin's use of "thought-
images" – that will illuminate the ontological immediacy of the
world as a place of images and powerful mechanical forces, in
short a utopia of the technical will. [17]

What better image could be found for the continuity of a world of transcendental homelessness within the longing for home and the security of ideological shelters than György Lukács's famous symphonic opening rendition of Kant's cosmo-logical longings in the *Theory of the Novel*:

> Happy are those ages when the starry sky is the map of all possible paths – ages whose paths are illuminated by the light of the stars. Everything in such ages is new and yet familiar, full of adventure and yet their own. The world is wide and yet it is like a home ... Kant's starry firmament now shines only in the dark night of pure cognition, it no longer lights any solitary wanderer's path (for to be a man in the new world is to be solitary). [18]

Lukács formed his poetical theory of the novel on the basis of a politics of nostalgia; he later discarded his romantic anti-capitalism as an anti-philosophy for a world already organized against any historical sense of continuity. However, it's important to understand that Lukács sided with Kant's cosmopolitanism that would carry the burden of a world into a world of universal peace – this world of "absolute sinfulness" of the hero condemned to solitude and "devoured by a longing for community" that had ceased to exist. For Lukács, models of reality had vanished: "Art, the visionary reality of the world made to our measure, has thus become independent; it is no longer a copy, for the models have gone; it is a created totality, for the natural unity of the meta-physical spheres has been destroyed forever." [19]

The mood of loss pervades the entire epoch and both loss *and the loss of loss* is expressed in the plaque that was placed at Kracauer's place of birth in Frankfurt: "For what has been formed cannot be lived unless what has fallen apart is gathered up and taken along." [20] Loss is emblematic of the times.

Kant asserts that "to write a general world history according to a plan of nature which aims at a perfect civic association of mankind must be considered possible and even helpful to this intention of nature." Lukács accepts the challenge of Kant's projection of the history of nature as the ground for a history of the novel. So when Kant writes, "It would seem that such a purpose could only produce a *novel*, but this idea might yet be usable if one could assume that nature and even the play of human freedom does not proceed without plan and intended end,"[21] Lukács concludes that it is the novel alone that can carry the "inner form" of the world-historical subject.

The "novel is the art form of virile maturity: this means that the completeness of the novel's world is an imperfection, and if subjectively experienced, it amounts to resignation."[22] The intent of the novel genre is immanent to its worldly cosmopolitan purpose. The world-historical individual becomes real in the novel through the reality-creating ethics and aesthetics of "the problematic individual's journeying towards himself," where the conflict between the Kantian is and *ought* "extends over a lifetime." The direction and scope and "the inner means of shaping" of a process, and of its material adherence to life and nature, is its finitude, its earthliness in a world without God, without natural boundaries, and without infinity.[23]

For Kracauer, however, along with writing that politicizes the intelligence, in Benjamin's formulation, it is not the novel but film that would carry the burden of the world-historical subject back to earth, in which the subject was now mere appearance. For Kracauer the rise of film revealed the world stumbling on its path to cosmopolitan peace – that is, the illumination and pacification of violence by the redemption of physical reality.[24]

Film is the realization of the hidden plan of nature. The spectators – the new collective agent in modern life – are strangers at home everywhere and nowhere. While the Cosmopolitan individual was vilified by Stalinism as a compilation of the bourgeoisie and the anti-national Jew who represents the declassed, alienated intellect, the Cosmopolitan for Kracauer becomes an emblem of modernity: the stranger. Simmel's stranger is a figure of the modern city – already a pariah in the nineteenth century – who arrives on the doorstep of the modern city to be allowed in only if not allowed to stay too long. [25] In Simmel's classic essay of that name, "The Stranger" laboured under the burden of paying a fixed tax, while the Christian citizens' tax burden "varied according to their wealth at any given time." [26] The stranger "intrudes as a supernumerary … into a group in which all the economic positions are already occupied." [27] The stranger, according to Simmel, is freed from the pain of subjectivity. The stranger sees the world in a disinterested, blasé fashion.

Yet, the stranger sees the world more dispassionately as an outsider. However, because Kracauer's saw in film a metaphysical sign of cosmopolitan homelessness, the nearness and farness of film-created reality both redeemed and made strange everyday life: homelessness may even appear to take on an aesthetic world view, exemplified in the aesthetic medium of the film. For example, the "homelessness" of antic comics like Charlie Chaplin, Buster Keaton, and Harold Lloyd carried the persona of the "stranger" into a world in which "the stranger" sets himself against objects in the world, which he brings to performance by remaining silent no matter the obstacles in the world which try to overwhelm us. [28]

The viewer-spectator appropriates the illusion of peace in order to overcome the shadowy existence of the urban life in which communal existence is deteriorating. The feeling of cosmopolitanism, then, is associated with the "stranger as a member of a group":

> As such the stranger is near and far *at the same time,* as in any relationship based on merely universal human similarities. Between these two factors of nearness and distance, however, a peculiar tension arises, since the consciousness of having only the absolutely general in common has exactly the effect of putting a special emphasis on that which is not common. [29]

This relationship to the film is erotic: the stranger is "an organic member of the group" while "being inorganically appended to it."[30] To remove the appendage would be the next step in purifying the organic body. This became a fascist political project which Kracauer already anticipated in his earliest essays and which formed his aesthetic politics, both in his life and his writing. In *From Caligari to Hitler*, which he began during his Paris exile, the first lines boldly state his life-project:

> This book is not concerned with German films merely for their own sake; rather, it aims at increasing our knowledge of pre-Hitler Germany in a specific way … dispositions predominant in Germany from 1918 to 1933 … which influenced the course of events during that time and which will have to be reckoned with in the post-Hitler era.[31]

This prophesies the future desecrations of the communal through the imposition of cosmopolitan otherness on the "degenerate" minorities under Hitler and Stalin. The art of minorities is violently annihilated in the name of faked national peace. Cosmopolitanism is an accusation; it is an attribute of world-historical intellectuals and underscores the decrees against bourgeois art, formalism, naturalism: "rootless cosmopolitanism" or any "aestheticizing anti-patriotism." "Inner life," Kracauer wrote in *Caligari*, "manifests itself in various elements and conglomerations of external life, especially in those almost imperceptible surface data."[32]

This became the fascist rallying cry against modern art, Jewish art, and cultural criticism; however, the struggle against neo-cosmopolitanism was already present in the Austria of Adolf Loos's anti-ornamentalism, and in Robert Musil's *The Man without Qualities* where modernity was seen as soulless. That Hitler saw in the city of Vienna the source of his urge to purge the city of its cosmopolitan mentality only shows how close the metropoles are to the imaginary world of a resentful anti-cosmopolitan mentality. Kracauer's 1920s studies of the metropoles are an inevitable consequence of his studies of the homeless, roofless city streets, assemblies, bars, hotel lobbies, and films which were places of interludes *in the flow of life* that was reproduced on the filmscreen. The struggles during the 1930s for a nationalist-oriented anti-cosmopolitanism led to the campaigns against all forms of avant-gardism. [33] The stranger, who is the hybrid of the cosmopolitan, carries the repressed ghost of the individual. The stranger becomes the emblematic grotesque inhabitant of the city and carries the uncanny memory of an idea of peace soon to be threatened by forces of great violence in "the state of nature" of social control. Kant's synoptic concept designed to overcome Hobbes's state of nature becomes a principle of second nature capable of being controlled. It was no accident that non-citizens – unemployed Jews and street merchants in Vienna – became the first to be rounded up and sent back to the "nations" that did not want them. Deracinated, non-citizens became the first victims of "homeless cosmopolitanism." [34] The group becomes a stranger to itself, an ornament of the mass. It becomes like an allegory of itself.

Kant's Second Principle

In man [*sic*] (as the only rational creature on earth) those natural faculties which aim at the use of reason shall be fully developed in the species, not in the individual. [35]

But what happens when one-dimensional Man becomes no-dimensional man? Outlawed from the polis and reduced to a dependent, state-owned citizen, Kant's challenge to the narcissism of European nationalism – who becomes the figure of Herbert Marcuse's one-dimensional individual – received its political death blow from the French Revolution's betrayal of the universal rights of man. For the romantic anti-capitalists like Lukács, Simmel, Kracauer, and Marcuse, the legacy of neo-cosmopolitanism migrated into the metropoles where the dream of a cosmopolitan peace was administered by advanced capitalism. [36]

Kant's ethical subject, whose values are predicated on axioms that would assure the integrity of the person was not violated, becomes more phantasmagoric than ever. This is the false universalism of ends over means also found in Nietzsche's *The Birth of Tragedy* and in Marx's alienation of the commodity from its roots in the division of labour. Under advancing capitalism, a new cosmopolitan world view is being created where exchange value is now cosmopolitan – a universal *marker* that transcends all nation-state traditions and local economies. The alienated group, the service-workers, become the tragic carriers of this False cosmopolitan spirit.

The new money economy, which is based on manufacturing, consolidated European culture as the superstructural transmission belt for imperial conquests of peoples who have existed in a no man's land within and outside of the "cosmos" of Europe: *Niemandsland* had no capital city. This was Kracauer's prophecy in the 1920s: reading films and the New Groups was like reading hieroglyphs that were signs of a desire for a "cosmopolitan" universal remedy for the decomposition of the white-collar worker's inner life, that in Kracauer's later formulation of redemption from physical reality would soon face the Nazi promises of apocalyptic redemption.

The ancient symbolic map of Europe from 1592 housed in Prague's Strahov Monastery shows Europe as a virginal woman perched on her side and whose navel is Bohemia and head is Spain. The iconic naïveté stamps a cosmopolitan imaginary onto the diversity of reality itself. But who are these peoples who do not inhabit the European cosmopolitan's very own class war? Nietzsche knew them as the latent Dionysian and Apollonian polarities of cultures of tragedy. Indeed, it is the "tragedy" of the *loss of the cosmopolitan* for Nietzsche that is revealed as the sign that the bourgeoisie's cosmopolitan peace was a fake peace: the war had been internalized into the tragedy of culture itself. And so Simmel saw the city through the eyes of the cosmopolitan world view in which we find ourselves at home in the illusions created by the modern metropolis, homeless in the urbanized world of the modern city.

Simmel's "The Stranger" describes these two streams and how they emerge out of the dialogue of exile and cosmos, the city and the tragedy of culture. One stream leads to mourning over the death of culture-as-a-refuge from society and follows directly from Kant's belief that nature becomes second nature – the will to find and make an "enlightened" culture. The other leads to what Simmel names the "unschematized individual expressions," which must allow for the "hatred of the money economy and the intellectualism of existence." [37] The linking of the money economy to a racialized Semitic origin would only need a short route to link both to the ideological use of cosmopolitanism in racist ideologies of history. This is the ideological principle that would be used as propaganda for the Third Reich's own version of its phantasmagoric, diabolical cosmopolitanism in the name of a grand scale revision of history in which all of political life would be reshaped in the "Luna Parks" of undiminished capitalism and state-building, each managing everyday life and the "imperceptible dreadfulness of normal existence." [38]

Kant's Third Principle

I name neo-cosmopolitanism, which is a transmission belt for Negative Socialization based on the elusive nature of happiness that is masked as self-esteem.

In many parts of the world, the year 2000 passed on without the protagonists noticing that it happened, but with the "guilt of the peoples of the metropoles" in not rebelling against war. Propaganda has become the prevailing ideology of the "globalicity" – that is, the cosmopolitanism of the global economy. This is the Weimar pathology that Kracauer, following Kant and Simmel, analyzed, in his continuous engagement with the *counterfeit cosmopolitanism of "the Masses," who were beginning to live at the beginning of an epoch that he would call the "No Man's Land of the social ornament"*:

> The position that an epoch occupies in the historical process can be determined more strikingly from an analysis of its inconspicuous surface-level expressions than from that epoch's judgments about itself. Since these judgments are expressions of the tendencies of a particular era, they do not offer conclusive testimony about its overall constitution. The surface-level expressions, however, by virtue of their unconscious nature, provide an unmediated access to the fundamental state of things. Conversely, knowledge of this state of things depends on the interpretation of these surface-level expressions. The fundamental substance of an epoch and its unheeded impulses illuminate each other reciprocally. [39]

For Kracauer, trained as an architect, film was an ornament of and for the masses. Films were the topography of the metropolis and the direct reflection of the collective mentality of an "anonymous multitude" – which is the functional equivalent of negative socialization. [40] His anti-millennial historical imagination is grounded in the surfaces of everyday life. Calendar time assimilates the idea of progress into beginnings and endings. The European peoples invent the idea of history as progress in order to salvage what they can out of the anxiety of the delayed redemption mediated by a church that cannot produce what it promises. We accept and propagandize the idea of progress in order to compensate for the sacrifices on the altars of history.

The "ornament of the masses" gives new meaning to modern mass culture and its consumer-spectator. It is difficult to avoid the banality of everyday lives at the end of the century which are coerced into belief in the superstition of numbers, even as many are said to believe in supernatural phenomena like spaceships, devils, creationism, telepathy, and astrology.[41] The power of the mortality of numbers terrorizes us into submission to systems that render the common person helpless in the face of the speed of economic change.

When Kant placed the Fifth Principle of universal history into a problem of our laws, he could not have imagined Kafka's parodies of cosmopolitan-universal citizenship in "The Great Wall of China" or "In the Penal Colony." Kracauer knew Kafka's work and saw how the individual is metabolized into a suffering compliance with the idea that, speaking philosophically in Kantian terms: "It is nature's intent that man should secure all these ends by himself" but the society "which not only possesses the greatest freedom and hence a very general antagonism of its members … also possesses the most precise determination and enforcement of the limit of this freedom." The parody of Kant's "highest purpose of nature" is not the "civic association" – the communality of free autonomous souls – but (the Sixth Principle) when a master, also themselves a human cipher characterized by Kafka in his parables of the city, can simply look out of the window and undercut their footing in the cosmos.[42]

In order to solve this problem of the laws of culture in the age of universal images in a world that was, for Kracauer, a world without ideological shelters – a world without boundaries – Kracauer saw the rise of film producing a new culture which would be a force both *Jenseits* ("the other side of") the culture, and yet within culture. Film is the universal medium for producing uniform mentalities that were mechanically and technically produced for the citizens of the modern city. The hired workers yearn for the resolution of conflicts in the world of now-democratized images of ideology as reality and reality as ideology that could mask Kant's cosmopolitan peace, which for Kracauer became the antechamber for "those who wait" – in the "*horror vacui* – the fear of emptiness – [that] governs these people."[43]

Film brings an epochal change. The film world brings us to the boundaries of the social and leaves us waiting there hungering for more; film carries our unfulfilled desire for a universal ethics into the feelings of homelessness without compensation other than the fantasies provided in the culture industry. The aesthetic space-time of the film form produces a feeling of the present and a crisis of personal time. Time stands still but also moves! Those who seek tolerance *and* recognition of their lives seek cultural evidence of other cosmopolitan world views *but also* the aesthetic mimesis of one's own "*horror vacui* – of one's emptiness."[44] This becomes the guiding principle of modern thought: those who wait cannot escape searching and finding an "idea for a universal history with a cosmopolitan intent" that is grounded on the loss of an *immortality* and the transcendence of the subjective into another realm. The transcendence releases the will from its dependence on forms; the individual should now be capable of maturity sublimated into a universal public realm where attempts, as we wait in the Antechambers of History, make us at once "subject and object, at once poet, actor and spectator" (Nietzsche's *Birth of Tragedy*) in which the spectator who is part of an anonymous multitude struggles with a new form of alienation below the dimensions of consciousness. The spectator, however, finds only the transitory and the fleeting.

Kracauer's studies of film illuminate the mourning for the loss of the universality of a world. The deterritorialization of modern life produced film as a mirror, as the "nature" or essence of reality.[45] This means that the inner world is a displacement of autonomy and this inner world is projected onto the surfaces of society where the spectacle-conditions of modern life are presented through new instruments that disclose in their very enclosure the brutal contexts of modern depersonalizations. In this sense, Kracauer is a paradigmatic modernist whose work follows directly from Kant and Simmel. The idea of a universal history has been assimilated into the very fibre of the modern, "cosmopolitan," metropolitan citizen.

Walter Benjamin tried to understand – while almost minimizing – this motive force in Kracauer. Benjamin described Kracauer as an ironic and laconic cultural "ragpicker" who, on his way to the "politicizing of the intelligence" in the grey morning of the revolution, reminded the newly possible revolutionary "we" of both the inner life of the human and of the objective conditions of life which stamped thought with the phantasmagoria of every-day life. [46]

Benjamin understood the literary intelligence of this mod-ernist who unprecedently burst upon the public scene by using modern life, mediated through film and cultural creation in every-day life, just as an ethnographer uses a native informant who speaks a unique language which the ethnographer *has to learn in order* to understand a culture that the ethnographer feels is familiar but is becoming stranger and stranger. The strangeness and uncanny qualities consist in discovering both its archaic qual-ities and something that was new just beneath the surfaces. To grasp the experiences beneath and alongside of the newly learned language, and to embody that process of learning in his own life became Kracauer's lifelong project, summed up in his exile reflec-tions that reconstructing history "as it really was" would be a futile endeavour.

Kracauer's construction of this exterior and interior world of the shelterless, anonymous spectator of historical forces defined the intellectual-imaginary worlds as the phenomenology of the impersonal.

Where Kant's notion of the autonomous person existed even as the external world was eliminating evidence of sociality and individual autonomy, Kracauer makes specific reference to the loss of communality and collective trust in the hidden workings of anonymous spectatorship. He applies this principle to his own life in both *Theory of Film* and *History: The Last Things before the Last*, where he argued that modern life should be understood in metaphorical terms as "the anteroom of history," a place "like that of photographic reality," "of a kind which does not lend itself to being dealt with in a definite way." This describes his own life in which as an exile he tried to live out the *horror vacui* of the memory of the destruction of the past by the fascist German forces of violence. He was one of those exiles who attempted to make a rough peace with the "banality of evil," by seeing in the rise of the Weimar film industry the same dangers, the same perversion of Kant, which Hannah Arendt saw in her *Eichmann in Jerusalem* (1963), *her* devastating portrayal of an empty "little man" who used the maxims of Kant to defend his bureaucratic innocence by proclaiming that he acted in such a way that if his leader, Hitler, knew what he, Eichmann, was thinking, his leader would have approved of his actions. [47]

To return once more to the world of the loss of cosmopolitanism as a utopic concept, we can remind ourselves that George Lukács described the "other" romantic-anti-capitalists like Adorno and Horkheimer as inhabitants of the Hotel Abyss of exilic conformity to despair. The question of Lukács's compliance with Stalinist anti-cosmopolitanism is not an idle one. On both sides of the Cold War, there was the struggle against the appropriation of the idea of the "cosmopolitan" by ethnic nationalism masking itself as internationalism. Arendt's Eichmann study, which opened the entire question of the destruction of European Jewry when it was unfashionable to raise the subject, also questioned the way Zionism acted like a cosmopolitan principle in the name of nationalism.

How does Kracauer write a book about history in the Cold War period that does not mention the unmentionable – the devastation of his homeland, his language, his relatives, his work, his friends – in a period when the historians of universals had not really faced nor answered the question of which view of history could explain the rise of fascism or the Holocaust? And why does Kracauer write a book about the failure of concepts of universal history? The answer may lie in Kracauer's return to Kantian precepts, which argues against Hegel's embattled "world-spirit" (*Weltgeist*) and the "natural history" of development and progress. If the totemistic and teleological spirit of the modern age is revealed through the transparencies of the film image of reality, then film is the negative transparency of forgetting. The film image recreates the terms of memory, which shows the world as it is in its phenomenal intelligibility. When Kracauer was writing his study of history, Adorno was writing *Negative Dialectics* (1966), which also described how the smallest cells of immanent negative moments outweighed all positive universals.

Beginning with the earliest details of Kracauer's plans to explain and delineate how hybrid forms of thinking must disclose cells of yet-unvisualized existence – the assemblage of moments which are caught in film as the form of expression that lies somewhere between art and history – we see how he continued to long for a concept of the dialogical relationship of hybridism in art and a humanistic cosmopolitanism in social thought. This would allow us to compose and configure the memory traces, not in mere montage, but in the intermediary areas between the visual and the organized collectives, which have not yet been fully recognized and valued.

Kracauer's lifelong struggle with Adorno over the nature of this utopian transcendence is an important and unexamined source of their conflict over what constituted a cosmopolitan outlook. Adorno and Benjamin had already noted in their attitudes towards Kracauer that this "ragpicker" of capital was in fact someone who was using the Marxian notion of false consciousness to show that the "Weimar spectacle" had channelled the cosmopolitan tendencies of the power-protected culture into a new kind of collectivity which was given a personality through the films of the times. The white-collar workers were being *anatomized* dramatically in Weimar films. The pathos of the masses had not yet found its literary or cultural form: film is the "redemption of physical reality" that created the legibility for modern life, even as the film form produced by its very nature the feeling of the uncanny penetration of physical reality.

In this, Kracauer follows Lukács and Simmel in their disillusionment that the democratic social movements would find their fearful expressions in the new agitational art movements of documentary, reportage, photomontage, vernacular idioms, or the images portrayed in the grotesque violences of Otto Dix, George Grosz, and John Heartfield. Yet there are more hopeful, autonomous specifics: the autocratic state's transformation into populist-welfarist ideologies that took place from Weimar to Russia, to America and England were recorded on film, which was the medium that appropriated and exploited the spectacle of the times and gave new life to the idea that in film a utopian chronotope had merged with the technical means that had surpassed the panoramas of the nineteenth century.

It was as if the European city had come onstage as the universe's unconscious. To bring the masses face to face with their own fate and the mystery of the visual was the new face of cosmopolitanism. It was not for nothing that art and culture historians like Erwin Panofsky, Rudolf Arnheim, Béla Balázs, Arnold Hauser, and filmmaker Sergei Eisenstein, and literary philosopher Viktor Shklovsky, who turned film towards literary and art history, were in essence constructing a socio-aesthetic as a new naturalism. The film axis of Budapest–Vienna–Berlin and the new experiments in book publishing and graphic design, which include the images of John Heartfield and Hannah Höch, gave radical art a sense of internationalism with a cosmopolitan intent of resistance. Yet this struggle to live within spectacle-consciousness could not eliminate the need to recover the intimate world, that world of "lost causes" and "unrealized possibilities" which defined modern life, and, eventually in exile, Kracauer's own life.

This Kantian "life" and "art" come together as an image of reality in Kracauer's film aesthetic and become a productive relationship of text and image. The relationship between text and image is resolved by Kracauer's recognition that the film image provided us with productive understanding, a product of the unconscious, which is shorn from internal reality but is experienced aesthetically by the photograph. [48] Internal reality can only be found again in a consciousness of the aesthetic of fragmentation, much as if a frozen image in a still photograph in an album depicts individuals who, when they are talked about by their family counterparts while viewing the photographs, suddenly come alive, and the relationship of memory to the present is illuminated in the interstices between history and speech.

Kracauer compares Marx and Kafka as the forerunners of this method of photographic literacy,[49] which he calls the "side-by-side" method of representation. In reality this is an aesthetic of the interstices, of the off-handed, the chronotope of an emerging historical materialism, which Kracauer had developed in his Weimar essays and had already measured against the age's economistic Marxism and spectacle capitalism.

The photographic image is an object of terror-filled beauty: redemption of physical reality is a cosmopolitan image of both hope and resistance: it is the pre-conceptual imperative of a visual composition, which Kant, for example, presumed was the bedrock of any concept of autonomy.

Following on Kant's notion of the sublime, Kracauer illuminated the Weimar topography of a modernity in which the subjects of modernity are aligned with the fate of the dreamer dreaming of itself with no hope of knowing itself, in the midst of sublimation as the mimetic dream in life itself. The dream, then, is a figuration, an expression of the unconscious life of the individual, but the dream, like film, contains non-conscious elements in the individual's delusions and obsessions: a life history is marked by the fate of memory and forgetting. The alienated, non-homogeneous structure of contemporary life illuminates Kracauer's own life as an exile. His life took on the form of a Kafka-Proust chronicle, rather than a philosophical mediation of philosophy, which for his friend Adorno was philosophy written as the history of unreason.

Kracauer was more interested in those left out of the tableau portrayal of the cosmopolitan, "those who are waiting" (*Die Wartenden*) in the transition from feudal social structures to democratic capitalism.[50] When Benjamin called Kracauer the "rag picker," he made him into the Baudelairean urban wanderer rather than as a Simmelian Marxist, or the Kantian analyst of collective mentalities. Kracauer uncovered the façades and portières, ornamental surfaces of deteriorating urban life being propped up with new phantasies of escape and control. Parallels are with Dickens and Dostoevsky, not just Baudelaire. In Kracauer's American exile, the struggle to "Americanize" his sense of the cosmopolitanism of his Weimar studies alienated him from Adorno. [51]

Kracauer did not publish his book on Georg Simmel. [52] His unyielding Kantian hope for a political ethics for the future is crucial to understanding one aspect of his thought: his attempt to bridge Marxism and its schisms with an alternative vision of something like a Kantian natural ethical anarchism, which is revealed in Kracauer's essay "The Hotel Lobby" where the artist in "giving form to life" renders life "bereft of reality" so that it has "lost the power of self-observation, may be able to restore [it] to a sort of language." [53] Kant's Eighth and Ninth Principles are realized as difficult passageways for a Marxist and socialist-utopic communalism. Kracauer's romantic anti-capitalism of hope for those extraterritorial inhabitants in modernity without a roof pushed Kant's ideas of a civic consciousness towards an anarcho-socialist critique of official social democracy as a really existing form of socialism. He understood that modern life had created a new kind of "unconscious" which formed and disseminated representations on a different level of wish and desire from those images we received from earlier cultures. The unconscious must be understood as a fabric of abstractions, of things, of thing-representations, which exist in consciousness through already reified images, but were controlled by a dream process whose erotic, libidinal energies came from unknown sources in culture. *Gemeinschaft* ("community") and *Gesellschaft* ("society") remain alive terms for him, yet they are loaded with the weight of suffering. These could not be understood simply as "community" or "society," respectively, nor can we use civil society as a simulacrum of Kracauer's references to finding life in the smallest objects where the unstaged invisible makes itself known. The film image for Kracauer redeems physical reality that lacks "any revelatory word." [54]

Transference from phantasy to consciousness is mediated by a range of intrapsychic social forces that revealed the nature of commodity fetishism inside of the pseudo-objective nature of the world. Film form freed the thing-representations, allowing the object to express the profound, heartless anxiety of a world saturated with "despised objects alienated from their purposes." [55] This full-frontal view of reality's surfaces on the skin of film enabled Kracauer to seek out and analyze (and defend) the harbingers of new social movements, whose traces he found in the American films of the 1940s and 1950s. [56] This links him to an incipient anarchist tradition of outsiders and lost causes against the various forms of fascism. When many artists and cultural critics in this period sought to hasten the decline of liberalism, Kracauer's historical-philosophical conditioning of the inner sensibility of a partisan, radical cultural critique created many ideological controversies which he wrote about: for example, over Brecht, Mann, and Scheler.

Kracauer realized the problem was how to account for immediate history and its relationship to forms of democratic aesthetics or culturist ideologies. Common fronts against fascism did not convince him, in the face of the new conformism, of the victimized masses. This meant confronting the way Soviet art ideology and avant-garde poetics came together in their scurrilous attacks on humanistic radical thought. Kracauer clearly realized that one problem for the partisan, aesthetically sensitive intellectual and for artists with a mindfulness towards the cosmopolitan was how to face the question of time-serving conformity, the *Einverständnis* (*agreement*), which in German means the accommodation and assimilation of the will to consent that also created the will to consume commodities, images, and state-run ideologies, which allowed everything to exist but permitted nothing to change.

Reading Kracauer reading society is to recognize the subworlds emerging in the phenomenal realities of film. American films seem to read themselves in a miasma of entertainment that illuminates the monumental suffering in which the victims of this phantasmagoric process of cultural conformity are suffering their own blindness. He sees both the subject matter and form of the expression of the subject matter dependent on reification of exchange value as the basis of cultural creation in capitalism.

The attempt to write the history of a cosmopolitan universal art history from the point of view of both the defeated in history and of their redemption in art and physical reality cannot be done. The full title of Kracauer's *Theory of Film: The Redemption of Physical Reality* equates to the "redemption" of physical reality, which means both "saving" physical reality for the future and the reparation of the damages to our understanding of suffering. Through recollection and reconstruction, reproduction and representation of memory, the photograph is ontologically both remembrance and reification, illuminating capitalism as the phantasmic and phantasmagoric form of spirituality in modern life. [57] The film form is technically a collection of photographs in motion.

The secularized outsider figures used as touchstones in Kracauer's *History* are variations on the mythological theme of Odysseus. Whether Orpheus, Erasmus, Ahasuerus, Proust, the historian Burckhardt, or Sancho Panza, these figures are chthonic, earthly gods who represent the artist as the nomadic parasitic anarchist, [58] masked as a photographer who "assimilates himself into the very reality which was concealed from him by his ideas of it." [59] Reality for Kracauer is "wonderous."

Kracauer's last work – in terms of his Weimar studies – may be an idiosyncratic work, a coming to terms with his distant and exilic past and present, and with his differences with Adorno and others who belong to the Hegelian tradition. In *History*, he outlines his answer towards Adorno's and Benjamin's philosophy of history as the mode of existence of the emergency ward. Kracauer turns to a cosmorama of social change based on a concept of experience that reads the new filmic construction of history in how we may define our quality-less selves by what is missing and immanent in the film form: "strange as it may seem, although streets, faces, railway stations, etc. lie before our eyes, they have remained largely invisible so far. Why is this so?" [60]

The spectator of the modern world is the new homeless cosmopolitan who is no longer the culture-bearer of former times. The new culture-bearer is the bourgeois spectator who is the carrier of history whose violence is inbuilt into the culture. This agent of history is not just a passive spectator but is conditioned by the reflexes that require escape into a Quixotic Universal History without cosmopolitan peace. This figure of the artist as the exiled photographer who has no "fixed abode" thus becomes the emblematic muse for our counterfeit-cosmopolitan times. While the photographer may be seen as an attractive aesthetic persona hiding behind the camera – because of the camera's ability to document, capture and interpret – the photographer also represents an abstract image of the psychology of the modern anonymous person. The photographed images represent the artist as an anonymous being who synthesizes the dissolution of reality into forms which cannot be rendered into essential or humanizable experience. The "man without qualities" is enshrined in the optical nature of culture itself as a form of present time. Film, one can say, is the secret history of the yet-undisclosed disclosures of modern man.

Because "the film screen is Athena's polished shield" [61] that permits us to see the expressions of the modern visualized horror of tortured humans, no longer taboo, Nazi concentration camps and the destructive acts which can be promiscuously simulated by the screen image, only to "redeem horror from its invisibility behind the veils of panic and imagination," [62] create a new aesthetics of the innermost image. It is the capacity to see ourselves reflected in Athena's shield. Kracauer identifies how we inhabit our lives on the burnished surfaces of the "abyss of everyday life."

Yet, having pointed to these aspects of Kracauer's struggle with cosmopolitan peace in film, one must ask why the politics and aesthetics of fascism, genocide, cruelty, murder, and organized evil do not make a more overt appearance in his post-humous opus, or in *Theory of Film*. If, as he says, historical ideas are objective precisely because of their indebtedness to the subject's unmitigated subjectivity, then the subject's personhood must be construed as an "active" subjectivity engaged with the liberatory details of history; and if these details puncture the screens that rationalize and separate us from truth, what then are these concrete-abstract ideas that he refers to? This "puncturing" of organic reality by transcendent, radical, undetermined subjectivity implies a creative source of knowledge for a modern art that radically challenges the artistic ideals from which the general historian – the failed thinker of universal history as it actually was – draws inspiration. Kracauer's metaphor for historical insight is in an important sense a sensual one, an erotic one, where radical moments occur in art as a spontaneous generation of thoughts and ideas – more in terms of John Dewey's phases of experience than Marxist rupture where contingencies break into a "seen-from-above" general history by non-contingent forces.

The sublimation of revolutionary Eros into sublime experience of the film form itself – film is conceived in Kantian transcendent terms as a sublime expression of what is missing but is there – relegates an experiential political or sensual quality to this eruptive moment of a *kairos*. This crisis of the moment is suffused by the ambiguity of Odysseus's journey from his impulse to escape from home. He becomes an exile and an apologist for bourgeoise culture, which was a theme in Kracauer's Offenbach study *Orpheus in Paris*, written during Kracauer's Paris exile. [63]

Adorno criticized the Offenbach study and wondered whether Kracauer could be taken seriously anymore and whether he should break off connections with him. Benjamin's response: that Kracauer had resigned himself, and ten years too late had aligned himself with the heroes of biographies – is a sign of an underlying disagreement about cultural politics that remained a feature in their personal lives but ignored the extreme situation of Kracauer fleeing into exile. [64] This led to a break in their friendship, in part created by Max Horkheimer's unwillingness to publish Kracauer's study of propaganda, which later appeared in an outline form in *From Caligari to Hitler*, arguably the first study of film that shows the double-sidedness of film as an extension of culture: a new form of cosmopolitanism of the lost in history is shown throughout Kracauer's analysis of Weimar's films.

This disagreement can be illuminated as a disagreement about the unstated dimension of sexuality and Eros, enunciated in Marcuse's and Adorno's aesthetic. If Baudelaire is for Benjamin a sign of a dissonant openness towards the world, or if dissonance becomes the sensual threshold for Adorno's aesthetics of music, this aesthetics of the contemporary must be analyzed as a crisis in interpreting the cosmopolitan who wanders in and out of the modern world in the way Chaplin or Keaton wandered in the world looking for an absent inner life. Both were favourite figures for Kracauer. Kracauer's photographic image can be understood aesthetically as a root metaphor for his theory of immanent reality and is related to his critique of abstract, desensualized experiences endemic to the modern world.

To become a spectator of the movement of history is the key to Kracauer's understanding of Kant's notion of universal peace as a lost cosmopolitan disposition and can be shown in two small studies on friendship written in 1917–1918 and 1921. Kracauer established there the ground on which a politics can be founded. As Karsten Witte notes in his afterword, "where the connection to the polis vanishes, thinking about friendship is taken along ... the private form of friendship as virtue is the public openness of society that is in keeping with reciprocity. In tyranny there is little or no friendship, which must be touched by freedom as equality." [65] Friendship is the *fundament* on which an anarcho-reciprocity can be built and is the basis on which Kracauer developed a theory of film that, as a world-historical form, became the counterpart to Kant's hope for a universal and intelligible language that would further the rights-based world that is not based on redemption or brotherly love, but on a notion that would require us, in Dieter Henrich's words which relate to Kantian ethics, "to restructure our conduct."[66] In Kracauer's words in "On Friendship": "Every human being is driven to snatch what is most valuable in his fleeting existence from the flood of time, to set it apart, and somehow to render it timeless."[67] That snatching from the flood of time and setting it apart is the basis of his method of reading film, memory, and history.

DOSSIER II – CHAPTER 2

Voices of Silence – Peoples of Invisibility: Joy Kogawa's *Obasan* and the Loss of World History [68]

I

World History and Exilic Memory: Unforeseeable Exile and Authorship in Canadian Writing

My memory of the other and of the other's life differs radically from my contemplating and remembering my own life ... Memory of someone else's finished life (although anticipation of its end is possible as well) provides the golden key to the aesthetic consummation of the person.

—MIKHAIL BAKHTIN, "Author and Hero in Aesthetic Activity"
  (ca. 1920–1923), *Art and Answerability: Early Philosophical Essays*,
  trans. Vadim Liapunov

World history might be said to begin for Western nations like Canada and the United States with the racism and imperialism that emerged after the Japanese victory over Russia in 1905, the first victory by an Asian nation over a European one. [69] From the point of view of the West, this was a loss that could never be allowed to happen again. The German–Japanese axis in World War II thus became the ultimate violation of all taboos against the "barbaric Orient." Now the Germans and the Japanese could become typed as arch examples of anti-democratic autocracy, representing two different versions of a feudalistic tyranny that challenged the hegemony of industrialism and colonialism in both the older British and the evolving American empires: the "classic" form of fascism typified in the German destruction of liberal institutions (which never existed in feudal Japan) and the Japanese attempt to reforge and expand an old empire were lumped together by the ideology of liberalism, a liberalism that was complacent about its own barbarism.

The political and culturally saturated images of the Japanese and the Germans were linked to their economies, but also to their military-industrial power; this bred a conception of their cultures as alien, hermetically sealed, and coldly violent. Put another way, both Germans and Japanese fit the stereotype of a strong and pure race. In addition, they were both characterized as "super-races," longing to be led by strongmen. [70]

Not only was this stereotyping of race and culture assisted by anti-communist sentiment in Canada and the United States after World War I, it reinvested the racist feelings with Christian pieties about the progressive and exclusive nature of Western democracy. Thus, the racial stereotyping of the Japanese put them below even the "uncivilized" Eastern or Southern Europeans, who were already subjected to postwar immigration quotas; interestingly, Germans in North America obtained a higher standing in the labour unions and factories than Southern and Eastern European immigrants. Asian people, therefore, were at the bottom of the labour scale – they were socially the "inferior race." In popular culture, the stereotype of the Japanese was perhaps even more virulently evil than the equally comic-grotesque "Nazi." The Asian in a uniform was more bizarrely a misfit. Consequently, the Canadian internment policies during World War II followed directly from immigration policies and their underlying racist attitudes from 1900, that reflected colonial, white-supremacist as well as labourist-industrial values that, when applied to so-called Orientals, who were considered beyond the pale of civilized behaviour, and allowed Japanese Canadians to be dispersed and resettled into "work" camps without much public protest – and, until the publication of *Obasan* in 1981, with hardly any public memory of this destruction of a culture. [71] Memory and forgetting is, then, the foundation of exilic authorship.

II

The Cassandra Complex: How to Speak and in Whose Mother Tongue?

Joy Kogawa's 1981 novel *Obasan* is a *representation* of the aesthetics of loss of memory, of loss of trust in the world. Its power for readers speaks to the feeling of the loss of memory and the loss of a desired community, in which consciousness is not depleted of enduring contact with a lost family. The author struggles with sentiment and emotion and attempts to reconstruct herself on the basis of the hybrid identity "given" her by two generations of Japanese enculturation: the Issei and Nisei. The Issei and Nisei, deracinated inside of the Canadian colonial culture, seem in Kogawa's view to have retained a lived experience of their own past, but this does not mean the novel affirms the "identity" of anyone, although it may wish to: the concept of a unified identity goes against the very grain of the aesthetics of loss in *Obasan*. The novel, written in polyphonic fashion, describes how the child Naomi faces her inability to mourn the loss of her mother and how this traumatic loss informs her so that she cannot – will not? – master the past, except in terms of her own creative undertaking to recover and give shape to that past. Kogawa's writing can itself be described as the struggle to write about her own unassimilated hybrid selves.

Put differently, this sense of loss might be named the "Cassandra complex" after Christa Wolf's 1983 novel *Cassandra*, where the mythical Greek woman, Cassandra, deprived of trustworthy speech by culture and authority, is doomed to represent herself not as a human being but as a prophetess who utters truths no one can or will believe. While being multivoiced, *Obasan* can also be read as a *critique of the concept of identity – identity as a no-place* itself, insofar as memory and the past are seen as constructs of both authority and the national traditions which Naomi must learn about in the new world of the Canadian state.[72]

In *Obasan*, the author presents the mimesis of this loss as speech that can only be performed in *written* form, thus giving the lie to the sentimental appropriation of the native, the immigrant, the minority, and the outsider as a "silent" victim or as a transgressive oral voice: it could be said that Kogawa writes by discovering and performing her own literacy in the act of writing her own hybrid history. Breaking her own silences and performing her own voices through writing becomes, to the critical reader, a critique of the silence of world-historical forces towards the dispersal and dispossession of an overwhelmingly silent people. Kogawa learned that personal silence and world history, the inarticulate and the articulated, interrelate: "It is, after all, that which exists in the silences and in the voicelessness, that which is inarticulate and not yet known, that which is victimized, manipulated, trivialized, and exploited, that which exists below the tip of the iceberg, that determines the drift of the ice-flow."[73] It was thus a kind of poetic justice that *Obasan*, a novel that includes voices of those who had been rendered voiceless by their own government during and after World War II, was quoted on September 22, 1988, the day of the signing of the Japanese Canadian Redress Agreement at the very place where the laws that created what Kogawa once called a "silence of pain" had been passed: in parliament in Ottawa.[74] What stories does *Obasan* tell? What voices does it allow to speak? To what silences does this prose poem of silence give names? And what reception is possible for it in a world having lost its world-historical voices?[75] From the standpoint of the territory of the emotional "place," it is a no man's land.

Shortly after the Japanese attack on Pearl Harbor in December 1941, about 22,000 Japanese Canadian men, women, and children, about three-quarters of whom had been born in Canada or had become Canadian citizens, were branded "enemy aliens" by their own government under Mackenzie King. Short-lived protests ensued, followed by a silence paralyzing the until-then-bustling Japanese Canadian community of British Columbia, a silence turning into stone: "We are the despised rendered voiceless," Naomi remembers as she finally confronts her suppressed and concealed history, and the "stone bursts with telling." During this painful process of remembrance that breaks open her past and for the reader explodes the complacency of Canada's self-ignorance about its complicity in cultural genocide, she discovers that the hostile attitude towards the Japanese Canadians had begun long before the narrator and her family were, in the course of World War II, "stampeded in the stockyards and slaughterhouses of prejudice." Racism was made official.

Racial prejudice against Asian and Indigenous people has been widespread in British Columbia ever since the establishment of this British colony in the mid-1800s. BC's immigrant population, overwhelmingly of European origin, saw its ideal of a white society threatened by Asian people, whom they considered unassimilable; consequently, they did everything in their power to prevent Asian people from integrating and prospering: Asian citizens and their Canadian-born descendants were denied the right to vote as well as the right to enter certain professions. When in 1905 Japan defeated Russia, the Japanese replaced the Chinese, who until then had been considered the greater danger, as a "main threat" to "white culture." The result: the civil rights of Japanese Canadians were even further restricted. About 80 percent of the Japanese Canadian fishing licenses, for example, were revoked in the twenty years *before* Pearl Harbor.

The remaining fishery fleet, as well as farms, houses, businesses, cars, and personal belongings, were confiscated after Pearl Harbor, allegedly to protect the nation against espionage and sabotage. There are still remnants of wartime fortifications in British Columbia facing westward towards the Pacific. In a fashion reminiscent of the Nuremberg Laws, the properties of the Japanese Canadians were held in trust, which amounted to nothing less than selling them without consent. Racism had now become a patriotic ethos governed by the motto "No Japs from the Rockies to the sea."

When the British Columbia Security Commission was established in March 1942 to oversee the removal of all Japanese Canadians from an approximately 150-kilometre-wide "security zone" along the West Coast, the militant advocates of a politics of racial hatred had finally achieved their goal: within six months, the culture of the Japanese Canadians was, by government decree, destroyed forever in a manner that reminded its victims and others of Nazi methods, suggestive of pogroms and trans-settlements of peoples in Europe and the Americas, the Soviet Union, and South Africa.

Against the express advice of the military and the RCMP, who at no time considered the Japanese Canadians a risk to national security, thousands of Canadian citizens were, despite their confidence in and loyalty to the Canadian parliamentary democracy, torn out of the context of their lives, temporarily collected in converted livestock stables in Vancouver's Hastings Park, and then "evacuated," as it was euphemistically called, into the most primitive internment camps and ghost towns all across the province. Many men were sent to work camps to build roads. In the words of Muriel Kitagawa, a politically active journalist in the 1940s whose writings Kogawa discovered in the National Archives in Ottawa and used as a model for Aunt Emily's journal entries, British Columbia had become "hell."

Whoever resisted the hellish orders was shipped to camps in Ontario without redress and put behind barbed wire. German prisoners of war were also placed in camps in Canada. To crown it all, Japanese Canadians, unlike the citizens of enemy nations who were protected by the Geneva Convention, had to bear the costs of their own internment – the humiliation was complete. Justifying this as "civilized" behaviour was necessary in order to maintain those factors of repulsion and distance so crucial to the behaviour of dominant classes, who represent the outsider as the polarity of the insiders' own internalized values of superiority. Charismatic capitalism, to paraphrase Max Weber, invents its own enemies in order to endow itself with the magical powers crucial to maintaining its cultural control over the economic means of production. The friend–enemy distinction is critical in maintaining the illusion that national unity is at stake.

In the spring of 1945, when the end of World War II was foreseeable, the "final solution" of the so-called Japanese problem in Canada was initiated. Mackenzie King, who confided to his journal that it was "fortunate the use of the [atomic] bomb should have been upon the Japanese rather than upon the white races of Europe," gave the Japanese Canadians already living in exile in British Columbia the choice of being deported to the eastern part of the country or of being "repatriated" to Japan as "missionaries of the Canadian way of living."[76] Demoralized, about four thousand "enemy aliens" reluctantly "agreed" to be exiled to a country that more than half of them had never seen. The remainder dispersed east of the Rockies. As a result of massive protests, the "repatriation programme" was finally discontinued, but it took until April 1949 – four years after the end of the war – for the uprooted Japanese Canadians to be granted full civil rights and to be allowed to return, after their nightmarish odysseys, to their former homes on the West Coast. Their community, however, was never again to regain its original vitality and its many voices.

III

The Silence of Inner Exile

There can be neither a first nor a last meaning; [anything that can be understood] always exists among other meanings as a link in the chain of meaning, which in its totality is the only thing that can be real. In historical life this chain continues infinitely, and therefore each individual link in it is renewed again and again, as though it were being reborn.

—MIKHAIL BAKHTIN, "From Notes Made in 1970–71," in *Speech Genres and Other Late Essays* (1971), trans. Vern W. McGee

The official, demagogic noise drowned, until long after the end of the war, the resigned silence of the dispersed and dispossessed victims of racial hysteria, while many of the Japanese Canadians believed that they themselves were to blame for their persecution. Small wonder that the injunction to be silent and invisible, as well as related shame, had been etched into the psyche particularly of those Japanese Canadians who at the time were "growing up": the Nisei. Kogawa describes this destructive indoctrination in an interview: "When I was a kid and I was made to feel that overall I was unworthy and inferior and ugly and so inadequate ... that was part of who I was for so long. That was just within me and I believed it all."[77] Similarly, she confesses that there is still a lot of Naomi in her because, as Aunt Emily put it, "the message to disappear [had] worked its way deep into the Nisei heart and into the bone marrow."[78] For the Nisei, the period of any consciousness of identity and being an autonomous person was therefore a period of culturally and politically created silence.

Kogawa describes knowing and not knowing:

> It is terrible not to know. But when you don't know that you don't know, it's not so bad. When you're in denial you can go on with your life – it's a great survival tactic ... You have to tear it away and that's the hard part ... You go into the flame and you will find that the safest place to be in a fire is to go directly into it, into the clearing where the ashes are. So that's what you do when you're no longer in denial: you go rushing into the thing, you get to the safe place.[79]

To disappear and to fall silent had been delivered to people who could look back on a long tradition of silence. It is this kind of silent understanding particularly noticeable between her mother and herself that gives the young child Naomi her unshakeable sense of security and protection. Primarily, however, this tradition of silence can also be characterized by a Confucian fatalism, a resignation governing, perhaps predominantly, the lives of the

Issei: Obasan, Uncle, and Naomi's parents. In order not to break, they were like bamboo bending in the wind, a wind that, in the 1940s, increased to hurricane force and whirled them and their families around the entire country and beyond. Submitting to what was experienced as shameful fate, they and their offspring carried on this destiny in the lee of the rock face of silence, in the shelter of forgetting.

For the girl Naomi, however, forgetting does not begin with the forced expulsion of her family – in her, speech had already begun to hide much earlier – watchful and afraid – in Old Man Gower's backyard where she is sexually violated as a four-year-old while, visiting the old man, when she feels shame for the first time. This secret of her terror and exhilaration is the one thing that separates her both from her mother and from herself as her mother's daughter who sees herself as a "rift." When her mother, the incarnation of silent knowing, disappears shortly afterwards – forever, as it turns out – Naomi is left speechless. Thirty-two years later, she still lives in what Freud named an "internal foreign territory," full of silence towards childhood memories, unable to give names to the shame of having betrayed her mother, to her feelings of guilt, unable to remember the wordless, painful disgrace brought to her, her family, and her community, and thus unable, as the voluble Aunt Emily once puts it, even to attempt to heal "the diseases, the crippling, the twisting of [her] soul." [80]

IV

The Remembrance of Silence

Dear father ... you let me learn about the most central event in your life from my grade twelve history book, which reduced your incarceration, property confiscation, and degradation to four lines.

—MARYKA OMATSU, *Bittersweet Passage: Redress and the Japanese Canadian Experience* (1992)

The desperate attempt by Naomi and her family – with the obvious exception of the political Aunt Emily – to forget the trauma of the war and postwar aftermath, to drown the memories of their violation and their shame in a "whirlpool of protective silence," is clearly a survival strategy. Resigning themselves to the dark past, they wanted to be done with their pain, to allow the wounds to heal, and to look towards a brighter future for the sake of future generations. While the events of the past may have been forgotten and deeply repressed, the spell of the past, however, was not broken. Beneath Naomi's scars, then, there is still poison, the poison of fear, of humiliation, of self-hate that had seeped deep into her body and soul, and there had become as hard as stone.

This petrification of the repressed past paralyzes Naomi without her realizing it: heavy like Uncle's bread, which she is unable to digest, a growth of silence lines her abdominal walls. The emotions do not subside, but ultimately, once she asks for it, are "extracted," one might say, by the political; Aunt Emily wakes her up after her almost lifelong childhood sleep; Naomi, deprived of her memory, begins her *recherche du temps perdu*. [81]

Just as for Joy Kogawa the confrontation with the past begins with shedding tears over Muriel Kitagawa and her tormented, passionate life, for Naomi the confrontation with history, with her story, begins with mourning her uncle and his stoically accepted exile. Soon, however, the focal point of her remembrance, of her search for her lost historical time, of her mourning work is the integrity of her own unlived life. [82] During the wake for her uncle she visits what Margarete Mitscherlich-Nielsen calls "tombs of self-formation." With no access to the sealed "vault of [Obasan's] thoughts," she burrows herself back into her own early memories, and she falls into Old Man Gower's demanding, sexual hands. Searching for her lost home ground, as it were, Naomi uncovers "fragments of fragments," splinters of a split-off life. She recovers this memory treasure of past experiences, these disowned "patterns of childhood" in front of our very eyes: the process of laying bare these "segments of stories" is nothing other than the fate of writing in the narrative itself. [83]

Naomi's autobiographical appropriation of the splinters of her identity thus becomes an act of self-repair: her consciousness evolves through "remembering, repeating, and working through" (as Freud would have put it) a reality hidden to herself. This process constitutes a step out of her non-identity and into her search for self-identity as a person in the making. Telling her stories, she opens up her previously inaccessible "internal foreign territory"; writing her story, she produces the experience of attempting to inhabit her unacknowledged, unmastered past. Naomi's return from the exile of silence, the past and the present, thus brings forth past and present.

By narrating herself back into her painfully alienated past, she narrates herself out of an agonizing ambivalence towards her enforced "identity" in the present; by tracing back present disturbances to past censored conflicts, and by recalling the past into the present, she turns the present into the past – and, then fictionally, the future becomes imaginable, at least minimally through telling the story. At the end of her story, when the stone has finally burst with telling, Naomi recognizes that the silence, which seemingly had protected her as a child, clearly damages her as an adult: "Gentle Mother, we were lost together in our silences. Our wordlessness was our mutual destruction." By acting out the remembering of what I name the "Childhood of Memory," Naomi prevents the memory of the dead, their continued existence in the act of remembrance, from being destroyed as well. Having returned to where she had begun her journey into the "silence of pain," the narrator sees splinters of the moon rippling in the water, sees "water and stone dancing." Finally, the question about the unfinished demand for the "freeing word" has been answered. The story of her speechlessness, of her voiceless non-identity has therefore bestowed upon Naomi the language she needs to come to herself. Through this language of non-identity, we understand that voicelessness means cultural invisibility for the

peoples of Canada officially dubbed "minorities." That became
the "ideological" basis for the reception of the novel.

V

Voices against the Silence

The level of articulation, the level of comprehension, the level of
awareness and the level of compassion that I heard in the words
of the speakers [of the Redress Committee] was music in my ears.
—ROY MIKI, *Justice in Our Time: The Japanese Canadian Redress*
Settlement (1991)

Aunt Emily's conviction that the past is the future thus proves
to be true at the level of cultural politics. However, by telling of
her untold despondency, Naomi gives this story a glimmer of
hope whose faint glow touches us too: "What draws us together
is not sermon, but story," Kogawa once said in a talk on human
rights and Japanese Canadians.[84] While the "word warrior" Aunt
Emily eloquently preaches justice for Japanese Canadians – and
thus becomes an allegorical representation of the liberal politics
of multiculturalism – Naomi, from her long years of teaching,
knows that "it's the children who say nothing who are in trouble
more than the ones who complain"; she must first of all allow
her cut-off tongue to be sewed back on.

The quiet, intimate stories of this healing, however, are more
moving and engaging than the engaged, political intelligence
of the publicly enraged Aunt Emily. And does Rough Lock Bill
too know the irresistible attraction of storytelling? This universal appeal of storytelling may be the reason why Naomi's lyrical
search for answers to the question "Who am I?," when senti-
mentally expressed, can't redress a nation's shame that had paid
almost no attention at all to Aunt Emily's pamphlets and her
documentary answers to the question "Who are we?," until the
politics of the Redress Movement became a historical moment.

Once Naomi has dug up the fragments of her buried identity, the soil has been prepared, towards the historical subject, and for Aunt Emily's orientation towards the silence of the collective to come together, in public, in the Redress Movement. What had begun tentatively in 1977 at the centennial of the arrival of the first Japanese immigrant in Canada, broadened out in the 1980s to a movement whose members had the courage to break the spell of silence, no longer hide from themselves the stories of their ostracism, and tell them in public.

They were spurred by the discovery of government documents, finally accessible thirty years after the war, that proved beyond any doubt that their internment and dispersal had not been motivated by security concerns but rather by political, racist expediency grounded in historical precedent. The historical memory of a pious democratic federalism was, in its national spirit of renewal, not unlike the federalism and constitutionalism of the Adenauer regime in Germany that became the basis of the conservative and social-democratic consensus on the Federal Republic's Basic Law (the *Grundgesetz*). The correlate national identity had become part of Pierre Trudeau's Liberal government. All the Naomis and the Stephens, who during their childhood suddenly found themselves to be "both the enemy and not the enemy," and who had deeply internalized this existential puzzle, now had it set in black and white that they had not been Canada's enemies, but rather that Canada had been their enemy. The negotiations between the National Association of Japanese Canadians and several successive federal governments lasted almost ten years. By reappraising and appropriating communally and (self-) critically their "silence of pain," as well as their pain of silence, people began after long years of voiceless alienation to approach each other again, to put an end to what Marcuse famously called in *One-Dimensional Man* the "nightmare of a humanity without remembrance." As if the two ideographs for the word "love" that Naomi had once seen were coming together, many Japanese Canadians were tying together the "long threads" of their stories, joining together in order to "act" by "telling" with their "hearts" and "hands" how to form a collective and yet not be a collective on others terms. [85] Naomi's memory-work becomes, in Bakhtin's understanding of language, a litmus test for how the past informs a future, or whether there can be a future.

When, in September 1988, only weeks after the US government had reached a redress agreement with the Japanese Americans interned in camps far from the Pacific coast, but not expropriated under Roosevelt, a settlement was signed in which the Canadian government apologized for injustices done in the past, vowed to do everything in their power to prevent anything like this from recurring in the future, and awarded Japanese Canadians individual compensations for their losses, Kogawa and with her the entire Japanese Canadian community felt that "after an awfully long labour" they were finally "being born." [86]

One of the dreams of the Redress Movement did, however, not come true: it was unable to secure a constitutional safeguard against any relapse into earlier mistakes and a guarantee of the right to equality of all Canadian minorities. And the promised national foundation for the battle against racism is still a long way from being established. Even though one may thus doubt that this movement has created conditions that will irrevocably lead to different behaviour patterns in "white Canada," it nevertheless provided crucial impulses for a freer political culture. The most important thrust has without doubt been the beginning co-operation with Canada's most inhumanely treated minority: the First Peoples. These "elective affinities" between invisible cultures are based on the rejection of a spirit of colonial subservience summarized by Kogawa: "No, we will not be subject to other people's definitions of us. No, we will not be marginalized. No, we will not be humiliated and made to feel inadequate." [87] *Obasan* and the Japanese Canadian Redress Movement tell the story of such a coming to terms with the past in a country guarded by red-coated RCMP officers, in which writers and dissidents search for a common tradition of resistance.

VI

Dissidence and Race

The novel in Canada is restless with traditions of dissidence; it does not know the grandiosity and mordant, racialized self-examination of culture that is displayed in many American novels like *Moby-Dick*, *The Sound and the Fury*, and *Invisible Man*. *Obasan*'s small challenge to the naturalistic tradition of the novel that dominates the Canadian novel gives us Kogawa's confessional aesthetic, which belongs to a minor literature with major consequences: *Obasan* enters a dissident tradition – whether she wants to or not. The "pain of silence" that Kogawa names fits into a world-historical genre of poetic remembrance, of the politics of dissidence – the search into world homelessness – whose many quiet voices and soft nuances insistently make themselves heard against the noise of the official stories that drown them out.

But Kogawa's novel also raises a larger question: What is a "world-historical novel"? We know the emancipatory tradition of Rabelais, Goethe, and Dostoevsky, read at the end of our century of total war and ethnic justification for wars, which began with two European "world" wars and comes back again and again with worldwide civil wars, extinguishing entire peoples. Where does a novel like *Obasan* fit in World Literature?

Today, world history and the world-historical novel must give us a sense of time and progression of a liberal humanism at war with itself. A place where world-historical consciousness has invaded the lifeworld of the individual. This invasion, which Hannah Arendt described as "world alienation," has created the stranger, the outsider, and the nomad, who, unable to be a citizen of the world, carries on weak shoulders the burden of estrangement from the world. This stranger lives inside as well as outside history and suffers the fate of being the "village idiot" who is the litmus test for the polis, who lives as a private self, but may in fact be the only truly social being. Fleeing and emigrating become joined. [88]

Obasan tells intimate stories about this outsider who moves in and among us. It is the discourse of the exile who can't return home. All over the world, universal strangers drag themselves to the borders where their irregular bodies are checked. Even if they are allowed in, they are by no means always welcomed into our "midst" because they have no will to power so necessary for living in our world that sweeps up selves into commodities called "identities." Thus the inland-outsider becomes a universal symbol of our times, rebuffing Kant's hope for a universal citizen by making the stranger one of the norms of world history, a stranger whose presence in contemporary novels from Kundera to García Márquez and Rushdie to Kogawa and Richler raises the question of whether national identity can ever be a basis for forming a living tradition, a sensuous aesthetic-cultural memory. In the *fin de siècle*, the politics of multiculturalism appears to be the only politics that people can grasp without falling into a faint from the sheer guilt at having to exercise their market selves in the polis of the world economy. This is world-historical exile of the surplus peoples.

Kogawa appears to write from this non-national perspective. She lives in two cultures and belongs to neither one. At the same time, she refuses, as she once put it, to "militantly claim the role of the victim as a right." [89] Her poetic inwardness is a struggle with nameless power which is continuous with the silent politics of the unpolitical: these politics reveal that, today, the world-historical victims are inevitably connected to the power of the affluent in the metropoles, who must separate suffering from their own self-understanding.

These new "Gods" of shame and guilt have produced a new accommodation and resistance to a world order that lets the self-consuming wound of perpetual guilt over our fear of the outsider's "otherness" fester in the "other" as stereotype. While the politics of the large, noisy world risks leading to our renunciation of the social, the litmus test of the voice finds a home in works like *Obasan*.

Yet we must acknowledge that although *Obasan* is a "minor work," it must be seen in the larger claims about inner exile and the fear of resignation in a world of exile and leaking high walls. Christa Wolf's *The Quest for Christa T.* and *Cassandra*, for example, or Václav Havel's *Letters to Olga* are also intimate and are speaking to a large meta-politics, too political for the official handling of the past. *What Remains*[?], Christa Wolf asked.[90]

Perhaps nothing more remains for the exile out on the streets than a bottom-drawer identity made up of scraps of letters, an essay here, a document there, photographs, slivers of poetry, all searching for the missing integrity of the person. In this aesthetic ghetto of the unpower of the powerless, little remains of the grand world-historical novels of the great bourgeois period, from *Elective Affinities* to *War and Peace* to *In Search of Lost Time*. Even the novels of the early twentieth century already shrink the outsider-exile to anonymity, preparing the way for Albert Camus's figure of the stranger, and the worlds of Musil, Mann, Kafka, Broch, or Woolf, where characters are struggling for poetic integrity – a different kind of exile. The modernist tradition allowed the creation of large works, but the world exposed in these works was small, narrow, and banal, and its heroes, robbed of any personal integrity, were estranged from any concept of the person as someone who might sense the breakdown of legal, cultural, and artistic traditions.

Kogawa's is a struggle for artistic integrity based on exile, race, and ethnic consciousness at the end of the twentieth century that required she transform her "identity" as an inland-outsider into a political education – but such an effort lacks definition and falls too easily into the ready, generalized truths of multi-cultural ethics.

As a consequence of its legal prerogatives (which Naomi bitterly summarizes when she says that the "government makes paper airplanes out of our lives and flies us out the windows"), the modern state defines the person as one in whose identity it can lodge itself through social pressures: "Ethnicity is something that got put onto me by the country," Kogawa stated.[91] No exile, not even an inner exile, no minority rights, no redress movement can change anything about the fact that Naomi's lifeworld is lost and the politics of hate have left scars of self-censorship which cannot be removed by anything that others can share. And when Naomi returns to the place of the crime, of the destruction of the private world, which we read through the psychological story that she narrates and reconstructs of her life and her memories, a sense of coming to terms with reality emerges. Remembering the history of her loss of self and of her transformation into the grotesque figure of the "enemy within" leads Naomi to give her guilt of silence the name of "political immaturity."

The "mature" Aunt Emily, on the other hand, rejects any silence: she attempts to build a political National Language of Multicultural Fairness out of the historical entanglement of self and history. As long as Naomi denies these politics, she remains immature politically, and we as pious multiculturalists are prevented from completely identifying with her character. But Naomi is also strange to herself, and for the conventional Canadian reader she will always be so: she can never "become" Canadian. The riddle of her origins gives the lie to the popular, conventional imagery attached to the "Canadian" landscape where, drowned out by the "multicultural piper's tune," Indigenous Peoples haunt the unmastered bad memory. In the sense that Kogawa searches for a multi-voiced personhood, the novel as art reveals how the riddle of "origins" becomes a litmus test for the ideal of origins.

Naomi thus emotionally embodies a shameful, depersonalized inability to fit in, which is so "familiar" to her that its language is spoken even by the inner voice nesting in her. In the relentless world-historical story of the political fugitive, however, there is no universal master plan for being "saved." The survivor struggles with the personal guilt of having to become the forgiver, of being too familiar with and too agreeable to the emergency measures taken to attempt to solve the problems of "outsiders," often called in the bold German language the *Fremdenproblem* – the problem of what to do with strangers.

In the noise of these emergency decrees, "the silence which cannot speak" can only be recomposed in a literature of soft dissonances. This prevents a present-day work about suffering from being grand or monumental.

The stereotype of the quiet, silent Japanese, the Japanese Canadians who feel like pariahs in *Obasan*, are thus prophetic of our dehumanized, world-historical reality where a new market order has produced a world of broken identities without integral "selves." In this way, Western societies fanatically maintain the illusion of freedom and equality by protecting their own security while shielding themselves against history. We condemn the art of memory to the cultural reserves of other tribes: the leftover nations, the limitless barrios, the *ghettos turísticos*, and the guest- worker enclaves over which world history casts its long shadow.

By the miracle of writing at all, Kogawa does not confuse her own shadow for that cast by the institutions of "home" and "nation" which supposedly housed and protected her. She represents the past through an internal dialogue by translating inner cultures into outer ones. Her fictional self-construction *Obasan* may, in fact, be a gift from another, *third* culture. It shows that language and images remain untranslatable unless the reader can imagine everyday situations that do away with those misunderstandings that have stripped language of its capacity to convey meaning and agency. This breaking of the spell of language is symbolized by the atomic destruction revealed at the end of the novel. Here the "silence of pain" and the language of world history come together, without our hearing of the deathly statistics.

VII

The Loss of World History

The Canadian reception of *Obasan* has, to be sure, capitalized on the silence in the novel, a silence that, as this essay attempts to show, constitutes a many-sided critique of the person subjected to cultural invisibility in a modern democracy.

For Bakhtin, the novel has a history of complex dialogue with society and culture. In this sense, *Obasan* is *mimetic* of silence without itself being silent, and its characters *represent* this silence in their struggles to *deal with* their victimization as enemies of the state. At the same time, these characters are litmus tests of resistance to reconciliation with nation-states that have deprived them of their integrity as persons. The characters' memories are fragmented into miniature stories and images, often of victimized animals.

Clearly, at one level, the internment of Japanese Canadians during the war is about human rights; but its world-historical aesthetic subject is mimetically "about" – is a depiction and figuration of dehumanization within contemporary history, examples of which have been brought to view. Today, this destruction occurs the world over: Poland builds steel mills over Kraków; Germany covers a former Jewish cemetery with a supermarket parking lot; Canada turns a Kanien'kehá:ka burial ground into a golf course; state-regimes build holocaust memorials while fighting off fascist or right-wing extremist regimes; a President Reagan and a Chancellor Kohl march on the graves of SS Officers at Bitburg; nation states develop constitutional guarantees for minorities only to relegate them to enclaves of powerlessness through economic misery and landlessness.

Of course, *Obasan* is a small novel, despite the awakening of the author to these problems, and does not, or cannot, do justice to historical exigencies such as those commented here; yet its author's aesthetic truths become, in the characters who suffer, ethical-critical images of feelings about the will to power because its language touches the chronotope of the inland-outsider identity. Sensitivity about identity is insufficient for memory to translate "identity" into the political realm of the psychological feelings of being outside of the dominant culture. [92] Small novels take on a life larger than their own aesthetic size.

The bilingual world of Canada is in reality a social amnesia towards any linguistic or cultural hybridism that would embody what Bakhtin calls the folkloric crossing-over of genres. Or, one has to say, brings the French- and English-speaking and -writing Canada into everyday confluence. [93]

In this regard, Canada is a place of subsistence cultures or of usurped identities because minoritarian culture is suffused with invisibility in relation to the dominant culture, and former anarchist or dissident political cultures – in particular the populist movements of the Prairies and maritime British Columbia – have been subsumed into the left traditions of many kinds of populism. The Latino model of popular culture, with its representation of Creole, mestizo, and Indigenous cultures, arguably takes different forms in Canada. [94]

In Canada, the anti-hegemonic forces that mobilized against American culture in the early 1970s were not equally mobilized against British colonial culture. Nationalist sentiment made headway against American cultural icons and symbols without establishing any civic nationalist consensus. Along with separatist nationalism in Québec and secessionist segments in the western provinces of Alberta and British Columbia, movements towards national unity have failed. Yet a form of economic and cultural federalism still dominates over transnational populism, and communitarian particularity, while growing, is not a strong influence on aesthetics or popular culture. [95]

Perhaps the problem of defining the hybrid aesthetic work can become clearer if we refer to the characters in *Obasan* as "inland-outsiders," because the ideological myth that the Canadian state is an immigrant land, like Australia, Argentina, or the

United States, disguises the inner realities of the cultural pressures towards homogenization. In addition, these other immigrant nations are also deeply polycultural, linguistically and vernacularly diverse cultures that have different ways to camouflage the origins of their historical memories of deracination. From the point of view of the Indigenous Peoples living in Canada, the term "foreigner" might refer to the Europeans as well as to the Asians or the South Americans, yet Asian and the Black people remain even lower, "more" outside of history than the European immigrants.

In aesthetic and political language, the characters are hybrids – inland-outsiders. Authorship itself lives inside the double bind of living in two cultures and not being able to be loyal to either, while facing into and outside of the histories of both cultures.

Kogawa seems to have stumbled onto the false enlightenment of religious redemption as a place of refuge and rejected it, even while calling for love of the world in the manner of heroic saints like Simone Weil. But this is not limited to Canadian redemptive desires, for this longing for redemption has become part of the postwar cultural mythology worldwide, as Christa Wolf showed in her novel *Cassandra*, where the term "foreigner" achieves a new consciousness of reified identities. Why? Because Cassandra's "identity" is represented in terms of the aura of the German nation's identification of *das Volk* (the People) with *die Heimat* (the Homeland). Wolf depicts the ancient tradition of world-homelessness in the war of the Greek peoples in terms of the ancient legacy of Greece and Rome – a second home for Germans in German cultural history – where the dissenter is honoured even when outlawed.

Kogawa represents at the least a cultural uneasiness with dissidence in a culture that has an insecure radical or cultural tradition from which to draw an inclusive politics of worldly multiculturalism, even though the official politics of multiculturalism might contain the basis for a cross-cultural politics. The secure European colonial-immigrant is easily able to translate residual ressentiment about perceived loss of status and loss of territorial-regional space into attacks on the official multicultural policy of the urban state. The spillover of the loss of ethnic legitimacy transforms itself into the exclusive view that the state has created strange creatures of no-identity, or anti-Christian monsters.

In addition, *the state is made into a magically coercive force that inhabits all immigrants,* who are turned into politicized subjects whether or not they in fact see themselves as political. Concrete experience is subjected to the rule of law. Who is a settler-person? Who is not? And the result, if *Obasan* is any proof, is that authorship becomes a problem of aesthetics and the politics of identity. There is a prerogative for avant-garde artists and writers to identify themselves as anti-racists or postcolonialists, or ethical humanist beings that can acknowledge the cross-cultural reality of their lives within the hegemony of a Canadian public sphere looking for a transition into a politically sensitive domination of the reality of everyday life.

Immigrants must identify as "good" survivors who, in escaping the tyranny of collectivism, at their peril, must recognize multiculturalism as another form of indoctrination, if not a conspiracy, organized by and for the Canadian state.

Thus, the search for an active cultural "hybridity" often conflicts with the official ideology of the mosaic and with quasi-assimilationist immigration policies. In this regard, a theory for a specific Canadian cultural aesthetic would have to inform a social movement that affects, among other things, the curriculum in schools and universities. Yet only by including the First Nations and their emancipatory agonies can a Canadian post-multicultural vanguard assume the scale of a social movement in the making, related to the integrity of "the person" that transcends mere semantic "multiculturality."

Naomi, with her struggle against what I am calling her "inner colonization" (insider–outsider), is being stranded on the shores of simple commemorative time, as a fragment of debris from the past. The official commemorative history of the Canadian State is inside the Japanese Canadian community to the extent that the fragments of memory available to her become tormenting reminders of the narrator's *inability to recover the past*. She is unable to "remember, repeat, and work through" her memories. Only an aesthetic reconstruction of the situation of the self is possible within the historically diverse chronotopes of exile, inner exile, inner emigration, nomadism, and dispersion of peoples. This is the message one must draw from this small novel on a world-historical subject.

But *Obasan* is a novel, not a tract or political manifesto, although it might be seen that way. I am drawing attention to Bakhtin's aesthetic of memory and to a literature which can open the novel to world-historical dimensions, small or large, that engages in the struggle to have a dialogue with the readers, both an inner and outer in dialogue. In short, *Obasan* is a *Bildungsroman*.

This sense of memory loss can only be conveyed as an "image of a language," not as language itself. In essence, the novel cannot affirm a concept of the "person" that is simply defined in legal terms, such as citizen, rights, or "visible" minorities – whose invisibility reminds us of the broken promises of civil society. Visibility in the hybrid novel of suffering is thus conceived as *invisibility*, in the way experience may be related only in popular culture. The prototype of this genre might be Ellison's *Invisible Man* which, building on the song-sermon ghetto chants of American Black people and the blues of its ghetto heroes, can be seen as an offspring of the world-historical novels of Melville and Dostoevsky, Ellison's acknowledged precursors. The salient point for exiles and surplus peoples is: To whom is the novel addressed? Bakhtin, who opened this essay, can be a rejoinder to the question that *Obasan* as novel is in search of a "super-addressee" which in this case is not God or the Nation. The super-addressee in this case is the search for what might be named the "lost human" of one human speaking to another, which can be framed by thinking of translation itself from one human to another. Caryl Emerson puts translation and the "image of language" into perspective; but what can be said with certainty is that, for Bakhtin, to translate was never to betray. On the contrary, translation, broadly conceived, was for him the essence of all human communication. Crossing language boundaries was perhaps the most fundamental of human acts. Bakhtin's writing is permeated by awe at the multiplicity of languages he hears. [96]

DOSSIER II — CHAPTER 3

W.G. Sebald and Exilic Memory: Photographic Images and the "Cosmogony" of the Aesthetics of Exile and Personal Restitution [97]

Exile is a shaping force in W.G. Sebald's essayistic novels, which are devoted to his personal and historical recollection of the catastrophe of World War II. In *Austerlitz* he inserts personal photographs that change how we think about memory and the construction of memory. For Sebald, the act of reading implicates the reader into the work of historical and personal memory. What has fallen into fragments is restaged fictionally as scenes of memory, as if memory carries an allegorical quality by working through how one takes an approach to one's own life in regard to others. Mikhail Bakhtin poses how an author is both writer and creator of a verbal-storied reality. Bakhtin is a guide in this essay on the genre of autobiography, in which the author is a figure in the work, who poses as a writer. Authorship becomes an imageless materialism in the story. The author-creator shapes the lived experience within the verbal-ideological nature of the story without always telling us directly who is speaking. The story, then, appears both apocryphal and fable-like, as do all fables. Thus *Austerlitz* as a novel is both allegory and fable. The character of Jacques Austerlitz is a "figure in the carpet."

Mikhail Bakhtin, the great Russian theorist of the novel and culture – the novelization of culture – is relevant to Sebald's chronicle-tableau of memory. Sebald tells his story by mapping the art of memory through storytelling, which becomes his aesthetic of memory, the classic storytelling aesthetic of the *Bildungsroman*. The *Bildungsroman* is writing that completes one's life in writing in order that a missing wholeness can be seen in the passing of time completing the life cycle of the individual:

> There lurks beneath the specific question of the propriety of glorifying oneself a more general question, namely, the legitimacy of taking the same approach to one's own life as to another's life, to one's own self as to another self. The very posing of such a question is evidence that the classical *public wholeness* of an individual has broken down, and a differentiation between biographical and autobiographical forms had begun. [98]

Sebald's prose, combined with his photographs, appears as if "found"; together they illuminate what in memory remains incomplete. They are restitutions of memory and unforgetting. Put another way, Sebald's prose photographs are memory in the making. His novels appear to take on a life of their own as he "inscribes" his memory onto his photographs. The photographs seem to appear from the darkness of memory, as if memory is an unresolved stigma. Sebald's photographs speak to us; they are a dialogical "gestus," which is a force beyond their presence in a story that winds its way through biography and autobiography by resisting, painfully, the dramatic effect of the memory of death.

If the apparently random gestures, the small gests, of Sebald's images appear to be banal, trivial, mere household pictures without compositional sophistication, they can remind us of the more conscious artists of the everyday in the German tradition of photography: Gerhard Richter, Jochen Gerz, Thomas Struth, or Jeff Wall, whose photographs appear to be random transitional objects. The viewer of the photograph sees memory and history as life that emerges in front of us by our very looking at such pictures and learning to make judgments about how memory and the starkness of "looking" are represented. The everydayness and ordinariness of life becomes a power in itself.

Sebald's photographs appear suddenly as we turn the pages, but without captions. It seems we are reading an authorless album found in a second-hand shop. The reader is suddenly placed into a dialogical relationship with the unconscious in memory revealed through the tableau nature of Sebald's novel. Memory becomes tableau. The exile lives in a world of fragmented selves that have lost the basic natural law of human habitation: the potential of a "public wholeness." The tormented absence of a "public wholeness" marks the difficulty of writing a traditional autobiography. The photographs appear as showing, telling, and making: the author struggles with authorship: scenes are containers of memory, as if the photographs are pictographs, only traces of memory like pictures on the walls of caves, markers that mean something personal to the person who makes them, but that exist as leftovers from some spectral past. They are photos that increase their meanings based on the literary context.

But let us also call them "pictograms," which make stories into visual events, not just representations. The pictogram, or story, shows the author struggling with authorship, with the relationship of representation to figuration. The relationship of author and writer is, then, the dialogical and the field of vision of the exile who emerges slowly in time and place. Emergence, Bakhtin writes, is exactly a problem of *showing* time:

> In such novels as *Gargantua and Pantagruel, Simplicissimus,* and *Wilhelm Meister,* however, human emergence is of a different nature. It is no longer man's own private affair. He emerges *along with the world* and he reflects the historical emergence of the world itself. He is no longer within an epoch, but on the border between two epochs, at the transition point from one to the other. This transition is accomplished in him and through him. He is forced to become a new, unprecedented type of human being. What is happening here is precisely the emergence of a new man. The organizing force held by the future is therefore extremely great here – and this is not, of course, the private biographical future, but the historical future. [99]

So then, I name Sebald's photographs "pictographs," which are memory traces like pictures on the walls of the caves; they are figures or markers that mean something to the "author" who makes them. They show time starting and stopping.

While they are photographs, pictographs have meanings based on context. Picto*grams*, however, are attempts to make pictographs into something more – material for and about making stories. It is as if they are an oral storytelling as literature speaking dialogically with, and to, the photographs. The effect is "digressive" writing. The photos, then, are in part allegorical representations of light and shadow. But collected together they are tableaux and compile scenes; yet they are also single figures because they are part of a whole story and they make sense in the entire novel in concert with the other pictures. While the story recounts a life lived with, and in memory, the pictures are enigmatic: Whose memory is this? Why is memory joined with places whose names haunt the author and the reader? Memory work recounts the life of the character Austerlitz who lives with the enigma of memory that is both in the past and is the unpast, literally and figuratively a "posthumous memory" that comes back again and again, but not always at the same place. We experience the enigmatic nature of art as a form of life by trying to find a way to solve a life problem through artistic measures that play with mimesis.

Sebald's writing is inextricably connected to what appears to be autobiography, yet asks: Can we really write autobiography? Almost as if he is thinking with Sartre who, in *Nausea*, writes: "This is odd: I have just filled up ten pages and I haven't told the truth – at least not the whole truth ... nothing new ... I admire the way I can lie." [100] Sartre's novel is really a figurative "Diary," as if it were collected from undated notebooks from a cardboard box, "published without alteration." Existentially, in the light of the events of Austerlitz's life, one needs a concept for a work that forms a "world" – tells the truth – and leaves memory traces that falls in the interstices of history and storytelling. I coin "cosmogony of memory" to show that Sebald struggles about writing as such. His work is about the situation of writing that resists writing. *It is an errant memory world, which becomes a cosmogony about writing and shows the breeding grounds of writing.*

I have given subtitles to the stages of exile – as stages of writing about exile.

I

Zones of Contact with the Childhood of Memory

Sebald's writing is both about memory and is a tableau of memory. The character named Austerlitz does not arrive in the scenes until page 123. Here he describes what the reader has been experiencing all along: an aesthetic of loss and reparation in which language, memory, and the European cities come together clashing as if

> some soul-destroying and inexorable force had fastened upon me
> and would gradually paralyze my entire system. I had already felt
> in my head the dreadful torpor that heralds disintegration of the
> personality, I sensed that in truth I had neither memory nor the
> power of thought, nor even any existence, that all my lie had been
> a constant process of obliteration, a turning away from myself
> and the world ... Whatever was going on with me[,] the panic I
> felt on facing the start of any sentence that must be written, not
> knowing how I could begin ... If language may be regarded as
> an old city full of streets and squares, nooks and crannies, with
> some quarters dating from far back in time while others have
> been torn down. [101]

Can it be said any better? Throughout the novel, language, fantasy, reverie, and transitional states of mind unravel the "unforgetting" of war and its aftermath that allow Sebald's novel to move within interstices of novelistic prose and the photographed image. The aesthetic, then, falls between author-ship and the decisive nature of the image that builds a tableau world of recollection, remembrance, and restitution of the past that is linked with Germans, Jews, Europeans, and exile. However, the aesthetic – what I call his "cosmogeny" – is the pastness of the past, in which the character Austerlitz goes through different devotional retreats into the chaos of the aesthetics of memory and exile. The expectation: that the reader accompanies the author and the riddle of the memory of exile and restitution. Austerlitz's life becomes a litmus test for our remembering and forgetting the past and the unpast.

The "cosmogeny" is paradigmatic of layers of historical remembrance and thinking about exile and return and no return. The "in-between" experience of transience creates a leaking boundary. Sebald comes into view on the waves of memory traces that flood the memory-saturated world of German and Jewish, and European exilic remembrance. There is no end to the diaspora of memories and the uncertainty of telling the same stories over again. What can they keep telling us that we do not already know? The "cosmogony" of memory is a world made of the remnants of the world of exiles, memory and photographic emblems of memory that come back again and again, often without a name. Memory-work becomes a quixotic quest and adventure, not only by recalling, but through *memoration* of what I name *the childhood of memory*. Memory is not just recollection, but is "memoration" as the consciousness of memory, because memory itself grows, retreats, and has a corporeal presence. Memory has a "childhood" in which memory is uncertain, plays with meanings and is often on the verge of a breakdown. In an essay on the Austrian writer Adalbert Stifter, Sebald writes:

> The decisive difference between the literary method and the same hunger for experience in an experience-shy technique of taking photographs, consists certainly in the description of memoration [*Eingedenken*]; photographing promotes forgetting. Photographs

are the mementos of a destruction process in a world seized with disappearance, painted and written images surrender to a life in the future and are to be understood as documentations of a consciousness, that is devoted to the continuation of life. [102]

Sebald's description of writing as "written images" should best be described as writing as "figurations" or as "colportage," as a struggle with symbolization and the agony of misremembering and forgetting images, which appears in the dark light of the subject matter of *Austerlitz* as an "eschatology" of fear of forgetting. The colportage is much like Pirandello's *Six Characters in Search of an Author* (1921) in which characters not only search for the author, but are "carrying" a play in search for the play itself.

By Sebald's aesthetic "colportage," we understand the dissemination of religious and devotional literature, manuals, almanacs, collections of folklore and popular tales, chivalric romances, political and philosophical works in inexpensive formats, carried by travelling pedlars carrying their wares on trays suspended from straps around their necks who wandered nomadically from city to city, from neighbourhood to neighbourhood carrying books as commodities. The unpredictability of memory is placed in Austerlitz's memory, in which fragments of memory come together in the writing, even as they have been fragmented in history and memory through writing and authorship as itinerancy verging on vagrancy.

Adorno can also be a guide to memory and vagabondage, which Adorno reads through Paul Valéry, who sees art as the struggle with chance and unmediated contingency. Valéry may have suspected the contingency of itinerant musicians whom he wrote of as

frivolous people, whose fleeting spectacle is no more stable, binding, reliably settled in space and immanent within order than the itinerants themselves. Not the least of Valéry's ideals is that of an art that has divested itself of its vagabondage and its social odium, no matter how well sublimated it may be. In fact, however, this element of vagabondage, this lack of subjection to the control of a settled order, is the only thing that allows art to survive in the midst of civilization. [103]

In the light of Valéry, we can see Sebald's characters guided by the Virgilian vagabond narrator, who guides Austerlitz through the odium of the history that wandering in memories is tracing. The characters only hesitantly begin to think on their own by learning to relate to new events, old traces, and unsuspected associations, as if their unconscious was suddenly released by some force of nature. Memory is coming to terms with the violence done to memory. Memory, then, in Austerlitz's journey, depends on the immanence of place, and the demolition of place, what happened and what didn't happen in the place: place itself carries memory.

The work seems diminutive where small, unknown people begin to live again in a world-sized magnification of exile, loss, and restitution of memory. In addition, Sebald's reception grows larger, more mythic, and puzzling when questions about his photographs cast a dark light on our perceptions that has the effect of allowing us to think the impossible: that Sebald's photographs must include the feeling that memory can also become "posthumous." Posthumous memories are the forgotten recollections that come alive again in the aftermath of forgetting, as if the remembrance happened to another person and that person comes alive again without a name: thus the name "Austerlitz" is a character, a train station, and a person in a place in time, at a crossroads, or station of memory, and a battleground in the Central Europe that haunts the novel.

The novel moves the reader from place to place, but the place is not always clear, just as "Central Europe" as a place has leaking boundaries and broken borders and is an imaginary geographical place where armies have rampaged and trampled cities from the time of the Thirty Years War and before.

It is as if Sebald is directly engaging Adorno's notorious terms of the incommensurability of a poetry after Auschwitz and knows that words alone cannot redeem the misunderstood Adornian claim about poetry after the destruction of the Jews and the devastation of Europe. Sebald avoids words like "Shoah" or "Holocaust" because his vagabondage traces a lost land of language, place, and memory. The question of how to transform the aesthetic itself through the aesthetics of "vagabondage" addresses what is misunderstood about Adorno's embattled polemic against kitsch and the abuse of historical memory by our constructing new genres of memory in other forms than what society allows in the lyric. It is as if exiles are like freaks of history that exist as inscriptions in opaque zones of contact with the photographed past.

The forms of culture that we relied on to transmit, not only our own memories, but the cultural memories of others, vanished against the images of death that come back again and again, like a landscape that includes brutalist architecture of libraries, train stations, dilapidated doorways, vaults, fairgrounds, baroque interiors – which for Sebald were way stations to concentration camps like Theresienstadt. We are left with Sebald's own "Minima Moralia" embedded in childhood visions and childhood memories, which frame Adorno's own exilic unconscious in his meditations, *Minima Moralia: Reflections from Damaged Life*.[104]

We also understand Sebald's aesthetic of memory and loss, past and unpast, through his essays on authors like Jean Améry, Primo Levi, and Joseph Roth, who are paradigmatic of the tortured captive for whom a post-Auschwitz exile was not even half a life. Améry and Levi are also vagabonds of a past that is also an unpast.[105] Sebald's uncompromising view of postwar Germany: "[Améry] is still the only one who denounced the obscenity of a psychologically and socially deformed society, and the outrage of supposing that history could proceed on its way afterwards almost undisturbed." Améry as a writer "knew the real limits of the power to resist as few others did … even to the point of absurdity." Through Sartre's influence, Améry takes his resistance to domination and power into the responsibility of the intellectual to render writing into a critique of power and domination. [106]

Sebald's construction of an exilic past through his reconstituting childhood memory means the restitution and reconstitution of the past are delivered through his essayistic, hybrid, part fictional, part autobiographical storytelling world in which the silence of the photograph plays so important a mediating role. The photographs constitute a tableau of facing the exilic unconscious, which is constituted both by the barrier between those who became stateless and by the permeable memory-membrane through which childhood struggles for assimilation somewhere. Exile is a shaping force for a never-ending impermeable inability to rescue the exile from the memory of exile.

When Sebald describes his alter ego – a created persona from Sebald's own spectral past – the persona, Austerlitz, searches for peace of mind that would be a refuge that would only become real when he could learn to remember the past, which the novel shows would become *the second breeding ground about the unthinkable*. Austerlitz-Sebald's restitution of memory takes place in a location that is "some place," a place of remembering but that has the body of having been already there, and yet it is unfamiliar. He searches for an architecture that would shelter the future from the past. During his pilgrimage, he encounters railroad stations, museums, libraries, archives, manor houses, old factories, which mirror the "impenetrable fog" of language, as well as the hospitals where he resists throwing himself over banisters, and instead he takes to wandering in remote parts of London where "Londoners of all ages lie in their beds in those countless buildings in Greenwich, Bayswater, or Kensington, under a safe roof, as they suppose …" all of which are shadowed by the fear of the corporeality of the past. [107]

The new library building, which in both its entire layout and its ludicrous internal regulations seeks to exclude the reader as a potential enemy, might be described as the official manifestation of the increasingly importunate urge to break with everything which still has some living connection to the past. Sebald's fictionalized characters and the authorial voice listen carefully to their shattered monologues screened through the character, Austerlitz, namesake of battlegrounds and train stations and of the exiled Napoleon himself. Austerlitz is the allegorical man in search of his memory of childhood, who takes the reader into a Virgilian-Dantesque epiphenomenal pilgrimage into the post-Auschwitz world spirit where the politics of remembrance are displaced by the silence of the photographs interlacing his personal journey. The reader encounters the photographs as interruptions and obstacles. They enact barriers. Photographs neutralize and assimilate. At unexpected moments, turning the pages of Sebald's "yarns," the photographs break the prose's rhythms into a mannerist, alienated, Kafkaesque mirroring of an inner turmoil of the author, interrupted by the uncanny refamiliarization of the prosaic, street wanderings where Austerlitz has been before. Concrete images of sinister architecture, people, or shabby scenes of vacant lots, vegetation, broken city walls, marshy meadows are the aura of the past embedded in the characters' memories. Ferber, one of Sebald's reluctant inner voices of the dialogical, recalls in *Vertigo* that history speaks through his Munich childhood in the aftermath of the new order in 1933; in 1939 his parents escape to the Baltic and the child is sent into exile in England as one of the many, many child transports. The memory of child transports from Central Europe is vivid, especially in the deep recollection of the event of departure and arrival for exiles and immigrants.[108]

The Sebaldian narrative and tableau of photographs are both *photographically and optically vivid*, because they recall those *transitional objects* lodged in memory and release meaning by simple storytelling: the generic limits are reached. The story hovers in a zone of contact between distance and proximity. The addressees of the exilic unconscious are the readers and listeners who, in different times and spaces, encounter the image of language in the limits of speech.

Exile is an ideological chronotope, yet prevents any self-glorification of the autobiographical self, because the biography of the exile shows that fragmented internalized selves have lost *both* the real and potential "public wholeness" common to autobiography. The world that is revealed to the reader in the photographs marks Sebald's conscious attempt to create a new space-time chronotope from the actual world of exile to one that disallows the fruits of a composed autobiography pretending the writer had at one time been a whole person. Sebald creates "pictured time." The author-creator of the story of others who poses as a real human being in the novel becomes a permeable membrane between exile as an ideological state of mind and exile in a verbally many-storied reality.

The transformations of the genres of autobiography into exilic frames of consciousness occur under the extreme circumstances of crisis embedded in the distant and proximate nature of threatening images. The photographs, therefore, function as transitional objects that reveal the surface exteriority of the individual within the public, composed world that proved to be a sham against the coming onslaught of the camps and exile. The photographs are verbal-ideological interventions into the mystery of the storytelling compulsions. They lurk beneath the story as image-traces and as fragments of a *missing wholeness* in the incomplete life cycle of an individual.

The photographs are saturated with the pathos of passing through time where we experience the transience of time and memory. We readers are strangers and guests of the image. Ferber recalls his father looking at a photograph in a newspaper clipping about the book burning in the Residenzplatz in Würzburg. Since it was dark on May 10, 1933, when the books were burned, the picture, Ferber's Uncle Leo recalls, had to be "some other gathering outside the palace." Ferber remembers this "fake" history and it gnaws at him the way a memorable photograph finds the story to be true. Sebald prints the photograph, whose smoke and fire even an amateur's eye could recognize as having been faked. What is important about this construction of a photograph image as *transitional object*, the picture of a book burning, is the suspicion that all memory is fake, that memory itself is unreliable, in particular the historical memory of events seen from the fragmented, exilic unconscious when we are looking at the photograph of memory. [109]

But the photograph is fake. Sebald's narrator finds the story improbable and tracks down the photograph in an archive in Würzburg. The boundary between historical memory and the public memory in the pictures lies in the zone of contact that Mikhail Bakhtin calls "the process of exchange," which "is a chronotope" of represented time, and in the narrator's "evolving contemporaneity," which includes many realms of literary experience semantically enriched by the photographs' silence in the face of the reader-viewer's facing both inward and outward towards the exile's own inner-outer world, in which the small world of the exile cannot yet see the large world of historical processes changing underfoot. [110] Bakhtin writes, relevant to Sebald's chronicle-tableau of memory:

> There lurks beneath the specific question of the propriety of glorifying oneself a more general question, namely, the legitimacy of taking the same approach to one's own life as to another's life, to one's own self as to another self. The very posing of such a question is evidence that the classical *public wholeness* of an individual has broken down, and a differentiation between biographical and autobiographical forms had begun. [111]

II

Photographing the Transitional Object

What is meant by my strange term "exilic unconscious"? I began this essay by focusing on the exilic memory as part of the unconscious and the forms of restitution that the characters long for, especially since Sebald's gallery of exiles includes the narrator-as-author Sebald, whose own emigration to England made him into a voluntary exile. Yet ostracism plagues Sebald and his writing. He confesses in his book of essays *Campo Santo* that cities, streets, and buildings since his childhood have been a private world

> that marked not only the beginning of my career as a reader but the start of my passion for geography, which emerged soon after I began school: a delight in topography that became increasingly compulsive as my life went on and to which I have devoted endless hours bending over atlases and brochures of every kind. [112]

Austerlitz, the paradigmatic exile, lives in a tradition of remembering places and geography. Ostracism and the distance from place, and the intimacy of place, allows Sebald's characters to see themselves in album-like depictions of their pasts. The album photographs have an aura of the archaic and the present.

Sebald collects photographs that provide images of the lost memory of the exilic as a condition of life. He constructs a family that canonizes the exilic as the chronotope of our time. His range of figures incorporates an almost biblical canon: Peter Weiss, Adalbert Stifter, Franz Kafka, Vladimir Nabokov, Jean Améry, and Thomas Bernhard – all those I am naming the "Marrones" and who appear in Sebald's *The Emigrants* (1992). [113] These writers are the stations of memory – the ghetto is a shadow that falls on all of his work.

So, his childhood passion for geography becomes his adult obsession with the memory of others' losses in the cities of Europe and later, on the streets of Terezín, the concentration camp just north of Prague, the city that ends and begins Austerlitz's "posthumous memory."

Memory is photographed in transitory locations; the travels of the characters and Sebald's intrepid research into the history of Jewish figures repeat this event of memory and transitional inner images of a place once whole, but which is now a place of deprivation and dilapidation: the stones and buildings have fallen and are now "de-lapidated." The photographs *are* those muted places of recall and research that preserve the childhood of memory as a place where the dispossession of childhood is emotionally constructed as both loss of the past and the fear of loss.

The tableau of the photographs, and the spell they cast over us, express the author's passion for repeating names of different places, streets, passageways, placeways, insects, flowers, and the scenes of impending departures; the exits are exilic moments; they give the reader the feeling that a crime has been committed.

In this way, the photographs contain and communicate the aura of intimacy, while neutralizing the violence of the acts that lead into exile.

III

The Town That Cannot Be Photographed: Terezín

Gavrilo Princip assassinated the Archduke of Austria and was imprisoned and died in 1918 in the Terezín fortress. The town was remote from major centres in the Austro-Hungarian Empire, although it was a crossroads, a way station to the East, the Slavic Lands, Poland and Russia, northern and western Germany: an Austro-Hungarian crossroads. Some reflections in the spirit of Sebald: The only trace of Gavrilo Princip today would be found in photographs, some of them possibly falsified; his name was unknown to my students that I taught in the Prague Field School for many years, although their great-grandfathers, maybe their grandfathers as well, were touched by his act of revenge. I thought of Gavrilo Princip at various times in my many visits to the streets and museums of Terezín and to the dilapidated cemeteries of Central Europe, many in little-travelled rural regions.

Often, we scrambled through the underground tunnels that ring Terezín's archaic fortifications; floods threaten to wipe them out along with the dungeons and cellars under the placidly standing blocks of apartment houses on the streets, graded flat and girded against memory of what happened there.

I thought of Princip as a "gestus," an emblem, for the entire process of remembering through photographs. Sebald places his own photograph in *Vertigo* along with a number of other blurry, archaic-looking images. Sebald had come upon an exhibition in Frankfurt of colour photographs of the Litzmannstadt (Łódź) Ghetto, "tinted with a greenish-blue or reddish-brown," [114] which had been discovered in 1987 in a small suitcase in an antique dealer's shop in Vienna. Łódź became Litzmannstadt, renamed after the German World War I general Karl Litzmann. These "found" photographs become for Sebald a topography of memory, images yet to discover a context: the photographer had recorded the "exemplary organization within the ghetto," the industry, the planning, the very false utopia of the modernized, feudalistic, factory-model towns that the German Reich was imposing on the eastern territories. "People are all around," he writes, but "strangely" deserted pictures, scarcely one of which showed a living soul, despite the fact that at times there were as many as 170,000 people in Litzmannstadt in an area of no more than five square kilometres. I also thought of these blurry pictures of heads and figures as photographic figurations, not representations, while thinking about Sebald's use of the silence of the photographs that resist self-glorification, while at the same time the photographs construct other people's stories, perhaps as if pictures had a memory of their own and remembered us as the figures in the frame are looking at us.

So then, Sebald creates a new chronotope of "pictured time," photographed memory. Without glorifying himself or his subject he focuses sharply on the biographical – a staple of German letters. Yet the urge to depict traumatic circumstances that define the photographic aesthetic interpenetrates his storytelling with researched facts.

In examining the Litzmannstadt pictures in *Vertigo*, Sebald's attention falls on three young women who sit behind a loom:

> The carpet they are knotting, and even its colours, remind me of the settee in our living room at home. Who the young women are I do not know. The light falls on them from the window in the background, so I cannot make out their eyes clearly, but I sense that all three of them are looking across at me, since I am standing on the very spot where Genewein the accountant stood with his camera.[115]

Genewein is the accountant and photographer who took and collected the pictures. Like all depictions of great pictures that inhabit a zone of emotional recognition of the truth value of a scene of recall, the image requires the reader's participation in the objectivity of the judgment on the scene of historical memory that a photograph might contain. Sebald uses the photographs as emblems of once-lived experience faced with the potential duplicity and inaccuracy, their lack of authenticity in the face of the aura of the viewers' memories. Their identities live as archival memory.

The authorial consciousness speaks to us from the road in *Campo Santo*, where the stories uncover new exiles, or places where exiles passed through, almost as if Sebald refuses any form of assimilation and seeks places where assimilation cannot happen, as if, identifying with Kafka, he "yearns for his own dissolution, to perish almost imperceptibly in fugitive images running inexorably away like life itself." [116] The photographs are not pictorial (as they are in Boltanski); they are fugitive images, homeless, extraterritorial representations of memory. Speaking of Nabokov, who was never a homeowner and lived, Sebald recounts, only in rented accommodations, Sebald refers to exile as a "looking-glass world of exile." [117] The enigmatic photographs reveal the enigmas of living with memory traces. I myself have experienced the same haunting extraterritoriality of place and time in the locations where Sebald finds himself, when he recalls the German towns and villages and the small villages behind the cities that surround the *Isenheim Altarpiece* of Matthias Grünewald's paintings. The towns are backdrops to Grünewald's tormented and tumultuous scenes of pain and humiliation. [118]

The town itself, with its eighteenth-century fortress, auratic and mapped with grid-like streets and low buildings, is unlike any other Central European town I know. It reminded me of American towns built on a pattern of rectangular blocks, wide enough so that wagons, horse-drawn machines, and tractors, and, if near a military base, trucks, artillery, or tanks, could rumble through.

Photographs of Terezín could not release the horror of memory of destruction of the Jews built into the streets, blocks, river, and old battlements: down several flights of stairs in an off-limits, semi-abandoned apartment house are dark hallways with dungeon-like doors and rooms with graffiti and Stars of David on dungeon walls, along with other unreadable scrawls and names – melancholic brutal mementos and tracks of obscurity on the doors and walls. The little eight-by-eight-inch windows in the doors with rusty hinges are like apertures, about the size of photographic plates.

Nearby was another hidden "place" that won't give up its secrets to the photographic scene. It was a garden, off limits to contemporary Terezín's Czech-speaking citizens, with a garage-like stucco structure where the interior walls were still visibly fading from the, even then, pastel colours with scenes of sacred places, the hidden prayer house of Jews who had constructed a holy place under the eyes of the Gestapo and certainly a long way away from the International Red Cross contingent that examined Terezín in June 1944 and pronounced it a healthy prison, a model camp complete with the accoutrements of culture and entertainment.

Terezín, the faceless town, has been photographed countless times. It is a place of tourism, and a shrine; international figures are shown on plaques as the board of directors that include Václav Havel and James E. Young. The two museums catalogue and display everyday life and the horrors. Visitors young and old scan the names on the walls for images of dead souls. Signs of any intimate sphere in the town are absent; it is an empty, incommensurable place, blurring historical memory into its many disguises.

The German title of Sebald's *The Emigrants* (*Die Ausgewanderten*) holds the meaning of "emigrant" more accurately than the Latinate "emigrant," because leave-taking – those who leave – is the shaping force for the photographs that deconstruct the shape of the always-incomplete restitution of memory work, the always-left-behind in the interior of the exile's wandering-out of home. Sebald's memory work poses the question of crimes against nostalgia of place and time. Leave-taking rather than "homecoming" is the "mutual immanence" of place left behind.[119]

Sebald's attempt to rescue the forgotten, exiled individuals parallels Adorno's attempt to rescue the individual from a blurred aspect of historical accounts where the distancing effect that accompanies the photographs brings the idea of loss of sight emotionally closer to us. The half-Jew Paul Bereyter in *The Emigrants* experiences this growing blindness, but continued to read "writers who had taken their own lives or had been close to doing so."[120]

IV

Turning Again to Photographing Memory: The Gestus

The photographs come upon the reader as the uncanny, a reminder that visualizing the past, as accurate and precise as the photograph yearns to be, cannot be complete without the storyline, the narrative, the resistance to the finality of photography. Siegfried Kracauer's astute comment clarifies the compilational-transitional nature of image and memory:

> Memory encompasses neither the entire spatial appearance of a state of affairs nor its entire temporal course. Compared to photography, memory records are full of gaps ... The meaning of memory images is linked to their truth content. So long as they are embedded in the uncontrolled life of the drives, they are inhabited by a demonic ambiguity; they are opaque, like a frosted glass, which scarcely a ray of light can penetrate. [121]

Photographs fetishize memory while showing the person who appears to us as both anonymous yet familiar-looking. [122] Kracauer writes:

> In order for history to present itself, the mere surface coherence offered by photography must be destroyed ... The two spatial appearances – the "natural" one and that of the object permeated by cognition – are not identical. By sacrificing the former for the sake of the later, the artwork also negates the *likeness* achieved by photography. [123]

One can find no better description of the aesthetic effect of Sebald's use of the photograph in the interstices of writing and the colportage of images and writing juxtaposed together.

Pathos and the Elegiac accompany the exile's search for reassurance that in the photograph there will be a legacy and remnant of memory – the *gestus* that stops the wheels in the head from turning over and over again with the incomplete project of the inner world of trauma and forgetting, of holding memory and loss as if the two were commensurable. Wheels turn in our heads; the photographs repeat themselves in Sebald's labyrinthine chronicles of the characters' everyday-forgetfulness. The photographs seem shabby obstacles to recollection; Kracauer, again: "In order for history to present itself, the mere surface coherence offered by photography must be destroyed." [124]

The light that bathes Sebald's sedimented and shabby photographic images does not wash the mundaneness away. The aura remains: the demeaning quality and power of the remembered details of trauma and the culture that did not provide a refuge from trauma. This is the dimmed light emanating from Sebald's chronicles of remembrance. The photographs do not bear witness, do not simulate the work of the prose, do not resemble or represent or appropriate the inner speech of the characters' monologues, or the author's working through, the agony of writing, but we experience the obstacles to remembering those whose memories are obsessing him.

Memory in Sebald's works is not portrayed as ordinary recollection, but is closer to the German *Eingedenken*, which is "to bear in mind, be mindful, and hold in mind," to risk the pathos of the loss of recollection, that is, regarding. Sebald's gestus of memory is the embodied *gestus* of the image that can look back at us with the falseness of familiarity and the peril of falling into the kitsch of remembering only what one wants to remember. [125] While the "other" of exile is in some respects suffering at home, the violence of the invasion of the person is ultimately dislodged from home by the aura of danger to the uncanny home that hovers over exile. Adorno's comment, perhaps even more mordant than his comment about Auschwitz, can be applied to Sebald's pictured depiction of his own childhood and a pre-exile existence, reminding us of some picturesque, wishful aura of a kitsch "happy end." Adorno writes: "Even the most stupid people have long since ceased to be fooled by the belief that everyone will win the big prize. The positive element in kitsch lies in the fact that it sets free for a moment the glimmering realization that you have wasted your life." [126] While pathos and the elegiac accompany memory of some reassurance about the past, for Sebald's personas and characters, home has betrayed the children.

At a pathos-ridden moment in Austerlitz's search for his origins in the children's transport from Prague, the breeding grounds where he began his cultural and personal myth of origins, as well as his obsession with architecture, railroad stations, streets, and squares, he hears his former nurse, Vera, say:

> When memories come back to you, you sometimes feel as if you were looking through a glass mountain, and now, as I tell you this, if I close my eyes I see the two of us as it were disembodied, or more precisely, reduced to the unnaturally enlarged pupils of our eyes, looking down from the platform on the Petrin Hill. [127]

And shortly after we see this image of the picturesque, kitsch, and postcard-like diorama of Prague, Austerlitz recalls a garden in Gloucestershire county of wildflowers – "shade-loving anemones" – that he had examined with a beloved, now dead, teacher, Hilary. The same flowers were lodged in his memory of childhood in Prague, but now, *only the aesthetic memory* emerges for the reader, who is following this chronicle from one European city to the next. Memory is muted, and pathos, which we need, hovers and forgives this emotional "gestus" in the way that great photographs are a gestus of feeling – a configuration of emotions, not only a representation of reality.

Memory in Sebald is both a gestus and a representation of spatial events that freeze time and appear again and again as an uncanny representation of the flight from death. This is both a representation of the dialogical nature of story, and, further, a revelation and depiction of intimate and private worlds: the aesthetic *depicts* interior space in story and picture.

V

Compilational Memory: The Riddle of Restitution and Exile as the Commonplace

Sebald's characters do not think of returning permanently to home, nor did Sebald return again to reside in Germany. The photographs as we see them are beckoning from the past; they speak of an innocence about the coming future of misery and the life of forced Aryanization. Such photographs could easily turn up in some shop where albums are sold, fading and stuck together in their anonymous resting place. Their existence as castaway objects is a colportage existence. And they are, like exiles, jettisoned.

In a poignant discovery in *Campo Santo*, Sebald finds a postcard of Stuttgart in a Salvation Army junkshop in Manchester; it shows the Paul Bonatz–designed railway station that he remembered from his childhood when he played the card game German Cities Quartet. The postcard was sent by a young girl visiting Germany, who writes glowingly of a festival with the Hitler Youth. She writes on August 10, 1939. Sebald is struck by the thought that on that very date his own father was on a convoy approaching the Polish border. The association with kitsch Hitler mania almost drives him mad. He then recalls and compiles memory traces about his childhood friend, Tripp the painter, who lived in Stuttgart. Sebald then describes his troubled conscious artistic method of writing. He keeps asking himself about the invisible connections that determine our lives:

What, for instance, links my visit to Reinsburgstrasse with the fact that in the years immediately after the war it contained a camp for so-called displaced persons, a place which was raided on March 20, 1946, by about a hundred and eighty Stuttgart police officers, in the course of which, although the raid discovered nothing but a black-market trade in a few hen's eggs, several shots were fired and one of the camp's inmates, who had just been reunited with his wife and two children, lost his life. *Why can I not get such episodes out of my mind?* Why, when I take the S-Bahn towards Stuttgart city centre, do I think, every time we reach the Feuersee Station, that the fires are still blazing above us, and since the terrors of the last war years, even though we have rebuilt our surroundings so wonderfully well, we have been living in a kind of underground zone? [128]

Passages such as these are related to atrocities committed by the Germans revenging the resistance in France. For example, Sebald follows Hölderlin to the locations where these murders had occurred; Hölderlin had been there on one of his exilic journeys before his period of exile in Tübingen, only an hour from Stuttgart.

Sebald's essayistic-/novelistic-like treatises are meditations as well on exilic consciousness and unconsciousness, and are composed from the standpoint of the Jews and the Germans and those in "Attempt at Restitution," whom he finds are living under the same stars as the rebuilt "Stuttgart," the Daimler factories, the constellation of stars "spreading all over the world." [129] "Why?" he writes, "wherever columns of trucks with their cargo of refugees move along the dusty roads, obviously never stopping, in the zones of devastation that are always spreading somewhere, in the Sudan, Kosovo, Eritrea, or Afghanistan ... can I not get such episodes out of my mind?" [130]

Sebald's "fresco"-like episodes relate to his personal reading of Grünewald's paintings, or those blurred and hurried photographs of suffering in the ghetto which we have come to see as disturbed historical memory. By including the map of Terezín in *Austerlitz* with the photographs that construct his compilational technique, Sebald is right: one needs to look at the maps, architectural and engineering drawings, city planning documents, and sanitation blueprints of the Reich's plans and protocols to turn Eastern Europe into a garden city for clean, industrialized "Planning and Reconstruction." [131]

However, the intimate world of Sebald's pictures of the search for restitution fit awkwardly into his own chronicle that is in history as exile, but searches for a form for the experience itself. Exile, in his text and image, interrelates two interpenetrating dialectical forces of opposition: on the one side, the Utopian desires to recover what is lost from the destruction of what we can call homeland; on the other, it desires to come to terms, to repair in the sense of reparation of the damaged life, created by the invasion of the material body, the Gestus, illuminated by the "laws governing the return of the past." [132]

The person in Sebald is invaded by the violence-making powers of the state against persons and the natural-unnatural history of the decomposition of the cities and the migration peoples, when the borders of states break down, and the poorest of the poor suffer *Ausgrenzung* (literally, "the fact of being placed beyond the borders"), as they move or are moved out into no man's land.

The end result: the "other" of exilic unconscious is the destruction of the everyday, replacing the everyday with vagabondage always inside of the structural inequalities of the world. The world is mapped by zones of contact with the ever-increasing number of peoples exiled, ostracized through shifts of political, cultural, and ethnic boundaries, and excluded from the possibility of a settled life. The United Nations' classifications of human-development indices, charters, and protocols have no limits on the way to describe the ways that departures and arrivals, movements of peoples from city to city are categorized, named, measured, counted, and labelled. The refugee carries the exilic consciousness that remains a shaping force, a zone of contact, with a rights-based consciousness that is the unthought, known within the "other" of exile: the exilic unconscious. It is clear that this author was having a continuous crisis over the question of the exile and the exilic.

The very title of Sebald's final book, *Unerzählt*, beautifully translated by Michael Hamburger, himself a German exile, as the "Unrecounted": told, foretold, and untold. "Unrecounted" becomes what I have called a "gest," an image, a pictograph, and imago, by expanding the situation of writing: compiling, telling unspoken thoughts, writing dispersive prose, the unthought of the unconscious we see in the pinpoint silences of the photographs, and yet there is wishful thinking towards the future.

Sebald set out to photograph this process, create an inner dialogue about it with his exiled character Austerlitz and his exiled, semi-fictional companions, vagabonds, in a world where capital now transects nations whose peoples are on the move throughout the world.

VI

A Postscript: Vagabonds, *Homo migrans*, Refugees, Squatters, and Asylum: The "Play of Mourning"

Really the chorus of tragedy does not lament. It remains detached in the presence of profound suffering; this refutes the idea of surrender to lamentation.

—WALTER BENJAMIN, "Baroque Play of Mourning," *The Origin of German Tragic Drama* (1928), trans. John Osborne

The UN High Commissioner for Refugees, the official conscience of our time, gives us figures of the movement of peoples into tent cities, encampments, flight, and resettlement. Sebald's photographs and essay-like novels create an aesthetics for an exilic consciousness of the always-existing presence of mourning among a chorus of exiles. His exiles have an inner border that crosses into potential madness. Exile becomes a paradigm for how to even *think about thinking* the deep aesthetic enactment of the writer's situation in his own time – about how historical memory still constructs the idea of exile as a power that neutralizes the memory of forgetting itself, here named "posthumous memory" in this study of Sebald's play of mourning. [133]

Behind the implementing of state violence on citizens lies warfare and displacement by force, rivalry, and revolution that cause the internal and then international migrations. Vagabonds and squatters: they search for employment often created by environmental disasters, degradation of the means of subsistence, upheavals to the home workforce caused by the increased production of resources and privatization of massive resources like oil, coal, minerals. The forced resettlement of the really existing settled and never-settled peoples, who are forced to make way for roads, dams, power plants, urbanization, not to say the "outsourcing" of work to poorer countries just across the borders of nation-states, or who live far away in the interstices of the hypernetted systems of communication, which has become the jargon of pseudo-authentic mobility.

Redrawing borders and territories are the new political realities, because exiles live with inner borders grounded on old symbolic ethnicities, or remembrances of cultural wars from "other" centuries, and grievances. Welfare structures decline and health, education, hospitals, disease control, population expansion, lack of farming supplies, infant mortality, HIV/AIDS, and malaria are the breeding grounds of the always-present exilic unconscious. It is the furiously improvised mobility of capital and *Homo migrans*. [134]

The proliferation of studies of memory, a memorialization of lost dimensions of culture, holocaust, and genocide studies, has displaced the classic studies of individual exile. The classic paradigm of the exile is deeply embedded with the violence of persecution, ostracism, banishment, expulsion, escape, flight, refuge, being welcomed as a guest, simply having someone to talk to, resettlement, and in some cases redress or restitution, but in a world with walls, in the flight to asylum. A restless conclusion: will the reception of Sebald's paradigmatic exilic writing be affected by the waning of the classic exile paradigm?

Exile has been refurbished into postcolonial studies as diasporic studies, and the proliferation of studies of memory and the memorialization of lost dimensions of culture and, while we speak of "diversity," the diversity of First Peoples' languages risks withering and dying. Perhaps holocaust and genocide studies have displaced the classic studies of exile for reasons that have as much to do with the overwhelming nature of the subject as they do with the overwhelming nature of the displaced peoples, migrant labour, and squatters that block our "enlightened" world view. [135]

The relocation, transformation, and movements of peoples into subsistence cultures in the cities, or into strategic parasitic existences in the margins of the metropoles, produce diverse forms of pauperization in the megacities, written about by countless writers. The abandoning of towns that have become superfluous, the decentralization of regions that have no regional autonomy, in short, the creation of vast regions of extraterritoriality have changed the way the classic forms of exile have to be understood. We know very well that the classic paradigm of the exilic is deeply embedded within Western culture and religion, and we know, now, notably with Sebald's digressive writing, that we live in a world where there are too many photographs, too many exiles. Sebald's archival memory of text, image, and story gives us a cosmogony of exile, an aesthetic world of photograph, essay, and memoration.

Sebald's archival consciousness, expressed through the compilational nature of memory as the experience of the unpast, uses the cosmogony of exile and restitution to photograph memory – again and again. He has become one of the paradigmatic writers about exile for our time when the word, when the frozen speech of the exile should be recounted and retold. Exile is here and will continue to stay around and be the reality of borders, and leaking boundaries for peoples who have lived like moths clinging to walls.

There will be more exiles, vagabonds, and refugees. There are many vagabonds-in-the-making.

DOSSIER II — CHAPTER 4

Kafka Is the *Stumbling Block*: The Person at the Crossroads between Law and Memory, or The Incommensurability of Law and Human Rights [136]

Our laws are not generally known; they are kept secret by the small group of nobles who have power over us. We are thereby convinced that these ancient laws are scrupulously administered; nevertheless, it is an extremely tormenting thing to be ruled by laws that one does not know ... Of course, there is wisdom in that – who doubts the wisdom of the ancient laws? – but also hardship for us; probably that is unavoidable.

—FRANZ KAFKA, "The Problem of Our Laws" (1931), trans. Willa Muir and Edwin Muir [137]

I

Before the Law in the Age of Oblivion

One is tempted to believe that the creature once had some sort of intelligible shape and is now only a broken-down remnant. Yet this does not seem to be the case; at least there is no sign of it; nowhere is there an unfinished or unbroken surface to suggest anything of the kind; the whole thing looks senseless enough, but in its own way perfectly finished. In any case, closer scrutiny is impossible, since Odradek is extraordinarily nimble and can never be laid hold of.

—FRANZ KAFKA, "Cares of a Family Man" (1917), trans. Willa Muir and Edwin Muir [138]

I begin with a parable that I wrote in Marbach am Neckar, in southwestern Germany, on the eve of the celebration of the Museum of Modern Literature's acquisition of the manuscript of Kafka's *The Trial*, for which a German consortium paid almost $2 million.

THE PARABLE AND THE FABLE

Joseph K. awoke one morning as a librarian. He looked at the familiar lines of the stacks and found the books were gone and in their place he found letters, not ones written from person to person, from A to B, but just letters; alphabets that looked for all the world like faces just as the clocks in Dickens's novels had faces. The world was deconstructed, the book censor said. The librarian went out into the world to seek the meanings that were lost. What is lost is the obstacle to reading. On this quest he became dimly aware that they who appeared to have meanings that were claimed were outmoded, exhausted, were more exhausted than He. Yet this made him ashamed for pursuing those meanings, which had disappeared. In process of reaching out to those who were in control, who always managed to recede from sight, he realized that there was only a partial truth in his feeling ashamed to not read the signs, as this was not the shame of anxiety or compulsion, almost a moral injury to not know; but he felt panic, experienced as a small death and the pathos of mourning of lost meanings. He mostly felt bad about the quest because those who observed him – including his hoped-for readers – understood what it was to feel so bad, since they had appropriated the powers of interpretation and had left none to him. The more truth disintegrated, the more degraded he felt. The more his mind left him in this retarded state, the more beautifully his feelings of pathos awoke. His sense of the imaginary did not depart – it grew until he entered the Great Baroque Church where he learned that pathos and partisanship for truth were not synonymous, and were in fact incommensurable. The Law and Human Rights had nothing to do with each other – a melancholy truth, he says, and he proceeds to disabuse himself of any claim to being a free and autonomous and recognizable person in this world. He learns about his death before it happens. However, he also learns that this kind of death is a violation of the *care for the integrity of the person* that is the figure of Odradek, the Person. Those who behead him act out of their belief that the law of the world is greater than the law of the person. It is they who are incommensurable, he thinks, as he glances sidewise at his head rolling into the sand and the blood takes on the shape of a book sinking into the sand and the book becomes devoid of letters. All great literature comes back to us phraseless, he thought; but now and then we get glimpses of it. He asks himself and Odradek, who has joined him on the journey: When does a parable become a fable and when does it become history as it really was? When does it become Law and when do we have faith in the law? [139]

In the aftermath of our century of global wars – called the century of "total war" by the Czech philosopher Jan Patočka – the post-Auschwitz, post-Hiroshima realities of everyday life were also proliferated beyond belief by fratricidal religious and civil wars that are so pathologically immune to reality that they can still be construed as wars for the right to self-determination. In Kafka's world, the "person" has vanished. For the minds stunned by European destructions of the Jews and the staying power of imperialisms, poverty, and genocide, it is inconceivable for humanity not to have a communicable image for rights based on negotiation and law. The brute realities of a post-apocalyptic age silently steal up on us with all the ambiguous sensitivity of a photograph of still another victim of carnage or mayhem. But photographs that flatten out reality also take away an image of language and the relationship of image to text. This fact of the absence of thinkable mimetic norms (and treaties) at the end of the century should give us pause, maybe tempting us to flee once again into stories of original sin, and certainly by repeating like a mantra Adorno's satanic pronouncement about the impossibility of poetry after Auschwitz. But this formed the basis upon which he would write *Aesthetic Theory*, allowing him to speak from a vantage point well beyond Weber's disenchantment with the rational.

For Adorno, deeply influenced by Kafka, speaking of rights after "our" very own collectivized genocides is to perjure oneself before a natural law that might provide a basis for protection against the barbarisms of authoritarian states, warlords, and leaders who are beyond the reach of peaceful traditions and who use the commodified laws of process and exchange to increase their powers. In the 1940s, Adorno began his only essay devoted to Kafka with these words:

> Kafka's popularity, that comfort in the uncomfortable, which made of him an information bureau of the human condition, be it eternal or modern, and which knowingly dispenses with the very scandal on which his work is built, leaves one reluctant to join the fray, even if it is to add a dissenting opinion. Yet it is just this false renown, fatal variant of the oblivion which Kafka so bitterly desired for himself, that compels one to dwell on the enigma. [140]

What is one to say of this enigma many years later as Kafka is assimilated into the cultural dictionary? What elements of his thought resist assimilation and require interpretation? This was Adorno's problem and is ours. But ours is worse because we live in a charismatic, cultic society which requires analysis in the age of deconstruction of the modern self that goes by the name of splitting the individual off from the social character into indeterminacy.

In fact, as monuments to the victims of the Holocaust are designed, built, and nationalized, and new fields like victimology are institutionalized in redemptive acts of memoration, a link is forged between the study of terror as an academic genre and the forgetfulness towards the person that is perpetuated by law and becomes an invisible norm of the violent public sphere, resisting collective memory through the cultic formation of cultural icons like "Kafka," "Jews," "Coke," "the Titanic," or anything else that in its ephemeral but cultic state will "survive" us all. Kafka writes of Odradek:

> In vain, I ask myself what will happen to him. Can he possibly die? All that dies has had some kind of aim in life, some kind of activity, which has had enough; but that does not apply to Odradek ... He harms no one that one can see; but the idea that he is likely to survive me I find most painful. [141]

This forgetfulness towards the idea of the person – in the parable the person is a star-shaped spool trailing tangled threads of wool always rolling down the stairs – is the pathos of memory that forgets history. Moreover, it is still overheard in one's memory, how the "Odradek" has spoken: "You put no difficult questions, you treat him, you can't help it – rather like a child." The Parable of Odradek asks: What is to happen to him? What is your name? "No fixed home." Adorno's reading: "Kafka sides with the deserters ... Instead of human dignity, the supreme bourgeoise concept," we "stumble upon the principle of individuation, the postulation of the self by the self, officially sanctioned by philosophy, the mythic defiance. Kafka does not glorify the world through subordination; he resists it through nonviolence." [142]

The ambiguity of the law in Kafka is grounded in the promise of European liberal compromises of the nineteenth century, which pacified religious and civil wars in order for nationalism to oversee and control the deeper, poly-cultural expressions of peoples whose histories became subject to annexation by more powerful traditions which in Kafka became prophecy that feels shabby and outdated, as if terror becomes obsolete the moment it is enacted, as if the individual simulacrum in "Odradek" has become useless at the bottom of the stairs where it lives and where the children play in safety.

Put another way, the constitutional protection of minorities certainly may legitimize individual as well as private, religious, and cultural heterogeneity, but it does so by establishing differences where there may be no differences, thus ensuring that the public sphere is an artificial creation of procedural laws or constitutions that do not guarantee an adequate participatory governing process. If it is true that modernity begins with "working through" the historical dispersion of peoples and ends with multicultural ideologies that sweep clean the hegemonic corners of the Kafkian "attics and taverns,"[143] then it follows that modernist works might open details, dissonances, and blind spots towards the incommensurability of law and rights. It follows also that opening up blind spots in art and literature cannot happen without having a zone of contact between the person who is capable of experiencing the full range of the aesthetics of self-creation and the laws of incommensurability that form the objective world.

Incommensurability between the law as an internalized ontological good and law as a process that defines the nature of the person who is reduced to a unit of the administration: this is that point in Kafka where the guilt imposed upon the individual begins the process of thinking about individual responsibility in the new public sphere.

It is also that point where reciprocity is at a standstill and *the law itself is placed on trial*. I raise the point of the incommensurability of law and human rights in order to point to a problem in contemporary neoconservative reading and viewing behaviours that have turned to the law as a metaphor defining the person in order to define by extension that there is no autonomous reader who is in the process of becoming a person. By depicting the experiential values that appropriate reality and by finding and exploring what is a possible representation of what is livable and permanent in transient experience, the interpenetrability of experience and memory is revealed. The shame of Joseph K.

is the feeling that his shame is imposed on him. He experiences this "shame" as a moral injury. [144]

The Kantian distinction between inner experience, or imagination, and outer experience is governed by a need for mimetic representation of the *relation between inner and outer life*. In the case of Kafka, representations are the force field, we might say, of the person's exploration of the mediating powers of memory that attempts to keep this relationship active. Speech is power over others. Inner speech, or language, is not subject to law.

Both Kafka and Kant explore the ideological or distancing representations of interior worlds that are commensurable with the view that reality can be known and is an active law-forming institution in the world, connecting the person to the social world: "This consciousness of my existence in time is bound up in the way of identity with the consciousness of a relation to something outside of me, and it is therefore experience not invention, sense not imagination, which inseparably connects this outside something with my inner sense." [145] The "readability" of the person, then, is not dependent upon the notion that the person can be reduced to a "text," or a tool, for interpreting and reading another reality in any which way we choose. This would suggest that such a person was a permanent victim of some ontologically predetermined higher law that colonizes the lifeworld of the experiencing individual. To be sure, this view of the Cartesian self is often wrongly equated to Kafka.

Not surprisingly, J. Hillis Miller perpetrated this form of reading in his 1987 book *The Ethics of Reading: Kant, de Man, Trollope, James, and Benjamin*. [146] He argues: "It is impossible to get outside of the limits of language by means of language. Everything we reach that seems outside language, for example sensation and perception, turns out to be more language." [147] This does not lead to the free play of meaning, something "indeterminate," or nihilistic, which of course would rule out the surrealist turn in both art and literature; on the contrary, this limitation on our reading experiences makes us post-ethical beings subjected to law, that places a "categorical demand" on the reader to "take responsibility for [each reading] and for its consequences in the personal, social and political worlds." [148]

De Man's "'impossible' task of reading unreadability" is in essence turning the person into an allegorized process of a de-aestheticized reading that becomes, for Miller, understandable through his use of Kafka's Joseph K., whose life among the lies in *The Trial* becomes emblematic of our colonized life-world among the texts.

But for de Man, this is not an emblematic truth of our condition, but cultic appropriation of Kafka for those ends that remind us of the destruction of the Jews. What for Joseph K. were palpable lies – the famous melancholy truth spoken by the Priest that "it is not necessary to accept everything as true, one must only accept it as necessary," which is quite clearly a critique of the world of domination and power – become, for Miller, and presumably his epigones, unreadable and impalpable truths, that is, truths that cannot be appropriated because they remain unknown, silent, and therefore taboo. The law is taboo because it cannot be appropriated. For Miller, Joseph K.'s answer, uttered after his wearying pilgrimage through the law's incommensurable "truth" that "turns lying into a universal principle" is that "Whether I intend to lie or do not intend to lie I lie in any case, by an intrinsic necessity of language." [149] This means that reading is subject not to the text as its law, but to the law to which the text is subject. This law forces the reader to betray the text or deviate from it in the act of reading it, in the name of a higher demand that can yet be reached only by way of the text. This response creates yet another text for the critic, which is a new act. So, for the critic, the "text" has a performative effect on yet other readers, which for the critic is of the same kind, for better or for worse, "as the effect the text it reads has on the reader … It does not transmit its own law or make its own law legible in it. Its law cannot be read within it but remains in reserve." [150] In this rendering of Kafka, the reader becomes helpless before the law of "reading."

This new law of language becomes – in Miller's socially forsaken, pathos-ridden world of solitary reading – a form of inverted liberation. In addition, Miller buttresses his argument by a misreading of Benjamin. Both Kafka and Benjamin become epigones of a position in which "all information, all languages ... all sense, all intention finally encounter a stratum in which they are destined to be extinguished." [151]

Miller's theologically induced ontological conformism is important to mention here, not least, because he argues that the mimetic identity of the world of the text and the world of the critic precede, in their divine lawfulness, an open-ended reading of a work, that any new pragmatic context which might give the world of the author some capacity to appropriate flesh-and-blood reality is cancelled out.

Miller ends by ontologizing the law. He invokes a putative aesthetic of the fragment, or difference, that denies the truth value any referential and discoverable meaning or information in the text, but affirms what once in the history of criticism would have been called "extrinsic ideals," or moral "form," or moral "imperatives," or the perversity of identifying with the ego ideal of authority to use psychoanalytical insight, or all of these. For Benjamin, this was an attempt to overcome the hegemony of non-aesthetic forms by reconstructing the shape of natural laws through the aura of the autonomous persons who were once capable of expressing now lost communal languages broken into force fields of power and domination by modernity. [152] And in Benjamin's writings on Kafka, this meant both the end of the idea of the book and the ending of any thinking about the creative will of the person of the author or character: both were now the broken fragments of law, history, memory, and reality constructions which, mimetically and palpably through empathy with the exchange process itself, give forth new information about the meanings of that which has appropriated the individual.

These fragments, which Kafka and his allies, Adorno and Benjamin, defend as the autonomy of the person, have been, for Miller and his epigones, reassembled into a new law, the legal obligations of a "higher demand," namely, the sovereignty of law as a primary act of nature. This is a theology of a new sovereignty, a state of emergency, an apocalyptic crisis of historical alienation.

Benjamin's anarchistic philosophy of the act, articulated in his essay on surrealism and worked out in his *Arcades Project*, does not give us a monadic position, as it were, where we are accused, "before the law of the ethics of reading, subject to it, compelled by it, persuaded of its existence and sovereignty by what happens to me ... When I read ... the experience of an 'I must' that is always the same but always different, unique, idiomatic."[153] This reduction of an aesthetic of self-creation to a new apocalyptic ethics of the divine will to power puts a dignified turn on a commonplace theological gesture, and becomes ultimately a new ethical command: "I still stand before the law of the ethics of reading, subject to it, compelled by it, persuaded of its existence and sovereignty by what happens to me when I read."[154] This infinite postponement of aesthetic judgment and satisfaction results in the identification of the reader's prelinguistic experience – the possibility of cognitive experiences based on a mimesis that objectifies the subjective totality of the person with the dissonant forms of remembrance – degrades the individual into a "case" which mirrors the melancholia of the particularity of the law's dismissal of universal needs. Institutional, bureaucratic forces are aligned with reading practices in the name of reading the suffering nomadic individual as sheer process of information. Kafka's characters, who function aesthetically as persons even though they are partial beings, are read out of literature in the name of the very law that Kafka has made visible in order to kill them off through critical theories that champion the vanishing of the individual. This is the bitter end of what Adorno in *Aesthetic Theory* names the "truth value of the work." "Odradek" will end up at the "Oklahoma Nature Theatre," where Odradek is a sideshow.

The *K*-word has become an adjective. The "-esque" suffixed part is not the aura of Kafka but the need to eliminate him by the American assimilation of the European experience. It's the fiction of the fiction of fiction that criticism can replace aesthetics, and the struggle of making this natural artist into a "cultural" icon will continue as we replace Kafka with criticism that refuses to recognize the referential contexts of his work. It is the loss of reality, the loss of referentials, that now has become the norm for all icons.

Once culture can be hypostatized as more important than speaking or writing or listening, we can say that illusions are gone. Those small, imaginary, Odradek-like events that are real and yet gone, and are real because posited by a speaker-reader of reality, do not count. The old evil that was inside of the transgressive grotesque vision – the power to face and confront the transgressive grotesque – has escaped the power of regression and repression by becoming naturalized in American culture. Mass culture has become a kind of visible unconscious that usurps the author's role as storyteller of his life as story.

Adorno, Arendt, and Benjamin established the groundwork for a social theory that was in essence built on the aesthetic superstructure of Kafka. One might say that their work responded to Lukács's criticism of Kafka's multiple dimensions of dispossession as a form of alienation on the grounds that the destruction of liberal democracy by German fascism and American mass culture, which created the demonic other of "communism," set the stage for the cultural appropriation of the world of Kafka and his way of reading the past and how we read – as he said of the novel as "the axe for the frozen sea within us." [155]

This ontological spontaneity that changes lives and perception of our own lives – "this life means this art" – is the cornerstone of modernist aesthetics, which is the great divide between the will to power, and the *Einverständnis* at the heart of classical realism, and the will to self-creation at the heart of modernism.

The sense of loss that pervades modernism, the various losses of the will to self-creation and how these are creatively forced back into the world of referentials – the loss of the book in Benjamin, the loss of the subject in Adorno, in Lukács the loss of the real and the loss of the bourgeois world that grounded the real – becomes the deepest loss of all in Kafka: the loss of the person, or, put more philosophically rather than psychologically, the inability to subjectify the objective through images of language.

Both Benjamin and Adorno referred to Odradek and reification and empathy with the commodity. But "commodity" means the degradation of the mind's capacity to imagine language – to see it in action, performed, albeit in the shape of pathos and retarded awareness. All of Kafka's characters suffer the anguish of retarded awareness – the subject thinks for the object while the object rejects that thought. This is the law of misunderstanding and misrecognition. The task at hand: to make this law an aspect of creation and therefore put the law on trial. Thus the incommensurability of law and person in Kafka.

II

The "Other" Way to Read Kafka: The Law and the End of the Idea of the Person

Here the excessiveness of the created is revenged mercilessly on the manufactured system. As booty for the sacrifice of reason, reason receives whatever falls within its region. Sacrificed reason governs as a demigod.

—THEODOR W. ADORNO, *Kierkegaard: The Construction of the Aesthetic* (1962), trans. Robert Hullot-Kentor

The social system has taken revenge upon the person and any communicable image of human rights. If texts and laws have appropriated the person, is it possible that the assumption that literature can provide experiences and information about the person can be reflected in really existing circumstances? I take as an example, that a "dialogical" reading of Kafka can illuminate what happens in our violent postmodern world where the Law is a stumbling block that gnaws at the heart of conscience.

This can be illustrated by the Israeli Supreme Court's 1993 decision not to convict the concentration camp guard Ivan Demjanjuk for murder and complicity in the deaths of Jews at the Treblinka death camp. The "Stumbling Block"[156] against unjust conviction in the minds of the judges who administered the law was the nagging presence of the law itself, neither higher nor more ancient, not handed down by a demigod, but something that "falls within its region." The justices noted the inner resistances that work against any transcendent concept of Justice, or against conviction by revenge without adequate textual or corroborating evidence that this man, Demjanjuk, was he whom his accusers claimed he was. The trial was, in its own way, a challenge to the world that takes away identities and demands identities.

The court, in reference to the evidence as to Demjanjuk's "identity," concluded that it did not know "how these statements came into the world and who gave birth to them." Further:

> And when they [the submitted statements about his identity] came before us, doubt began to gnaw away at our judicial conscience – perhaps the appellant was not Ivan the Terrible of Treblinka. By virtue of this gnawing – whose nature we knew, but not the meaning – we restrained ourselves from convicting the appellant of the horrors of Treblinka.[157]

The notion of humanity's *representation* of conscience is dramatized by the tribune's inclusion of a statement about the law's helplessness towards the "meaning" of the Jewish State versus Demjanjuk. Their utterances show how their consciences and the law come together to create a really existing "stumbling block" against righteous vengeance taken against this identity-less figure, represented in the press as "from Cleveland," and whom the media has now enshrined with the bloated, culturally fashioned name of "Ivan the Terrible." Doubt gnawed away at them they said, using an animal image as a kind of Golem to *depict* the law's inner soul. This is not unlike Freud's claim that Kant's categorical imperative is a simulacrum of the rights-based laws, which must constantly be treated as both taboo and ethical, both vengeful and untrustworthy. However, the strength of the superego is weakened and also is conditioned by a sense of individual justice that brings doubt and dissonance together in this Kantian framework where means and ends establish a judicial law that is higher than the declared procedural law that has determined the conflict around *legal identity* and the demand for righteousness.

Not only were Demjanjuk's "rights" upheld, but the meaning of those rights was re-embedded in the concreteness of a non-sacrificial concept of rights. Put another way, rights are not sacrificed to the laws of resignation, those laws that Miller in his reading of Kafka announced as a "higher demand."

To readers familiar with Kafka's profound treatment of the law – where the "Odradeks" live at the bottom of the stairs as reminders of the individuum of the individual – the hybrid of animal and child, which, in Kafka's view of the law and the Israeli tribune's judgment, can remind us of Kafka's story "The Burrow," where the personified human-animal hears the sounds of an outer power gnawing away at its abstract "home." [158] Kafka's parable "Before the Law" becomes the guide to why and how:

> Our laws are not generally known; they are kept secret by the small group of nobles who have power over us. We are thereby convinced that these ancient laws are scrupulously administered; nevertheless, it is an extremely tormenting thing to be ruled by laws that one does not know ... Of course, there is wisdom in

that – who doubts the wisdom of the ancient laws? – but also hardship for us; probably that is unavoidable.

Kafka's "buried" animal is unable to construct an image of what a human being might be: Is it a beast who is plaguing it? A divine rescuer, or another perhaps-friendly animal? The burrow-builder's self-obliteration is so frightening that it constructs an image of savagery that is all the more brutal for being seen through the "loss of the subjective." [159] The sound the animal hears is the sound of the ambiguity of Law in its just and unjust imagelessness, even as it reminds us of the sounds of the adults who approach the bedrooms of children.

The struggle inside the burrow is the struggle against the overwhelming power of loss of memory, which is itself tied to the law – unwritten, verbal, consensual, and not just legal, processive, or textual. However, in terms of the argument I am advancing, the sound is also an image of the modern world's loss of an image of natural rights. One might render this loss in terms of the "eschatology of the impersonal," [160] which has become one of the dominant scars left over in the debris of modernism.

In the absence of any rational theories of human rights applicable to the murdered and the dead, the meaning of the Israeli court's verdict is not self-evident. The court is saying that they only had eyes to see and read, and that they must resist examining the human heart and mind of the accused: the court was not present at the event of the murders of the innocent. No text exists to convince them of the truth of history. To the outside world now addicted to the notions of the sovereignty of the individual and to total justice, this judgment is an impediment, a stumbling block: it looks perverse. Indeed, in moral-historical terms, it is perverse because, for the entire world, Ivan Demjanjuk was just the person his victims said he was. However, in the court's willingness to use the norms of the inviolable integrity of the self it seeks a different, Kafkian-Kantian, truth: it honours the many selves killed by a regime which did not honour individual selves and which saw itself reflected only in cultural myths. It therefore interpreted the living as those who did not have this chance to speak the truth of the subjective being. The court did not subjectivize the objective but objectified the subjective judgment of the victims as rounded beings whose subjective selves were still in a formative stage of subject-making.

The judgment condemns a society that would have only one moment in which truth is revealed – a redemptive society. The murdered must not end up on the ledger books of history as Gogolian "dead souls" who could be bartered away for incomplete truths. The judges closed the matter by saying that the *case* was incomplete: "The complete truth is not the prerogative of the human judge." Yet, in the verdict's novelistic illumination of truth, there is the nagging presence of the other violations which are orbiting this particular trial and which will be forgotten as soon as they are covered up by exchanging the human subject for case law. These are the war crimes against the human person being committed against innocent non-combatants and against whole peoples throughout the world *at the moment of the trial*.

The information society provides us with no perspective from which to depict this interrelationship of law and rights, since the information society disclaims any responsibility for "authoring" an image of human rights that might link the atrocities to historical precedence. But this lack of perspective Habermas calls the *neue Unübersichtlichkeit* (the "new confusion," a world without place from which to stand). Wolf-Dieter Narr has more precisely described this new world with no overview as the world of conditioned reflexes; this is not, of course, caused by the literary products of postmodernity: but it is a product of the culture of risk, fear, and invasion of rights that has been with us long since states have constructed official ethnic identities in order to legitimate the state's monopoly of violence. [161] This becomes the civilizing process of the cultural genocides that Kafka, in his parable-novel *Amerika* or *The Man Who Disappeared*, relates to the disappearance of Indigenous people in the parable of "The Oklahoma Nature Theatre" at the end of the novel.[162]

Kafka illuminates, through the two very different parables about law and incommensurability in our time, the most terrible problem of "the laws" of our time repeated across world literatures. I can turn to Ivo Andrić's 1945 novel *The Bridge on the Drina* seen through Kafka's "The Cares of a Family Man" and "The Problem of Our Laws." In Andrić's parable-like novel, fratricidal violence always threatens to make the victims "forget … the reality of the moment which might sweep them all away." Andrić includes a description of the impossibility of any real emancipation from violence. This description could serve as a prophetic image of the Cold War and the Yugoslav Wars that follow, where the peculiar combination of loss of reality, loss of image of rights, and denial of the capacity to depict and represent the "other" has become so familiar a feature in the dogmas related to postmodern thought. Andrić writes:

> So the night passed and with it life went on, filled with danger and suffering but still clear, unwavering, and true to itself. Led on by ancient inherited instinct they broke it up into momentary impressions and immediate needs, losing themselves completely in them. For only thus, living each moment separately and looking neither forward nor back, could such a life be borne and a man keep himself alive.[163]

This description depicts – in 1945 – what it would feel like to live in a "deconstructed" reality. What is meant by "ancient inherited instinct"? This is the passion to keep the integrity of the individuum of the individual alive: the self is broken up into fragments in order to survive. And so we are face to face with really existing postmodernist unreality embedded in the experiences of violence against the person, violence against the law of our "Odradekian" instincts for minimally keeping the self alive.

This loss of the concept of the person means a loss of reality, that which the law has both enabled and reduced to a world in which "Odradek" is the last figure in Kafka's figurative world. Attempts to create an anti-humanistic discourse, which would be beyond the reach of the legitimating mythologies upon which any understanding of the law depends, contribute to this loss of reality.

Is this a question of language? Perhaps. If literature has become "transcultural" or "cross-cultural," then theory lags behind it, because literary modernism long ago posed a concept of an emancipatory human rights as an ethic of obligation and answerability, a view that recognizes the tension between the individuum and the constituting powers of production. These emerged in early capitalism and are reflected in the Hobbesian apologies for the transcendent powers of mediation and authority, lurking always, and residing in the ideological shelters of sovereign states' inbuilt violence of constitutional authority that enables war and sacrifice and the destruction of Indigenous Peoples – a postulate of both Kafka's stories and Benjamin's theoretical work. [164]

Perhaps the conflict continues, beneath the critical jabber about techniques of "ethical" or ethicized reading practices, in places where appropriation, mediation, and constitution of forms searching for "the law," as the creature in the burrow is doing, faced with the shame and humiliation of the moral insult of "the Burrow." The "burrower" is the incommensurable individuum that has assimilated the "individual" into the ideal of a collective law that exists without a universal concept of the autonomous person or a dialectical-dialogical concept of autonomy that could become the basis of a critical aesthetics informed by Kafka's elegiac parables. We are "standing by ruins," watching the destruction of universals and with it the sacrifice of particular and concrete humans to the law of the state, which is itself on trial in the incommensurability of law and rights. [165]

"Foreclosure" – to bring into the testimony a word from contractual law – or the property of the human, and an ethics of man-made law mediated by a deconstructive ethics that rejects a concept of the live creature of the "human," would correctly situate us as little more than living out the moribund, mimetic reflections of a world that has lost its collective mind.

DOSSIER II: ENDNOTES

CHAPTER 1

1   This essay is slightly revised from the one published under the title "Siegfried Kracauer's Cosmopolitan Homelessness: The Lost Cause of an Idea in the Film Age" in *Cosmopolitans in the Modern World: Studies on a Theme in German and Austrian Literary Culture*, ed. Suzanne Kirkbright (Munich: Judicum, 2000). Siegfried Kracauer became known for his books on film: *From Caligiari to Hitler* (1947) and *Theory of Film: The Redemption of Physical Reality* (1960). Kracauer went into exile in 1933, first to Paris and then to New York. He was known as a sociologist of material life in the manner of George Simmel. His writing on film is a materialist history of modern times and what he called a "material aesthetics" that existed beneath the ideological planes of everyday life. His writing style was uniquely poetic. He saw everyday life through a theory of history and film as redemption of physical reality and memory of the contemporaneity of the "just-past." His *Theory of Film* is written as the redemption of material reality, in which he argues that "material phenomena elude observation under normal circumstances ... the camera reality discloses unstaged reality and thereby the falseness of staged reality" (in *Theory of Film*, originally published as *The Nature of Film*, a more appropriate title). Kracauer was preoccupied with the flow of reality from the time of his "feuilletons" essays in the Weimar 1920s until his death in 1966 when he was finishing *History: The Last Thing before the Last* (1969). In his exile, working on a lifelong project of an aesthetic of film at the Museum of Modern Art, he was also researching and writing on propaganda and refugees from the communist-controlled nations who had emigrated to the United States: *Satellite Mentality: Political Attitudes and Propaganda Susceptibilities on Non-Communists in Hungary, Poland, and Czechoslovakia*, with Paul L. Berkman (1956). See also my essay on Kracauer's exile related to his writing on film and memory, "'The Reparation of Dead Souls': Siegfried Kracauer's Archimedean Exile; The Prophetic Journey from Death to *Bildung*," in *Exile, Science, and Bildung: The Contested Legacies of German Emigre Intellectuals*, ed. David Kettler and Gerhard Lauer (London: Palgrave MacMillan, 2005), as well as "Exterritoriality: An 'Open Letter' to Siegfried Kracauer, or The Last Letter Not Lost in the Dead Letter Office in the Game of History," in *Crossing Borders: Essays in Honour of Ian H. Angus, Beyond Phenomenology and Critique*, ed. Samir Gandesha and Peyman Vahabzadeh (Winnipeg: Arbeiter Ring Publishing, 2020).

2   For a start one could look at Gil Elliot, *Twentieth Century Book of the Dead* (New York: Ballantine Books, 1973). Elliott counts the magnitude of deaths from military action, death by privation in camps, disease, public terror, civil wars, famines. He looks at total war machines like chemical, air, and mechanized warfare.

3   Trans. Quintin Hoare (London: Verso, 1998).

4   Kracauer, *Theory of Film*, 15.

5   Kracauer wrote two novels: *Ginster* (1928) and *Georg* (1934). The latter appeared in Paris during the first stage of his exile. His study *Orpheus in Paris: Offenbach and the Paris of His Time* (1937) was written while in Paris in his flight from Germany (in

English: Alfred Knopf, 1938). The Offenbach study is in essence a biography of an epoch in which the superficial, satire, and the disintegration of the Napoleonic epoch is portrayed by the operettas of Offenbach's Paris.

6   Kracauer, *History: The Last Thing before the Last*, ed. Paul Oskar Kristeller (Princeton, NJ: Markus Wiener, 1995), 84. Kracauer's last study, which was published posthumously, mirrors his early writing in Weimar, when "seeing" into both the present and the past creates a "state of mind of the impact of involuntary memories." Inner life remains out of reach, yet is revealed in the presence of the camera lens (Kracauer, *Theory of Film*, 15). Visible here are the influence of Proust and "cinematic memory," enabling the viewer of both film and personal historical memory to "embark on a journey whose end is hidden from [them]" (91).

7   George Simmel, "The Stranger," in *Georg Simmel on Individuality and Social Forms*, ed. Donald N. Levine (Chicago: University of Chicago Press, 1971).

8   See Kracauer, *History*, 4: "This discovery made me feel happy for two reasons: it unexpectedly confirmed the legitimacy and inner necessity of my historical pursuits; and by the same token it justified, in my own eyes and after the event, the years I had spent on *Theory of Film*. This book of which I had always conceived as an aesthetics of the photographic media, not less and not more, now that I have penetrated the veil that envelops one's most intimate endeavours, appears to me in its true light: as another attempt of mine to bring out the significance of areas whose claim to be acknowledged in their own right has not yet been recognized. I say 'another attempt' because this was what I had tried to do throughout my life ... So at long last all my main efforts, so incoherent on the surface, fall into line – they all have served, and continue to serve, a single purpose: the rehabilitation of objectives and modes of being which still lack a name and hence are overlooked or misjudged. Perhaps this is less true of history than of photography; yet history too marks a bent of the mind and defines a region of reality which despite all that has been written about them are still largely *terra incognita*."

9   Walter Benjamin, "An Outsider Attracts Attention" – published as an appendix to *The Salaried Masses*. A more accurate title would be "An Outsider Makes His Presence Felt." Translated as "An Outsider Makes His Mark," in Benjamin, *Selected Writings*, vol. 2, part 1, *1927–1930*, trans. Rodney Livingstone and others, ed. Michael W. Jennings, Howard Eiland, and Gary Smith (Cambridge, MA: Belknap Press of Harvard University Press, 1999), 305.

10   Kracauer, *History*, 5.

11   Georg Simmel, "The Metropolis and Mental Life," in *On Individuality and Social Forms: Selected Writings*, ed. Donald N. Levine (Chicago: University of Chicago Press, 1971). Kracauer studied with Simmel during the time he was studying architecture.

12   This is the basis on which Lucien Goldmann used Kant, Lukács, and Piaget to develop a theory of cognitive universals that were transformative of the dialectic of class consciousness and cultural creation. See Mitchell Cohen, *The Wager of Lucien Goldmann: Tragedy, Dialectics, and a Hidden God* (Princeton: Princeton University Press, 1994).

13   The 1971 German edition uses Benjamin's review of Kracauer as the "Politisierung der Intelligenz" (the politicizing of intelligence).

14   Kracauer, *The Salaried Masses*, 94.

15   *The Salaried Masses*, 48.

16   Later collected in *Das Ornament der Masse [The mass ornament]* (Frankfurt: Suhrkamp, 1963). Kracauer's work is prodigious. The standard bibliography by Tom Levin lists over 2,100 entries: Thomas Y. Levin, *Siegfried Kracauer: Eine Bibliographie seiner Schriften* (Marbach am Neckar: Deutsche Schillergesellschaft, 1989).

17   See Walter Benjamin, "A Different Utopian Will," in *Walter Benjamin, Selected Writings*, vol. 3, *1935–1938*, trans. Edmund Jephcott, Howard Eiland, and others, ed. Howard Eiland and Michael W. Jennings (Cambridge, MA: Belknap Press of Harvard University Press, 2002), 134.

18   Georg Lukács, *The Theory of the Novel: A Historico-Philosophical Essay on the Forms of Great Epic Literature*, trans. Anna Bostock (London: Merlin Press, 1971), 29.

19   Lukács, *The Theory of the Novel*, 38.

20   In the original, "Denn das Gestaltete kann nicht gelebt werden, wenn das Zerfallene nicht eingesammelt und mitgenommen wird" (remembrance plaque at Sternstraße 29, Frankfurt).

21   Kant, "Idea for a Universal History with a Cosmopolitan Purpose," in *Collected Essays* (New York: Modern Library, 1994), 129.

22   Lukács, "The Inner Form of the Novel," in *The Theory of the Novel*, 71.

23   Kracauer's sociology must be seen as a new literary sociology, a materialist ethnography of the contemporary. This is the aesthetic of his untranslated two novels, *Ginster* and *Georg*. The novels were praised by Thomas Mann.

24   Kracauer, *Theory of Film: The Redemption of Physical Reality* (Oxford: Oxford University Press, 1960).

25   See Hannah Arendt, *The Origins of Totalitarianism* (New York: Schocken Books, 1951), and Arendt's understanding of the pariah and nation-state domination of the autonomous citizen who is reduced to the role of the spectator without capacity for judgment. See also Arendt, *Lectures on Kant's Political Philosophy*, ed. Ronald Beiner (Chicago: University of Chicago Press, 1982). Arendt's views on the *aesthetics of politics* are influenced by Benjamin.

26   Georg Simmel, "The Stranger," in *On Individuality and Social Forms*, 149.

27   Simmel, "The Stranger," 144.

28   Kracauer refers to Chaplin often in *Theory of Film*. Kracauer's essays on Chaplin, Keaton, and Harold Lloyd remain untranslated and can be found in Siegfried Kracauer, *Kino*, ed. Karsten Witte (Frankfurt: Suhrkamp Verlag, 1974).

29   "The Stranger," 148.

30   "The Stranger," 149.

31   Kracauer, *From Caligari to Hitler: A Psychological History of the German Film* (Princeton: Princeton University Press: 1947), v.

32   Kracauer, *From Caligari to Hitler*, 7.

33   See Matthew Cullerne Bown, *Art under Stalin* (New York: Holmes and Meier, 1991), and Boris Groys, *The Total Art of Stalinism: Avant-Garde, Aesthetic Dictatorship,*

and Beyond (Princeton: Princeton University Press, 1992). Also: Edward Timms, "Images of the City: Vienna, Prague and the Intellectual Avant-Garde," in *Decadence and Innovation: Austro-Hungarian Life and Art at the Turn of the Century* (London: Weidenfeld and Nicholson, 1989). I have discussed this form of aesthetic culturalism in its present-day hybridism as a form of anti-cosmopolitanism in "Vindicating Popular Culture in Latin America: A Response to García Canclini," in *Canadian Journal of Latin American and Caribbean Studies / Revue canadienne des études latino-américaines et caraïbes* 23, no. 46 (1998): 133–154.

34   Kracauer's psychological history of Weimar films in *From Caligari to Hitler* carried on this analysis.

35   Kant, "Idea for a Universal History with a Cosmopolitan Purpose," 131.

36   Marcuse's *One-Dimensional Man* reformulates the conceptual demands of Kant's cosmopolitanism as a normative ideal of justice understood as the pacification of nature, Marcuse's repressive desublimation of capitalist culture. Marcuse deconstructs the "one-dimensional" man who is a stranger to himself because "the individual identifies himself with the existence imposed on him" and ideology becomes reality and reality, ideology; see Herbert Marcuse, *One-Dimensional Man: Studies in the Ideology of Advanced Industrial Society* (London: Routledge, 1964), 11.

37   Simmel, "The Metropolis and Mental Life," in *On Individuality and Social Forms*, 329.

38   Kracauer, *The Salaried Masses*, 105. See Benjamin's "Central Park," preparatory notes for his studies on Baudelaire, and his *Arcades* as a "Luna Park": *Selected Writings*, vol. 4, *1938–1940*, trans. Edmund Jephcott and others, ed. Howard Eiland and Michael W. Jennings (Cambridge, MA: Belknap Press of the Harvard University Press, 2003), 162–199. Kracauer and Benjamin discovered how the dialectical image is allegorical and labyrinthian and how its destination is the marketplace.

39   "The Mass Ornament," in *The Mass Ornament: Weimar Essays*, trans. and ed. Thomas Y. Levin (Cambridge, MA: Harvard University Press, 1995), 75. Kracauer began his study of propaganda and fascists in 1936. The study appeared as a supplement, "Propaganda and the Nazi War Film," to *From Caligari to Hitler*. My essay "Propaganda" in *Encyclopedia of the Essay*, ed. Tracy Chevalier (Chicago and London: Fitzroy Dearborn Publishers, 1997) follows Kracauer in pointing to how propaganda became an epochal expression in our displaced lives.

40   See Kracauer's introduction to *From Caligari to Hitler*, 8.

41   Cited by Alan Sokal and Jean Bricmont in *Fashionable Nonsense: Postmodern Intellectuals' Abuse of Science* (New York: Picador, 1998). The figures cited are: "47% of Americans believe in the creation account of Genesis, 49% in possession by the devil, 36% in telepathy, and 25% in astrology" (203).

42   See Kafka's parables, for example, "The Street Window," "On the Tram," or "The Wish to Be a Red Indian." Kracauer saw films as parables for our time, but I cannot explain the full range of this shift of genre-chronotope for Kracauer, whose essays on Kafka show Kracauer's theory of history in Kafka's parables.

43   Kracauer, "Those Who Wait," in *The Mass Ornament*, 132.

44   Kracauer, "Those Who Wait," 109.

45 Kracauer's *Theory of Film*, written in exile, was originally entitled "The Nature of Film" since it is not "a theory" but a way of seeing.

46 The famous lines by Benjamin are accurate for both Kracauer and also for Benjamin himself: "So by right this author stands there at the end – all alone. A malcontent not a leader. Not a founder, but a spoilsport. And if we wish to visualize him just for himself, in the solitude of his craft and his endeavour, we see a ragpicker at daybreak, lancing with his stick scraps of language and tatters of speech in order to throw them into his cart, grumblingly, stubbornly somewhat the worse for drink, and not without now and again letting one or other of these faded calicoes – 'humanity,' 'inner nature,' 'enrichment' – flutter ironically in the dawn breeze. A ragpicker at daybreak – in the dawn of revolution." (Benjamin, "'An Outsider Attracts Attention': On *The Salaried Masses* by S. Kracauer," in Kracauer, *The Salaried Masses*, 114).

47 I refer to Arendt's controversial and devastating portrayal of Eichmann's perverse use of Kant to mean that he, Eichmann, was only a "law-abiding citizen" doing his duty, but not merely doing one's duty but acting as if "one were the legislator of the laws which one obeys." In Arendt, *Eichmann in Jerusalem: A Report on the Banality of Evil* (New York: Penguin Books, 1975), 136–137. Arendt's book was published in 1963 and appeared originally as a series of articles in the *New Yorker* in 1961. The catastrophic irony is not lost on Arendt.

48 See Kracauer's seminal essay "Photography" in *The Mass Ornament*. The essay is a critique of historicism which would be a "giant film depicting the temporally interconnected events from every vantage point" while "photography grasps what is given as a spatial (or temporal) continuum; memory images retain what is given only insofar as it has significance ... and truth content" (50). Truth lies in what is revealed.

49 See Kracauer, *History*, 215–216. The view of Kracauer and Kant that I am advancing here suggests a rights-based aesthetic and is influenced by Dieter Henrich's *Aesthetic Judgement and the Moral Image of the World: Studies in Kant* (Stanford: Stanford University Press, 1992). Kracauer's radical humanism stems from Kant and this is passed on to Adorno: Kant pervades Adorno throughout Adorno's *Critical Models: Interventions and Catchwords* (New York: Columbia University Press, 1998). Adorno thought to become a journalist in the Kracauer model rather than becoming an academic. The "elective affinity" between Kracauer and Adorno is clear from their correspondence.

50 See Kracauer, "Those Who Wait," in *The Mass Ornament*.

51 Adorno's testament to Kracauer, "The Curious Realist: On Siegfried Kracauer," did not please Kracauer, because Adorno objects to Kracauer's "incommensurable hope" for the sufferers; see *Notes to Literature*, vol. 2, trans. Shierry Weber Nicholsen, ed. by Rolf Tiedemann (New York: Columbia University Press, 1992), 58–75. Adorno did not see that an anarchist stream in Kracauer's thought could be hope for another way.

52 Kracauer studied with Simmel and wrote a book-length study, which is unpublished. A 1920 essay on Simmel is in *The Mass Ornament*.

53 "The Hotel Lobby," *The Mass Ornament*, 173.

54 "The Hotel Lobby," 173.

55 Adorno, "The Curious Realist," *Notes to Literature*, vol. 2, 75.

56　In *Theory of Film*, which he conceived during his Paris exile and completed in New York, using the Museum of Modern Art as his base of support, Kracauer references hundreds of films – American, European, Japanese, Indian – that enable us to touch ideology as reality and reality as ideology on the screen by touching "reality with our fingertips," and yet feel in loss of continuity the "chimerical character of these efforts" (*Theory of Film*, 298).

57　For sure this approach to Kracauer's work on film and the construction of spectators shows how "cultural studies" is embedded in Kracauer, who is a forerunner of this now-fashionable trend. The photographed reality in movement of images becomes the most radical of cultural reconstructions of perception in culture. Kracauer's early work was clearly an influence on Walter Benjamin's thinking about film.

58　This term is from Wayne Burns's *Journey through the Dark Woods* (Seattle: Howe Street Press, 1981).

59　Kracauer, *History*, 93.

60　Kracauer, *Theory of Film*, 299.

61　Kracauer, *Theory of Film*, 305.

62　Kracauer, *History*, 306.

63　Kracauer, *Orpheus in Paris: Offenbach and the Paris of His Time* (New York: Vienna House, 1972).

64　The critique of the Offenbach book is discussed in various letters of Adorno and Benjamin. I believe their critique is couched in not a little bad faith, since both of them knew the reasons why Kracauer had written this book: not only to save his skin financially, as he had no external source of income in Paris, but also to characterize his own life as a journalist now in exile from a falling regime. However, for Adorno and Benjamin to read the book outside of Kracauer's own life is tantamount to their not reading him at all, and therefore not to understand him. In Paris in extreme hardship after 1933 until his emigration in 1941, Kracauer was in weekly intense correspondence with his aunt and mother in Frankfurt about their daily lives under the Nazi regime. I described Kracauer's letters as a laboratory for exile and survival in my essay "Zeitgenossen without Genossen: The Contemporary without Friendship or History; Exile and Community in an Age That Denies Exile," in *Contested Legacies: The German-Speaking Intellectual and Cultural Emigration to the United States and United Kingdom, 1933–1945; Essays from the "No Happy End" Workshop*, ed. David Kettler (Annandale-on-Hudson, NY: Bard College, 2001). Kracauer's mother and aunt were transported to the Terezín concentration camp in 1941 and then to Auschwitz just as he was beginning his exile in the United States. The Offenbach study should be seen almost as a scenario for a film on Offenbach's life in Paris.

65　Karsten Witte, "Nachwort," in Kracauer, *Über die Freundschaft: Essays* (Frankfurt: Suhrkamp Verlag, 1986), 99; see Kracauer's essay "On Friendship," trans. Michael Mundhenk, in *Anarcho-Modernism: Towards a New Critical Theory in Honour of Jerry Zaslove*, ed. Ian Angus (Vancouver: Talonbooks, 2001), 359.

66　Dieter Henrich, *Aesthetic Judgement and the Moral Image of the World* (Stanford: Stanford University Press: 1994), 64.

67　Kracauer, "On Friendship," *Anarcho-Modernism*, 361.

CHAPTER 2

68   This essay has a history as an event about memory and exile in Canada and Germany. It was initially published in *Multiculturalism in a World of Leaking Boundaries,* ed. Dieter Haselbach (Munster: Lit Verlag, 1998). Subsequently Michael Mundhenk translated *Obasan* into German and the essay here, co-authored with Michael Mundhenk, became the afterword to the German edition, which was published after the fall of East Germany amid the subsequent unification of the two Germanys. I was doing research in Germany on Kracauer and his exile at the time and engineered the publication of *Obasan* with Reclam (Leipzig, 1993). Essays on exile, Sebald, and Kracauer appear elsewhere in this volume. Exile and authorship are central to Bakhtin's work, a chronotope of time and space, streets that go somewhere and elsewhere in an always-changing hybridity in literary form. Further amplification of this essay in the light of Bakhtin's work is entitled "Memory's Children and Redressing History: Critical Reflections on *Obasan* by Joy Kogawa," in *Unforeseeable Americas Questioning Cultural Hybridity in the Americas,* ed. Rita De Grandis and Zila Bernd (Amsterdam and Atlanta: Rodopi, 2000), also translated into Portuguese.

69   By the end of the nineteenth century, Canada had in part become an immigration nation of settlers from Western European cultures, the European diaspora sending over a million settlers into the territory of Canada. The dominant trend of immigration and settlement restricted entry of Black people, South and East Europeans, as well as Asians, and, during World War II, Jews. This was established as domestic policy. Looking back to the beginning of the century from the view of the shorelines at the end of the millennium, the admission of Asian people to Canada at the beginning of the twentieth century for the purposes of cheap labour brought Canada face-to-face with soon-to-become-racialized strangers. By 1986, Canadian residents from the "Third World" consisted of 30 percent of all foreign-born people. By the 1990s, the restriction patterns that had once favoured immigration from Europe and the United States limited these regions to one-quarter of the total. Asian immigrants accounted for 53 percent. See Valerie Knowles, *Strangers at Our Gates: Canadian Immigration and Immigration Policy, 1540–1990* (Toronto: University of Toronto Press, 1991).

70   Our approach illuminates the historical-philosophical context of what has been called the "friend–enemy polarity" which underlies the historically violent, adversarial opposition of the "civilized" behaviour of North Americans to the "barbaric" behaviour of other races and cultures; which is why this struggle on the part of minorities for their search for recognition, this resistance to the degradation of identity emerges in the later part of the twentieth century. The search for "identity" is grounded both in the history of labour's emancipation of the human being *into* labour within the assimilation of immigrants into often remote regions and territories. However, Canadian history is unlike that of the United States since the official national Canadian multicultural policy – the protection of cultural differences – has remained an entrenched, albeit controversial, ideal in the Canadian multicultural psyche. Canadian theorists whose work is grounded in large part in the German and Canadian philosophical traditions place the modernist problem of the self into the framework of the recognition of the autonomous self. Liberal self-interests conflict with collective moral values in the work of Canadians theorists Charles Taylor and Will Kymlicka, and of Axel Honneth in Germany.

71   This kind of stereotyping continues: Hockenos reports that of all the violent attacks in Germany, 90 percent "occurred against foreigners, particularly asylum applicants and their accommodations" (Paul Hockenos, *Free to Hate: The Rise on the Right in Post-Communist Eastern Europe* [London: Routledge, 1993], 319).

72   *Cassandra* was published in 1983 along with four essays on Christa Wolf's struggle for political and literary autonomy.

73   Joy Kogawa, "Some Random Thoughts from a Novel in Progress," in *Visible Minorities and Multiculturalism: Asians in Canada*, ed. K. Victor Ujimoto and Gordon Hirabayashi (Toronto: Butterworths, 1980), 323–327.

74   Magdalene Redekop, "The Literary Politics of the Victim," *Canadian Forum* (November 1989): 16.

75   In its obsession with loss, mourning, and grief, *Obasan* should be read along with Wolf's *Patterns of Childhood, Quest for Christa T.*, and *Cassandra*. Both authors reveal their despair over resentment within cultural identity that dominates the aesthetic drive towards integrity, recognition, and autonomy. However, Wolf had to negotiate the political crises in her life and face *the incommensurability of the aesthetic and the political*. In *Obasan*, this struggle is resolved in part by the child's sense that her identity relies on living with *language-that-is-not-yet-language*: the shame of having no language: childhood and the language of exile. Hope is rooted in repulsion and distance, loss and shame, which indict nationalism, colonialism, and the patterns of exclusion that existed long before World War II in the cultural attitudes of Christianity towards the Jews in Europe and in Canada towards the Japanese internees. Kogawa's struggle with the Christian ethics in her family is therefore as problematical as is Wolf's struggle with socialist political ethics. Both are inner exiles.

76   Thomas Berger, *The Banished Canadians: Mackenzie King and the Japanese Canadians* (Vancouver: Clarke Irwin, 1981).

77   Joy Kogawa with Karlyn Koh, "The Heart-of-the-Matter Questions," in *The Other Woman: Women of Colour in Contemporary Canadian Literature*, ed. Makeda Silvera (Toronto: Sister Vision, 1995), 24.

78   Interview for *Writers & Company*, CBC Radio (April 26, 1992).

79   Kogawa, "The Heart-of-the-Matter Questions," 38.

80   Freud, "Remembering, Repeating, and Working Through," trans. James Strachey, in *The Standard Edition of the Complete Psychological Works of Sigmund Freud*, vol. 12, *The Case of Schreber, Papers on Technique and Other Works* (London: Hogarth Press, 1948), 147–156.

81   Described by Alexander and Margarete Mitscherlich-Nielsen in *The Inability to Mourn: Principles of Collective Behaviour* (New York: Grove Press, 1975). The "inability to mourn" also applies to Christa Wolf's title character in *Cassandra* learning how to be silent in the face of disaster and failing.

82   A generation of poets and cultural critics like Joy Kogawa, Roy Miki, and Fred Wah thus experience the fate of language as the burden of modernity within their own lives, however in very different ways and against mainstream Canadian culture with its official multicultural policies, which gives an aura of liberalism to an officially bilingual society. Miki is elegiac and critical, Wah comical and mythical about how the hybridity of their poetic language emerges in the enactment of writing itself.

83   Kogawa describes this change: "After writing *Obasan* and in a way being forced into
      public situations, the Naomi character that was within me, who basically could not
      talk, and which is really the way I used to be, got more and more transformed, and
      the Aunt Emily voice came out." In *Sounding Differences: Conversations with Seventeen
      Canadian Women Writers* (Toronto: University of Toronto Press, 1994), 30–31.

84   Kogawa, "Is There a Just Cause?," *Canadian Forum* (March 1984).

85   See Adorno, "Education after Auschwitz," in *Critical Models*, trans. Henry W. Pickford
      (New York: Columbia University Press, 1998): "People who blindly slot themselves
      into the collective already make themselves into something like inert material,
      extinguish themselves as self-determined beings" (198). This confusion is internal
      to the author's attempt to find the way to a self-determined authorship not burdened
      with shame or what I would call moral injury. See the essays in dossier II for further
      discussions of exile. Utopia and the utopian Will is the basis of Ernst Bloch's *The
      Principle of Hope* (1954, 1955, and 1959). Bloch's "upright stance" (*aufrechte Gang*)
      is the upright gait of a person's uprightness which Bloch writes eloquently about in
      volume 3 of *The Principle of Hope*.x

86   Interview for *Writers & Company*, CBC Radio (April 26, 1992).

87   Kogawa, "Guest Editorial," in *Gatherings*, vol. 2 (1991): 9.

88   Arendt, *The Human Condition* (Garden City, NY: Doubleday Anchor, 1959), 225–233.

89   Kogawa, "Interview by Magdalene Redekop," in Linda Hutcheon and Marion
      Richmond, eds., *Other Solitudes: Canadian Multicultural Fictions* (Toronto: Oxford
      University Press, 1990), 16.

90   Roy Miki continued the work of memory at a time in Canada when redress and
      reparation emerged. Cases of Holocaust deniers like Ernst Zündel and James Keegstra
      were well publicized. In 1983–1984 both were charged and then brought to trial under
      the Canadian federalist "hate speech" codes. These white supremacists were fed by
      anger and anxiety produced by the historical reality of immigration and recent waves
      of Asian immigration, as well as heavy publicity about the redress campaign that
      concluded in a financial settlement with the "enemy" within, the Japanese Canadians.
      On the redress settlement, see Roy Miki, *Redress: Inside the Japanese Canadian Call
      for Justice* (Vancouver: Raincoast Books, 2005).

91   Kogawa, "Interview by Magdalene Redekop," 16.

92   In Jean Morisset's words, these are "usurped identities" (*L'identite usurpée: L'Amérique
      écartée* [Montréal: Nouvelle Optique, 1985]).

93   The "folkloristic" search for "joyful relativity" and the "carnivalesque" is the mark
      of Bakhtin's aesthetic of the novel. While Kogawa's novel does not aspire to the
      carnivalesque or Menippean satire, the confessional destruction of "ethical norms"
      of belonging brings the novel into the orbit of Dostoevsky. See Mikhail Bakhtin,
      Problems of Dostoevsky's Poetics, trans. Caryl Emerson (Minneapolis: University of
      Minnesota Press, 1984).

94   This touches on the problem of how Canadian avant-garde artists and writers who
      identify themselves as anti-racists and postcolonialists see themselves as having
      already obtained a cultural politics that acknowledges the cross-cultural reality of their
      lives within the hegemony of a Canadian public sphere that has yet to be translated
      into a politically sensitive reality. Thus, the search for an active cultural "hybridity"

often conflicts with the official ideology of the mosaic and with quasi-assimilationist immigration policies. In this regard, a theory for a specific Canadian cultural aesthetic would have to inform a social movement that affects, among other things, the curriculum in schools and universities. Yet only by including Indigenous Peoples and their emancipatory agonies can a Canadian post-multicultural vanguard assume the scale of a national social movement that transcends mere semantic "multiculturality."

95   Attending a Commonwealth literature conference in Germany in 1988, Kogawa compares the experiences of visible minorities in America and Canada: "In my brief journeys through Californian Japanese American communities I've seen a lot more political consciousness among the people. They seem to exist even more strongly as identifiably separate groups there than we do here. This seems to be a contradiction. We're the people who have the mosaic and they're the melting pot, and yet I experienced it the other way around completely; in the Canada I grew up in we were supposed to become English. I found many Asian Americans thinking of themselves as a political unit, especially in the artistic community – the Chinese, Japanese, Filipinos. There was a feeling that they needed to be together in their big White country. In Canada the multicultural program gives a grant to this or that group, and that's the pie. We fight each other to make sure we get our grant, and our voices are kept distinct and separate from each other, controllable, smaller, and less united. That seems very destructive." In a later interview, she had this to say about the 1994 Writing thru Race Conference in Vancouver: "What I felt at Writing thru Race was that this is not a place of inadequacy, this is a wonderful community of people and there is power here, tremendous power. And it's not just the power of originally bright people, it's the power of people who have something extremely important to say and who have been through the crucible, they've been through the fires, and because of that there's something that has been purified" (Kogawa, "The Heart-of-the-Matter Questions," 25).

96   "Image of Language": see Bakhtin, "The Bildungsroman" and "The Problem of the Text," in *Speech Genres and Other Late Essays*.

CHAPTER 3

97   This essay is abridged from *Journal of the Interdisciplinary Crossroads* 3, no. 1 (April 2006), titled "The Limits of Exile" and edited by David Kettler and Zvi Ben-Dor, and later included in *The Limits of Exile* (Berlin and Madison, WI: Galda Verlag, 2010). It reflects on courses and writing I have done on Primo Levi, Imre Kertész, and Central European writers who lived through World War II and beyond. Sebald's *Austerlitz* was also central to my course "Reading the City Reading Us." I translate the German noun *Eindenken* as "memoration," the work of memory that comes back again and again as traces without a name. Sebald's is an elegiac world in which mourning – in psychoanalysis – is the experience of the *après-coup*. The retarded awareness is saturnine. This aesthetic is explored in Sebald's *The Rings of Saturn*, trans. Michael Hulse (New York: Vintage, 2002).

98   Mikhail Bakhtin, *The Dialogic Imagination*, trans. Caryl Emerson and Michael Holquist (Austin: University of Texas Press, 1981), 133.

99   Bakhtin, *Speech Genres and Other Essays*, trans. Vern W. McGee (Austin: University of Texas Press: 1986), 21.

100 Sebald, *Nausea*, trans. Lloyd Alexander (Norfolk: New Directions, 1950), 18.

101 Sebald, *Austerlitz*, trans. Anthea Bell (New York: Alfred A. Knopf, 2001), 123.

102 Sebald, *Die Beschreibung des Unglücks: Zur österreichischen Literatur von Stifter bis Handke* [*The description of misfortune: On Austrian literature from Stifter to Handke*] (Frankfurt: Fischer Verlag, 2003). The word *Eingedenken* is not a phase of "memoration" that means "recounting and accounting for what one recalls": it is a thinking into memory, perhaps best reflected upon as an illumination of memory.

103 Theodor W. Adorno, *Notes to Literature*, vol. 1, trans. Shierry Weber Nicholson (New York: Columbia University Press: 1991), 149.

104 Trans. E.F.N. Jephcott (London: New Left Books: 1974). Sebald's vision of postwar Germany became known with his collection of essays *On the Natural History of Destruction*, trans. Anthea Bell (Toronto: Random House, 2004).

105 See Sebald, "*Verlorenes Land: Jean Amery und Osterreich*" [*Lost land: Jean Amery and Austria*], in *Unheimliche Heimat: Essays zur österreichischen Literatur* [Uncanny homeland: Essays on Austrian literature]. Levi is tormented by exile and his own vagabondage: "the exodus of scientific minds from Germany and Italy ... [who] 'gave birth to nuclear bombs' ... and the [desperate] Jewish survivors in flight from Europe after the great shipwreck [of survivors who] ... created in the bosom of the Arab world ... a portentous palingenisis of Judaism, and the pretext for renewed hatred": in Levi, *The Drowned and the Saved* (New York: Vintage Books, 1988), 201. Levi refers to Stalin's slave labour as the basis of the extension of the German state into the work camps in which he survived. For a thorough political and economic analysis for the establishment of the slave labour camps and the transportation and ultimate extermination of Jews, Sinta and Roma peoples, dissidents, socialists, and communists, see Adam Tooze, *The Wages of Destruction: The Making and Breaking of the Nazi Economy* (London: Penguin Books, 2006). Also among countless studies see Götz Aly, *Why the Germans? Why the Jews? Envy, Race Hatred, and the Prehistory of the Holocaust*, trans. Jefferson Chase (New York: Henry Holt and Company, 2011).

106 Sebald, *On the Natural History of Destruction*, 155–156,

107 Sebald, *Austerlitz*, 124.

108 Sebald, *Vertigo*, trans. Michael Hulse (New York: New Directions, 2000), 181.

109 Sebald, *Vertigo*, 183.

110 Bakhtin, *The Dialogical Imagination*, 181.

111 Bakhtin, 254–255.

112 Sebald, *Campo Santo*, trans. Anthea Bell (London: Hamish Hamilton, 2005), 207–208.

113 Sebald, *The Emigrants*, trans. Michael Hulse (New York: New Directions, 1997). See the book's blurry photographs on pp. 248–253, some of which are reproduced from the film on Theresienstadt; Sebald's own photograph as a child in costume appears on p. 183: "as if pictures had a memory of their own and remembered us" (182). We can compare *Austerlitz* and the photographs to the very different use of photographs of exile in Christian Boltanski's archival obituaries "The Reserve of the Dead Swiss" (1990), which are newspaper reports of the anonymous dead. The 1944 Nazi propaganda film *Theresienstadt* was "famously" made to show Red Cross visiting examiners the "good life" in the camp. See, among numerous studies: Karel

Margry, "'Theresienstadt' (1944–1945): The Nazi Propaganda Film Depicting the Concentration Camp as Paradise," *Historical Journal of Film, Radio and Television* 12, no. 2 (1992): 145–162.

114 Sebald, *The Emigrants*, 235.

115 Sebald, *Vertigo*, 237.

116 Sebald, *Campo Santo*, 153.

117 *Sebald*, 153.

118 Sebald throughout his essays refers to writers who have thought about suicide or have taken their own lives or whose writings were burned by the Nazis: Ernst Toller, Klaus Mann, Walter Benjamin, Arthur Koestler, Arnold Zweig, Ludwig Wittgenstein, Kurt Tucholsky.

119 See E.V. Walter, *Placeways: A Theory of the Human Environment* (Chapel Hill: University of North Carolina Press, 1988), 41. Walter's concept of "mutual immanence": physical intimacy and social experience create textures of homogeneous life spaces which, when destroyed by war, famines, disease, or natural disaster, turn once-living *placeways* into "cacotopias" (chap. 2, "Topomorphic Revolutions").

120 Sebald, *The Emigrants*, 58. Paul Bereyter in the novel experiences growing blindness but continues to read the works of writers who have taken their own lives or considered suicide.

121 Siegfried Kracauer, *History: The Last Thing before the Last* (New York: Oxford, 1969), 50–51.

122 Kracauer, "Photography," in *The Mass Ornament: Weimar Essays*, trans. and ed. Tom Levin (Cambridge, MA: Harvard University Press, 1995), 50–51.

123 Kracauer, "Photography," 51–52.

124 Kracauer, 51.

125 Sebald's "memory work" as exile and return or no return is influenced throughout by Benjamin's *The Arcades Project*. Benjamin's own memory work carried out in the emerging post-Weimar fascism constructs the city of the past and present into the unpast, which for Benjamin is the phantasmagoria of the unassimilated passages of memory sedimented into the contemporary. The fear of Kitsch hovers over memory.

126 Adorno, "Quasi una Fantasia," in *Essays on Modern Music*, trans. Rodney Livingstone (London: Verso, 1992), 50.

127 On Prague's Petřín Hill still stands the Petřín Lookout Tower, a small Eiffel Tower replica made for Prague's World Fair Exposition in 1891, when Prague was still in the Austro-Hungarian Empire ruled through Austrian bureaucracy. Tourists and weekenders long for the high view to peer across the city, geometrically constructed in part on Cartesian principles. The "Exposition Hall" constructed also at the end of the nineteenth century for exhibitions and large events is the hall where Jewish people and others were assembled for transport to Terezín. That architecture speaks and is not lost on Austerlitz. There is also an image of the neo-baroque building that housed the Prague City Archives; it is a bizarre building with surveillance-like arcades and balustrades that reminds Austerlitz of monasteries, riding schools, opera houses, and lunatic asylums, or, in the framework of the exilic unconscious of this

troubled character, of passengers waving from a steamer. Today this building has been refurbished as a location for music recitals (see Sebald, *Austerlitz*, 158).

128 Sebald, *Campo Santo,* 200. Italics mine.

129 Sebald, "An Attempt at Restitution: A Memory of a German City," *New Yorker* (December 13, 2004).

130 Sebald, *Campo Santo,* 210.

131 These chilling plans that looked to the future and the aftermath of the war, which Germany planned to win, are collected in Debórah Dwork and Robert Jan van Pelt, *Auschwitz: 1270 to the Present* (New York: W.W. Norton & Company, 1996) and show the "blueprints of genocide." The plan of Terezín/Theresienstadt appears on pages 234–235 with all the "hieroglyphic" compound names of sections that crammed sixty thousand people into an "extraterritorial place" with prisoners from every corner of Europe, from cities and soon-to-be defunct communities, to work in shops, imitating real life, even providing entertainment and a string orchestra. Terezín/Theresienstadt was a way station to extermination camps further to the east. Sebald examines the charts and illustrations of railway lines as if they are "Egyptian hieroglyphs."

132 Sebald, *Austerlitz*, 185.

133 See Peyman Vahabzadeh, *Exilic Meditations: Essays on a Displaced Life* (London: H&S Media, 2013). Sebald is clearly following Benjamin's struggle with the power of Chronos devouring time and "how it might be possible to discover for oneself the spiritual powers of Saturn and yet escape madness" (*The Origin of German Tragic Drama*, 121).

134 The Canadian experience of destabilized citizenship and extraterritorial, fragmented selves in regard to restitution is similar to what happened in many nations, although redressing the Canadian experience destabilized citizenship and fragmented persons into statelessness. The Japanese Canadian internment during World War II became part of the collective bargaining and negotiating of how the state redresses crimes of the state and grievances against the state. See, among other studies, Roy Miki, *Redress: Inside the Japanese Canadian Call for Justice* (Vancouver: Raincoast Books, 2005). In the light of this study of Sebald, Miki's book is also about the objectification of "identity" into a historical subject, who is "subjected," not only to the violence of the state, but also to the state that encloses and changes our very concept of the "person." Life becomes little more than the power of everydayness and the eschatology of the unpast.

135 Among many studies of the kind, see Robert Neuwirth, *Shadow Cities: A Billion Squatters, a New Urban World* (London: Routledge, 2005).

CHAPTER 4

136 This essay was published as "Odradek and the Mimesis of the Person: The Incommensurability of the Law and Memory," in *Journal of the Kafka Society of America* 18, no. 1 (1996). It was presented at a Kafka Society of America conference with photographs of Jeff Wall's backlit lightbox pictures *The Stumbling Block* and *Odradek*, which the reader can view online.

137 Translation slightly modified by me.

138 *Sorge* is here translated as "cares," but the word also carries the meaning of sorrow and worry and careful attention to what one cares for.

139 This parable illuminates the fate and history of Kafka's manuscript of *The Trial*, which was the subject of several trials about the ownership of the manuscript, and its subsequent afterlife in the hands of Max Brod, who owned the rights to the manuscript. The publicity in regard to the destiny of Kafka's "unburned" papers, letters, and manuscripts was great. For a complete account of the (for me) sordid story, see Elif Batuman, "Letters: Kafka's Last Trial," *New York Times* (September 22, 2010).

140 Adorno, "Notes on Kafka," in *Can One Live after Auschwitz? A Philosophical Reader*, trans. Rodney Livingston and others, ed. Rolf Tiedemann (Stanford: Stanford University Press, 2003), 211. See also Adorno's study *Kierkegaard: Construction of the Aesthetic*, trans. and ed. Robert Hullot-Kentor (Minneapolis: University of Minnesota Press, 1962). The key idea is the "constitution of inwardness" that Adorno relates to both Kafka and Kierkegaard, where inwardness is forced to become "objectless inwardness"; in this case, the Law becomes mythical and bloody. Inwardness becomes the Law and any semblance to reality lived under "the star of reconciliation burns in the abyss of inwardness as an all-consuming fire. It is to be sought out and named in this abyss, if the hope that it radiates is not to be forfeited by knowledge" (*Kierkegaard: Construction of the Aesthetic*, 67). See *Can One Live after Auschwitz?* for the correct understanding of Adorno's often misunderstood statement. Adorno explains his comment in a number of essays about "working through the past" and "education after Auschwitz." Section 4 in the reader is entitled "Memory of Suffering," which is the moral and aesthetic basis of Adorno's comment about a life of writing and reading after Auschwitz.

141 Kafka, "The Cares of a Family Man," in *The Complete Stories*, trans. Willa Muir and Edmund Muir, ed. Nahum N. Glatzer (New York: Schocken Books, 1976), 427. Translation slightly modified by me.

142 Adorno, "Notes on Kafka," in *Can One Live after Auschwitz?*, 237.

143 Adorno, "Notes on Kafka," 258.

144 My approach to Kafka among other commentators is reflected by Eduard Goldstücker, who wrote about Kafka in the Cold War when Kafka's works were officially banned: "The decisive turning point, though, was World War II. The similarity between the Nazi world and the world of Kafka's works is only a superficial reason for this burst of interest. More basic was the growing realization on the part of writers that during a period in which Europe and the entire world were being ground up by the terrible mill of history in an unprecedented way, the significance of events could no longer be grasped by conventional literary means. Kafka demonstrated the tremendous possibilities of expressing the phenomena of modern life in a parable-like manner. Furthermore, all established ideologies had proven disappointing and had lost their credibility and this formed another bridge to Kafka, who was also unable to find a satisfactory solution, to his problems in any system of ideas offered by his era." In *The Politics of Culture*, ed. Antonin J. Liehm, intro. Jean-Paul Sartre (New York: Grove Press, 1972), 281. In many respects the Cold War Kafka is a more genuine "Kafka" than that of the phase of Kafka's penetration into European and world literary consciousness, which is connected to French existentialism; now it was the existentialists' turn to consider Kafka as a spiritual antecedent. Of course, the existentialists made the error

of regarding Kafka as a philosopher, which he wasn't, rather than as the artist that he truly was.

145 Immanuel Kant, "Preface to Second Edition," *Critique of Pure Reason*, trans. Norman Kemp Smith (London: Macmillan), 35.

146 J. Hillis Miller, *The Ethics of Reading: Kant, de Man, Trollope, James, and Benjamin* (New York, Columbia University Press, 1987).

147 Miller, *The Ethics of Reading*, 59.

148 Miller, 59.

149 Miller, 38.

150 Miller, 120–121.

151 Miller, 123.

152 Others of my essays in this collection refer to the struggle of "natural law" and "man-made law" that reflect a common thread of an anarcho-utopian outlook. See as well my essay "Constitutional Law and Epics," in *Public* 9 (Spring 1994), "Reading our Rights," ed. Andy Payne, as well as Edward McWhinney, Jerald Zaslove, and Werner Wolf, eds., *Federalism-in-the-Making: Contemporary Canadian and German Constitutionalism, National and Transnational* (The Hague: Martinus Nijhoff Publishers, 1992). These are informed by Ernst Bloch's quote: "Social Utopian thought directed its efforts towards human happiness; natural law was directed towards human dignity. Social utopias depicted relations in which toil and burden ceased, natural law constructed relations in which degradation and insult ceased" (Ernst Bloch, *Natural Law and Human Dignity* [Cambridge, MA: MIT Press, 1986], xxix). Also see this book's last dossier.

153 Miller, *The Ethics of Reading*, 121.

154 Miller, 127.

155 "Letter to Oskar Pollak," January 27, 1904, in *Letters to Friends, Family, and Editors*, trans. Richard and Clara Winston (New York: Schocken Books, 1977), 15–16.

156 I am referring to the enigmatic picture *The Stumbling Block* by Jeff Wall as a parable-like picture in a Kafka-like manner of interiorizing and creating a figurative story. The photograph is viewable on the web. A fable, in fact, this picture brings into the foreground of a hyper-urban scene an image of the incompatibility of love (or romance) and justice. I see in the picture an "elective affinity" of love and justice – which stands at the heart of Kant's view of the person as well as Nietzsche's trans-erotic fear of close affinity with others. Perhaps mine is a bizarre interpretation of a bizarre scene that is depicted, I believe, in the way the picture is a study of both impersonality and fantasy, which are combined in the Dürer-like melancholy and solitude of the strange creature who is itself studying the event. It is also perhaps "mannerist" in a way that we can think of Nietzsche's self-confession of the secretive nature of his solitude and his inability to establish solidarity or understanding with others. The oddness of the picture provides insight into the aggravated sensitivity to counterfeit versions of modern culture appearing as the emptiness in all ideals of social justice and understanding the enigmatic nature of obstacles. Wall's pictures continue the traditions within radical modernism where modern art, including classic movements of avant-garde art, began as the working of hybrid forms through various mimetic traditions, which

bring images of social justice and peripheral cultural experiences into proximity with each other without completely sacrificing deep longings for universality. In order for this universality to become visible once again in terms of a universal sense of social justice, the institutions, whose ideological traditions are constantly being undermined by economic forces, would have to find new sources of insight into what makes this society an "essentially historical society." See Claude Lefort, "Genesis of Ideology in Modern Societies," in *The Political Forms of Modern Society*, ed. David Thompson (Cambridge, MA: MIT Press, 1986), 185.

157 "Acquittal in Jerusalem: Summary of Court Ruling," *New York Times* (July 30, 1993), A8.

158 For a treatment of the mixing of the tabooed animal-human paradigm with civilized cruelty and honorific human qualities, see Marian Scholtmeijer, *Animal Victims in Modern Fiction* (Toronto: University of Toronto Press, 1993).

159 The "loss of the subjective" is Adorno and Horkheimer's phrase, used in the essay "Elements of Anti-Semitism," in *Dialectic of Enlightenment*, which examines anti-Semitism as a moral and social pathology of bourgeois civilization itself but also as a moral injury, reminding the reader of humiliation and shame and adapting and accommodating to power and projecting catastrophe onto other peoples and blaming them for the falseness of the society itself. A sentimental appropriation of their and Kafka's approach to the neutralization of violence inside of civilization can be recognized in Art Spiegelman's 1973 pictorial fable *Maus*, which uses rodents to relativize the horror of the story he tells about his father and Nazi persecution. Using the naive techniques of propaganda and entertainment, which control horror by repressing the grotesque and phantasmagoria of modernity, Spiegelman's work calls attention to the mimetic without releasing transcendent meanings; on the other hand, the work repeats the tragedy of culture by reducing history to images of childhood which cannot possibly overcome the horror, and in this sense Spiegelman extends a technique of the comic-grotesque.

160 Václav Bělohradský, cited in Václav Havel, "Anti-Political Politics," in John Keane, ed., *Civil Society and the State* (London: Verso Books), 387.

161 Wolf-Dieter Narr writes on human rights and the artistic and activist strategies in making human rights visible when faced with "the stumbling block" of the structural impossibility of a universal concept of human rights, the struggle to bring the Kantian view of human rights into an activist framework in which the sovereign law of the state and the use of law illuminates the aporias of human rights: "Therefore, the permanent dialectics between dominant powers and emancipatory ones shape history. All of us are part of this dialectic" (Wolf-Dieter Narr and A. Belden Field, "Human Rights as a Holistic Concept," *The Human Rights Quarterly* 14, no. 1 [February 1992]: 1–20).

162 *Der Verschollene*, Kafka's first novel written between 1912 and 1914, is usually translated in English as *Amerika*.

163 Ivo Andrić, *The Bridge on the Dina*, trans. Lovett F. Edwards (London: Allen & Unwin, 1959).

164 See Benjamin's "Critique of Violence" (*Selected Writings*, vol. 1, *1913–1926*), in which he tries to find the commensurabilities of sacred violence, mythical violence, and law-constituting violence and revolutionary violence. Their inseparability is the subject

of Benjamin's anarcho-utopic vision of a world without violence in which a world of "Odradeks" would become lost. The postulate of state-owned violence that replaces the "primitive" with civilization is configured in Kafka's stories "The Great Wall of China," "Josephine the Singer or the Mouse Folk," "A Report to an Academy," and "In the Penal Colony."

165 The phrase "standing by the ruins" has been borrowed from Ken Seigneurie, *Standing by the Ruins: Elegiac Humanism in Wartime and Postwar Lebanon* (New York: Fordham University Press, 2011).

Streets and Borders: Vancouver and Elsewhere

About places, classrooms, and teaching in "Untimely Places," and the configurations of the always-present place. *Pictographs* are images or representations or figurations, tableaux found in books, configurations, memory traces like drawings on cave walls, markers that mean something to the one who makes them. *Pictograms* are graphic images / stories. These essays are about places and the immanent realities of places and configurations.

The construction of life is at present in the power of facts far more than of convictions, and of such facts that have scarcely ever become the basis of convictions. Under these circumstances true literary activity cannot aspire to take place within a literary framework – this is, rather, the habitual expression of its sterility. Significant literary work can only come into being in a strict alternation between action and writing ... Opinions are to the vast apparatus of social existence what oil is to machines: one does not go up to a turbine and pour machine oil over it; one applies a little to hidden spindles and joints that one has to know.
—WALTER BENJAMIN, *One Way Street and Other Writings* (1979),
    trans. Edmund Jephcott and Kingsley Shorter

The cardinal principle of imaginative projection is what Freud calls *Darstellbarkeit* ... [or] presentability ... *Darstellbar* means capable of presentation ... or "exhibitable."
—SUZANNE LANGER, *Feeling and Form: A Theory of Art* (1953)

DOSSIER III – CHAPTER 1

Ten Fables for the Heroic Future:
Picture Fables[1]

Some author's comments are in order here for a series of picture-fables whose meaning may not be immediately realized in the prose itself. Heroes fly about like angel-demons, flapping their wings against baroque ceilings, while the rest of us watch under the shelterless sky trying to catch a glimpse of these demonic cherubim as they occasionally leave the security of the church and perform their magical feats in the open, on the battlefields, flying by the winds of our spectacular gazing. What will bring them to Earth? As we wear ourselves out watching them, we also construct some fables in the hope that their wings will come undone and they will be seen for what they are: disembodied beings of great danger. "Fables" are used as picturing, or depicting, following a tradition used by Walter Benjamin, for example in his "Theses on the Philosophy of History," or other essays presented as theses, which are influenced by the German storytelling and fable tradition exemplified for Benjamin in the writing of Johann Peter Hebel's riddles, stories, almanac-household advice and anecdotes. Bertolt Brecht also used fables as a storytelling form, for example his *Stories of Mr. Keuner* which are dialogues about the theatre and political forms of telling stories. (See my Fable X about the Angel with wooden wings.)

No concept of heroism can escape the power of the term itself, which is embedded in the very culture in existence since the Enlightenment. This heroism is destructive of everyday life because it claims to defend everyday life by setting necessary limits on the power of the others. Meanwhile, the heroic, in its Napoleonic and post-Napoleonic stages, allows capital to control everyday life. In the name of defending the masses, everyday life, from the total domination of capital and theology, the heroic allows capital to free itself from both labour and theology. Hero and capital thus have a lot in common as they skydive above our heads. Capital frees itself from labour and goes on to the greater heights of accumulating and storing wealth, power, and energy amid dazzling records, deeds, and facts. The power of the others becomes the dominant reality, not the necessary limits of human coping.

At the same time, no concept of heroism can escape the sentimentality, pathos, and banality of the term itself, which causes us to forget the victims, sacrificial offerings, and triumphant marches over and through the ghost of the past. These ghosts are evoked by the hero of the bourgeois revolution which magisterially raises the bourgeois class itself above the degraded nature of the world: the conquering of theology and myth in the name of progress and destroying the shelterless place where the victim stood. "No vision inspires the destructive character," writes Walter Benjamin in "The Destructive Character" (1931), "he [sic] has few needs, and the least of them is to know what will replace what has been destroyed." In contrast, for Theodor W. Adorno the hero of everyday life is the combination of King Kong, the movie gorilla, and the suburban barber, extracted by Adorno from Chaplin's portrayal of Hitler in *The Great Dictator* as the parody of everyday life. On the other hand, the heroes of everyday life are the sorrowful adversaries of the collective dream, those who seek resistance and those who "pay for the increase of their power with alienation from that over which they exercise their power" (Adorno and Horkheimer, *Dialectic of Enlightenment*).

Fables can be understood as resistance to the proxy dreams of heroic actors. The phony natural power of processes speeding their way into the future is slowed down. The diminishing of reality by postmodern academicism is implicated as well, for the indifference to feeling and motivation that runs through the backbreaking struggle for existence in modern capitalism is mirrored in the mediocrity of postmodern criticism that bases authenticity of analysis on the name-dropping of Heroes of Criticism, as if everyday life could be identified with the demonic laughter of fragmentation and renunciation – an old trick of culture heroes who claim to speak for the silent. There is also an authoritarian technique: to find legal or quasi-legal means to establish the rules of the game. The relationship between the species-altering activities of humans destroying other humans in the name of the heroic ideal of keeping everyday life going by whatever means possible corresponds to the extroversion of the heroic fantasies of those who build palaces on the "empty space, the place where the thing stood or the victim lived" (Benjamin, "The Destructive Character").

The future belongs to the proxy dreams of those who build railroad stations where the trains run on time: into the past and future, carrying disembodied beings, the victims of the decomposition of the bourgeois revolutions and institutions of the last two centuries. Arising like a cheesy phoenix from the ashes come the heroes of modern times, the self-appointed survivors. At the site of those ashes, speakers and listeners who share stories and tales and by extending their subject matter into the artist's world, create fables in the continuing effort to explain the hero, to demythologize nature. The inversion of the public into the spectator, and the extroversion of the public world into a spectacular, theatrical façade is more difficult to speak about than to denounce the heroic itself; nevertheless any attempt to represent the heroic must in some way participate in the fabulous reality that divests the flights of heroes of their gravity-defying lies and also counters the official records left behind through which the future is rendered plausible and rational.

Fable I

Reality Atop Tall Buildings Seems Heroic

Heroism is a character mask of the economic system that, in freeing itself from reality, worships itself in countless stereotypes produced by the culture industry – stereotypes for the future that mask the sacrificial victims of the past. Stereotypes become surplus reality. Adorno called stereotypes "the all-powerful reality." Stereotypes, once a historical problem of conceptualizing authorities from below, have become the absolute mode of thinking of the authorities themselves. King Kong is the surplus of reality without insight into the "powerless subject," and the weight of the monster is secondary to the weight of the real pessimism of those who feel that reality has become unreal. Heroism slays the subject by making reality lifeless, inert, and evil. The pessimistic intelligentsia takes over and accuses the masses of indifference, despair, and intellectual sloth: they identify with "the all-powerful reality." But people are not just lazy masses. As powerless subjects, they reflect the bad dreams of the rabbits of technical progress who reproduce their own kind while emancipating culture by producing a reality beyond the grasp of the subject. This is the new feudal integration of masses to heroes – a new welfare state where we are all heroes of everyday life and those who run the show make no distinction between the culture of everyday life as abstract relations and the struggle for everyday existence. Beyond the grasp of knowledge, the future forgets the sickness, war, disease, poverty, and violence spread along the trade routes of the Black Plague used by fleas, rats, sailors, businesspeople, and migrating peoples. The blind search for causes – who poisoned the fountains? – continues today in the shadows of the rising states where we look for scapegoats.

Fable II

Crisis Management Is No Vision of the Future

Crisis is the new narcotic. The "disproportion between the all-powerful reality and the powerless subject" (Adorno, *Aesthetic Theory*) emerges at the very moment when insight fades into reified images, which aren't at all funny (as the demonic laughter of postmodernist gurus and careerist stand-up comedians of the void proclaim). The hidden power in modern life relies on a higher network of financial forces and a higher interdependence of abstractions, which distribute the goods produced by surplus itself. The rich states propagandize the "privilege" of living and working in the shelterless open spaces of post-ideology. They monopolize security, preventing insecurity from becoming a useful tool for investigation into the all-powerful reality. Instead, insecurity becomes the drugged-prolonged moment before therapy or before work: both are tools of a third, unknown force. The manager is the heroic unknown.

Fable III

Fingerprinting the Mind

There is a modern miracle. The one we live in. A culture that not only worships itself, but also assumes it is greater than any culture in time and history. This is a culture of decomposition and fragmentation, bursting apart with the screams of the routed millions who have been shattered by their efforts of work and who lie tattered along the roadside worn out by the war of attrition between culture and time-splitting diversions that pound away inside their heads as if the brain were made of pieces of vermillion atoms. The revolution of production has created a culture of displaced persons which has wiped out cultural differences – imperishable differences sprayed like moisture beads into the void. Technology itself has replaced culture and holds the atoms together without the will or motivation to find out whether there is any cultural compatibility between the friendly users and the millions of un-users whose future lies in having their minds fingerprinted for the one and only one really existing future. The exhausted life-worlds lying at the roadside are reproduced in the communications model, a middle-class system which has no inner life.

The hope that one day the unfulfilled potential of a bourgeois lifeworld might be realized is gone forever, gone into the future where, like technological progress itself, a culture of symbols rules. Subjective culture leaps into the postmodern age without ever passing through the period between modernism and postmodernism. When did it happen? Where did it go? How did those symbols become a culture without passing through a stage of nature where human hands were revealed as part of the process? The future fools us and is merely a grammatical feature of the modern tense. The past is merely a nuisance to these heroes who read our minds.

Fable IV

The Dream of the Collective: Motives and Motivations to Speak

Can technological progress contain images and realities that also carry the burden of the insulted and offended? Work, communications, procedures, administration, consumption, and bureaucracy are all sublimated into the clarity of the daydream. Yet we have another miracle coming to us after religion's last miracle, where the lame were made blind and the lame lead the blind. We have one more religion coming to us, too, where the blind, having been made lame, lose their voices.

Fable V

Middle-Class Heterodoxy Is One Culture: Adidasology

The middle class always gets one more chance. Its claims to heterodoxy go by the name of democracy. It makes nothing new, but it packages bulky goods in slick and streamlined containers carried by ships to the four corners of the reinforced computer-marvelled world, where the electronic secular heroes believe they are literate. The literate past and the utterances of oral cultures are dispersed throughout the corners of the globe in the form of brand products like Adidas and Nike, washed up on the Galápagos Islands, or in the trees of Borneo, or in the cemeteries of Prague, where they lead an extraterritorial existence. The Adidas sole is the imprint of the future, the sole of the new man and woman, the spirit which turns always-impending poverty into new factories in the Brazils of the world, where advanced consumer science for citizens and athletes of superior capabilities can work on behalf of the winners – the middle-class team. If everything is middle-class, maybe there is nothing but the business of its life anyway. On the other hand, the middle classes in all industrialized countries of this world where there is no other world often demand another chance for themselves. Just one more election and we will have it all down pat.

Yet we know that the trans-avant-garde techniques of persuasion display light and speed that eliminate the subject of it all, because the person is already reduced to the point on the screen, the anti-pixel, from where no light emanates.

Fable VI

A Negotiable Future Based on Work Only: Heroic Censorship

The dream of a participation society based on play – that is the untapped potential of the culture of the unfulfilled subject turned into labour. In postmodern criticism within the Academy, it has turned into strenuous exercise with the rules of hierarchy and domination. The acid wash of hyper-industrialization bathes the reproductive elements, the graphic plates of consciousness, in the codes of the pregiven, of one language, of the authoritarian science of semiotics. These censors of the future are the last censorship we have coming to us: the one which removes expression by changing the basis on which expression and play are negotiated. The performance of the system is the new morality play. On the level of work, the control and distribution of money take place without disturbing the legal system, which lives there above the entire process, while the location of poverty shifts from one place to another. When money magic is performed by the system, and not by the authors of enchantment, we have work and censorship dancing together. Not only the avant-garde live well in the bedrooms, but the censor is there in the bed too.

Fable VII

Heroic Architecture

Secularization of the world in hundreds of places all at once – designing scenes and strategies. We walk through mass culture as well as being in it. However, from the perspectives of those who sit outside of the centres of mass wealth in America, Japan, Western Europe, mass culture appears on the shore as the coming Americanization. Waves upon waves of it. In opposition, we find nationalisms. Within nationalism, there are new groups and cultural movements that make networks of relationships based on new needs created by the system. These are needs that require immediate fulfillment, immediate emancipation, and immediate care. How closed, redemptive, and ecstatic are these networks? They cut welfare costs. They provide therapy and theatre, teach language and literacy to immigrants and fugitives from the countrysides; they enhance childhood, rescue delinquents, deliver food and medicine – yet all this within the societies that create the needs and break apart the networks, the vernacular architecture: "Pity the land that needs Heroes," Galileo said when he was censored – not because of what he discovered, because the authorities can always use the critical insights of the intellectuals – but because he wrote and spoke in the vernacular. This language of anarchism is the task of designing *solidary* human beings, of which there may be many models already that used to be "good enough" but not perfect. The task of designing an economic confederation is more difficult.

Fable VIII

Eternal Youth

Bureaucracy is the process of pre-established aging and passes the torch of civilization on to younger bureaucrats, those who have made it in the system. So the torch of civilization has passed away in a long relay race from powerful males, prophets, wizards, explorers, tradesmen, rationalists, colonizers, soldiers, philosopher-warriors, patrons, exporters, race traders, identity makers, revolutionaries, priests, entrepreneurs, money hoarders, shipbuilders, magnates, engineers, sweet-living celebrities, philanthropist families, muckrakers, mythmakers – and now to entrepreneurs and bureaucrats whose aging and sagging bodies have been tolerated east and west.

Aging democracy passes its bad breath too – the old bodies of the voters aged prematurely by the cynicism that means never voting at all (United States, Chile, Switzerland), or voting a lot (West Germany, Romania, Nicaragua). Youth cultures are outside of this process, just as youth is worshipped as the unpoisoned fountain of resources. Once upon a time, before the last war, there were young cultures and a fantasy of a last war before the last, but the last is not the last. America, Russia, exiles, immigrants, dislocated peoples, genocides, Auschwitz, classes blind to themselves who dreamed they carried the burning torch for a democratic, co-operative "civilization" with the hopes for a human-sized labour process and equal rights that are human rights or there are no rights at all.

Who would have dreamed that the myths of Prometheus would have produced the businessman and bureaucrat as the models of the heroic? Had Orpheus not turned his head, he would have brought back the women and not the aging dreams, imitations of reality. Did Marx also turn his head to look around? What prophecies did he make?

Fable IX

Beyond Condoms: The Last Taboo Is the Heroism of Science

Innovation seems heroic; it all fits in the condom: psychology, engineering, programming, genetic restructuring. Sexual advice and business advice: take one in the morning and repeat as needed. The luxury of thinking, we have broken with theology and determinism.

First, God's presumed laws were violated by the universal laws of reason. So Hegel told us; we were not Pariahs but could reason. Second, God's laws were ignored by the redemptive values of progress. Third, God's laws were violated by history itself, where unknown laws determining action and choice were exposed and demystified. Marx helped in this new lawmaking labour. This was heroic intellectual labour. What is left now for the rest of us? The indeterminacy of science, the organization of production, the restructuring of desires, the monopolization of persuasion by those in the know. In short, action and choice are reserved for those at the top. The conscience of science shelters us from the fallout – from pieces of information that appear on a screen where light comes from no man's land. The strengthening of the taboo on thinking that all evil can become good continues to exist in the laws of science that design out the sensual incompatibility of humans with systems.

Fable X

Taking Risks: Sport on Stage

Redeeming the masses is a full-time job and employs a cast of millions. The flight into repression on a large scale has never found an art form which could adequately express the enactment of the movement of history itself. The anonymity of the masses opens a new sense of the utility of history, but no redemption of the whole. Utopian and collective allegories can be photographed as fragmented and captioned reminders of the whole, as film did in its formative, naive stage. There we saw and used for a few brief moments the astonishments, risks, gambles, insights, spectacles, creaturely pleasures of photography, and of what is seen, the physical, the newly made, the left out, the visible, the wealth of images and memories yet unorganized by "cinema": all this was there to be picked like flowers and placed in the pages of material life, to be remembered in history even when, like dried flowers, the scent is gone forever. These silent flowers reproduce themselves in nothing today, for film cannot again recapture the naive childhood of memory, except in lands where official censorship exists and one nourishes a critical culture where "Nothing is absolutely dead: every meaning will have its homecoming festival ... the problem of Great Time" (writes Mikhail Bakhtin in an important text, "Towards a Methodology for the Human Sciences," collected in *Speech Genres and Other Essays*).

Homecoming today is the cold presence of war and athletic combat, the one substituting for the other.

DOSSIER III – CHAPTER 2

Carrall Street: The Last Snapshot of the Vancouver Intelligentsia [2]

> Intellectual currents can generate a sufficient head of water for the critic to install his power station on them.
>
> —WALTER BENJAMIN, "Surrealism: The Last Snapshot of the European Intelligentsia" (1929), *One-Way Street and Other Writings,* trans. Edmund Jephcott

> Despina can be reached in two ways: by ship or by camel. The city displays one face to the traveler arriving overland and a different one to him who arrives by sea.
>
> —ITALO CALVINO, *Invisible Cities* (1972), trans. William Weaver

I

Prologue

What follows here is an open letter to the participants in Althea Thauberger's one-night performance, "Carrall Street." The performers are live creatures who have arrived in many ways to the city of Vancouver and come from elsewhere in modern times as wanderers have always ended up in Vancouver, at the edge of the continent. This letter is addressed to the Actors, Agents, Writers, Artist-Photographers, Bystanders, Mercurians, Apollonians, and Cultural Apparatchiks who participated in the Scene of a Crime – the Search for Who Wrecked Vancouver, a Once-Beautiful Town. In this "open letter" I give names to the city blocks that describe what it feels like to be alive in this part of town. These names describe the city and reveal how the contemporary turn to the city as subject matter is related to the symptom of the crisis about art in the city and art that is about the city.

II

Culture Shock Avenue: Encumbered Space?

I am writing as someone who wandered into Carrall Street by land, like Calvino's camel driver who "sees, at the horizon of the tableland, the pinnacles of the skyscrapers coming into view, the radar antennae, the white and red windsocks flapping, the chimneys belching smoke, he knows it is a city, but he thinks of it as a vessel that will take him away from the desert,"[3] and I have experienced a form of culture shock where a few square blocks of what has become known by the popular media and academics as the Downtown Eastside, who see it as an opportunity for study and grants, has been transformed into a movie set. The culture shock was the suddenness of becoming a part of a "we" in a street theatre without an apparent subject. Because Vancouver is the incarnation of a colonial dream that parades itself as modern and has become populated by subjectless "subjects" full of the self-consciousness of being in a *Gesamtkunstwerk* – a total work of (urban) art – one lives with the illusion that Vancouver as a city is unique.

Althea Thauberger's Felliniesque street scene constructs a text on the street. It is a text that should allow us to hear the footsteps of the ghosts of nomads of the past in this depiction of what I would name *Carrall Street Now*. The work is an intervention into a city that itself aspires to be seen as a work of art. The primitive and raw edge of experience at the poor terrains and buildings surrounding Carrall Street remains willfully invisible to the city's other borders; older and traditional neighbourhoods are now blurred by the network of streets and arteries that cut through the city like razor blades. The artist as ethnographer builds a total work of art on dramaturgical principles constructed in the heart of Gastown.

The work is staged in Vancouver with clusters of people meandering through a city block; these are eddies of snapshots that claim to make this planned convergence of people as a happening into a "profane illumination" of the really existing, yet extinct, neighbourhood. "Extinctness" is the essential condition of forgetting.[4] The recasting of the Street as a text is a minimalist construction because it reduces "the city" to a series of random performative incidents that create the illusion of the city as a total work of art. The performance is an event without an author. The city as a lifeworld of artifice dramatizes itself by performing itself, by sacrificing art as such to the idea of the city. City works, as they were in the age of Baudelaire, Dickens, Kafka, and then the great city photographers, who saw the city as a foundation of neo-modern thinking. Now the city has become a profane illumination that can explain the rise and fall of the urban.

The profane sacrifice is important to this analysis, because by acting out the dramatic or theatrical blurring of the performance's boundaries through the street life that is itself enacted by interactive scenes, we valorize the mundane as the everyday without the art's intervention. We see situations as the profane commonplaces that we do not recognize, which is different historically and artistically from the documentary as a witness of the everyday. Put another way, commonplace situations are raised to the power of a dialectic, allowing us to see artistic work on the city as the entanglement of surface and depth, the near and the far, and the interconnectedness of phenomenal reality with the people who build the reality. If autonomous art is sacrificed to experience as such, and the framing of experience becomes a loose array of frozen, sociologically interesting moments in time which are yet memorable, but fleeting, because we are in the domain of another kind of artistic movement – the theatrical performance becomes almost a series of transient acts.

I refer here to Walter Benjamin's critique of surrealism by pointing out that in Carrall Street – which I name an enclave – the air of the city has been sucked out by the glass ghettos of the uptown shops of the commercial centres to the west and north of the enclave of Carrall Street. This leaves this area to the "reader, the thinker, the loiterer, the flâneur ... the illuminati just as much as the opium eater, the dreamer, the ecstatic ... not to mention that most terrible drug – ourselves – which we take in solitude." [5] Benjamin, Georg Simmel, and, in his own time, Siegfried Kracauer all realized that the city exhausts the individual of resources of resistance. The individual is reduced to the tumbledown interior of this self whose solitude recalls those others, which in the case of Carrall Street, are the Mercurians and Indigenous Peoples and dead readers who have no shrines, who once walked here at the edge of experience, the edge of the Potlatch, now measured not by contemplation of wealth and its origins, but by the irradiations of the consumer-capital that make those who can't buy the products into its human repositories walking among abandoned warehouses. Mental energy is reduced to poverty or sickness or both.

The inconspicuous Carrall Street exists as a threshold street rather than a thoroughfare or crossroads. It is a gateway to a crime, namely that, after one hundred years of heavy investment in real estate and brutalist development, Vancouver has become a city that is not more unique than any other continental pioneer settlement becoming an urban modern place, but is modern precisely because it has managed to build a city where most of us have become observers, analyzers, and willing and obedient participants in a placeway that is a failed illumination of the historical sources of the changes. In this sense it is no wonder that the turn of the performance as a *"text" is a form of art as communication* that turns to historical reminders that imitate historical reconstruction.

The placement of Stan Douglas's forty-four-foot mural for the atrium of Westbank's project in the adjacent Woodward's complex at the corner of Abbott and Cordova frames culture shock into historical idioms that remind some of us of the riots, streets, and police intervention. Is culture shock ameliorated by the artwork? Maybe. Maybe not. The heavy mural encumbers the space allotted for it.

III

Walter Benjamin Square

Walter Benjamin criticized the nervy surrealists for failing to bring their "profane illuminations" into the "materialist, anthropological inspiration" promised by their orientation towards the city of Paris.[6] The strength of the surrealist Breton was that

> he was the first to perceive the revolutionary energies that appear in the "outmoded," in the first iron constructions, the first factory buildings, the earliest photos, the objects that have begun to become extinct, grand pianos, the dresses of five years ago, fashionable restaurants when the vogue has begun to ebb from them. The relation of these things to revolution – none can have a more exact concept of it than these authors. No one before these visionaries and augurs perceived how destitution – not only social but architectonic, the poverty of interiors, enslaved and enslaving objects – can be suddenly transformed into revolutionary nihilism.[7]

Benjamin is not only referring to the aging of the city seen through the profane optics of a camera keen to see the phantasms of the past in the present, but he also sees how the immediate aging of the surrealist intelligentsia that becomes his subject will become part of the landscape of the city. Their mental energies lead to "collective innervation."[8] Benjamin's collective innervation should have been a banner over Carrall Street. And then I would have understood the culture shock of wandering into a street named "Hidden Dialectical Street" where the destitution of the surrounding neighbourhood and revolutionary nihilism of capital come together around property and boundaries, borders and zones of contact disappearing into nothingness, not action. But ethnography or historical narratives as art are not about action, but about texts. Maybe or maybe not.

IV

Georg Simmel – Culture Shock Laneway

Simmel is the great German philosopher and sociologist of the city, money, and the inner structures of the metropolis-self. Simmel used the city of Berlin as the benchmark for modernity. He portrayed the countless ways in which the city became the source of modern nervousness. Being alive in the city was an everyday culture shock without end, as if the city spoke to the inhabitants in their sleepless sleep, perhaps in the manner of Dziga Vertov's phantasmagoric filmic ecstasy of the city, *Man with a Movie Camera*, that opens and invades every nerve ending of the city, while the Chaplinesque cameraman does himself in nervously trying to find the totality of the city. He is exhausted and frenzied, at the same time proving Simmel right about nervousness created by the metropolis.

Simmel's prophecy about the nervousness of the abstract individual wandering in the modern city foretold a future of the individual created by and through the weakness of the self's defences against the revolutionary energies of capitalism that transformed the village and towns of Europe into urban enclaves of inner lives where the inner life had to learn to read new forms of references and signs pointing towards a new reality. And then there are the abysses of the city. Learning the art of relativity towards the absolute of capital was needed in order to maintain any modicum of social control over modernity. The industrial power that transformed the nineteenth century into

the unprecedented movement of peoples into the city and transformed migration, immigration, exile, and dislocation augmented
the growing traumas of the middle classes under siege by the
forces of industrialization, and the struggle over private property right into the desire to turn public space into utopic, surreal
landscapes. This created the conditions for massive migrations
to the New World and the ecstasy of city-building that became
the modern city surrounding the Island of Carrall Street. Simmel
and Calvino would understand each other!

V

The Vampires' Picnic Grove

In 1991 Jeff Wall created a backlit Cibachrome titled *The Vampires'
Picnic*, depicting a group of people in diverse poses and guises
in a *mise en scène* that gives one pause. Who are these people? I
would call them "Mercurians." This is a metaphorical name that
refers to those who exist alongside the powerful Apollonians who
escaped Europe and Asia and migrated into civil society. We look
in astonishment at the refugees of the modern age. Astonished
that they have not joined the modern age. They are invisible. They
are the modern world's baroque angels who harm no one and are
influenced by or become nomads, strangers, and gypsy types and
in general are those who make do within the city. Thauberger's
city block is a "Hermes," a "One-Way Street Interchange" for
the city block that includes these people who have secrets. The
figures in Wall's *The Vampires' Picnic* are in a dark wooded grove
having a picnic. They can be actors, nomads, exiles, readers, and
spectators of a city and, in the case of the forest that surrounds
this grove in which the picnic takes place, it can be a place like
Vancouver; but it is also any settlement that has been excavated
again and again out of the forests adjacent to oceans and rivers.
The atmosphere is the subject, but the cast of characters are like
extras in a film; they are mournful. The characters sit on the earth

in poses of ease, unease, and maybe disease; they peer in various directions and appear abstracted in the bloody aftermath to a picnic. The baroque allegory of the picture can be compared to Walter Benjamin's sense of an aftermath to a great tragic event that has become a comic ruin. We are filled with the need to know who these people are and to learn their stories. What do they represent? Some process, economic or political, has rendered them soulful and reflective, as well as stunned, about the fate of becoming vampires who feed on each other. What better, albeit comic-grotesque, allegory of capitalism could there be?

The exchange process that turns people towards destructive violence and force, and invades the integrity of the person's insides, takes place with a silent appeal to the absent gods that have ruled over the individual's desires. This force also transforms the individual into a money person whose desires are sublimated into the use of edible others and the fetishistic accumulation of goods. Can dressing up for a picnic alleviate the misery of exchange value? The theatricality of the photograph remains operatic and melodramatic. The scene is well lit by floodlights.

How this inbuilt violence of an exchange economy affects the geography of perception and experience of the city is another story in itself, about Mercurians and settlements that have been displaced by the city as a force for land holding and development.

Using the backlit Cibachrome photograph gives the illusion of reality, but also intensifies the reality via artifice. The macabre picture shows us how it is possible to manipulate our vision with the image-making powers that extend the prosthetic technology everywhere in the city. Suspicion is built into the spectator until the flatness is made into a haptic experience of touch and depth through critique, memory, and story. The theatricality of the vampire picnickers joins with the hidden theatricality of money as blood money; both are artificial constructions insofar as both are invisible. The theme is possession and value and money, all of which can reduce others to means and to stunned silence over the hiddenness of desires.

Vampirism uses theatrical illusions that increase the possibility of creating images that are uncanny – memory-like, almost real, but subreal – and in effect, the photograph of areas of the city as settlements, which are not neighbourhoods. Our inner map of the city, we experience through the symbolic nature of the forms of the city that we have internalized in order to get around. There is no way to "see" the city, except through the high view or the art of photography to create a total impression of a city.

Vampirism sucks the blood out of symbolic places. When this happens – the destruction of the symbolic – certain rescue operations in culture occur in order to repair the loss of experience. The loss of experience of the city is also reparation of our memories of it. Staging the city for city builders is one stage in the aesthetic formations of the avant-garde. We reach out for the phenomenological understanding of our modern condition and this comes in the search for a total work of art that the city seems to promise. The theatricality of art shadows the objects we experience in daily situations; the street becomes a movie-like, theatrical ensemble of effects without an author, all of this replacing the ornamental interiors of once-great movie theatres that gave us the city: the film palaces had names like Strand, Loews, Palace, Bijou, Ritz – these are movie theatres of my own typical childhood in a small mercantile and industrial city.

Simmel writes that "money provides the technical possibility for the creation of the correlation in basic social relationships ... [However] the result had to be subjective in the worst sense of the word – an arbitrary, inadequate valuation that made a momentary constellation into a fetter for future developments." [9] Money is a power that flows upward and downward in daily life, he writes, that ultimately forms an invisible totality, a total work of society that governs the invisibility of diverse interests. Unless one has a theory of class conflict, *The Vampires' Picnic* is about the loss and maybe the absence of a theatre of desire, the displacement of actors from the theatre, into nature. The next stage is letting the characters whose images live in the movie houses escape, and then removing the roof of the film palace from the shelter of the imagination. The vagabonds are exposed to the elements.

Alongside the event on Carrall Street stand the façades of new, expensive urban housing as well as ornamental lampposts and iron gates. The mastery of the street belongs to the relationship of private property to those civil institutions haunted by the presence and absence of vagrancy and homelessness. The Vampires' Picnic is this grove where the topography of fear is domesticated into a picnic. Everyone can have a picnic, even vampires. The inbuilt violence of a money economy affects the geography of perception and the experience of the city. However, the story about "Mercurians" and settlements displaced by the vampiric growth of the city as a force for land holding and development can be *depicted*, but it is difficult to tell.

VI

Exposition Boulevard – Fairs, Clienteles, Crowds, Architects

Do we really read Vancouver globally? I doubt it. The provincial dominates. Having to maintain the fiction of the global, we don't want to see how the city is "in us" through developments that hide visible, and invisible, contradictions of class, inequality, accumulation of wealth, incommensurable communities, and power mediated by imagery. The photographs taken about Vancouver from the age of Philip Timms and Leonard Frank in the early half of the twentieth century, and then after 1950 by Fred Herzog, reveal the invisible holes in the cities, streets, settlements, and common situations. They do not reveal the names of the traders and investors from afar; the Streets spoke the history. Today Hong Kong, Iran, Holland, Germany, the United States, and names like Bentall, Wosk, Block, Bronfman, Marathon Reality, British Pacific, Birks, and all the railroad builders who built Vancouver through land speculation, which has been running rampant from the beginning of the century all the way into the 1970s and 1980s. And corporations like the CPR bought and sold land so that property values could balloon. Malls replaced settlements and streets become routes to further land speculation all the way out to industrial parks in Langley and to the US border. The streets become "archetypical places" and developers provide amenities to the neighbourhoods. The newspapers join in the development of a city and report about it as if the city were a creature roaming through unfettered land claims. [10]

Street photography, and the journalism that makes the newspaper the storytelling sponsor of the city, is part of the process of building the consciousness of the city as a gigantic arcade. The manias of collecting, examining, ornamenting, decorating, and re-presenting a past through the dramaturgical use of a site that never was permanent, or could be, is imagined and symbolically orchestrated by city planners to produce new breeding grounds for the city as a mediating and objectifying power in the marketplace society. Photography becomes both the agent provocateur and documentary agent for showing the city, for providing a high view (Berenice Abbott and others), and the inside view of the city (Jacob Riis), and ultimately the challenge is to camouflage the anxiety and fear that are revealed in the photographs of Eugène Atget.

Commercial photography emerged in the Paris of the Second Empire. Mass-produced portraits were made possible and one can say, metaphorically, that the frontal landscape of the interior of the city is shown in portraiture. Important photographs of famous people attracted crowds of onlookers who looked at the personages close at hand in the photograph; these were people they had only seen, if at all, from a distance in ceremonies and parades on grid-like streets. Financiers, politicians, groups of dignitaries and social adventurers, entertainers and businessmen could be produced in large-format pictures (two feet high) until the photographer André-Adolphe-Eugène Disdéri started to make mass portraits a few inches in size. These are the city builders.

Architects are city builders, too, and become celebrities. The architect Gregory Henriquez, the architect of the new Woodward's reconstruction, speaks about his vision and finds an archetype in the Woodward's development. His explanation makes the point of Althea Thauberger's "Carrall Street" and Walter Benjamin's "profane illumination" of architecture that celebrates the intoxicated raptures of city-building amid poverty:

> It is a public–private partnership in the best sense of the word. The public is representative of the public. We have a community advisory council involved in the design process. The City of Vancouver is taking a real leadership role. We also have enlightened developers who want to do the right thing. Together … you can create inclusive communities, which aren't ghettos. For Woodward's you won't have ghettos for the wealthy … You have a city where everyone shares a common ground while having their own space at the same time. Everyone is part of the same complex … that [is] a win–win for everyone. [11]

There's that word "community" again, emptied of any meaning. The total work of art is the total inclusive "community." No ghettos allowed.

VII

Settlement Street 1900

Who were the workers and tradesmen who made up this settlement society? Does Henrique's idealism and his sociology tell us enough about community governed by developers' and planners' "win–win" values and tell us enough about the "other" people I call Mercurians who can be identified around Carrall Street? These are invisible to the naked eye because they are types, stereotypes who don't live here or anywhere; but classes? Elites? In 1900, they were visible immigrants and adventurers and those in flight from persecution, or famine or unemployment, or wars or plagues, who left the Old World but carried it within them as strangers, then as creators of surplus, and then settled in the several square miles within the vicinity of Carrall Street: *farmers, carpenters, tinkers, domestic labourers, brewers, druggists, doctors, pharmacists, hatters, butchers, hunters, fishers, shoemakers, loggers, commercial travellers, pedlars, bakers, tailors, metalworkers, potters, soldiers, photographers, typesetters, printers, soldiers, brewers, blacksmiths, plasterers, storekeepers, chandlers, surveyors, police, miners, teamsters, coopers, carpenters, entertainers, accountants, fire brigadiers, engineers, "gentlemen," teachers, ministers, newspaper editors, bankers, speculators, and realtors.*

These people are not just "figures" or "fixtures": they are the bearers of culture who flee the old world and arrive in the city in order to remove the settlement mentality from the wooden sidewalks and build over it an urban worldly place. Beneath the wooden sidewalks and the landscape, Christos Dikeakos mapped the salmon streams under the streets by showing us the land's games. [12]

Buying and selling land begins immediately. It is the engine of the habitat that is dismembered piece by piece through both money exchange and cultural means like Territorial Education Acts and Indian Agents.

VIII

Hermes One-Way Street Interchange [13]

These are culture-shock troops for those outside their domains of the Nomads, Mobs, Crowds, Masses, Mercurians, which are the *homines rationalistici artificiales,* hybrids and composites which consist of service workers, those of chimerical nationality, strangers, intelligentsia, teachers, ministers, ex-soldiers, students, apprentices, who change jobs and become other than their pasts, exiles, who do not carry the national canons but begin to seed the cultural memory of regions and settlements with new combinations of culture; for example: insiders/outsiders, dropouts, prostitutes, dancers, actors, opium smokers, squatters, homeless vagrants, panhandlers, land clearers, musicians, spiritualists, promoters, anarchists, utopians, visionaries, mystics, actors; caricaturists show them as dangerous or comic or as just plain outsider-strangers; the culture begins to be built out of popular and traditional forms of entertainment and the crossover of literacy and the public world of shifting and leaking boundaries. The dominant British, Scottish, and German population controlled the public sphere of a rapidly growing population of over one hundred thousand by 1900. The Chinese, Japanese, Indian subcontinental peoples became the new foreign peoples displacing the pre-political pagans, the barbarians, the Indigenous Peoples, who lived by fishing, sea and land hunting, and whose houses and boats, receptacles for food, laws and alliances, languages and religions, Shamanism, and Potlatches could not be understood by the settlers. Simmel describes the "life-crisis" mentalities of the Europeans in the new Metropolises. The mental life of the cultured city dweller comes closer to the fears carried by the primal mentalities of those strangers the Indigenous Peoples displaced by urban growth; the European could not grasp the new "life crises" of the Indigenous Peoples whose own complex life-crisis rituals were displaced.

The transfer and transmission of collective memory from one civilization to another is the most difficult of all dramaturgical and theatrical processes framed by art and memory.

So, the installation recalls a life-crisis ritual in the way we might describe Beckett's plays. The "Carrall Street" production, then, is an art that takes up a kind of anthropology and ethnography because the artist no longer feels comfortable with a secure relationship to autonomous art. Art is extended to new subject matter and searches for reinforcement of the now as an event or performance. But the "moral injury" to the persons who are displaced onto the street comes along, too, as a phantom reality.

This disorientation brings one face to face with the distance and nearness and intellectual relativity associated with the money economy of the metropolis. Simmel calls this "the wave-like motion," that extends the metropolis "over a broader national or international area."[14] The ruins and pathos of attending to the transient nature of a city's landscape brings the "taste" or "feel" of a sharp sense of loss or disorientation – a shock to one's memory of another photograph or another city. Crossing borders is an example of culture shock. Coming to Carrall Street might be a form of culture shock for those who don't live there because the street camouflages those who do not share in this property-based, rights-based civil society that benefits the growing numbers of the few.[15] Private property determines who is a stranger and who is not and who stays today and tomorrow based on who owns the land.

Post culture shock: the city is a hunting ground, a place to scavenge impressions, food, clothing, and survival tools of both the tourist and the stranger to a neighbourhood. It is culture shock to be entertained by klieg lights that blot out the sky and point to the high view that dominates the enervated centre of uptown Vancouver. The city reproduces itself in the mirrored glass and light that might have shocked the viewer looking at photographs of the city. It might be comforting to wander into Carrall Street stagecraft, but the boundaries are the primitive edge of the experience of the strange affair of the Downtown Eastside and the symptomatic crisis of art and politics in the post-autonomous art age as it relates to Indigenous immiseration.[16] The result is "we," spectator-agent-counterfeiters of the new, become like the inhabitants of Samuel Beckett's *Footfalls*, or *Not I*. In the latter play, a mouth speaks and reduces those beggars, strangers, and pedlars among us to the "Not I," who are the simulacra of the Simmelian adventurers in the city, the exiles, homeless, wanderers of humanity. The sojourners become shoppers.

The ancient art of pedlars, who were also booksellers, and experts at colportage and itinerancy, may be the origin of the intelligentsia. Pedlars knew no borders. They lived by their wits and traded news and objects – a form of literacy transmission that cannot be seen in the "total work of art." The realm of the storekeeper and department store usurped this regime of pedlars. The pedlars, as Laurence Fontaine writes in his *History of Pedlars in Europe*, were scapegoats that the State, according to police documents, "used to ease the tensions between divided communities ... In return the pedlars exploited their marginal position which protected the freedom that was essential to their continuing wealth – or even just to their survival – and tricked their way out of all attempts to register their status, evaluate their fortunes, uncover their business connections or unravel their activities, leaving the historians battling with blank documents."[17] Carrall Street is a ruin of this devalued culture. Benjamin describes such questions as my "What happened to Vancouver?" as based in the "humiliating sobriety" that has lost the battle of living in the city "on the morning before a battle or after a victory."[18]

IX

Not a Detour: Being Outfitted for a "Topography of Terror" Walk; The Built World over the Hidden Street Scene

Architectural styles and forms contribute to the cultural memory of encroaching gentrification; it produces the security of construction that cannot reproduce the stately homes and public buildings that existed around the city before and after fires caused the reconstruction of cities and planning for growth, only to quickly cover over the land bulldozed and trucked into the outskirts. Modernity hides the past and creates normative (inevitable) approaches to history. Development transforms settlements into modern cities or "urban" enclaves. Development has made of Vancouver the city it now is – both myth and spectacle and yet a reality marked by the illusion of permanence. The city thrives after more than a century of being little more than a resource-based marketplace. All this promises to renew, revitalize, and reward those who live here and move here. Are there counter-myths?

Is there a counter–"myth of self-creation" about this city? Is it in fact a fictional city? It would seem that Althea Thauberger and a new generation of artists working on the city, including older and recent photographers, believe that new forms of dramaturgical theatricality can show the city as if a Situationist Guy Debord–inspired drama where the "collective drift," to use a Situationist International term, can outfit us with an inner resistance to one hundred years of capital development and land grabbing. The lower depths, the Trickster-Mercurian existences that are the hidden, not-so-invisible defences created within the city's "pathways" of consumerism and development, remain attractive as theatrical illusions.

Vancouver tries hard to be a spectacle which can be described by using Italo Calvino as my guide. I will follow Calvino, who writes: "the city … [that] repeats its life, identical, shifting up and down on its empty chessboard. The inhabitants repeat the same scenes, with actors changed; they repeat the same speeches with variously combined accents; they open up identical yawns. Alone, among the cities of empire, Eutropia remains, always the same. Mercury, god of the fickle, to whom the city is sacred, worked this ambiguous miracle." In the city "we do not know what is inside or outside." Our "eyelids," Calvino writes, are what separates the "wasteland covered with rubbish heaps, and the hanging garden of the Great Khan's palace." [19]

From caves and shrines and the adaptive forms of living that gave natural selection its name to cultures that survived, to villages and settlements, to sacred cities, to Renaissance urbanity, to cosmopolitan centres of European expansion – the city has become the most visible evidence of spectacle and masquerade and the home of the live readers and artists as the intelligentsia who look into the receptacles and holes where memory might glow. At the same time the city can be used as a symptom and weapon of the crisis of present-day art, because cities converge with popular art, mass communications, and institutions in decline. At a touching point in *Invisible Cities,* Calvino observes that those who arrive by sea, in contrast to those of us who arrive by land, discern in the "coastline's haze … the form of a camel's withers, an embroidered saddle with glittering fringe between two spotted humps … he [*sic*] knows it is a city, but he thinks of it as a camel … taking him away from the desert of the sea … Each city receives its form from the desert it opposes; and so the camel driver and the sailor see *Despina*, a border city between two deserts." [20]

Calvino's image of the camel and the sea forms an image of itself between fate and destiny, fate being the given land, and destiny what we do with it, making the built world. Calvino's image not only evokes the arrival of explorers, vagabonds, immigrants, and outcasts to inland dynasties like the Great Khan's, and the towns and cities of the Realms, it evokes the arrival of those who come to northern shores, the other shores, of the western part of the North American continent over land and from other seas, those who bring with them the modernity that has resulted in Vancouver as it exists today, and also tomorrow.

DOSSIER III – CHAPTER 3

Cultures of Market Terror: Nomadism and Nemesis at the Borders[21]

The reflection in speech relations among people, and their social hierarchy. The interrelations of speech units. The keen sense of one's own and someone else's speech life. The exceptional role of tone. The world of abuse and praise (and their derivatives: flattery, toadying, hypocrisy, humiliation, boorishness, caustic remarks, insinuation ... the erasure of boundaries between the terrible and the comical in images of folk culture (and to a certain degree in Gogol). Between the mediocre and the terrible, the ordinary and the miraculous, the small the grand.

—MIKHAIL BAKHTIN, "Notes Made in 1970–1971," *Speech Genres and Other Late Essays* (1979), trans. Vern W. McGee

Only with the experience of the loss of justice do we become aware of justice as such. It is with the loss of home that we become cognizant of home as such. Exile, then, is primordially an epistemic rupture in that which has been matter-of-course. The genuine experience of exile forever denies us the nostalgic return to our pre-exilic life since the experience of exile is the experience of our homebound essence in the loss of home.

—PEYMAN VAHABZADEH, *Exilic Meditations: Essays on a Displaced Life* (2012)

Néstor García Canclini illuminates the Mexican *mestizo* and peasant popular cultures by showing that the fate of popular culture lives and dissolves into capitalist market economies. Craft and fiesta rituals and artisanal works are responses to what I name "nomadic capitalism" that restructures nomadic lives through their individualized life experiences, the everyday life of communal experience. These experiences are created against the grain of the museum, or boutique culture in the metropolises. Bakhtin's writing on folk culture and the everyday speech discourses of parody and the comic-grotesque informs how I see the culture of nomads, exiles, and migrants. García Canclini is influenced by Antonio Gramsci. Global crossing of borders, lands, empires, and ecological damages of cultures already on the margins are the "inner borders" where boundaries are erased. Supranationalism replaces internationalism through the integration of the capitalist system of profit enhanced by the state planning that exists alongside the market system. Provinces and distant lands are the borderless worlds needed for expansion of agriculture, mining, resources, and markets. The intellectual on the road to class power is enlisted in this project: Appeal to efficiency, discipline, leadership, faith in work, mass production, and toil is made into dignified work for the good of the whole society. Here we encounter the antagonism of culture and intellectuals which represent external or independent knowledge, and other forms of collective imaginaries within modern art forms. The depiction of alternate realities means no one escapes the material needs over ideas. In short, "nomadism" as a form of culture touches what we call populism.

Nomadic migrants act out their hybrid values at the borders. I argue that the anthropological use of artisanal creations continues the European avant-garde's defence of popular arts as a struggle of the symbolic against the economic. García Canclini vindicates popular culture by arguing that "Cultural Studies" as an academically derived politics cannot alone transform social policy or political attitudes towards a critical, democratic lifeworld. We need to look more closely at the anarchistic-communalist basis of artisanal cultures in order to understand the ethical bases of individual responses that pervade nomadic, capitalist modernization. The commercial violation of communal norms of those who arrive at official borders as migrants and immigrants illuminates the internal unofficial boundaries where one might say lies a "natural history" of movements of peoples. [22] Peyman Vahabzadeh refers in *Exilic Meditations* to "the experience of our homebound essence in the loss of home." [23]

I

Nomads in the Market – Cultural Norms and Spreading Popular Culture

Néstor García Canclini's writing on popular culture and modernity is primarily available to English readers in North America in *Transforming Modernity: Popular Culture in Latin America*. [24] I extend and elaborate on his post-Gramscian perspective on what constitutes popular culture at the congested divide of North and South America.

This is the divide where culture and politics, artisanship and craft, language and literacies collide under the spell of capitalist rapid modernization. Incommensurable modes of production in Latin American cultures collide and are dispersed at the borders: peasant, communal, national corporations exist under the spell of the overwhelming global markets. Here is a cathartic traffic jam. Europe and Latin America meet, and radical culturists like García Canclini attempt to understand this "non-country." [25] Like many of his modernist predecessors, Brecht, Borges, Kafka, Bakhtin, and Paz, popular art and the artisan-created works and styles that were created by unnamed artisans fascinate García Canclini, especially as he knows there is no homogeneous art style that can eliminate the resistances that the artwork manifests through the individual as the only "viable agent of history ... [whom] one must recognize ... as the source of inexhaustible, ever-fresh spontaneity if one is to see him [*sic*] in the proper light." [26]

García Canclini creates a new border region between critical anthropology and the politics of culture. At the same time, his approach to popular culture is critical of the hidden assumptions about literacy and modernity, namely, whether the history of domination of oral, preliterate cultures by nationalist regimes can be revised by a simple affirmation of the popular culture. Romantic populism or academic scientism cannot disguise the prevailing class alienation and cultural liaisons with conservative nationalism that steals cultural property in order to appropriate the wealth of artisans and Indigenous Peoples. His approach to the use value of artisan styles and the organization of community does not rest solely in describing a generalized peasant economy and *mestizo* ritual celebrations. He shows how the singular "gesture of the producer as an individual," who introduces stylized effects in the work, also becomes alienated from the communal and the stereotypical. The work that accommodates itself to the national economy is no longer communally directed; it becomes an individual, expressive (speech) genre that is more like a grotesque gesture and alienated utterance as a moral category, than it is a statement about "ethnicity." [27]

This raises the question of a political basis for popular art, which has been on the cultural agendas in Western countries since the beginning of the twentieth century. Marxists and anarchists took on vanguardism's role in articulating the struggles between realism and popular art, and engaged art and high art. Engaged art, or partisan art, had a propagandistic, agitprop, and oppositional objective in Europe and Latin America. The adversary was contemplative or autonomous art. Ultimately, as a result of the Spanish Civil War, Stalinism, and the rise of fascism in Germany, Italy, and France, the role of folk art or popular art was reduced to a footnote of mass culture during the period after the war. The period of de-Stalinization and the Cold War gave the war between realism and peoples' art a faint, post-utopic odour of the mausoleum. This fascinating debate has been raised again, today; however in a different form. The question of an art of everyday life, studied by ethnographers and anthropologists and critical art historians, builds upon a continuous text of life and art that is caught between stagnation and development, monetary economies and forms of exchange based on solidarity and co-operation. In this spirit, García Canclini raises questions about artisanal culture that expresses everyday life through the making of artworks that are measured not by their use only, but by the meanings they express in their attempt to adapt to contemporary life. The ambiguities in the struggle of art and life are not solved, but illuminated. Thus, peasant and *mestizo* cultural artworks become paradigms of how we measure any critical adaptation to the terrors of the market. Art seen through *mestizo* culture cannot be reduced to the level of mere information for a field called "cultural studies" when the artist is illuminating the historical experience of memory and forgetting in the art of the people.[28] The relationship of urban and rural and culture and history shows what the cultural anthropologist V.J. Walter names "mutual immanence," where shared expressive space also has a utopian quality.[29]

The dichotomy that exists between utilitarian objects of art and the nomads' marketplace overdetermines objects of art. The explosive art styles that emerge along with a spreading mercantile economy become problematic when artisans are unwilling to talk about their work or what they know: they resist talk of their individuality precisely because they know that the speed of change drives the solitary and nomadic producers to adapt and accommodate to hybrid modern cultures.

This dialectic of accommodation asks us to become aware of the power of mass culture that lies in wait, disguising meanings and masking the desire to conceal that is at the basis of a capitalist commodification of culture. It is in this tradition of postmodernism, and against the background of what once was labelled "primitivism" or folk art, that García Canclini's study of popular art should be placed in an art history without names.

However, behind the culture of popularity, publicity, tourism, and commerce lurks the question of whether the critical intelligentsia in emerging economies in Latin America, which traditionally supports social movements, are themselves implicated in the dissolution of the ethnic into the national state?[30]

How we read the emerging social movements through the production, circulation, and consumption of craft-commodities was a salient feature of the European avant-garde movements and also belongs to the Latin American intellectual's lived historical experience. García Canclini is deeply aware of pre-Hispanic and *mestizo* cultures and "border narratives" as lived experiences that produce improvised art from conventions. In the first four parts of this commentary I want to defend García Canclini's approach, and then I want to indicate where turning to cultural studies as a framework for a critique of contemporary nomadic capitalism falls short of his expectations.

García Canclini approaches modernity through the hybrid styles that are the mark of mass culture: on the one side, there is technical reproduction and commodification of culture; on the other is the intellectual who wants to unmask the concealed meanings behind objects of art. He does not ignore the relationship of popular art to populism and utility, the "Brechtian" aspect of living at the class borders where identity is changed by crossing the street into a different culture of class. García Canclini speaks for the artisans whose works are bought and sold for reasons that have little to do with their autonomous creation. This turns the works of artisans into alienated objects. The detachment of artisanal works from the point of production is a double-sided alienation: the work is socially alienated, but so are the intellectuals and cultural apparatchiks of the dominant classes, who set the standards of judgment about art, and who long to understand the living cultural communities whose spontaneity is reflected in the reception of the art.

However, the alienation of the artisans themselves, who continue to search for a livelihood by using the conventions and styles familiar to their subjects, are constricted by their social circumstances. We might say that at this *cultural borderland* there is a "semiotic flood" that is waiting to be unleashed once the dammed-up artistic conventions are exposed to the world of commerce. In other words, the border is a leaking border.

This is one reason popular art is so attractive to anthropologists, because a handed-down art form appears to be art, not anti-art, and artisanal art can appear to be surrealist in the similar sense that surrealism played with the idea that art can become anti-art.

The partisan and democratically inclined intellectual is attracted to folk and popular art. In addition, the intellectual uses the "scientific" freedom of research to turn the works into new knowledge about intercultural relations. This is also a way to defend artisans from the neoliberal market economies that embed poverty, dependence, and misery among the Latin American artisan cultures. The irony is that the work of artisans is often treated as entertainment, as if it has no permanent value, and yet this work survives the deterioration of the social order while appearing to be both transitory and permanent, and yet appeals to the market. Entertainment, however, is a delivery system, too.

García Canclini argues that modern capitalism isolates the objects of production from the engine that forces the producer to assimilate into the culture of capitalist modernity. Capitalist modernity in turn colludes in this isolation by "unconsciously, with the dislocation and concealment carried out by the economic system ... separat[ing] production from circulation and both from consumption." Any analysis "of the changes in meaning as they pass from producer to consumer, and their interaction with the culture of the 'elites'" has to recognize that the system of commodification requires individualization of the craft – it becomes both "artistic" and decultured – in order to satisfy the demands of a boutique, globalized marketplace.[31] The individual object mirrors the lived nomadic life of the youths who migrate, leaving those who must "remain behind in the changeless villages."[32] Both the artistic object and the nomadic worker are doubly alienated. However, in order to "abrogate this choice between art and kitsch, we must vindicate popular culture, the most diverse products, and their most heterodox usages."[33]

By preferring to speak of culture broadly as a form of knowing that precedes institutional rationality, and instead of simply isolating popular art as a convention-imprisoned artifact, García Canclini uses the styles and conventions of popular art to open up the entire field of the politics of culture to a critique of the counterfeit and hybrid populism that informs our experience of mass culture that mixes bad art and good art.

In essence this provides us with a dynamic framework for identifying just what is "mass" about "mass culture": its role is to spread a developmental and technocratic ideal of the popular that decorates and sentimentalizes market capitalism. This creates a specifically "capitalist" art style which destroys memory, detaches creation from meaning, and imparts the aura of self-sufficiency and nomadic transferability to the life of the object. Popular culture becomes the ideology of mass culture, and ethnicity becomes one of the ways we can preserve national identity as ethnic identity.

For García Canclini, it is important to vindicate popular culture through cultural studies, which allows for the study and protection of the independence of Indigenous forms. The gigantic mistake is to divorce the economic and the symbolic. Put another way, art becomes invention and production, and is sold and sentimentalized just like the nomadic, "nameless" workers at the borders are sold and sentimentalized. Any solution that takes into account only one of these forces, the symbolic or economic, cannot resolve the conflicts inside of the cultural identity that needs to be constantly rejuvenated by the market in order to rescue popular cultures for profitability and from stagnation. [34] The very title of García Canclini's essay, "Narratives of the Border," mirrors this story that links making things to impoverishment.

So, to speak of borders in these times obliges us to speak of an alien popular culture. If it is true that the global market has created a Kafkaesque, market-like prison (see Borges's 1976 poem "Ein Traum"[35]) in which everything is a transaction in a transcultural global market, then popular culture cannot escape the evils which are the products of globalization. While the "ethnics" wage wars of territorial identity throughout the world, the domination of free trade increases the hold of sovereign states over other sovereign states, even over the heads of those engaged in territorial struggles, for example, Israel–Palestine, Bosnia–Serbia–Kosovo, Québec–English Canada, and others. Thus, finding a paradigm of an emancipatory popular culture, rather than an assimilationist one, allows García Canclini to understand how culture can become *an experientially alive force* for productive understanding that reveals the strengths of social organizations.

Clearly, as a social anthropologist, he is resigned to seeing modern culture in terms fated to express both symbolic and economic alienation. He asks whether, beneath his call for a communally based social policy, there is an adequate theory of community, which can account for, while witnessing, a new form of globalized romantic nationalism emerging throughout the domestication of the popular. Ethnicity becomes the ideology of the nation in the "reduction of the ethnic to the typical."[36] This idea is reflected in his central thesis in "Narratives of the Border": "To recuperate a polycentric perspective it is necessary to include intercultural tensions in the analysis of globalization." At the same time, paranoia in the wealthy northern states takes the form of despising all things big and powerful that at one time assisted in developing the autonomy of the person through welfare and civic-enlightenment ideals, enabling academics and artists to tour the world for examples of the grassroots-popular arts – "grass-pop"? – that appear to resist incorporation into the hegemonic state.

García Canclini refers to Marcos Ramírez Erre's double-headed Trojan Horse, a statue placed at the border of Mexico and the United States, which is emblematic of another reality, the "universal modified symbol." However, the statue is not "a work of national affirmation" but parodies borders and affirms border people. The question: Is the Trojan Horse an emblem of resigned passivity or a symbol of a future engagement with the political conditions at the border?

The popular seen in this way risks becoming a way of loving the systems we live in, as if the system could correct itself and, by becoming cross-cultural, humanize its motives. Because the popular expresses the desire to escape from spiritual conquest by dependency and acculturation to the market, it appears to be the universal culture we all long for. But this is a counterfeit version of resistance and escape. Is the typicality of objects merely picturesque? The typical has assimilated the threadbare social aspects of manual and intellectual labour that are the mark of work and production in global, urban worlds. Cultural studies as a discipline names and renames the popular, while at the same time new forms of romantic nationalism emerge behind the back of the popular through the coercive market.

An example of the idealization of the popular can be seen in the influence of Mikhail Bakhtin on Latin American cultural critics. Bakhtin supports a critique that explains how the cross-cultural, intersubjective relationships that occur in vernacular styles give us a clue to the way genres of the popular also inform the high-art modernists (Mexican muralists, for example). Bakhtin shows that popular genres reverse the border between vernacular language and a living ethnography or *semiosphere of culture* – what García Canclini names the "Chicanization" of Latin Americans [37] – and ultimately overdetermine the forms of culture inside of vernacular societies that cannot hope to escape the pressures of colonization. [38]

Cultural interaction releases surplus energy that shadows the oppressive totality taking place behind the back of liberal pluralism. However, the reconstruction of cross-cultural forms into "identity politics" perpetuates colonization by another name. Thus, García Canclini's work touches on the borders of anthropology and aesthetics. Alienation rises to the top of culture, symbolized in the terror of Erre's two-headed Trojan Horse, straddling the Mexican–US border. This comic-grotesque emblem of the Trojan Berlin Wall symbolizes both the nomad and the inner exile. This border-person lives both inside and outside the horse of culture. The border is corporate and impersonal.

Corporations have the right to challenge and displace national sovereignty. Neoliberalism in the US has increased the number of billionaires, reduced the minimum wage, privatized until McDonald's owns all the cows, while new forms of romantic nationalism emerge in the wake of the New Border Cold Wars. But the border is not an ecstatic fiesta of pleasure: it is the flight from death. [39] In the same way we internationalize incommensurable cultures, we mediate incommensurability through theories of popular culture that make everyday life into a place that is Beyond Liberalism. Here is a transcultural realm where the overwhelming nature of national sovereignty is mediated by the apparatus of commerce that colonizes weakened and emerging sovereign states. García Canclini's essay turns modernization on its side, but not on its head, in an effort to see the borders as places of doubleness, or "corporate borders."

In the US, corporations are now treated as persons that can legally process information and money behind the back of labour, and can be protected by sovereignty and the legal apparatus. This is one face of a neo-colonialism that looks deceptively like "polycentrism," but is really more like the dark side of the double movement of globalization. While it weakens borders for trade, there is a complementary field of forces that exports people to work "elsewhere" in a remittance culture that turns labour into products and the circulation of people into other "borderlands."

In an immigrant society like the United States and Canada, where a large percentage of the border immigrants are inhabitants of both European and non-European descent, the existence of incommensurable cultural borders and the hybrid values that emerge from face-to-face encounters is a reality that will not go away. Capitalist modernization does not separate "modernity" from capitalism but hides modernity as a terror-filled separation of material, fragmented, specialized production of cultural styles, in which the loss of economic ownership is embedded in the ecstasies of capital expansion. García Canclini softens the representation of the "border" as a threshold filled with distanced memories and displacements of the economic and symbolic. If this is an imaginary border for most immigrants, then where is the reality of the border that has created the pariahs falling into the abyss between past and future?

The current debates about popular culture try to answer this question by isolating autonomous artistic culture from residues of folk, mass, and administered culture. Yet, in a culture based on commodities, this effort to distinguish mass culture from an authentic culture is fated to reveal the inner contradictions of modernity: the confusion over whether popular culture is the same as mass culture, or whether we can actually define "mass culture" as a counterfeit culture mediated by groups, crowds, mobs, audiences, or classes. Capitalist mass modernity attempts to disguise a traditional normative culture that is rooted in hidden class power but is then mediated by symbols of national identity.

We are witnessing a resurgence of interest in borders and popular culture that has not happened since the beginning of the twentieth century in Europe when the dispersions of the class-cultures of the previous century created a frenzy of centralization of national identities around territories whose boundaries were ultimately settled by war and whose borders disguised historical cultures. We can remember that this is the subject of Kafka's tale "The Great Wall of China," Conrad's *Heart of Darkness*, and other masterpieces that described the uprooting and dispersion of peoples. Today we see just one of the effects of this dispersal of local cultures in the failure of the West to understand how and why the once-dominant Arab civilization is now – from the point of view of the West – a "lost" culture. In turn-of-the-century theories of historical decline, decadence and devolution of culture ran into utopic modernism's ideal of progress represented in the vividly regenerative art movements of techno-futurism, cubism, surrealism, and muralism. These movements assimilated the artisan cultures of agrarian and craft peoples for the purposes of industrial and interior design and decoration of façades of buildings, furniture, etc.

This fusing of cultures produced what we call modernism. For example, the primitive/civilized polarity was deeply internalized into attitudes towards the popular and appears in particular in the way photography was used both as a tool to document everyday surfaces and to expose the hidden traces of history. Today we are seeing the same exaggerated faith in technical renewal and cultural regeneration, but the strains of hope are sung to a different arrangement than at the beginning of the twentieth century. Today, behind the doors of the board rooms, we know that a "cynical" false consciousness is in reality a synonym for an "enlightened" false consciousness of depressed, embattled tycoons. [40]

The corporate sector and the private sector are merged into a battle against welfare-state entitlements in the northern states, while, in the southern hemisphere, bourgeois national identities are locked into multiple cultural traumas over the export industry of crime, drugs, and violence. The borderland dreams of the future are stencilled over with millennial fantasies that imagine that Democratic Vitalism will end history, although not in something like the utopic socialism of the nineteenth century, which mirrored the artisanal *Gemeinschaft* (community) of labour in the service of solidarity. Today we face the apotheosis of the commodity into what García Canclini calls "transnational communities of consumers."

II

García Canclini's Dilemma and Our Dilemma

García Canclini's dilemma is to explain how Latin American societies are composed of the dual legacy of pre-state societies that had some form of self-government and local associational communications and bonding with the conflicting, morale-depleting institutions that are set up by centralizing states. He knows that simply to assert that human beings live in groups is a banal commonplace, hardly worth uttering. That humans are subjects, and that subjects are ethically involved individuals who are persons, is more complicated, but also a commonplace. What is *not* a commonplace is the self-questioning and internalization of mass culture into something like an autonomous culture that has become the object of study in Latin America right at the moment when communities are weakened and when manufacturing from the north invades.

The communities where artistic problems are worked out, negotiated, remembered, and recreated have themselves become inner-border regions.

The border that separates a culture of voluntary artisanship from commodity cultures is saturated with the demands of national identity; the will to make art is dominated by the aura of shame and the economic necessity to conform. The idea of the formation of any solidarity as the essence of the public sphere has been fragmented into a Kafkaesque purgatory where publicity, tourism, propaganda, and audience manipulation mould feelings and desires. In the north, the most familiar form of public coercion has always been the war-making rhetoric and political propaganda common to secularizing nation states; but today the dissemination of popular art through all avenues of television and film reveals the capitalist hunger to assimilate others and asks whether this can stop at the borders.

Jürgen Habermas referred to this transformation of publics into the capitalist unification of the public and private. For Habermas, transformation occurs through a combination of "sentimentality towards persons and corresponding cynicism towards institutions," which curtails "the subjective capacity for rational criticism of public authority." This reinforces García Canclini's observations about the transformations of artisanship within the Latin American public sphere into cultural consumption among the highest urbanized, upwardly mobile status groups in need of cultural power and legitimation.[41]

If Erre's double-headed horse means anything, it should be seen as a grotesque hybrid monster – a Goyaesque, disorderly creature. Where Habermas emphasizes how the propertied intelligentsia forms the basis of an apolitical, pseudo-public sphere by first separating and then merging the private and public, García Canclini emphasizes how landless peasants and Indigenous peoples must find alternative forms of subsistence in order to flourish in a global marketplace by making their passage from propertylessness to wage-labour through participation in a market that has disintegrated their past communal affiliations and symbolic repertoires.

III

From Nomadism to Homelessness

Nomads are at home everywhere. Strangers may be as well. But the exile is at home elsewhere in an imaginary world. Or so it seems. We theorize in an affirmative way about the hegemony of popular art by using the latest trends that celebrate popular culture as a homeland for displaced migrants or intellectuals at odds with nationalism and capitalism.

García Canclini's position has difficulty answering how the effects of globalization create homelessness and unemployment. It is no wonder, then, that it is easier to turn to the study of popular culture, as if there were everywhere in Indigenous forms a paradigm for a new populistic-public participation in politics. This raises the questions: to what extent does popular culture exhaust the utopian potential of the political? And to what extent is communal culture also communitarian and able to withstand the powers of globalization? This is the question of our attitude towards the utopian, which may have a bad name.

García Canclini's utopian outlook calls for a form of cultural fellow-travelling and partisanship for art from below. He argues for methods of archival study to locate oral histories, examination of vernacular languages and conventions that parody and imitate.

The underlying *ethic* is the argument for the recognition and respect deserved of those cultures made up of women and children and nomadic workers, and as well to affirm the critical spirit of the declassed, organic, village intellectuals who are trying to interpret the cultures of the village to fragmented audiences in the cities. [42]

Behind market populism is the dream of a more political popular culture: a socialism that does not have the aura of the museum or the corporate boardroom. There is always the risk that we idealize ethnic cultures as if they were actually rooted in national social formations. Yet, it would appear that no cold sovereign nation can exist without this warm ethnic stream as a form of both the exilic and the utopic.

We noted that García Canclini's critique of aesthetic typicality is also a major part of his perspective. He sees how dangerous it is to conclude that Indigenous artisanal productions are simply conventions typical of the past. He objects to a "History" turned into a simulated memory of the past. Preservation of typicalities covers up amnesia and submerges the fragility of unforgiving memory into a history of conventions. At the same time, history is seen as the struggle with collective memory and iconic conventions that prevent us from idealizing popular cultures as spontaneous cultures. This is one of the lessons of *Transforming Modernity*, where García Canclini shows that Indigenous artisanship parodies the power of the commodity and irreverently uses the spirit of commodities to produce artifacts that are demonic transactions with the impersonal consumers, symbolized best by the silence of the objects in the modern supermarket, which has replaced the noise of the marketplace where seller and buyer communicate freely. [43] Erre's Trojan Horse looks towards both the kitsch of the north and south, and illuminates the regressive element in culture. Yet, the regressive element in kitsch also acts as a utopic element in the sense of Adorno's gloomy, yet strangely elegiac and positive, statement that "the positive element of kitsch lies in the fact that it sets free for a moment the glimmering realization that you have wasted your life." [44]

The translucently shifting marketplace commodities take on a life of their own as they float from manufactured object to consumption, and then to a second life in which they are purged of their use value by being transferred from one social context to another, accompanied by the boom box or by kitsch music. The commodity is akin to nomadic workers: both take on a life of their own as *migrating objects* shuttling between museum, market, and boutique. Nomadic existence lies inside the life of the illusory object.

We know that the artistic movements of the twentieth century show us that this doubleness of mystification has two sides. On the one hand, there is the romance with "fiesta culture," in which the celebration of making autonomous objects conflates aesthetic culture with material culture. On the other hand, the "national" artifacts of popular culture parody the collection mentality at the root of any genuine aesthetic culture; but where autonomous art consciously separates itself from the political in order to challenge the society that would limit, if it could, art's didactic and revolutionary qualities, and yet looks at the sources of its spirit in experience, popular art escapes the social and migrates to us as entertainment, market goods, or museum artifacts.

IV

Border Persons Are the Nemesis of Culture

We might say that the formation of civil society in Latin America is just as typical of the most progressive aspect of the "northern" societies' modernist project; this is not theorized in García

Canclini and does not seem to interest him. Instead he focuses on popular art in a manner reminiscent of anarchists who register communal decline through the objects of popular art mocking the ideological goods peddled by the dominant – in this case Christian and capitalist, culture. The traumas of urbanization are mirrored in the self-defeating nature of hybrid cultures. Carnivalized forms of culture are absorbed into mass culture as spectacles that do not reveal the communal protections that underlie the economies of the security-based institutions of villages and towns. The cultural studies, paragons of hybridism, that want to make "resistance" the unexamined norm of popular culture, not only ignore that hybrids do not produce new offspring but ignore that a by-product of hybridization in cultures of modernity is the excavation of the interior of the individual. The individual is overwhelmed when the forms of recognition are withdrawn from intersubjective experience that might lead to political awareness: naïveté becomes a virtue. Nomads, whether immigrants or exiles, live at the leaking boundaries of their many-sided lives.

What remains is also a discarded spirit of place. Human-animals "naively" roam the world like dogs in libraries sniffing the once-living texts, possibly also raising a leg to urinate on the monuments at the borders. The Kafkaesque, post-everything world has left a political-theoretical vacuum filled with various cultures of pseudo-belonging. The border is also a boundary where the deep intrasubjective worlds of the person-in-the-making is also the traumatic border of modernist aesthetics described by the romantic anti-capitalist cultural critiques of an Ortega y Gasset, a Borges, a García Márquez, or a Paz. An earlier discourse for a cultural criticism that sought a legitimate basis for a liberal civil society based *on already existing multiculturalism* in the trading-industrial worlds may be very different from that impure – hybrid – form of it which exists in the Mexican world that García Canclini describes.

We can argue for the differences in the many-sided worlds by reminding ourselves that *modernism was never pure,* was never politically settled: it was essentially a cultural-aesthetic movement based in art and literary nomadism, transitory, learning about hybrid cultures. Modernism explored both the pathological and utopic dimensions of the mass age in which societies appeared to fall apart, although the traditional elements appeared to remain intact insofar as they were useful shields against social decay.

In the world of capitalist *modernity*, traditional elements are on the move, can be trashed and sold, can end up in boutiques or in murals. In many of Borges's parables, for example, he describes the case for a "gaucho-esque" form of nationalism for Argentina, where the individual is inside and outside the artificial constructions of culture. Anthropology knows that culture was against individuals. Images of social deterioration appear in Borges as parables of hope for the hopeless, as the not-yet, through which we see glimpses of a second nature to be found only in books, or more accurately in pieces of books – books as the end of books in history, because books become symbolic of the erosion of the self by the traumatic forces of European historical time. The lesson of Borges lies in his Argentinian outsiderness and European insiderness. This is the border where the forces that create self-destruction are conditioned in the nameless and territory-less places, places of admonition to anyone who claims authority over the utopic imaginary of escaping into a better life.

The kind of person I see trapped in García Canclini's vision of the border narrative must essentially be framed as a critical model similar to an anarcho-aesthetic person, not a shadowy liberalistic individual. This is a dropout person who realizes that by being formed in the image of the group, entry into the phantasmagoric world of modernity is assured. This anarchist type lives in the world as an immigrant-migrant-nomad who understands that one may become less than human, and that this may happen very quickly. The speed of change is a function of being globalized. The border person is the anarchistic "nemesis" to culture and national identity.

García Canclini does not fully explain how the cultural authority of institutions is transferred to the cultural authority of the border, the nomadic masses. He doesn't have to. If hegemony is the domination of cultural reproduction over the masses, it cannot be understood that it arises outside of the circulation of culture that is independent of capital. On the other hand, modern hegemony functions best when dominant groups coerce consent *without* using obvious propaganda or techniques of persuasion that can be recognized as coercive. Civil society requires the consent of the governed, but it also requires that the organic intellectual mediates between institutions and symbolic systems, between art and the lifeworld. But art-minded intellectuals in Latin America, like García Canclini, Paz, or Borges, perhaps articulate a utopic communitarian aesthetic. This aesthetic works against the millennial conditioning of time characteristic of both Christian religious ideals and ideals of progress which create an aura of redemption. Culture will win this game. A communitarian-rich civil society would look different from the ones that are dependent on legality and universalistic norms established by liberal institutions whose economic motives dominate and control artisanal productions.

The person who is formed out of the grotesque social matrix of borders and markets is living out what the Greeks called "nemesis," the irrational principle in culture. Nemesis, the goddess at the border of the consciousness of animal-man-culture, is embodied in the works of the dispossessed artisans who face the "nemesis" of irrational death, which, as García Canclini shows, is integrated into fiesta culture itself. Fiesta culture is a way of coming to terms with the violence of social death and the loss of faith in traditional beliefs. Death is the next-to-nothing-poverty that drives the nomad from forms of social disintegration and hopelessness into the borders where immigration laws are used to protect the labour market in the home countries. Nomads must risk the consequences. We should see the goddess Nemesis as a dialectical goddess of popular culture who shows us the *pathos* of the artisan culture that attempts to order the market, both around resentment at the loss of community and hope for social justice. The artisanal culture becomes a paradigm for conscience and indignation, anger at what is unjust, and righteous anger towards borders themselves: this paradigm allows one to express one's sense of failure at becoming totally acculturated. [45]

For García Canclini this alienated artisan culture is represented through an iconic world of conventions, pastiches of identities, and as a still photograph for the soon-to-be assimilated culture of solitary communities into the phantasmagoria of the market, where exchange value is so commodified that no single commodity can express the totality of culture. A souvenir made by an artisan is a reminder of what can be done by others, of what one makes oneself and leaves behind. But nostalgia for the past also becomes the philistinism of the present. What for modern sociology was the tragedy of culture is today tragic for the persons living in a dying communal culture, which in our capitalist modernity invites us to send those persons who do not belong to the trash heap along with the exhausted conventions of popular culture.

Exile is about leaving home; emigration is remembrance of home, and "no return" means living with an endless departure and arrival of the memory of "an original injustice." Peyman Vahabzadeh writes:

> If exile is expulsion from the realm of justice – which is utterly an injustice – then the realm beyond the existing borders is an expansive realm which the exile travels in search of a lost justice. But that is not possible unless injustice first reveals itself in an epistemic way ... life in complete justice is needless of knowledge, of an awareness of the sovereign's borders and finally of self-consciousness. [46]

V

From Popular Culture as Social Criticism to an Anarchist Ethics

I want to turn to what I believe is a blind spot in García Canclini's hopefulness about cultural studies: how to theorize within a bad, global culture about individuals who are suffering moral injuries in their everyday lives. García Canclini writes:

> In order to abrogate this choice between art and kitsch, we must vindicate popular culture, the most diverse products, and their most heterodox usages. I am not suggesting an indiscriminate aesthetic vindication, like populism ... What I mean is a scientific and political vindication, abolishing the criteria for inclusion imposed by art histories, aesthetic doctrines, and folklore, opening those disciplines to a critical, unbiased analysis of popular tastes and uses according to their representativity and social value. [47]

If imperialism and colonialism formed capitalist modernity, how can the stable institutional cultural forms of a village economy recreate the various emancipatory and counter-hegemonic responses to a market form of colonialism? García Canclini hopes that cultural studies will lead to a postcolonial model of resistance to both kitsch and populism. His problem: How do we get out of capital-C Culture without falling into academic versions of popular culture?

Postmodernism in its deconstructive phase does not necessarily lead to socialism or communitarianism or anarchism, although in Latin America anarcho-communitarian impulses have historical roots that García Canclini approaches. García Canclini takes a more academic approach, concerned more with migrant society than with the effects that loss of home has on the individual; yet his approach to cultural policies pays attention to critical participation in society by artisans. In anthropology, this is viewed as an attempt to replace the historical person with the term "the subject position." However, when theory moves from person or individual to "subject position," theory risks reifying the individual by ignoring the person-in-the-making who has been traumatized by moving from a class culture to a mass culture. In a world where boundaries leak and persons are rendered into fragments, the "subject" atrophies in the face of the laws of the state-owned citizenship machines of the political boundaries and borders of multiculturalism as antidote to the "exilic rupture … decisive for the emigrant."[48]

Borders are flooded with new people but are quickly plugged up. The academy intellectual who believes in the virtues of popular culture as a social movement has moved modernism's critique of mass culture aside, censoring how modernism defended the authenticity of the person who was living at the borders of culture and society. Inserted here are the politics and ideology of multiculturalism on the premise of the "absolute foreigner."[49]

If borders are now controlled by corporate national states that can "organize, process, store, retrieve, and disseminate information,"[50] these borders not only entrench corporations as legal entities simulating the corporate "citizen" as a person with rights, but extinguish the difference between corporations and historical persons who carry memories and make value through their experiences that carry their nomadism into new territories. The ideal "neo-person" of our postmodern capitalism is the one who creates wealth and assimilates information at a fast-enough pace to live with and for the system. However, the multiple selves who carry several histories to the borders of the United States, Mexico, and Canada give liberal, civil society spasms because these selves may not be adaptable to the neo-nationalist and neo-global movement of trade, where their value on the labour market is determined by their capacity to accept being poor. Of course the border people are not completely unlike the classic generations of proletarian and immigrants and exiles, but now their emancipation from labour servitude and impoverished villages can only be gained if they become part of the labour economy that is itself unstable, and whose powers are mediated by a society that is unaware of its own assumptions that lie behind the spell of consumption and consumerism. Thus, to work is one thing, but to plug up the holes in the market economy, as immigrants have always done, is another; only now there is an endemic distrust of the forms of society and the emotional reality internal to the reality of being a social being. The prevailing identity machine is more powerful than ever.

One of the classic, modernist critiques of culture as a market prison stems from the Weberian and Kierkegaardian legacy of Theodor W. Adorno's sociology. Adorno did not deny that culture was the place of crossroads, boundaries, emergences, intrasubjective purposefulness, trust, familiarity, and frankness that allowed us to establish a sense of place and direct face-to-face speaking in history and memory. The passionate struggle to climb over imposed moral boundaries and cultural self-personifications marks Adorno's attitude towards pseudo-culture, in which the entire society stands under the law of exchange, of the "like for like" of calculations, which leave no remainder, and in which experience, like reason itself, is liquidated as a kind of irrational element.[51]

Adorno's critique of the false autonomy of the modern economic human also defends a concept of the popular: the person who would not be affected by propaganda, state-owned symbolism, and museum culture that collects the expressions of racialized peoples and turns the alliance of culture and leisure time into a humanly negative place distant from everyday life.

García Canclini shares this idea that the "popular" is a fragile condition not defined by its origin, but by its use.[52] This is the Kantian-ethical, anarcho-autonomous person, who, when faced with the nemesis of culture, can only turn back to an ethics based on societally motivated norms, which are internally felt to be social emotions. This raises the spectre of the double bind of culture against the individual, also described in the work of

Pierre Bourdieu, who refuses, along with Adorno, to ascribe to the masses any form of resistance, precisely because the pseudo-culture has hired artists and managers to direct the education of the senses and to depoliticize the popular. The popular is a fragile zone of suffering.

Modernism as a cultural movement in Latin America has historically intersected with discussions of rituals as "reifications" of labour and labour as a category of expression of the popular. In García Márquez's novels, death and moral injury inflicted by church, state, and commerce are endemic. Social terror occurs when communal obligations for others vanishes. This critique leads us to ways to measure plebeian and Indigenous people's histories as a confrontation of memory with standardization – the deathly amnesia of culture industries where coercive behaviours, magical systems, centralizing and marginalizing forces in mass societies enforce needs and desires. Are intellectuals complicit in the neo-colonial management of Indigenous cultures and labouring cultures?

Sociability, consociation, trust, living at a distance from power, concern about means instead of ends, montagist and colportagist techniques of displaying and witnessing life narratives, the return to an awareness of the performative modes of self-creation that intuitively precede the legal and civil ones, all are clearly on the agenda in the recent surge of immigrants to the borders and cities of rich northern nations in the Americas and Europe with long histories of local settlement and service industries.

Here, rights-based race theories, multiculturalism, and post-colonial social movements vie with one another for the space left by the retreat of capitalism from the modernist vision, which was to understand the moral norms that were adequate to the humanizing needs of the person-in-the-making and to remove the "protective coloration" or camouflage that covers the individual.

What kind of "anarchism" can be suggested by this person-in-the-making? Is it simply a more liberal version of the asocial, self-interested individual? I cannot pursue this difficult question here, but one question still stands: whether García Canclini faces the question of the individual closely enough in the profit-loss schema of modern culture in terms of his call for a new "task for cultural studies ... to reformulate the stories of globalization and Americanization by incorporating the complexity and the ambiguity of contradictions, the fragile mobility of borders" ("Narratives of the Border"). [53] The same care which cultural critics devote to the objects of popular culture can also be applied to the normatively controlled realizations of the self as legal and civil beings on the road to becoming "persons." Legal and civil values – often pejoratively called "humanist" or "enlightened" – must be extended to understanding the commonly shared values and intersubjective lives that allow one to understand the incorrigibly irreplaceable "me" as a hegemonic construction of others, who are like me but are not me.

This intersubjective theory of moral recognition has been framed by the Frankfurt philosopher Axel Honneth, who comes quite close, although unwittingly perhaps, to an anarchist theory of values. He argues: "The extent to which the social integration of societies is normatively dependent on a shared conception of the good life is a question that lies at the centre of the debates between liberalism and communitarianism." [54] Here is another new political border, where the autonomous "person" recognizes others as persons with histories and pasts and is held to be communally liable for others, *and* for worlds that may be as much like ours as they are unlike their own. This form of recognition occurs *inside* the communal order that preserves the "utopic" time of progress against capitalist forms of regression. García Canclini's border looks as though he expects that the future will be based on a rights-based framework; yet it is without an obvious politics, except the one that liberates the individual from the "shame" of being homeless and from enduring the *pathos* internal to the tragedy of modern culture with memories of injustice and no return: memory's children.

Borges's short poem "Ein Traum" ("A dream") could well have served as postscript to this chapter, and as counterpart to Erre's two-headed horse. The horse exists in frozen border time, just as Borges poem exists in alienated Kafka parable-time. Each head of the horse is philosophically resigned to the "border"; the Trojan Horse heads seem contained and passive and yet are combative. They may be seen as disruptive or reactionary, if one hates their anarchist isolation, about how to remember injustice in a progressive, satirical manner, because their heads test the limits of the illicit nomad. To grasp this, the ethnographic spirit of Borges's "gaucho" anarchism must be felt. [55]

The "she" in Borges's poem ("She was Kafka's companion") may be the female-nation who seeks to become a culture-nation by incorporating the voices of the popular as the self-justifying idea of the group, as an unhomely, uncanny collective of no-names. The new Nation is the reality of both pre-state conviviality and the post-state fear of conformity that comes into being when the group becomes dependent on the state and must fight for its integrity or flee to the borders.

The pre-state group protects against the violence inherent in the state's anger towards all fugitives from the group: the immigrants and border jumpers. The State asks: "Who makes up this group?" But wait: "I determine that!" says the State. So we ask: Is the group at the border made up of exiles, displaced and unemployed migrants, feudal artisans, itinerant professionals, or simply gatherers, lovers, dropouts, and poets who form a public world around the debris of the commodities piled at the borders of powerful sovereign states where the nomads cross and recross?

DOSSIER III – CHAPTER 4

Geological Poetics: A Triptych for Kladno and the Similkameen Valley[56]

I

The Continental Drift

> It was the kind of horse they have in mines – he must have worked underground somewhere because his eyes were so beautiful, the kind I would see in stokers and people who worked in artificial light all day or in the light of safety lamps and emerged from the pit or the furnace room to look up at the beautiful sky, because to such eyes all skies are beautiful.
>
> —BOHUMIL HRABAL, *I Served the King of England* ([1971] 1985), trans. Paul Wilson

The artistic illumination of the continental landscapes of the Middle and Far West on the continent I live on came of age historically when artists began to show the ruins and excavations of geological forces that seemed to have a life of their own. The images themselves are archaic residues, yet are modern in the way they looked at the world of form and eliminated the image of the persons who inhabited the land of such monumental scale. The inanimate landscape became alive due to the chemical processes of photography.

Robert Smithson's anti-lyrical earthworks came later and were an answer to lyrical photographers like Ansel Adams, Edward Weston, and Minor White. Theirs was a terrible beauty, purged of anthropomorphic invasions. They did not show the *geological poetic* of the landscape being invaded by the mining industries with their inner triptych of Pioneering, Prospecting, and Refining the glacially pressurized rocks that could be found by ferocious digging, first by hand and then by hydraulic and diesel machines. *They did not accuse.* Their lyrical and beautiful images did not show the moment when the purification of the metallic ores underground in nature had been put on trial by the mythical powers of industry in order to force the physical resources of modernism to work.

Mining is not often seen as a space-time chronotope. As a geological poetic it is the loophole in modernism's attempt to define itself as progressive development. Because of its downward transcendence, mining, excavation, and ferocious digging are the negative transcendence of modernism's utopian hopes to avoid the disaster of being left behind. Along with the devastation of the forests, mining-polluted waterways, left-over chemicals and cyanide poison that gave wealth to the many who lived in the far-flung cities like Vienna, London, Berlin, New York, Chicago, and now to the stable and emerging metropolises of today's narcissistic cities. We worship the skylines, and the higher the high view, the more expensive the property. Even today, in my homeland, Canadian mining industries flourish in Chile, Mexico, Argentina, the United States, Burma, and Peru: gold, copper, bismuth, zinc, heavy metals, uranium, and *always* the tailings. From the Baia Mare mine in Romania to mining accidents in Sweden, China, Peru, and Papua New Guinea, modernism continues to excavate and drain tailings into rivers. In the neocolonial worlds of Africa and subcontinents and islands south of Asia, the "tailings" of money continue to produce dependence on the outside world. Hrabal's almost blind, wide-eyed horses that haul the ore no longer emerge from mines, but we the inhabitants of the world live next to the urban landfills, which contain the debris of the always still-useful metals. Modernism recycles itself.

II

Where is Hieronymus Bosch or Caspar David Friedrich?

Someone will strike a match made with the phosphorous of my body.

—BOHUMIL HRABAL, *I Served the King of England* ([1971] 1985), *trans.* Paul Wilson

In the US and Canada, the traces of modernism are the last utopia of progress. The pioneer mining towns have become vacant. This gives us an image of the past and future and allows the New World a sense of history creating itself. There had been history of the here and now, but now we look with nostalgia at the remains: lost towns, ghost towns, degraded and left-over machinery, piles of dirt, burned-down towns, nomadic peoples still hanging on, often in trailer parks. The European ancestral landscape with its inbuilt ruins of castles, fortresses, monuments, walled cities, ruins of towns, geo-morphemic settlements is not the landscape in the New World.

Historically, we come of age only as juveniles. We situate ourselves in the landscape in regard to the ruins of farms, mining towns, the broken fences of once-surveyed land. Land is always for sale here. The saturnine pathos-ruins of the degraded and humiliated industrial cityscapes where industries once thrived, typically worked by European or Asian immigrants, are left standing. In the rural outlying regions, we build "industrial parks." In the west of this continent where the towns were founded by mining prospectors, hordes of gold and silver seekers sold their claims and moved on; then the combines of railroad and town-builders came together to found smelters, clinics, theatres, hotels – and the lung diseases that were researched and cared for often by company doctors who came from Toronto medical centres to do research.

Today many of these formerly prosperous towns are gone. They lived on rivers. The landscape barely remembers them. Or people live there in the shadows of poverty – the Harlan Counties of West Virginia and Appalachias of the soul. In my immediate vicinity of British Columbia, the nearly ghostly towns of an eroded past: Cumberland, Britannia, Hedley, Greenwood, Sandon, Lemon Creek – many were once among the largest copper, silver, or gold-producing mines of the world. Copper prices decline after wars. Gold is hammered down into the interior of the all-consuming desire of the measureless economy. The smelter at Trail, BC, is still producing, and as in the European New-Old world the corporation (Canadian Pacific) family owns the mines and smelters. Why not conjecture that the origins of modernism that lie in this sense of impending degradation came of age in the paintings of Hieronymus Bosch?

Bosch was the first landscape painter to understand that there was a *geologic unconscious*. The meaning of "conflagration" in the burning landscapes shines on all the inhabitants of a hellishly divine countryside in northern Europe. White disaster. His iconography illuminates the terror we live in as "nature-bound man," in our fright at the en-caved inwardness we live with. Not until much later in modernism does this inwardness become visible in the digging, excavation of the surfaces, the skins of life adulterated by the chemical affinities of objects for other objects, transmutation, emulsions, intervention of the hand and eye into the intuitive inscape and outscape of Bosch's hermetic view of the world: his eschatology.

Bosch begins the journey underground that mines the geological poetic and brings the everyday to the surface. I thought of his works of negative transcendence when I walked through the ruins of smelters in Kladno, Czech Republic. I thought: What would Bosch have done with this scene of vagabond students and teachers walking through this iron machinery that encloses us as if we were hermit crabs left over from some disaster?

I wandered in the ruins of Kladno's steel mills as if walking into Goya's or Bosch's saturnine ruins. I walked up and down in one simultaneous direction, like Bosch's landscapes, which were not only paintings with the aura of religious iconography, but were also knowledge maps – epistemological excavations – of industrial, agricultural, hermetic, fleshly engravings, astrological signs, and religious epiphanies. Moments of happiness occur, however, in the comic ruins of desire, the anarchistic sense of a judgment over what we deserve when all this falls apart. Then there is the fiery landscape we see when we emerge from the mined-out, exhausted caves whose shadows come from inside of us that we carry when we leave them. The comic subverts the making of things into sheer abundance that become scrap, surplus, unrecyclable batteries that power our prosthetic commodities that have become extensions of ourselves.

We emerge from the smelters, like Bohumil Hrabal's blind horse in his novel *I Served the King of England*, with widened eyes, touched by the extreme labour of the constant repetition of excavation, digging, shoring up, and looking upward like the miners with our necks straining towards the wet walls of civilization's stones – the wet walls of the mines dripping with sediment and water, and then trucking out the surplus stones that will be made into objects, large and small, not yet polished and shining full of light. We are as much the ornaments of the process as the objects are the ornaments of the masses. [57]

There is no adequate language for the iconography of the light that is contained inside of these rocks that children collect and label. When Bosch sees the universe as a transparent ball of glass, he has discovered the very non-conscious itself: the seamlessness of the inside–outside of yet-to-become-conscious geologic time. The "seams" of the mines lead further and further into the earth until they play out and we lose the image of the world. The unconscious must once again become that ball of glass where we see outside of the images of terrestrial events that are inside of us, un-mined. Inside the mines of the fires of fierce work we imagine how to melt the stones into the worldly place which watches us in anticipation of the collecting practices that bring surplus wealth. The eyes watch and grope for an image of the future. The future is only heard, not seen. [58]

One crazed statistician calculated that, had the seven million tons of aluminum cans in the ten-year period between 1990 and 2000 been recycled, they would have produced enough aluminum to make 316,000 Boeing 737 airplanes. This was twenty-five times larger than the worldwide commercial fleets at the time. [59] So Bosch predicts how crazy statisticians really are. Numbers are the infinite taxonomy.

III

The Alchemical Tailings of Cultural Objects

I wanted to be a world-citizen after death, with one part of me going down the Vltava into the Labe and on into the North Sea, and the other half via the Danube into the Black Sea and eventually into the Atlantic Ocean.

—BOHUMIL HRABAL, *I Served the King of England* ([1971] 1985), trans. Paul Wilson

Yet the same unearthed materials also create the musical instruments – the harp, the organ, the mandolins – that dig into our inner chambers in some beautiful act of pure vengeance against taking too lightly the way we devour the earth. Perhaps Bosch in his Flemish landscape lived near mines and furnaces and rocks and birds and iron machines. The alchemical nature of the geological non-conscious produced, of course, the most modern of all artistic inventions: photography. Photographic techniques and processes opened the loopholes in painterly traditions, just as the geological tailings that come from the crushing of stones gave painters material for colours. With photography, the next generations of modernists documented the repetition compulsions of industrial societies that permanently scarred the earth by constantly and relentlessly digging beneath it to extract the ores and rocks that would make us all into sturdy mechanical beings. Our terrors lie like veins beneath the surface of our Boschean bodies.

We extended our powers as the gods did by turning rocks into objects. No wonder the poetry of industrialization mesmerized modern consciousness.

Photography is the outcome of chemical processes. The processes allow us almost mystically to locate space and to show our way through our culture's indifference to cultural memories that are so familiar to us in the everyday. The stony images of fallen industries no longer shine or burn their fires in the dark, leaving some residues of hope for the next day.

Caspar David Friedrich, at the beginning of the industrial era and in his encounter, both imaginary and real, with the geological formations of the Old World, produced the kind of negative transcendence that is the downward movement of the mind into the absolute indifference of nature: repetition and monotony, earth reaching towards the sky, and ice formations that are gazed at by friends who notice the indifference of nature to human aspirations to make objects that last.

This may be the Kierkegaardian longing for both the inwardness of feelings about God and a northern rejection of mediation in favour of the purity of the geological formations over history and progress. Rather, look for a direct encounter with nature on the other side of nature. Friedrich's *Man and Woman Contemplating the Moon* (1824) or *The Abbey in the Oakwood* (1809–1810) show the geological formations of the earth in a friendly manner, illuminated by the overexposed "photographic" sky. In a Kierkegaardian mood, *The Sea of Ice* (1924) also includes the friendships that any one person can make in the world of relationships to stones and gothic ruins. We see traces of comradeship with inanimate objects that cultural works mine even in the ruins. Friedrich may be the first to discover that the formation of Gothic moods in nature, and his construction of transcendence, came as a result

of the desire to imitate stone and rock formations and to celebrate
the use of stone through the power of human-made objects to
rise to new heights in order to transcend the downward direction of the luminous reality of the ravines, clefts, fallen trees, and
rock fortresses that were the homes and shelters of early peoples.
The coming age of mines, smelters, and factories would not be
friendly towards nature. [60]

IV

The Geological Unconscious and a "Kladno Tryptych"

Over 60 percent of the world's mining companies are based in
Canada. In 2003, roughly 45 percent of the $12.7 billion in equity
capital raised around the world was for the mineral exploration
and development of companies listed on Canadian stock exchan-
ges. At the end of 2003, Canadian companies held a portfolio
of more than 6,400 mineral properties located in Canada and
in a hundred other countries ... Canada, in 2003, remained the
country where the world's mineral exploration companies were
the most active. [61]

This is the aftermath of an all-pervasive industrial eschatology. The European revolutionary attempts to adapt industry
to the Napoleonic wars of liberation in Europe was historically
dialectical because of the internal colonization of Europe. First,
to dig into history for the codes of historicism and the laws of
progress, and then to transcend those codes and then make new
objects that would pretend to last forever. The Old World would
in fact vanish quickly, to be replaced by new versions, new valued
objects, and new alloys that would fertilize and inspire the desire
for commodities.

The nineteenth century moved the geological unconscious
to the surface in impressionist art, in order to paint the surfaces
of life with flatness, on the one hand, and cubist solidity on the

other. Depth, if it existed in the anxious beholder who desires to become emancipated in the cities, would have to turn to forms of consciousness in-formed by psychology or forms of Enlightenment that were linguistic, rational, instrumental. Wittgenstein's utopian desire for the destruction of surplus and ornament by transforming language into both clarity and silence, *in order to dissolve subjectivity, in fact,* may have its primal origins in digging into the obscurity and ambiguity of the geological veins of the non-conscious, the not-yet-conscious.

The ruin was not an object of attention in the New World until the transmigration of peoples brought the reality of the distant view of the landscape into the near view of the destroyed spaces inhabited by peoples who were not "us."

This view of the purged environment is part of a modern Canadian view of the landscape of the city. The photographic artists Jeff Wall, Roy Arden, Christos Dikeakos, and Edward Burtynsky have turned to the landscapes of excavation, clearings, digging – makeshift spaces that tear into the surfaces of the earth as a kind of exegesis of the abandoned memories of now-forsaken places that were once the playgrounds of other peoples, other workers, or were their homes and streets. [62]

The New World has obsolete vistas and camouflaged anonymity, which not only corresponds to the industrial age, but displaces itself onto other nations where labour is cheaper. The gigantic scale of the northern part of our continent requires that the photograph resist the idyllic and the picturesque. This requires a geological non-conscious, as in Jeff Wall's "Prague" picture, *Odradek, Tàboritskà 8, Prague, 18 July 1994,* which is related to Kafka's fable "Troubles of a Householder." While not a picture of the earth, the inner world's forsaken object is shown as an identity-less quality hidden silently at the bottom of a staircase. This can be related to the eschatology of the sacrifice of childhood to the depths of memory whose veins we tap into. Memory is the quarry where one excavates not just particular concrete memories, but the memory of memory itself. In this process of photographing memory lies the origin of the need for a geologic aesthetic that calls up both the ruins of the once-active world that has gone underground and the restitution of historical concretion in the present – that is, in how the world works to reveal and restore its own veins, arteries, nerves, and skin. Otherwise we might ask: Why be interested in the earth and the machines that tunnel into it?

In British Columbia there is a little town that stands still in time. There are many such towns as Hedley, a former gold-mining town that sits in the interior of the province about five hours east from the metropolis Vancouver. It sits on Nlaka'pamux and Syilx Territories, and Indigenous pictographs are not too far away. The people are the Upper and Lower Similkameen First Nations, who live on either side of a beautiful river with that name. The "modern" Indigenous people are progressive and entrepreneurial. One band has rebuilt a road to the top of a mountain to an old gold mine with the name of "Mascot"; they plan to have a bed and breakfast and tours there. Seen from below, the ruins of the mine, which are now being rebuilt, are reminiscent of an existing Mayan ruin. The local museum caretaker explains that a Swiss consortium would like to build a gondola from this gold mine to another mountain across the gorge. The views are astonishing from there. But where is "there"?

This is the "Californication" of Canada. Neo-panic by developers smoothes over the rough capitalism of the earlier wild developments that settled the country. Development covers over all traces of suffering and the wounds of resistance. But this violent modern digging into cultural memory echoes another form of violence that invades the integrity of people with another kind of "tailings": many First Nations children and their families are victims of drugs – crack cocaine and methamphetamine, drugs that eat away the brain – chemical concoctions, which have penetrated even here from the cities – in the Rural Slums that exist far from the ornamental cities and have become similar to cities in other places on the Boschean globe.

The schools and initiatives of popular education that are being developed in Vancouver by artists and cultural planners are very primitive if compared to the initiatives found in the artistic installations and practices of Kladno that inspired this essay. They try to provide some human and humane image of the world, while "globalization" is the larger story that consumes parts of us. But globalization and the mining and marketing of metals are an old and long chronotope of an ongoing globalization story. Hrabal knew the story from his outpost in Central Europe. In *I Served the King of England*, Hrabal's character, Ditey, tries to save himself by buying a "Hotel in the Quarry" – a baroque palace. Hrabal mined the veins of memory inside and outside of Kladno, which itself has become a city with not just a many-sided past that once upon a time quarried and smelted the products of mining, but now exists in its ruins with a silent past. I don't know whether it has time to remember its past. For Hrabal, the past is a quarry to be mined.

Perhaps one can create a saturnine "Kladno Triptych" on the model of Bosch's *Triptych of the Temptation of St. Anthony*? The left panel could show "Gnostic Capitalism." The right panel would try to show "Pagan Communism." The middle panel, a revolving circular stage with the town portrayed by the temptations of the future, a "Garden of Earthly Delights." There would have to be goblins that inhabit caves and mines and an allusion to Andy Warhol's *White Disaster* (1963).[63]

DOSSIER III – CHAPTER 5

Talking Through: This Space around Four Pictures by Jeff Wall [64]

If you can believe in its depictorial quality, a photograph can be a valuable means of a thesis, antithesis and communication. It has a clear language, one that speaks openly not only about its subjects, such as people, architecture, and landscape ... but also very much about the attitude of the photographer towards these things. In this regard, a photograph is always objective.

> —THOMAS STRUTH, "Artist's Statement," quoted in Ann Goldstein,
> "Portraits of Self-Reflection," *Thomas Struth, 1977–2002* (2002)

What has been formed cannot be lived unless what has fallen apart is gathered up and taken along.

> —SIEGFRIED KRACAUER, "Gestalt und Zerfall" [Figure and ruin],
> *Aufsätze (1915–1926): Schriften* (1990), my translation

The following dialogue developed in collaboration with Glen Lowry. We were editors of *West Coast Line*, a Vancouver cultural / literary journal that chronicled and developed interdisciplinary cultural production relevant to the vanguard traditions of the West Coast – the western region of Canada, which we describe as a watershed feeding into the Pacific Ocean, roughly the province of British Columbia. [65] In keeping with my essay "Faking Nature and Reading History: The Mindfulness towards Reality in the Dialogical World of Jeff Wall's Pictures," we have created a dialogue that came out of our shared interest in photography and cultural memory that has involved various projects, including a series of interviews with Jeff Wall and Fred Douglas on photography in Vancouver in the book *Unfinished Business: Photographs of Vancouver* (edited by Bill Jeffries, Glen Lowry, and Jerry Zaslove, Presentation House, 2005). The sections below are distilled from approximately six hours of transcribed discussion, spanning three meetings that took place in October 2004 in the office of *West Coast Line* at Simon Fraser University. The images that accompanied the original publication, courtesy of Jeff Wall, are the following transparencies in lightboxes: *Swept* (1995); *Morning Cleaning, Mies van der Rohe Foundation, Barcelona* (1999); *The Storyteller* (1986); *Bad Goods* (1984). I refer to them in my comments sometime as "figurations" or "tableaux." The dialogue is published in *Locating Memory: Photographic Acts* (edited by Annette Kuhn and Kirsten Emiko McAllister, Berghahn Books, 2006).

GLEN LOWRY: There appears to be a fundamental shift in Jeff Wall's work, notably in the work in his exhibition at Vienna's mumok (Museum moderner Kunst Stiftung Ludwig) and in the book by Göteborg's Hasselblad Center, both entitled *Jeff Wall: Photographs*. A key aspect of this shift, for me, has to do with an increasingly photographic bent in Wall's work. In particular, images that Wall made during the mid-to-late 1990s – the *Diagonal Composition* series, *Clipped Branches, East Cordova St., Vancouver*, and *Swept* – suggest a movement away from the earlier, more cinematic or painterly work for which he is famous towards something that suggests a direct engagement with the early history of photography. As such, this work presupposes a different way of relating to history and to cultural memory. Paradoxically, it seems much more personally invested and immediate. As a lead-in to our discussion of this work, I wonder if you might say something about "Faking Nature and Reading History," and about some of the changes you see in the critical climate surrounding Jeff Wall's work. Looking at the reproductions in *Jeff Wall, 1990* (Vancouver Art Gallery, 1990), your monograph on Jeff's work, it seems to me that the images that were under consideration are of a different type or category from the ones we're talking about here. *Swept*, for example, is much harder to relate to conceptual art, or to an art-historical discussion of Wall's work. In a profound way, this work seems to initiate a complex dialogue with scholarship or epistemology vis-à-vis the relationship between history and art-making. I'm interested in the way his work negotiates with the irony you set up: that after Adorno one has to be "mindful" of memory formations while, at the same time, there is a proliferation of "memory work" across disciplines and cultural locations.

JERRY ZASLOVE: My monograph *Jeff Wall*, 1990 explored Wall's pictures and my response to their complexity that his work and technique evoked with me in his using a different "delivery system" in photography and representation; among other matters, I wrote that an inner strand of his work was confrontation with the baroque. We are faced with the Enlightenment's break with neoclassicism and the "illusionistic" representation of baroque's opulent capitalism. For example, Jacques-Louis David's post–French Revolution paintings and its claim to fresh subject matter in the paintings of Delacroix and Géricault shows how a new stage of modernism had emerged. Already with Bruegel the Elder, then with Goya, Manet, and Courbet, new subject matter brought new framing devices – figurations, we must say – that brought the spectator into a critical, self-reflective, *empathic* position in regard to the origins of art in social controversies.

Following this, photography brought on the emergence of a new realism that focused memories of revolutionary violence and the violence of the everyday as new, formative cultural forces. Baudelaire, Dostoevsky, then Freud and Proust, gave this cultural force, simmering on the surfaces of the nineteenth century's millennial fevers, a new grounding in the dialectics of the mimetic powers inherent in memory-based art-making. This fuelled the effort to recall a violent past through new, consciousness-breaking formations and new meaning. Photography's capacity to simulate reality, copy it, gave the mimetic impulse a sense of invasiveness that threatened the integrity of copying reality. We might say that if reification is a form of forgetting, then photographic depictions of reality provide a form of remembering how reification works *at* us, in front of us, facing us.

In my 1990 Wall monograph, I addressed the aesthetic idea that photography had to be "mindful" towards reality because not only did it bring about a new mode of realistic *depiction*, but it also brought the spectator into the magical world of re-presentation in a manner that broke with its yearning for origins and fixed beginnings.

Today, the uses and abuses of the memory wars dominate much of the discussion of cultural politics, yet it appears that, as spectators, *we* are indulging in the architectonics of memory (remembering) without a very deep knowledge of the way memory works as a dramatic representation of the images in the unconscious. We seem to be telling stories about memory without always or clearly understanding that memory is not a trustworthy representation of chronology in history. Memory is asynchronous.

When I wrote the "Faking Nature" essay, the wars around monuments, memorials, and commemorations had not yet hit us the way they have today.[66] Levinas expresses somewhat what I am saying: "The presentation of the face, expression, does not disclose an inward world previously closed, adding thus a new region to comprehend or to take over. On the contrary, it calls to me above and beyond the given that speech already put in common among us ... Everything that takes place here 'between us' concerns everyone, the face that looks at it places itself in the full light of the public order, even if I draw back from it to seek with the interlocutor the complicity of a private relationship and a clandestinity."[67]

GL: We might connect this to Wall's particular form of image making, his use of lightboxes, which you suggest in your monograph engage the audience by illusionistically making surfaces disappear. Standing in front of Wall's large-scale lightboxes, one tends to slip into the space of the photograph, becoming tangled up in a very authoritative way in its aesthetic production. I think this is the reason some people are resistant to Wall's work: in front of his images, you are unwittingly brought into the space of representation in an unnerving way. Through their seductive texture, the lightboxes script us in; in so doing, they destabilize our relationship to the cultural object, or to the quotidian particulars the object appears to represent. Contrary to the theatrical performance depicted in many of Wall's larger works (many of which use Vancouver or the West Coast as a backdrop, forcing us to recall specific streets, buildings, and personae, often already carrying a politics with them into the photograph), an image like *Swept* depicts a different relation to space, one that has been swept clean of human subjects or obvious geographical references. *Swept* looks like a crime scene to me – the photographer cleaning up after himself. It presents an obsession with orderliness that I am tempted to relate to the artist's historical specificity or being, and at the same time it moves in much more closely on the subject matter, divorcing it from a larger social context. *Swept* reeks of the psychological energies that would go into producing such an image. At the same time, it gestures towards more conventional notions of photographic media – silver prints, smaller photographs, found images – that rely on a different psychic drama connecting viewer, image-maker, and object.

JZ: This is a terrifying picture for me. It's a dirt floor that really can't be swept clean. This room will never be "clean." This picture smells. Its sensual surface is musty, dank. This picture is also about the play of light. It is a Spartan image about the problem of origins, which, as I have suggested, is very much the problem of cultural criticism in modernism: Where is the origin of fragmentation and the ruins, as Kracauer says? The problem of origins is by definition a problem of how a generation identifies itself with the past. It therefore fits into the institutional struggles we've been talking about. It's not only disappearing, it's gone: Wall's craft has cleared the space. And the catharsis is in the clearing.[68]

GL: This space is waiting for the arrival of something. It's ready for the next tenant – tenants being a key motif in Wall's work. While I'm struck by the austerity of this image, I worry about my own interest in these photographs that are empty of personae. There seems to be a dangerous safety in moving away from representations of individuals (and of their social relations with other subjects). But I'm not sure that this is what's happening here. In fact, I see the reverse happening: in emptying the frame of personae, the image allows in the subjects – Wall's, the viewers' – in an immediate way. In this sense, *Swept* explores in a new way the question of surface discussed earlier: paradoxically, it does so by becoming a space of play of subjectivities that are more *and* less historically determined.

JZ: The daringness of this image is the risk it is taking with our sensibilities. We see the aggressive and violent invasion of the integrity of the person in this work – violence that pervades modernity, nihilistically; ethnicity has to start all over again and gender sensitivity has to start all over again, then cultural criticism has to start all over again. This is not a sublime act: it is a repressive act. You have to start thinking in hard terms about what you are doing and whom you are affecting. In terms of cultural criticism, the implications of what you are doing are crucial: in art, one can be much more aggressive. That's why I am suggesting that Wall establishes a "feelingful" relationship with the form: in experimentation one experiences form as a figuration, the totality of the work. The work assimilates the subject matter, even if it's horrific. The location of memory depends on an orientation to the familiar cultural objects in one's world. Proustian reveries are a form of free association: the early Picasso or cubism provides a rough engagement with memory as a stark disengagement with traditional forms of representation. Likewise, with photography it was more difficult to come to terms with form or innovations in form, because as Kracauer suggests, photography is like a sponge that absorbs too much of the world, placing the viewer in a reciprocal relationship with distance and closeness – the memory problem.

GL: If certain photographic images demand a knowledge of the history of photography, then, in terms of your expressed desire to develop a psychoanalytic approach to Wall's work, might we not also say that the photographer, as opposed to this other figure of the artist who uses photography, is better suited for psychoanalytic readings? A photographer is an embodiment of the technology, whereas the artist who uses photography still has a distance from it. For the conceptual artist, the mode of seeing is not the photographic per se. But when you start to think of Wall as a photographer, respecting the depth of his knowledge and engagement in photographic praxis and history, then desire and a much closer relationship between the machinery and the individual become more entangled.

JZ: I would agree with that, but the way you get at the identity question, which again goes back to the invasion of the person by technology as well as the prosthetic extension of the person into the real, is that you start by acknowledging that the person is made up of multiple selves. I mean, this is why the dream analogy is so interesting in terms of memory work. [69]

GL: The notion of sweeping up – of simultaneously remembering and forgetting the relationships between the photographer or spectator, or photographic subject and object – is at the core of Wall's remarkable image *Morning Cleaning, Mies van der Rohe Foundation, Barcelona*. It seems to me that this categorically different type of image brings together many of the issues we've been discussing – international modernism, labour, social

history, cultural location or position, representation, globalization – while returning to a number of Wall's important ideas
or themes.

JZ: This picture has the same depictorial qualities as *The Giant*
(1992), where the interior of a public space, an architecturally
opulent space, brings international modernism right into ordinary view. Like *Swept*, it depicts a space cleansed of any people.
The architecture has a neoclassical and yet baroque quality, which
might be strange to think about, but this is Wall's trickery – it
works against and with the illusion of inside and outside. The
image connects with Wall's earlier pictures where mirroring and
doubleness are given primary significance as the plane in which
the viewer is shocked into feeling a kind of disorientation. There
is the utter ordinariness of the scene. It hasn't got a lot of drama.
But there is also this amazing texture of the walls and again,
a consciousness about the light: as in many of his interiors, it
sweeps across the scene (here, from left to right). For Jeff Wall,
who does not take many pictures of architectural interiors, this
image is uncanny: it evokes the return of the repressed. In the way
Freud uses the term, the uncanny is a place where the home, the
hearth, and the secret come together. In German, *unheimlich* can
mean "secret." It also means "homely eerie, uncanny, unfamiliar"
and "mysterious." It is a place near you where you tell and make
up stories for children. You would teach them about another
world – of gremlins and spirits and so forth – with the uncanny.

GL: Your point about this being a space for stories raises an
interesting question about the function of this room. It is one of
those wonderfully modernist spaces that is almost dysfunctional
in its functionalism. The chairs are too far apart, the design of
the room is too rational. In the scene depicted here, the conversation is no longer taking place. Juxtaposed with the work
of the cleaner, the nature of last night's discussion exists as a
secret, hinging on a separation of an administrative class from

the labourer who arrives in the morning and is gone before anyone notices his presence. Against the austerity of this artificial space, the cleaner's body and labour represent something of a secret or unacknowledged aspect of its design. On another level, the long vertical line splits the scene while connecting the domestic worker and the statue of a nude woman. The image balances the labourer with the abstracted female form in a manner that suggests an uncanny haunting of the rational order of this room. What remains outside this room and looking in on it are both the material relations of the work and the sexualized image – the labourer's body and an idealized female form.

JZ: In conversation the uncanny resides in the comfort of home. In Freud's wonderful 1910 essay on the double meanings of words, "The Antithetical Meaning of Primal Words," he suggests that words carry archaic meanings – as in the word *unheimlich* that has double and reversible meanings of "home" and "secret." For Freud and early psychoanalysts, including Melanie Klein or even Jung, the unconscious must include images and prelinguistic forces. The relevance here is that the unconscious is symbolic as well as animistic, insofar as it calls into existence, through poetic language or the act of naming, objects whose use and function can change with the name changing. In other words, language does change reality. In fairy tales and fables, language is constantly mutating and disappearing. The notion that when you change language you change reality is one of the basic principles of therapeutic analysis: the repressed returns in a context that is normal. This relates to what I think is going on here at the level of reification, social change, and the social exchange of space and image. It is a process that started out with the displacement of space into image – a commodity in the contemporary world which you can do anything with.

GL: That idea of language changing reality is also a Marxist concept, and it might be a point of intersection between the psychoanalytical and the sociological, which in relation to Wall's work – this photograph and *Swept* – seems to be a border that you and I are moving across. Figuratively, this image is about the skirting or framing of the gaze. In this sense, this line enacts a separation of sociological and psychological elements of the work. On one side, there is the cleaner; on the other, behind the veil of the window washing, the statue. Semiotically, this photograph breaks itself in two.

JZ: One of the gaps in the literature on Wall's work is an interest in his deep understanding of the social history of art.[70] I'm a follower of Arnold Hauser's ideas; I'm fascinated by the use of intelligence in Wall's work, its connection with those art historians who see the social through the holes in the history of modernism: Alois Riegl, Herbert Read, Meyer Schapiro, Michael Baxandall, T.J. Clarke, and Michael Fried, each a social historian and an art historian. Once you denude the photograph of social history, you lose the belief systems that function historically and that lie behind its creation of audience. I am speaking of the sociological tradition of Simmel, Kracauer, Weber, or, for that matter, Hegel. Wall's pictures aren't only part of art history but also of an art history of photography, and it is his mindfulness about new dialogical values that needs to be brought out.[71]

GL: This room is mausoleum-like: as you have suggested, it is a space of social death. Yet, this is very specifically named. We know it is "Barcelona." And we are looking at the Mies van der Rohe–designed German Pavilion for the 1929 World Exposition, a building that had no practical purpose: No functional programme determined or even influenced its appearance. No part of its interior was taken up by exhibits: the building itself was the object on view. These famous Barcelona chairs, which were designed specifically for this building (as thrones for the Spanish royalty during the opening ceremony), are the only "objects" in the building. And in a sense, this building doesn't really have an inside: its secret past is that it has never housed anyone or anything. The question about who is more at home here is really useful: after all, is it not the figure of the cleaner who actually inhabits the space? This ironic turning inside out of the monumental built environment invests it with life and memories, but with those of the cleaner, who might be connected historically with globalization and the movement of bodies from the Americas back to Europe.

JZ: Wall's black-and-white photograph *Housekeeping* (1996), which depicts a maid on the threshold of a hotel room's bathroom, is another image about a domicile or shelter. This image depicts a room that is so reproducible; it represents every motel room anywhere. Again it suggests something of domestication carrying out the logic of the secrets, but it is also demystifying the secrets, making them public, talking about them. The home is the place of political economy: the household is the economic core of all social systems. So if there's intrusion from the outside to the "inscape" of the home, this has to be contained. In classic Marxism, you have to ensure that the surplus that is created at home through craft, not factory work, cannot be alienated, estranged; which is another way of talking about the uncanny, as maintaining the economic at home without having it robbed of its meaning.[72]

GL: There is an element of familiarization in the cleaning being depicted in these works. In the "making strange" of these images we are reminded of domestic labour in a space that is supposed to already be sanitary, untouched by human hands. The presence of the housekeeper reminds us of the lives and memories of others – their dirt and disorder – which must be forgotten each night. In this way, inhabiting a hotel room is analogous to taking and looking at family photographs, which depend on our ability to see ourselves or take ourselves out of the flow of social habits – to see ourselves at home in the utterly clichéd snapshot.

JZ: How do you alienate something that's already alienated in this way? Maybe one has to say that this is a cultural location, a place in which cultural, artistic, and architectural activities take place; where you build culture, a laboratory for modern culture. The irony is that it was a style that became a vision of the modern at a time when the modern was being destroyed by fascism. This is similar to the notion that dreams give you a sensual relationship to the spatial; that they're infused with touch. You can feel them because they're in your body. It's a body-based insight that comes out of experiences you had before. Your temperature goes up, and your heart beats. Dreams simulate real life. Your point is really a good one.

GL: What I see in some of this later work is that the photograph itself, even though it always already was a gesture, a gesture of gestures, is displacing itself into the social act of making the image. I read this image as a more personal, but incredibly nuanced, understanding of the photographic gesture, and consequently of remembering.

JZ: There's a mistake in thinking that classic Freudian dream theory is only visual. In a dream there is the illusion of mortality and time, as well as spatial material. Freud differentiated between the manifest and the latent content of a dream: the manifest is what we talk to ourselves about in everyday life; the latent content is interpretable in dream work. In dreaming and talking about the *mental event* of the dream when you wake up with the sense that something happened to you which, even philosophically, is an event. A dream is haptic; it also has rhythm, a pulse, emphasis, and blank moments. If you try to recreate the dream by writing it down, you lose its auditory quality, which still exists in talking about it. You need to have a voice, *your* voice, speaking the dream; otherwise, it remains fully internalized with the qualities both of being exposed and of feeling that we are hiding out because dreams disguise our emotions – we mistakenly call this "invisible" because we are so used to thinking in images. Freud developed the "talking cure" as a way of recreating voice through talking about dreams or memories, recreating the voice of one's parents. In the process, one is actually projecting a voice that may or may not be one's own but may have echoes of other people in one's intimate life. This idea is important for memory work because it involves the three stages of memory: remembering, repeating, and working through. "Remembering" in classic psychoanalysis is really best translated as "insight" or "inscape" (the German is *Erinnern*). Thoughts are in your body as images and thoughts that have been floating; we make them repeatable through reverie. [73]

GL: So, in this sense, the photograph, or more precisely the point of intersection it provides between the act of photographing and looking at the photograph – which is also between the psychic and the social – bridges the gap between remembering and repeating. In the case of *Morning Cleaning*, this process might be said to be an uncanny event because it remembers and repeats something that wasn't supposed to be seen happening. It shows us something of the quotidian, internal, almost secret life of the foundation.

JZ: The third phase is the working through – the phase of transference in classic Freudian analysis. This involves thinking beyond concepts, not reducing the dream to simple ideas or themes that allow one to say, "Well I had a dream and I know exactly what it meant." You can't know what it meant, because you can't entirely commit the dream to consciousness. You may have some ideas about what it meant, but it doesn't mean that you have actually come to terms with it. By working the dream "through" and perhaps remembering it later on, you come to terms with the dream structure; the actual specific meanings of those dreams might be ultimately irrelevant. The objective of dream work is to have some affective response to the process, to have a sense that you've got to where you want to be. Demystifying the structure, you are no longer in it: in working through, you're in a process of working on totality, in Adorno's sense that "all reification is a forgetting."[74] You begin to see the relationship of the totality of the dream process, the dream structure, to an experience of totality, but not in its *reified* form. Thus, the room in this photograph is a perfect representation of an overdetermined vision of style or design. Wall may see a certain kind of beauty in the space, but for me this image depicts an alienated totality or beauty. I could sit in this room and talk, but it's not a very comfortable environment. The gestural aura is forbidding and aggressively modern. Your words will echo.

GL: The traces of desire – of individual intention, perhaps – seem to me to mirror very complex social memories and Jeff Wall's engagement with history. The history of this building, for example, suggests a link between the built environment this image places us in and the desire to reconstruct a modernist past. The building was disassembled after the 1929 Barcelona Exposition and then reconstructed in the 1980s. Its existence performs a kind of historical rewriting that not only glosses over the radical shifts in how and what the Pavilion means, but also over the historical rupture between the building and the rebuilding. After the Spanish Civil War, Franco, World War II, the Cold War, and the emergence of globalization, its rebuilding frames a radically different geo-historical reality. What is the link between international modernism and the material history alluded to in the image? How do we read parallels between the arrival/position of the labourer in this structure and the remembering of Wall's image? This image grapples with abstraction – as opposed to or in addition to mimesis – as an aesthetic process, a physical process or as bodily gestures. This image, in a sense, demands a stronger questioning of embodiment, of the particularity of the photographer's embodied eye, or his subject.

JZ: This is what I mean by empathy with form. "Internalizing" is the more appropriate word for remembering in the psycho-analytic context, because it is more closely linked to knowing. Knowing means regaining some affect over the memory: not as an "abstraction," that's the wrong word, but by making it particular again, which you can't do automatically because the "consciousness-raising" aspect of memory requires this repeating of form. Freud's concept of memory needs the verb *wiederholen*, which is to "call back again." It's oral: a call-back, which means to literally "go and get the voice": to call. We go over a memory again and again because it is opaque: this type of repetition may be a compulsive act. We go over the same dream until it feels part of our character – and we don't know why. It is habit, as in the German sense of *Erfahrung* – "experience": it happens to you and you are digesting it, constantly assimilating it. You histori-cize because that's the process of memory. You take a hundred photographs, snapshots, and the repeating wards off the image, rather than taking one picture and looking at it again and again because it's meaningful. I think this is the "creative will" inside Wall's pictures: they approach the sense of a painting, as one picture you go back to again and again, and you're not exactly sure why, but it has such important signifying qualities because it is in part "haptic."

GL: Wall's work offers complex interpretations of the gaze, but it does so in reference to highly specific social situations. In a number of images, Wall more or less provokes the viewer, demanding a critical engagement with the politics of looking, his and ours. Faced with well-known images like *Picture for Women* (1979), *Woman and her Doctor* (1980), *Diatribe* (1985), and *The Drain* (1989), which represent women and girls in relation to psychoanalytic themes; *Mimic* (1982), *Trân Dúc Vân* (1988), and *Outburst* (1989–1991), which engage with the culturally charged representation of racialized subjects; or *The Storyteller* and *Bad*

Goods which enter into questions regarding Aboriginality, one is forced to think about the relation of the artist to the subject matter. But in so doing, we need to pay attention to the disjunction between the visual and the oral/aural.

JZ: According to the classic Freudian view of dream work, voice is translated into visual material in the dream but the voice is never gone. In my reading of Lacan, the voice is gone and the universality of method prevails, whereas in classic Freudian analysis there is more room for culturally specific contexts. The speaking voice in the psychoanalytic dialogue is gone in Lacan, and what is left is primarily "opticality," or mirroring. But we know the importance of voice already through observing mothers with children and children playing. One assimilates the voice of the other's body into one's body. But in the translation of the process from sheer optical vision to seeing, listening, and recognizing, there's a crucial disfiguration underlying the transparent surface. Seeing is a distancing mechanism, listening is much more intimate. A vital aspect of the psychoanalytical break from psychiatry that used hypnosis, water cures, and other violent therapies that made the patient look crazy was the decision to actually listen to the individual's words. Lacan was good at listening to the displacements, condensations, and reflections, but he was not so good at listening. In terms of film, we might say he was interested in the words that "bounced off the screen" but not the words that penetrated the screen. I think this is why film critics pick up on Lacan so wonderfully. In the traditional psychoanalytical paradigm, the radical act was the listening act, which would obviously entail watching body gestures in order to understand what the unconscious was doing. In that respect – and this is something I feel strongly about – psychoanalysis did not always translate well from one culture to another. Psychoanalysis had to invent new founding myths wherever it found new soil, whether in Italy, Argentina, Japan, or France; it often had to reinvent itself in the new culture, as it did in France. Thus the problem with Lacan, at the theory level, is that it appeals to those who want a universal method more than a critical cultural sense of reality. Lacan wants to make the figurations of the unconscious the norms of discourse. This is my bias, of course.

GL: We might say the same about photography as memory work: it reinvents itself as it moves across borders, cultures and times. Jeff Wall's work demonstrates, almost obsessively, the paradox of photographic representation: his extremely high-resolution images record a richness of realistic detail and information even as they empty it of temporal and spatial specificity. Thus his images hinge on an almost instantaneous remembering and forgetting of historical time. To put it another way, they foreground and destabilize the space of reception and the act of viewing. This is a point that you suggest needs to be understood in terms of social history – *of* art, but also *as* art. I would add that it is this aspect of Wall's work that seems to have dramatically shifted in the past decade. Time seems to be propelling Wall's oeuvre into an ever more complex engagement not only with the illusionist practices of Renaissance and baroque painting but also, as I have suggested, with the history (and prehistory) of photography itself. It provides a return to the relationship between representation and one's experience of the photographic act. The question of aura invoked by these images is linked to the auditory/aural space – to what is no longer being heard or spoken. Drawing attention to the intersection of public and domestic spaces – the ironic issue of "housekeeping" or "cleaning" as public acts – his images raise fundamental questions about the specificity of cultural interpretation. I'm fascinated with how particular images function for those of us working and living on the West Coast, for whom the issues of First Nations' entitlements and anti-Asian or anti–Asian Canadian racism (to pick two recurrent themes in Wall's work) are deeply embedded in both the social history and the academic cultures of this place. Wall's work depicts the remembering and representing colonial anxieties of settlement and Indigenous anxieties which have been both fed and mediated by a long history of photographic ethnography that dates back to the 1850s and the beginnings of photography itself. I have in mind the (in)famous images of Edward Curtis, but also those of early Chinese Canadian and Japanese Canadian frontier photographers, such as C.D. Hoy in Barkerville or the Hayashi/Kitamura/Matsubuchi Studio in Cumberland. Images like Wall's *The Storyteller* or *Bad Goods* seem extremely important in this light, especially in the way they bring something akin to what you have referred to as folkloristic time into collision with modernity, international traffic, or commerce.

JZ: Social reality is always in dispute in great pictures. Some of the most compelling discussions are around Dutch painting and its social history; as in, say, Rembrandt's *Anatomy Lesson of Dr. Nicolaes Tulp* and his still lifes like *Slaughtered Ox*, where the role of the beholder is depicted in the picture. The experience of storytelling, of "facticity," can be related to Walter Benjamin's essay "The Storyteller." The storyteller is at home in distant places as well as in distant time because the storyteller embodies two "archaic types" of storytelling: the resident master craftsman and the itinerant journeyman; the story is infused with "both the lore of faraway placed and the lore of the past, such as is manifested most clearly to the native inhabitants of a place." Through the storyteller, we become *enmeshed* in the weave of disparate times and spaces. The figures in Wall's image are dressed in a way that suggests they are in modern time, but they have gathered in this almost ghettoized place beneath the bridge. It is a beautiful bridge, by the way – suggesting that they are part of another, perhaps archaic, time. To add to this, a Bakhtinian notion of genre reminds us that where you tell the story, as well as to whom you are telling it, changes the story's lifeworld. That's a positive dimension of Jeff Wall's pictures, and I don't know to what extent it has been talked about. Although it might be seen as a kind of sentimentality, or an overly romantic interpretation of the situation, it's vital to remember that, traditionally, stories change depending on who is telling them and who is listening.[75] Jeff Wall's 1986 The Storyteller depicts what I am formulating here as the living materiality of story.

GL: As in Morning Cleaning, The Storyteller depicts a complicated segmentation of space. There are various listening groups, making it difficult to locate the story or point of focus. Above it all, this bridge, which functions as a trope of a dominant modernist time and a well-developed network of spatial relations, suggests the provisional nature of a much older scene. The elements of image – the clothes and bridge design – placed as they are within a depiction of the all-but-lost craft of the storyteller, destabilize the dream of modernity, symbolized by the bridge. I say it is a dream because there is this unique obsession, prevalent here on the West Coast, with modernity as something that never really takes place historically. In terms of the cultural history of this place, remnants of modernity remain as reminders of the incomplete incorporation of this colonial space into the temporal logic of a dominant nationalism. This beautiful bridge might frame the discourse, but what's interesting is happening just below and off to the side of it. In terms of globalization and the cultural struggles that persist here, one might say that this image can also be read as a reminder of the failure of colonialism, of the nationalist project that grows out of it, of modernity's claims to completely subsume the contradictions of the past into the look of the present. Indigenous Peoples and their cultures survive. In terms of the cultural politics in British Columbia, the question of ownership, property, and land claim has everything to do with the relationship between story and fact, orality and textuality. It is not too reductive to say that culture is owned by those who govern time and that the creation stories owned by the First Nations, for example, might provide the basis for juridical knowledge and action. At the same time, storytelling is an alternative mode of knowledge production and distribution that exists at the limits of bourgeois culture and capital. The notion that stories are property or, conversely, that Ancestral Lands might be other than property in the sense that real estate is property, these are concepts bourgeois culture has never been comfortable with here. They are antithetical to bourgeois notions not only of land, but also of the future. Thus I might place *Bad Goods* in relationship to memories of historical Potlatch ceremonies, which for colonial British Columbians represented an "outrageous" practice of abundant giving, but that has now been partially lost, elided beneath the rationaliz-ation (or naturalization even) of "trade" as universal practice.

JZ: Typically, in the Freudian paradigm, or even in a Marxist paradigm, the taboos that appear to be so petrifying to bourgeois society also exist in archaic societies. However, in a craft-based agricultural society, fear of the other tends to be more common-place and less traumatic, unless placed under the spell of taxation. In modern society, these fears are much more worrisome and are part of the memory wars. Just think of the controversies over monuments commemorating the Holocaust or the Vietnam War. This is something in Wall's pictures: the taboos – let's say sexual taboos, restrictions, incommensurables – appear to fall away as in a dream and liberate us from the power of institutional forces; they come back again, in many other forms. Today we have the pursuit of memory by a generation that did not participate in the horrors of the wars: the Holocaust, the Hiroshima bomb-ings, or the Vietnam War. Yet the repressed come back again in another form, as if they have changed, but they may not have changed. Or then again, the experience of seeing them come back again can liberate us from their powerful attachments. *The phantasmagoria of memory may depoliticize the present!* This is something interesting about Lacan; I think these images suggest the compulsion to repeat and the preoccupation with memory as a lingering around death. But, in terms of memory work, it might be better to consider more classical approaches to analysis, such as in D.W. Winnicott's or Melanie Klein's work, that deal with the power of transitional objects. *Stories as transitional objects* might be then connected to how we establish new relationships. To properly deal with the ogre, parent, or powerful institution, one must begin to deconstruct it, and through telling or listening to a story, we defuse the originally overwhelming experience. Thus, the transitional object is a very important aspect of our postmodern world. When a new group intersects with dominant ethnic or racial identities, it reminds us that the world may itself have become a transitional object by virtue of alien people who are threatening. Society does all sorts of scrambling and dancing around to make sure that aliens are not going to be heard without first paying the price of official forms of tolerance organized by the state that leads to political and institutional forms of tyranny – indeed, fascisms. [76]

GL: *Bad Goods* highlights the way that whiteness in the space of British Columbia has been a source of intense anxiety since its transition from a British colony to a province of Canada in 1871. What's remarkable about Wall's depiction of space – the geography he seems so compelled to represent (I wonder how European audiences might understand this differently) – is that it resonates with the repressed memory of white settlers. They never managed to establish the pure "white colony" they so fervently desired. The First Nations did not "die out" with modernization; instead they have used the Canadian legal system to make Land Claims and demanded compensation for the abuse that three generations of their children have undergone at Christian residential schools. Non-European migrant workers did not return to their homelands after they finished building the province's economic infrastructure from the late 1800s to the mid-1950s: instead, they stayed in what was to become a multicultural Canada. I'm interested in going back to your comments about the return of the repressed, but specifically I'm interested in how "what returns" has in fact actually been present throughout the cultural history of this province.

JZ: The repressed returns in a context that is always normal – the more normal, the more irrational the return of the repressed feels. This is the basis of the aesthetic of the grotesque. The dominant culture understands this as the Nietzschean eternal return of the same, treated as myth. This can also be understood as the bourgeois way of recapitulating history as the eternal development of something they've always owned and will own forever. The return of the repressed could be experienced as class struggle. *However*, in terms of exile and the nomadic lives of people, we might say that on arriving at the shores of a new dominant culture, some European immigrant groups found that, contrary to their expectations, they could not escape the repressed of their homelands. Instead, "difference" kept "returning," but from the origins of a history they never owned. Many European peoples who came here believed that they were making history in a way that it had never been made before; but in another sense, depending on their class, religion, or the persecutions they fled, they were just recapitulating European history. When they met others from Asia or South America, or when they began to share the spaces with Indigenous Peoples, history became a problem: there was no coherent story they could fall back on. It is important to remember, however, that many immigrants to Canada had a sense of history from *an exilic position of loss of homeland*. For example, the Ukrainians in the Prairies or Scots in Ontario or Atlantic Canada had an exilic relationship to their past as ethnic outcasts from sovereign nations, Colonial Russia and Empire England.

GL: The fragmented persistence of folkloric time that is carried forward in the historical anxieties of the European subjects who have settled here seems to be linked to Wall's intricate engagement with twentieth-century vanguard art and the histories underwriting it. When we talk about Indigenous subjectivities within the history of a Canadian nation, there is a long tradition of resistance to the temporality of European history, to the documentation of European history and its means of historicizing. I'm interested in the way Wall's work resonates with this other socio-political consciousness. [77]

JZ: If you look at the image carefully, you'll see that the box says this is "iceberg lettuce from Salinas California, product of the USA," suggesting issues of large-scale industrialization, or even globalization. Don't forget that Wall did a picture, *The Storyteller*, which addresses the question of the landless and un-landed. If you look at *Bad Goods* or *The Storyteller*, the figures are composed and attentive. In the former, the figure is choreographed to stand in such a way that his face is neutral, looking straight at the viewer. Together, we approach "the bad goods" in the centre of the frame in a kind of "face-off," as Kaja Silverman has suggested. [78] Yet when this picture was made, the problematic epistemology of colonialism and modernity had already been exposed. We know everything we need to know about this kind of exploitation. So why are we looking at it again? What is new and controversial, and why this is a great picture, goes back to voicelessness; to our inability to penetrate the gaze of this subject, to use Lacanian terminology; to find (or place) its voice.

To return to your discussion about modern time – in Lacan and Freud, the unconscious has no explicitly developed concept of time, and it is questionable whether it has a notion of space. Arguably, Lacan gives the unconscious a notion of space based on language and the fantasies inside of the optical; but to understand this relationship one would have to interrogate his notion that the unconscious is structured like a language. For Freud, however, language is a culturally specific condition imposed by the superego in the name of culture – not just of the father – and of the ego's defence mechanisms that reify culture. As such, language cannot be ontologically separated from the institutions of family, school, culture, and so on. Languages and emotion, or "affect," move into the aesthetic dimension of memory. Future work on memory needs to go back to questions of time and space, because without the principle of time there is no psychoanalysis of space. Time brings with it all of the experiences, fragmented as they may be, that make up the life of the individual subject and "subject" within what Adorno calls "power-protected inwardness" in his 1933 study of Kierkegaard, which became the basis of his work on aesthetics. His aesthetics can be said to be based on the incommensurability of the ethical and the aesthetic. The ethical self "vanishes into truth whose trace reaches the self by aesthetic semblance in the ephemeral images of which the self's mighty spontaneity is powerless [and is] lost in sacrifice." The autonomous self "survives in its transience by making itself small … [to] the exclusion of the incommensurable."[79]

GL: The argument that you are making is not simply that you want to open up Wall's work to new psychoanalytic interpretations. Instead, you are saying that this work might challenge the basis of psychoanalytic theory. In terms of the bigger project of the "location of memory" this suggests to me that if we are going to go back and reclaim psychoanalysis or Freudian engagements with the issues of temporality, then time has to be re-spatialized or re-historicized within different geo-historical and epistemological terms. It seems to me that we are moving towards a number of key questions about how scholarly discourse and art practice are linked. In the fallout of the Cold War and the dissolution of the nation state as a dominant cultural-economic order, notions of interiority and exteriority have given way to new returns and new thresholds that bring to light troubling incarnations of the uncanny. In this respect, Wall's work is provocative. Memory, in its most radical form, here breaks down binary oppositions that lock the other into rigidly defined caricatures of "Us" and "Them." Here, memory presents other possibilities: the ways that lives cross racial and class boundaries through conflicts and collaborations that neither deny the violence of these interactions nor accept their inevitability. The radicality of this form of memory is spoken in the nuances of Jeff Wall's photographic practice and in the critical discussions it seeds.

DOSSIER III: ENDNOTES

CHAPTER 1

1   This essay appeared initially within the installation *HEROICS: A Critical View*, curated by Daina Augaitis and Helga Pakasaar at the Walter Phillips Gallery in Banff. It was later republished as "Ten Fables for the Heroic Future" in *Vanguard* 17, no. 4 (September/October 1988): 16–21, with images chosen by the editors.

CHAPTER 2

2   This essay was a contribution to Canadian artist Althea Thauberger's installation *Carrall Street*, a street event, almost a carnival, on one of Vancouver's oldest streets, at one time a "skid road" on which logs were rolled to the waterfront. The event was staged in 2008 outside of the Artspeak Gallery on Carrall Street, Vancouver. The essay was later published as part of *Carrall Street: Althea Thauberger*, edited by Melanie O'Brian and the artist (Vancouver: Artspeak, 2009), under the title "The Last Snapshot of the Vancouver Intelligentsia: An Open Letter to the Participants of Althea Thauberger's *Carrall Street*." One inspiration is Italo Calvino's novel *Invisible Cities*, a dialogue between explorer of cities Marco Polo and builder of empires Genghis Khan. They argue over whether the city is an organic life of place and time or whether the city harbours the origin of dynasties, desire, and memory. Each city that Marco Polo visits bears the name of a woman. Vancouver is not mature enough as a city to have names of women as founding playful godesses. So, by renaming the streets I use other emblems and names for Vancouver streets. I name them after writers who wrote about streets and cities, writers who have carved places through me. Marco Polo is a poet-explorer who loves cities and sees them as Places in time. The Great Khan loves diagrams and mathematics and wants cities to be timeless. Staging the city, then, and seeing the unstaged is Calvino's aesthetic. The other inspirations: George Simmel and Walter Benjamin.

3   Italo Calvino, "Cities and Desire," in *Invisible Cities*, trans. William Weaver (New York: Harcourt Brace, 1974), 17.

4   "Profane Illumination" refers to the aesthetic foundation of Walter Benjamin's *Arcades Project*, which is based on the city as an archaeology of culture laced with signs of former and forgotten violence and signs of the deterioration of economic forces.

5   Walter Benjamin, "Surrealism: The Last Snapshot of the European Intelligentsia," in *One-Way Street and Other Writings*, trans. Edmund Jephcott and Kingsley Shorter (London: New Left Books, 1979), 237.

6   Benjamin, "Surrealism," 227.

7   Benjamin, 229.

8   Benjamin, 239.

9   Georg Simmel, *The Philosophy of Money*, trans. Tom Bottomore and David Frisby, ed. David Frisby (London: Routledge, 1978), 317.

10   See Donald Gutstein, *Vancouver Ltd.* (Toronto: J. Lorimer, 1975).

11   Interview with Ian Chodikoff in *Canadian Architect* (January 22, 2009).

12   See Christos Dikeakos, "A Vast and Featureless Expanse: The Car Rides and Street Scans, 1969/71," in Bill Jeffries, Jerry Zaslove, and Glenn Lowry, eds., *Unfinished Business: Photographing Vancouver Streets, 1955 to 1985* (Vancouver: Presentation House Gallery and West Coast Line, 2005).

13   The "Hermes One-Way Street Interchange" and *homines rationalistici artificiales*, or hybrid people, is a reference to Yuri Slezkine, *The Jewish Century* (Princeton: Princeton University Press, 2004), which is about peasants and others whose cultural and social lives were transformed by migration and immigration into the lives of entrepreneurs, urbanized intellectuals, cultural intellectuals, etc.

14   Georg Simmel, "Metropolis and Mental Life," in *Selected Writings* (Chicago: University of Chicago Press, 1978 [1903]), 335. In the same volume, see "The Stranger," "The Adventurer," and "The Ruin."

15   See Simmel, "The Stranger," in *Selected Writings* (143): "The stranger will thus not be considered here in the usual sense of the term, as the wanderer who comes today and is gone tomorrow, but rather as the man who comes today and stays tomorrow ..."

16   See Jeff Wall, "Depiction, Object, Event," *Afterall* 16 (Autumn/Winter 2007).

17   Laurence Fontaine, *History of Pedlars in Europe*, trans. Vicki Whittaker (Durham: Duke University Press, 1996), 204.

18   Benjamin, "Surrealism," 229.

19   Calvino, *Invisible Cities*, 64–65.

20   Calvino, 17.

CHAPTER 3

21   I am grateful to Rita De Grandis of the University of British Columbia for the invitation to respond to Néstor García Canclini's *Transforming Modernity: Popular Culture in Mexico*, trans. Lidia Lozano (Austin: University of Texas Press, 1992), in *Canadian Journal of Latin American and Caribbean Studies / Revue canadienne des études latino-américaines et caraïbes* 23, no. 46 (1998): 133–154. The original title of this essay was "Vindicating Popular Culture in Latin America: A Response to García Canclini."

22   My term "natural history" is influenced by W.G. Sebald's *The Natural History of Destruction* (1999), which takes on the question of the memory of destruction of peoples and the aftermath of exile and war. Sebald is in turn influenced by Benjamin.

23   Peyman Vahabzadeh, *Exilic Meditations: Essays on a Displaced Life* (London: H&S Media, 2012), 40.

24   An altered translation of the original title, *Las culturas populares en el capitalismo*. References to "Latins of Americans: Narratives of the Border," are referred to as "Narratives of the Border." Underscoring García Canclini's sympathetic and critical analysis of fiesta celebrations of surplus and preservation of the ordinary in the face of commercial violation of communal norms is that "fiesta" is "the death of the belief in death" as a transformation of old death into new life (García Canclini, *Transforming Modernity*, 100). On the relationship of historical violence and popular adaptation, see also Michael Taussig, *The Devil and Commodity Fetishism in South America* (Chapel

Hill: University of North Carolina Press, 1980) and *The Magic of the State* (London: Routledge, 1997).

25   I borrow the provocative idea of a "non-country" from Jean Morrisset in order to call attention to how different the world of Latin America's Indigenous multiculturalism is from American and Canadian multiculturalism, which is grounded in an assimilationist ideology, determined to remake its own identity in terms of the ideology of globalism and separatism. On the one hand, pillaging the world's wealth while on the other hand, not knowing how to maintain its own guilty separation from the effects of globalism. See Jean Morrisset, "The Native Path and its Trance-Cultural Connections," in Dieter Haselbach, ed., *Multiculturalism in a World of Leaking Boundaries* (Münster: Lit Verlag, 1998), 103.

26   See Arnold Hauser, "Art History without Names," in *The Philosophy of Art History* (Evanston, IL: Northwestern University Press, 1958), 197–199.

27   The demonic character of everyday life is emphasized by Mikhail Bakhtin in *Speech Genres and Other Late Essays*, trans. Vern W. McGee, ed. Carole Emerson and Michael Holquist (Austin: University of Texas Press), 154. Bakhtin's "anarchistic" theory of language underscores García Canclini's ideas about culture and the experience of crossing and erasing boundaries. Bakhtin elaborates "the erasure of boundaries between the terrible and the comical in images of folk culture in Gogol's writings.

28   See Arnold Hauser, "Folk Art and Popular Art," *The Philosophy of Art History*. Folk movements search for new conventions, like films in similar periods of upheavals. There is a turn to conventions, which can fall into allegory and repeatable conventions, but often the experience behind the use of the conventions is lost.

29   See E.V. Walter, *Placeways: A Theory of the Human Environment* (Chapel Hill: University of North Carolina Press, 1988). The chapter "Road to Topistics" describes the "topistic imagination" and the mutual immanence of both slums and urban dwelling shaped "by a process of exclusions, enclosures and dissociations … [which] shaped physical intimacy, and social distance in everyday life."

30   García Canclini, *Transforming Modernity*, 60.

31   García Canclini, 62. For Canclini's critique of Gramscian approaches to popular culture, see pp. 21–27. Ultimately, his position is closer to Bakhtin than Gramsci, since the products of artisan culture are also a moral and ethical response to subordination and dependency, and in Bakhtin's sense are more like linguistically expressive speech genres which are stories or narratives; they are not neutral statements.

32   García Canclini, 110.

33   García Canclini, 108.

34   García Canclini, 110.

35   Jorge Luis Borges, *Twenty-Four Conversations with Borges: Including a Selection of Poems*, trans. Nicomedes Suarez Arauz, Willis Barnstone, and Noemi Escandell (Housatonic, ME: Lascaux Publishers, 1984), 137.

36   García Canclini, *Transforming Modernity*, 65.

37   See also Serge Gruzinski, *The Conquest of Mexico: The Incorporation of Indian Societies into the Western World, 16th–18th Centuries* (Cambridge, UK: Polity Press, 1993), for a view of writing in the Christian colonization in Mexico.

38   See Alberto Moreiras, "Afterword: Pastiche Identity, and Allegory of Allegory," in *Latin American Identity and Constructions of Difference*, ed. Amaryll Chanady (Minneapolis: University of Minnesota Press, 1994).

39   See chap. 6, "Fiesta and History: To Celebrate, to Remember, to Sell," in García Canclini, *Transforming Modernity*, 87–104.

40   Peter Sloterdijk, *Critique of Cynical Reason* (Minneapolis: University of Minnesota Press, 1987), 10.

41   Habermas, *The Structural Transformation of the Public Sphere: An Inquiry into a Category of Bourgeois Society*, trans. Thomas Burger (Cambridge, MA: MIT Press, 1989), 172–174.

42   See García Canclini's "Conclusion: Towards a Popular Culture in Small Letters," in *Transforming Modernity*, 105–114.

43   García Canclini, *Transforming Modernity*, 73.

44   Theodor W. Adorno, *Quasi una Fantasia: Essays on Modern Music*, trans. Rodney Livingstone (New York: Verso Books, 1992), 50.

45   Nemesis is the Greek goddess, the daughter of Night, who is also female, daughter of Chaos. Nemesis breeds "conscience" as force and is a deity because she is a goddess of retribution for evil deeds done, or undeserved good fortune. She is a personification like Hermes who exists at the borders and boundaries.

46   Bakhtiyar Vahabzadeh, *Exilic Meditations*, 40.

47   García Canclini, *Transforming Modernity* 108.

48   Vahabzadeh, *Exilic Meditations*, 115.

49   Vahabzadeh, 115.

50   Jody Berland, "Angels Dancing: Cultural Technologies and the Production of Space," in Lawrence Grossberg, Cary Nelson, and Paula Treichler, eds., *Cultural Studies* (London: Routledge, 1992), 49.

51   Adorno, "The Schema of Mass Culture," in *The Culture Industry and Other Essays on Mass Culture*, ed. J.M. Bernstein (London: Routledge, 1991). See Pierre Bourdieu et al., *The Weight of the World: Social Suffering in Contemporary Society* (Stanford: Stanford University Press, 1999).

52   García Canclini, *Transforming Modernity*, 106–107.

53   Néstor García Canclini, "Latins or Americans: Narratives of the Border," *Canadian Journal of Latin American and Caribbean Studies / Revue canadienne des études latino-américaines et caraïbes* 23, no. 46 (1998): 117–131.

54   Axel Honneth, *The Struggle for Recognition: The Moral Grammar of Social Conflicts*, trans. Joel Anderson (Cambridge, MA: MIT Press, 1996), 91.

55   García Canclini refers to Borges's *A Universal History of Infamy* at the conclusion of *Transforming Modernity*, 110.

CHAPTER 4

56   This essay was originally published in another form for an installation about the art and social practices in the city of Kladno, Czech Republic; see "Geological Poetics: A Triptych for Kladno," in *Kladno+Zaporno* (Prague: Muzeum Poldi Kladno, 2005).

Kladno, a former centre of steel production, is now a ruin. Uranium deposits were left underground until the Russian and Czech governments cleaned up the refuse. The essay in the original Czech publication was accompanied by images from Vancouver artists Jeff Wall, Christos Dikeakos, and Roy Arden, which I interpreted as the artists' geological vision. It then appeared in Bill Jeffries, Glen Lowry, and Jerry Zaslove, eds., *Unfinished Business: Photographing Vancouver Streets, 1955 to 1985* (Vancouver: West Coast Line and Presentation House Gallery, 2005).

57   Siegfried Kracauer, *The Mass Ornament: Weimar Essays*, trans. Thomas Y. Levine (Cambridge, MA: Harvard University Press, 1995).

58   See Bosch's drawing "*The Trees Have Ears and the Field Has Eyes*," where eyes watch an owl in a tree.

59   Quoted from World Watch Institute, *State of the World 2003: Progress towards a Sustainable Society* (New York and London: W.W. Norton, 2003), 126.

60   On Kierkegaard and "power-protected inwardness," see Adorno, *Kierkegaard: Construction of the Aesthetic*, trans. Robert Hullot-Kentor (Minneapolis: University of Minnesota Press, 1989), chap. 2, "Constitution of Inwardness."

61   From Canadian Intergovernmental Working Group on the Mineral Industry, *Overview of Trends in Canadian Mineral Exploration* (Ottawa: Natural Resources Canada, Minerals and Metals Sector, 2004), 149. While these figures are now old news, Canadian mining industries still pervade worldwide.

62   See my essay "Unfinished Landscapes: Smelting the Tailings from the Riches of the Canadian Landscape," *Topia* 21 (Spring 2009), a review of John O'Brian and Peter White, eds., *Beyond Wilderness: The Group of Seven, Canadian Identity and Contemporary Art* (Montréal and Kingston: McGill-Queens University Press, 2008).

63   That Andy Warhol's family migrated from Mikó, Austria-Hungary (now Miková, in north-eastern Slovakia) to Pittsburgh, a US coal mining and steel producing capital, was not lost on Hrabal.

CHAPTER 5

64   See the chapter's introduction for this text's original source.

65   Glen Lowry was associate dean for outreach and innovation at the Faculty of Art at Ontario College of Art and Design. He specializes in creative-critical collaborations, working with artists and writers.

66   See "Jeff Wall and Fred Douglas: An Interview by Jerry Zaslove and Glen Lowry," in *Unfinished Business: Photographing Vancouver Streets, 1955–1985* (Vancouver: West Coast Line and Presentation House, 2005). Fred Douglas was a Vancouver artist whose installations of photographs, tableaux, bookworks, and prints have been exhibited and collected at galleries throughout Canada. He taught at the University of Victoria for many years.

67   Emmanuel Levinas, "Ethics and the Face," in *Totality and Infinity: An Essay on Exteriority*, trans. Alphonso Lingis (Pittsburgh: Duquesne University Press, 1969), 212.

68   This point is reinforced in Camiel van Winkel, "Jeff Wall: Photography as Proof of Photography," in *Jeff Wall: Photographs*, ed. Gunilla Knape (Göteborg, Sweden:

Hasselblad Centre, 2002); see also Jeff Wall, "Frames of Reference," *Artforum* 42, no. 1 (September 2003): 188–192.

69   In *Jeff Wall, 1990*, I wrote: "Jeff Wall's early pictures can be understood 'aspectually' – as emerging chronotopes – feelings of time-space … by which I mean they stage an attitude towards contemporaneity within the contemporary empathy towards the commodity function of photographed images – *the exchange process itself* … dialogical relations between genres, historical periods, and works of artwork to release material from the melancholy calcification of alienation theories … A new emergence and hybridization of speech and image might negate the always-present montage and minimalist laws. Bakhtin makes the case that in Russian formalism the dialogical attitude is not a dramatic dialogue between two monads, or monological entities, but it is a dialogue taking place in time and space within the historical combinations of forms that makes up the resistances to centralized power … The creative chronotope encounters alienated modernist perspectives in the late 1970s. Dialogism pervades Jeff Wall's pictures even to the point of people engaging with speech" (Zaslove, "Faking Nature and Reading History: The Mindfulness towards Reality in the Dialogical World of Jeff Wall's Pictures," in *Jeff Wall, 1990*, 86).

70   See Arnold Hauser, *Mannerism: The Crisis of the Renaissance and the Origin of Modern Art,* trans. Eric Mosbacher (New York: Alfred A. Knopf, 1965). Hauser's work for me is important in the way I contextualize Jeff Wall's pictures in terms of art in history and the philosophy of art in dialogue with the institution of art and art-making.

71   See, in particular: Alois Riegl, *Historical Grammar of the Visual Arts,* trans. Jacqueline E. Jung (New York: Zone Books, 2004); Herbert Read, *A Concise History of Modern Painting* (London: Thames and Hudson, 1974); Meyer Schapiro, *Theory and Philosophy of Art: Style, Artist, and Society* (New York: George Braziller, 1994); Michael Baxandall, *Patterns of Intention: On the Historical Explanation of Pictures* (New Haven: Yale University Press, 1985); and T.J. Clarke, *Farewell to an Idea: Episodes from a History of Modernism* (New Haven: Yale University Press, 1999).

72   This point is reinforced in Camiel van Winkel, "Jeff Wall: Photography as Proof of Photography." Also see Wall, "Frames of Reference," *Artforum,* and Michael Fried, *Art and Objecthood* (Chicago: University of Chicago Press, 1999).

73   This is more directly conveyed through the "photo-paintings" of Gerhard Richter; see: Benjamin H.D. Buchloh, Jean-François Chevrier, Armin Zweite, and Rainer Rochlitz, *Photography and Painting in the Work of Gerhard Richter: Four Essays on Atlas* (Barcelona: Consorci del Museu d'Art Contemporani de Barcelona, 2000). The visual "figurations" of memory work as the enigmatic representations of the past are discussed in *Gerhard Richter,* ed. Benjamin H.D. Buchloh (Cambridge, MA: MIT Press, 2009).

74   Adorno to Benjamin, letter, February 29, 1940, in Theodor W. Adorno and Walter Benjamin, *The Complete Correspondence, 1928–1940,* trans. N. Walker, ed. H. Lonitz (Cambridge, MA: Harvard University Press, 1999), 321.

75   Walter Benjamin, "The Storyteller," in *Illuminations: Essays and Reflections,* trans. Harry Zohn, ed. Hannah Arendt (New York: Schocken Books, 1969), 144.

76   See Adorno and Horkheimer's "Elements of Anti-Semitism," in *Dialectic of Enlightenment,* trans. John Cumming (New York: Continuum, 1972), 168–208.

77   On the cultural, ethnic, and racial diversity of British Columbia at Confederation, see Adele Perry, *On the Edge of Empire: Gender, Race, and the Making of British Columbia, 1849–1871* (Toronto: University of Toronto Press, 2001); and Wayde Compton, "Introduction," in *Bluesprint: Black British Columbian Literature and Orature,* ed. Wayde Compton (Vancouver: Arsenal Pulp Press, 2001), 17–40.

78   Kaja Silverman, "Total Visibility," in *Jeff Wall: Photographs* (Vienna: Museum moderner Kunst Stiftung Ludwig Wien, 2003), 64.

79   Adorno, *Kierkegaard: Construction of the Aesthetic,* trans. Robert Hullot-Kentor (Minneapolis: University of Minnesota Press, 1989), 128.

Exiles, Pedlars, Tricksters, Utopians, and Mercurians on Other Shores

These are some of the Authors Who Always Come Along with me because of their "colporteur" quality of mind and work.

Everyone carries a room about inside him. This fact can even be proved by means of the sense of hearing. If someone walks fast and one pricks up one's ears and listens, say in the night, when everything round about is quiet, one hears, for instance, the rattling of a mirror not quite firmly fastened to the wall.

—FRANZ KAFKA, *The Blue Octavo Notebooks,* trans. Ernst Kaiser and Eithne Wilkins ([1919] 1991)

Every morning my landlord enters my room on tiptoe. I can hear his footsteps. The room is so long you could ride a bicycle from the door to my bed. My landlord leans over me, turns, signals to someone in the doorway, and says: "Mr. Kafka's here."

—BOHUMIL HRABAL, *Mr. Kafka and Other Tales from the Time of the Cult* ([1965] 2015), trans. Paul Wilson

Silence, Counterfeit, and Aesthetic Act in Alex Morrison's Vision of "Academic Freedom as Academic": Installations of the Phantoms of a Utopian Will[1]

A photograph of the Krupp works or of the AEG [Allgemeine Elektricitäts-Gesellschaft] reveals almost nothing about these institutions, tells us nothing about these institutions. Actual reality has slipped into the functional. The reification of human relations – the factory, say – means that they are no longer explicit. So something must in fact be *built up*, something artificial, posed. We must credit the Surrealists with having trained the pioneers of such photographic construction.

—BERTOLT BRECHT, *The Threepenny Lawsuit* (1931), quoted in
 Walter Benjamin, "A Little History of Photography" (1931),
 trans. Edmund Jephcott

Alex Morrison has created a compilation of aesthetic objects that illuminates the dour words "academic freedom." The expression may appear to be an abstract, even an exotic subject, since we think we live in a time when cultural institutions like the gallery, the museum, the library, and the university would seem to have no need to worry too much about "academic freedom" not related to a specific figure or works challenged because of offending some organization or cause. When such formidable cultural Institutions find themselves supported by civil society and liberal democracy, that by and large pays their bills through grants and foundations and, in the case of universities, through student tuition, students who are deeply in debt to their future, it is possible that one might view academic freedom with a jaundiced eye or even as an annoyance. The freedom to express dissident views would seem to be outmoded as a worrisome problem. The avant-garde does not really worry. Certainly "academic freedom" is not a force for revolutionary thinking or acting. The aura of something archaic hovers over the seven memorializing objects in Morrison's small pantheon of objects. And that is just the point. One should look carefully at how the archaic hovering over these works serves a not-yet-conscious effect – a mimesis effect – of how architecture has become an object itself that illuminates a graveyard of something vanished. What may appear as abstract in the works is in fact an important aesthetic and ethical act for the here and now.

The politics underscoring these aesthetic objects shows how difficult it is for a new generation to figure out where the university is in the public realm. The president of Simon Fraser University opened SFU's new School of Contemporary Arts, a large part of a redevelopment scheme to refurbish the Downtown Eastside, Vancouver's poorest quarter, with the words: "This investment in arts education will further support our economy by helping attract and create the creative class that is powering many of the world's most dynamic cities." Academic freedom for the "creative class"? The class unconsciousness in these words shrieks out in Morrison's 2007 figurative installation *Proposal for a New Monument at Freedom Square*. The other works become a scenic chorale dialectically related to *Picture for a Glass Tower (New Dawn Rising)*.

Picture for a Glass Tower reveals the inner shape of the new generation's destiny. Together with a companion piece, *The Poetics of Grey (No. 6)*, with its coloured triangle atop a bent-over pinnacle, we see a utopic mirror image of an anticipatory illumination of an abstract future. Like a conning tower overlooking the nameless grey architecture, the immanence of an era passes into a wasteland of space. Arthur Erickson's concrete pylons leave no room for the flâneur, the loiterer, the straggler, the messenger, the huts, or the palaces. Class itself is blocked out by a devotional piety to style. And the era of "academic freedom" belongs to the lost legacy of the utopian will that produced the social movements mediated through universities, which began, not in the 1960s, but with the critiques of the military-industrial complex in the 1950s, with the witch hunts in the universities for communists and others who did not sign loyalty oaths. These legacies are clamped together in a short film, *We Dance on Your Grave* (2007), where we watch a counterfeit rendition of that past, which slacks into merely empty ornamentation. One can't help but extend this view of these gravediggers into a longer view of the past. We are looking at a generational expression from an artist who stands upright looking unflinchingly towards the monopoly capitalism that has engulfed the university today. His treatment of the university as a set of objects suggests that the university is a means of production that is architecturally concealed and screened by the "grey on grey" of the architectural scenarios. These objects do not invite us to revolt against the history that made them what they have become in the new millennium, but invite us to see the pathos of the generation that wonders what this "academic freedom" thing is all about: the University now lurks in the grey fog of the cipher in joining itself through a mimetic effect that joins it to the culture at large. The contours are gone. Countless studies about the university have produced a grey-on-grey journalistic oeuvre that has changed nothing. Morrison's aesthetic objects are not deaf to his generation's resistance to specious sentimentalizing of the past. Architecture of walls and corners eliminates even the Minotaur-like labyrinths that would harbour crowds and mythical beasts, instead of the barricade-less spaces.

Aesthetic objects, how artists think, the public realm, social movements – these cannot avoid being placed against the ideological project of the refurbished cultural institutions that have marked the period since the formation of Simon Fraser University in 1965, when the university became a modern scene of progressive education that framed a would-be vocabulary of cultural change. This theatrically inbred scene of buildings high up on a small mountain highlights an age when building universities made reputations and future fame for the founders. Many other universities from the early and mid-1960s now lastingly wave at us from a generation ago. Even the cultural institutions that have orbited around the ideals of post-1960s cultural reforms have assimilated the very core of the avant-garde artistic and intellectual movements of the middle of the last century. *Arriviste* and avant-garde, they popularized the idea of knowledge-for-all in a form that has now become commonplace and harmless. The core of both the gallery and the university may have been at the time synonymous with the turn in artistic thought towards a new artificialism with all of the originality of manifesto-intense art forms asserting the compilational potentials of art and poetry, image and language as a technology of means and end.

The great montage artists of the generation on the wane, like John Heartfield (d. 1968), Hannah Höch (d. 1978), and George Grosz (d. 1959), had long before inserted "academic freedom" into the public discourse. Artistic form criticized the idea of "progress" in culture and art by conflating both with mass consciousness and propaganda. They condemned, not condoned, the bourgeoisie's holding on to the culturally dominant institutions. The energies of insurrection were everywhere, not just in surrealism. The notion of progress in education and the arts also lead to a new form of narcissistic, institutional self-identification with progressiveness as a form of freedom in the name of the metropolitan values of the avant-garde. The self-appointed vanguard universities continued to woo culture by gambling with philanthropy and mass-cultural institutions. This reveals the inner logic of accommodation to the capitalist experiment of mastering monopoly capital at all costs by harnessing institutions to idyllic views of the landscape. Mastery is the name of the game. Great moments of modernism would not exist without it. But yet.

The nature of this form through which the institutions dominate culture is the pretense embedded in the architecture of cultural suburban settlements like Simon Fraser University, where the culture makers see themselves as natural outgrowths of their will to perform in a vanguard-like fashion; they do not administer transient historical institutions at all, but in fact secure reality as the only constituted social form because they have answered the call of the showpiece – the buildings – and in that way hide the mediations related to its existence. The students, then, become petty bourgeois apprentices waiting for entrance into the middle class that they richly deserve. The architecture says so.

Alex Morrison's route into this generationally transitory world arrests the trek into the future and stops time for a brief moment in order to catch a glimpse of the falsification of the institution as a "polis" that is signified by the vanguard architecture. His is a view of the university as a phantom-like emblem of the avant-garde on the road to corporate identity. University Reform in a modern sense historicizes itself as a generational rupture with the past, and in this way is characteristic of art movements revising themselves. The architectural building styles become partners with a new collectivity in the quest for a unified polis envisioned through the designed cult manias of architecture as monuments in which the users, as Walter Benjamin writes, are "the distracted masses [who] ... absorb the work of art into themselves. This is most obvious with regard to buildings. Architecture has always offered the prototype of an artwork that is received in a state of distraction and through the collective."[2] Where is the independent thinking, and where the autonomous groups and independent artists who struggle both with the dematerialization of art and the incorporation of art into the cultural institutions – the museums and universities? The Faustian bargain made, universities became the bellwether institution that would define the future of culture by giving culture a name: progress in the name of semblance – faking classical architecture. A critique of semblance or imitation would be the underlying meaning epitomized by Morrison's compilation of seven objects.

Yet because the "post" generation has been labelled with so many different identities, one should be cautious of falling into the trap of thinking about generations themselves as a clear expression of any new utopian will or collective identity. The power of forgetfulness in regard to the nature of the university's direct route into its corporate persona is such that one almost believes that the power of the university ever did lead to the unblocking of the possibilities in the human being's immeasurable powers and that this place of unblocking would be the settlement of a community of intellectuals and students. This is the illusion that it would lead to something other than the curse that now inhabits all of society, not just the individual in the university: namely, the isolation, dissociation, and loneliness of being found inside of a counterfeit polis atop Morrison's tower.[3]

❋ ❋ ❋ ❋

Already immanent in Arthur Erickson's "Concrete Polis of Monumental Architecture" is the melancholy of desire that reminds us of the loss of the totality of previous historical movements. The melancholy core of the very being of today's students and professoriate is compromised by grief, regret, and powerlessness – that is, by the unfinished nature of the grey inner world, a kind of homelessness. This also represents the falseness of even the higher cultural kitsch found now in the joyfully willful message of the new architecture of the Royal Ontario Museum by Daniel Liebeskind. One needs to keep reminding oneself that the museum and the professoriate are the most privileged segments of a class society, and yet do not express their roles directly in the brutal class and cultural struggles of one of the most deeply exploitative periods of history. Autonomy may be a good if it remains independent. All of this is expressed in the greying of the architectural massifs that look to me, as a former historical participant in this particular university, more like expressionist sets from Robert Wiene's *The Cabinet of Dr. Caligari*, a habitat without people, like a haunted architecture are seen through the melancholy object of desires unmet.

In the film *We Dance on Your Grave*, the documentary view of Simon Fraser's fortieth anniversary party is transformed into a slow-motion silent video of pathos-ridden dancing on the premises of Arthur Erickson's imitation of the 1851 London Crystal Palace Mall, which celebrated industry, mechanical production, and glass. Morrison prepared the video by filming the celebration of a fabricated public sphere. The video reveals no genuine joy or celebration of the origins of a university in 1965 in the muddy construction site of the time but reveals a form of stupidity about the players' amnesiac actions. It is fake. It mimics the dropout culture by dropping in. This is the kind of stupidity that comes with the erasure of history and the substitution for historical consciousness – displacing any class consciousness – with ersatz, carnivalesque posturing. This is not a celebration of individual memories but of the taboos on "academic freedom" that appear artistically as a strange concoction of exotic costumes that imitate the now-mythical "sixties." In the context of the entire installation, this integrates the objects into figures of loss. The camouflaging of the legacy of academic freedom across the centuries becomes reified nonsense commingling with a question of "Why are we here at all?" It suffers from the veneer of coerced participation in a pop-cultural event. In another room in the gallery, there is the crew-necked, bearded academic artist manqué with a large head and spindly legs – *Proposal for a New Monument at Freedom Square* – screaming madly about nothing we know about into the void of the art gallery. The figure looks like a fugitive from Red Grooms's *Ruckus Manhattan* (1975–1976) or from an Edward Kienholz installation. It also reminds me of Karl Marx's tomb in Highgate Cemetery in London. There, Marx's oversized head sits on a small podium, almost mocking the class struggle by saying, "I'm just the big head and no body." Mockery lurks behind Erickson's architecture, which functions as mere punctuation marks for a memory that dwells nowhere. But what mocks what? One thinks of iconographic statuary of Stalin and Lenin, or even of the Palace of Soviets that received proposals from Gropius, who later protested the final results, and Le Corbusier. Tatlin's Tower, or "Monument to the Third International" (1919–1920), might well be reflected in Morrison's glass tower – a parody of the Bauhaus movement.

We Dance on Your Grave installs capital-*M* Memory in the abstract. The creative class dances. Unknown to these dancing participants, their movements reverberate with a Norman Rockwell – or Carl Spitzweg – folksy aura of the homey. They are in a happening taking place in some place – no place – that is at some time, somewhere, but we don't know what it is or where, but we know what it feels like – kitsch – because in coming closer to it, we hear the melody of a sentiment for nostalgia attached to the beating heart of the common person who reduces life to the median. The student as commoner. No elitism here. No class. We all dance together to the same tunes. The populist university created in 1963 by the Social Credit visionaries in modernist splendour had every intention of intervening in the public sphere with the values of modernism. Arthur Erickson's architecture offered pastiche modernism of weathered concrete that would make it possible to imagine the future. Yet something is wrong with the party and the vision: somnambulism. Morrison understands this aesthetically by presenting the fortieth anniversary party through the technically sharp images that combine silence and imitation of movements all in the name of miming emptiness. The figures are blind to knowing what it is. The concluding scenes of Antonioni's *Blowup* (1971) come to mind. Mimesis is the other side of blandness and mute silence.

What is the university both as agent and actor located in the public sphere? Can it be conveyed by a collection of objects? This is the critical and aesthetic challenge. The crisis of the nature of the university as a modern place of assembly is built into the distant views of the wilderness and the city, dominated by the geometrically rule-bound architecture. It must serve as both a house of learning and a socially engaging space. In my experience of living and working in Erickson's allegorical house of learning, it utterly fails in its purpose to be a socially engaging place. The anodyne corners always obstruct the possibility of even a minimalist sociality. The architecture buries the private realm in the false image of an artificially picturesque public realm. Resistance to the social is internalized in the obstructions created by the grey concrete. The medieval idea of the university, on which empathy with learning is based, lies in the capacity to reflect and also resist the social world that gives it meaning. It is, as Morrison recognizes, based on a view not only of the freedom of academics to be learned, but on whether they can defend this idea against the outside of the walls, as well those who would ruin it internally by the seductions of religious, political, or, today, corporate sponsorships that mirror the commercial needs of society. Whether we like it or not, this implicates the university as a place in the struggle for the emancipation from reactionary forces of anti-enlightenment. Put more philosophically, the university struggles with, and personifies, the great Hegel's notion of the unhappy consciousness, the institution and constitution of the alienated soul struggling for autonomy between the earthly world of existence and the spiritual, or "Geist," which for Hegel also means the cultural "aura." Here the cultural aura is represented by the university seen through today's counterfeit culture.

For Alex Morrison's generation, this struggle does not appear to be totally meaningful as a struggle. The *memorial* of his *Folk Riot* (2007) construction shows the truth of the utopian nature of the 1960s' failed revolution. It all falls in lapidary fashion to the field of forces seen in the emblems of a failed avant-garde institution. "Academic freedom" is a hollow phrase. Growth dominates. Yet the intellectual pogroms, censorship, political trials, burning of art and books in fascist celebrations of anti-modernism, the exiling of intellectuals in the 1930s, and then the witch hunts of the 1950s, and then the rise of student opposition to the Vietnam War – all have become largely mythology for the current generation of students. Whitewashed by the counter-revolutions of universities in the 1970s and 1980s, the grey on grey has been ornamented by the Multiversity Wal-mart of everything under one roof.

While protests wane and the intellectuals become greyer, the term "radical" comes to mean literally nothing when one tries to situate it today by imagining that the university is a social move-ment. Even the "war on terror," with its attacks on free speech and its surveillance mentality, does not galvanize the professor-iate out of institutionally defined roles. I see, then, in Morrison's work a sense of a work about generational literacy at the edge of history, not the mantra of the End of History preached, perhaps self-importantly, by the crew-necked model who protests to the air in clay and wood. This *Proposal for a New Monument on Freedom Square* is also about how the weak, class-conscious movements that sought to bring public universities into historical view have become phantoms of immanence, manically transcendent only to be left to the abstract beauty of Morrison's *Picture for a Glass Tower (New Dawn Rising)*. The new monument moves from bitter to cynical in the way the revolution as idea moves to commodity from its original allegorical model of the melancholy of desire.

Seen historically, portraying the idea of a university through visually sensual means has rarely been attempted. Learning has been portrayed through the reading and writing of books, or observing scientific experiments, or through the death of mar-tyrs like Socrates, but often through culture seen through the ruins of architecture. Even the self-portrait is a mode of learning that represents knowledge outside of institutions. Architecture becomes an allegorical viewpoint in the way panoramas of classic architecture reveal the ruins of older civilizations. One thinks of Giovanni Paolo Panini's *Ancient Rome* (1758) or interior images of the great libraries of the universities and monasteries of the West. Put another way, the physical image of the university as a location is deeply embedded in the historical weaving of secular, royal, and bookish mediations of knowledge into an arcade in the older sense of knowledge as a threshold – a library between worlds. One might even think of reading itself as an image of threshold learning, for example in the collection of photographs *On Reading* by André Kertész (1971), or Jeff Wall's *The Giant* (1992), a photomontage which shows a posed, nude, older woman in a reading room of a library standing upright and reading from a slip of paper. The pose and the tableau create an ethical sense that the architecture is supposed to be meaningful.

Turning to the theme of architecture as an arcade-like reference point for this generation, one wonders whether a generation-that-comes-later is perhaps sick to death of architectural immanence in their lives. This to me is prefigured in the image of Abstract Beauty in the triangular structure of *Picture for a Glass Tower*.

✳ ✳ ✳ ✳

But first we must deepen this sense of generational transmutation of ideas through the aftermath of aesthetic objects.

Walter Benjamin himself was caught in the struggle of generations. He teaches us that all art is an unfinished project and that the next generation that comes after the deluge of capitalism and war, and the neutralization of violence into myth and force of law, cannot necessarily be trusted to complete the project of the Enlightenment without sacrificing itself to the overwhelming forces that required enlightenment in the first place. What is the nature of that sacrifice? In his writing he became the artist consuming himself by using his life as an allegorical paradigmatic model of the very story he was telling about his generation. In this way Benjamin's work is a phenomenological excavation of the sources of his own thinking – that is, of how artists think. The end result is Benjamin's conceptual history of concepts where he searches the scarified history of art and literature for evidence that the Kantian ethics that underscores his independent anarcho-modernism can be architectonically compiled into a Marxian, arcades-like concept of the present. This is just one of the backgrounds to Benjamin's *Arcades Project* (1927–1940).

This view of the present will enable us to experience what Benjamin refers to as "nowtime," or the utopic, conceptual, revolutionary organization of the field of forces that became modernity. Modernity, however, also became, in its duplicity, an adjunct to the spectacle that capitalism has also become; what is needed is a range of aesthetic objects that speak to that duplicity. The pseudo-polis of the university, emblematically Simon Fraser, is that duplicitous adjunct to capitalism.

The immanent nature of Morrison's generational view of the 1960s dematerializes the generations and, aesthetically, reveals through a process of excavation how the architecture is a graveyard in which the past is embalmed. Morrison's dramaturgy, if I may call it that, expresses both the calamity of the process of playing with academic freedom as if it were merely academic, and the difficulty that the recalcitrant nature of his material has in speaking on its own about this melancholy of desire. In this regard the materials he uses, the compilation of it into an arcade-like system of colportage without a pedlar, or flâneur, or student, speaks to the actual state of affairs of thought about the university today: not only is it a failed avant-garde institution, but a headless monstrosity that has cannibalized itself so that only phantoms exist – the shadows that sit inside of and around the architectural field in "Grey on Grey."

Simon Fraser's architecture used as historical emblem speaks to the architectonic rendering of the counterfeiting of a scholarly settlement and the erasure of the past. In this sense, then, the university's glamorous architecture does us a service in announcing itself without knowing itself as a cultic happening, shown in Morrison's art, which is what the inhabitants would dearly wish it could be, since the cult of the past announces itself by denying the terms of its existence in the hidden struggle of classes that lies deep in the underbelly of this society.

The startling beauty of the abstract triangle that is *Picture for a Glass Tower (New Dawn Rising)* lies in its fractured light, its aura, and its colour, and is thus a utopic moment waiting for an event to reveal itself as a need that does not go away. This could also be a way to remind those who would interpret it this way, as a monument to the invisibility of the future and, as well, to the spell of the veneer that casts a sense of futility towards the university in the minds of a younger generation.

DOSSIER IV – CHAPTER 2

The Insurance Man: Kafka in the Penal Colony[4]

In Vietnam, when the corpse disappeared from the battlefield the thread of griefwork snapped at its origin ... Grief turns the attention of the survivor *to* inward feelings, memories, and imagined what-if scenarios; attention to the present sensory world is largely shut down.

  —JONATHAN SHAY, *Achilles in Vietnam: Combat Trauma and the Undoing of Character* (1994)

The "colportage phenomenon of space" is the flâneur's basic experience ... Thanks to this phenomenon, everything potentially taking place in this one single room is perceived simultaneously. The space winks at the flâneur: What do you think may have gone on here? Of course, it has yet to be explained how this phenomenon is associated with colportage.

  —WALTER BENJAMIN, "The Flâneur," *The Arcades Project* (1927–1940), trans. Howard Eiland and Kevin McLaughlin

I

Clearing the Room of Interpretations

The installation *The Insurance Man: Kafka in The Penal Colony* recreates Franz Kafka's 1919 story-fable in an art gallery that happens to be in an academic setting. Kafka is the author of "A Report to an Academy," a 1917 short story where a captured ape lectures his audience: "I imitated people, because I was looking for a way out, and for no other reason." We might respond that an academy is exactly the place where Kafka's protean sense of the pervasiveness of bureaucracy ought to be seen.[5] The installation is formed in part from materials that I have collected over the years with the idea of creating a colportage "reading" of Kafka. This reading is an extended metaphor. Fragments related to the pre- and post-history of the penal colony story bring the viewer into Kafka's spatial, territorial, and temporal world, and into the vexed problem of understanding the "torment machine" at the centre of the penal colony story. Walter Benjamin's phrase, "a category of illustrative seeing," [6] could describe projects such as this, consisting of collections of objects in a setting that is more typical of archival displays, like those created by the Deutscher Werkbund and other museum and archival institutions in Germany that display the texts and the authorship of literary texts by placing the work with materials related to the text, giving the viewer a contextual understanding of the author or artist. [7]

This is a Brechtian–Benjamanian, *mise en scène*-type installation, assembled as a colportage of materials; in this case, I am the collector of the materials, texts, objects, and images that populate the fable-allegory's central visual metaphor of a bizarre claptrap apparatus, an amalgam of machines that eventually destroy themselves. The *mise en scène* allows us to see the execution as an everyday affair. The conviction, persecution, and sentencing to death of an ordinary soldier who has ignored a command to "OBEY THY SUPERIORS," and whose body is inscribed with the words "BE JUST," takes place in a room that Kafka would have recognized. I have, in this sense, built the room.

In this room we see the commonplace objects that constitute the pre-history of Kafka's tale of a South Seas penal colony. The notoriety of those colonies, as well as events like the French Third Republic's Dreyfus Affair (1894–1906), whose aftermath rocked France and Europe for many years, and the trials of innocent Jewish villagers in Central Europe for the "blood murders" of children, embedded the deportation of prisoners into Europe's collective memory. [8] Kafka's working life was focused on factory safety and accident prevention, and he had an interest in, and heard lectures as a law student on, the deportation and trans-portation of criminals; factory labour and convict labour were close by. Work camps for vagabonds, allegedly antisocial individ-uals, Marxists, anarchists, or the unemployed were well-known lock-up phenomena. Deportees to prison camps that were often disguised as utopian resettlement camps – forerunners of the Nazi forced labour and concentration camps – included psychi-atric patients who were often convicted as degenerates and then deported to a territory where they could not "contaminate" the home country. Colonies were the subject of widespread juridical discussion in Europe, especially in the Weimar Republic; Kafka read *Journey to the Penal Colonies* (1913) by Robert Heindl, a lib-eral criminologist and jurist who toured the colonies of the South Seas, ostensibly to report back to the German colonial ministry. Heindl returned from the South Seas prison colonies and wrote his report. Graphics and statistics from Heindl's study of New Caledonia, the Andaman Islands, and Ceuta appear in the instal-lation, along with travel books owned and favoured by Kafka.[9]

I attempt to break the spell of the mystifications around Kafka as a writer whose ambiguities have moved the bound-aries of interpretation into the popular arena of what Adorno labelled "false renown."[10] Kafka's stories quote from his diar-ies and letters. All of his writing includes commonplace scenes. The stories rewrite themselves; they are amalgamations of key motifs. I highlight "ROOMS," "WRITING," "PHOTOGRAPHS," "BEDS," "CHILDREN," "WINDOWS" that occur in the manner in which Kafka becomes the pedlar who wanders into a city, going house to house as a "pedlar" – *Hausierer* in German, *colporteur* in French – who carries his domestic wares, gossip, and news. My pedlar's archive consists of Kafka's diaries, notebooks, epi-grams, aphorisms, and documents that relate to the pre-history of the torment machine in the "Penal Colony." In this respect the installation shows the "itinerancy" of Kafka's own wanderings in Prague by my "museumizing" of Kafka's own journeys in Prague and to the factories and workplaces he examined as a legal officer of a Workers' Accident Insurance Institute. He wrote reports on dangerous health and working conditions. The "spirit" of the installation is about Kafka as a literary pedlar, diarist, letter writer, aphorist, and one condemned to the torment of writing.

The Penal Colony machine in the installation is portrayed having a secret memory function that transforms a command into a life of writing. Writing merges into writing that can only be known through the shortness of life itself – Kafka's short life. The connection of writing to the sentencing of the prisoner, combined with how the Officer cannot avoid his petty-bourgeois desire for a leader, are two key sub-real aspects of the story. [11] In the exhibition, we construct the tormenting machinery of beds that ink words on the body of the soldier. Writing is portrayed as Kafka's secret nightmare. It is Kafka's own private insurance policy that keeps him sleeplessly alive in the face of the grinding indignity of the bureaucracy and the inadequacy of his writing to exhume the torment he sees in the world. The rays of light from the outside world seen through the window of his inner territory, the rooms he inhabits described in his diaries and letters, preserve his memory of a faraway world that will not vanish. What remains are the fragments and traces of memory embedded in the torment machine of his consciousness that comes with reading the world as if the world were himself, and he cannot trust himself. He articulates how one reads and writes in a letter to Oskar Pollak in 1904:

> Altogether, I think we ought to read only the kind of books that wound and stab us. If the book we are reading doesn't shake us awake like a blow to the skull, why bother reading it at all? So that it can make us happy, as you put it? ... What we need are books that hit us like misfortune that pains us, like the death of someone we loved more than we love ourselves, that make us feel as though we had been banished to the woods, far from any human presence, like suicide, a book must be the axe for the frozen sea within us. That I believe. [12]

"In the Penal Colony" echoes the feeling of "being banished to the woods," just as Kafka's letters and diaries have been subjected to countless readings on the nature of the "wound and stab" of writing. The first, by Wayne Burns in 1956, drew out the affinity to Octave Mirbeau's *The Torture Garden* (1899). Burns points out that Kafka may have been aware of the anarchist ideas in Mirbeau, Tolstoy, and Kropotkin, but had applied anarchist ideas artistically, which is what this installation tries to do. [13] Burns wrote, to the actuality of where we live, in a "world closer to dream than to surface actuality ... the sub-real world we live in when ... the I has no choice but to conform – either that or be destroyed." [14] But Kafka's secret was to cleanse Mirbeau and "the remarkable apparatus" of their ornamental, melodramatic elements and recover its spectral nature, the sub-real, as well as its domestic, everyday actuality. This installation likewise tries to capture the sub-real beneath Kafka's realistic account of a visit to a penal colony as an everyday event.

Kafka's story redeems the objects in the world of their physical reality – the ladies' handkerchiefs, for example, or the ladder leading down into the pit, or an ordinary bucket – by presenting the reader-spectator with a torture ritual that defies the understanding of the narrator, the Explorer, until he must leave just when he appears to understand where he is but is not able to explain what it is that is happening before his eyes. The story poses the Explorer/Kafka as an ethnographer of the real.

At the end of the story, the Explorer and the reader enter an inn where the furnishings are impersonal, yet have the archaic quality of the shabby Austro-Hungarian/European bureaucracy. [15] The bureaucratic sublime of Kafka's world opens to the inner territory of the selves being watched, ever capable of returning to reveries of hope while under the siege of bureaucracy. The sub-real worlds of banal, commonplace situations emerge. The apparatus itself is a simulacrum of the story; it is *furnished* and dressed up with explanations that hide its secret – the bureaucratic uncanny, the ecstasy of the impersonal, whose origins lie in the almost human apparatus that embodies documents and official decrees. The machine noisily grinds itself with clumsy precision into silence, then breaks down when the memory of violent acts become incommensurable with the explanations of the Officer. The idiotic machine never overcomes its grotesque relationship to the almost-inarticulate Officer. Kafka's technical mastery of machines and his curiosity about them in his investigative work is clearly alive in his almost comical description of the Rube Goldberg–like contraption of the Apparatus that debases us as spectators, especially when the Officer-operator charged to maintain the machine submits to it at the end of the story in a sacrificial embrace of slave consciousness and identification with the machine itself. [16] The Apparatus is made of a stylus, a harrow, and a bed that the story describes as "correspond[ing] to the human form." The execution of the prisoners on the Island has a long history and typically takes place before hundreds of spectators, celebrities, and common people alike, and, Kafka notes, especially in front of children. [17] The relationship of the writing on the body to documents relates to the myths and oral histories associated with juridical sentences and executions; supposedly the Explorer sees this curiosity as an eternally returning violence that has no name.

II

Colportage Endlessness: Digging in a Quarry

Kafka read the penal colony story aloud in Munich on November 10, 1916, at a salon, "Evening for New Literature," in Munich's Galerie Neue Kunst, in the art quarter of Schwabing. The reading in the avant-garde bookshop – not a favourite of the Munich police – was risky and adventurous. The title of the story was itself inflammatory in the period of the war during which atrocities, mob violence, and pogroms accompanied grisly warfare and fear of subversion. The proprietor of the Galerie advertised the story with the changed title "Franz Kafka: A Tropical Fantasy." The irony of the change of title is not lost on how the installation used material on prison islands that looked innocuous in keeping with Kafka's innocuous prose. It was the only reading of his work that he ever gave outside of Prague. He was very reluctant to read the story, not being sure of how the Munich public or the censor would receive his work. He decided to read the unpublished "In the Penal Colony." Rainer Maria Rilke was present at the reading and was very taken by Kafka's reading. Three newspapers reviewed the reading: one reported "he was a lecher of horror"; another criticized Kafka for going on too long and not being entertaining enough. A reviewer in Munich's *New Reporter* (*Münchner Neuesten Nachrichten*) wrote that it was a very poor example of his work and spoke on behalf of the listeners:

> Kafka read the "Groteske." The material should have been treated more efficiently in order to bring out a more artistic impression. But in spite of the technical failures, the detailed description of the torture machine and the psychically pathological love of the officer for the machine were understood by the listeners. The grotesque death of the officer as the last sacrifice of the machine made the story's endlessness slowly subside.[18]

Kafka agreed to the ending. Others found it to be a psychological case study. One thousand copies were printed, taking ten years to sell. Kafka's books, including this edition, were banned, burned, and buried by the Nazis as "non-Aryan degenerate" literature.[19] The citizens who were Kafka's Munich listeners and spectators at the reading appear as imaginary figures in the installation via my personal collection of photographs and paintings of Kafka's Prague contemporaries.

Picturing Kafka is not for the faint of heart; Kafka cautioned the publisher of *The Metamorphosis*, Kurt Wolff, not to illustrate the insect Gregor Samsa. Equally, it would be incommensurable with the art of "In the Penal Colony" to reconstruct the machine according to either the Officer's description of it or the Commandant's diagrams that the Explorer can barely make out when he tries to decipher them. Kafka's secret about the apparatus is that he artistically takes out a risk policy on the instalment plan of his own writing and life in order to protect his memory from the implications of the machinery that damaged factory and quarry workers; the latter apparatus he examined carefully and conscientiously in his own office writings for the Bohemia Workers' Accident Insurance Institute that was known all over Europe. The coded blueprint of the machine carries childhood memory traces, such that "the Commandant in his wisdom ordained that the Children should have preference" in observing the execution, since the idea that watching the radiance of the tormented prisoner would reveal the secret message in the torment. The Old Commandant is portrayed as the keeper of the tradition of watching something that reminds us of a ritual murder. Kafka marvelled that the workers who came to his office to "redeem" their grievances and resolve insurance claims arrived cap in hand rather than storming the office out of revenge for the injuries they had endured.

There have been many portrayals of Kafka in film, serious as well as kitsch. One should always heed Adorno's warning that adaptations of Kafka "should be reserved for the culture industry."[20] Odradek, the creaturely figure in Kafka's "The Cares of a Family Man" (1919), silently inhabits "the zone in which it is impossible to die," and, Adorno writes, represents the "no-man's land between man [sic] and thing."[21] The Odradek in this installation is the apparatus itself – the beds that care. The images that look to it do not see it as description or illustration, but as a recording device that does what Walter Benjamin hopes can be done by

> blasting a specific life out of the era or a specific work out of the lifework. As a result of this method, the lifework is preserved in this work and at the same time cancelled; in the lifework, the

era; and in the era, the entire course of history. The nourishing fruit of the historically understood contains time as a precious but tasteless seed. [22]

Memory "blast[s] a specific life out of [an] era." [23]

Siegfried Kracauer's classic Kafka-influenced essay "Photography" (1927) agrees: "From the perspective of photographic representation, memory images appear to be fragments – but only because photography does not encompass the meaning to which they refer and in relation to which they cease to be fragments." [24] "In the Penal Colony" compiles Kafka's stockpile of memory traces from his diaries, writing, letters, and documents filtered through the sub-reality of the penal colonies' Sovereign Law. Here is the logic of a civilization built on emigration; Empire transports its convicts, while judiciously managing land revenues and its "quarries," to promote "an immediate and extensive emigration of virtuous and industrious families and individuals." [25]

III

Scripting the Penal Colony

This production/installation shows Kafka's texts in one room, perhaps like an album in an attic filled with photographs of Prague's cultural celebrities. Portraits from the Langhans Gallery Prague watch the proceedings. There are also portraits from the Academy of Fine Arts that were in Prague at the time of the writing of the story. The models lived in the vicinity of Kafka's many Prague homes, but here they are viewing the beds of the machine. Other objects are specimens directly related to the story.

By the end of the story the noisy machine goes silent. The photographs and paintings are wordless, like the word and figure of Odradek and the songs in "Josephine the Singer, or the Mousefolk" (1924). Thus, the story-installation should be understood as a compilation relating both cultural memory and personal memory to the reality of a silent place. Gestures of memory function as markers for storytelling. The in-piction of the inner life of our labyrinthine memories is redeemed by images that transmute the senses of time into objects and space. We reader-spectators are distant from the torment machine and are yet inside it, as an X-ray reveals the contours of the body, illuminates the inside, and at the same time cancels both.

IV

Vertigo and X-Ray

There are seven beds: "writing," "marriage," "sleeping," "office," "hospital," "machinery," and an unnamed bed. The Officer's tormented fantasy of his perfect machine causes the Explorer to feel the vertigo of being thrown into the pit with the machine. He experiences *Schwindelerfahrung*, "vertigo." The fear of living with perpetual fear of a "diagnosis" that no X-ray could reveal creates the vertigo of a disembodiment. In Kafka's world, beds are soft objects surrounded by space and the view of the "Hunger Wall" is placed above them. The Hunger Wall still exists on Petrin Hill. It was a make-work project for the unemployed. It has no purpose and becomes still another sardonic image for Kafka's stories like "Before the Wall" or "The Great Wall of China," even for the Law itself. Spacelessness and vertigo are an event, a fragment, a book, something read about or imagined. Memory, assisted by photographs, is more Heraclitean than fixed. Memory fragments appear in bizarre corners of the world, signalling the extraterritorial body punished by Sovereign Law – Kafka's novels *The Trial* and *Amerika*, whose original title is *The Man Who Disappeared*, reach into the corners of his body and were conceived and written at the time Kafka was working on "In the Penal Colony." In the case of our Explorer, the scenes seemingly deport him into the territory of an unmasterable future.

For Kafka, the city of Prague was a gigantic room where his wanderings brought him into contact with people of all classes and stations. Prague became a territory surrounded by "The Great Wall of China" (Kafka's story of that title), a prison that contained the conflicts and convergences of traditions, languages, and uprooted ethnic peoples caught in the early twentieth century's apocalyptic fear of decline. Cities trumpeted industrial progress in the machines, factories, mines, and technical advancements that gave machinery an aura of sublimity while World War I brought brutal violence inside the walls.

European cultures beckoned to Kafka from behind the walls of the Austro-Sovereign Empire's Bureaucracies and their archives, records, and texts. The Austro-Hungarian Empire, the French and Belgian Empires, the Russian and Turkish Empires spread to the corners of the globe and exported their prisoners to the South Seas, to Siberia, and then under the Nazis to the Theresienstadt Ghetto (Terezín), a fortress-prison since the eighteenth century only sixty kilometres outside of Prague that was to become a labour camp for further transportation to Auschwitz-Birkenau and other camps in the East. Kafka's sisters Valli, Elli, and Ottla were imprisoned there and subsequently transported and murdered in Auschwitz. Other imperial corners of the globe included Devil's Island off the coast of French Guiana, New Caledonia, and the Andaman Islands off the coast of India. Ships regularly embarked throughout the nineteenth century from Bengal to these South Pacific prison colonies. These "utopian," fabricated colonies housed Asian and European prisoners ranging from petty criminals and murderers to political dissenters and revolutionaries. Kafka knew that the plantation class, like the factory owners he studied and documented, would supervise the colonies. His imagination turned to a series of travel books, especially ones like *Schaffstein's Little Green Books* series (early 1900s), *Letters of a Coffee Planter: Two Decades of German Labor in Central America* (1913), and others.

The Explorer-Researcher enters a self-sufficient world emptied of signs of the past. He sees a sophisticated machine that exacts retribution from a man sentenced to humiliation, shame, and pain for refusing to obey. The machine implicates the reader in many levels of punishment for both the Explorer and the Storyteller: both, although for different reasons, are onlookers when the bizarre machine trembles, when it writes words on the body of the sentenced man. Kafka's calm "voice" is written into how the storyteller and the Explorer tell the story. The watchful reader listens to the story and hears how both the Explorer and story characterize the Officer. The story is, then, double voiced.

We learn about the Explorer's liberal attitude towards the aesthetics of violence in his embarrassment about watching the machine, we see the growing panic of the Officer, and we note the Explorer's bewildered resistance to the Officer lovingly naming the parts of the machine – from technical jargon to popular nicknames. The condemned man carefully imitates the Explorer's watchfulness and hopes for his help. The Prisoner has a comical, clown-like face that reminds us of the toys Kafka saw in factories, or of the actors in the Yiddish theatre that he loved and incorporated into *The Trial* and *The Castle*. Faces meet the facelessness of the machine.

Kafka records in his diary that while travelling through the countryside, his friend saw a bunker with its artillery camouflaged by both the landscape and foliage and commented on how beautiful the guns looked in nature; Kafka agreed but said that this could only be true from the point of view of the quadruped. The beds in the installation camouflage violence and Kafka's dreams about violence. The inner workings of the tribunal-like scene at the site of the sentence reveal not a dream, but a parable of ancient human relationships turned lawfully violent.

V

Furnishing – *Einrichtung* – "The Machine Operates on Batteries"

The centre of the story is the pit that houses the machine that is run on a battery. The room in this installation is "furnished," summoning up images of books, pictures, plants, carpets, uniforms, women, armour, detritus, equipment, and household furniture and devices. The German word *Einrichtung*, "furnishings," also implies bringing the evidence of a crime into the courtroom where we find ourselves "furnished" with justifications for an act of solitary and unreliable witnessing. We see Kafka's texts on the walls, the walls of the writing machine, and the walls inside our head where writing is composed. We also hear the music of children's voices from outside the walls and the infernal inner machine that constantly forces us into the commotion of reading and rewriting one's own work as if it is a strange occupation. [26] Kafka's story reminds us of the common saying that "it all runs on its own"; the bureaucracy, "the machine direct[ing] itself on batteries," is rendered here in the folk saying that one "cannot direct oneself to make both ends meet." In Kafka's story-fable, the Explorer says, "One can't make oneself fit into this situation," and then the "I" that doesn't fit in disappears.

An Open Letter: Tracing Roy Miki's Aesthetic and Political Literacy[27]

Everybody praises their favorite day. / But few know what they're talking about. / Sometimes a day can be a stepmother. / Sometimes it can be a mother. // Happy and blessed is the man / who knows all this lore / about all these days, / but who still does his work with piety every day, / giving no offense to the immortals. / This man judges truly / what every flight of birds / is aiming at: / deliverance from evil.

—HESIOD, *Works and Days* (700 BC), trans. C.S. Morrissey

From this story it may be seen what the nature of true storytelling is. The value of information does not survive the moment in which it was completely new. It lives only at that moment; it has to surrender to it completely and explain itself to it without losing any time. A story is different. It does not expend itself. It preserves and concentrates its strength and is capable of releasing it even after a long time.

—WALTER BENJAMIN, "The Storyteller" (1936), *Illuminations*, trans. Harry Zohn

The true nature of storytelling may be that it provides information without footnotes. The listeners become the footnotes. This "open letter" traces how I think about Roy Miki's openness to a generation that has learned from him and how I have learned from him as well. His political and poetic world view changed how many of his generation faced a racialized Canada. But this commentary is also about the marriage of "reflection and shipwreck" and those who came ashore by sea or land to the Pacific side of the Canadian Coast. This speaks to my own experience of the underground generation that emerged when Simon Fraser's English department burst upon us when a new generation of poets and writers, critics and teachers fearlessly rendered the immanence of modernism into a way of thinking about the cultural politics adjacent to the territorial settlements of colonial Canada.

But to whom do we speak now?

Theodor W. Adorno wrote, in *Kierkegaard: Construction of the Aesthetic*, that "the genuine writer moves between the 'necessity' [of the marriage of reflection and shipwreck]," which, for Kierkegaard, risks moving from "objectless inwardness" to potential "shipwreck" on a "romantic island where the individual undertakes to shelter his [*sic*] 'meaning' from the historical flood … Only at particular instants do person and history come into contact. At these moments, however, the historical dimension shrivels."[28] It is this feeling of reflection, shipwreck, and shrivelling of history that I want to convey here in how I see Roy Miki's aesthetics and politics.

Mapping the demise of literary and cultural politics in the age of the university's capitulation to capitalism is one side of how we try to represent the power of culture; the other side is the fragile institutions collapsing and needing to pretend to grow under the sign of the money economy. The need for legitimation pervades modern institutions of culture. The duplicity about the official representation of minorities exploded into a range of historical stories after Simon Fraser University opened in 1965. The foundational myths of modernism had barely settled before the academic institution became fractured by poetic and social dissent. Here was a new generation inserting experimental poetics into the question of race and ethnicity, creating a maelstrom in which one had to think about and through the incommensurability of aesthetics and cultural narratives. The legitimation of the "contemporary" or the "contemporaneity" of the non-contemporary, the feeling of being "contemporary" could not be severed from the past without the past becoming the "unpast" where the historical dimension withers. This reflected the incommensurable community-in-the-making and its origins traceable to a small English department that took on the question of the exilic while the national emergency of the state was tracing official multiculturalism into the modernism of the future. [29] At the same time, the changeling city of Vancouver saw how race, ethnic identity, and new class wealth could no longer hide behind colonial façades. Colonial places, the "stepmother" of Hesiod's *Works and Days*, were now in the position of watching for "bird signs." They assimilated the diasporic worlds of the exiled Japanese Canadians and the lived experiences that were emerging from their dislocated memories. This became the "works and days" of Roy Miki's and many others' beginnings in the academy, which was coming of age itself. A new cultural intelligentsia was on the way at a time of deep modernizing of the academy. At the time, my own studies, informed by anti-fascist exiles, were, as Hesiod beautifully puts it, "watching all the bird signs, and keeping clear of transgression." [30] This was the time of the trickster and the ambivalence of the gods of culture towards Hermes the Thief who lived at the borderlands of the other shores of cultures. But one does not keep clear of transgression; one crosses that threshold and enters the unknown public sphere where, as Roy Miki's struggles against the duplicity of "representation" have shown in his work, the necessity of remembering how "the marriage of reflection and shipwreck" was at a pre-political stage in an academy unsure of its own reality in a traditional public, colonial public sphere.

Out of this, Roy Miki's work suddenly emerged as political, beyond the allegory of race and identity, where the trickster crossroads of culture, politics, and poetry faced into the identity machines that subsumed the devastating nature of the politics of racialized identity machines into its executive organs. In my courses on the "City in History: Reading the City Reading Us," I used several propaganda films that "represented" the eviction and relocation of Japanese Canadians and Japanese Americans transported into the interiors of Canada and into eastern California. In addition, I showed the classic photographs by Dorothea Lange which were taken at the request of the US President. The photographs were later banned. It was all being documented, but was not understood as the brutal transgression of the rights of people being herded out of modern urban cities as if they were dangerous wildlife.

The "representation" and documentation countered the propaganda of a crisis of the state needing protection from The Enemy who might destroy our cities from within and without. Nation-building by sanitizing the city is internalized as the fate and destiny of emergency patriotic acts that lead to incarceration, masked as the building of sustainable towns in the "interior" of a nation. The "city" of aliens is made up of those who are excluded from the city, and films are portrayed as geography lessons: the coast is fate and nature; topography becomes the built cities; the city is destiny. The camps are "utopian" solutions to the security of the state. Films and photographs represent the city where property and land, that is, *real estate*, were in danger of losing their "modern" identity if Japanese Canadians were allowed to live on the "coast." Where was the coast?

The films show whole peoples transported "elsewhere" while their property, memories, and futures were stolen from them, dis-placed, un-placed. Everything is framed in terms of denaturalizing the white settlements of racialized peoples. The terms of exclusion, force, and law are cast in militarized emergency measures. The state of emergency is built into the construction of the emergency and presented as neutralized documentary evidence that proves that the force of law must prevail and that peoples can be transported to some "interior" or inward place. That was the official story of renaturalizing the city as a pristine place of security. Racialized people are turned into melancholy allegorical figures. [31]

Adorno poses the critique of the construction of the aesthetic in extreme times as the struggle against sheer inwardness. A definition of this outcast generation would help: History is being written as the "last thing before the last." Generations become immanent historical realities in the making. I name this as "epochal" or "generational" time. "Epochal time" – a phenomenological or experiential concept – struggles against and within cultural institutions where a span of time and the power of tradition and the literacy associated with inbuilt learning becomes a foundation for further creative work. In the case of Miki, his aesthetic illuminated the times when lying about race and exclusion was normal behaviour. No wonder that this post-foundational, "epochal" generation turns to memory, photography, and the archive in order to guard against the strong institutions surrounding us that claim to represent history as it actually is. [32]

For Benjamin the mechanization of the means of producing art described in the much quoted "The Making of Art in the Times of Technical Reproducibility" – my awkward, but more accurate way to translate the famous title – is not just about the consequences of the ideology of progress through technical means, or the rapid dissemination of art or literature to new audiences by aesthetics, spectacle, and allegories of mourning the past. It is about finding a way to become conscious of and knowledgeable about how the phantasmagoria of modern life uses visible means to reduce the distance of history and the magical powers of reification by focusing on the new mediations and the machines used to exploit "identity" as a necessarily democratic concept. It is no accident that Miki uses, as an epigraph to his *Redress: Inside the Japanese Canadian Call for Justice*, one of Benjamin's astute statements regarding the historicizing of generations: "The events surrounding the historian, and in which he himself takes part, will underlie his presentation in the form of a text written in invisible ink." [33]

I have myself written essays on the "invisible ink" of the ruins of the city and the university, reflecting on the time when coming to Canada meant escaping the US and its nationalistic capitalism. The first poem I published in Canada in the early 1970s reflects something of my own generational leap into the unknown, and it came when Canada was turning towards a visible nationalism by institutionalizing missing elements of the past. But in whose memory? In terms of Hesiod's memory as labour, the poetic movements that moved within Simon Fraser University as a new beginning of language were mythical and epical, yet trickster-like in the sense that Benjamin draws between the storyteller, the novelist, and "profane illumination." [34]

Benjamin's distinction was for me creatively alive and can be combined with Bakhtin's "image of language" or "prosaics," which gives us a longer view of time derived from the startling combination of Bakhtin's Menippean satire and utopic thought as a form of history-thinking that is a time–space (Bakhtin's "chronotope") of time and memory. Time is conditioned by labour, by memory as remembrance, a cosmogony of labour, in which language is not derived only from gods, who themselves go berserk, but from the inner demands of the labour of making stories in the built world, where the origins of created time exist through resistance to empire and colonization. The world is turned upside down and inside out. By working within the surplus of culture, we find that the basis of culture is storytelling, farming the culture inside the city, so to speak. Literacy means the writer dreams the dream of the free-thinking reader and relates the craft of writing to the relationship of surplus – building others' language and questioning ownership of the means of production. That is, I see in Roy Miki's struggle an older cosmogony of writing related to farming and city building, being aware of how the colonialized slaves really are the human surplus, are commodities in the making.

One could go so far as to say that the origin of writing begins with slaveholding and the consciousness of the master–slave dialectic that required putting laws onto paper. This is not new. This "revolutionary" position regarding the dialectic of work, power, and domination by sovereign myth asserts a different cultural logic than sovereign myth does and suddenly illuminates fate and character, user, teller, beholder as living history. I used Roy Miki's poetry in a course on exile along with other works (and days), trying to show how the chronotope of the "exilic" writer and Hegel's master–slave dialectic shadows the fate and destiny of the writer in Canada.

Behind the exilic is the work of mourning for both fate and destiny, as articulated by Benjamin in his 1920–1921 essay "Fate and Character":

> ... (for insofar as something is fate, it is misfortune and guilt) – such an order cannot be religious, no matter how the misunderstood concept of guilt appears to suggest the contrary. Another sphere must therefore be sought in which misfortune and guilt alone carry a weight, a balance on which bliss and innocence are found too light and float upward. This balance is the scale of the law. The laws of fate – misfortune and guilt – are elevated by law to measures of the person ... All legal guilt is nothing other than misfortune.[35]

Fate then also has a double: destiny. Destiny is the working out of fate, in this case of the exiled internally and externally eradicated Japanese Canadian West Coast community: the law is on trial and the "pagan" subject (see Benjamin) must regain speech which the law has robbed from them.

In Bakhtinian terms this is the chronotope of the visible and invisible secret of the always-lurking exilic that is of not belonging. I have posed this aesthetic-political question in many essays on memory, photography, and the city where I speculated that the city is inside of us as spatial experience. It is real estate made into partially destroyed inner objects today accompanied by the destiny of city-building, where a once beautiful city has become a commercial stronghold. In Vancouver we have the prototype of a future phenomenon that has no name, a "western" city where experiments in community are going on that also have no name; or when names are given to new constellations of race or identities that do not adequately describe how the new generation of social thinkers and artists are struggling for a sense of continuity with the past, and a sense that the forms that their work takes are inside encumbered geographical spaces – what Benjamin describes as "profane illuminations" of the past. I think Roy Miki's "theory of knowledge" gives history a "physiognomy" in Benjamin's sense of working out the fate and destiny of race and ethnicity as a "primal history."

The university became one of the *encumbered spaces* that plugged up the breathing holes and loopholes of city-building with culture-building. But that is what it is supposed to do! Universities not only build into their "identity" an image of a monument, like the desiccated concrete of Simon Fraser's architecture, but also join the quest for a cultural identity that will enable institutions to be part of the international cultural marketplace of the knowledge industries that have become the object of desire of postwar expansion. Universities have become the "adjacent reality" to the new globalism or "world government" that is determining the future of civic society and the fate of young people. Yet ...

Cities and universities do provide students with an image of the globalized, cosmopolitan world, where we know that fifty-one of the world's one hundred largest economies are corporations, providing 70 percent of world trade. [36] One can enumerate such Hesiodic-inspired figures without realizing that the poor live in feudal-like states in terms of their exilic lives. Universities mirror this new reality by way of serving the accelerated development model that governs university culture as both theatre and necessity.

But a final word on a generation as an incommensurable community. If generations see their own history as "destiny" on the thresholds of a future of culture if there is to be a future at all, the encounters, the crossing-overs, the *kairoi* of experience that moves art into other terrains of the exilic, the lapsed and forgotten, the camouflaged in the cities incapable of predicting the outcome of the future character, or "fate" of the moral order. Out of the world of the senses comes the fall of the world into the ruins of allegory or pathos of institutions. The racialized public spheres, Miki's battles in his day job, have emerged in a dialogical reciprocal community that is both *time-bound* and *out of time*. The incommensurable communities dream of social justice against the time-bound historical process of capital as theatre, as spectacle. The generation that finds itself assimilated into historical movements, where the artist or critic had previously felt it necessary to make big statements, lives now within an imaginary typology searching for a working cosmogony of the present. The present is then the Nemesis of the Generations, its destiny to be understood through movements in art and culture that become a school, a group around a manifesto-like sense of affinity with movements, and assert their influence and, in its particularized sense of historical experience, work to inspire others and infect others with their presences. Poetically speaking through Mikhail Bakhtin, the nature of dialogue is about language and contiguity, as in Benjamin it is about mimesis and invasion of the integrity of the person by capital and sovereign law; both Bakhtin and Benjamin showed that dialogism is an encounter, an argument, in the works-and-days places where the now so-called imaginary community is a chronotope of space and time, formed by the experience of resistance to even wanting to be included without creating its own fate and destiny, its own character. That space and time in the present reveals itself in phantasmagoria, surreal combinations, dislocations of art and culture, is a sign that the generation lives under, Benjamin's "sign" of "profane illumination."

A new satellite intelligentsia needs to stand apart and be dissident, refuse to become artists and teachers assimilated into the Institutions. The New Intelligentsia already knows that historical vanguards and dissident intellectuals comprised themselves around journals, neighbourhood places, cafés, non-traditional movements, and these often included exiled strangers who had not yet been seen or become famous, yet were identified by their works, technical skills, brains, and commitment to cultural politics, but whose fate was to fall outside the networks of apparatchik cultural managers.

Against institutions, they formed new institutions based on emergent values, but they were also defined by other "generations" who had the belonging game all sewed up, were being assimilated and operating in the social scenes. The attempt to participate in this imaginary association based on lost identities brings culture into view as a typology of mental life that can at least try to remain incommensurable and grow and germinate. But above all, this kind of incommensurable, self-reflective grouping must, if it is to work against the grain of embedded traditions, also be diagnostic and interpret the modern age. This is Benjamin's historical-aesthetic project of profane illumination.

In the mid-1960s, there was no generation working on the issues that I describe here in this sketch, but they became the inside and outside of Miki's work and poetics, and that of others like him. Everything was embedded in the settlement of Vancouver and was assumed to be ready to merge with new institutions. The settlement town was a city of living neighbourhoods and enclaves that had been clearly defined by the colonial, elite-class-based tradition, a Matthew Arnold struggle of culture, of anarchy, of traditional, and inbred and almost confident, class-bound, racialized culture. The prospect: streets and buildings would soon become remnants of the past. The city would become urban. The Arnoldian assumption of tradition could be mined, however. Benjamin, Brecht, or Mallarmé also mined this tradition by measuring force and law, violence, and the contiguities of capital with surplus, the throw of the dice, measuring the city as a place where the forces of property joined the force of law. Culture was surplus and could be inclusive of the emerging voices that Simon Fraser's English department brought together willy-nilly.

At every step of the way in forming this new university, the weight of the previous "generation" weighed in with the Culture of Arnoldian assumptions critical to English Canadian English departments. Race, class, aesthetic experimentation, and cultural hybridism were barely subsumed into a yet-to-be articulated cultural nationalism. As an intellectual child of the 1950s, I was more of a hybrid Marxist-anarchist modernist, a radical Benjamanian in the making with roots in Russian and European movements, so this staging of cultural invention was not new to me. At the time it might have been all a form of cultural bungee jumping where one is pulled back to the thought that this might not last – something was always in the wind, the Mercurian-trickster mentality was the most stable ethos in one's life. There was always a sense of being a stranger, in the way Georg Simmel with deft sociological poetics described the "potential wanderer":

> The stranger ... not in the sense often touched upon in the past, [as] ... the wanderer who comes today and goes tomorrow, but rather as the person who comes today and stays tomorrow – so to speak, who, although he [sic] has not moved on, he has not quite overcome the freedom of coming and going ... he brings qualities into it that are not, and cannot be indigenous to it. [37]

"The Stranger" is a chronotope, both a figure and a representation that brings a new way of thinking about space and time. The Stranger carries emergent time and is a figure of exchange-relationships circulating anonymously. [38] I believe that this is where Miki landed in his own form of bungee jumping that later on landed him in the Redress Movement fighting "representation" tooth and nail, and this is why I felt comradely towards Miki and his *works and days*: the work that resists being a form of empathy with the cultural commodities that lie like seeds beneath the soil, and has the courage to speak the difficult truths embedded in aesthetics and politics – perhaps one could put it in the way that Brecht put it in the dark ages of 1935 when he wrote "Writing the Truth: Five Difficulties" at a writer's conference about authorship, in times when it was difficult to think about "truth":

> Nowadays, anyone who wishes to combat lies and ignorance and to write the truth must overcome at least five difficulties. He [*sic*] must have the courage to write the truth when truth is everywhere opposed; the keenness to recognize it, although it is everywhere concealed; the skill to manipulate it as a weapon; the judgment to select those in whose hands it will be effective; and the cunning to spread the truth among such persons. These are formidable problems for writers living under Fascism, but they also exist for those writers who have fled or been exiled; they exist even for writers working in countries where civil liberty prevails. [39]

DOSSIER IV – CHAPTER 4

The Literacy of the Spectacle: The Legacy of Walter Benjamin and the Production of Performance [40]

Technologization, the extended arm of [the] nature-dominating subject, purges artworks of their immediate language. Technological requirements drive out the contingency of the individual who produces the work.

—THEODOR W. ADORNO, *Aesthetic Theory* (1970), trans. Robert Hullot-Kentor

The spectacle cannot be understood as an abuse of the world of vision, as a product of the techniques of mass dissemination of images. It is, rather, a *Weltanschauung*, which has become actual, materially translated. It is a world vision, which has become objectified. The spectacle, grasped in its totality, is both the result and the project of the existing mode of production. It is not a supplement to the real world, an additional decoration. It is the heart of the unrealism of the real society.

—GUY DEBORD, *The Society of the Spectacle* (1967), trans. Donald Nicholson-Smith

Mankind, which in Homer's time was an object of contemplation for the Olympian gods, now is one for itself. Its self-alienation has reached such a degree that it can experience its own destruction as an aesthetic pleasure of the first order. This is the situation of politics, which Fascism is rendering aesthetic. Communism responds by politicizing art.

—WALTER BENJAMIN, "The Work of Art in the Age of Mechanical Reproduction" (1935), *Illuminations*, trans. Harry Zohn

I

The Crisis of the Everyday: A Dialectical Fairyland?

This essay discusses Walter Benjamin's struggle to understand the fate of revolution in his times and how he never swayed from seeing how cultural creation in its most problematic forms turned during his own lifetime into the ideology of the spectacle in which ideology became reality. Benjamin saw the anxiety of the artistic object now facing the process of the technical reproduction, and the enigmatic relationship of the aesthetics of the spectacle converging into "Aesthetics" of Performance. Suddenly the life history of the fragmented subject was dreaming itself within the culture of the spectacle. The epic drama: to become a player-spectator in the new fascist mass culture. The aura of the object is the subject of his "The Work of Art" essay. The aura reveals remembrance which is a doubleness in the form that the experience of art leaves for us, is similar to how a dream leaves behind aural images that I see and which see me. It is the experience of the uncanny loss of the object's origin that haunts capitalism itself and leaves traces of scars on our "capacity for attentiveness." [41]

Benjamin's romantic anti-capitalism becomes influenced by Brecht's own emerging Marxism. In the mid-1930s, both were looking for the preconditions for a new political literacy in times of fascism and militarism. A new "literacy of performance" is a critical materialist anthropology of the everyday that is the legacy of representation and performance. The famous "aura" in Benjamin's essay is the concealed history of the pathos of "critical emotion" in the creation and reception of the artwork, and the reverie as an aesthetic is central to the exchange of letters between Benjamin and Adorno. [42]

The fascist breakup of the bourgeois struggle of cultural politics and aesthetics shadows the loss of aura. The struggle is the condition under which art communicated an aesthetic – not merely through the history of cultural ideas – but as a marketable experience in the phantasmagoria of the dangerously evolving fascist present:

> The commodity economy ... arms that phantasmagoria of sameness which simultaneously reveals itself, as an attribute of intoxication, to the central image of illusion ... the price makes the commodity equal and identical to all those other commodities which could be purchased at the same price ... And it is precisely in this respect that the *flâneur* accommodates himself to the commodity; he imitates it utterly ... he makes himself thoroughly at home in the world of saleable objects. In this he outdoes the whore; he takes the abstract concept of the whore for a stroll, so to speak. It is only in the final incarnation of the *flâneur* that this concept is totally fulfilled: as the man with a sandwich board over his head. [43]

Both Benjamin's and Brecht's adversaries were the surrealists who also saw performance as a form of artistic and political praxis. The goal: to regain the pathos of aura as social concept, as well as an art idea; the cultural *authority* of modernism must be questioned at those points where it presumes to speak for all of cultural creation as such. The loss of aura was both an attraction and repulsion to the terror of the newly organized apocalyptical turns in history. For Benjamin this was an "epochal" change in how to measure the modern as experience and how to write a conceptual history of the turning points of the exhibition of suffering and the deference to political authority. [44]

Benjamin's concept of history is an "epochal concept" about time, progress, decline, and the effects of what is missing in how "destruction is idealized; in the transfigured face of nature we fleetingly realized the light of redemption." [45] The loss of "aura" is the loss of that which is no longer reproducible. Writing cultural memory from the standpoint of the history of the victors is equally an archaeology of a history of the vanquished. This is the basis of his understanding of the *epoch* of the spectacle. The "spectacle" as a concept of historical and contemporary experience is a historical concept about timing that continued his thinking from the "Baroque Play of Mourning," which goes beyond his 1919 doctoral dissertation at Bern on "The Concept of Art Criticism in German Romanticism."

Modern cultural production transforms everyday life into the spectacle, which needs bureaucracy and industrialization as *forms* of political culture that will enable the "vanquished" to see themselves as contemporary; this pathos of seeing enables what they could imagine on their own. The legacy of patronage, enlightened bourgeois taste, and mass audiences, along with the assimilation of the intelligentsia into bureaucracy, have made politics and culture virtually indistinguishable. Cultural capital expands with the appetite of capitalism for crisis and spiritual renewal through the commodity. Performance no longer signifies the struggle of the subject for critical autonomy, freedom, or the authentic and concrete knowledge of experience; performance plays out the intervention of the spent and speechless cultural forms of property which stand in the modern world as an inhabited emptiness and "epic forgetting." [46] Dispossessed and then annexed, the means of production of modern cultural literacy, which would criticize everyday life in fact, reproduces its muteness. [47]

Benjamin's essays were a turning point in understanding the problems of the production of cultural literacy in modern mass culture. The canonization of Benjamin as one of the patron saints of the intelligentsia's post-Vietnam radical culturism parallels the attempt after World War II to find authors who took the measure of their times; one thinks of Sartre or Orwell. We wanted to find the author who directly faced the heroic but failed movements and who had intellectual authority in the period of the struggle against fascism and the aesthetics of the spectacle. What kind of art criticism is possible? Benjamin's essays speak to that critical age dominated by the cultural authority of strong cultural ideologies.

In 1927 Benjamin wanted to write a work that would illuminate the origins of capitalism and the commodity culture by using the city façades from the Arcades of Paris, Berlin, Milan, and other metropolitan centres, which emerged from baroque architecture and its cityscapes. Here the "masses" were formed, who were yet to see themselves objectively illuminated and performed, but *not yet* represented by art that would reveal itself as both "natural" and artificial and ready-made for consumption. Consumption of and in culture is the key to understanding what the "technical" means of production means when liquidation is experienced as transience in search of an ideological form of life.

These arcades are glass-roofed, marble-panelled corridors extending through whole blocks of buildings, whose owners have joined together for such enterprises. Lining both sides of these corridors, which get their light from above, are the most elegant shops, so that the arcade becomes a city in miniature. This phenomenon of transience Benjamin names "Dialectics at a Standstill" or "Parisian Arcades: A Dialectical Fairyland."[48] Benjamin returned to this project in 1934; however, he had already been in discussion with Brecht about how "to refunction" (*Umfunktionierung*) art and politics to show how the working class accommodates the everyday under the sign of labour. This "refunctioning" of perception was influenced by Siegfried Kracauer's writing about the streets of Berlin, Russian theatre, and Erwin Piscator's experimental theatre; Brecht's emerging theatrical practices were understood as a mode of teaching performance in real time: "The film is the first art form capable of demonstrating how matter plays tricks on man [*sic*]. Hence, films can be an excellent means of materialistic representation."[49] We also "construct an alarm clock that rouses the kitsch of the previous century to 'assembly.'"[50] In other words, authenticity is foregrounded as shock drawing the beholder into history.

Benjamin's "alien thinking" about the passages from past into the present eventually became his long-unpublished *Arcades Project*, a collection of colportage quotes and fragments that visually and conceptually represent the imaginary city as a construction of "Passages," in which we feel how the world of the commodity becomes the *phantasmagoric* world of capital and commodity and the transition to another kind of perception that erases the past of the work and "liquidates the function of the very thing itself." Here, capitalism, fascism, and communism, as well as esoteric views of the future, were emerging and competing for political and imaginary space in the streets and dreamworld of the everyday. [51]

The Arcades Project is a dramaturgical production, just as Brecht's theatre practices were dramaturgical theatrical presentations (*Darstellungen* in German), which foreground the aesthetic as "constructions" beyond representation. Both struggled with the "aesthetics of commitment" in order to foreground the ethical and political dilemmas posed by commitment to the Communist Party. This is the severity of the objectives of Brecht's *Lehrstücke*, or "teaching plays," which are about the political will in theatre and art; put simply, a struggle exists between Bruegel the Elder and Malevich. [52] The *Arcades* years are turning points in Benjamin's engagement with Brecht's plays and their literary-political experiments. Benjamin's thinking and writing about political change and art in this period consumed him. Restless with surrealism's accommodation to the machine age, which was creating new "beholders," he saw Spectacle aesthetics and the futurist movement appearing in the same "epoch" as contemporary mass movements. [53]

Benjamin saw aesthetic form as "political," wherein the suffering masses and their masters were ripe for the object to be pried "from its cultural shell to destroy its aura." The destruction of the city after World War I is the background that exposes the resemblance of the object to reality, and the spectacle of violence pervading the city in history that preoccupied Benjamin.

He becomes a chronographer of history's losers in the crisis of modernity where we live in confusion and terror in a state of violence – the kind of violence that Benjamin attempts to unravel in his essay on "Critique of Violence" (1921),[54] in which he traces how violence is done to the experience of violence itself through the penetration of mechanical equipment into reality. The new epoch is fed by the eschatological question: Who writes history – the victors or the vanquished? Benjamin writes that the "epoch" is now revealed in the stations of time: "The biological historicity of the individual" reveals *the stations of suffering* in the "baroque, secular explanation of history. The Passion of the world ... resides solely in the stations of its decline."[55] The Weimar phantasmagoric film exposes the decline and the confusions over suffering and war: "All efforts to render politics aesthetic culminate in one thing: war."[56]

Inbuilt violence is exposed to the phantasmagoric confusion of a historicism of progress in which depersonalization and negative socialization shatter confidence in historical time as progress. Time is understood as the non-contemporaneity of the contemporary. Christian cultures gave to perpetual violence the "divine" laws that deferred the redemption of violence until a final "justice" will be redeemed and distributed into performance of the masses, and the masses *are now embedded* in a mode of reality that transcends writing, the book, the symbol, and the text. *The masses should be understood as if they are a modern delivery system.* The masses live out the historical tragedy of living out the consequences of historical inevitability of the falseness of "progress" as the impossibility of redeeming suffering.[57] Thesis number three in *Theses on the Philosophy of History* puts the struggle over what is lost enigmatically:

> The chronicler, who recounts events without distinguishing between the great and small, hereby accounts for the truth, that nothing which has ever happened is to be given as lost to history. Indeed, the past would fully befall only a resurrected humanity.

Said another way: only for a resurrected humanity would its past, in each of its moments, be citable. Each of its lived moments becomes a citation *à l'ordre du jour* – whose,day is precisely that of the Last Judgement. [58]

Benjamin rearranges our historical understanding of the crisis of loss in history and culture by showing that the presentness of life rescues and redeems the aura of the hand–eye aesthetic of performance. One might even describe the historicity of loss as "the loss of loss" in which "transitoriness and eternity confronted each other most closely." [59] Brecht is also politically preoccupied with a new aesthetic of performance that will bring the material conditions of art-making both closer to us and farther from us, which would defend against the distractions of the spectacle and the theatricality embedded in the architectural and constructed forms of the quotidian. In other words, Benjamin discovers how the war-remembering masses play out Benjamin's baroque play of mourning; the masses are signs of the times and are ready-made to be reduced to resignation and despair and awareness of a guilt-laden atmosphere of past and future ruins. Benjamin hoped that technical reproducibility would reveal the private consumption of art and the new art market now playing out the conditions of technical production, which could shift cultural production to the author as producer.

Authors join collectors, connoisseurs, advisers and create journals. Benjamin's awareness of the social history of art mediated by the production of culture means that art is seen now as an institution: slave owner, merchant owner of capital, guild expert, patron of the arts, salon visitor, and *flâneur* and the now-emancipated bourgeoisie all come into the free market through pushing at the back door of culture. In this dialectic of the production of art, Baudelaire becomes the iconic carrier of the enigmatic artist who sufferers emotionally from the loss of aura and who lives in the preserved ruins of the past. [60]

The public is caught within the old institutions of collecting, buying, and selling; a collectively, critically receptive art public just doesn't exist. An unambiguously defined bearer of culture will experience distance and proximity as both critique and sorrow, alienation and utopian longing; in short, the "baroque" individual re-emerges inside the masses where "class consciousness" expresses itself as false consciousness. Here again is the genesis of the allegorical, in Benjamin's sense of the pathos of culture and the suffering of the observer-spectator.

The loss of the aura of totality is not just any loss but the "loss of Loss" that accompanies a *productive alienation* which is the interior of the art of making over the ruins; finding a new "language as such" means that the allegorical reveals the transitional, fleeting sense of the fragment and complexity of the fragmentary. The fragment lies in the structure of the whole that Benjamin pursues in *The Arcades Project* and his Baudelaire studies. The anxiety of the object is its aura. Through empathy with the commodity, the commodity itself acts "modern" and seems to show "progress"; the end of the commodity is in the mediating form that the exchange process takes on as if it is autonomous. The commodity becomes the "allegorical personification [that] has always concealed the fact that its function is not the personification of things, but rather to give the concrete a more imposing form by getting it up as a person."[61]

II

The Spectacle and History as Exposé: Benjamin and Brecht, "The Archimedean Point Is in the Political Will for Commitment"

The allergy to aura, from which no art today is able to escape, is inescapable from the eruption of inhumanity. This renewed reification, the regression of artworks to barbaric literalness of what is aesthetically the case, and phantasmagoric guilt are inextricably entwined.

—THEODOR W. ADORNO, *Aesthetic Theory* (1970), trans. Robert Hullot-Kentor

The Spectacle becomes a historical concept: history as Spectacle is a dizzying critical concept. The loss of "aura" is "epochal"; it is a fundamental break with the past and is the brute reminder of living in a world of decline, catastrophe, and exhaustion of subjectivity in the experience and expression in art. Benjamin is framing the present and the unpresent as the mark of what he calls "now-time," the feeling of transience and impermanence. Benjamin uses the word *Wirrwarr* ("jumble") for the phantas-magoria that turned the exchange and commodity world into spectacle, which foretells the admixture of the magic spell of com-modity and exchange value that does violence to remembering "experience" (*Erfahrung*). This leads to the loss of aura, which under the spell of capital can no longer be a rescuing agent in the epoch of the technical reproduction of art. The aura throws a veil of materiality of "lived experience" (*Erlebnis*) over the art object. The idea of a proletarian-inspired community can't be abandoned but can be reconfigured to show that the art object that lives in an "epoch" of reproducibility means we are experien-cing in the long present a transitional period of a mode of lived experience in a time of remembering and forgetting of terror and catastrophe, which has become the epochal period between fascism and communism after the catastrophe of World War I. Benjamin constructs a concept of what I would call "aesthetic memory" or "body-based memory" – insight-made body – what he calls *Eingedenk ("mindful" or "mindfulness")*, a form of think-ing-in memory, presence of mind, a hovering memory that opens into memory as a moment of awakening to bring things near, the memory that comes back again and again without a name. Things themselves carry memory in regard to our mindfulness or our bearing-in-mind or our holding the living moment.[62]

The essay "The Work of Art" was neither programmatic nor hermeneutical. He is restating what he writes in other essays: how "aura" holds memory and how technical reproduction refocuses our attention onto "things." This enables the optical in the modern technical reproduction of the world of "things" which become objects that carry both the loss of memory and the enigmatic present. The essay was formed during discussions with Brecht on the aesthetics of epic theatre that saw how the present means seeing into things differently. Benjamin believed this was a new "theatrical epoch." [63]

However, the spectacle is also violence in the making. One should be clear that, for Benjamin and Brecht, genocidal fury was being readied in the fascism of the Hitler state's monopoly of violence. Reverie and dream struggle against reification and the fetish of the commodity, which is deathlike worship of the object that "calls to us." The objects and the masses live in this epoch of transience and radical discontinuity.

In this sense the spectacle becomes life in a transitional zone of anxiety and attachment to domination. Our attachment is also to the *delivery system of technical reproducibility*, which means that our "silence" conditions our fear of being appropriated by complicity with the violence of the emerging fascist state. This anticipatory anxiety is in surrealism, that foregrounds that silence when reverie and distraction touch on madness and play with insanity. Surrealism shows us the enigmatic, but surrealism becomes part of the problem, not its solution. Compliance and complicity are the subtexts in this zone of transition between fascism and communism. It is beyond the capacity of institutions to account for this transition zone, which "technical reproducibility" displays in what Benjamin calls exploiting its "exhibition value." Benjamin writes:

This suggests that the degree of auratic saturation of human perception has fluctuated widely in the course of history. (In the baroque, one might say, the conflict between cult value and exhibition value was variously played out within the confines of sacred art itself.) While these fluctuations await further clarification, the supposition arises that epochs which tend towards allegorical expression will have experienced a crisis of the aura. [64]

Benjamin, Kracauer, and Adorno responded to the need for a theory of technical reproducibility at the heart of mass culture's worship of "things." Any political aesthetic had to find a historical view of mass culture, where the reification of "things" and the suffering of the masses became the basis of a theory of the epoch of the spectacle. Corporate fascism is the key political issue. Who controls capitalism? The debate included the actuality of communism, socialism, and anarchism, and the fear of the necessity of a union of capital with a state form of fascism: Why did the proletariat not perform the revolution and yet lived with the violence of the state? And, if they could have performed it, what about social democracy and communism? One could not escape this question of the relationship of art to politics and the liquidation of the past of the auratic artwork and its history of reception as "fine art" with the emotions they arouse now as objects of transitory experience. [65] Yet: "Fascism sees the salvation in giving these masses not their right, but instead a chance to express themselves." [66]

On the left and right, capitalism was the foe. The fear: that the historical process would lead inevitably to state control and to the industrialized, technical reproduction of all of life in the future. A central state was now the prerogative of politics. Faith in the state was a requirement for the fascists who needed to create a public sphere that addressed political life by creating a symbolic mass whose deference to authority camouflaged ethnic and class struggle by masking itself as a socialism en route to a class-based *institution* of industrialized mass culture that would "perform" itself through the naturalization of violence as part of everyday life, as if everyday life would become allegorical, full of signs and symbols expressive of power and domination over the very *historicity of the individual itself.*

So, Benjamin's critique of the immanent reformation of the bourgeois public is in all respects a critique of feudal capitalism that disguises the terror of the market. Capitalism as spectacle is protective coloration of the Third Reich's violence and war-preparation. Mechanical reproduction effectively and thoroughly, even by enlisting the avant-garde, reveals the destruction of historical consciousness of the aura in a world in ruins which, under the fascists, will ultimately "experience its own destruction."[67]

Benjamin means the "aura" is a "matrix" that brings art to performance through the historical modes of production, that is, the culture's delivery systems. Although the historically product-ive modes do not create the work of art, nor do they signal exact meanings, they embody the creator and audience as forms of lived experience and *actions* and class outlook of cultural behold-ers in real time. "Time" then becomes both delivery system and experience. Film becomes a productive understanding of the real world. The emergency: Film can move the masses into position to merge with the fascist state. The double-sidedness of labour and toil turns our mental and physical work into commodities which the new technical forms like radio and film can reproduce and disseminate, so, on the one hand, the mechanical reproduction as assembly-line violence, and on the other hand, the loss of aura and the need for a new materialism.

The new "delivery system" that follows World War I is marked by inflation and the political bankruptcy of the bourgeoisie who are yearning for the dictatorship of the one party over soci-ety. Easy to do! What is the "matrix" – Benjamin's word – of mass culture?

The formal structures of the Bismarck state and Weimar Social Democracy levelled differences in the name of the prop-erty system and industrial expansion as German universities were filling with anti-democratic agitation, nationalism, and conservative hostility to Weimar. The economic crisis and the preparation for war amid desperate poverty – guns or butter? – were parodied in John Heartfield's illustrations. The pursuit of an Aryan German society, war fever, the vicious rampages against Jews in the pogroms of reprisals against the Jews of Central Europe and in Germany, until then unparalleled, drove Benjamin and Brecht into flight and then exile. However, the old wealth, status, power, class, were becoming incorporated into the new consciousness-forming power of cultural capital. The legacy of Hegel's master–slave haunts the essay. Benjamin would have to include how ideology becomes reality and reality becomes ideology. Culture was always where ideology merged with domination, but now that technical reproduction delivers and disseminates reproducibility, there is a new frontier for political aesthetics.

Baudelaire, Flaubert, and Proust replace Goethe as the epigone of the "elective affinities" of capitalism and intellectual culture, traditionally understood as *Bildung,* and are the same cultural capital for both the older intelligentsia and the new white-collar and working classes. [68] Self-cultivation in bourgeois materialism meant that "great thinkers" shaped reality and that cultural political nationalism would both protect culture against the masses and would also provide a sanctuary for the cultivated individuals' moral qualities, identified as "Germanness" for everyone: Jews, Socialists, or any class who were advocates of a Kantian Enlightenment.

Benjamin and Brecht joined forces by thinking about *Umfunktionierung,* or "refunctioning," – rethinking literary form through a technique of distancing the *institutional means* of production. The Kantian relationship of author and public exist in a functional relationship to culture and the arts, and centrally to the need for an aesthetic form that shows and also "denies consideration to modern man's [*sic*] legitimate claim to being reproduced … the film industry is trying hard to spur the interest of the masses through illusion promoting spectacles and dubious speculations." [69] Film, narrative, the iconic are principles of modes of performance that incorporated, but had not yet replaced, the "book" and the "state" and the organs of culture which encoded the old political culture without understanding the "permeation of reality with mechanical equipment, an aspect of reality which is free of all equipment. And that is what one is entitled to ask from a work of art."[70]

No literary form, from tragedy to pamphlet, to tract or sermon, songs, ballads, or polemics would be left outside of how analogues throughout art and literary history traced how mechanical reproduction created "audience" and "spectator" and the *auratic* conditions for reception. Influences came through Freud, Rudolf Arnheim, Sigfried Giedion, Brecht, Chaplin, Russian film, and Kafka, not to say Lenin, in forming a materialist theory of expression that would count as both a genuinely revolutionary *attitude* and as an emotional experience of both political pathos and intellectual critique, "beyond the stage of reverence of works of art as divine and deserving our worship."[71] Meant here is that the work of art carries the seeds of resistance and the pathos of the mass's inability to "organize and control themselves in their reception."[72]

Thus, the dialectical connecting of thought, theatre, and the possibility of a political revolution leads him to theory of performance that maintains a relationship to older narrative forms in which pathos, allegory, and the social function of art struggle with the cult value of art; yet cult value cannot simply be liquidated. To relate stories of the war was absent for Benjamin – the silence after the World War and domination by capital and the commodity was the last will and testament of the work of capital. The objective: to show the cult value of art as a form of life and to reconstruct a new literacy of social performance that can intervene conceptually and sensually into the crisis of everyday lives while the rapidity of fascism is being entrenched into everyday life.

New art forms would reveal the latent political dimensions of the readers' receptivity. Like Lukács and Adorno, Benjamin identified narrative with the crisis of the nineteenth-century bourgeois class; however, he saw in the eighteenth-century novel and baroque theatre the origin of class consciousness in the Enlightenment where pathos, exhibition, and revolution are lured into the restoration of Kingship. Dictatorship competes for a "theological-political-juridical" solution to the haunting idea that catastrophe is around every corner. The concept of an all-encompassing "epoch" fits Benjamin's theory of allegory.

Developing Brecht's realism, not how real things are, but how things really are, Benjamin wrote of film: "The equipment-free aspect of reality … has become the height of artifice; the sight of immediate reality has become an orchid in the land of technology."[73] The "orchid" represents the living conditions of action, class, character, memory, history, and knowledge which rise from the world of modern existence screened by clerical obscurantism and philosophical idealism. Marx's "German ideology" hides a melancholy that is the core essence of the baroque cultural melancholy, where sterile flowers of obscurantism rise from the cells of living history: the new performance ideology would celebrate the now as history in the making. Here, Benjamin rethinks the technical nature of art, which we are aware of and is common to painting, music, and architecture, but not to writing and authorship; however, the "technical" nature of writing should now involve writers in a discussion of innovation, the nature of realism, and the popularity of forms in finding new readers in times of political emergency.

Benjamin, following Marx's *Eighteenth Brumaire of Louis Napoleon* (1852), suggests that the city seen through the screen of the film is stained with the images of persecution and sorrow; we see the countless relationships in which the individual produces *concrete, humanly*-made objects which also now include how images are made. Images have momentum and are "figures" and screens of memory beyond representation.

Film opens lived experience to our "equipment-free bodies," while the form of technical reproduction extends over the power of the crowd to see itself represented, which under fascism risks turning into the haunted phantasmagoria, the *Wirrwarr*: here can be a change in the making of a critical "receptivity" towards images! The spectators assembled before a screen that contained a "theological archetype," he comments, can embody the collective to "shake off clerical tutelage."[74]

The unconscious impulses of society *revealed* in the film form are organized in film images, which allows us to "go travelling" amid the ruins of our "prison world" of "metropolitan streets, our offices and furnished rooms, our railroad stations and our factories [which appear] to have us locked up hopelessly."[75] The "necessities which rule our lives" are made visible in a form that I name here "productive literacy" that for Benjamin is subsumed into a *situation* where storyteller and listener share the material means of expression and reach a productive understanding of the origins of story in material conditions. *Film must regain an aura that shields its own concreteness* from the spectacle.

The *epoch* of modernity is then marked by the *loss of the aura*: transience, impermanence, and the exhaustion of older forms of art lie in ruins. The former time-bound communal and nation-state forms of culture collapse into new spatial arrangements which are inbuilt into the city as we know it. Modernity as an *epoch of catastrophic changes* must account for loss and dilapidation – the "de-stoning" of structures in the physical and spiritual ruins of war. As Hegel wrote, the worshipping of art is no longer the purpose of art but goes beyond into "spiritless stupor of the soul."[76] For the modern mass-individual, the prototype of reception is architecture, which "has always represented the prototype of a work of art, the reception of which is consummated by a collectivity in a state of distraction. The laws of its reception are most instructive."[77]

III

The "Arcaded" City and the Film Form as Tableau

The aftermath of city-building gave us impressionism, cubism, futurism, and colportage movements of art-making that emerge from the city. This is clearly visible in the photographs and films in the new technological age of reproduction. It also illuminates the past as the "unpast," the work of remembrance: the "aura" of the past and the not-yet-past is the immanence of the "passage" of time in the "arcaded" city, which can now best be seen through the film form and the aesthetics of technical reproducibility, what Kracauer in his exile in America called "The Redemption of Physical Reality." [78]

The city simultaneously performs energy, monumentalism, experimentalism, and compilational film; for example, Dziga Vertov opened new "passages" for photography, film, and surrealist and technical experiments with images. This epoch is a "diachronic" time of time past and time future moving and mobile; it is also "synchronic" time, as well, where everything in the present telescopes into "now-time." The pressure of the present time only appears to us to be "homogeneous," *yet feels like dream time and dream space*. This is a new architectonics at the dawn of a dream world of revolution where Benjamin sees Kracauer (and himself) writing on "the road to a politicization of the intelligentsia." [79] Both are showing how the politics and psychopathology in the phantasmagoria of everyday life needed to be "isolated and made analyzable ... [as] things which had heretofore floated along unnoticed in the broad stream of perception." [80]

The bourgeoisie perform in the streets but do not see how they are the homeless anxious *objects* who are becoming allegorical objects, ruins, that are entangled in the decomposition of life itself. Events display the conditions in which the wealth of states and classes, the powers of liberal humanism, and the dreams of the intelligentsia are on display through the power of distraction, patronage, culture, and entertainment. Exhibition has aesthetic value, but also impoverishes.

Through the ontology of the film experience we see how the ambivalences inherent in all cultural creation confuse the *common experiences* of people with the *common situations of history* which could give those experiences objective meaning; but auratic literacy is lost and the spectacle triumphs through the demolition of aura and the disintegration of the "origins" of the work of art. New delivery systems for art produce unprecedented political and artistic resources and pervade the states of emergency by integrating the psychic lives of individuals into genres, forms, and forces of production. The "spectacle" constructs the now-time, the contemporary, which is the measure of the new instrumental means of reproduction in radio, film, technology, propaganda, the new literacy. Adorno and others were frightened by how the masses were becoming hypnotized by the living execution of "aura" applied by the Third Reich. One had to see the "auratization" of politics in the apparatus of the *Kulturstaaat*, the Culture-State.

The masses long for distraction, long for performances, for events, for transformation of needs that respond to the voices of authority, to the sight of symbols of authority. They become "subjects." The allegorical force of the spectacle transforms everything it touches into the enigmatic medium that hides immanent barbarism. This ambivalence towards authority is the enigmatic origin of the violence inherent in cultural-political power and the revolutionary potential of the new technical mediums; the potential to confront our common political situations requires a new politics and new performers who can break through the proletariat's relationship to wealth production. Technology magically distributes itself! Yet: in the streets, demonstrations, police murdering demonstrators, over five million unemployed, book burnings celebrated, and thugs are breaking Jewish store windows!

The great bourgeois psychological form of the novel gave way to film; already prepared in Baudelaire, Flaubert, Proust, Céline, Kafka, and Joyce, the novel had departed from a purely realist analysis to one that enabled the work to perform *beyond the level of hopelessness* into which we had plunged. The unbroken flow of life that was poured into the novel of the nineteenth century, and which saw society as a *place* of change, character, and labour, gave way both to the cultic posturing of *spectacle consciousness* and *the tableau*. What is, then, the "tableau" that attracted Benjamin and Brecht?

The *spectacular* real and the *exotic* real of film combine in the desperation of consumers and the anxiety of producers that Benjamin named "phantasmagoria." Life had become a labyrinthine stock exchange where images *separate* the lives of spectators from each other. Capitalism not only forces us into the production system but leads us into a fantasy world divorced from the historical pathos of a new "Baroque Play of Mourning." The film simultaneously reveals and illuminates the enigmatic performance of the everyday that promises deliverance and emancipation from the spectacle's hold on the beholder-spectator.

Surrealism, futurism, Lang's *Metropolis*, Reinhardt's theatre, Griffith's films, and the new "genre" films reproduce the cultural-melodramatic traditions, which historically are expressions of a dying world view. New forms of society seem incapable of performing themselves, arguing that would continue the critique of *aura* on the supply side of culture. Benjamin knows now that "Fascism seeks to give … the masses an expression while preserving property. The logical result of Fascism is the introduction of aesthetics into political life."[81] There is no salvation in our secular versions of crisis, and those modern forms of cultural creation simply proliferate spectacle consciousness by assimilating class-consciousness into the cultural dilemmas of the bourgeoisie's anxiety about property and culture. Capitalism requires crises, states of emergency, war, vigilante politics, new markets, standardized production, and the capacity to distribute, market, and accumulate goods.

Benjamin's *Arcades Project* was constructed during the period of "The Work of Art" and intended as an assembly of materials and quotations, in short, a performance, a tableau. Benjamin wants to see revolution as an epoch of life that "sloughs off form."[82] In his "Theses on the Philosophy of History" (1940), he writes about historical subjects who are representatives of new *situations*, not only as expressions of a class-cultural point of view. History blasts the agent of the spectacle out of the spectacular firmament of the formalistic, bureaucratic apparatus in order to free the object from its state of tragic ambivalence – its life in the phantasmagoric when fascism is threatening Europe and Benjamin fears the collapse of any resistance, especially when the Popular Front in France collapsed. Through performance, the subject is *reconstituted* by the subject matter of art, and by means of the *aura-deprived*, dehumanized, iconophobic, and atomized languages; the spectator sees itself collectively in its origin *in labour*.

Shortly following the writing of "The Work of Art" and his reading of history as the history of the victims of historicism, that is, history as progress which culminates in the endtime of a universal history, the German army invaded Poland. Benjamin had fled to France and was interned in the Clos Saint-Joseph in Nevers, near the Pyrenees, in a camp for fugitives who had fled Germany. The camp, originally set up for fugitives from the Spanish Civil War, now housed Germans, Austrians, those Germans from the French annexation of the Saarland, and Jews who had fled Hitler's plan for a "Jewish-free Germany" (*Judenfrei Deutschland*) and who, hoping for safety in France, were rounded up, labelled as "Inner Enemies of France," suspicious. Benjamin, as if anticipating the future in the past that holds the future, had written, as if prophetically, of his "epochal" life, his famous "History is written by the victors":

Universal history has no theoretical armature. Its procedure is additive: it musters a mass of data to fill the homogeneous, empty time. Materialist historiography, on the other hand, is based on a constructive principle. Thinking involves not only the movement of thoughts, but their arrest as well. Where thinking suddenly stops in a constellation saturated with tensions, it gives that constellation a shock ... The historical materialist ... recognizes the sign of a messianic arrest of happening ... As a result of this method, the lifework is both preserved and sublated *in* this work, the era *in* the lifework, and the entire course of history *in* the era. The nourishing fruit of what is historically understood contains time in its *interior* as a precious but tasteless seed. [83]

"Messianic time" is nothing more nor less than redemptive time gathering the fragments of history lost in time. Spectacle is the enemy of time. Spectacle is frozen time. The film form cannot provide the kind of contemplation we can have towards a painting. The film's auratic world contains the shock, that sudden change in perception that requires a "heightened presence of mind" to contain the shock of our change of perception. [84] Benjamin writes in "The Storyteller": "All great storytellers have in common the freedom with which they move up and down the rungs of their experience as on a ladder. A ladder extending downward to the interior of the earth and disappearing into the clouds is the image for a collective experience to which even the deepest shock of every individual experience, death, constitutes no impediment or barrier." [85] Film *dislocates the storyteller from the material of the story* and reminds us of stories that affect us by "assuming transmissible form at the moment of ... [a] death." [86] Benjamin poignantly writes that, "Just as a sequence of images is set in motion inside a man [*sic*] as his life comes to an end – unfolding the views of himself under which he has encountered himself without being aware of it, suddenly in his expressions and looks the unforgettable emerges and imparts to everything that concerned him that authority which even the poorest wretch in dying possesses for the living around him. This authority is at the very source of the story conceived in 'remembrance' of a life lived and unlived." [87]

A sequence of images, then, is the massing of aura in *the epoch of reproduction*. The death of aura is enacted by and through the new masses who are becoming the new historical agents: the collective *as if they are participating in a dumb show that film can show them in the embrace of a destructive power*. In film we see spread out on the screen an *aura* of politics without redemption; indeed we witness both the "collective" mentality and the release of the capacity for the "masses to organize and control themselves in their reception." [88] Performance is political stagecraft, a place where galleries, salons, libraries are displaced through the luminescent everyday.

Everything and anything can be "represented" by the promiscuity of images; yet internal space is compromised because the intentions of the actors in time and place are governed, still, by the structures of space that are invisible to the eye or experience.

Depiction, not representation, now overshadows the urban, which is the one form of reality that we know and can see. The Arcades, then, are the city reading us and are the mythical location where modernity takes up its final place in history of perception as a form of experience.

IV

The Inner Political Aura and How We Live Retrospectively

Corresponding to the form of the new means of production, which in the beginning is still ruled by the form of the old (Marx), are in the social superstructure, wish images in which the new and old interpenetrate in fantastic fashion ... The utopian images which accompany the emergence of the new always, at the same time, reach back to the primal past … in the dream in which each epoch entertains images of its successor, the later appears wedded to elements of its primal history.

—WALTER BENJAMIN, "Exposé of 1935, Early Version" (1935), *The Arcades Project*, trans. Howard Eiland and Kevin McLaughlin

To build an analogy with Benjamin's epoch in which the history of annihilation lies behind the spectator's everyday existence, Benjamin lives with war and the immanent rise of fascism. Arnold Hauser, influenced by the same conditions of the loss of aura in our contemplation of art, writes in his search for a sociology of art that would be able to understand that:

> it was the collapse of liberal humanism which gave present-day art the decisive impulse towards its problematic nature. The materially conditioned productive forces of developing capitalism and the methods of production which correspond to them could not stop the benevolent effect of humanism and liberalism on art and culture. The individual only loses his [*sic*] dignity and sovereignty in mass society, and the work of art forfeits its aura of individuality and irreplaceability only when it becomes a technically reproducible commodity. [89]

The aura of the artwork's recovery of the "individuality" of expression lies concretely and aesthetically in showing how the "aura" of renunciation, sacrifice, and strangled feeling for life becomes compressed into images of secularism, plebeian world views, the decomposition of time into space into montage, the victimhood of the small man, gangsterism, the assimilation of women into the industrial workplace, and the mobilization of education against children. [90] Melodrama, farce, music, ritual, and fashion merge into film and challenge visual and literary symbolism, intellectualized techniques in the poetry of surrealism, and all forms of the cultural collaboration of art with society. In short, the social ingredients of film narrative do what the novel had traditionally done as a form of public literacy: both artist and audience were schooled by prosaic reality. It is also the confusion of the will to self-creation and the demands of the technological will.[91]

In Benjamin's "A Different Utopian Will," there are two "wills." One is driven by *Willkür*, our first nature, the will to self-creation and the *demands* of the ego; and one is driven by the "Immanent will," or aesthetic mimesis, which is "the higher demand for the technical mastery of elemental forces." Benjamin means that these are "revolutionary" forces in the making: both against and for the ones driven "by the bodily organism of the individual human being ... These demands, however, will first have to displace the problems of the second nature in the process of humanity's development."[92] Technical reproducibility will show spectators this "development" almost as if the technical development is a new spoken language no longer concealing meaning which written language hides.

The novel, the storyteller, and film are the utopian modes of performance corresponding to the specific historical activity which governs modes of mass reception and assimilation of the collective into the blind laws which *annex* the individual to modes of domination by the technological will. Arnold Hauser is right to say that "film is absolutely not a form which is particularly suited to symbolic expression. It is essentially a form of art, which is true to nature, and the symbolic references inside its realistic framework usually have a rather painful effect."[93]

The epochal background is the historical *Gleichschaltung* *("equalization")*, the *annexation* of the proletarian into the spiritual and political *history* of a whole people forced into the state-built culture. This is the final political form that the spectacle takes when culture assimilates aestheticized politics. Aura-less culture is the tapeworm that eats its own being. So, when Benjamin looks to the "proletariat" as the agent of fate and destiny and the film and photograph that will carry a new technical praxis, he dreams of a new utopian technological will.

The prophecy: the modernist tendency to "forcible conquest" in politics will be exposed through the new technological will to construct a different kind of experience of art. [94]

Performance is the delivery system of cultural formations. Performance is put on trial because it belongs to dictatorship, administration, and bureaucracy; this is what Cornelius Castoriadis refers to as the unification in culture of "formalism and the Universal Museum" and the bureaucratic mediation of the intrinsic tendencies of capitalism to be "consumption for consumption's sake in private life, and organization for organization's sake in collective life." [95] This is the spirit of capitalism – its aura is inside of its bureaucratic core. The administrative core in fascism is the prerogative of the state's intrusion into everyday life and is reproduced in mass culture by any means that bring nature and culture together. Mass culture allegorizes and symbolizes itself in a mythology of cultural capital: myth, religion, and artifacts of history stashed in the museumization of history that has become the essential core of fascist everyday life.

Performance is a cultural force, the *tertium datur*, the "third force" of the patriarchal, liberal, and administrative state that performs law and order. The objective: economic nationalism and production and preparation for war. It was the fundamental cooperation of the military and bureaucratic state-made institutions during the period 1918–1934 which made the National Socialist dictatorship capable of ruling through the law and edicts whereby the state became the *prerogative* of all performances. [96] Patriarchy and democracy, industry and shopkeeping, religion and economy, conquest and empire, art and entrepreneurship, charisma and burning art – these were the conditions under which a post-Weimar will to "democratic" performance eventually became the crucible for the Third Reich's creation of a state-owned capitalism, a German version of American and Western capitalism's extroversion of Max Weber's "iron cage." [97]

The "new character," the victim crying for "help," cries from inside the heart of expressionist films that appealed for a rebirth of law and order. Peter Lorre's character in Fritz Lang's 1931 melodramatic film *M*, in a twentieth-century "parody" of Ivan Karamazov, plaintively cries for sympathy and a fair trial, but not a new world or resistance against this one. The onlookers see themselves in him. The audience and the jury are spellbound by the pathos of the aura of resignation.

The unfreedom of spellbound pathology in Lorre's performance illuminates the sub-real, grotesque mobilization of police, populace, and crime world in Lang's classic film about the "people" and the hunted. The vigilante morality portrayed in Gustaf Gründgens's performance of the chieftain from the Preußische Geheimpolizei (Prussian Secret Police) answers to the anxious desires of Weimar victims and leaders, audience and spectators for a ritual conclusion to what will become a new war that Brecht and Benjamin saw coming on the verge of their exile: Brecht's flight to America and Benjamin's race to his suicide in Spain.[98] The pauperized middle classes were soon to perform the fantasies of fascist rulers, allowing Benjamin to write in 1936 in "The Storyteller" that: "With the [First] World War a process began to become apparent which has not halted since then. Was it not noticeable at the end of the war that men returned from the battlefield grown silent – not richer, but poorer in communicable experience? … In a field of force of destructive torrents and explosions, was the tiny, fragile human body."[99]

Benjamin and Brecht formed a close friendship, if to some of Benjamin's friends an improbable one. Brecht's anarchist-like poetic, along with the undertow of Benjamin's anarcho-messianic revolutionary critique of the state and capitalism, brought them into mutual understanding about the phantasmagoria of the catastrophe of the fascist abyss-dreamworld.[100] Ultimately it was Brecht's repudiation of bourgeois theatre and his writings against the state that gave Benjamin a sense of the immediate possibility that their attitudes towards schools of modernism, their openness towards many aesthetic genres of writing, either in the theatre or in essay writing, had deep understanding about what was being lost in the fascist Spectacle and what kind of "awakening" was needed. Benjamin, as to the "dialectical structure of awakening":

> The new, dialectical method of doing history teaches us to pass in spirit – with the rapidity and intensity of dreams – through what has been, in order to experience the present as a waking world, a world to which every dream at last refers ... Therefore: remembering and awakening are most intimately related. Awakening is namely the dialectical, Copernican turn of remembrance. [101]

The debate had to include the reality of communism, socialism, and anarchism, mediated by the horror of the spectacle of capital merging with fascism: Why did the proletariat not perform the revolution, and if they could how could they achieve it? On the left and right alike, capitalism was seen as the enemy on the principle that some higher historical process would lead inevitably to state control and to some form of industrialized future and war.

The fascists were creating a new "people" through a new "blood Sovereignty" by forcing a symbolic shock effect of a new mass out who would defer to the authority of the spectacle, while the Communist Party camouflaged ethnic and class cleansing of social-democrats and socialism en route to its own version of mass culture and corresponding new means of production.

So Benjamin's critique of technical reproduction is enigmatic in regard to the formation of both a proletarian and bourgeois public sphere that was already, in all respects, a continuation of feudal capitalism that disguised the terror of the market. The protective coloration of violence required for technical reproduction effectively and thoroughly camouflaged the end, even by enlisting the avant-garde in the destruction of historical consciousness by creating an aura of a world in ruins through the techniques of montage and collage.

Similarly, Brecht, in this period of technical reproducibility, is developing his theatrical principles against the bourgeois auratic theatre and into trickster, carnival, Chinese, and Russian traditions. Contemporary to this moment, Kracauer was conceiving his monumental study of Weimar film, *From Caligari to Hitler: A Psychological History of the German Film*, that showed the contradictions of Weimar in a new light. Kracauer's 1920s Weimar essays were influential in Benjamin's "The Work of Art." The study follows Kracauer's analysis of the mass behaviour in Germany through an "auratic" concept of "the anonymous multitude," constructed aesthetically and psychologically through the film's "visible hieroglyphs" of the inner world of the spectators at a particular time when a nation "firmly rooted in middle-class mentality," in economic shifts, mass unemployment, and the "shadowy being" of the army, big landowners, and moneyed classes, and the despair that was taking hold in a national emergency, refused to take Hitler seriously. [102]

Kracauer's study identified in Weimar films those film qualities that undercut the overt nature of the director or the heroic expressionistic styles, because the photographic image also has an aura of the business of film-making and the "fortuitous considerations" that reveal how it is made; it carries the "unstaged reality" – the aura of the photographic image. The film could not be completely controlled by its style or message or its "beautiful semblance." [103] The "cult of the movie star fostered by the money of the film industry preserves not the unique aura of the person, but the 'spell of the personality,' the phony spell of the commodity." [104] The formal ingredients of the culture hero who played on the registers of violence, ecstasy, wizardry, priestcraft, and the collective soul – the total mobilization of "the aura" – became the *object* of Brecht's withering critique of the "heroic" and the function of his theatrical stagecraft. As Brecht dissolved his political commitment into the *artistic agents* – gangsterism, dandyism, speech, hymnal and choral music, sentimentality, hack and profound verse, invention, athleticism, plasticity and speed, work and triumph, Supermanisms and archaic styles of acting – he created a new stagecraft which would not only serve the new cause of performance but would create a new conception of *historical literacy. Benjamin saw in Brecht the new spectator.*

Brecht's bitterness about bourgeois melodrama insisted that art derive from reality and experience, and his now famous statement that "he who laughs has not yet heard the bad news" parallels his defence of realism as a *literacy*: "Nothing prevents Cervantes and Swift, realists that they are, from seeing knights joust with windmills and horses found states." [105] Both statements ground "realism" in the trickster literacy of revolutionary authorship and political struggle. Benjamin's storyteller and Brecht's trickster are both the gods of a new literacy. [106]

Benjamin's difficult 1928 study of the *Origin of the German Trauerspiel*, or "tragic drama," conceived as a metaphysical analysis of a *cultural form*, parallels Brecht's attempt to delimit and delegitimize "tragedy" and parallels Freud's 1920 *Beyond the Pleasure Principle, which located death worship in the culture itself.*

Benjamin's work of art essay comes almost as footnote to the *"Baroque Play of Mourning."* Melodrama was the art form of the middle classes who were attempting to salvage a cultural form from their marketplace literacy. Brecht's *Threepenny Opera* combined the cultural aspirations of the bourgeois class with the desire for kingship and sovereign authority. Melodrama was the art form that expressed the bourgeoisie. This class permeated humanistic culture from the time of the baroque, yet its reading and viewing public did not fully control the values and taste of art until the emergence of propitious market conditions and of a literate reading public. The estrangement of the middle classes from the dominant art preserves – the museums, patronage, stage, and courts – were slowly transformed into a fluid estrangement informed by the worship of the intimate problems of the private individual.

While agrarian capital and bourgeois democracy provided the basis for the worship of both nature and competition among the various renunciatory philosophies and ideologies, as well as the *Drang nach Osten* (the drive to colonize the East for its agricultural lands), questions for the bourgeoisie were still whether there is a "God" or whether there is a "god" in the works.

Benjamin saw how these political anxieties of the impersonal mechanism of the market are experienced as the natural disasters of social institutions, including the psychological power of sexual relationships as moral dilemmas, which are seen as universal experiences. When character, culture, and property emerge as ideal *and* material qualities, new forms of consciousness, new objects of revolutionary intent must undercut melodrama and popular reading habits. Yet the popular in the populace calls.

But in spite of the novel and Brecht's aesthetic and his theatrical experiments, melodrama continued to sustain itself. The public grew more and more to identify with the state, or national aspirations, and identified the private with self-interest and the hope for an enlightened critique of and faith in the business, educational, and professional intelligentsia. In the world of melodrama, the popular mass arts, and older folk arts, ecclesiastical idioms, monumental and heroic vocabularies split apart and were never again united in a common literacy.

The mood of fragmentation prepared the way for the agonized soul and body in flight from guilt and mental turmoil that even in the torments of expressionism became the subject matter of both high and middle art forms – Ibsen and Mallarmé, as well as Hardy and Gautier, Lang and Pabst, are forced to use symbols and myth because their radical visions are weakened by the coming of the forces of social reaction.

The refuge would be in the utopian dream of a new mode of performance of art and society; without a "breakthrough into performance," there will be silence about the "technical reproduction" that had become part of the rootless, homeless, fugitive, marginal, or stratified world and technically, artistically, aesthetically, and linguistically conceptualized into the common currency of words without historical presence.

As priests, Shamans, magicians, and warriors have always controlled and established the idioms and conditions of writing – the conventions, codes, repertoires, and materials used in cultural creation – and eventually determine what is allowed and what is deemed legitimate as a cultural-*universal* literacy, a new form of art-making would challenge the bourgeoisie's cultural property. Imposing on cultural literacy the *logic* of their destructive needs, the art that survives, in bourgeois ideology, becomes the horrible, grotesque work that only barely survives the mutilation of its own creative materials. Kafka's "A Hunger Artist" (1922) parades his beauty and truth to the spectators who gawk at him; the artist does not know, but Kafka does, that performance will become the lie that transforms into a new world order.

For Benjamin, then, reading films, and the artworks forged in this sub-Promethean crucible of industry, capitalism, and bureaucracy, means finding how the legacy of narrative, with its accompanying characteristics and features – memory, character, unconscious intention, atomized totalities, material reflection of the real world – meets the spectacle head on and creates the concept and activity *performance* as a "meta-theatre" and *a new history of political consciousness.* The hunger artist is the new prototype.

Brecht, in a heroic act of reconstruction, attempted to stage the epic of the rise and fall of historical narrative on a theatrical stage where *making* replaced the world of cultural spectacles. Finally, the superego *in* society personifies the political revolt of the masses against the superego itself and against those false intimacies masked as sexual yearning and longing. Arnold Hauser writes that the material changes during the nineteenth century produced what Benjamin named "residues of a dream world" that "in dreaming precipitates its awakening": [107]

The superego is for psychoanalysis personified society: the organ of the strongest bond and of the most powerful revolt of people in relation to one another. It combines within itself everything, which we understand by conscience, ethos, moral authority, and absolute divine authority. In contrast to the Christian idea of God, however, it is a force which is always the source only of duty, pain, and sorrow, which burdens the subject with … an apparently intransigent force – the unconscious. This is for the most part a pointless and hopeless struggle and in spite of that the only one which in the present unheroic skeptical world gives some deeper meaning and tragic seriousness to human existence. [108]

We soon recognize that where our own voice superimposes itself on the material of the struggle and vanishes as in a dream into the estranged "languages" of surrealist styles, that we are being made to perform this act, that we can and do inhabit *more* than one world at the same time. While alienated from this world, we never leave it behind; thus, Freud recognized that the speech of his patients was the speech of the many in the solitude of the one. History and dream speak to each other. Benjamin saw in the "boldness of the camera" what psychoanalysis shows in the labour of the ego that imposes our formal participation *in* society but makes us spectators of our own consciousness. [109] Everyday life produces both dream and desire for power; our performances dominate our waking lives, giving us the power of technical reproducibility without possession of the means to organize and use the power. The radical element in psychoanalysis and Kafka gives the dreamer a sense of discontinuous time, a present that lives both for and against the past. Kafka's clear and simple language and his application of a "silent" screen language to a *world* that is obscure shows how our everyday speech and thought are overdetermined by an inner narrative that mechanically reproduces the ideological quality of life itself. Josef K.'s "trial" – his *Prozess* (trial, disease, and inability to know who is judging him) – lies in the reference to the spectator of his own awakening into a consciousness of the spectacle. For Benjamin the spectator awakens to the epoch in which "film ... [is] the art form that is in keeping with the increased threat to his [sic] life which modern man has to face."[110] The Stalin Trials are political performances that Benjamin and Brecht had to face in the historical force field of their emerging exile.

Performance, then, *is* the dialectical, social struggle that contains the means of materially creating a new audience out of the ruins of modern life. For Benjamin, surrealism was a symptom of the phantasmagoria. In the "film age," however, performance co-exists and is continuous with a desire to destroy form as well as to deepen already-existing legacies. In the film form we see the illusion of the mass soul with its relationship to industrial organization: time and space as heterogeneous phenomena.

The history of performance as a principle makes historical consciousness visible and makes visible the invisible by creating spectatorship that is politically conscious. Performance, or in Benjamin's and Brecht's words, working out the relationship of politics and aesthetics, must be understood as "gesture" and the theatrical "gest."

Generically, then, film works on us as performance, that is, as more than "film"; the everydayness of film responds to the forms of capitalism and culture that have crushed the individual and replaced the crowd by annexing needs to the need to have spectacle. What gives voice to this process of assimilation and accommodation to those who are not being quoted? Benjamin's "book of quotations," *The Arcades Project*, is then in essence a theatrical project in which Benjamin exposes the ideology of a civilized character structure when at this point in history the industrialists were already preparing for the next war just as the demonstrators were in the streets, and the numbers of unemployed were growing every day to almost five million by early 1931.

V

The Grotesque Angel of Everyday

Make no mistake about Benjamin knowing that the Power of Mechanical Reproduction is a Violent Power. Simply conceptualizing this power around a culturally loaded term like "performance" does not in itself create a new culture, or a political organization, or an innovative aesthetic technique. Benjamin places performance into film as the vehicle of the modern grotesque. There is still the ambivalence of a neutral technology of the emotions, yet performance of repeated shocks forms time and the body into reminders of our mortality. The film age is the age of shock, recollection, of the multitude in all of its simultaneity with aura-less solitude. René Char's advice "to put off the imaginative part until later" in *Hypnos Waking* (1956) means to hold the literary in readiness as resistance to fascism. Char's poetry, as is Paul Celan's, is a counterpart to Benjamin's aesthetic.

However, the literary public cannot be fully trusted. While they may respond to surrealism and montage and to fantasy and commercial art in the feuilleton, the growing proletarianization of "modern man" produces fascism as a logical result, along with the introduction of aesthetics and the Führer cult into political life.

Did Benjamin sense that a well-disciplined revolutionary vanguard party corresponds to the logic and materialism of modern art? As if the measures to be taken in history correspond to art within the expanding, post-Dada uses of literacy for political ends? Not really. Yet maybe. Benjamin's work teaches that film cannot be mystified and glorified through prescriptive use of montage and arbitrary techniques of film language, because these absolutist, meta-approaches to film-performance reduce the live, plastic, historical qualities to fashion, to blind laws, to baroque forms of mourning, in short, to allegory.

Film is yet a propagandist medium, a shock to the system; it is also an immediately adaptive cultural creation. Unlike reading, writing, and speaking, film is *not* part of everyday life, but like historical consciousness and storytelling it gives us the illusion *that there is somewhere a performable, reproducible totality*. For Benjamin the film was fated to be a weapon that, like the angel of history, contained a double power of weeping and teaching, teaching and weeping. The film form cannot turn its back on pathos. Film is a form of dreaming that unfolds both the dream and awakening as an *intérieur* and reproduces itself as a commodity. The cunning of history wins because both the "dream kitsch" overcomes the aura, because "only with cunning, not without it, can we work free of the realm of the dream." [111]

This holds imagination in readiness for coming attractions and, as Adorno puts it in the quotation at the head of this essay, the question is whether or how "technologization, the extended arm of [the] nature-dominating subject, purges artworks of their immediate language ... [and whether] technological requirements drive out the contingency of the individual who produces the work." [112]

The Public Spheroid: Following the Paths in the Millennial Wilderness, or "Lost without a Utopic Map" in the Spheres of Hannah Arendt and Robin Blaser[113]

The discovery that the human mind has ceased, for some mysterious reasons, to function properly forms, so to speak, the first act of the story with which we are concerned here.

—HANNAH ARENDT, *Between Past and Future* (1961), trans. Jerome Kohn

From this bridge to the next we walked and talked of things my Comedy does not care to tell; and when we reached the summit of the arch we stopped to see the next fosse of Malebolge and to hear more lamentation voiced in vain: I saw that it was strangely dark!

—DANTE ALIGHIERI, *Inferno* (1320), canto XXI, trans. Mark Musa

The three-part title to this essay on Robin Blaser's aesthetic brings his poetic into a relationship with what I see as the three sides to Robin Blaser's thought and writing. First, there is Hannah Arendt's public sphere, in which poetry is an active world of "Homo Faber," which means humans making their world in poetry. Humans are not merely "Homo Laborans" who make their world through labour. In addition, Blaser followed paths through Dante-like millennial wildernesses, looking for the "utopic maps" that would guide us in the comedies of everyday life, which can appear to us as allegories of everyday life. Of course, "spheroid" is my way of saying that the modern world shrinks our understanding and the world becomes flatter. For Blaser's aesthetic found in Arendt in the 1950s some answers and a witness to his political concerns, but then his poetic practice takes on a life of its own.

It is difficult to find the right tone that establishes the ethos in which a comprehensive poetic mind turns to poetry rather than the novel or philosophy. In these meditations I am imagining an inner conversation that might have occurred between Hannah Arendt and Robin Blaser at a particular location in 1950s America. In writing the three pathways to this location I avoid as much as possible adopting the literary critical language that has always lived at the boundary of the professionalized literary studies – in the bureaucratic sense of the term – known as the literary critical movement. "New Criticism" set up the new pedantry. The new-New Criticism had all the pretense of a vanguard movement without the confidence of basing its criticism on specific literary works that might stand for thinking about the future of what Hannah Arendt called "the human condition" – surely unacceptable language today. This is a "clear the ground" essay which takes on a particular period in time when building a poetic practice and aesthetic understanding of poetry as such, and a fearlessness towards language in times when the aesthetic seems to demand personal history and passionate attention to the world around the poet.

Since English departments have adopted a humanistic self-understanding that they are politically expert and relevant to the establishment of a democratic public sphere, it is difficult to measure the role that mindfulness towards thought plays in making poetry of the kind that Robin Blaser's poetic nerve creates. [114]

For Arendt, it was the poets who thought philosophically – one thinks of Arendt's deep familiarity with René Char, but also Bertolt Brecht, Walter Benjamin, and Franz Kafka – those who reached to the limits of poetic praxis. At the same time this polarity of personal and public illuminates, almost in a religious sense, the unadulterated violent connection between law and justice, sacrifice and martyrdom in the face of thought internalized as a permanent, Cartesian doubt that erased the Archimedean point of balance between private and public – "this spiritual condition which is everybody's language / of the world is not finally as small as my own solitaire."[115]

Martyrdom, in the way I use it here following Arendt, means that we must observe how violence resides inside of the sacred and that we bear witness to those unable to speak. How innocent it is to believe that if you construct a public world by leaving the private behind, you enter a world of rich discursive reflection about violence, exclusion, and the real! How naive to believe that the world would be more humane and that a utilitarian notion like "happiness" could become the foundation of a public sphere, and that you could understand the meaning of happiness only in this sense of making a humane world! Indeed, this is Arendt's notion of action – the search for an enlargement of the world – and a politics that maps the world and shrinks alienating space so we can recognize again its human size. It is clear to me that this can be interpreted not just as a rejection of politics – what do you actually do in that newly created world in which life forces are released and that has so much disrespect of others? This is the struggle of a poetics to see in philosophical anarchism a public philosophy. The political is defined by the danger of acting into nature, of redesigning nature through physics, and by making the inbuilt world into a "natural world."

The philosophical ideal here relates to the influence of Hannah Arendt on Blaser's aesthetic of the public world. The influence of Arendt on the poetic of "the real" is based on learning about the world from the Archimedean point of the history of totalitarianism, the Nazi "revolution," the Soviet state-dictatorship, and the American consumer revolution that transformed how we think about work and labour, and thinking and writing as intellectual labour. In this reconstruction of world-alienation – Arendt's term – we find in Arendt's critique a challenge to the modern masses that *were made unpolitical in the deepest sense of denying the political in everyday life.* By turning the political over to the banal everydayness of the Eichmanns, who were radically evil just because they denied the political, we distance the citizen's right to happiness, and ultimately sacrifice the private to the deformed public, preordained to the glorification of necessity through labour.[116]

Arendt's critics would see in her thought European elitism, denial of representation, even denial of revolution and social movements, and a strange interpretation of Aristotle's ideas of poiesis as political *praxis* in the making. However, the basis of Arendt's idealization of the "polis" republicanism is in the council republics that sprung into life in pockets of Europe. Poets with an anarcho-social bent will, however, see this as an opening to rethinking the politics of the public in which the lost past of the life of poetry as the life of the mind in action resides: this is citizenship and this is also pathos and suffering (martyrdom) expressed in the language of the politically dispossessed. This view of the political has influenced Habermas's and postwar German philosophy, which, for the Frankfurt School political philosophers, was about whether there can be a post-Enlightenment Marxist civil society and on what basis can the hegemony of mass culture and the scientific-technological turn spare humankind from becoming obsolescent.[117]

However, in the 1950s there was a sense of this double negation of speaking about a deathly world of conformity and a false omnipotence regarding the establishment of an authentic public sphere. But this was almost pre-intuitive, since the feelings denied longing for a future while idealizing utopic thought, in the sense of a visionary community, which for the poet one finds in Charles Olson's *Maximus Poems*, or making up something like a Marxist republic during the Cold War. Were there any examples of a hybrid public sphere? By the 1950s, socialism was a dead-duck choice for politics. So dead that the Marx Brothers' 1933 parody of democracy in *Duck Soup* seemed to fit Artaud's sense of a political future. Any public culture would have to be clumsily made up of fragments of lost poleis, mythical remnants of stories of vanished places and details that held stories of sacred reminders and traces lost in collective memory. Historiography was on the agenda precisely because of the sense of loss. The world could be best described as a phantasmagoria.

Hunting for an appropriate audience on leaving the polis-harbour and wandering to the America of the 1950s would not be an ideal journey. The ideal America is a poetic place of bridges and ships, but it is a dangerous place, in the sense of Dante's *Inferno*, canto XXVI, which scurrilously ends in an image of the troubadour, Bertran de Born, bearing his "head cut off from its life-source / which is back there, alas, within its trunk," where the severed head bears witness in retributive justice – *contrapasso* – to the loss of a natural poetics. Dante's vernacular modernism laments that poetry does not end in democracy and a Godly-civic society whose communality cares for the already lost and soon-to-be-lost souls. The Augustinian sacrifice of the body to the damnation of a world without God is for Dante a world alienation without civic poetry. The underbelly of earth lies martyred at the feet of anger and pathos.

It is the uncoerced voice that is being hunted, spoken, and heard that, in Arendt's public world, is the basis of a dialogical ethics. But in the world of deconstruction that searches constantly for missing voices, we have ended up in "language and death," not even the luxury any more of the death of God. Necrophilia rules, we might say, but this is not the case; for example, in Agamben's interpretation of Heidegger, we get the confirmation that voice cannot be maintained, negated, or even shown. The death of language is the death of the subject in search of the chimera of language and poetry – for example, Paul Celan's or César Vallejo's retreats from collective necrophilia: "You're all dead. / What a strange way of being dead. Anyone would say you aren't. But, truly, you're all dead." [118]

I have always seen the poet's deep modernism as a post-modernism before postmodernism was "invented" – facing up to the problem of loss, the loss of the book, of eternity, and of the recovery of a number of ethos-rich worlds where the unconscious existed behind the back of every gesture. Here is almost the loss of loss, but recoverable by the always insistently relentless personal project of discovering language again and again. Arendt's private realm, where the weak community of poetry writers conquers the strong political state, is a crossroads. In short, poetry celebrates the anarchism of the body and the bitterness of the mind in the will to self-creation, but in travelling away from Nietzsche's solitary will discovers images of others. This is the private searching for a public that is willing to travel this route.

But in literary-historical terms, this means that Blaser's extraordinary talent for reperiodizing and rethinking literary history by crossing the bridges that always exist between authorship and new reading possibilities, and which will bring various poetic conversations into a relationship with the present itself, is a way of bringing the modern world of conflicting publics into dialogical relationships with the voices that have been lost in the academic desert of English departments. Let me now dispense with English departments quickly in one Golem-like blow: starting in the 1950s, English departments began the long road to obsolescence in which they now reside in their doldrums. This is an indefensible personal thought, but for now let me simply say that in connecting the dots of this invisible picture of poetry and politics in the public sphere, we can imagine a Gerhard Richter image that becomes clearer and then fades away as one searches the photograph for the source of the picture in reality. For, if Arendt's philosophy of loss is to contain a philosophy of the future, then there have to be categories of thought that still exist in the place "between past and future."

If English departments have a future, I am not aware of it, nor would I recognize it today. [119]

I

Anarchism after the 1950s

This essay may be a form of fiction, because I have imagined that my relationship to the book *The Holy Forest* and its tree-poems constitutes an orientation point for the labyrinthine relationship that subtly indoctrinates us with the idea that, between aesthetics and ethics in this poetry, there is the possibility that indoctrination into the public world is not as bad an idea as we have been taught to think.

In Arendt's world the relationship of private to public is worked out in the Medusan relationship of aesthetics to ethics. In the "connect the dots" map that emerges from *The Holy Forest*, I also have imagined that these avant-gardist poems have been written in an age of earthly dismemberment of the social. They can teach us to survive the millennial thinking emerging in the rush to make the nation-state into a global prison.

Since the end of the Cold War that gave birth to the anarcho-spirits of the Duncan–Ginsberg–Spicer–Blaser axis in modern poetics, a public world for poetry and ethics did not emerge into any boundlessly public world; although we can see the struggle between, on the one hand, earnest Habermasians and other civil society post-Marxists, and, on the other, the Deleuzians, Foucauldians, or Lyotardians who conceive of the lifeworld as a series of black symbolic boxes which can be decolonized and disenchanted of their inner-rational pathologies. The ethics we hear are not the echoes of the old "collectives," but the gas tank being filled up at the neoliberal nation-state gas station, topping up the engines of capital with surpluses understood by Batailleans as a lifeworld that exists beyond any Nietzschean hope for a millennial end to bourgeois politics. Since I have considerable sympathy and affinity for the anarchist turn in these movements against the state, I cannot excuse myself from the curse of believing in an aesthetics and ethics as the lost parents of Autonomy and Individuality. But these parents, too, are fictitious renderings of the past, because none of us has experienced an age of economic stability and political peace necessary to the survival of the utopic idea – autonomous art. On the other hand, not all dissonance is liberating.

A careful study of the American avant-garde of the 1950s and early 1960s (Ellison, Pynchon, Spicer …) would show that the movement struggled to advance beyond a romantic anti-capitalism that always threatened to fall into the very phantasmagoric techniques that the autonomy of art was trying to escape. This means that American poetics in the 1950s suffered in the Dantesque pathos and anger, grounded in the world of American kitsch and consumer culture – that never allows us to awaken from the psychology of the interior: this is Arendt's private sphere, made up of phantasmic, mindless configurations.

Modernism had felt the losses of tradition as the loss of mindfulness towards reality – for example, Lukács's notion of the novel as the epic of an age of absolute sinfulness mourns the loss of an integrated world whose character produced the novel and the problematic character. [120] At the same time, the interest in the psychology of the creative process recovered a feeling of absence of a world which would represent the loss of a "world" as personal and creative loss in the period when "romantic anti-capitalism" was growing as an aesthetic world view. Capitalist cultural forms absorbed the age of absolute depersonalization and mimicked the phantasmagoria of *homo faber*, which works against the system that produces *social action as mindless politics*. Arendt points out that "even if the historical origin of art were of an exclusively religious or mythological character, the fact is that art has survived gloriously its severance from religion, magic, and myth." [121] This statement, with its magisterially overstated "gloriously," is not only an idealistic defence of the autonomy of art, but a call for engagement with the world: this call is radical at mid-century and full of problems in our millennial *fin de siècle*. Why?

Arendt's public world has not survived the ritualistic sacrifice to the banal magic of the commodity, where freedom lies in our desiring to be the slaves of the mirror. But as there are two Arendts – the one obsessed with love in speech and the other disgusted by the convergence of state and violence – so here there are two poets: the one who pronounces on the public sphere and the loss of speech and the other who makes speech. Oriented by the poet's poems, we can understand the lament and provocations that occur in the post-utopic "meataphysics-pata(ta)physics" of the aesthetics of the poor – a scarcity that exists in the forest – a disparity that lies between the poverty of the world's images and a surplus of poetic paradigms in search of images. [122] The poet caught inside different traditions could create a baroque world that to many readers would appear like digressive writing which would require a "syntax" of ethics, mourning, and utopic thinking as Archimedean points.

II

Vanguardism, Ethics, and Aesthetics

Equally important to this Kantian-sublime dream of a disinterested social justice would be a discussion about the ethics of the practices of the aestheticized avant-garde. Academic criticism and the cultural industries have absorbed and aestheticized modernism. The avant-garde remirrors and simulates the techniques as lampoon-art. How does one understand avant-garde practices today? How do we keep these techniques alive in reality and memory without feeling guilty at every turn that these avant-garde practices have become the staple of propaganda, advertising, and public-spinning relations? Today, the avant-garde does not direct its Baudelairean spleen against society itself – which was the principle of modernist practices – but has turned against art itself and, in the process, sneers at authorship as simply a mode of production. Art as anti-art speaks on behalf of the philistine spirit embedded inside the techniques of reproduction that have been so influenced by the practices of photography. The Russian, French, German, and Italian avant-gardes drew their ethical energies from the attack on the bourgeoisie and the critic-philistine who promoted kitsch and themselves by seeing reality as a manipulatable aesthetic phenomenon in which the aesthetic dimension could be eliminated in favour of productivist values. Today it is fashionable to point out that these older modernists are themselves guilty of being reactionary, autonomous, detached, Bolsheviki or fellow travelers of anarchism. The highway today is littered with rapprochements with mass culture; critics no longer see mass culture as the other of modernism; but now see it as the sublime to which we are all accountable. The grotesque – once the home of the nomadic visitor from the irrational – now becomes the Archimedean point in the exchange process which, by eliminating the voice of the public, follows the path of violence into the process of perception itself. Since communism and anarchism are discredited as thinkable social movements, and socialism is taboo, only democracy as the productive other of capitalism can provide an ethics or soon-to-be-realized ethics. That this is the ethics of bourgeois ways of thinking is forgotten.

Boris Groys, in his study of the Russian avant-garde, points out the truth that goes beyond Stalinism: that any study of the avant-garde must be historical because aesthetics hides its own particular ethical component – for example, the Nazi Degenerate Art Exhibition and the assimilation of the Russian avant-garde to Stalinism. Here is the formula: the totality of the artwork presupposes a relationship to the past and then destroys these conditions – a specific social context – by claiming that art cannot be properly understood without formalizing these destructive tendencies. To be sure, this means that every discussion of ethics and aesthetics must be grounded in a study of the practices of creation, reception, assimilation, and elaboration of the work in society and how this immanent totality of experience alienates the very present in whose name this destructive alien-reality occurs. [123]

III

Authorship and Ethnography of the Real

The critic as an alchemist practising the obscure art of transmuting the futile elements of the real into the shining, enduring gold of truth, or rather watching and interpreting the historical process that brings about such magical transfiguration – whatever we may think of this figure, it hardly corresponds to anything we usually have in mind when we classify a writer as a literary critic.

—HANNAH ARENDT, "Walter Benjamin: 1892–1940," in Benjamin, *Illuminations* (1969), trans. Harry Zohn

The American 1950s reinvented the romantic idea that authorship foregrounded "writing" itself as an aesthetic subject. An ethnographical, materialist aesthetic was in the air, and it was possible to see it in many thoughtful authors whose influence on writers were part of the poetic public sphere: Stanley Diamond, Paul Goodman, Marshall Sahlins, Paul Radin, Kenneth Burke, John Dewey, Alfred North Whitehead, Suzanne Langer all broadened the intellectual horizons and showed how an ethnography of the real could be recreated in and by the poetic world. The history of the intellectual renaissance in the 1950s would show that a non-violent, dialogical reciprocity of voices in action could combine with a post-symbolic partisanship into what Arendt terms "making" – *homo faber*.

While it is difficult to extract an aesthetics as such from Arendt, her politics evoke a philosophical attitude towards art production as a communal activity. There is the dimension of her thinking that places the author at the centre of the private, the household – a lay person's private space – where the person lives among books and in thought. This is typical for modernism's attempt to rescue the personal project from the retreat to liberal subjectivism. I believe much of Arendt's problematical politics (as described above) lies behind some of the most poignant and enigmatic images in Blaser's *The Holy Forest*. The poet's echoes of Arendt's feeling for her own "era" are not conceits, but images or thing-representations, thought in motion, which are grounded in thoughtfulness and take great risks with revealing and then building on "the urge towards self-disclosure." [124] This aesthetics of the private is framed in a realm and discourse of the "poor," since the poetry takes risks with its own survival. Why do I use the idea of the "poor" as a linguistic framework? Precisely because the poet is showing the personal poetic sphere, even the intimate sphere as with the public sphere, hoping for good luck in the Greek sense that marks off politics from the realm of permanent necessity of aesthetic disclosure of dialectics of the personal and public. Here *poiesis* destroys action because it is only personal – "a wordy prison does not make a house." [125] The effort to escape into a utopic polis using a map is structured in the title, *The Holy Forest*, because the search for the polis allows for a "remedy for the futility of action and speech." [126] Poems co-exist with the dying politics and ethical demands inside the public spheroid that we are in, rolling away from the public. Another way of saying this is that the aesthetics of *The Holy Forest* suggests that we discover a counter-modernism to the pseudo-Rousseauian social contract grounded in the will of the state and find our way back to another form of republicanism, grounded in a different vision of a city – in an older imaginary city. [127]

IV

Redress

In a hallway conversation of the English department, nestled in the interstices of the architectural extravaganza of Simon Fraser University on Burnaby Mountain, the poet once opened up a difficult problem to me which can be characterized as such: "The problem with the Marxists is that they have no theory of language." I thought: Another problem that Marxists had a lot to answer for was the apartheid imposed on sexual identity and the inability of the public world to take in the sexual itself. That was the early 1970s, at the time of *Image-Nations*. But now that Marxists and sexual identities have become part of the human condition and the "public sphere" after living in the closet, the challenge to the Marxist oyster then was to open it up to theories of language: Where are we now?

I am not sure. Who is sure? But then I was taken aback by the poet's challenge to a politics that had a critique of fetishism and reification at its foundation, because from my own anarchist perspective on Marxism I had assumed that the language of the poor in conflict with the social was an emergent language, one that the poets, intellectuals, and outsiders were writing yet not speaking directly to any official audience. While the social – in Arendt's sense of a public world – was eroding public speech by an earthbound alienation stemming from modern capitalism's call to throw off the chains of religion and take up the commodity – against which "wealth accumulation and expropriation are of minor significance" – the poets were attacking the very idea of culture as the pseudo-public sphere. [128] For me, who understood Marx's theory of history, Marxist theory of culture was insufficiently anthropological or materialist and missed how cultural forms were as great a determination of the prison of the industrial lifeworld, equal in power over everyday life to class or the state. [129] The task was to redress the historical innervation of public culture through the rediscovery of the roots of language, where a dividing line was being drawn between a social praxis which could map a return to the "primitive" polis and the uses of the word "culture" to mean hegemonic "civilization." To be sure, this is romantic anti-capitalism with a vengeance.

The problem becoming very clear in the 1950s, seen through anthropological insights into culture, was that we had constructed a civilizational logic that had incorporated the idea of the "primitive" as an adversarial concept. We had thus constructed and monopolized the definition of the primitive. This *Kulturkampf* meant that to redeem language *we had to redeem philosophy away from culture and away from philosophy*; and perhaps that road went through the anti-philosophy of Husserl, Heidegger, and Whitehead more than Derrida.

This loss of a worldly language in the modern age did not mean it was possible, simply and academically, to *recover* an ancient unspeakable language through some Arnoldian mediation of cultural polarities like Hebraism and Hellenism. The road went through the *consequences* of totalitarianism, and this was expressed by the anti-nationalistic politics of Arendt, whose work was a kind of miner's lamp in the mid-century wilderness of figuring out nation-building and colonialism.

The mapless road that led out of colonialism had to find a way to the relationship between experience, which took place in the household, and the choices that were to be made in the public world that was rapidly becoming a permanent warfare state. While the critiques of Arendt's work centre on her way of proposing an anti-politics within the institutions of civil society, it is forgotten that she was one of the first to bring a concept of the *anti-colonial* into the Marxist, *anti-imperial* world view, which saw class struggle dominating us until the end of history. This boundary world where we are not dominated by either the products we make or the experiences of production itself appeared to augur a new aesthetics that challenged the labouring person as the normative concept for a world of work. The economic society that would redeem labouring humanity was deeply wounded as a concept, because, exiled from home into work, humans were made shelterless and ideologically homeless, as they were lost in the world of the Hegelian spirit of the commodity. Arendt's devotion to Benjamin lies in this corrective to Marx's belief that work will turn into a classless culture of equals in which distribution of surplus and wealth would not only create new "persons," but also new images of language and understandings of aesthetics; this aspect of Arendt inspired Robin Blaser's poetic praxis.[130]

The force field of "ethicality" in the growth of the individual, who lives within the experience of recognizing the nature of the present times in which one lives, cannot wait for a magical leap into future consciousness. This leap must happen thaumaturgically through the will to self-creation that rids us of the residue of the will to power. The philosopher of the self, Charles Taylor, may confuse the self with "identity," and romanticism with the expressive act, in such a way as to limit modern poetry to mere expressiveness. His view of poetry suggests that by eroding the will to action we reduce the utopic sphere of heroic, creative discourse to the everyday, which can be made experiential and utilitarian. In this sense it is debatable whether Taylor's construction of an ideal democratic state can co-exist with the aesthetic of a deconstructive poetics that reflects more adequately the abject poverty and loss of recognition of those who live in the subsistence culture of modernity.[131]

Arendt's concept of making comes closer to a love of liberty and happiness that is paradoxically grounded in the idiocy of a public opinion, which is, for her, always manipulated by the powerful elites that deny their complicity in horror – to convey the notion of communal liability as the basis of the political taught by Karl Jaspers, her teacher. Put another way, collective social guilt leads to redemptive violence and the sacred conditioning of force through racism and colonialism; communal liability leads to the discovery of responsibility for others.

The polarity of collective guilt and communal liability was most active in the 1950s, when Arendt wrote *The Human Condition*. We poor who survived the war were faced with the alternative of becoming political conformists: splitting the household and its precarious existence into private consumer acts of commodity desire – "To each according to his desires" – or to redressing the war, Auschwitz, Hiroshima, Stalinism, national-ethnic civil wars, and the segmentation of the population into what was left of the social state, where private happiness forgets any remembrance of the lost world in which poetics might take place. This is the loss of the *imago mundi*.

V

Loss of Loss – Incommensurability and Reversal of *Homo Laborans*

Often an era most clearly brands with its seal those who have been least influenced by it, who have been most remote from it, and who therefore have suffered most.

—HANNAH ARENDT, introduction to Benjamin's *Illuminations* (1969), trans. Harry Zohn

The great radicals of modernism were always tempted to understand how the loss of tradition was the loss of something that allowed us to feel loss – the loss of a world that Arendt claimed was already here.

Already in the 1950s the self-reflexive attack on modernism in arts and letters had begun with the attempt by modernist writers and painters to unlink art from the social by putting the social outside of the personal in the name of an Eliotian poetics of the impersonal. Yet Eliot was "the" poet! At the same time, it was a principle of modernism to make art into an *alternative* public world that only *seemed* to deny the social. The debates over modernism were heard often in the *Partisan Review*, for example, where the debates over kitsch and American mass culture claimed to determine what was the truly autonomous culture and what was a truly engaged autonomous art that would confront conformist mass culture.

This oppositional gesture fought against the triumph of the Americanist liberal ideology of belonging, which for Arendt did not mean a simple critique of conformism, but rather an exposure of the loss of reality itself. However, these debates did not accurately reflect how modernist aesthetics phrased the social. All of modernism did not necessarily end up in "irony" or the New Criticism, or with Eliot's churchly separation of poetry and politics. Modernism arrived at this stage by going through the personal project, which documented the incommensurability of the creative self with the social self – the one falsely built, not on "each according to his [sic] needs" but on "each according to his [sic] desires." The scent of this ideology of reality that assumed the separation of poetry from politics had begun to rise up in the halls of power and legislatures in the Cold War 1950s.

In *The Origins of Totalitarianism*, Arendt argues that the nineteenth-century separation of the political life of societies and individuals from economic power created the framework for imperialism. Imperialism became the economic arm of the nation-state and permitted the bourgeoisie to emancipate itself from politics in order to pursue business and commerce. Deprived of political rights, the home-based individual is divorced from the economic engine that drives commerce and finance:

> What imperialists actually wanted was expansion of political power without the foundation of a body politic. Imperialist expansion had been touched off by a curious kind of economic crisis, the overproduction of capital and the emergence of "superfluous" money, the result of oversaving, which could no longer find productive investment within the national borders. [132]

Native bourgeois financiers took over from the free-floating Jewish pioneer financiers. Her thesis: The need to create stabilizing forces by incorporating the political and the economic, and by seeing that imperialism must be considered the first stage in the political rule of the bourgeoisie rather than the last stage of capitalism. The individual is deprived of political rights even while constitutions regulate public affairs through bureaucracy and control of dissent, race, and minorities. This is accomplished by the alliance of mob and capital. Thus, military control is a *sine qua non* extension of the already-existing inner colonization and the "never ending accumulation of capital." These processes were furthered through what in the 1950s were understood as the American cultural industries and institutions that determined cultural ideals in order to "combine domestic and foreign policy in such a way as to organize the nation for the looting of foreign territories and the permanent degradation of alien peoples." [133]

In nuce, this is a theory of making people into "trash," of the degradation and humiliation of peoples in the name of the economic. Arendt's story: Race consciousness is embedded in cultural identity and is "politically speaking, not the beginning of humanity but its end, not the origin of peoples but their decay, not the natural birth of man [*sic*] but his unnatural death." [134]

The connection of this line of thinking to the American and British *misère* of the Cold War 1950s is not clear today and may, in fact, not be understandable from the standpoint of the 1990s when ethnicity and democracy are assumed to be linked, without acknowledging that racism and imperialism are extensions of the economic and political. In this way, the cultural hegemony of inner colonialism is maintained. Arendt argued that America was unique among nations in knowing less about the psychology of the masses and mob formation than any other country in the world. [135] Her comment that the masses that "grew out of the fragments of a highly atomized society whose competitive structure and concomitant loneliness of the individual had been held in check only through membership in a class" [136] is tantamount to saying that America had created a unique cultural condition. The American bourgeoisie had become the leaders of a new crowd formation that had escaped the class-based realities of the class-ridden nation-state. Institutions of resistance were on the march. The analogy to the Nazi-fascist powers is clear, but what is not clear is that Arendt develops more than a politics of passive, force-fed, and coerced masses. *She describes the way a radical politics of consent enabled the masses to join with elites in order to create an imaginary classless society*, first by taking over the public sphere with totalitarian propaganda conveyed through the transmission belts of literacy, and then by manipulating belief systems so that elites could claim that perceptions and imagination are superior to facts. Arendt wrote:

> The effectiveness of this kind of propaganda demonstrates one of the chief characteristics of modern masses. They do not believe in anything visible, in the reality of their own experience; they do not trust their eyes and ears but only their imaginations, which may be caught by anything that is at once universal and consistent in itself. [137]

A hybrid of nationalism and economics and labour is created and is based on the cultural ideology of security, popularity, vicarious participation, exorcism of death in spectacles, sublimation of violence and sexuality by charismatic males, display of sexual identity, and creation of institutions that would worship state-run science and technology. Arendt's central thesis about the Modern Age is the reversal of contemplation and action and, within what she calls the *Vita Activa*, the victory of the *Vita Laborans*, and then the victory of the principle of happiness, or "life as the highest good," with subsequent conquering of life by the *Animal Laborans*.

Arendt condemns science for becoming the mouthpiece, the organ of the *zeitgeist*, that contributes to the elimination of the public world, and which reverses thinking into the counterfeit of acting and doing – the betrayal of the *Vita Activa*: "the *reversal* within the *Vita Activa* and the Victory *of Homo Faber*," she writes, was the separation of the ability of "making what he [*sic*] wanted to know" from understanding the new that was being made. Bureaucracy was for her a more powerful instrument of repression than class. This reminds us that science gives us acting without action, and instrumental symbols, not worlds. Science does not allow each of us a place for acting on life or for disinterested ethical observation, for science unmasks truth without taking responsibility for the revelation. [138]

The modernist turn for the poet recognized that art competes with science, and that the shadowy communalistic powers of the public sphere are based on the reifications and permanence and durability of the object of contemplation. Science is not the enemy: the uses and reification of science are. I believe the poet means this when he opens *The Holy Forest* with the idea of a journey from ancient to modern: "The whole thing: just trying to be at home. That's the plot." [139] The poet turns to a complex set of passages, where Arendt argues that Thought is related to feeling and transforms its mute and inarticulate despondency: exchange transforms naked greed of desire and usage transforms the desperate longing of needs – until all are fit to enter the world and to be transformed into things, to become reified. [140]

Society that regressed to nature was a way of justifying that this holy society had become second nature.

Well, this plot of homeland is the exile's territory. The *Image-Nations* poems are an intellectual's ethnographic parable of an imaginary community, a kind of paradigmatic story and ethnography of the modern which retains a link to the hidden angers and promises of the last gasp of modernist aesthetics. The attempt to maintain the desire to find a utopic, postwar ethics in the post-1950s is an imaginary world in which the separation of economics and politics is not allowed. This, of course, was also the terrain of Ezra Pound. If Arendt is right that philosophy suffered more from science than from any other intellectual field, it is also true that philosophy committed suicide each time it opened its mouth by turning its back on the poets who refused to fall into the toothless cavity. They fought being turned back to the social by way of the fetish of production. [141]

It is not possible here to be the cultural historian necessary to bring out the inner struggle in 1950s poetics that would show how the struggle of poetics with science and philosophy marked the age. This is the period that produced Paul Goodman, Herbert

Marcuse, Norman O. Brown, C. Wright Mills, the "Howl-ers," and others, like Christopher Lasch, who attacked the CIA infiltration of the intelligentsia.

The period also produced the combative, anti-romantic modernism of the New Criticism and the academic sellout to the morality of America, which marked the beginning of the end for American universities, whose enclaves of free thought in America were mutilated by the McCarthy–Cold War politics. Those entered every phase of cultural and political public life and education as technological "training institutes." In 1958, Arendt discussed the changing way we think about "the person" in the exchange market and the "idolization of genius" as the "degradation of the human person" and "the conviction of *homo faber* that a man's [*sic*] products may be more and essentially greater than himself." [142]

The many intellectual traditions inside Arendt's work cannot be isolated in order to explain the intense connection of these traditions to her idea of a communal politics of inclusion. The point here is that I believe her work has influenced the poet's sense of the radicality of republican traditions which became obscure to the intellectual preoccupations of the New Criticism that reflect an emerging "Archimedean point" in American culture that Melville knew about: the desire to jettison Europe in order to create an exceptional culture that in being fair and tolerant and wealthy became philistine and narrow. But the mind throws off influences and dons a jaunty hat and dances away into the carnivalesque "thousand hearts" of loving and loveless matter. [143]

Yet it is the mass culture of the 1950s which we cannot get away from, and the version of trash or kitsch which is celebrated in our degraded world was not just invented by Arendt. It was on Melville's, Pound's, Lawrence's, and Faulkner's minds, but not just. Arendt's meta-critique and search for the turning points, the Archimedean points, alien from Hegelian syntax, radiates disaster and war. Every line is saturated with martyred contemplation of genocide and statelessness, with anger against sacrificing the good of the many, and disgust against the Lutheran power of the state and law. In this period, Adorno and Horkheimer formulated their dialectic for and against Enlightenment, recognizing that there was a process of domination in the creation of a form of society that regressed to nature as a way of justifying what this holy society had become, as if there was always an existing second nature of cultural capital that is on the rise.

But Arendt did not abide a Hegelian redemption of fatalism even as all recognized that the consumer industry exchanged the aura of a culture that saw itself as "divine" for the notion of the thing, thus incorporating *both* God and death into the spell of the commodity. Where Adorno and Horkheimer focused on the destructiveness of Western cultures, Arendt regarded the latent social movements as untapped territory. When nature collapsed into the thing, history's utopic trajectory became that thing – became that "thing," what I name the "spheroid" – which is why she saw the invention of the space capsule as symbolic of our alienation. Arendt's notion that art is the history and memory of suffering is light years from the American technical conscious-ness, framed in the ideals of progress and driven by the Engine of Calvinism: *Do it yourself and do it to yourself if you can.*

In America, enlightenment became myth and myth became reality as ideology mimicking Odysseus's flight from himself: regression in the service of the displaced ego means to become everyone and no one at the same time. When Odysseus is con-fronted by words that mean many things – the ambivalence of thought at the moment of duplicity before its own unmasking by his bourgeois spirit – he realizes that language is being demyth-ologized of its roots in magical spells, and that he must work through and create his own meanings; instead he does what the cultural industries demand, he sacrifices his own ego on the altar of the status quo. This pilgrimage of the naive bearer of enlighten-ment is also the pilgrimage of people in dark times who, Arendt found, spoke in the opaque music of dissonance as thought that encountered the demons of mass culture which flew around in an ungrounded liberalism.

Adorno, for example, concentrated his anger on the social function of music just because music produced a *semblance* of sociality and uncoerced freedom and spontaneity, a complexity of the inner musical composition that in reality resists sameness and boredom through the mimetic repetition and mirroring of familiarity with suffering. Empathy with the commodity overcomes the paranoiac overwhelmingness of modern life at the expense of political action. This apparently unpolitical aestheticism marked the language of the real that Arendt felt was lost from modern life. Popular music becomes the sign of America and the pylon around which we fly: the power of America exists in its openness to its own innocence, which kept it from seeing that the real power of mass culture is that people are moved to act against themselves while fully aware that they are being deceived, thus dramatizing all the depth psychology advertising needs.

Not only is this a loss of the semantic and critical powers of the unconscious; the sense of loss displaces the self by manufacturing the shined-up memory of satisfaction or happiness. Unfortunately, this has been misunderstood in the American reception of, for example, Arendt's book on Eichmann. Understanding little of German social theory, American readers assumed that she was blaming the Israeli justice system. The impulse to describe Eichmann's evil as "banal" was not "mandarin" thought or pop-art, modernist caricature: it was the opposite. As Adorno does not prefer art to society, so Arendt does not prefer the private realm of condemnation of genocide to the public display of righteousness.

For Adorno, art can only be experienced in emphatic art and phatic continuity with society. As Robert Hullot-Kentor has noted: "The point of all his writing on art, in fact, is that aesthetic importance is defined by the intensity of its social content," which composes history from the point of view of the present and what is lost or gained from the past. [144] After Adorno left America, he gave little thought to popular music, but revised his views on the culture industries because he had to revise his thoughts about whether the uneducated masses, disoriented by mass culture, could be rescued from total manipulation. The older Adorno became, the closer he came to Arendt's position regarding institutions, or put more accurately, the closer they might be seen if their personal disputes are discounted. Arendt, on the other hand, attempted to uncover the flaws of the republic, and noted that

> To live an entirely private life means above all to be deprived of things essential to a truly human life: to be deprived of the reality that comes with being seen and heard by others, to be deprived of an "objective" relationship with them that comes from being related to and separated from them through the intermediary world of things, to be deprived of the possibility of achieving something more permanent than life itself. It is with respect to this multiple significance of the public realm that the term "private," in its original privative sense, has meaning. [145]

This Augustinian-Kantian concept of public obligation to an ethically active transcendent concept of the human "condition" is Arendt's way of describing the mass society of our day: and every culture has mass coercive societies that seem to guarantee that the deprivation of objective relationships in the world not only destroys the public realm *but the private as well.* Arendt's understanding of the loss of an inner shelter, even the shelter of ideology, is the mark of the contemporary power of kitsch that connects her Heideggerian world alienation of *irreparable* loss to her Kantian ethics of mutual recognition. Her politics are a corrective to Hegel and Marx's millennial sense of the end of the political in labour and the myth of history ending in the myth of happiness as a form of action. Her prophetic sense of earthly alienation – the atomic destruction which would be the end of all alienation – was implicit in the new-age science that was unfolding in the "fifties" when combined with the new bureaucratic world order of sovereign states divvying up the earth. The seeds of the new world order were exhibited in the Eichmann trial.

The Cold War dream of the end of ideology marked the beginning of the nightmare of the worship of the mass-minded private at the core of the American culture and the new "Dark Times." Arendt saw the signs of the Dark Times in the poetry of Char, Brecht, Kafka, Benjamin, and in Melville's *Billy Budd*; in this novella, Melville saw into the banality of the Hobbesian evils: the literary world saw the condition of being modern more clearly than philosophical realism could do. But the radical evil was in the way of modern technology: for example, the euphoria of space exploration allowed us to lose track of objective reality.

The conquest of space changed the nature of "man": the prologue of *The Human Condition* announces that the modern age began with the scientific revolution of the seventeenth century, but that the modern world began politically and with a catastrophic sense of fear with the atomic explosions and then the launching of "Heisenberg's Man" as the prototype of the future: "In 1957, an earth-born object made by man [*sic*] was launched into the universe, where for some weeks it circled the earth according to the same laws of gravitation that swing and keep in motion the celestial bodies – the sun, the moon and the stars." [146]

No Prometheus is going to meet anything beyond himself, and we will ultimately be devoured by political life and the market that replaced slavery by establishing the category of "work" that dominates over contemplation and creativity. Work, for Arendt, does make one free both to end the world and to "trace world alienation, its twofold flight from the earth into the universe and from the world into the self, to its origins" at the very moment when it was overcome by the advent of a new and yet unknown age. That is where the mapping begins in the path of the Millennial Wilderness.[147]

This is where kitsch man, mobman, *banausic* man as Superman, is flying his capsule, wearing the smile of the swindler's traces of the realization that he has wasted his life and ours. This figure has become a permanent feature of our landscape where we are all intruders in the dust of any memory of where it all began.

Of the many references to this demonism of the "irreal," the mediocrity of the real, when ideology appropriates and becomes reality and reality no longer expresses the loss of reality, for the poet "public life has fallen asleep / like a secret name   the wrong-reader / will say he has pity for others / where the thought is born in *hatred / of pity*, which is *only feeling*   the action / we are only images of   hates pity / and its *reduction of horror to sentiment // wordlessness   no thing is so simply // personal.*"[148]

VI

Forces of Reparation

Without following this ellipsis of the personal to its bitter poetic conclusion in the always impending loss of Eros, it is important to stress that it is this reparation of the personal that emerged out of the ruins of the war and the experiments of the avant-garde of the 1950s, which was the last great attempt to rescue the aesthetic as a philosophy of art without leaving home, without abandoning the social in the blind faith that we would not be buried alive by the apotheosis of mediocrity of the political. This burden of modernism has been mercilessly attacked by post-structuralists, who like Dante's souls hanging from trees might be addressed by the poet's "masked procession / *through 'you' I conceal my loneliness from myself / and make a way in to the multitude and into love / by lies, for my heart cannot bear the terror, and / compels me to talk as if I were two.*"[149]

The American modernists were constructing an ethnography of the inside and outside, its relationship to ancient forms of poetry, when poetry is cut short by violence and violations of the voice that we can describe as the revenge of the world on the poetic. I describe here the loss of the world as the pathway of an *imago mundi* in the empathy for the will to self-creation as an aesthetic problem of life itself and against the will to power. This seems to me to be how Blaser understood and used Arendt.

At the end of the twentieth century, the earth became flatter, seemed to begin and end in nowhere. Through the struggle of ethics and aesthetics, the weak ethics of experimentation, and the strong possibilities of the historical avant-garde speeding towards the end of the road, we can see in the rear-view mirror the traces of the Arendtian disappearing public world. The narcissist mirror-people, for Arendt, are left with opening the images to reifications and the return of the repressed. Looking back to the now for me not so dark 1950s, the idea of a tragic public world, as expressed by Arendt's collapsing Augustine, Marx, and Heidegger together into an image of the end of the public world in "world alienation," formed the basis of a poetic. In Arendt's remapping of the public world, anarcho-modernist poets like Blaser come alive in a poetic of reparation.

We intellectuals and artists have lost the battle. The old Marxists have become hopefully and properly infatuated with transforming civil society without a revolution; community and earth seduce the Heideggerians. We still find it difficult to see how the eschatological millennialism of capitalism that causes so much suffering creates ineluctable damages to the inner speech of the inner world. Our very own millennial answer is the search for the chimera of community – a last-but-one supper – in order to create forms of self-repair – communal ethics – that might help us ... once again. But in world-historical alienation, where the loss of reality can no longer be politically measured, the poet needs more resources than to will a concept of community that, as in classic modernism, depends on this utopic social for sources in the old, Nietzschean will to self-creation. Arendt writes in *The Human Condition* that "No matter what sociology, psychology, and anthropology will tell us about the 'social animal,' men [*sic*] persist in making, fabricating, and building, although these faculties are more and more restricted to the abilities of the artist, so that the concomitant experiences of worldliness escape more and more the range of ordinary human experience." [150]

At the end of *The Human Condition*, Arendt quotes Cato the Younger: "Never is he more active than when he does nothing, never is he less alone than when he is by himself." Perhaps this is a personal anarchism which keeps some poets and other human persons alive even as the will to power is attacking the juridical bases of collective rights – the public's and government's treatment of Indigenous Land claims, new "Berlin Walls" at the borders between rich and poor lands, civil wars that are surrogates for global wars – at the same time as states have posed the ethnic as the nationalist-ideological terrain of the future by turning global economic powers into larger-than-life sovereign states.

We know what happens when juridical rights are eroded in the name of the soaring heroic state, and we know what happens when the state becomes defensive and then becomes obsessed with using the ethnic to define its power. Arendt saw how it leads to the legal "populocide" and the ethnicides that mark our century. Meanwhile the poet remains stuck at the crossroads – the *kairos* – as the Greek-French philosopher Cornelius Castoriadis has written so beautifully, asking for something we cannot always hear, because no poet can every time heal the world he has lost with that one more poem. [151]

The modernist sensibility posed the great question of our time: the incommensurability of the will to self-creation as a private world against the will to power that became the mark of the public; poems that celebrate that quality of incommensurability, while exploring the personal project, carry on Arendt's philosophical quest to investigate the changing sense of the person that marks modernity from previous forms of the social.

VII

...

We need a new map: here's a beginning.

> It is Divine Justice that spurs them on,
> Turning the fear they have into desire.
>
> —DANTE ALIGHIERI, *Inferno* (1320), canto III, trans. Mark Musa

DOSSIER IV: ENDNOTES

CHAPTER 1

1   Originally published in Catriona Jeffries, ed., *CJ Press: Anthology of Exhibition Essays, 2006–2007* (Vancouver: CJ Press, 2008).

2   Benjamin, "The Work of Art in the Age of Its Mechanical Reproduction" (1939), in *Selected Writings*, vol. 4, *1938–1940*, trans. Edmund Jephcott and others, ed. Howard Eiland and Michael W. Jennings (Cambridge, MA: Belknap Press of the Harvard University Press, 2003), 268.

3   "Revolutions are innervations of the collective – attempts to dominate the second nature, in which the mastery of elemental social forces has become a prerequisite for a higher technical mastery of elemental natural forces. Just as a child who has learned to grasp stretches out its hand for the moon as it would for a ball, so every revolution sets its sights as much on currently utopian goals as on goals within reach. But a twofold utopian will asserts itself in revolutions … these demands, however, will first have to displace the problems of the second nature in the process of humanity's development …" From Benjamin's fragment "A Different Utopian Will," in *Selected Writings*, vol. 3, *1935–1938*, trans. Edmund Jephcott, Howard Eiland, and others, ed. Howard Eiland and Michael W. Jennings (Cambridge, MA: Belknap Press of Harvard University Press, 2002), 135.

CHAPTER 2

4   This text accompanied an installation of the same name, created and installed in 2008 for the Simon Fraser University Art Gallery, and was published separately in a book, *The Insurance Man: Kafka in the Penal Colony* (ed. Bill Jeffries and Jerry Zaslove, Vancouver: Simon Fraser Gallery and Linebooks, 2010).

5   On Kafka's story "In the Penal Colony" and how it is related to "A Report to an Academy," see my article "A Report to an Academy: Some Untimely Meditations Out of Season," *ESC: English Studies in Canada* 38, no. 1 (March 2012): 27–50.

6   Benjamin, *The Arcades Project*, trans. Howard Eiland and Kevin McLaughlin (Cambridge, MA: Belknap Press of Harvard University Press, 1999), 419.

7   The Werkbund was a group of artists and architects similar to those of the Bauhaus that brought principles of design, function, and avant-garde practices into relationship with new materials and techniques of display.

8   The "blood libel" referred to Jews accused of murdering Christian children to use their blood to make matzos. The trials linked nationalism and anti-Semitism with the blood libel superstition. The Czech statesman Tomáš Garrigue Masaryk became prominent in defending the accused. Kafka was aware of these trials.

9   For example, Oskar Weber's 1914 *The Sugar Baron: The Adventures of a Former German Officer in South America* and 1913 *Letters of a Coffee Planter: Two Decades of German Labor in Central America*. Kafka liked to offer travel books to his sisters as gifts.

10   Adorno, "Notes on Kafka," in *Prisms*, trans. Samuel and Shierry Weber (Cambridge, MA: MIT Press, 1981), 245.

11   Benjamin, "Conversations with Brecht," in *Understanding Brecht*, trans. Anna Bostock (London: New Left Books: 1973), 111–112. "Sub-real" is there defined as "a return of the unreal into a place rendered so normal as to defy the imagination." Benjamin and Brecht are describing their premonitions of the coming war that they are planning for the next thirty thousand years. They also converse about Kafka and a "tribunal before which [Brecht] is questioned" and how Kafka's parables see what is to come.

12   Kafka, *Letters to Friends, Family, and Editors*, trans. Richard and Clara Winston (New York: Schocken Books, 1977), 15–16.

13   Authors Kafka quoted in letters or diaries and whose books were in his personal library: Kafka's library has been reconstructed after many years of research. See Jürgen Born, *Kafka's Bibliothek: Ein beschreibendes Verzeichnis* (Kafka's Library: A Descriptive Index) (Frankfurt: S. Fischer, 1990). The reconstructed library is housed in Prague with a replica of Kafka's desk and chair. Not a tourist attraction, but an archive and museum.

14   Wayne Burns, "'In the Penal Colony': Variations on a Theme by Octave Mirbeau," *Accent* 17, no. 1 (Winter 1957): 45–51.

15   Portrayed as an archaic, Dickensian bureaucratic sanctum in Richard Eyres's film, written by Alan Bennett, *The Insurance Man* (BBC Production, 1986).

16   Kafka's "day job" was at the Workers' Accident Insurance Institute. Among the writing on Kafka that comes closest to showing his comic roots is Peter Demetz's *The Air Show at Brescia, 1909*, describing Kafka's visit and subsequent essay (in the Prague newspaper *Bohemia*, September 29, 1909) on the airshow in northern Italy that he visited with his friends Max and Otto Brod.

17   The comic-grotesque quality of the scene appears often in Kafka. Reiner Stach, author of the most comprehensive biography of Kafka, writes that he "derived pleasure" from "the distressing link between man [*sic*] and technology, years before the introduction of the assembly line and decades before the invention of the industrial robot." Stach further notes Kafka's interest in mime. Stach points to Chaplin's *Modern Times*, which Kafka saw, and the relationship of the inhuman machine to the twitching body in Chaplin's film. Kafka's 1912 *Amerika* (*Der Verschollene*) carried this construction to dark levels of prophetic understanding. See Reiner Stach, *Kafka, The Decisive Years*, trans. Shelley Laura Frisch (New York: Houghton Mifflin Harcourt, 2005).

18   November 10, 1916. Max Brod would also read during that evening. Fifty people attended. The Gallery was poorly lit and unheated. On the walls were drawings, paintings, watercolours by Maurice de Vlaminck, Kees van Dongen, and Auguste Herbin. The account of the reading by Kafka's friend Max Pulver (translation mine) describes Kafka's voice as modest but sharp as a knife that drew the listeners into the story; each word of the story was read as if it were a judgment delivered to the bed of the martyred soldier. Poetic justice was in the reading as it was in the story when the Officer himself dies on the machine. Some newspaper reports of the reading found him calm, modest, fully composed, very natural, and the story disturbing enough that several people left the room. See Max Pulver, "Walk with Franz Kafka," in Jürgen Born, ed., *Franz Kafka: Kritik und Rezeption zu seinen Lebzeiten, 1912–1924* (Frankfurt: S. Fischer, 1979).

19　The first serious attempt to place the story into a historical and political context was by the author and publisher Klaus Wagenbach. Although many biographies and pictorial histories are indebted to Wagenbach, Kafka's life is often treated as if he is a quarry to be mined.

20　Adorno, "Notes on Kafka," 263.

21　Adorno, 263.

22　Walter Benjamin, "Theses on the Philosophy of History," in *Illuminations*, trans. Harry Zohn, ed. Hannah Arendt (New York: Harcourt Brace, 1968), 265.

23　Benjamin, "Theses on the Philosophy of History," 263. It bears remembering that Benjamin's philosophy of history owes a sense of time to Kafka.

24　In Kracauer, *The Mass Ornament*, trans. and ed. Thomas Y. Levin (Cambridge, MA: Harvard University Press, 1995), 50–51.

25　See John Dunmore, *Transportation and Colonization, or the Causes of the Comparative Failure of the Transportation System in the Australian Colonies, with Suggestions for Ensuring Its Future Efficiency in Subserviency to Extensive Colonization* (London: A.J. Valpy, 1837).

26　During some periods of the installation, but not all the time, we used music in very low tones from the 1938 children's folk opera *Brundibár* by the Jewish Czech composer Hans Krása, performed in 1943 and 1944 in the Theresienstadt Ghetto by children who were there.

CHAPTER 3

27　Originally published as "An Open Letter: 'Dear Generation' – Works and Days Tracing Roy Miki's Generational Literacy in the University and the City," in Maia Joseph, Christine Lim, Larissa Lai, and Christopher Lee, eds., *Tracing the Lines: Reflections on Contemporary Poetics and Cultural Politics in Honour of Roy Miki* (Vancouver: Talonbooks, 2012).

28　Adorno, *Kierkegaard: Construction of the Aesthetic*, trans. and ed. Robert Hullot-Kentor (Minneapolis: University of Minnesota Press, 1989), 37.

29　On the vexed question of race, aesthetics, and authorship, see dossier V. Companion essays related to the aesthetics, ideology, and politics of race are my "Memory's Children and Redressing History: Critical Reflections on *Obasan*, by Joy Kogawa – The Case of a Northern Hybrid Novel," in *Unforeseeable Americas: Questioning Cultural Hybridity in the Americas*, ed. Rita De Grandis and Zilà Bernd (Amsterdam: Rodopi, 2000), and the "Afterword" by Jerry Zaslove and Michael Mundhenk, in "Voices of Silence Hybrid Streets – Peoples of Invisibility: Joy Kogawa's *Obasan* and the Loss of World History," in the German translation of *Obasan*, trans. Michael Mundhenk (Leipzig: Reclam, 1993). Also see my elegy for Roy Miki, "Exile and Culture Pre-Tending (After a Talk from Coach Barnholden)," in *West Coast Line* 57, vol. 42, no. 1, "Miki," ed. Fred Wah (Spring/Summer 2008), which I introduce with Benjamin: "This is the voice of the will to symbolic totality venerated by a humanism in the human figure. But it is something incomplete and imperfect that objects stare out from allegorical structure" (*The Origin of German Tragic Drama*, trans. John Osborne [London: New Left Books, 1977], 186).

30   Hesiod, *The Works and Days*, trans. Richmond Lattimore (Ann Arbor: University of Michigan Press, 1991), 117.

31   Benjamin: "Allegorical personification has always concealed the fact that its function is not the personification of things, but rather to give the concrete a more imposing form by getting it up as a person" (*Origin of German Tragic Drama*, 187). Dorothea Lange's photographs show the cruelty behind the assembling of an "alien" people. The photographs are emblematic of the silence.

32   Further discussion about "History" as the "Last Thing before the Last" can be found in other essays in this collection, in particular my essays related to Kracauer, Benjamin, and Sebald.

33   In convolute N, "On the Theory of Knowledge, Theory of Progress," of his *Arcades Project*, Benjamin writes of the need for political and aesthetic categories to overcome or "clear the undergrowth of delusion and myth" in the ruins of historicism and ideals of progress. The full passage, quoted in Roy Miki's *Redress: Inside the Japanese Canadian Call for Justice*, reads: "The events surrounding the historian, and in which he himself [*sic*] takes part, will underlie his presentation in the form of a text written in invisible ink. The history which he lays before the reader comprises, as it were, the citations occurring in this text, and it is only these citations that occur in a manner legible to all. To write history thus means to *cite* [Benjamin's emphasis] history. It belongs to the concept of citation, however, that the historical object in each case is torn from its context" (*The Arcades Project*, trans. Howard Eiland and Kevin McLaughlin [Cambridge, MA: Belknap Press of Harvard University Press, 1999], 476). Benjamin's theory of history means that the "historian should no longer try to enter the past; rather he should allow the past to enter his life." A "pathos of nearness" should replace the vanishing empathy, which is the "awakening from the dream of the nineteenth century" of a "dream-filled sleep" of forces that were hidden on the surfaces, but were covered over with dreams of progress as "profane illuminations" which are the "invisible ink" that I believe Roy Miki is addressing in his writing.

34   In his 1936 essay "The Storyteller," Benjamin brings writing, telling, work and labour, and moving from place to place under conditions not of one's own making into view, and, moreover, how storytelling brings counsel and usefulness to the productive relationship of listeners to teller. See Benjamin, *Illuminations*, trans. Harry Zohn, ed. Hannah Arendt (New York: Harcourt, Brace and World, 1968).

35   In Benjamin, *Reflections: Essays, Aphorisms, Autobiographical Writings*, trans. Edmund Jephcott (New York and London: Harcourt Brace Jovanovich, 1978), 307.

36   Data of 2000.

37   Simmel, "The Stranger," in *Georg Simmel on Individuality and Social Forms*, ed. Donald N. Levine (Chicago: University of Chicago Press, 1971), 143.

38   The "story" is both experience and epistemology – a form of knowledge about the fetish of the abstract and how the enigma of the commodity enters intellectual thinking. See Alfred Sohn-Rethel, *Intellectual and Manual Labor: A Critique of Epistemology*, trans. Martin Sohn-Rethel (Atlantic Highlands, NJ: Humanities Press, 1978).

39   In *Brecht on Art and Politics*, ed. Tom Kuhn and Steve Giles (London: Methuen, 2003), 141. The Stalinist left criticized the "utopian" nature of Brecht's position. Brecht and Benjamin had formed a close relationship in the mid-1930s, described in

moving detail in Erdmut Wizisla, *Walter Benjamin and Bertold Brecht: The Story of a Friendship*, trans. Christine Shuttleworth (London and New York: Libris, 2009).

CHAPTER 4

40   This essay appeared in *Open Letter 5–6*, 5th series, special issue (1983), edited by Bruce Barber. The approach to Walter Benjamin in this essay comes in large part from my teaching a course for several years on "The Aesthetics of Performance: Weimar to Hollywood, 1945" in the School for Contemporary Arts at Simon Fraser University. The approach was through Benjamin, Brecht, and Kracauer. Thus, the emphasis in the title on the aesthetics of "performance." Benjamin's now hyper-famous essay was written in the period when his engagement with Brecht's theatrical ideas and poetry and his friendship with Brecht became important to Benjamin's aesthetic and Brecht's emerging theatrical performance-practices of "epic theatre," the comic and music theatre, and the aesthetics of alienation technique (*Verfremdung* in action) pointing towards the controversies of politically engaged poetics. See Benjamin, *Understanding Brecht*, trans. Anna Bostock (London: New Left Books), 1973.

41   In "On Some Motifs in Baudelaire" (1939), Benjamin writes: "To perceive the aura of an object we look at the means to invest it with the ability to look at us in return." He means the relationship of an inanimate, created object is experienced in the distance of the object from the viewer or reader and is a lived fragile perception that will become lost in a "forest of symbols," and recede into the distance. In *Illuminations*, trans. Harry Zohn, ed. Hannah Arendt (New York: Harcourt Brace & World, 1955), 190.

42   Theodor W. Adorno and Walter Benjamin, *The Complete Correspondence, 1928–1940*, trans. Nicholas Walter, ed. Henri Lonitz (Cambridge, MA: Harvard University Press, 1999).

43   Benjamin to Adorno, letter, February 23, 1939.

44   Benjamin's *Ursprung des deutschen Trauerspiel*, translated as *The Origin of German Tragic Drama* by John Osborne (London: New Left Books, 1977), is the foundational work that lies behind Benjamin's *Arcades Project* and "The Work of Art." Both prefigure his discussions of allegory, loss of aura, mourning, seeing the world in fragments, melancholia, suffering, and ruins. Both Benjamin and Brecht were sensitive to loss and mourning in cultural productions, including comic performances, detective fiction, the films of Chaplin, and other literary forms like folktale and story. For the "melancholic," loss is emblematic for the "profane illumination" of an inwardness that has lost power. Life is transitory, and becomes dream, phantasmagoria, and a dumb show. Benjamin's essay, however famous it has become, is often misunderstood. "The Work of Art" is written during the time of his contact with Brecht's ideas and aesthetic. He met Brecht in 1929 in Berlin one year after Brecht founded the Theatre on Schiffbauerdamm. Here was the original *Threepenny Opera* and other plays of Brecht's. Brecht and Benjamin planned to edit a journal together which would be directed towards Marxism and Aesthetics. The name of the journal would have been "Krisis und Kritik." The journal never appeared. "The Work of Art" appeared in 1936 in the *Zeitschrift für Sozialforschung* (Journal of social history), under the editorial direction of Adorno and Horkheimer. Of equal or more importance, in terms of my approach to Benjamin, is Benjamin's and Adorno's discussion in this period of Adorno's study *Kierkegaard: Construction of the Aesthetic* (1931), the critique of "power-directed inwardness" that disguises suffering

while appealing to suffering. This work was published in 1933 on the very day that the Hitler regime took power and anti-Semitic boycotts intensified. Adorno began his own academic career with a lecture on Benjamin's study of allegory and mourning, *The Origin of German Tragic Drama*, which influenced Adorno throughout his own writing on aesthetics and politics. Benjamin and Adorno had already met in Berlin in 1923. Adorno had read Benjamin's *Origin of German Tragic Drama* in manuscript at the time. Benjamin knew of Marx's use of "phantasmagoria," which Marx used to describe the phantasmic aura in the commodity that conceals the human labour in the "thing" existence of the commodity. See Adorno, *In Search of Wagner*, trans. Rodney Livingstone (London: New Left Books, 1981), 85. The chapter "Phantasmagoria" is clearly indebted to Benjamin's use of the term; the term, in Benjamin and Adorno, not only disguises labour but also the power of death and the escape from human suffering. The influence of the study of mourning pervades Adorno's thinking throughout his writing.

45   "Allegory and Trauerspiel," in *The Origin of German Tragic Drama*, 166.

46   Adorno's comment in this letter is central: "This raises the question of how far this forgetting is one that is capable of shaping experience, which I would almost call epic forgetting and how far it is a reflex … in connection with this question of reification, i.e., of unfolding the contradictory moments that are involved in such forgetting; or one could say, of formulating a distinction between good and bad reification" (Adorno, *Complete Correspondence*, letter 29, February 1940, 321). This is one of the last letters in their exchange. Benjamin fled Paris with his sister for the south of France to Lourdes in the middle of June as the German army invaded Holland, France, and Belgium. Benjamin's *Arcades Project* and other manuscripts were left with Georges Bataille in Paris. He carried a small suitcase with a manuscript and some personal items. The manuscript may have been "Theses on the Philosophy of History," but this is disputed.

47   The reader may wonder about the word "literacy" used in this essay. It is used in a particular way to include, yet to go beyond, "ideology" as the single most important principle of a materialist theory of expression and cultural performance. Ultimately the history of "literacy" and its formalization into pedagogy, classroom culture, and the technologies of communication used by the modern intelligentsia should be understood to relate to the affliction of normative approaches to reading, writing, and seeing: *Bildung* in German. Other essays in this collection pay attention to literacy, as Benjamin did, attending to cultural production and readership. The essay on "Technical Reproduction" is in effect a manual on literacy. Benjamin and Brecht, Erwin Piscator's theatre experiments, Kracauer's essays on film in the 1920s and his study *From Caligari to Hitler*, which includes an appendix on propaganda, all saw that radio, film, broadsides, and newsprint, for example John Heartfield's montages, Russian film like Dziga Vertov's 1929 *Man with a Movie Camera*, Eisenstein's films, as well as Brecht's "learning plays" (*Lehrstücke*), would make use of the new technical capacities in film, graphic arts, broadsides, and radio, and are referred to as "weak weapons" like human rights and pacificist literature banned by the Nazis. The means to reach the workers and the unemployed and those subject to violence in the streets and the Hitlerian edicts and decrees related to everyday life, one needed all the weapons one could muster.

48   See Rolf Tiedemann, "Dialectics at a Standstill: Approaches to the *Passagen-Werk*," in Walter Benjamin, *The Arcades Project*, trans. Howard Eiland and Kevin McLaughlin (Cambridge, MA: Belknap Press of Harvard University Press, 1999), 932.

49 Benjamin, "The Work of Art," 248.

50 Benjamin, *The Arcades Project*, 205.

51 Benjamin, "The Work of Art," 248.

52 In 1973 I created and directed with students from a Brecht seminar a production of *The Measures Taken* in the Simon Fraser University Theatre. The stage was a boxing ring with Bruegel the Elder slides as a backdrop. The scenes intended to show the limits of sacrifice to an abstract moral or utopian commitment to a communism of precarious existence between the catastrophe of World War I and fear of another war. Accommodation to fascism as a form of "agreement" or *Einverständnis* and complicity with the State and authority was also a prevailing theme of Brecht's poems, in which he expressed his struggle over in his own political commitments which he carried into his exile in America.

53 See Erdmut Wizisla, *Walter Benjamin and Bertold Brecht: The Story of a Friendship* (New Haven: Yale University Press, 2009). About their closeness and mutual relationship: "The meetings between Benjamin and Brecht up to 1933 are characterized by 'extended and extremely stimulating conversations' and more and more new plans, the most interesting of which was the project for the journal *Krise und Kritik* … Benjamin attributed his interest in this collaboration to Brecht, whose writings were, he said, typical of the questions posed by the left-wing critical intelligentsia in general" (40).

54 In "Critique of Violence" (1921) Benjamin had already raised the question that the "expiatory of violence is not visible to men" because, like the "equipment free element of violence" in film, violence hides from view different forms of violence: Divine Violence, Mythical Violence, Sovereign Violence, and Law-Preserving Violence embedded in constitutions allowing legal use of violence. Exposed to view: revolutionary and mass violence. In Benjamin, *Reflections*, trans. Edmund Jephcott (New York: Harvest Books, 1978).

55 Benjamin, *The Origin of German Tragic Drama*, 166.

56 Benjamin, "The Work of Art," 243.

57 See Peter Bürger, "Walter Benjamin's 'Redemptive Critique': Some Preliminary Reflections on the Project of Critical Hermeneutics," in *The Decline of Modernism*, trans. Nicholas Walter (Philadelphia: Pennsylvania University Press, 1992).

58 Benjamin, "Theses on the Philosophy of History," in *Illuminations*, 256.

59 Benjamin, *The Origin of German Tragic Drama*, 224.

60 Benjamin's approach to genre and art history influenced Adorno on where to place the origins of "modernity" in art. Benjamin's study opens up the entire question of the origins of modernity, which can be found in Dürer, Bosch, Bruegel the Elder, Riemenschneider, Giotto, Rembrandt, and the Northern baroque, when the artist felt free to express and exhibit emotion, or what Benjamin refers to as the "aura" that pervades the conventions portraying reality; the "breathing holes" in the art of the conventions or the received styles are the suffering within the work itself or the execution of the work, which is pictorial and reproducible through the institutions available to the patronage of the Church or have mercantile exhibition value. Reproducibility did not just occur when the modern technologies of reproducibility became available. The aesthetic demands of a problem in a work cannot simply be

delivered over to the means of its reproducibility, which must remain immanent to the truth value in the work's critique of form and style; the critique may not be comprehensible to everyone. This can account for the "enigmaticity" of the artwork which expresses the loss of aura. On the "enigmatic," see Adorno on enigmaticalness, truth content, and metaphysics in *Aesthetic Theory*, trans. Robert Hullot-Kentor (Minneapolis: University of Minnesota Press, 1997), 127. In Adorno "aura" became the pathos of "enigmaticalness," which is an aspect of the phantasmagoria as well.

61   Benjamin, *The Origin of German Tragic Drama*, 187.

62   This is the central aspect of the struggle between Adorno and Benjamin over the nature of just what kind of memory is lost in times when reification under capitalism is a form of forgetting, if memory can no longer "shape experience" – Adorno names this "epic forgetting," not "reflex forgetting" – or the problem of "recall" in Freud's *Erinnerung* and *Gedächtnis* (remembering?). (Adorno to Benjamin, letter, February 29, 1940, 323.) Benjamin's reply refers to Proust and *mémoire involontaire* (May 7, 1940, 326). The matter of memory – in psychoanalysis a "working through" of memory – is related in my reading of Benjamin to "the dialectical image" which memory "illuminates" when the beholder realizes the art work is a figuration, an autonomous work, a dialectical image which "recalls" the phenomenon of a childhood memory and the afterlife of memory.

63   This reflects the literary debates in the 1930s between "realism and formalism" and how a future for any self-emancipation of humanity could be portrayed. The arguments were deeply engaged with the political will of how to overcome the "Faustian" bargain with Stalinism. The Moscow Trials are a backdrop.

64   Benjamin, *The Arcades Project*, 365.

65   Benjamin turns to Hegel, who sensed that the relationship of "emotion and devotion to the exhibition value of the painting would hinge on where the painting would be located" ("The Work of Art," 248).

66   Benjamin, "The Work of Art," 243.

67   "The Work of Art" concludes (*Illuminations*, 244) with Benjamin's discussion of the "epoch" of the New War Imperialism that "abolishes aura in a new way" by making war "aesthetic." See my discussion of violence and aura in note 54 above.

68   Benjamin's friendship with Kracauer, and Kracauer's essays on film, Berlin streets, and understanding of the new spectators for film is a source of inspiration for Benjamin's essay. See Kracauer's *The Salaried Masses: Duty and Distraction in Weimar Germany*, trans. Quintin Hoare (London: Verso Press, 1998). The title of Kracauer's study in German is *Die Angestellten*, best translated as "clerks" or "hired workers" or "personnel." These constitute the backdrop of the new moviegoers. Benjamin's essay on Kracauer is an appendix and is translated as "An Outsider Attracts Attention," better translated as "An outsider makes their presence felt," or, as Benjamin identifies them, as "A malcontent makes themself known." The meaning in Benjamin's essay is, "bitterly" said, that Kracauer is a "ragpicker at daybreak – in the dawn of the day of revolution" (114). Both are looking at fragments and ruins.

69   On the question of Kant and education for "Bildung," see George L. Mosse, *German Jews beyond Judaism* (Cincinnati: Hebrew Union College Press, 1997).

70   Benjamin, "The Work of Art," 236.

71   Benjamin, 247, quoting Hegel's *The Philosophy of Fine Art*.

72   Benjamin, 237.

73   Benjamin, 237

74   Benjamin, 252.

75   Benjamin, 238.

76   Benjamin, 247.

77   Benjamin, 241.

78   Benjamin, *Theory of Film: The Redemption of Physical Reality* (Princeton: Princeton University Press, 1960).

79   Benjamin, "An Outsider Attracts Attention," in Kracauer, *The Salaried Masses*, 113.

80   Benjamin, 237.

81   Benjamin, 243.

82   Lukács, *History and Class Consciousness* (London: Merlin Press, 1968), 208.

83   Benjamin, "Theses on the Philosophy of History," 207.

84   Benjamin, "The Work of Art," 240.

85   Benjamin, "The Storyteller," *Illuminations*, 102.

86   Benjamin, 94.

87   Benjamin, 94.

88   Benjamin, "The Work of Art," 237.

89   Arnold Hauser, *The Sociology of Art* (Chicago: University of Chicago Press, 1982), 666.

90   Hauser, *Sociology of Art*, 666.

91   See Benjamin, "A Different Utopian Will," in *Selected Writings*, vol. 3, *1935–1938*, trans. Marcus Bullock, Howard Eiland, and Gary Smith (Cambridge, MA: Belknap Press of Harvard University Press, 2002), 134–136.

92   Benjamin, "A Different Utopian Will," 134.

93   Hauser, *Sociology of Art*, 633.

94   Hauser, 675. Also see the chapter "The Film Age."

95   Cornelius Castoriadis, *Modern Capitalism and Revolution* (London: Solidarity, 1974).

96   See Karl Dietrich Bracher, *The German Dilemma: The Relationship of State and Democracy* (New York: Praeger, 1975), 55–56.

97   See Goran Therborn, *Science and Class Society: On the Formation of Class and Sociology in Historical Materialism* (London: New Left Books, 1976), 315.

98   Walter Benjamin in *Understanding Brecht*, trans. Anna Bostock (London: New Left Books, 1973).

99   Benjamin, "The Storyteller," 83.

100 See Gershom Scholem, *Walter Benjamin: The Story of a Friendship* (London: Faber and Faber, 1982). Scholem, a friend of Benjamin's since their Berlin days, bitterly complained that the concept of aura, which Benjamin had used in a different way

before, was now corrupted by his Marxist politics influenced by Brecht and the circle around the Institute for Social Research (206–207).

101 Benjamin, "The Arcades of Paris," in *The Arcades Project*, 884.

102 Kracauer began his study of Weimar film during his Paris exile. He left Germany in 1933 before the full Nuremberg Laws were in place. He completed it in New York at the Museum of Modern Art.

103 Benjamin, "The Work of Art," 231.

104 Benjamin, 233.

105 Brecht, "Breadth and Variety in the Realist Mode of Writing," in *Brecht on Art and Politics*, ed. Tom Kuhn and Steve Giles (London: Methuen, 2003), 226. The disputes over "realism and expressionism and formalism" marked Marxist and anarchist debates in the mid-1930s, along with inner battles with party hacks, ideological disputes about fascism, anti-fascists, communists, disputes with and about György Lukács and "realism" and naturalism and Soviet socialist realism, the struggle against Hitler, etc. Benjamin's "The Work of Art" changes the landscape.

106 See "Conversations with Brecht," in *Reflections: Essays, Aphorisms, Autobiographical Writings*, trans. Edmund Jephcott (New York and London: Harcourt Brace Jovanovich, 1986), especially Benjamin's reflections on Brecht's clarity about the coming of the Hitlerian war as "a force acting on … [him] that was equal to that of fascism; a power that has its source no less deep in history than fascism" (218).

107 Benjamin, "Exposé of 1935," *The Arcades Project*, 898.

108 Hauser, *Sociology of Art*, 673.

109 Benjamin, "The Work of Art," 250.

110 Benjamin, 252.

111 Benjamin, *The Arcades Project*, 907. In "The Work of Art," Benjamin remarks: "Before the rise of the movie the Dadaists performances tried to create an audience reaction which Chaplin later evoked in a more natural way" (252). This coincides with Brecht's view of Chaplin as well.

112 Adorno, *Aesthetic Theory*, 60.

CHAPTER 5

113 Originally published in Robin Blaser, Edward Byrne, Charles Watts, eds., *The Recovery of the Public World: Essays on Poetics in Honour of Robin Blaser* (Vancouver: Talonbooks, 1999).

114 This claim of mine is meant to indict the anti-humanist literary discourse of the tail end of my generation, which in its zeal to eliminate the individual and the self advances a pure exteriority of language; various hermeneutic approaches of a post-structural hybridism lead to strange critical monstrosities. The turning points and the struggle between poetry and philosophy goes on in this dossier. A personal note: Robin Blaser came to SFU's English department with a background in European literature different from but somewhat like my own. He was one of the few who had that background. He could understand how literature and the political, tradition and modernity formed a difficult world in which to teach. In many respects I saw him as a Baudelaire figure who wrote poetry in a time of crisis. In Walter Benjamin's words: "If it can be said that

for Baudelaire modern life is the reservoir of dialectical images, this implies that he stood in the same relation to modern life as the seventeenth century did to antiquity" (Benjamin, "Central Park," in *Selected Writings*, vol. 4, *1938–1940*, trans. Edmund Jephcott et al. [Cambridge, MA: Harvard University Press, 2003], 161).

115 Robin Blaser, "lake of souls (reading notes," in *Syntax* (Vancouver: Talonbooks, 1983), 43. In her frequent use of "Archimedean point," Arendt likes to cite Kafka's aphorism about the "Archimedean" point that exists between the inner and outer world; she introduces the last chapter of *The Human Condition*, "The Vita Activa and the Modern Age," with it. Arendt argues that life at the Archimedean point has become interiorized as mere processes, mere behaviourism, and we have become as if alien objects seen from outer space, existing without thought (Arendt, *The Human Condition* [New York: Doubleday Anchor Books, 1959], 295). Arendt joined political thought and literature in the European tradition; she saw the "turning points" in literature and the forces breaking into the public realm. She saw these turning points by championing Benjamin's work when she arrived as an exile in the United States. Both were interned in the Gurs internment camp in the French Pyrenees.

116 Arendt's controversial *Eichmann in Jerusalem* (New York: Viking Press, 1963). Arendt's reflections on Kantian duty and obligation and Eichmann's distortions of judgment is the foundational principle of her study of the "little man" who accommodates himself to the "banality of evil"; the nature of the trial itself is an event that brought to mind questions of the relationship of power and domination to "forgetting" the human condition. Her closeness to Benjamin's work on violence is a filigree inside her thinking.

117 The "obsolescence of mankind" and the earth as our only "dwelling place" in regard to the atomic bomb, which was experimented on humans, in which "the laboratory" for the bomb is coextensive with destroying the earth. Arendt's reference to Günther Anders's *The Obsolescence of Mankind* (1956) is more telling in German: the "antiquation" of the human.

118 César Vallejo, *Trilce*, trans. Clayton Eschleman (Middletown, CT: Wesleyan University Press, 2000), 199.

119 I wrote this comment in 1999, but I don't know that I have changed my mind since. The comment is in part inspired by the critical movements during the 1950s that inform Blaser's struggle to find his aesthetic. Alfred Kazin, an American essayist who was friends with Arendt, is a case in point. Kazin's views of the narrowness of American criticism is an example of the ferment in the 1950s about criticism and the rewriting of the past and present: Which writer from the past would be relegated to the posthumous? Kazin was one who was at home both in American and European literature. See *Alfred Kazin's America: Critical and Personal Writings*, ed. Ted Solotaroff (New York: HarperCollins, 2003) for his critique of American criticism in the period of the "New Criticism." Arendt's *The Origins of Totalitarianism* (1951) was an important controversial continuation of the Cold War background to aesthetic modernism. Compare Adorno's "all reification is a forgetting" and the "gap between us and others was the same as the time between our own present and past suffering; an insurmountable barrier ... [The] loss of memory is a transcendental condition ... All objectification is a forgetting" ("Le Prix du Progrès," in Horkheimer and Adorno, *Dialectic of Enlightenment*, trans. John Cumming [London: Alan Lane, 1972], 230).

120 See György Lukács, *Theory of the Novel*, trans. Anna Bostock (London: Merlin Press, 1971).

121 Arendt, *The Human Condition*, 147.

122 Blaser belongs to the American avant-garde of the 1950s. For a review of the issues pertinent to discussions about the 1950s, see my entries under *"Partisan Review"* and "Propaganda" in *The Encyclopedia of the Essay*, ed. Tracy Chevalier (London and Chicago: Fitzroy Dearborn, 1997); also, my essay on Herbert Read and anarchist modernism in this collection.

123 See Boris Groys, *The Total Art of Stalinism; Avant-Garde, Aesthetic Dictatorship, and Beyond* (Princeton: Princeton University Press, 1993).

124 Arendt, *The Human Condition*, 173.

125 Blaser, *The Holy Forest*, ed. Stan Persky and Michael Ondaatje (Toronto: Coach House Press, 1993), 322.

126 Arendt, *The Human Condition*, 176.

127 The importance of the aesthetic of romantic anti-capitalism is clearly an influence in the San Francisco "City Lights" poetic movement and the "Drunken Boat" aesthetic of poetic visionaries. See *Revolutionary Romanticism: A Drunken Boat Anthology*, ed. Max Blechman (San Francisco: City Lights Books, 1999), and *Drunken Boat*, ed. Max Blechman (New York: Autonomedia, 1994).

128 Arendt, *The Human Condition*, 240.

129 That Arendt's *The Human Condition* struggles between work and labour and the domination of mass political action over everyday life speaks to the tragic dimension of when work and labour become synonymous and exchange value dominates everyday life.

130 In this regard, the dispute between Adorno and Arendt about who owned the "posthumous memory" of Benjamin and how to understand Benjamin was important to Arendt in her own understanding of where "Kritik" (critique) as "truth value" fitted into the public world. Her comment in *Illuminations* that Benjamin cannot be described merely as a "literary critic" I take as apropos of Blaser's sense of himself as poet and writer engaged in the everyday world. Arendt describes Benjamin as being "unclassifiable" as a literary "critic" (*Illuminations*, 5). Benjamin's *The Origin of German Tragic Drama*, "with its counterpoint of allegory of previous ages of conventions and the world of the contemporary" in which "any person, any object, any relationship can mean absolutely anything else ... with this possibility a destructive, but just verdict is passed on the profane world" of the past in the present as the unpast can be applied to Arendt's politics and Blaser's aesthetic ("Allegory and Trauerspiel," in *The Origin of German Tragic Drama*, trans. John Osborne [London: New Left Books, 1977], 175). Benjamin's study puzzled the professoriate because it appeared unclassifiable, whether it is literary criticism, art history, or philology.

131 Blaser was critical of Taylor's view of the Self in poetic discourse. In "The Concept of History: Ancient and Modern" (in *Between Past and Future*), Arendt anticipates deconstruction by arguing that modernizing societies must eliminate historical consciousness (58). The presence of "loss" marks Arendt's *Between Past and Future*, even to the extent that the loss of a feeling for loss marks Arendt's sense of living in the "in-between": "What perhaps hitherto had been of spiritual significance only for

the few now has become a concern of one and all. Only now, as it were after the fact, the loss of tradition and of religion have become political events of the first order" (*Between Past and Future: Six Exercises in Political Thought* [New York: The Viking Press], 93). The offending work was Charles Taylor's *The Sources of the Self: The Making of Modern Identity* (Cambridge, MA: Harvard University Press), 1989.

132   Arendt, *The Origins of Totalitarianism* (New York: Harvest Books, 1968), 135.

133   Arendt, *The Origins of Totalitarianism*, 143.

134   Arendt, 157.

135   Arendt, 316.

136   Arendt, 317.

137   Arendt, 351.

138   Arendt, *The Human Condition*, 268–269.

139   Blaser, *The Holy Forest*, xix.

140   Arendt, *The Human Condition*, 148.

141   Arendt, 268.

142   Arendt, 189.

143   Blaser, *The Holy Forest*, 142.

144   Robert Hullot-Kentor, "The Philosophy of Dissonance," in Tom Huhn and Lambert Zuidervaart, eds., *The Semblance of Subjectivity: Essays in Adorno's Aesthetic Theory* (Cambridge, MA: MIT Press, 1997), 321.

145   Arendt, "The Private Realm: Property," *The Human Condition*, 53–54.

146   Arendt, *The Human Condition*, 1.

147   Arendt is making clear that indifference to suffering is a given in the modern world. In this regard, while she and Adorno shared little political common ground, they both raised the radical Kantian question: "How does one live after Auschwitz with poetry," not that, as Adorno says, "you could no longer write poems." Adorno and Arendt both mean that "the inhuman part of it, the ability to keep one's distance as a spectator and to rise above things, is in the final analysis the human part, the very part resisted by ideologists" (Adorno, *Negative Dialectics*, trans. E.B. Ashton [New York: Continuum, 1973], 363).

148   Robin Blaser, "Image-Nation 9 (half and half," *The Holy Forest*, 167.

149   Blaser, "Image-Nation 12 (Actus," *The Holy Forest*, 181.

150   Arendt, *The Human Condition*, 296.

151   *Philosophy, Politics, Autonomy: Essays in Political Philosophy*, ed. David Ames Curtis (Oxford: Oxford University Press, 1991), 220. Castoriadis points out compatibilities in his political philosophy with Arendt's in *A Society Adrift: Interviews and Debates, 1974–1997*, trans. Helen Arnold (New York: Fordham University Press, 2010).

Postlude: An Anarchist Manifesto

A postscript and postlude that continues from this book's prelude. It is a breviary for the Plague years, an anarchist manifesto announcing the danger of summarizing or gathering up by a *Last Mohican* in the choking hammerlock of capitalism, with a note that describes the three curated installations I have produced in my effort to take my writing as *colportage* and writing as labour. It is not by chance that we write about what they are planning, nothing small, the monstrous synthesis that we all participate in as one indomitable whole.

Others decided, "Let's be outsiders. The only place for us is the fringe of society." They did not stop to think that society has no fringe, that no one is ever outside it ...
—VICTOR SERGE, *Memoirs of a Revolutionary* ([1951] 2012),
　　trans. Peter Sedgewick

He'd been working in Interpretation for nearly three weeks. For the first fortnight he'd been attached to some of the older hands, to be initiated into the secrets of the department. Then one day his boss came and said, "You've learned enough now. From tomorrow on you'll be given a file of your own." "So soon?" said Mark-Alem. "Am I really up to working all on my own?"
—ISMAIL KADARE, *The Palace of Dreams* ([1981] 2014), trans. Jusuf
　　Vrioni and Barbara Bray

And its tawny caricature and tawny life,
Another thought, the paramount ado ...
Since what we think is never what we see.
—WALLACE STEVENS, "What We See Is What We Think" (1949)

DOSSIER V — CHAPTER 1

Postscript: A Breviary for the Plague Years [1]

> The inferno of the living is not something that will be; if there is one, it is what is already here, the inferno that we live in every day, that we form by being together. There are two ways to escape suffering it. The first is easy for many: accept the inferno and become such a part of it that you can no longer see it. The second is risky and demands constant vigilance and apprehension: seek and learn to recognize who and what, in the midst of the inferno, are not inferno, then make them endure, give them space.
>
> —ITALO CALVINO, *Invisible Cities* (1974), trans. William Weaver

> Victor Serge said: "I followed his argument
> With the blank uneasiness which one might feel
> In the presence of a logical lunatic."
>
> —WALLACE STEVENS, "Esthétique du Mal," *Transport to Summer* (1947)

Anarchism is both phantasm and reality – and a common thread in *Untimely Passages*. It is anarchism as the letter *a*. I have claimed that there is an overarching architectonics, an umbrella named "anarchism" in these essays, but I do not want to define anarchism there or here. I do not refer to anarchist political theory as such, but point out features of anarchism that continue to be active in my essays about reading, but primarily in the lives of individuals and authors who speak, read, and create for each other, but who can fall apart, go berserk not only in their political, pedagogical, or cultural work but in their poetic writings too. How do they survive? How did I survive with the spirit of Sancho Panza hovering over me?

My essays dream of the insurgent spirit of resistance against what Mikhail Bakhtin referred to as the "alibi of being," that which forces us to fall silent when faced with institutionalized violence. For better or worse, these essays are encounters in the name of a "prophetic utopianism," or romantic anarchism as a radical humanism; not least they fall into the tradition of Marx's *Economic and Philosophic Manuscripts of 1844* with their bedrock of different forms of alienation: estrangement, defamiliarizing, dispossession, the walling-off of reality, immiseration; in short, ideology as reality and reality as ideology, finding us circling the loss of any trust in the world. Finally, we face right i"nto our sublimation of desires and into objects that haunt us and come back again and again in our dreams, leaking through the boundaries of the phantasmagoria of everyday life. Thinking psychoanalytically about sublimation and reification, the thing-world of the unconscious lurks in the background.

The essays could be described, were I a Brechtian *Moritatensänger*, as a tableau, which, in fact, the Breviaries that follow are. In some ideal world a simulacrum of "anarcho-syndicalism" comes to mind – that would be a world worth living in.

So then, we have a problem if we try to find a "community" in which to translate the different publics, cultures, world-historical movements, that come into the university to be studied, and there we try to make one conceptual whole.

We go to the "other shores," trying not to do everything that the culture wants us to do without making really clear discriminations about where the ideological positions of the universities are: sometimes they're class, but they are institutions that work against "barbarisms" or they are not democratic institutions at all. But there is one more illusion to thoroughly understand, both ideologically and historically: the "enemy" is not always on the outside of the Myth of the Happy University; the enemy is also inside if we understand how the University loses its way when bureaucratic administrations believe that there is historical progress gained by eliminating or rejigging the humanities according to what appears to be the exigencies of the moment without understanding our own ideological moment.

Peter Weiss, in his magnum opus, *The Aesthetic of Resistance*, is a literary *Guernica*, which I have referred to in my Kafka installation, *The Insurance Man: Kafka in the Penal Colony*. Peter Weiss drew his title and inspiration from the Pergamon Altar in Berlin's Pergamon Museum, for him a foundational image of the founding of Western culture on warfare, ethnocide, and violence which are illuminated in the tangled "brittle fragments" in every detail of the sculpture – the aftermath and detritus of warfare and the discarding of people. People are obsolete. Weiss's work is a monument to understanding our difficulty with difficult authors – one of the titles of the dossiers in these pages. It is the difficulty of thinking about how and where we know domination and its effects everywhere and nowhere when we try to grasp the causes.

Simone Weil's 1939 *War and the Iliad* is an inspiration about how to write about "force" and violence that touches every fibre of our beings; there is no alibi for it: In these few words (by Hector, prince of Troy): "Chastity appears dirtied by force, and childhood delivered to the sword." The foundation at the gates of Troy becomes an object of poignant nostalgia when Hector runs by, seeking to elude his doom: "In the old days of peace, long ago when the Greeks had not come ... past these did they run their race, pursued and pursuer." The whole of the *Iliad* appears under the shadow of the greatest calamity the human race can experience – the destruction of a city. This calamity could not tear more at the heart had the poet been born in Troy. But the tone is not different when the Achaeans are dying, far from home. [2]

So then, these thoughts bear on my continuing reflection on the role of anarchism as a way of seeing a world and opening that world to a rights-based vision of human relationships. How artists think is crucial to this anarcho-communitarian sense of how people have survived against systemic violence and systemic delusions and the inbuilt violences of the swollen, overly complex societies that pretend to be democratic. Clearly this obsession with what I call "overwhelmitude," a term I use to describe the internalization of the system at the end of the centuries – words in which "regeneration," "revolution," "reform," and "renewal" struggle against the consequences of thinking about historical decline. "Decline" also means a string of "*de*-words": "degeneracy," "disease," "displacement," "defeat," and "devolution": the *re*-words against the *de*-words – modernity in full bloom.

But if we believe we always and only live in some bridging or saddle-time, then we do what the systemic violence wants us to do: give up imagining a future and accept the illusions that are prepared for us now through cybernetic apparatuses and algorithms that become our nerve endings.

Let us pause to consider: The anarcho-community is a direct and many-sided relationship between members of a self-regulating "group," and this activity of the "intentional" or dialogical community militates against specialization and expertise and centralization, which belong to another level of society, itself always centralizing and monopolizing power. A dialectical sense of how society operates is therefore necessary – often for me through Marx and Hegel's dialectics and what has become known as the Frankfurt School of culture criticism and aesthetics.

But dialectics end up in the mind. Dialectics can also be frozen in time and, by becoming locked into the unconscious, formed into what psychoanalysis calls "thing representations." The unconscious is a time–space world in which, for the anarchist who understands psychoanalysis and aesthetics, the unconscious is a form of reciprocity and mutual aid, but at times blocked from its desires, which are the basic foundational social values, even as the principle of mutual aid takes many forms. Mutual aid should be understood as co-operation, sharing and listening, resisting the impingement of the Hobbesian-mediated power relations grounded in competition, bureaucracies, and systemic patriarchy. Here, indeed, rule the bureaucracies and systemic patriarchy and meaningless work of millions of the "Mercurians" and workers that build against the death narcissism that has come into their lives, no matter what form it takes. There are many names for these resistances: libertarian socialism, anarcho-syndicalism, mutual aid, or communitarian once-in-a-while temporary organization. *Anarchists of the world, unite!*? (For a little while.) [3]

Let us pause to consider: the anarcho-community is not based on eschatological or revealed religion. The future – if there is one – will have to account for the rise of cities that will number, according to predictions, twenty-five million people and up – Dhaka, Lagos, Karachi, México, Tokyo, New York, Berlin, Rome, or London. At the same time, a sense of common values is required in order to counteract how the state assumes it will always be eternal and even sacred, based on the still-existing shadow of Kingship and the use of force, and is the only way humans can protect what they have made and then excuse the domination that is inside their lives. Domination expresses itself in forms of time, sacred time, and immanent forms of expression that are the artistic genres, enactments, embodiments, and figurations in art and literature that cannot be framed by representations in mass-cultural formations.

In my essays, whether related to literature, culture, the city, or teaching, I have worked within paradigms like these. We might name them a "finale of seem," or a utopian-materialist architectonics of the new. They follow here in an anarcho-playful postscript titled "A Small Manual of Piety and a Curriculum for the Plague," which brings the dossiers to a close. It is a mock proposal for a course in the spirit of the first stanza of Wallace Stevens's *"The Emperor of Ice-Cream"* (1922) – or a "finale of seem":

> Let the wenches dawdle in such dress
> As they are used to wear, and let the boys
> Bring flowers in last month's newspapers.
> Let be be the finale of seem.
> The only emperor is the emperor of ice-cream. [4]

DOSSIER V — CHAPTER 2

A Small Manual of Piety and a Curriculum for the Plague: After Bertolt Brecht's *Die Hauspostille*, or Breviaries [5]

Es steht nicht mehr bereit. [6]

—BERTOLD BRECHT, *Aufstieg und Fall der Stadt Mahagonny* (*Rise and Fall of the City of Mahagonny*) (1930)

A Guide to the Use of This Curriculum of Breviaries, or Individual Lessons for a Short Course on Plagues [7]

Why a Breviary? An instruction manual allows the freedom for revelation and fragmentariness that reminds of prayer and supplication. The Breviaries come into existence in dark times of obfuscation and debased discourse that covers over the now-visible and forbidden-to-speak-of class conflict and the division of labour rearranged as if a pandemic is new news. It is new-old news. Breviaries are devotionals for the everyday when in the Plague the "division of labour" becomes "essential services" and emergency measures, as if everyday life under market capitalism was not already an emergency, with fire alarms ringing in our ears.

The arrangement of my Imaginary Course of Readings with several images tracks my "devotional" readings in a lapidary arrangement of Lessons – both a Primer for an Untaught Course and scenes for a "Songplay" influenced by Brecht and Weill's *City of Mahagonny*, the utopia where everything is allowed and nothing is permitted.

The Breviaries are conceived as both course readings and as the script material – a tableau yet without music to accompany a performance of the Breviaries. So, the *Singspiel* is a Schema for Partisan-Anarchist Thinking, reading and writing and planning against the "colossal crimes" of what appears to the innocent and experienced alike to be an epoch without history. [8]

Again, breviaries are devotionals, instructions we should not be without. The danger: the return to a universal religion or universal death wish. On the other hand, when push comes to prophecy and disaster, as it does with certain tribes when they experience disaster, stories are constructed about a time when hunter-gatherers thrived; but when warfare and pandemics occur, the entire economic system of surplus and exchange is discovered and laid bare for all to see, and prophets, wizards, and failed chiefs will emerge as salvationists, attempting to answer the alarm bells. [9]

Breviary I

First Lesson: Epochs of Phantasmagorias

Readings:
Giovanni Boccaccio, excerpts from *The Decameron*
Walter Benjamin, "The Storyteller"
Image:
Pieter Bruegel the Elder, *Dulle Griet* (*Mad Meg*)

Measuring history by Epochs of Time. So then, Time suffers and then Time and the Phantasmagoria plague us. Artworks are our evidence of the difficulty of understanding how the dialectic of time moves through "suffering time." We long for "progress," but views of history that claim "progress" lead to the death of others. We count them. One is too many. The interpretation of meanings given to time are diverse and are passed on to others, not just through "ideas" but through images of ideas in society. To "know thyself" (and "nothing human is alien to me") begins the search for the forms of human expressiveness and critical feelings. I teach the history of critical emotions. The study of the humanities typically begins with timelines and how we measure change and continuity. The European traditions give us many timelines and ways we measure time: cycles of nature, myths, legends, heroic figures, epochs, periods, great men, martyrs, heroes, battles, wars, inventions, revolutions, social movements, cultural changes, breaks and ruptures, generations. Don't forget: modus = measurement = movement, floating, transience, flowing, fading and recovering memory, and forgetting. Institutions create "official" memory and then the humanities emerge willy-nilly as a critique of institutions and the official forms of memory – that is tradition. Plagues arrest the flow of time. "Now-timer" reveals the frozenness of time. Frozen speech is the speech of absolutists, says Rabelais in *Gargantua and Pantagruel* (book 4, chap. 3). The European consciousnesses of time: the archaic, messianic, eschatological, redemptive, millennial, and utopic maybe gives us a sense that our experiences are part of a larger *flow* of "epochal time" – that is, time as a function of space and nature – the cosmological? We know, too, that "humanities" includes "science" and that the "humanities" do not protect us from barbarism: thus, here, the Breviaries.

Breviary II

Second Lesson: Measuring Time

Reading:
Walter Benjamin, "Theses on the Philosophy of History"

The *messianic* lets us know of a break or coming break in time and prophesizes a "new time," when a new set of beliefs startles us with a figure or movement that represents new time. The old beliefs are "transvalued" and lead to a new equality or social justice or realms of freedom. *Redemptive* time means that past acts or events are recovered in time and are recreated by forgiveness or by overcoming mourning or the violation of a taboo or deep code or even beliefs that were imposed by an outside force. *Eschatological* time predicts the coming events based on signs from the past, and then history begins from the point of that prediction. *Millennial* time invites us to look back for a time when history begins and periods end. In *apocalyptic* cultures one awaits signs of "end time," or breaks, or "profane illuminations" like revolutions, or hidden signs that "apo-" – the nearby – is no longer "secret" but is now "revealed" ("-calyptic"), but it has been, without our knowing it, there "side by side" with us all along and we haven't seen it. Turns our heads inward! The fear we have lies in the emptiness of prognostication and time.

Breviary III

Third Lesson: Why Are We Afraid of Revolutions?

Readings:
Bertolt Brecht, *Mother Courage and Her Children*
Hannah Arendt, *On Revolution*
Karl Marx, *Economic and Philosophic Manuscripts of 1844*

The *utopic* or *anarchic* is an imaginary placeway where we become conscious of the ways we work out our communal identifications and break free from coerced ends and beginnings, powers and dominations. Typically, one might even "force freedom," which gets us into trouble, for the good of the communal or the People or Nation. Often the utopic or anarchic is marked by free association, self-regulation, and the admission of fantasy to everyday life (imagination), and we abolish the division of labour and act out in the name of self-expression. However, there's also Social Death where we measure time by catastrophes.

Breviary IV

Fourth Lesson: Brecht and Benjamin

Readings:

Walter Benjamin, *Conversations with Brecht*

Charlotte Beradt, *The Third Reich of Dreams: The Nightmares of a Nation, 1933–1939*

Franz Kafka, *"In the Penal Colony"*

Jaroslav Hašek, *The Good Soldier Švejk*

Images:

Bertolt Brecht and Kurt Weill, *Rise and Fall of the City of Mahagonny*

The National Socialist German Workers' Party (NSDAP) made itself into a "workers' party state," so they attacked the unions first and then the independent associations, whether religious, cultural, academic, or professional. Why? To incorporate them into the state or to isolate them from "natural law," which the state would pursue. The German political-economic theorist Franz Neumann named the German concept of *Lebensraum* the "Leviathan State," which was a Labour State in which private economic activity had to be subordinated to the bureaucracy and normative administrative state. Lucky that an already existing Bismarckian bureaucracy and modified welfare state existed, so the Nazi Party only had to install party members into the fabric, or ensure that workers became party members. In addition, a surveillance structure was installed. The military expanded into a vast spy network, bringing thugs into the street breaking the windows of Jewish storekeepers. This was well known and feared by the common citizen and, for Jews, ended up we know where – not only in their dreams and nightmares (which Charlotte Beradt recounts in *The Third Reich of Dreams: The Nightmares of a Nation, 1933–1939*). The work of the party ensured that the economic forces and the political state were coordinated by an elaborate legal framework. That created big problems for the corporations, many of which needed Jewish money and international finance, which they were loath to abandon. The struggle: to ensure that everything was outwardly legal but remained capitalist, while the "worker state" became the *Kulturnation*. The *Kulturnation* "naturalized" everyday life into the Terror State. Fear turned up everywhere and so were social security and armaments brought together in the heroic New Individual. The 1935 Nuremberg Race Laws extended the legal "Prerogative, One-Party State," named correctly by Ernst Fraenkel, that embedded a racialized normative legal system into labour and the class war. The Nationalist ideology of the Party State gained and held power at all costs. Costs are nothingness. This, then, was the "Fascist Public Sphere." Robert Ley, Nazi Minister of Labour, organized "shop troops" in the factories and bureaucracies, ensuring that the Nazi labour organizations did not become communist through the ideology of worker solidarity. A worker-contra-worker regime ensured that labour was celebrated by the Party's staged rallies. Schismatic religions like Anabaptists, Quakers, Jehovah's Witnesses, Mennonites, and eventually Jews, Roma, gay people, atheists, anarchists, pacifists, and Marxists and their "civil" organizations, were deracinated because religious sects were a danger to the prerogative State. The State appropriated the financial resources of the churches and synagogues.

The radical Protestant labour movements were watched carefully. Rule by emergency declarations was the norm. The Nuremberg Laws among other decrees separated, banned, and eliminated Jews from everyday life; this was just the beginning of the plague over everyday life. The Enemy: the Weimar Constitution, bourgeois labour law, Jewish-owned businesses, fear and envy of Russian Communism. [10]

Breviary V

Fifth Lesson: Peter Weiss's *The Aesthetics of Resistance* and Scattergrams of Plague: Who Are You to Speak of Plagues?

Images:

Peter Weiss and Peter Brook, *Marat/Sade,* or *The Persecution and Assassination of Jean-Paul Marat as Performed by the Inmates of the Asylum of Charenton under the Direction of the Marquis de Sade*

Jeff Wall, *Dead Troops Talk (A Vision after an Ambush of a Red Army near Moqor, Afghanistan, Winter, 1986)*

Pergamon Altar at Berlin's Pergamon Museum

Peter Weiss, in *Aesthetics of Resistance*, writes his own history of resistance that brings together his readings on art (Delacroix, Bruegel the Elder ...), which is also his own autobiographical account of his wanderings and exile in and out of revolution and friendship with revolutionaries, also visiting Brecht and his family in Svendborg, Sweden. I here paraphrase the opening of volume one:

> When we see all around us the bodies rising out of the stone, crowded into groups, intertwined or shattered into fragments, hinting at their shapes and the strangleholds of their twisted figures and so ... Like stones on a field reaching to the horizon there are symptoms, symptoms, symptoms, a gigantic primitive agony, a scattergram of symptoms like any and all plagues and states of war. Genocidal processes: millions of people starving to death; millions of children without homes or shelter; refugees around the world crammed into overcrowded cities in poverty-stricken countries; mass unemployment in rich countries; ecological catastrophes, violent and anomic actions of and against the state ... Who are You Authorities to speak of Plagues ... ?

Breviary VI

Sixth Lesson: From Benjamin's "Theses on the Philosophy of History"

"To historians who wish to relive an era, Fustel de Coulanges recommends that they blot out everything they know about the later course of history. There is no better way of characterizing the method with which historical materialism has broken ... The nature of this sadness stands out more clearly if one asks with whom the adherents of historicism actually empathize. The answer is inevitable: with the victor. And all rulers are the heirs of those who conquered before them. Hence, empathy with the victor invariably benefits the rulers. Historical materialists know what that means. Whoever has emerged victorious participates to this day in the triumphal procession in which the present rulers step over those who are lying prostrate. There is no document of civilization which is not at the same time a document of barbarism. And just as such a document is not free of barbarism, barbarism taints also the manner in which it was transmitted from one owner to another. A historical materialist therefore dissociates himself from it as far as possible. He [*sic*] regards it as his task to brush history against the grain."[11]

Breviary VII

Seventh Lesson: The Relevance of Freud: From *New Introductory Lectures on Psychoanalysis*

During the June 2016 Institute for the Humanities forum on "Psychoanalysis and the Trump Phenomenon," I spoke about the immanent fascist movements coming alive in the liberal-democratic capitalist world: "The Fascist Public Sphere" grew and enabled the election of a demagogue whose malignant narcissism and clinical alexithymia – the inability to feel or relate to the emotion or plight of another person – showed a character disorder that should have opened a discussion about psycho-analytical understanding of authority and delinquency in group formations and right-wing formations and the anxieties and fears of terror-filled groups around the world. Group formations are under siege. Militarized elites, monied brokers called "oligarchs," exist everywhere, and racialized groups pump their anxieties onto scapegoats. This leads to what Wilhelm Reich named in his 1933 classic study *Character Analysis* "the emotional plague," and what Freud restlessly referred to as the death drive that emerges when our ego-ideals fail us, and our omnipotence of thought turns our emotions into abstractions that promise us release from terrors. The terrors appear, not as man-made, but magically as acts of nature, floods, earthquakes, disease. Plagues appear to us as if nature has a second nature; we believe that wars, economic collapse, revolutions are not man-made, but are created by unknown forces not subject to analysis. Faced with the disintegration of the "ego" and the phantasmagoria of the forces of destruction in the natural world, the omnipotence of thought when faced with death turns our face away from already-existing *administered death*.[12] Those who create and then exploit nearby anxiety draw upon a political cult of death that is nearby.

So then, Freud, in his old age, writes a brief history of the ego:

> No wonder that the ego so often fails in its task. Its three tyrannical masters are the external world, the super-ego and the id. When we follow the ego's efforts to satisfy them simultaneously – or rather, to obey them simultaneously – we cannot feel any regret at having personified this ego and having set it up as a separate organism. It feels hemmed in on three sides, threatened by three kinds of danger ... it strives too to be a loyal servant of the id ... to remain on good terms with it, to recommend itself to it as an object and to attract its libido to itself ... observed at every step ... which lays down definite standards for its conduct, without taking any account of its difficulties from the direction of the id and the

external world ... if those standards are not obeyed, punishes it with tense feelings of inferiority and of guilt ... the ego ... obliged to admit its weakness ... breaks out in anxiety – realistic anxiety regarding the external world, moral anxiety regarding the super-ego and neurotic anxiety regarding the strength of the passions in the id.[13]

Breviary VIII

Eighth Lesson: Bakhtin's *Rabelais and His World* ... of Language at the Edge of the Plague Turning the World Upside Down: We Can Say Nothing More But Speak through the Pathos of the Invective!

Bakhtin and the Menippean diatribe-vituperative-billingsgate-scurrility-abuse-rant-bombast-rodomontade-fustian-tirade-diatribe-jeremiad-philippic-harangue-denunciatory:

> In the Renaissance, laughter in its most radical, universal, and at the same time gay form emerged from the depths of folk culture; it emerged but once in the course of history ... and entered with its popular (vulgar) language the sphere of great literature and high ideology.[14]

> "Even this must have a preface – that is a literary preface," laughed Ivan, "and I am a poor hand at such things. You see my story takes place in the sixteenth century. At that time, as you probably learned at school, it was customary in poetry to bring down heavenly powers on earth. Dante was not the only one to do this."[15]

Breviary IX

Ninth Lesson: Bruegel the Elder's *Two Chained Monkeys* (1562)

There's pathos in the idea of painting these monkeys at all *as worthy subject matter* and isolating the painting from any larger whole! One monkey is looking at the painter. The other monkey, we really aren't sure. There is starvation in the scene. There are several "frames" in the painting, so we are framed both as spectator and participant. One, the window, and the other the window to the viewer. Why were they captured and why are they chained? That's an estranging device because we don't know; so, there is an interrogation in the picture, a judgment in the question of the Picturing and Depicting itself. But we know that monkeys were kept for entertainment and street fairs! So, "devices" are also "interrogating" gestures. The scene outside is peaceful. The natural life of labour and the economy. The "utopia" of work and harvest. Yet, there is the fate of the monkeys, like the "fall" of Icarus to blind fate. Bringing the spectator into the "scene" – Bruegel the Elder constructs the enigmatic. The painting functions like music about the end of any utopia. The painting *moves by showing* the figurative. The madness of the world is criticized but the world "moves." There is fear, deadness, and the reminder of violence: the "monkeys" have lost what they are through their domestication into entertainment. This is a reminder of what "we" humans do. The painting engages long time and short time: the "contemporary," the humanist "revolution" of the ethically engaged spectator in the present: painters and writers engage everyday life, the grotesque, madness, terror, and the sublime. Nothing escapes the Plague of Everyday Life when the *division of labour is revealed to us as "essential labour."*

Breviary X

Tenth Lesson: A Restitution-Destruction Fantasy and Fascism's Distorted Public Sphere

Readings:
Walter Benjamin, "Theses on the Philosophy of History," IX
Theodor W. Adorno, *Minima Moralia: Reflections from a Damaged Life*[16]

Image:
Paul Klee, *Angelus Novus* and other "angel paintings"[17]

Theodor W. Adorno's reflections on his damaged life associates his exile with the phantasmagoria of modern life when

> The dreamer encounters his own image impotently, as if it were a miracle, and is held fast in the inexorable circle of his own labour, as if it would last for ever. The object that he has forgotten he has made is dangled magically before his eyes, as if it were an absolutely objective manifestation. Governed by the logic of dreams, the phantasmagoria succumbs to its own particular dialectic[18]

Benjamin chronicles the emergence of the fascist Spectacle and how fascism created a public sphere and institutionalized the forms of everyday life into the Nazi Party that, in turn, enforced a distorted and deranged concept of the "public" – a fake public sphere of reality as ideology and ideology as reality. The Feudal Volk existed alongside of Enlightenment ideals of the German-Jewish-European ethical and humanist Parnassus; however, the "fascist public sphere" was intended to be a dictatorship over everyday life in which human rights as democratic rights and democratic rights as human rights were no longer emancipatory rights and obligations. So then, the Nazis rearranged the idea of a public sphere against all palpable evidence that the actuality of the degeneration of a public could be enforced. A public was administered through laws against imaginary plagues from within and beyond the German Reich's borders, where pogroms flourished. Smothered and masked in laws and decrees, the People become both Plague and Publicum ruled into Law by the *Plague of Emergency Measures*. Fascism as corporate-military-bureaucratic capitalism needed a concept of revolution to inspire and defraud the public. Wait: can't we describe this "form" of life psychoanalytically, as a restitution-destruction fantasy? Estrangement and alienation merge into a non-objective form of being: power-protected inwardness – a non-objective being which is a non-being. Albert Speer's architecture and slave labour camps lie behind and in the future of *being as such*. The future of being *forecloses being as such*, because we are in the present now staring into a *plague-like* catastrophe that is beyond denial or repression, and which some have experienced every day even before the plague.

Breviary XI

Eleventh Lesson: A Supplication

Assignment:
Write a meditation on counting virus deaths. How can we become up to date?

But wait! A meditation on counting makes me feel unclean.

> I.
> speaking of counting
> Jews or not
> Armenians or not
> Others or not
> they are pointing out that the number of COVID deaths
> outdied Vietnam deaths
> Hey!
> Fallacy of undistributed middle

But it makes a certain point
Wait in the undistributed middle
How many Vietnamese died?
This is the minefield
One is too many.

II.
Forgot
Better look it up
2 million civilians and 1.5 million soldiers

Breviary XII

Twelfth Lesson: Class Becomes a Chorus
Reading: "The Manual of Piety Which Is
Intended for the Reader's Use. It Should Not Be
Senselessly Wolfed Down" [19]

—

Breviary XIII

Postscriptum: The Dramaturge Speaks

The Plague discloses our feelings of absence and mourning, but
it's even the loss of mourning – the "loss of loss" comes with the
feeling of total abandonment, when even "loss" is not a possible
human feeling or consolation for deathly uncertainty. Loss is
replaced by the "phantasmagoria" where there is no consoling
for what is missing. We pick up the fragments that are strewn by
the wayside. Or are picked up and made into another delusional
camouflage of ideology as reality, reality as ideology. The canonization of death and the cults of assorted forms of fascism emerge.
But wait. This course is about a time to stop thinking about death

on "their" terms. That's exactly what "they" don't want us to do: to think about death as ideology as reality and reality as ideology. Adorno, again: "Thinking no longer means anything more than checking at each moment whether one can indeed think."[20] And Benjamin, in *The Origin of German Tragic Drama*: "It is indeed characteristic of the sadist that he humiliates his object and then – or thereby – satisfies it. And that is what the allegorist does in this age drunk with acts of cruelty lived and imagined."[21] A note from the Dramaturge's Notebook for the Course and the Production: *The rear projection screens show Mahagonny and other cities burning. Then the columns of demonstrators set off, chaotically criss-crossing and confronting one another, continuing right until the end.*[22] The allegorist is comfortable with tableaux that show the epoch of capitalism in mock epic form … Stage directions for scene 20 of *Rise and Fall of the City of Mahagonny*: *And amid increasing confusion, inflation, and hostility of all against all, in the final weeks of the Capitol Cities, those who had not yet been killed demonstrated for their ideals – having learned nothing.* Science? The science of counting? Noam Chomsky, in an interview published in *Media Control*, poses questions in a mordantly Brechtian fashion:

> How many Vietnamese casualties would you estimate that there were during the Vietnam War? The average response on the part of Americans today is about 100,000. The official figure is about two million. The actual figure is probably three to four million. The people who conducted the study raised an appropriate question: What would we think about German political culture if, when you asked people today how many Jews died in the Holocaust, they estimated about 300,000? What would that tell us about German political culture?[23]

DOSSIER V: ENDNOTES

CHAPTER 1

1   (Previously unpublished.) Through the years I have created three art installations. This "Breviary for the Plague Years" would be the fourth; it is here created as an imaginary script for a performance. In 1973 I created, with the students of a class on Brecht, Brecht's politically controversial play *The Measures Taken* in the Simon Fraser University Theatre. In 1984 the Carnegie Centre in Vancouver, the classic 1903 Vancouver building at the corner of Main and Hastings Streets which was originally a library, housed my installation *Dialectical Postcards 1948/1984*. I constructed a house-room surrounded with photographs from the years 1948/1984, of Orwell's *Nineteen Eighty-Four* significance. Nineteen eighty-four was also the year of a conference on Orwell that took place in Vancouver in a hotel at English Bay, far from the impoverished communities of Main and Hastings. In 2008 I created another installation, *The Insurance Man: Kafka in the Penal Colony*, at the Simon Fraser University Gallery; see Jerry Zaslove and Bill Jeffries, eds., *The Insurance Man: Kafka in the Penal Colony* (Vancouver: Linebooks and Simon Fraser Gallery, 2010).

2   Simone Weil and Rachel Bespaloff, *War and the Iliad*, trans. Mary McCarthy (New York: New York Review of Books: 2015), 31.

3   I have no illusions that this utopia of means has an end in sight. I'm referring to the tradition of hope for the hopeless – the work of Ernst Bloch being referred to in various essays in this book. The novels and memoirs of Victor Serge are other exemplars; see *Memoirs of a Revolutionary* (New York: New York Review of Books, 2012). Serge portrays his life through the formation of his many-voiced lives that move through his writing.

4   Wallace Stevens, *The Collected Poems of Wallace Stevens* (New York: Vintage Books, 1982).

CHAPTER 2

5   This "Breviary" first appeared in *Contours* 10 (Fall 2020), an online publication of the Institute for the Humanities edited by Ted Byrne, Alessandra Capperdoni, and Hilda Fernandes. The issue, titled "In a Time of Plagues," was devoted to essays on the COVID-19 pandemic. See www.sfu.ca/humanities-institute/contours/issue10 .html (accessed February 2022).

6   "There's no life after this, nothing significant awaits you." Brecht's and Kurt Weill's *Rise and Fall of the City of Mahagonny* is a mordant utopia where everything is allowed, and nothing permitted except songs about the pieties of capitalism. Songplay (*Singspiel*) combines song and talk, projected images, stage sets (in this case of an imaginary utopian city), opera motifs, even an onstage audience, and references to archaic texts and satires of authors who may appear in the play in disguise. The *Mahagonny* songplay was written at the same time as the *Threepenny Opera* was being composed. Both productions were attacked by right-wing agitators. Both productions are founded

on Brecht's aesthetic and dramaturgical "functional" theatre. The present "Breviaries for the Plague" are adapted for the functional classroom.

7   See Bertold Brecht, *Manual of Piety: Poems by Bertolt Brecht,* trans. Eric Bentley and others (New York: Grove Press, 1966), 9.

8   See Walter Benjamin, *Understanding Brecht,* trans. Anna Bostock (London: New Left Books, 1973), 120.

9   See Pierre Clastres, *Society against the State,* trans. Robert Hurley (New York: Zone Books, 1989), in particular pp. 212–218.

10   See Ernst Fraenkel, *The Dual State: A Contribution to the Theory of Dictatorship,* trans. E.A. Shils (Clark, NJ: Lawbook Exchange, 2010).

11   Walter Benjamin, "Theses on the Philosophy of History," in *Illuminations,* trans. Harry Zohn, ed. Hannah Arendt (New York: Harcourt, Brace & World, 1955), 258.

12   Theodor W. Adorno, "Phantasmagoria," in *In Search of Wagner,* trans. Rodney Livingstone (London: New Left Books), 91.

13   Sigmund Freud, Lecture XXXI, "The Dissection of the Psychical Personality," in *The Complete Introductory Lectures on Psychoanalysis,* trans. James Strachey (New York: W.W. Norton, 1966), 521. That lecture is only a "primer" of Freud's and is included in the "Breviaries" to indicate that a "Breviary" about the terror of death must include Freud's view that the taboo on death and the origin of the "omnipotence of thought" and "wishful thinking" is the beginning of the dialectic of culture and civilization expressed in Freud's *Civilization and Its Discontents.*

14   Mikhail Bakhtin, *Rabelais and His World,* trans. H. Iswolsky (Bloomington: Indiana University Press, 1984), 6.

15   Ivan Karamazov's preface to his tale of "The Grand Inquisitor," in Fyodor Dostoevsky, *The Brothers Karamazov,* trans. David McDuff (London: Penguin, 2003).

16   Adorno, *Minima Moralia,* trans. E.F.N. Jephcott (London: New Left Books, 1951). Phantasmagoria is a feature in several essays in this collection and in the prologue.

17   See also Boris Friedewald, *The Angels of Paul Klee* (London: Arcadia Books, 2016).

18   Adorno, *In Search of Wagner,* 91.

19   Bertold Brecht, *Manual of Piety (Die Hauspostille),* trans. Eric Bentley (New York: Grove Press, 1994), 9.

20   Adorno, *Minima Moralia,* 197.

21   Benjamin, *The Origin of German Tragic Drama,* trans. John Osborne (London: New Left Books), 184–185.

22   Bertold Brecht, *Rise and Fall of the City of Mahagonny,* trans. Steve Giles (London: Methuen Drama, 2007), 58.

23   Noam Chomsky, *Media Control: The Spectacular Achievements of Propaganda* (New York: Seven Stories Press, 1995), 10.

Publisher's Acknowledgments

Talonbooks acknowledges and is grateful to the many journals, publishers, and collaborators for the permissions to use the previously published material appearing in this book. In all cases, slight or substantial revisions were made to the texts by the author. See the initial notes to individual chapters for information on their bibliographic source.

INDEX

First Nations 229, 364, 382, 384, 386. *See also* Indigenous Peoples, First Peoples, Native American Peoples

First Peoples 220, 259. *See also* Indigenous Peoples, First Peoples, Native American Peoples

Flaubert, Gustave 452, 458

For a New Novel (Robbe-Grillet) 130

Forster, E.M. 128, 130

Foucault, Michel xii, 93, 94, 101, 103–105, 481

France 255, 331, 381, 382, 415, 459

Franco, Francisco 379

Frank, Leonard 319

Frankfurt am Main 7, 10, 183, 185, 247, 353, 478, 522

Frankfurt School 10, 478, 522

Frankfurter Zeitung 7, 183

Fraser River 41

French Guiana 424

French Pyrenees 459

French Revolution 158, 189, 368

French Third Republic 415

Freud, Sigmund xi, 106, 116, 121, 123, 126, 127, 129, 132, 142, 145, 154, 156, 157, 215, 217, 274, 298, 368, 373, 374, 377, 378, 380, 381, 385, 388, 389, 453, 468, 471, 531, 532

Fried, Michael 375

Friedrich, Caspar David xi, 357, 361

Froissart, Jean 141

From Caligari to Hitler (Kracauer) 188, 205, 467

Frye, Northrop 103, 143

G

Galerie Neue Kunst 419

Galileo Galilei 306

Gandhi, Mahatma 154

García Canclini, Néstor 328–330, 332–343, 345–349, 351, 353

García Márquez, Gabriel 222, 345, 352

Garden of Earthly Delights, The (Bosch) 365

Gargantua and Pantagruel (Rabelais) 234, 526

Gastown, Vancouver 312

Gautier, Théophile 469

Geneva Convention 212

Géricault, Théodore 368

German National Library 37

German people and culture xii, 6, 10, 13, 24, 28, 31, 37–40, 92, 158, 177, 188, 196, 201, 207, 212, 225, 228, 233, 237, 247–250, 252, 254, 257, 262, 271, 299, 315, 323, 373, 375, 378, 380, 416, 424, 426, 442, 444, 451, 452, 454, 459, 464, 467, 468, 478, 484, 497, 528, 536, 538. *See also* Germany, East Germany

Germany 7, 26, 37–40, 178, 183, 188, 219, 226, 240, 246, 254, 262, 307, 319, 331, 415, 452, 459, 467. *See also* German people and culture, East Germany, West Germany

Gerz, Jochen 233

Gestapo 40, 250

Giedion, Sigfried 146

Ginsberg, Allen 481

Godwin, William 137, 141, 154, 157

Goethe, Johann Wolfgang von 221, 452

Gogol, Nikolai 15, 17, 38, 79, 276, 328

Goldberg, Rube 419

Golding, William 153

Golem 274, 480

Gombrich, Ernst 34

Goodman, Paul 485, 494

Goody, Jack 98, 104, 110

Gouldner, Alvin 88, 96, 99

Goya, Francisco 342, 359, 368

Graff, Harvey J. 103

Gramsci, Antonio 123, 329

Great Dictator, The (Chaplin) 300

"Great Wall of China, The" (Kafka) 193, 339, 423, 424

Greece 44, 180, 182, 228. *See also* Greek people and culture

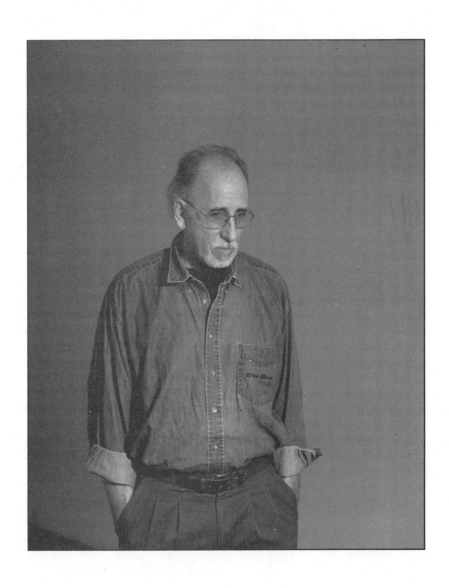

PHOTO: JEFF WALL

Jerry Zaslove was a teacher and writer in the fields of comparative literature and the social history of art. His most important work includes the installation and book *The Insurance Man: Kafka in the Penal Colony* (with Bill Jeffries), the monograph *Jeff Wall, 1990* (with Gary Dufour), and numerous essays and articles written over five decades on the place of the university in society, exile and memory, and the city in history. He taught at Simon Fraser University from its opening year in the Departments of English and Humanities and was the founding director of the Institute for the Humanities. He passed away in 2021, before *Untimely Passages* was published.